CHAPTER 12

53. Understand your personal strengths and weaknesses. 348
54. Consider a just-in-time team. 349
55. Find a mentor. 352
56. Decide who's in charge of what. 359

CHAPTER 13

57. Prepare a letter of inquiry. 373
58. Study a business from the outside. 373
59. Study a business from the inside. 375
60. Probe the depths of ill will. 384

CHAPTER 14

61. Conduct secondary research on franchising. 401
62. Investigate the franchise system by interviewing franchisors and franchisees. 402

CHAPTER 15

63. Write a cover letter for your plan. 423
64. Write an executive summary. 426
65. Describe your product or service. 428
66. Describe the market and the target customer. 428
67. Describe your major competitors. 431
68. Describe your marketing strategy. 432
69. Show off your location. 433
70. Introduce your management team. 433
71. Describe your personnel. 434
72. Project your cash flow. 436
73. Project your income statement. 437
74. Project your balance sheet. 442
75. Construct a PERT chart, and go for it. 444

SmallBUSINESS
an entrepreneur's plan

Seventh Canadian Edition

Ron Knowles

Chris Castillo
Algonquin College

NELSON / EDUCATION

NELSON EDUCATION

Small Business: An Entrepreneur's Plan, Seventh Edition

by Ron Knowles and Chris Castillo

Vice President, Editorial Higher Education:
Anne Williams

Acquisitions Editor:
Alwynn Pinard

Marketing Manager:
Dave Stratton

Senior Developmental Editor:
Elke Price

Photo Researcher:
Julie Pratt

Permissions Coordinator:
Julie Pratt

Content Production Manager:
Claire Horsnell

Production Service:
MPS Limited

Copy Editor:
Kate Revington

Proofreader:
MPS Limited

Indexer:
Shan Young

Senior Manufacturing Coordinator:
Joanne McNeil

Design Director:
Ken Phipps

Managing Designer:
Franca Amore

Interior Design:
Cathy Mayer

Cover Design:
Cathy Mayer

Cover Image:
Dim Dimich/Shutterstock

Compositor:
MPS Limited

Library and Archives Canada Cataloguing in Publication

Knowles, Ronald A., author
Small business : an entrepreneur's plan / Ron Knowles,Chris Castillo. — Seventh Canadian edition.

Includes index.
ISBN 978-0-17-650967-5 (pbk.)

1. New business enterprises—Planning. 2. Small business—Planning. I. Castillo, Chris, 1969-, author II. Title.

HD62.5.K568 2013
658.1'141   C2013-901984-7

ISBN-13: 978-0-17-650967-5
ISBN-10: 0-17-650967-4

Credit lines for icons: E-Exercises (hands typing): Varijanta/Shutterstock.com; Action Steps (stairs): Jupiter Images/Thinkstock.

Brief Contents

Preface   xv

Chapter 1
Your Great Adventure: Exploring Your Options   1

Chapter 2
Spotting Trends and Opportunities   33

Chapter 3
Positioning Yourself as an Entrepreneur for Market Opportunities   67

Chapter 4
Profiling Your Target Customer   93

Chapter 5
Learning from the Competition: Your Competitive Intelligence   119

Chapter 6
Marketing: Pricing and Promoting Your Product or Service   143

Chapter 7
Marketing: Distribution and Location   173

Chapter 8
Legal Concerns   199

Chapter 9
Risk Management Issues   239

Chapter 10
The Power of Numbers   261

Chapter 11
Financing Your Business   307

Chapter 12
Building and Managing a Winning Team   339

Chapter 13
Buying a Business   369

Chapter 14
Buying a Franchise or Franchising Your Business   397

Chapter 15
Pulling the Plan Together   419

E-Modules

Please go to www.nelson.com/knowlescastillo7e.

E-Module 1
Exporting: Another Adventure Beckons   M1–3

E-Module 2
Fast-Start Plan   M2–1

E-Module 3
Business Plan Outline, Templates, and Examples   M3–1

Glossary   449
Index   457

Contents

Preface   xv

Chapter 1

YOUR GREAT ADVENTURE: EXPLORING YOUR OPTIONS   1

Learning Opportunities   1
Building Your Road Map   4
The Age of the Entrepreneur   6
    WHAT DO THE NUMBERS SAY?   6
Small Business Entrepreneurs   8
Characteristics of Entrepreneurs   8
    OTHER IMPORTANT CHARACTERISTICS
        OF ENTREPRENEURS   8
Rev Up   11
    WHY DO YOU WANT TO BE AN
        ENTREPRENEUR?   12
    WHAT DOES IT TAKE TO BE AN
        ENTREPRENEUR?   13
What Is a Social Entrepreneur?   14
What Is an Intrapreneur?   14
"Inc." Yourself   15
What Is a Small Business?   15
Green Business   17
The Downside to Being an
    Entrepreneur   18
Your Chances of Success   18
Beat the Odds—Write a Business Plan   18
    CREATING A BUSINESS PLAN—
        WHY BOTHER?   19
    WHAT DOES A PLAN LOOK LIKE?   19
Beat the Odds—Do Your
    Research   20
    PRIMARY RESEARCH   20
    NEW-EYES RESEARCH   20
    SECONDARY RESEARCH   21
    HARD DATA   21
Innovation—An Entrepreneur's
    Tool   24
In a Nutshell   25
Key Terms   25
Think Points for Success   25
Action Steps   26
Business Plan Building Block   30
Checklist Questions and Actions to Develop Your
    Business Plan   30
Case Study: Mechanic To You®   30
Notes   31

Chapter 2

SPOTTING TRENDS AND OPPORTUNITIES   33

Learning Opportunities   33
Recognizing Opportunities   35
    BRAINSTORM YOUR WAY INTO SMALL BUSINESS   37
    BE A TREND WATCHER   38
Globalization   40
Technology   41
    INTERNET AND E-COMMERCE   42
The Boomer Trend   45
The Splintering of the Mass Market   47
    SOCIAL MEDIA TRENDS   48
    TRENDS CREATE OPPORTUNITIES   49
    THE LIFE-CYCLE STAGES   52
Watch for Market Signals   53
How Deep Is Deep?   54
Segmentation and Gap Analysis   55
Know Your Real Business   55
    DEFINE YOUR BUSINESS   57
Develop Your Pitch   58
In a Nutshell   59
Key Terms   59
Think Points for Success   59
Action Steps   60
Business Plan Building Block   62
Checklist Questions and Actions to Develop Your
    Business Plan   64
Case Study: Trends and Opportunities   64
Notes   65

Chapter 3

POSITIONING YOURSELF AS AN ENTREPRENEUR FOR MARKET OPPORTUNITIES   67

Learning Opportunities   67
Your Vision and Values   70
Welcome to Opportunity Selection   72
    STEP 1: IDENTIFY YOUR BUSINESS GOALS   73
    STEP 2: LEARN MORE ABOUT YOUR FAVOURITE
        INDUSTRY   75
    STEPS 3 AND 4: IDENTIFY PROMISING INDUSTRY
        SEGMENTS AND PROBLEMS THAT NEED
        SOLUTIONS   76
    STEP 5: BRAINSTORM FOR
        SOLUTIONS   78

STEP 6: MESH POSSIBLE SOLUTIONS WITH
  OPPORTUNITIES IN THE MARKETPLACE 79
STEP 7: TAKE STOCK OF, AND FOCUS ON, THE MOST
  PROMISING OPPORTUNITIES 80
Business Mission Statement 80
  YOUR BUSINESS MISSION 81
  YOUR BUSINESS STRATEGY 82
  THINKING ABOUT YOUR BUSINESS MODEL 84
In a Nutshell 86
Key Terms 86
Think Points for Success 86
Action Steps 86
Business Plan Building Block 89
Checklist Questions and Actions to Develop Your
  Business Plan 90
Case Study: Shopify—An E-Commerce
  Alternative 90
Notes 91

Chapter 4

PROFILING YOUR TARGET CUSTOMER 93

Learning Opportunities 93
  MOBILE APPS: THE ULTIMATE ONE-ON-ONE
    MARKETING 96
The Power of Profiling 97
  PRIMARY CUSTOMER 97
  SECONDARY CUSTOMER 98
  INVISIBLE CUSTOMER 98
  CONSUMER, OR END-USER, PROFILE 99
  DEMOGRAPHIC PROFILE 99
  PSYCHOGRAPHIC PROFILING 101
What We Can Learn from Media
  Sources 103
Business-to-Business Profile 105
  THE SOFTWARE SCHOOL INC.: B2B TARGET
    CUSTOMER EXAMPLE 107
  B2B OR B2C: WHICH ONE
    WILL IT "B"? 107
  PRIMARY RESEARCH CAN HELP TOO 108
Field-Interviewing Target Customers 108
Surveying Target Customers 109
  VISUALIZE YOUR NEW BUSINESS AND TARGET
    CUSTOMER 111
In a Nutshell 112
Key Terms 112
Think Points for Success 112
Action Steps 113
Business Plan Building Block 115
Checklist Questions and Actions to Develop Your
  Business Plan 115
Case Study: Customer Profiling 116
Notes 117

Chapter 5

LEARNING FROM THE COMPETITION: YOUR COMPETITIVE INTELLIGENCE 119

Learning Opportunities 119
Who Is Your Competition? 122
  COMPETITIVE INTELLIGENCE 123
  COMPETITIVE TOUCHPOINT ANALYSIS 123
Scouting the Competitive Landscape 125
Developing Your Competitive Strategy 127
  NICHE, OR FOCUS, STRATEGY 127
  DIFFERENTIATION STRATEGY 128
  COST LEADERSHIP STRATEGY 128
  COMPETITOR ANALYSIS STRATEGY 128
  COMPETITIVE PRICING STRATEGY 129
The Competition Life Cycle 131
  YOUR COMPETITIVE POSITIONING STRATEGY 132
Forming Strategic Alliances with Competitors 134
  CREATING UNIQUENESS THROUGH CHANGE 135
You Can Do It 136
In a Nutshell 136
Key Terms 136
Think Points for Success 137
Action Steps 137
Business Plan Building Block 139
Checklist Questions and Actions to Develop Your
  Business Plan 139
Case Study: My Virtual Model 139
Notes 141

Chapter 6

MARKETING: PRICING AND PROMOTING YOUR PRODUCT OR SERVICE 143

Learning Opportunities 143
  PRICING YOUR PRODUCT OR SERVICE 145
Four Common Methods of Pricing for Small
  Business 146
  1. COMPETITOR-BASED PRICING 146
  2. PROFIT-BASED, OR COST PLUS, PRICING 146
  3. INDUSTRY NORM, OR KEYSTONE, PRICING 147
  4. CEILING, OR PREMIUM, PRICING 148
Other Pricing Strategies 148
  YOUR PRICING STRATEGY 148
Promotion—Your Way of Connecting with the
  Customer 149
The Promotional Mix 150
  YOUR PROMOTIONAL CORNERSTONES: CUSTOMER
    SERVICE AND QUALITY 151
Other Marketing Strategies 151
  PAID MEDIA ADVERTISING 151
  BUSINESS CARDS 152

POINT-OF-PURCHASE DISPLAYS 153
PACKAGING 153
CATALOGUES 153
DIRECT MAIL 154
MONEY-BACK GUARANTEES 154
FREE INK AND FREE AIR 155
FREEBIES 155
PERSONAL SELLING 155
TRADE SHOWS 157
INDUSTRY LITERATURE 158
WORKING VISIBLY 158
DISCOUNT COUPONS 158
BRANDING 159
ONLINE MARKETING 159
SALES REPS AS CONNECTORS 162
COURTESY AS PROMOTION 162
NETWORKING 163
Planning Ahead 164
DON'T KEEP YOUR BUSINESS A SECRET 164
PROMOTION AND MARKET RESEARCH 164
ASK CUSTOMERS QUESTIONS TO HELP DEVELOP YOUR
    MARKETING STRATEGY 165
ATTACH PRICE TAGS TO YOUR PROMOTIONAL
    STRATEGIES 165
In a Nutshell 165
Key Terms 166
Think Points for Success 166
Action Steps 167
Business Plan Building Block 169
Checklist Questions and Actions to Develop Your
    Business Plan 170
Case Study: 1-800-Got-Junk? 170
Notes 172

Chapter 7

**MARKETING: DISTRIBUTION AND
LOCATION 173**

Learning Opportunities 173
Distribution Channels 176
What Is Your Best Location? 177
A Location Filter 178
RATING IMPORTANCE (1–10) 179
Home-Based Businesses 181
WHAT HOME-BASED BUSINESS IS BEST FOR ME? 183
Getting the Information You Need to Find the Right
    Location 184
LOCATION INFORMATION USING SECONDARY
    RESEARCH 184
LOCATION INFORMATION USING PRIMARY
    RESEARCH 185
Some Things You Must Know About Leases 187
ENTREPRENEUR, READ YOUR LEASE 188
ANTICIPATE THE UNEXPECTED 189

HOW TO REWRITE A LEASE 190
In a Nutshell 193
Key Terms 193
Think Points for Success 193
Action Steps 194
Business Plan Building Block 195
Checklist Questions and Actions to Develop Your
    Business Plan 196
Case Study: QuestVest 196

Chapter 8

LEGAL CONCERNS 199

Learning Opportunities 199
Legal Forms for Small Business 200
Sole Proprietorship 200
Partnership 202
THE SHOTGUN 203
Corporation 204
REASONS FOR INCORPORATING 204
POTENTIAL DISADVANTAGES OF
    INCORPORATING 207
THE PROCESS OF INCORPORATION 208
WHO CAN BE A DIRECTOR? 209
MUST A COMPANY HAVE SHAREHOLDERS? 209
Cooperative 212
Additional Legal Structures for Social
    Entrepreneurs 214
Your Business Name 216
Patents, Copyrights, and Trade-marks 217
TEN THINGS YOU SHOULD KNOW ABOUT
    PATENTS 217
TEN THINGS YOU SHOULD KNOW ABOUT
    COPYRIGHTS 219
TEN THINGS YOU SHOULD KNOW ABOUT TRADE-
    MARKS 221
Protection Strategy for Social Media IP 223
More Red Tape 223
THE BUSINESS NUMBER (BN) 223
PAYROLL DEDUCTIONS 224
FEDERAL INCOME TAXES 225
GST/HST 226
PROVINCIAL SALES TAXES 227
Get a Lawyer and an Accountant 228
A PARTNER'S UNFORESEEN DEATH 228
Get a Will 229
Succession Planning—Especially for the Family-
    Owned Business 229
Bankruptcy 230
In a Nutshell 232
Key Terms 232
Think Points for Success 233
Action Steps 233
Business Plan Building Block 234

Checklist Questions and Actions to Develop Your
  Business Plan   234
Case Study 1: Your Pal, Steve   234
Case Study 2: It Was a Fatal Accident   235
Notes   236

Chapter 9

RISK MANAGEMENT ISSUES   239

Learning Opportunities   239
Developing a Plan B   240
Insurance Planning   244
Workplace Health and Safety   249
  OH&S GOVERNMENT, EMPLOYEE, AND EMPLOYER
    RESPONSIBILITIES   250
  JOINT HEALTH AND SAFETY COMMITTEES   250
  WORKPLACE HAZARDOUS MATERIALS   251
  DUE DILIGENCE   251
Theft and Fraud Prevention   252
Getting Advice   253
  PLANNING AHEAD: 12-MONTH START-UP
    CHECKLIST   253
In a Nutshell   255
Key Terms   255
Think Points for Success   256
Action Steps   256
Business Plan Building Block   257
Checklist Questions and Actions to Develop Your
  Business Plan   257
Case Study: Your Business Idea   258
Note   259

Chapter 10

THE POWER OF NUMBERS   261

Learning Opportunities   261
Your Financial Fitness   263
  FORMULATING A PERSONAL FINANCIAL VISION   263
  GETTING FINANCIAL ADVICE   264
Estimating Your Start-up Costs   265
  THE OPENING BALANCE SHEET   265
Assets—What the Business Owns   267
  CURRENT ASSETS   267
  FIXED ASSETS   269
  OTHER ASSETS   269
Liabilities—What the Business Owes Others   269
  CURRENT LIABILITIES   270
  LONG-TERM LIABILITIES   270
  OTHER LONG-TERM DEBT   270
Equity—What the Business Owes the Owner   270
Key Balance Sheet Ratios   271
  LIQUIDITY RATIOS   271
  SOLVENCY RATIOS   273

Cash Flow and Income Statement: Important
  Projections   273
  CASH FLOW PROJECTION   273
  WHY IS A CASH FLOW PROJECTION SO
    IMPORTANT?   274
Five Steps to Creating a Start-up Cash Flow   275
  STEP 1: CALCULATE YOUR OPENING BALANCE   275
  STEP 2: CALCULATE YOUR PROJECTED SALES FOR EACH
    MONTH—PROJECT MONTHLY SALES (LINE 3)   278
  STEP 3: FORECASTING RECEIPTS   279
  STEP 4: FORECASTING DISBURSEMENTS   280
  STEP 5: SUMMARY OF CASH FLOW
    (LINES 35 TO 39)   281
Pro Forma Income Statement   284
  SALES   286
  COST OF GOODS SOLD   286
  GROSS PROFIT   286
  OPERATING EXPENSES   286
  OTHER EXPENSES   288
  NET PROFIT (BEFORE TAXES)   288
Key Income Statement Ratios   288
  GROSS PROFIT MARGIN   288
  PROFIT MARGIN   289
  INVENTORY TURNOVER   289
  GROSS MARGIN RETURN ON INVENTORY
    INVESTMENT   291
The Closing Balance Sheet   291
  ASSETS   291
  LIABILITIES   293
  OWNER'S EQUITY   293
Key Ratios Based on the Balance Sheet and the Income
  Statement   294
Break-Even Analysis   294
  1. UNIT METHOD   295
  2. BREAK-EVEN USING GROSS PROFIT MARGIN
    (REVENUE METHOD)   296
In a Nutshell   299
Key Terms   299
Think Points for Success   300
Action Steps   300
Business Plan Building Block   302
Checklist Questions and Actions to Develop Your
  Business Plan   302
Case Study 1: Financing Your Business—Getting
  Started   303
Case Study 2: DISCovery Books and Magazines Inc.—
  Financial Statements   303
Notes   305

Chapter 11

FINANCING YOUR BUSINESS   307

Learning Opportunities   307
Before You Shake the Money Tree   309

WHAT IS YOUR CREDIT HISTORY? 309
HOW MUCH UNSECURED CREDIT DO YOU HAVE? 310
DEVELOP A PERSONAL BALANCE SHEET 313
CHART YOUR PERSONAL MONEY FUTURE 313
ASSESS YOUR RISK TOLERANCE 315
Informal Sources of Financing—Bootstrapping 315
SELF-FINANCING 316
FAMILY AND FRIENDS 316
Formal Sources of Funding 317
Banks and Financial Institutions 317
Other Sources of Start-up Capital 322
ANGELS 322
SUPPLIERS 322
CUSTOMERS 323
EMPLOYEES AND EMPLOYERS 323
MICRO-LENDING PROGRAMS 325
GOVERNMENT PROGRAMS 326
VENTURE CAPITALISTS 326
NONPROFIT FUNDING 326
COOPERATIVE PARTNERSHIP 327
Will That Be Debt or Equity? 327
ADVANTAGES OF DEBT 328
DISADVANTAGES OF DEBT 328
ADVANTAGES OF EQUITY 328
DISADVANTAGES OF EQUITY 328
Primary Types of Debt Financing 329
SHAREHOLDER LOANS 329
CANADA SMALL BUSINESS FINANCING (CSBF) LOANS 329
OPERATING LOANS (LINE OF CREDIT) 331
TERM LOANS 332
Primary Types of Equity Financing 332
COMMON SHARES 333
PREFERRED SHARES 333
CONVERTIBLE DEBENTURES 333
In a Nutshell 334
Key Terms 334
Think Points for Success 334
Action Steps 334
Business Plan Building Block 336
Checklist Questions and Actions to Develop Your Business Plan 337
Case Study: Financing Your Business—Getting Started 338
Notes 338

Chapter 12

BUILDING AND MANAGING A WINNING TEAM 339

Learning Opportunities 339
The Basics of Managing Your Team 341
Leading 341
ORGANIZING 343

Teamwork 346
THE FOUNDING TEAM 346
MANAGEMENT TEAM PROFILES AND OWNERSHIP STRUCTURE 346
BOARD OF DIRECTORS OR ADVISORY TEAM 346
HUMAN RESOURCES REQUIREMENTS 347
BUILDING BALANCE INTO YOUR TEAM 347
Non-traditional Teams 349
THE "JUST-IN-TIME" TEAM 349
GOAL-ORIENTED PARTNERSHIPS 350
THE INDEPENDENT CONTRACTOR OR ASSOCIATE 350
EMPLOYEE LEASING 351
THE MENTORING RELATIONSHIP 351
Hiring Your First Employee 352
STEP 1: JOB ANALYSIS 353
STEP 2: JOB QUALIFICATIONS 353
STEP 3: JOB REQUIREMENTS 354
STEP 4: STAFFING DECISIONS AND RECRUITMENT 354
Recruitment 354
SELECTION 356
TRAINING AND DEVELOPMENT 357
COMPENSATION 357
WHAT DO EMPLOYEES REALLY COST? 358
Managing an Aging and Multicultural Workforce 358
HR Best Practices 359
In a Nutshell 359
Key Terms 360
Think Points for Success 360
Action Steps 360
Business Plan Building Block 361
Checklist Questions and Actions to Develop Your Business Plan 363
Case Study: Management and Teamwork at MSM Transportation 363
Notes 365

APPENDIX 12.1 366

The Personality Analysis 366
Group 366
FILLING IN THE PERSONALITY GRID 366
INTERPRETING YOUR RESULTS 367

Chapter 13

BUYING A BUSINESS 369

Learning Opportunities 369
Why Purchase an Ongoing Business? 371
How to Buy and How Not to Buy 372
GETTING THE WORD OUT 372
Investigate the Business from the Outside 373
LEARN FROM OTHERS' MISTAKES 373
KNOW WHEN YOU NEED OUTSIDE HELP 374

Investigate the Business from the Inside   375
DEALING WITH BROKERS   375
How to Look at the Inside of a Business   376
STUDY THE FINANCIAL HISTORY   376
COMPARE WHAT YOUR MONEY COULD DO
ELSEWHERE   378
EVALUATE THE TANGIBLE ASSETS   378
GET A NONCOMPETITION COVENANT   379
ANALYZE THE SELLER'S MOTIVES   379
Examine the Asking Price   379
NEGOTIATE THE VALUE OF GOODWILL   380
LEARN WHETHER BULK SALES ESCROW IS
NEEDED   381
AN EARNOUT SUCCESS STORY   381
The Decision to Buy   381
PREPARE FOR THE NEGOTIATIONS   383
Protect Yourself   384
Negotiating the Price   384
1. ASSET-BASED VALUATION   384
2. ABILITY-TO-PAY VALUATION   385
3. EARNINGS-ASSETS VALUATION   387
The Contract   391
Expect Some Pleasant Surprises   391
In a Nutshell   392
Key Terms   393
Think Points for Success   393
Action Steps   393
Checklist Questions and Actions to Develop Your
Business Plan   394
Case Study: A Passionate Leap   395
Notes   396

Chapter 14

**BUYING A FRANCHISE OR FRANCHISING
YOUR BUSINESS   397**

Learning Opportunities   397
What Is a Franchise?   399
FRANCHISE SYSTEMS   399
FRANCHISE NETWORKS   400
Why Buy a Franchise?   400
WHAT THE CUSTOMER GETS   400
WHAT THE FRANCHISEE RECEIVES   400
WHAT THE FRANCHISOR ASKS OF YOU   401
Investigating Franchise Opportunities   401
The Franchise Agreement and System   403
THE PROCESS INVOLVED IN PURCHASING A
FRANCHISE   403
Buyer Beware: Some Pitfalls of Franchising   406
ENCROACHMENT   406
GROUND-FLOOR OPPORTUNITIES   406
RENEWAL PERIOD   406
VERBAL AGREEMENTS   406
MINIMUM FRANCHISE LEGISLATION   407

SIGNING PERSONALLY   407
AVAILABILITY OF INFORMATION AND FRANCHISING
REALITIES   407
Evaluating a Franchise   408
CHOOSE YOUR PRODUCT OR SERVICE WITH CARE   412
Reasons for Not Buying a Franchise   412
Can You Franchise Your Idea and Become the
Franchisor?   412
A Final Word About Franchises   413
MEMBER-OWNED BUYING GROUP: AN
ALTERNATIVE   414
In a Nutshell   414
Key Terms   414
Think Points for Success   415
Action Steps   415
Checklist Questions and Actions to Develop Your
Business Plan   416
Case Study: Franchise Shows   416
Notes   417

Chapter 15

PULLING THE PLAN TOGETHER   419

Learning Opportunities   419
How to Start Writing Your Business Plan   421
THREE-PART STRUCTURE: WORDS, NUMBERS, AND
APPENDICES   422
OUTSIDE ASSISTANCE IN WRITING A BUSINESS
PLAN   423
REMINDERS   423
THE COVER LETTER   423
THE TABLE OF CONTENTS   425
THE EXECUTIVE SUMMARY   425
SECTION 1: DESCRIPTION OF THE BUSINESS   427
SECTION 2: FINANCIAL SECTION   435
Epilogue: Act on What You Know   443
In a Nutshell   445
Key Terms   445
Think Points for Success   445
Action Steps   445
Checklist Questions and Actions to Develop Your
Business Plan   448
Note   448

E-Module 1

**EXPORTING: ANOTHER ADVENTURE
BECKONS   M1–3**

Please go to http://www.nelson.com/knowlescastillo7e.
Learning Opportunities   M1–3
The Start-Up Fundamentals   M1–4
Motivations for Exporting   M1–4
SWOT Analysis   M1–6

INTERNAL STRENGTHS AND WEAKNESSES M1–6
HUMAN RESOURCES M1–6
FINANCIAL SITUATION M1–6
OPERATING HISTORY AND TRACK RECORD M1–7
External Opportunities and Threats M1–8
Key Points You Need to Know for Export
    Start-Up M1–9
Finding Information and Advice About Your Target
    Market M1–10
DEPARTMENT OF FOREIGN AFFAIRS, TRADE, AND
    DEVELOPMENT M1–10
OTHER FEDERAL GOVERNMENT
    DEPARTMENTS M1–11
TRADE COMMISSIONERS M1–11
PROVINCIAL GOVERNMENTS M1–11
BUSINESS ASSOCIATIONS M1–11
FOREIGN EMBASSIES M1–11
BILATERAL BUSINESS COUNCILS M1–11
INTERMEDIARIES M1–11
DATABASES M1–12
EXPORT ADVISORS/EXPERTS M1–12
INTERNET M1–12
Choosing an Entry Strategy M1–12
INTERMEDIARIES M1–12
FOREIGN DISTRIBUTORS M1–13
TRADING HOUSES M1–13
DIRECT SELLING M1–13
PARTNERSHIPS M1–14
Pricing Your Product or Service M1–16
DOMESTIC COST PLUS MARKUP M1–17
FULL-COST PRICING M1–17
MARGINAL-COST PRICING M1–17
Promotional Strategies M1–18
PROMOTING SERVICES M1–18
PACKAGING M1–18
PROMOTIONAL OPTIONS M1–18
PROMOTIONAL MATERIALS M1–19
TRADE FAIRS AND EXHIBITIONS M1–19
PROMOTING IN THE UNITED STATES M1–19
Export Financing M1–20
METHODS OF INTERNATIONAL PAYMENT M1–20
ENSURING PAYMENT: TYPES OF SECURITY M1–21
CREDIT MANAGEMENT M1–21
MANAGING EXCHANGE RATE RISK M1–22
Getting Your Product or Service to Market M1–22
EXPORTING A SERVICE M1–22
EXPORTING A PRODUCT M1–23
Culture and Communication M1–24
A Final "Export-Ready" Checklist M1–26
Export Plan Outline M1–27
In a Nutshell M1–28
Key Terms M1–28
Action Steps M1–28
Think Points for Success M1–29
Notes M1–29

E-Module 2

FAST-START PLAN M2–1

Please go to http://www.nelson.com/knowlescastillo7e.
Learning Opportunities M2–1
Quick Checklist M2–2
Structuring Your Plan M2–3
Great Dream Equals Great Business M2–3
What Business Are You Really In? M2–4
Who Are Your Competitors? M2–5
How Much Should You Charge? M2–6
PROFILE YOUR TARGET CUSTOMER M2–6
HOW DO YOU MAKE THAT CUSTOMER
    CONNECTION? M2–7
WHAT ARE YOUR START-UP COSTS? M2–7
CHARTING YOUR SALES GOALS FOR THE FIRST THREE
    MONTHS M2–8
EXPENSE FORECAST M2–10
ASSUMPTIONS M2–10
FINAL PASS M2–12
TO-DO LIST M2–13
LIST OF NECESSITIES BEFORE OPENING DAY M2–13
Model Business Plan: Yes, We Do Windows M2–14
1. BUSINESS DEFINITION M2–14
2. WHAT BUSINESS AM I REALLY IN? M2–14
3. COMPETITION M2–14
4. PRICING M2–15
5. TARGET CUSTOMER M2–16
6. PROMOTION PROGRAM M2–16
7. START-UP COSTS M2–17
8. SALES GOALS AND EXPENSES—FIRST THREE
    MONTHS M2–17
9. TO-DO LIST M2–17
In a Nutshell M2–19
Think Points for Success M2–19
Action Steps M2–19

E-Module 3

BUSINESS PLAN OUTLINE, TEMPLATES, AND EXAMPLES M3–1

Please go to http://www.nelson.com/knowlescastillo7e.
Business Plan Outline M3–1
FIRST PART OF A BUSINESS PLAN M3–1
I. DESCRIPTION OF BUSINESS M3–2
II. FINANCIAL SECTION M3–5
APPENDICES M3–6
Business Plan Templates for Various Plan
    Components M3–6
COVER SHEET TEMPLATE M3–6
EXECUTIVE SUMMARY TEMPLATE M3–7
I. DESCRIPTION OF BUSINESS TEMPLATES M3–7

II. FINANCIAL SECTION TEMPLATES M3-10
    APPENDICES TEMPLATE M3–11
Business Plan Examples M3–11
Annie's Business Plan Proposal for Specialty
    Chocolates and Candy Concession at Sea World
    Encounters M3–12
    COVER LETTER FOR ANNIE'S M3–12
    ANNIE'S BUSINESS PLAN PROPOSAL M3–13
    EXECUTIVE SUMMARY M3–13

MANAGEMENT AND STAFFING M3–14
STORE OVERVIEW M3–16
MARKETING M3–18
STORE OPERATIONS M3–20
FINANCIAL MANAGEMENT AND FINANCIALS M3–21
ANNIE'S APPENDICES M3–25

Glossary 449
Index 457

Preface

Welcome to the Seventh Canadian Edition of *Small Business: An Entrepreneur's Plan*. This book and our extensive online resources were created for the thousands of dreamers like you who want to create their own ventures. Most first-time entrepreneurs start out with little more than an idea. By combining your talents, passions, and ideas with a practical approach, as we outline here, you will be able to take your idea, form it into a functional business plan, and succeed in realizing your dream.

Every great adventure begins with a map. This book serves as your map and your navigator. The Action Steps and the Business Plan Building Blocks provide you with direction and tasks to accomplish along the way, while the vignettes and case studies offer you a first-hand look at the trials, tribulations, and successes of other entrepreneurs.

By following the Action Steps and Building Blocks, you'll learn how to develop a business plan from the inception of an idea, how to find your target customers, and how to market to them successfully.

Fasten your seatbelt, hold on tight, and prepare to embark on your great entrepreneurial adventure!

ORGANIZATION

TARGET THE CHAPTERS THAT CALL TO YOU

This Seventh Canadian Edition contains fifteen chapters that will guide you along the way to owning or managing a small business. Within the pages of Chapter 1, "Your Great Adventure: Exploring Your Options," to Chapter 15, "Pulling the Plan Together," the textbook presents seventy-five Action Steps, as well as a number of Building Blocks.

- Chapters 1, 2, and 3 help you focus on yourself and your ideas; they explain how to develop and test your ideas in the marketplace before you spend any money. If you are just exploring entrepreneurship, concentrate on these chapters and the accompanying Action Steps and online exercises. Keep in mind that you are designing not only a business plan but also a life plan.
- Chapters 4, 5, and 6 help develop, locate, and satisfy the key to your success in small business—your target customer and knowledge of your competition. Here, you'll learn how to profile your target customer; develop a competitive strategy; and price, promote, and market your product or service.
- Chapter 7 helps you develop your distribution strategy and find a location—at home, on the street, or online.
- Chapter 8 helps you untangle and understand the legal red tape of starting and running a business. We help you decide which legal form (sole proprietorship, partnership, or corporation) is best for you and your business, help you understand bankruptcy and its danger signals, and show you how to find the right lawyer and professional advice.
- Chapter 9 prompts you to think about protecting yourself and your business. It considers matters such as insurance, health and safety, employee fraud, and the basic principles of patents, copyrights, and trade-marks.
- Chapters 10 and 11 plunge into the numbers. You will learn how to formulate a personal financial vision, ensure that your personal finances are in

order, and determine how much money you'll need to start your business and finance it. By the time you finish Chapter 11, you'll understand financial statements and be able to put together a financial plan to start and run your business.

- Chapter 12 steers you toward thinking about basic management functions, organizational structure, and leadership. It helps you begin to build a winning team.
- Chapter 13 offers tips and advice if you want to buy an existing business. If you want to join the franchise movement, though, read Chapter 14 first. Franchisees are on every corner, but as we caution you, not all of them are happy with their lot. If your goal is to be a happy franchisee, then be sure to complete a business plan for your specific franchise location. You'll need that to determine whether it will work for you.
- Chapter 15 asks you to gather up all of your Action Steps to form the basis for your business plan. One detailed business plan is provided as an example.
- Three comprehensive online instruction modules will further assist you as you enter the world of small business. You'll find the following support modules on our CourseMate site at http://www.nelson.com/knowlescastillo7e.

  - *E-Module 1—Exporting: Another Adventure Beckons* Many of you have expressed interest in the export market. And yes, exporting your product or service is an adventure you might want to think about before you start your business. In this module, we provide the start-up fundamentals and encourage you to become export ready.
  - *E-Module 2—Fast-Start Plan* If your business idea is simple or short term, perhaps you don't need a fully developed business plan. Consider completing a fast-start plan early on to determine if your idea warrants you going forth.
  - *E-Module 3—Business Plan Outline, Templates, and Examples* If you decide to "take the plunge" and write a detailed business plan—and we strongly recommend that you do—you'll need to follow an outline. In this module, we provide a detailed outline of a business plan, including all the questions you must address. If you follow this template and address all the questions, you will be ready with a solid plan that will guide you through your first year of operation. It also showcases Annie's Business Proposal for a specialty shop featuring fine chocolates and candy as a concessionaire for Sea World Encounters.

KEY FEATURES

These features help you stay on track and focus on the task at hand. At the beginning of each chapter, Learning Opportunities identify the learning outcomes of the chapter. Margin definitions help you build your business vocabulary. Other key features include the following:

ACTION STEPS

Our road to success in small business is marked by seventy-five Action Steps and supporting E-Exercises. Taking these steps should significantly improve your chances of reaching your business goals. If you view the world of business as a maze—a series of challenges and obstacles—then you can also see the Action Steps as a way designed to lead you through. Each Action Step is an exercise that accompanies an explanation of a particular portion of the maze.

ENTREPRENEURIAL VIGNETTES

At the beginning of each chapter and throughout the text, we present you with brief case studies full of strategies, real-world applications, and lessons that provide insight into entrepreneurial minds and ventures. We have modified the stories for simplicity and clarity. Some vignettes are composites of several case studies, and others are purely fictional.

E-EXERCISES AND ENTREPRENEURIAL LINKS

As we move through the book, we offer many current Web links. We also encourage linking to the Web in our E-Exercises. Here, you can test your entrepreneurial wisdom through personal assessment, trend analysis, number crunching, and even business plan preparation. These boxes provide you with the most up-to-date information on small business.

All of the links in the text are provided on the book's CourseMate site at http://www.nelson.com/knowlescastillo7e. As we all know, websites come and go. As a result, we will update the sites on a regular basis.

CHECKLIST QUESTIONS AND ACTIONS TO DEVELOP YOUR BUSINESS PLAN

At the end of each chapter is a series of questions to answer and actions to take. These prompts will help you to apply chapter theory and put it into practice as you begin to build your Business Plan.

OPENING WINDOWS

In each chapter, figures, tables, and online resources provide useful information and concepts to illustrate the text. Examples include Internet databases (throughout the book), tips for developing strategic alliances (Chapter 4), the best places to set up your booth at a trade show (Chapter 6), and a strategy for selecting your mentor (Chapter 12). All of these offer the new entrepreneur windows onto the world of small business.

COMPREHENSIVE CASE STUDIES

At the end of each chapter we provide a comprehensive case study to help you put into practice the key learning outcomes. Here, we help you understand and learn from successful entrepreneurs, such as Tobias Lütke in Chapter 3 or Robert Murray and Mike McCarron in Chapter 12. By researching the cases and answering the case study questions, you will learn the keys to small business success.

NEW AND REVISED FEATURES OF THE SEVENTH CANADIAN EDITION

New resources and websites have been identified throughout the chapters, and many of the entrepreneurial vignettes have been updated or replaced with new information and profiles, such as those on Matt Turner, founder of Mechanic

To You, and Doug Burgoyne, founder of FrogBox. We have also made several design improvements with the goal of ensuring that *Small Business* is the most exciting, current, comprehensive, and useful small business and entrepreneurship textbook available.

To reflect the changes in our society, this Seventh Canadian Edition emphasizes the importance of having a global perspective and of being Internet savvy. We have expanded our discussions on social media and social networking within a broader global perspective and added to our coverage of the importance of innovation. There are also new technology-related discussions of mobile apps and e-commerce, and text focusing on the growing field of green business.

Chapters 2 and 3 highlight many new trends and opportunities for entrepreneurs, featuring hot topics such as social media trends and e-commerce. We also explore the market potential created by aging baby boomers and how to manage a multicultural workforce. You will find updated information on future trend opportunities for entrepreneurs.

Chapter 4 covers the ultimate one-to-one marketing strategy of mobile applications. Many entrepreneurs are jumping onto the mobile app development bandwagon by developing their own business apps. In Chapter 6, the section on social media tactics in online marketing has been expanded to provide you with strategies to help promote and build your brand. Updated data on direct sales are included. Chapter 8 has the most current information available on how entrepreneurs can protect their Intellectual Property (IP).

Chapter 12 includes expanded coverage of best practices in human resources and also recognizes the importance of leadership by highlighting the key qualities of top leaders.

Chapter 14 recognizes the many entrepreneurs who decide to purchase a franchise. We have expanded information on franchise shows and incorporated research findings that provide updated insights and data on the world of franchising.

THIS BOOK IS FOR YOU: TO DREAMERS AND BEGINNING ENTREPRENEURS

As you're reading the book, keep your computer or pencil and paper close by so that you can take notes or jot down ideas. Get used to brainstorming and mind-mapping. The inspiration that you get from a highway billboard 400 kilometres from home might be the seed from which your winning business grows. Our point is that this is *your* book. Use the CourseMate site and the book in whatever way suits your needs. Make notes in the margins; mark up the text with a highlighter. Use the book as a handbook, a textbook, or both. This small business package is designed for a wide range of creative, energetic people who want to own their own business, and somewhere in that range of people is *you*.

We hope you open one of the three entrepreneurial doorways: starting your own business, franchising, or buying a business. We encourage you to find success along with the thousands of budding entrepreneurs who have followed the Action Steps provided. Good luck!

ANCILLARIES

INSTRUCTOR ANCILLARIES

The **Nelson Education Teaching Advantage (NETA)** program delivers research-based instructor resources that promote student engagement and higher-order thinking to enable the success of Canadian students and educators.

Instructors today face many challenges. Resources are limited, time is scarce, and a new kind of student has emerged: one who is juggling school with work, has gaps in basic knowledge, and is immersed in technology in a way that has led to a completely new style of learning. In response, Nelson Education has gathered a group of dedicated instructors to advise us on the creation of richer and more flexible ancillaries that respond to the needs of today's teaching environments.

The members of our editorial advisory board have experience across a variety of disciplines and are recognized for their commitment to teaching. They include the following:

Norman Althouse, Haskayne School of Business, University of Calgary

Brenda Chant-Smith, Department of Psychology, Trent University

Scott Follows, Manning School of Business Administration, Acadia University

Jon Houseman, Department of Biology, University of Ottawa

Glen Loppnow, Department of Chemistry, University of Alberta

Tanya Noel, Department of Biology, York University

Gary Poole, Senior Scholar, Centre for Health Education Scholarship, and Associate Director, School of Population and Public Health, University of British Columbia

Dan Pratt, Department of Educational Studies, University of British Columbia

Mercedes Rowinsky-Geurts, Department of Languages and Literatures, Wilfrid Laurier University

David DiBattista, Department of Psychology, Brock University

Roger Fisher, PhD

In consultation with the editorial advisory board, Nelson Education has completely rethought the structure, approaches, and formats of our key textbook ancillaries and online learning platforms. We have also increased our investment in editorial support for our ancillary and digital authors. The result is the Nelson Education Teaching Advantage and its key components: *NETA Engagement, NETA Assessment, NETA Presentation,* and *NETA Digital.* Each component includes one or more ancillaries prepared according to our best practices and may also be accompanied by documentation explaining the theory behind the practices.

NETA Engagement presents materials that help instructors deliver engaging content and activities to their classes. Instead of instructor's manuals that regurgitate chapter outlines and key terms from the text, NETA Enriched Instructor's Manuals provide genuine assistance to teachers. The Enriched Instructor's Manuals answer questions like these: *What should students learn? Why should students care? What are some common student misconceptions and stumbling blocks?* They not only identify the topics that cause students the most difficulty, but also describe techniques and resources to help students master these concepts. Dr. Roger Fisher's *Instructor's Guide to Classroom Engagement (IGCE)* accompanies every Enriched Instructor's Manual. (Information about the NETA Enriched Instructor's Manual prepared for *Small Business: An Entrepreneur's Plan* is included in the description of the *Instructor's Resource CD* below.)

NETA Assessment relates to testing materials. Under *NETA Assessment,* Nelson's authors create multiple-choice questions that reflect research-based best practices for constructing effective questions and testing not just recall but also higher-order thinking. Our guidelines were developed by David DiBattista, a 3M National Teaching Fellow whose recent research as a professor of psychology at Brock University has focused on multiple-choice testing. All Test Bank authors receive training at workshops conducted by Professor DiBattista, as do the copyeditors assigned to each Test Bank. A copy of *Multiple Choice Tests: Getting Beyond Remembering,* Professor DiBattista's guide to writing effective tests, is included with every Nelson Test Bank/Computerized Test Bank package. (Information about the NETA Test Bank prepared for *Small Business: An Entrepreneur's Plan* is included in the description of the *Instructor's Resource CD* below.)

NETA Digital is a framework based on Arthur Chickering and Zelda Gamson's seminal work "Seven Principles of Good Practice in Undergraduate Education" (AAHE Bulletin, 1987) and the follow-up work by Chickering and Stephen C. Ehrmann, "Implementing the Seven Principles: Technology as Lever"(AAHE Bulletin, 1996). This aspect of the NETA program guides the writing and development of our digital products to ensure that they appropriately reflect the core goals of contact, collaboration, multimodal learning, time on task, prompt feedback, active learning, and high expectations. The resulting focus on pedagogical utility, rather than technological wizardry, ensures that all of our technology supports better outcomes for students.

INSTRUCTOR'S RESOURCE CD (IRCD)

Key instructor ancillaries are provided on the *Instructor's Resource CD* (ISBN-13: 978-0-17-655890-1; ISBN-10: 0-17-655890-X), giving instructors the ultimate tool for customizing lectures and presentations. (Downloadable Web versions are also available at www.nelson.com/knowlescastillo7e.) The IRCD includes the following:

- **NETA Engagement.** The Enriched Instructor's Manual was written by author Chris Castillo, of Algonquin College. It is organized according to the textbook chapters and addresses eight key educational concerns, such as typical stumbling blocks students face and how to address them. This manual contains sample lesson plans, learning objectives, lecture outlines, suggested classroom activities and guest speakers, suggested solutions for Internet exercises and end-of-chapter case studies, and a resource integration guide to provide the support you need to engage your students within the classroom.

- **NETA Assessment.** The Test Bank was written by Cheryl Dowell of Algonquin College. It includes more than 440 multiple-choice questions written according to NETA guidelines for effective construction and development of higher-order questions. Also included are 524 true/false, 121 completion, and 103 short answer questions in the Test Bank. Test Bank files are provided in Word format for easy editing and in PDF format for convenient printing whatever your system.

  The Computerized Test Bank by ExamView® includes all the questions from the Test Bank. The easy-to-use ExamView software is compatible with Microsoft Windows and Mac OS. It allows you to create tests by selecting questions from the question bank, modifying these questions as desired, and adding new questions you write yourself. You can administer quizzes online and export tests to WebCT, Blackboard, and other formats.

- **NETA Presentation.** Key concepts from *Small Business: An Entrepreneur's Plan* are presented in Microsoft®PowerPoint® format, with generous use of figures and short tables from the text. The PowerPoint® presentation was created by author Chris Castillo, of Algonquin College. NETA principles of clear design and engaging content have been incorporated throughout.

- **Image Library.** This resource consists of digital copies of figures, short tables, and photographs used in the book. Instructors may use these jpegs to create their own PowerPoint presentations.

- **DayOne.** Day One—Prof In Class is a PowerPoint presentation that you can customize to orient your students to the class and their text at the beginning of the course.

VIDEOS (ISBN-13: 978-0-17-655891-8; ISBN-10: -0-17-655891-8)

Available in DVD format, these all-new and exciting CBC videos from the highly acclaimed CBC television show *Dragons' Den* explore many of the issues relevant to small businesses in Canada and bring the real world of the entrepreneur into the classroom. These video segments were selected by author Chris Castillo to stimulate a lively discussion. He has chosen relevant videos based on the entrepreneur's presentation skills, ability to persuade potential investors, and the viability of the business ideas.

The videos are also supported by a video guide, which includes a synopsis of each video, teaching notes, and case study questions with solutions.

SMALL BUSINESS COURSEMATE

Small Business: An Entrepreneur's Plan includes Small Business CourseMate, a complement to your textbook. Small Business CourseMate includes:

Engagement Tracker

How do you assess students' engagement in your course? How do you know your students have read the material or viewed the resources assigned?

Good practice encourages frequent contacts between students and faculty: With CourseMate, you can use the included Engagement Tracker to assess student preparation and engagement.

Use the tracking tools to see progress for the class as a whole or for individual students. Identify students at risk early in the course. Uncover which concepts are most difficult for your class. Monitor time on task. Keep your students engaged.

Interactive Teaching and Learning Tools

CourseMate includes interactive teaching and learning tools, including
- quizzes,
- flashcards,
- videos.

The variety of tools in CourseMate reflects respect for diverse ways of learning and gives students ample opportunity to actively engage with course concepts. Students receive prompt feedback, which helps them to focus their learning efforts on concepts they have yet to master. Time plus energy equals learning, and CourseMate offers an engaging way for students to increase their time on task.

Interactive e-Book

In addition to interactive teaching and learning tools, CourseMate includes an interactive e-book. Students can take notes, highlight, search, and interact with embedded media specific to their book. Use this resource as a supplement to the printed text, or as a substitute—with CourseMate, your students can choose.

LIVEPLAN PRO (ISBN-13: 978-0-17-667981-1; ISBN-10: 0-17-667981-2)

LivePlan helps entrepreneurs build dynamic business plans and pitches that evolve with their businesses, then syncs their accounting data to their forecast, providing insight into just how well their business is doing. LivePlan turns a business plan into an actionable business management tool that helps entrepreneurs grow their businesses faster and answers the question, "How's my business doing?"

- Easy, error-free financials guaranteed. LivePlan makes it easy to put together your financial projections. Write your whole plan without ever having to look at a spreadsheet.
- Real business plans to inspire you . LivePlan includes an extensive library of over 500 real sample business plans.
- Illustrate your financials with automatic charts. LivePlan's automatic charts will make your plan look great and save you a ton of time.
- Expert guidance at every step. LivePlan is packed with easy-to-follow instructions, helpful advice, additional readings, and video from renowned business planning expert Tim Berry.

SMALL BUSINESS ON THE WEB

http://www.nelson.com/knowlescastillo7e

This Seventh Canadian Edition is supported by our comprehensive support website to help you as you begin your entrepreneurial trek. Here, you'll find self-study questions, E-Exercises, key terms with definitions, PowerPoint® slides, Internet links, and more. Downloadable versions of the Instructor's Manual, PowerPoint® presentation, and Instructor's Video Guide for the small business videos can be accessed from the password-protected instructor's page of the companion website.

Cengage Learning's Small Business CourseMate brings course concepts to life with interactive learning, study, and exam preparation tools that support the printed textbook.

ANCILLARIES FOR STUDENTS

SMALL BUSINESS COURSEMATE

Small Business CourseMate includes

- an interactive e-book, which allows you to take notes, highlight, bookmark, search the text, and use in-context glossary definitions,
- interactive teaching and learning tools, including

  – quizzes,
  – flashcards,
  – videos, and
  – e-modules.

ACKNOWLEDGMENTS

We couldn't have written this book without significant contributions from a number of people. The book is built on a foundation of case studies, and the Action Steps are taken from real-life tactics in the marketplace. Many entrepreneurs have succeeded in the real world, and we have sought to tell you how they've done it.

Ron Knowles (1947–2007) was a husband, father, brother, professor, student mentor, and great friend and colleague at Algonquin College, Ottawa, Ontario. He was the consummate entrepreneurial thinker. His ground-breaking textbook, *Small Business: An Entrepreneur's Plan*, now in its seventh edition, is read by thousands of business students and professionals worldwide who want to learn how to fulfill their dream of becoming a successful entrepreneur.

As well as being a successful author, back in 1987, Ron was the pioneer of the Small Business Management program at Algonquin College. Just as he did with his passion for gardening, Ron planted the seeds, tended the program with care, and watched it grow. Ron believed that the lessons learned in business could be applied to lessons in life: be enthusiastic, share your knowledge with others, and always remember to have fun or, as he liked to say, "Shake that money tree!" Ron left us much too early, but his entrepreneurial spirit continues. We are grateful to him for sharing his knowledge through his publications and his years of dedication to teaching. His unique insights will continue to influence future generations of business students, entrepreneurs, and business professors worldwide.

We are also truly indebted to our colleagues who graciously devoted time, made helpful suggestions, and gave thoughtful comments to shape this edition:

Mark Fletcher
Georgian College

H. Douglas MacDonald,
Mount Royal University

Robert Greene,
Niagara College

Mario Pascucci,
George Brown College

Lina Jaglowitz,
Seneca College

Chris Roubecas
SAIT Polytechnic

Knud Jensen,
Ryerson University

Special thanks, also, to former Commander David Newing, founder of the Canadian Youth Business Foundation (CYBF), and to Kimberley Cunnington-Taylor, not-for-profit and charity lawyer.

And finally, this new edition could not have been completed without the endless help, guidance, and advice of the Nelson Education staff, notably Elke Price, senior developmental editor; Alwynn Pinard, acquisitions editor; Claire Horsnell, content production manager; Dave Stratton, marketing manager; and Kate Revington, copy editor.

I hope you enjoy your small business adventure.

Chris Castillo
Algonquin College, Ottawa

A NOTE FROM THE PUBLISHER

Thank you for selecting *Small Business: An Entrepreneur's Plan*, Seventh Canadian Edition, by Ron Knowles and Chris Castillo. The authors and publisher have devoted considerable time and care to the development of this book. We appreciate your recognition of this effort and accomplishment.

Instructors may have questions on how to make this course come alive in the classroom so we invite you to send your questions directly to author Chris Castillo at chris@chris-castillo.com.

Chapter 1

Your Great Adventure: Exploring Your Options

At the end of each chapter, you will begin a preliminary draft of what will become a complete and free-flowing business plan.

Jupiterimages/Comstock/Thinkstock

LEARNING OPPORTUNITIES

After reading this chapter, you should be able to

- identify the role, skills, and characteristics of successful Canadian entrepreneurs;
- discover why you might want to become an entrepreneur;
- identify your entrepreneurial quotient;
- understand what it takes to be an entrepreneur and intrapreneur;
- understand the meaning of the terms *micro business* and *small business*;
- use mind maps to help you decide on the life you want;
- discover what success means to you;
- understand the rationale for a business plan and list the main components;
- improve your research and information-gathering skills.

ACTION STEPS PREVIEW

1. Keep a 24/7 Adventure Notebook.
2. Find out why you want to be an entrepreneur.
3. Assess your interests and abilities.
4. Expand your self-assessment.
5. "Inc." yourself.
6. Interview entrepreneurs.
7. Take your "new eyes" into the marketplace.
8. Begin your industry research.

MECHANIC TO YOU®

After making the decision to be his own boss, Matt Turner, a licensed auto mechanic, looked into the regulations for opening a mechanic shop. He faced obstacles, though. Turner says, "I just really wanted to work for myself and have the satisfaction and recognition of my own work being done," adding, "not to mention the huge benefit of making more money as a self-employed person." He also noted that he thought he could achieve more than what he could as an employee. For these reasons, Turner decided that it was time to launch his own business.

After speaking to the City of Ottawa to inquire about getting a business licence, Turner was devastated to learn that, in Nepean, Ontario, no more permits to open an automotive shop were allowed unless the shop was built from the ground up. "After learning this," says Turner, "I wasn't sure how I was going to get all the money needed to build a building from the ground up."

Turner decided to have a business consultation with Chris Castillo, who is a business coach. After thinking about the obstacle together, they came up with a new opportunity. "If we can't build a new mechanic shop," they said, "then why don't we go to people's homes to fix their cars? What if we can do this?"

By asking a simple "What if" question, they gained a new business idea: an idea that proved to be brilliant since it allowed Matt Turner to start his business with low overhead and low start-up costs. Turner quickly turned to researching how to outfit a van so it could serve as a mobile automotive shop and what his competition would be. After doing some research, he confirmed that he could turn a van into a mobile automotive business.

So, together, Matt Turner and Chris Castillo launched Mechanic To You® Inc.

"Customers love the new approach to service," says Turner. "Customers have the ability to now save time and the hassle of driving their car to a mechanic shop. They also save money because customers now don't have to pay for towing to the shop, and because labour is 35 percent cheaper than other shops." The business's Core Benefit Statement, "We Come To You," firmly communicates the benefit of using this service.

"It really is a win-win situation for everyone," says Turner. "The customer gets automotive service to their door, they save money and time, and I have realized my dreams of being my own boss."

The marketing for Mechanic To You® has been made easier by driving the van. "The van is a moving billboard," says Turner. "People see the van drive by, take down the phone number and website, then call. Or, when I am working on a neighbour's vehicle, other neighbours enquire about the service.

"What's most satisfying for me is having the ability to drive around town working on customers' vehicles and meeting new and interesting customers each day," says Turner.

This business model—of a mobile automotive repair business—has proven to be a winner. Now, Mechanic To You® Inc. is growing by offering franchises. With two new franchisees and more on the way, Mechanic To You® Inc. is a true Canadian success story of a bootstrap-begun business.[1]

Why did Mechanic To You® Inc. become a huge success story? The reasons are as varied and as complex as the entrepreneurial mind, but here are four major factors.

PASSION

Like most successful entrepreneurs, Matt Turner had passion—in his case, to pursue working on cars—and he turned his passion into a business. Never giving up, even with the challenges of obtaining a business licence, he acted on the belief that his new and innovative way to service vehicles as a mobile auto mechanic could create a truly competitive advantage.

OPPORTUNITY SEEKING

Matt Turner had the ability to recognize a market opportunity and do something about it. The opportunity Turner saw was that customers wanted the convenience of staying at home or their place of employment while a mechanic worked on their vehicle. Offering this flexibility was a huge benefit to customers since many preferred to have their cars fixed while going about their daily routine.

PERSISTENCE

Matt Turner was persistent. He never gave up. He wanted to pursue the dream of owning a business even though obstacles were placed in his way. But the challenges he faced made him a stronger and more determined entrepreneur. These characteristics helped him to sustain his goal of starting and growing a successful business.

BUSINESS PLAN

Matt Turner worked on a comprehensive business plan to start and operate his business. His success in business is attributed to the importance of the development of a comprehensive business plan. In this business plan, Turner worked out what kinds of licences and permits he needed to start the business. He also looked into how to market his business and to ensure that he gains enough customers to make the business profitable. He planned out how he was going to get parts delivered or picked up while working throughout the city of Ottawa. Finally, as well as projecting sales, costs, and profits, he worked out a financial plan to see how much money he needed to start his business. The comprehensive business plan was a key part of his success.

Your time is precious to you. You want to make sure you're achieving what you desire, while having fun, making money, and being the best person you can be. So, how do you do that?

Many Canadians, such as Matt Turner, do it by going into business for themselves. These people are **P**assionate, **O**pportunity seeking, and **P**ersistent. They have what we call "POP." Keep this simple acronym in mind. It will remind you of what you need to be successful when you take the plunge and start your business. Beyond having these qualities, successful business owners do research and have a comprehensive business plan showing exactly what they're going to do, how they're going to do it, when they're going to do it, and how their idea is going to translate into a benefit for them, their customers, and their investors.

Our vision is to help you navigate your entrepreneurial road to independent business and, like Matt Turner, take pride in and be content with that career decision.

BUILDING YOUR ROAD MAP

This book, with its Action Steps and Business Plan Building Blocks, can be your personal road map to success in small business. Beginning with Action Step 1, we will guide you through the bustling marketplace—through trends, target customers, and promotion; through shopping malls and hushed, grey bank buildings; through franchise opportunities and independent businesses that are for sale—all the way to your new venture.

Along the way, you will meet people and have fun. Furthermore, by completing the Action Steps and Building Blocks, you'll be drawing a customized road map (Figure 1.1) for your small-business success. The Action Steps will give you direction, and the Building Blocks will provide the foundation. The complete business plan you develop will clearly evaluate and illuminate your opportunity for entrepreneurial success.

Figure 1.1 Entrepreneurial Road Map

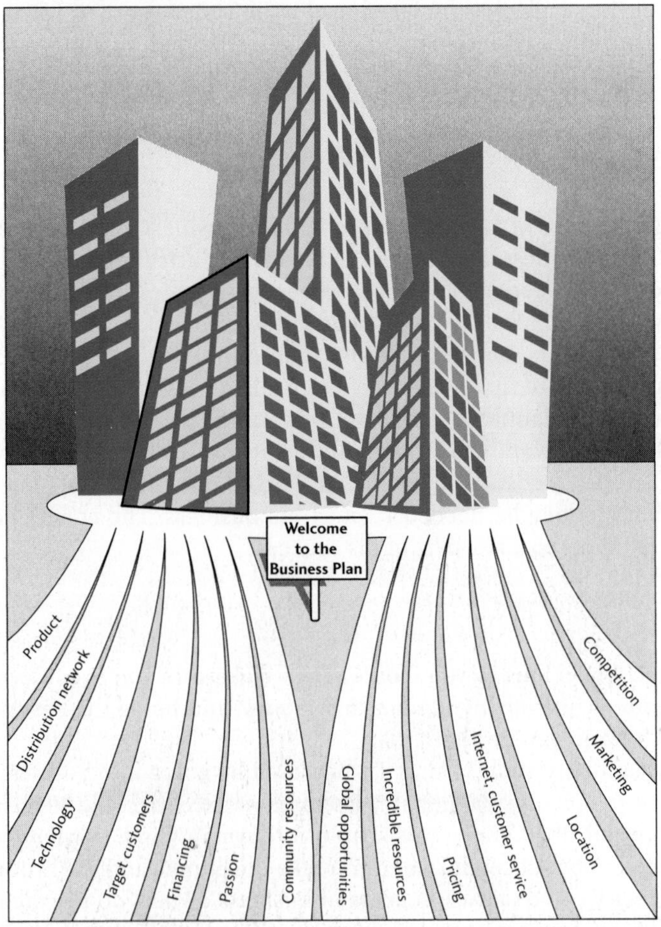

This road map displays how the different chapters and action steps in this book lead to the overall development of a business plan.

You'll begin your journey by taking a careful look at yourself and your skills. What kind of work pleases you? What internal drive makes you believe that you are an entrepreneur? What do you value? What do you like to work with? Whom do you like to work with?

Next, you'll step back and look at the marketplace. What's hot? What's cooling down? What's going to last? Where are long lines forming? What are people buying? What are they not buying? What distinguishes the up-and-comers from the down-and-outers?

Once you've got all of this information, you'll position yourself to take advantage of market opportunities. We'll encourage you to brainstorm a business that will fit into an industry niche, toss around numbers to get a feel for how they turn into money, and keep having fun.

Next, you'll need to profile your target customer; assess the competition; figure out clever promotional, pricing, and distributional strategies; and scout out possible locations. We'll be continually emphasizing the need to research your industry, marketplace, target customers, competition, and so on. Then, we'll encourage you to do more research and chart your business future with numbers, address your legal concerns, and form a winning team.

Along the way, we'll investigate three major doorways to small business ownership: buying an ongoing business, franchising, and—our favourite—starting a new business from scratch. By the time you reach Chapter 15, you will have gathered enough material to write a complete business plan for showcasing your business to the world—that is, to bankers, vendors and lenders, venture capitalists, credit managers, key employees, and your family and friends.

But first things first. We are convinced that, without passion, you won't succeed. The reason: If you're not passionate about your business, you'll have trouble coping with 10- to 14-hour workdays, few vacations, stress and tension, employee problems, misplaced cash, bank loan turndowns, and countless other frustrations. Throughout the text, we have profiled many entrepreneurs who, like Matt Turner (in the opening vignette), are passionate about what they do. We urge you to read their stories and learn from their experiences. That's why we've provided a case study at the end of each chapter. We encourage you to work through these studies. We want you to believe in yourself and fuel the passions that will help you achieve entrepreneurial success.

It might take you a few years to get your business off the ground, so now is the time to get started. To get your creative juices flowing, go to Box 1.1 and visit some of our favourite websites. Meet others who, like you, have decided to investigate the entrepreneurial option.

In this first chapter, we will help you begin to address these types of questions and explore your options. We hope that you'll share our passion for independence and decide to start your own business. But we know that, if you travel this

Matt Turner, Mechanic To You

entrepreneurial route, a business plan is a must, so we'll encourage you to begin looking at some plans. We'll also provide you with research tools to help you get started on your plan to join some 2.6 million Canadians who now own their own businesses.[2]

THE AGE OF THE ENTREPRENEUR

Welcome to the age of the entrepreneur. With the explosion of high technology, communication technology, and the Internet, it is now easier for people of entrepreneurial spirit to become their own bosses. And with the Internet as a key place to start and promote your own business, it is now commonplace to see entrepreneurs source their products from China, have Vietnamese programmers code their e-commerce site, use virtual assistants from India to take orders, use Skype to talk to customers from Europe, and use social media tools such as Twitter and YouTube to promote their business.

But even as technology and communications tools make it easier to be an entrepreneur, the global recession of 2008 has made people realize that their secure "jobs" aren't as secure as they once thought. Suddenly, being an entrepreneur is not viewed as a luxury, but as a necessity. Because of either economic necessity or the technology and communications tools available, many people have taken an interest in being an entrepreneur.

And Canadian entrepreneurs are leading the way! World-class companies such as Yahoo!, eBay, Research In Motion, Sierra Wireless, and Red Hat were all founded or cofounded by Canadians. In fact, Canada is an entrepreneurial hotbed. We have twice the percentage of self-employed people than the United States. According to *The World Competitiveness Yearbook 2012*, Canada has the sixth most competitive economy in the world.[3]

If you're thinking about controlling your destiny and starting a business, you're not alone. Almost 45 percent of Canadians who want to start a business are motivated by the desire to seize an opportunity as the economy recovers from the recession. According to the report *Canadian Entrepreneurship Status 2010*, Canada is undergoing an entrepreneurial revival that has been triggered by the economic crisis that broke in 2008 and the recovery happening in 2012.[4] The report, presented by the Business Development Bank of Canada and prepared by the Fondation de l'entrepreneurship, concluded that, in short, entrepreneurship is a good way to get richer in Canada.[5] According to the study, there are more business owners who earn more than $80 thousand per year compared to people involved in other phases of the entrepreneurial process and the general population. But, even if you do become your own boss, will you be content with this decision? There are never any guarantees, of course, but according to one report, about 80 percent of entrepreneurs say that starting a business was the best decision they ever made.[6]

WHAT DO THE NUMBERS SAY?

- According to Statistics Canada's *Key Small Business Statistics—July 2012*, there are about 2.622 million self-employed persons in Canada, of whom about 35 percent are female and 65 percent male (see Table 1.1).
- During the past 15 years, the number of self-employed with a postsecondary education more than doubled. Currently, about 60 percent of self-employed Canadians have a postsecondary education (*CIBC World Markets*).[7]
- About one-third of our small business owners are *serial entrepreneurs*—they own or have owned more than one business (*CIBC World Markets*).[8]
- According to Statistics Canada's *Key Small Business Statistics—July 2012*, Ontario, at 889,621, has the most number of businesses registered (see Table 1.2).
- According to Table 1.3, 78.6 percent of the service producing sector is in the category of 0-4 employees.

Table 1.1 Total Number of Self-Employed Persons (Thousands) by Gender, Yearly, 2007–2011

Year and Quarter	Total Self-Employment	Self-Employment as % of Total Employment	Male Self-Employed	% of Self-Employed	Female Self-Employed	% of Self-Employed
2007	2615.0	15.5	1703.2	65	911.9	35
2008	2629.6	15.4	1719.7	65	909.9	35
2009	2,701.7	16.0	1,742.3	64	959.4	36
2010	2,669.8	15.7	1,736.3	65	933.5	35
2011	2,670.4	15.4	1,719.7	64	950.8	36

Source: Statistics Canada, *Labour Force Survey*, April 2012. http://www.ic.gc.ca/eic/site/061.nsf/eng/02724.html

Note: Figures for men and women may not add up to total due to rounding. Differences between these data and those published in previous versions of *Key Small Business Statistics* are due to revisions made to data from the *Labour Force Survey*.

Table 1.2 Total Number of Business Locations and Number of Locations Relative to Provincial/Territorial Population and Gross Domestic Product, December 2011

Provinces/Territories	Total	Indeterminate[1]	Employer Businesses	No. of Establishments per 1,000 Population	GDP per Business Establishment ($ thousands)
Newfoundland and Labrador	26,014	8,690	17,324	51	1,084
Prince Edward Island	10,359	4,384	5,975	71	484
Nova Scotia	53,933	23,397	30,536	57	674
New Brunswick	41,756	15,868	25,888	55	705
Quebec	494,673	250,183	244,490	62	646
Ontario	889,621	497,301	392,320	66	688
Manitoba	77,458	41,002	36,456	62	700
Saskatchewan	96,367	56,964	39,403	90	660
Alberta	340,027	187,484	152,543	89	775
British Columbia	368,879	195,290	173,589	80	551
Yukon Territory	2,955	1,298	1,657	85	788
Northwest Territories	2,465	924	1,541	57	1,905
Nunavut	816	232	584	24	2,151
Canada Total	**2,405,323**	**1,283,017**	**1,122,306**	**69**	**675**

Source: Statistics Canada, *Business Register*, December 2011; National Income and Expenditure Accounts 2010; Estimates of Population by Age and Gender for Canada, the Provinces and the Territories, Q1 2012. http://www.ic.gc.ca/eic/site/061.nsf/eng/02715.html

[1] The "Indeterminate" category consists of incorporated or unincorporated businesses that do not have a Canada Revenue Agency payroll deductions account. The workforce of such businesses may consist of contract workers, family members, and/or owners.

On average, small businesses accounted for about 27 percent of our gross domestic product in 2010—a key measure of economic production.[9]

SMALL BUSINESS ENTREPRENEURS

SMALL BUSINESS ENTREPRENEURS

Agents of change—doers who see a market need and satisfy that need by translating it into a successful business

Small business entrepreneurs are the fuel of our private enterprise system. They provide the competitive zeal; create jobs, new ventures, and opportunities for others; and improve our economic growth and social fibre. They are visionary self-starters who love the adventure of a new enterprise. They have chutzpah, providing a spirit of energy, initiative, and potential for progress. Above all, they are agents of change who are passionate, opportunity seeking, and persistent—doers who see a market need and satisfy that need by translating it into a successful business.

CHARACTERISTICS OF ENTREPRENEURS

Hundreds of research studies have sought to determine the common skills, personality, and behavioural traits of successful entrepreneurs. The simple deduction from all this research is that entrepreneurs cannot be cloned. They tend to defy stereotyping and broad-brush labelling. "I have seen people of the most diverse personalities and temperaments perform well in entrepreneurial challenges," concludes business guru Peter Drucker.[10]

Nevertheless, if generalizations must be made, we can say that most entrepreneurs display "POP" characteristics:[11]

- **Passion.** Entrepreneurs are driven by a compelling vision.
- **Opportunity seeking.** Entrepreneurs are idea generators with a great capacity to dream up and carry out projects. They see problems as opportunities for creative solutions.
- **Persistence.** Entrepreneurs don't give up easily when things look bleak.

OTHER IMPORTANT CHARACTERISTICS OF ENTREPRENEURS

- **Vision.** Successful entrepreneurs have learned to visualize. They have a complete mental picture of where they and their ideas are going. Steve Jobs, cofounder of Apple Inc., is an example of a visionary entrepreneur. Apple Inc. was founded on April 1, 1976, after Jobs and Steve Wozniak saw the computer revolution starting.
- **Goals.** Entrepreneurs set short- and long-term goals, and many successful entrepreneurs strive to achieve them. Goal setting is important as it enables them to "keep score" on how they are doing relative to the goals set.
- **Independence.** Entrepreneurs have a need for freedom—a need to control their destiny and "be their own boss." For Matt Turner, this was the driving force to turn to entrepreneurship.
- **Idea generators.** No matter where they are or what they are doing, entrepreneurs see opportunities everywhere. As a result, they continuously generate ideas, and this ability to spot and create opportunities will help entrepreneurs on their journey to success.
- **People orientation.** Entrepreneurs are not loners. They have to like people—after all, people drive business. Arlene Dickenson, owner of Venture Communications and a Dragon on CBC's *Dragons' Den,* says that she attributes much of her success to the key people around her.

Table 1.3 Number of Private Sector Employees by Industry and Size of Business Enterprise, 2011[1,2,3]

Industry (Ranked by Number of Employees in Small Businesses)	Size of Business Enterprise (No. of Employees)									
	0–4	5–19	20–49	50–99	Small (<100)	100–299	300–499	Medium 100–299	Large (500+)	Total
Percent in Service-Producing Sector	78.6	77.4	74.9	73.8	76.2	69.0	66.0	68.2	76.5	75.1
Percent in Goods-Producing Sector	21.4	22.6	25.1	26.2	23.8	31.0	34.0	31.8	23.5	24.9
Industry Aggregate Total	917,175	1,816,860	1,399,277	1,024,975	5,158,287	1,251,661	461,265	1,712,926	3,918,759	10,789,972

Source: Statistics Canada, Survey of Employment, Payrolls and Hours (SEPH), April 2012, and calculations by Industry Canada. Industry data are classified in accordance with the North American Industry Classification System (NAICS) at http://www.ic.gc.ca/eic/site/061.nsf/eng/02719.html.

Industries in the goods-producing sector account for 24.9 percent of total employment in the private sector and 23.8 percent of employment in small businesses.
[1] SEPH data exclude self-employed workers who are not on a payroll and employees in the following industries: agriculture, fishing and trapping, private household services, religious organizations, and military personnel of defence services. The data breaking down employment by size of firm also exclude unclassified industries.
[2] Besides data excluded from the SEPH, the data shown in this table also exclude employment in public administration, public utilities (water, sewage, and other systems), postal services, public transit, educational services, and institutional and other government-funded health-care services, but include employment in the CBC, private practices (physicians, dentists, and other health practitioners), and beer and liquor stores. A technical note on the separation of public and private sector employment is available upon request by contacting the Small Business Branch of Industry Canada at SBB-DGPE.
[3] By conventional Statistics Canada definition, the goods-producing sector consists of North American Industry Classification System (NAICS) codes 11 to 31–33, while NAICS codes 41 to 91 define the service-producing sector.

- **Desire to share.** As old-fashioned as it sounds, entrepreneurs believe in sharing. Many of them feel empowered by having their own business so they want to share this feeling with others.
- **Ability to get things done.** Entrepreneurs are doers and invariably identify their primary motivations as "seeing a need and acting on it." Finishing what has been started is a key characteristic of an entrepreneur.
- **Willingness to take moderate risks.** Successful business entrepreneurs are moderate risk takers. They gather as much information and support as possible before making a move. In this way, they build a safety net and decrease the amount of risk involved.
- **Enjoyment.** Successful entrepreneurs enjoy the work they do. They translate their enjoyment into a business. Richard Branson, in *Like a Virgin: Secrets They Don't Teach You at Business School,* tells entrepreneurs that, "if you don't enjoy it don't do it." He emphasizes the importance of enjoying the work because it can give passion and fuel to run the business.

Table 1.4 Typical Employee Thinking versus Master Entrepreneur® Thinking

Typical Employee Thinking	Master Entrepreneur® Thinking
How much do I get paid per hour?	How much profit do I make per sale?
I want job security.	I can count on myself to create my own security.
I need to …	I want to …
I get paid when I work.	I get paid when I create value.
I wish things were like it was before.	I have a guiding vision.
Thank God it's Friday.	It's Friday already?
I work hard for my money: "With my $500, I will purchase [an item]."	My money works hard for me: "With my $500, I will start a business that will purchase [my item]."
I'm looking for a job.	I'm looking for customers with unmet needs.
I need to learn the skills of a painter.	I need to hire a painter.
I need to stay on the boss's good side.	I'm my own boss!
Why?	Why not!
Not my department.	How can I solve the problem?
I don't like taking risks. That's why I'm an employee.	I like taking calculated risks where the downside is protected. Being employed is more riskier because your economic well-being is dependent on someone else.
I prefer the merry-go-round, it's a safe ride.	I prefer the rollercoaster—it's an exciting ride!
I stay in my comfort zone …	I expand my comfort zone.
I wish I would have …	I have no regrets!
My life is unfulfilled and uninspiring.	My life is fulfilling and inspiring.
I need money to make money.	I create money with no money.
I have doubts and no confidence.	I have courage & strength of character.

Source: Copyright © 2006, 2009 Chris Castillo

- **Focused on sales.** Nothing happens unless a sale is made. Sales pay the bills for a business and bring profit to the owner. Successful business entrepreneurs are focused on making sales because they are what makes the business world go round. Zig Ziglar, a sales and motivational guru, stressed the importance of sales. In a famous quotation on sales, he said, "Timid salesmen have skinny kids."
- **Hard working, smart working.** Successful entrepreneurs are hardworking people. Nothing comes easy. Working hard is part of the game. Entrepreneurs know that they need to work hard *and* work smart.
- **Competitive.** Entrepreneurs are competitive. They always strive to perform at their best and beat their competitors. This competitiveness drives many entrepreneurs to success. Many not only compete with others, but also compete with themselves. They constantly try to improve themselves against the goals they have set out to achieve.

In a groundbreaking PROFIT 100 study of successful Canadian business entrepreneurs, Rick Spence, editor of *PROFIT Magazine,* concluded that most of the above entrepreneurial traits represent behavioural characteristics, which can be learned.[12] A recent study and extensive survey by the CFIB (Canadian Federation of Independent Business) came to the same conclusion—"entrepreneurship styles are more learned than innate."[13] According to these two studies of successful growth firms, most entrepreneurs are *made,* not born. This is good news for the thousands of Canadians who don't think they have innate abilities to start a business on their own.

Some characteristics of an entrepreneur can be learned. According to http://www.masterentrepreneur.com, a Master Entrepreneur® is defined as a "world-class person of consummate personal and business skill." These skills include learning to spot and create opportunities, developing a high level of confidence, and committing to personal and business excellence. In addition to skill, having the right mindset is a key to success.

Table 1.4 shows the different mindset that exists between someone who is a typical employee and someone who is a Master Entrepreneur®.

REV UP

"If life is a tree, find the passion to play on the ends of the branches and beyond. That's our passion. It has kept my husband and me going and made us successful." So says Adrienne Armstrong, owner of Arbour Environmental Shoppe, a small business in Ottawa, Ontario, that keeps on growing.

Armstrong's business goal is to help others respect the earth with planet-friendly products—an idea that took shape in the late 1980s. "While studying in France, I saw many small stationery stores selling recycled paper. These were little stores with pride and strong ties to the environment. I felt at home in these businesses. Even back then, I knew where I belonged and what I wanted to do. I kept a diary. I called it my **24/7 Adventure Notebook.** I would wake up at night and mind map my ideas like crazy. I remember writing letters to a friend—now my husband and business partner—Sean. The idea of protecting the environment consumed me, and I could not wait to get started. Fortunately, I married a man who shared this same vision."

Adrienne and Sean spent months writing and fine-tuning their business plan. "That was our first road map, and we wanted to get it right," she recalls. "Today our plan has become fluid, almost alive. Every three

24/7 ADVENTURE NOTEBOOK

A storage place in which to organize your personal and business ideas months we revisit it. If we are on target, we celebrate. If we are drifting off course, we get to work and correct it. Over the years, our first plan has changed gradually as we discovered new opportunities, grew our business, and moved toward our planet-friendly vision."

Today, Arbour Environmental Shoppe is a successful retail outlet which has earned a host of environmental and community service awards. "I'm very proud of these awards," says Adrienne Armstrong. "They remind all of us at Arbour Environmental Shoppe that we are making a difference … We display all our achievements behind the cash desk for everyone to see. We call this our 'Eco Wall of Fame.'"[14]

ACTION STEP 1

Keep a 24/7 Adventure
Notebook. (p. 26)

If you're thinking about owning a business like Adrienne Armstrong does, come along with us! We'll help you accomplish your vision by showing you how to build a road map. But to decide which road to take, you'll have to do some research and define your personal goals.

You can start the process by getting organized. Some people believe that getting organized stifles creativity. "No way," says Armstrong. "My 24/7 Adventure Notebook was and still is the place where I can organize and channel my thoughts and get creative. As a matter of fact, I woke up one night thinking 'Why are we not on the Web?' In my New Ideas section, I started scribbling down all the things I'd need to do. It took a while; I even had to take a course at a local college. But we did it. Arbour Environmental Shoppe is now on the Web (http://www.arbourshop.com). E-commerce has given our small business tremendous global exposure and has resulted in new sales. Just over 20 percent of our retail sales are Internet generated."

Now it's your turn to get organized and start your creative juices flowing by completing Action Step 1.

WHY DO YOU WANT TO BE AN ENTREPRENEUR?

After racing for Canada in the Summer Olympics and winning 150 times worldwide, cyclist Louis Garneau realized it was time to do something else. He still had a passion for cycling, and so, using his experience in sports and interest in art as a basis, he started his own company.

As with most start-ups, the launch was modest. Garneau began with a sole proprietorship, working out of his father's garage. When the time was right, he moved out of the garage and incorporated. Today, the Louis Garneau Group (http://www.louisgarneau.com) is a multimillion-dollar company with six factories and more than 400 employees.[15]

Self-employment allowed Louis Garneau the freedom to pursue his interest in art and cycling. For Adrienne Armstrong, becoming a "planet-friendly" entrepreneur was a lifelong dream. Matt Turner, in the opening vignette, wanted to pursue his passion to be a mobile automotive mechanic. According to a CIBC survey, most small business owners (about 60 percent) consider themselves "lifestylers," whose primary reason for "opening up shop" was to do something they loved.[16] They value their independence and choose the small business career path to pursue their passion and interests—be it building bicycles, saving the planet, or servicing automobiles at the clients' convenience.

However, there might be all kinds of other motivations for taking the entrepreneurial plunge. Some of you will choose to become an entrepreneur because you want the potential to earn a huge income, build a legacy, or experience the thrill of developing an innovative service or product. We want you to begin thinking about your entrepreneurial motives. Completing Action Step 2 will help you do this.

Now we want you to try this line of thought: What do you want to be doing in the year 2015? in 2020? What's the best course of action for you right now? What might be the best business for you? What are your strengths? What skills will you need? What do you want out of life? What are your dreams? Most of all, what are your passions?

WHAT DOES IT TAKE TO BE AN ENTREPRENEUR?

As we found out earlier, entrepreneurs cannot be cloned or replicated. Even so, certain characteristics are associated with entrepreneurial success. Action Step 3 (see page 15) will help you discover whether you have what it takes to make it in small business. Remember, though, entrepreneurs are made, not born, so if you find that you are lacking in the skills department, you can always make a plan to learn and gain more experience.

To discover more about your personality profile, complete the short questionnaire in the E-Exercise, Box 1.1. Once you've done so, assess what you've learned about yourself. File the results of this E-Exercise in your 24/7 Adventure Notebook. As you work your way through these exercises, remember that you won't be a perfect entrepreneurial (or "E") fit—there's no such thing.

Now, armed with this self-knowledge, you are ready to try your hand at Action Step 4 (see page 17).

ACTION STEP 2

Find out why you want to be an entrepreneur. (p. 26)

Box 1.1   E-Exercise

Do you have a "Type-Entrepreneurial" personality?

If you're thinking about starting a business, online self-assessments are a great place to test your entrepreneurial quotient. To learn more about yourself, check out the following Web pages.

- **Entrepreneurial self-assessment** (Business Development Bank of Canada [BDC]): http://www.bdc.ca/EN/advice_centre/benchmarking_tools/Pages/entrepreneurial_self_assessment.aspx#.UWGOSaCDTdk —A 50-question yes-or-no assessment will help you learn more about your personal background, behaviour patterns, and lifestyle factors.

- **Are you the entrepreneurial type?** (BDC): http://www.bdc.ca/EN/advice_centre/articles/Pages/inner_entrepreneur.aspx#.UL_oGIN_tLc —This article looks into the aptitude and skills that are common among entrepreneurial types.

- **Self-assessment** (Canadian Foundation for Economic Education): http://www.mvp.cfee.org/en/—Three online assessments help you to find out how you measure up and to learn where you have to improve and how you can build on your strengths.

- **Replacement Business Start-Up Quiz:** http://www.yesmontreal.ca/yes.php?section=entrepreneurship/tools/quiz—Are you ready for self-employment? Take the Youth Employment Services interactive entrepreneurship quiz to find out! Answer the questions honestly, then click "How'd I Do?" to find out whether you're ready to become an entrepreneur.

- **Take the TypeE Quiz:** http://www.typeepersonality.com/typeequiz.htm—Alex Giorgio is a practising psychotherapist and CEO/founder of The Giorgio Group. According to Giorgio, "TypeEs who are out of balance in their lives are often mislabelled as having a Type 'A' personality." Do you have a Type "E" personality? Take this simple 10-question assessment and find out.

WHAT IS A SOCIAL ENTREPRENEUR?

SOCIAL ENTREPRENEURS

Agents of social change; doers with innovative solutions to society's most pressing social challenges

Do you want to start a business that does social good? a business that provides innovative products and services for the betterment of people and the planet? Then maybe you want to be a social entrepreneur. **Social entrepreneurs** are similar to small business entrepreneurs in that they are agents of change. But in the case of social entrepreneurs, they are agents of social change. They are doers with innovative solutions to society's most pressing social challenges.

Social entrepreneurs start various businesses that do good for society. Some of the more famous social entrepreneurs include Muhammad Yunus (founder of Grameen Bank) who provided small loans (microcredit) to poor entrepreneurs who otherwise would not have qualified for traditional bank loans and Peter Dalglish (founder of Toronto-based Street Kids International) who teaches street children how to improve their lives.

Maybe you, too, want to be a social entrepreneur and start a nonprofit or charity organization that provides

- assistance to people with low income,
- awareness of environmental conditions in other parts of the world,
- unity and understanding of different religious beliefs.

Chapter 8 will discuss in more detail how to form a nonprofit organization or charity organization that will help you innovatively solve social challenges.

WHAT IS AN INTRAPRENEUR?

Let's assume that you've just graduated. You decide to put your plans for a small business on hold for a while and find employment with a large national firm. Better still, let's suppose you start your own business and your entrepreneurial venture takes off. A few years down the road, you find yourself heading up a 300-employee multinational firm. By now, your business has become established, and the growth rate begins to level off a little. For either of these situations, does that mean you are no longer an entrepreneur? Not at all. We are now fully entrenched in a "change" economy. To grow and compete, you will still have to foster entrepreneurship in a larger company—whether you own it or work for it. This process of making change in a large company is called "intrapreneurship."

INTRAPRENEURS

Agents of change who own or work in small, medium-sized, or large organizations

Intrapreneurs are agents of change who own or work in small, medium-sized, or large organizations. The skills intrapreneurs must acquire are a little different from entrepreneurial skills, but the prime objective stays the same. The main objective of an intrapreneur is to take a new idea and translate it into a profitable product or service. As an example, if you are an employee for a business, you might want to think about how your employer's business can benefit from a profitable business idea that you have. You could even suggest that you take the initiative and maybe start a business as a spinoff from your employer's business!

Managing and stimulating people to make change will be one of your major preoccupations. Here's a brief list of the sorts of things you'll be doing in your new intrapreneurial role:

- encouraging and rewarding individual and team risk taking,
- looking for opportunities arising out of failure,
- disseminating to everyone the vision and goals of your company,
- rewarding employees who make changes,
- encouraging brainstorming and new idea generation,
- empowering teams to make decisions and rewarding them when they do,
- encouraging teams to take ownership and work together as their own small business,

- encouraging employees to set goals and share their vision of company's future,
- encouraging employees to take ownership of their ideas,
- openly encouraging innovation and news ideas.

"INC." YOURSELF

So far, you have explored why you want to be an entrepreneur. You've reviewed your skills, accomplishments, and passions. It's now time to think about what success means to you. Think of yourself as a product you want to create. To help you think of yourself as a business—to "Inc." yourself, figuratively speaking—we will introduce you to a technique called "mind mapping." A **mind map**—also known as a spoke diagram, a thought web, or a cluster diagram—is a sketch that features circled words connected by lines to form units. Mind mapping is a form of doodling, only it has a purpose—to generate ideas. It works like this:

1. In the centre of a page, you write your main theme (e.g., your vision or goal), then draw a circle around the word.
2. Every time you get an idea related to your main theme, you write it down, circle it, and draw a line connecting it to the theme.
3. You keep adding new ideas to your mind map. Before you know it, you have a gigantic spider web or an idea tree full of opportunities.

Most entrepreneurs do mind mapping naturally. Entrepreneurs are visionaries, and mind maps help them picture what they want to become. A mind map that might have been devised by Adrienne Armstrong, owner of Arbour Environmental, is presented in Figure 1.2. To create your own mind map, along with a success checklist, go to Action Step 5. Once you have completed the first five Action Steps, you will be ready to enter the small business arena of entrepreneurism—the engine of our economy.

MIND MAP

An idea-generating sketch—also known as a spoke diagram, a thought web, or a cluster diagram—that features circled words connected by lines to form units

ACTION STEP 3

Assess your interest and abilities. (p. 27)

WHAT IS A SMALL BUSINESS?

If entrepreneurs are the fuel or driving force of the third millennium, **small business** is the engine. About 15 percent of our labour force is self-employed—that is, they earn an income directly from their own business as opposed to a salary or wage from an employer. According to Statistics Canada, about 135,000 new corporations are established each year.[17] Statistics Canada's July 2012 *Business Register* reports that there are about 1,112,306 million employer businesses in Canada; about 55 percent of these firms have 1 to 4 employees, and most of these small businesses provide services.[18] For example, the service-producing sector houses almost 80 percent of all micro businesses.

So exactly what is a small business? Do you define a business as small by the number of employees? Are small businesses those that are run by people classified as "self-employed"? Strange as it might seem, there is no standard Canadian definition. Most Canadian institutions define small businesses in terms of their particular needs, such as financing or exporting. Here are four interpretations.

- According to Industry Canada, a small business is any firm with fewer than 100 paid employees in the goods-producing or manufacturing sector and fewer than 50 paid employees in service-producing firms.[19]
- The Canadian Bankers' Association classifies a business as "small" if it qualifies for a loan authorization of less than $250,000.[20]

SMALL BUSINESS

Any venture with spirit, any business you want to start, or any idea you want to bring into the marketplace

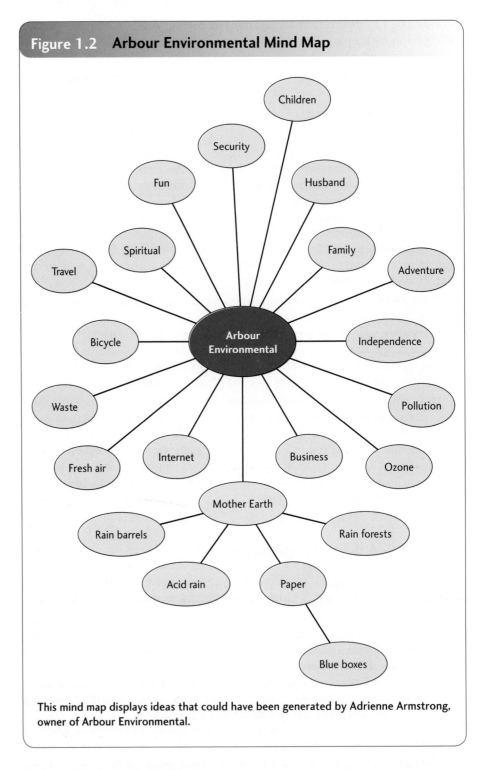

Figure 1.2 Arbour Environmental Mind Map

This mind map displays ideas that could have been generated by Adrienne Armstrong, owner of Arbour Environmental.

- The *Canada Small Business Financing Act,* which pertains to one federal government small business program, defines an eligible small business as one that has annual revenue of less than $5 million.[21]

Over the past few years, we have begun hearing about **micro businesses** and **SMEs (small and medium-sized enterprises).** According to Industry Canada, micro enterprises are most often defined as businesses with fewer than five employees, and the term *SME* normally refers to businesses with fewer than 500 employees. Firms with 500 or more employees are classified as "large" businesses.[22]

> **Box 1.2   Business Plan Outline**
>
> When you start a business, you are wise to create a business plan. Your plan should contain the following broad components:
>
> - Cover Sheet
> - Table of Contents
> - Executive Summary
> - Description of the Business
> - The Product or Service
> - The Market and the Target Customer
> - The Competition
> - Marketing Strategy
> - Location
> - Management and Form of Ownership
> - Personnel
> - Financial Section
> - Projected Cash Flow (monthly, first year)
> - Projected Income Statement
> - Projected Balance Sheet

As for defining *small business*, we tend to like the rather open definition provided by the BC Chamber of Commerce, which describes a small business as "a firm which is owner-managed and/or operated by an entrepreneur and is not dominant in its field of endeavour."[23] A typical small business owner, then, would employ anywhere from 1 to 20 employees. This description applies to at least 85 percent of all businesses in Canada today.[24]

The small business we are talking about in this book is any venture with spirit, any business you want to start, or any idea you want to bring into the marketplace. It might be part-time, something you do at home, something you try alone, or something you need a team for. The ideas for a small business are almost limitless.

GREEN BUSINESS

Businesses that are considered "green" provide an amazing business opportunity for entrepreneurs who are concerned about the environment and want to provide environmental change. Not only is this industry growing, but it is also a great way for entrepreneurs who care about the environment to become "green agents for change."

Green entrepreneurs are developing business products and services that provide the following solutions:

- solar heating, which provides a great way to cut energy costs;
- products made of recycled material, for example, recycled plastics or rubber materials;
- products that are eco-friendly—cleaning products among them;
- scooters and bikes, which are low-cost, low-emission transportation alternatives;
- green consulting, whereby companies are helped to adopt "green solutions."

ACTION STEP 4

Expand your self-assessment. (p. 27)

GreenIndex (http://greenindex.ca/) provides consumers with an easily searchable directory of green businesses in Canada.

THE DOWNSIDE TO BEING AN ENTREPRENEUR

Being an entrepreneur is not as glamorous as the media make it out to be. There are many stories of entrepreneurs becoming overnight successes and instant millionaires; however, the path to success is full of obstacles and challenges that people need to be aware of before embarking on an entrepreneurial journey. Knowing the downside to being an entrepreneur is just as important as understanding the upside to being an entrepreneur.

One downside to being an entrepreneur is the amount of hours put into building a business. The hours for business entrepreneurs are often long and sometimes lonely. For example, a study by the Canadian Federation of Independent Business (CFIB) found that 25 percent of small business owners worked more than 60 hours a week, and 30 percent worked 50 to 59 hours a week.

Another downside to being an entrepreneur is the amount of vacation time taken. Only half of the small business owners surveyed had taken a one-week vacation more than twice in the previous three years. And because entrepreneurs are focused on building a successful business, there isn't much time for family and friends either. About 90 percent said that running a business was stressful.[25]

Despite the downside of long hours and stress, however, entrepreneurs appear to be a happy lot. A 2009 CIFB report shows that people who own their own businesses enjoy the highest levels of life satisfaction.[26]

YOUR CHANCES OF SUCCESS

Do some small businesses fail? Of course they do—just like some students fail a course. Failure is a part of life. In the first part of this decade, about 8,000 bankruptcies occurred in Canada every year. We should note, however, that this number is relatively small considering the number of businesses.[27]

Studies have shown that slightly more than 85 percent of small businesses survive their first year. The rates then decline as each year goes by, with 70 percent of small businesses surviving year two, 62 percent surviving year three, and 51 percent surviving for five years. What allowed these small businesses to survive at least five years? They were able to sustain a competitive advantage in their respective markets.[28]

The cold, hard fact is your idea might flop. That's why we want you to work through the chapters of this book. If you do your research and prove your business idea on paper first—in your business plan—there's a good chance you'll beat the odds and be successful.

BEAT THE ODDS—WRITE A BUSINESS PLAN

ACTION STEP 5

"Inc." yourself. (p. 28)

The average small business does not make it past the six-year barrier. But successful companies such as Mechanic To You®, featured in our opening vignette; Arbour Environmental, described above; and many more exciting companies highlighted in this book have beaten the odds. They have jumped beyond the average survival rate. A major reason? In each case, they have armed themselves with a comprehensive business plan and followed their plan with passion and persistence.

Entering the world of small business and surviving demands a carefully designed **business plan**—words and numbers on paper that will guide you through the gaps, the competition, the bureaucracies, the products, and the services. A business plan is a written summary of your business goals, what resources you need, and how you intend to organize these resources to meet your personal and business objectives. It's the road map for operating your business start-up and for measuring progress. Your finished business plan will provide an overview of your industry, attract potential investors, demonstrate your competence as a thoughtful planner, and serve as a means of channelling your creative energies.

BUSINESS PLAN

A blueprint or road map for operating your business start-up and measuring progress

CREATING A BUSINESS PLAN—WHY BOTHER?

By the time you reach Chapter 15, you will have gathered enough material to write a personal business plan that will showcase your business to the real world. Your completed plan will be a blueprint for your business, whether it's a start-up or an expansion. Here are a few other reasons a business plan is important:

- **It lays out goals.** A written business plan provides an orderly statement of goals for ready reference at all times. It clarifies what you want to achieve and helps you work toward these goals.
- **It provides an organizing tool.** A plan, when completed, will provide you with the guidance to manage your business and keep it on track. It will help you discover the types and skills of the employees you'll need.
- **It acts as a financial guide.** You'll know before you start your business how much money you'll need and how much you're going to earn.
- **It will help you obtain advice.** A plan will help you find your board of advisors or directors. It will also provide you with a structure and format to get advice from your bankers and other outside advisors.
- **It will help you secure investment.** A well-written plan will help you get much-needed start-up capital. It will also help you obtain financing from other sources, such as credit from your suppliers.

WHAT DOES A PLAN LOOK LIKE?

The particular format and content of a plan will depend on a number of factors, such as the kind of business you want to start, how much time and patience you have, and who's going to be involved with your business—that is, your target customer. If you're planning to go into business alone, or if you're in a hurry or can afford to lose a small investment, you might want to consider a fast-start plan (See Box 1.3). If, on the other hand, you have some time to think about it and other people (such as bankers, investors, and advisors) are involved with your business, you will very likely have to write a comprehensive plan like the one shown in Chapter 15. Our template for this kind of detailed plan is provided in Box 1.2 on page 17.

Although we've provided you with one particular format—one that has worked for us over the past 10 years or so—there are all kinds of business plan variations. For example, the major chartered banks and accounting firms provide their version of a business plan to their customers. To find a format that suits your particular needs, check out the Web pages listed in Box 1.3. We'll add to this list in Chapter 15.

> ### Box 1.3   Business Plan Resources
>
> The following online resources will help you prepare your business plan:
>
> - BDC (Business Development Bank) Business Plan Templates http://www.bdc. ca/en/advice_centre/tools/business_plan/pages/default.aspx—The business plan templates contain two sections: a word section and a financial section. A glossary and a user guide are included to help you along the way. Sample plans are also provided.
> - Canada Business Plan Network. Government of Canada, http://www.canada-business.ca/eng/page/2865/
> - RBC Royal Bank Business Planning Resources http://www.rbcroyalbank.com/ sme/create-plan.html
> - About.com Business Plan Online: The Writing of a Business Plan Series http:// sbinfocanada.about.com/cs/businessplans/a/bizplanoutline.htm
> - Fast-Start Business Plan: http://www.nelson.com/knowlescastillo7e

Now it's time to talk about research.

BEAT THE ODDS—DO YOUR RESEARCH

To discover the right opportunity for you, you will need plenty of market research. Research opens doors to knowledge. There are three approaches to research—primary, new eyes, and secondary. Which is the most important type of research? They are all important. You'll need a combination of the three to make it big in small business.

PRIMARY RESEARCH

PRIMARY RESEARCH

Interacting with the world directly by talking to people (networking)

Primary research is carried out by interacting with the world directly or by talking to people, perhaps interviewing them. Primary research also includes talking to people "virtually," over the Internet. Some entrepreneurs refer to primary research as networking (see Chapter 6). You might ask small business owners questions like these: Where were you when the entrepreneurial bug bit? Whom do you bank with? How did you choose your lawyer? your accountant? Knowing what you know today, what would you do if you started up tomorrow? You might also ask customers questions, for example: Is there something we don't carry that you need? How else can we be of help to you? How did you learn about our business? Vendors and suppliers may be asked questions like these: What advertising works best in a business like ours? What products are hot? What services are being offered?

Throughout this text, we'll be encouraging you to practise your primary research skills because this is how most entrepreneurs stay informed and keep on top of their business. Action Step 6 will help you get started.

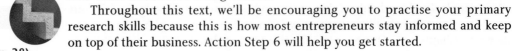

ACTION STEP 6

Interview entrepreneurs. (p. 28)

NEW-EYES RESEARCH

NEW-EYES RESEARCH

Using your intuition and powers of observation to learn about the marketplace

New-eyes research provides a variety of fresh ways of looking at a business. In carrying out this type of research, you use your intuition and observation skills to learn about the marketplace. Many successful entrepreneurs continuously conduct new-eyes research. Some of the successful entrepreneurs we have met over the years call it "sole" searching. They put on a good pair of shoes and go out into the marketplace with an open mind, looking for opportunities. In the opening case study, Matt Turner used new-eyes research to examine the way automobiles are serviced. By thinking differently, he developed a unique way to service vehicles.

In new-eyes research, you might look at your industry—say, automotive shops, as was the case with Matt Turner—or play detective and become a "mystery shopper." When **target customers** appear, you observe them so that you can profile them later. You might stand in a supermarket and, trying not to look nosy, watch what people put in their shopping carts. For example:

Steak + Beer + Veggie tray + 12-pack of cola = Party time

Cereal + Dog food + Diapers + Baby food = Family with young children

New-eyes research is fun. By doing it along with using the Internet, studying books, magazines, trade journals, and publications such as *PROFIT* magazine, and talking to people, you'll be able to develop a credible and valuable business plan. Remember, however, the business plan can become your guide to success—or it might show you that your idea isn't worth any more of your time. That's why research is so important.

It's time to practise new-eyes research. Complete Action Step 7.

SECONDARY RESEARCH

When you read secondhand what someone else has discovered, you're carrying out **secondary research.** The Internet might be your main source of secondary information, or you could go to the library and look up "small business" in the Business Index. Locate and read magazine and newspaper articles that contain information you think will be helpful. Databases and information from trade associations are also good secondary sources of information. You'll find data on sales that will help you project how much money you can make in small business. Good techniques here will save you lots of footwork.

Now we're going to introduce you to some valuable secondary research sources that you can use for gathering hard data. You will very likely need some of this information as we head into Chapter 2.

HARD DATA

Newspapers

Study the local newspaper, starting with the classified and display ads. For a bigger picture, read *The Globe and Mail, the National Post,* or the business section of your local paper.

Magazines

The list of great magazine reads is almost endless—*PROFIT Magazine, Maclean's, Canadian Business, Inc., Success, Omni,* and so on. Remember to study the ads. They tell you what's hot and where the money is flowing. In Chapter 4, you'll read about Mina Cohen, who found a niche in the travel business. Her idea germinated from a great deal of soul-searching and reading *Equinox.* The point

TARGET CUSTOMERS

Customers with the highest probability of buying your product or service

ACTION STEP 7

Take your "new eyes" into the marketplace. (p. 29)

SECONDARY RESEARCH

Reading about someone else's primary research

is, keep reading with your new eyes. Look for articles on new trends, ideas, and opportunities.

Trade Journals

These are a valuable source once you know what industry and business you're in. Use your new business letterhead to write to trade associations and ask for key information on your industry, such as trends, sales, and projected growth of the industry. You can find these listed at your local library. You might also want to try, for example, Canada's Information Resource Centre, the *Encyclopedia of Associations*, or the *Gale Directory of Publications and Broadcast Media*, also available at most libraries.

Banks

Banks are in the business of lending money. Banks have economists, marketing experts, and individuals who evaluate, research, and write forecasts and reports about economic trends. Ask to see those reports. Most major banks also have a number of free publications and brochures on starting and operating a small business.

Planning Offices

Cities and regional municipalities employ planners to chart the future and plan for growth. Check the city and regional offices listings in the phone book to find out where these offices are. Ask for a copy of the profile on your city. For the best service, however, you'll need to visit the office, make friends with the staff, and be pleasant and patient.

Reports from Colleges, Universities, and Investment Firms

Many colleges and universities publish annual and semiannual reports on economic conditions in the province. You can probably get copies of these by writing to the university public relations office. Reports are also published by private institutions of higher learning with special interests in business.

Real Estate Firms

Large commercial and industrial real estate firms have access to developers' site research. The more specific you can be on what you want to know, the easier it will be for them to help you. Familiarize yourself with the dynamics of the area. What firms are going into business? What firms are leaving business? (For more details on this, see Chapter 7.) Real estate agents can also supply you with a listing of rental space in your community.

Business Development Bank of Canada (BDC)

BDC publishes all kinds of materials of interest to small business. It also provides a wide range of financial alternatives (see Chapter 10) and sponsors numerous seminars on small business. For information, call or visit your nearest BDC office. You can also write to Business Development Bank of Canada, 5 Place Ville-Marie, Suite 400, Montréal, Quebec H3B 5E7; or visit the BDC website (http://www.bdc.ca).

Industry Canada

Industry Canada (http://www.ic.gc.ca/ic_wp-pa.htm) has specific federal responsibilities in the area of small business. Canada Business Network should be one of your first stops for small business information. There are 11—one located in each province and the Northwest Territories. Key activities of each Canada Business include toll-free telephone help; websites (see discussion below); resources and information, with in-person service, directories, publications, and access to external databases; a toll-free, fax on-demand service; and *Pathfinders*—brochures organized by topic, with overviews of services and programs.

Statistics Canada

Statistics Canada (http://www.statcan.gc.ca) produces a large volume and variety of statistics that are available to all Canadians. For most subjects, Statistics Canada will probably be one of your major sources of secondary information. How reliable is this information? *The Economist* asked a panel of experts from various countries to rank statistical agencies. All agreed that Canada has the best statistics in the world.

If you haven't used Statistics Canada before, you might find it overwhelming. Our advice is to persist—it's well worth the effort. You might want to start with its Catalogue No. 11-204, which provides a guide listing more than 1,000 reports and documents, as well as numerous electronic databases. (Check http://search.library.utoronto.ca/UTL/index?N=0&showDetail=first&Nr=p_catalog_code:1235759.)

Internet Sources and Computer Databases

The Internet has become a predominant source of secondary business information. There are hundreds of websites that can help you start and run your business. Here are some major sites.

- **Industry Canada:** http://www.ic.gc.ca/ic_wp-pa.htm—Industry Canada, in partnership with the business community and universities, has created the largest, most comprehensive business information website in Canada. It contains more than 75,000 reports, 600,000 pages of text, and two gigabytes of statistical data. You can also get updated information ranging from business diagnostic and benchmarking data to all of the government forms you need to incorporate.
- **Canadian Company Capabilities:** www.ic.gc.ca/eic/site/ccc-rec.nsf/eng/home—This database of more than 50,000 Canadian company profiles allows you to search for a firm by product, geography, or activity. You can also register your company and promote your products or services worldwide online.
- **Contact! The Canadian Management Network:** http://strategis.ic.gc.ca/sc_mangb/contact—This is the primary Canadian source on the Internet for business management information and advice. It gives access to a full range of small business support organizations in Canada and provides a

wide range of educational materials and tools to help entrepreneurs start a business.

- **Canadian Technology Network:** http://publications.gc.ca/site/eng/277174/publication.html —Here is a site that helps Canadian businesses find technological assistance. Advisors work with individual entrepreneurs to identify needs and to find the right source of assistance for almost every technology imaginable.
- **Business Development Bank of Canada (BDC):** http://www.bdc.ca— According to the BDC, this is a cyber-destination that small and medium-sized Canadian businesses can call their own. The website includes hundreds of links to small business resources, coast to coast.

Following are some other secondary research online sources.

- Canada's Information Resource Centre (CIRC): http://circ.greyhouse.ca/
- Nielsen (tracks retail store sales movement to consumers): http://www.nielsen.com/ca/en.html
- Canadian Company Capabilities: www.ic.gc.ca/eic/site/ccc-rec.nsf/eng/home
- Federal Corporations Data Online: https://www.ic.gc.ca/app/scr/cc/CorporationsCanada/fdrlCrpSrch.html?locale=en
- Industry Canada, Business Information by Sector: http://www.ic.gc.ca/eic/site/ic1.nsf/eng/h_00066.html?OpenDocument&%3fcategories=e_bis
- Industry Canada, Canadian Industry Statistics: http://www.ic.gc.ca/cis
- Trade Data Online: http://www.ic.gc.ca/tdo
- Canadian Importers Database: http://www.ic.gc.ca/cid
- Statistics Canada, Canadian International Merchandise Trade Database: http://www.statcan.gc.ca/trade-commerce/data-donnee-eng.htm

Now is a good time to start researching your chosen industry. Complete Action Step 8.

INNOVATION

A new idea, method, or device; the process of creating, changing, modifying, or improving a product, service, or business process with the purpose of creating value

INNOVATION—AN ENTREPRENEUR'S TOOL

One cannot talk about entrepreneurship without discussing **innovation**. Innovation is the act of creating change. It is an essential tool for entrepreneurs because they use innovation to make things better, different, and more effective. Innovation is used to create value; value is created when the lives of customers, employees, suppliers, and the community, as a whole, are improved in some way. In turn, customers might be willing to pay for this improvement if the value they receive from an innovation is worthy of exchange.

Successful entrepreneurs continuously look for better ways to satisfy their customers with improved quality, durability, service, and price offerings. They are always on the lookout for better ways. Sometimes, better products, services, and processes are produced intentionally but most of the time, unintentionally. In other words, improvements are made by accident or trial and error. To be innovative, you need to think in different ways. Ask yourself, can you make a product, service, or business process

- better?
- faster?
- cheaper?
- more convenient?

Although innovation involves risk taking, its results can be very rewarding. Obtaining answers to the questions above can result in a breakthrough for your business or in your industry, perhaps giving you a competitive advantage.

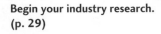

ACTION STEP 8

Begin your industry research. (p. 29)

In a Nutshell

It is the age of the entrepreneur. Small business owners are the fuel of our private enterprise system. Our goal in this book is to encourage you to join the ranks of some 2.6 million self-employed Canadians. To begin, we asked you to get organized by creating a 24/7 Adventure Notebook. Next, we advised you to test your entrepreneurial quotient. To help you find out whether you are prepared to live the life of an entrepreneur, we encouraged you to take a good hard look at your dreams and passions, your interests and abilities, your strengths and weaknesses. Ultimately, we want you to think of yourself as a future product—that is, to "Inc." yourself.

If you take the entrepreneurial highway, there can be wonderful personal and financial rewards. But you'll also pay a price. You'll work long hours and face your share of disappointments. Are you prepared to take this roller-coaster ride? Or do you need a 9-to-5 job and some semblance of security? We'll help you come to grips with these types of questions.

If you decide that becoming a small business entrepreneur is the right option for you, you'll need to develop a business plan that is backed up by primary, secondary, and new-eyes research. Your success as an entrepreneur cannot be guaranteed, but a business plan will improve your chances of success. This book will provide you with a business plan road map and the ideas and tools to succeed … but the research and the challenge are yours!

Key Terms

24/7 Adventure Notebook	secondary research
business plan	small business
innovation	small business entrepreneurs
intrapreneurs	SMEs (small and medium-sized
micro business	enterprises)
mind map	social entrepreneurs
new-eyes research	target customers
primary research	

Think Points for Success

✓ Change is accelerating everywhere, and that includes the world of business. Change creates problems. Problems are opportunities for entrepreneurs.
✓ To find the doorway into your own business, gather data and keep asking questions.
✓ Be creative on paper, organize your ideas, test your assumptions, and develop your business plan for the marketplace. Create and maintain a 24/7 Adventure Notebook and a Mind map. Confirm your venture with numbers and words before you enter the arena.
✓ Even though you might not be in business yet, you can intensify your focus by writing down your thoughts about the business you think you want to enter. Stay flexible.
✓ Be clear on who you are and what you want to become.
✓ Develop a business plan.
✓ Do your primary and new-eyes research. Get out and talk to people. That's the way most entrepreneurs learn.

✓ Do your secondary research.

✓ Always be on the lookout for opportunities.

✓ Above all, follow your passions.

Action Steps

ACTION STEP 1

Keep a 24/7 Adventure Notebook.

If you're a typical aspiring entrepreneur, you probably write 90 percent of your important data on the back of an envelope. That might have been fine in the past, but now that you're doing this for real, get yourself some kind of container, perhaps a shoebox, briefcase, or folder, to put those envelopes in. Even better, compile a 24/7 Adventure Notebook, ideally using something with pockets so that you can keep track of small items, such as brochures. You may wish to use a notebook computer or a personal digital assistant (PDA) like a mobile phone to organize data.

Your 24/7 Adventure Notebook should include

- 12-month calendar

- appointment calendar

- priority list of things you need to do

- your name, phone number, and email address—at the front, in case you leave it somewhere

- new ideas list, to which you can add ideas throughout your search

- mind map section to help you picture new opportunities

- new-eyes list for keeping track of successful—and not-so-successful—businesses you come across, as well as notes about the reasons for their success or failure

- list of possible team members: Who impresses you and why? What are their key attributes?

- list of possible experts to serve as resource people when you need them, a lawyer, an accountant, some bankers, and successful businesspeople among them

- articles and statistics that serve as supportive data

- list of helpful websites

- list of potential customers

ACTION STEP 2

Find out why you want to be an entrepreneur.

1. In your 24/7 Adventure Notebook, list all of your reasons for wanting to become an entrepreneur. Think about your personal and professional lifestyle, as well as your social, spiritual, financial, and ego needs.

2. Prioritize the items on your list. Spend a few minutes right away, and many more hours in the next few months, reviewing how several businesses would fit into your prioritized list. What fits? What doesn't?

3. If you have a job, review your current situation. Is your job secure? Are you happy or excited about going to work each day? Is there something else you'd rather be doing? If you didn't need the money, would you quit your job? As you explore various businesses, use these lists and questions to determine whether your selected business ideas meet your entrepreneurial focus and passion.

4. Make a list of all the reasons you do not want to become an entrepreneur—your roadblocks. Review the list and think about what you can do to minimize these obstacles. When you honestly review the advantages and disadvantages of being an entrepreneur, you'll discover they are the flip side of each other. For example, many people want to become entrepreneurs in order to be their own boss, only to discover that they will have many bosses—customers, suppliers, and investors!

Be as realistic as possible as you refine these lists during your exploration of different businesses.

ACTION STEP 3

Assess your interests and abilities.

Do you have what it takes to make it in small business? To find out, profile yourself as an entrepreneur. You won't be a perfect fit—no entrepreneur is. Nonetheless, you will get much more out of this book if you can picture yourself in the role of a successful entrepreneur. Keep your mind open and your pencil sharp. Opportunities are unlimited.

- How would your best friend describe you?
- How would your worst enemy describe you?
- How would you describe yourself?
- How much money do you need to survive for six months? for a year?
- How much money can you earn in your present position in three years? in five years?
- What is the maximum potential of your earning power?
- Are you comfortable taking moderate risks?
- Are you constantly looking for newer and better ways to do things?
- What can you do better than most people?
- Where do you live now? (Describe your home, residential area, geographical area, amenities, etc.)
- What changes would you like to make to any of the above?
- Do you enjoy being in control?
- How do you spend your leisure time?
- Do you look forward more often than backward?
- How important is winning to you?
- Do you know anyone whose strengths complement some of your weaknesses?

This Action Step will help you assess your abilities and interests, and get your creative juices flowing. Make sure that you file this information in your 24/7 Adventure Notebook. You will probably come back to this step several times.

ACTION STEP 4

Expand your self-assessment.

Use your information from Action Steps 2 and 3, and Box 1.1 to build on your self-assessment by compiling a list of

- things you love to do,
- skills you have acquired through the years,
- things you are good at,
- the times you were happiest in your life,
- your achievements and failures,
- your passions,
- your past dreams and dreams for the future.

In Action Step 5, you will be pulling together all your information. Keep your answers in a "Me" section of your 24/7 Adventure Notebook. Add new information whenever it occurs to you, and continue to refine your answers as you work on your business plan.

ACTION STEP 5

"Inc." yourself.

Mind map your way to a picture of what you want you to become, your product—yourself (see Figure 1.2). There is no such thing as a wrong idea or a wrong direction. So far, you have looked at why you want to be an entrepreneur and what success means to you. You have reviewed your skills, accomplishments, and passions. Now it's time to mind map the life you want.

Review your answers to Action Steps 2 through 4 and define success for yourself by reviewing the checklist below.

Success Checklist

Do you measure success in dollars? If so, how many?

Do you measure success in other ways? Examples of success might be

- being able to enjoy a certain lifestyle;
- dealing with friendly customers who appreciate your service;
- enjoying power, recognition, maybe even fame;
- being able to live and work where you want;
- providing employment and training for others;
- being the best business in your area;
- having time to enjoy your children and hobbies;
- participating in teamwork;
- building a legacy;
- retiring early;
- making people's lives safer and better; or
- helping others directly or indirectly.

Now draw a circle in the middle of a piece of paper. Write your name inside the circle. Close your eyes for a few minutes. Visualize and allow your imagination to take over. Think of yourself as a product. In 5 to 10 years, where and what do you want to be? What do you want your product—you—to be? What do you want—personally, socially, spiritually, financially, for your family and friends, as hobbies or lifestyle—and what are your material wants and needs? You can predict your future as well as anyone else can; all you need to do is mesh information with your imagination and go for it!

ACTION STEP 6

Interview entrepreneurs.

Successful entrepreneurs love to tell the story of how they made it. Interview at least three people who are self-employed. If possible, one of them should work in your area of interest. It's time to start practising your primary research or networking skills. More help on networking can be found in Chapter 6. You might want to take a look at that section before you begin.

Make appointments with your interviewees at times and places convenient to them. Taking notes during the interview is a good idea. If you want to record the interview instead, be sure to ask permission first.

Open-ended questions are best because they leave room for elaboration. Here are some suggestions to start you off:

- When did you decide to start your own business?
- What was your first step?
- Do you remember how you felt?
- If you were able to do it all over again, what would you do differently?

- How large a part does creativity play in your particular business?
- Are your rewards tangible or intangible?
- What was your best advertisement or promotion?
- What makes your business unique?
- How important is price in your business? Would a price war increase your customer base?

Think of these first interviewees as sources of marketplace experience. Depending on how you get along with them, you might be able to turn to one or more of these entrepreneurs for advice when you start to assemble your team—your lawyer, accountant, banker, and so on.

ACTION STEP 7

Take your "new eyes" into the marketplace.

Your community and workplace are your marketing labs. It's time for you to open your mind to all of the information around you. Time to head out!

First stop (large bookstore with lots of magazines): Select and read five distinctly different magazines that you've never read before. What did you learn? Did you read about a target market that you didn't know existed? Next, review the top 10 bestsellers: fiction, nonfiction, children's, trade, and paperbacks. What do they tell you about your current world? Any new genres?

Second stop (music store): What's hot? What's not? Are there any new music styles?

Third stop (local mall): What new stores are opening? Which department store has the best service? highest prices? best selection? Which restaurants are hot? Where are the longest lines?

Fourth stop (your favourite store): Compile a list of the products and services that weren't there a year ago (if you are visiting a computer store, shorten the time to three or six months). Can you guesstimate shelf velocity? What's hot?

Fifth stop (television time): Spend an hour watching CNN World Report. Make a list of the stories. Did any surprise you? Are there any opportunities?

Final stop (Internet): Log on and surf the Internet for at least two to four hours on topics you know nothing about.

Your brain should now be in high gear—and suffering from information overload! Use this information as you continue to explore opportunities.

ACTION STEP 8

Begin your industry research.

1. To locate the names of trade associations in your area of interest, consult the *Gale Encyclopedia of Business and Professional Associations* or visit Canada's Information Resource Centre online: http://circ.greyhouse.ca. Note the associations, addresses, phone numbers, and websites. Contact the associations that interest you and request information and membership details. Mention that you are a student—they might surprise you by providing you with information you hadn't thought to ask for. You can go further on this assignment by getting into contact with associations that your potential suppliers and customers might belong to.

2. Locate a chapter of a national association and attend a meeting as a guest.

3. Visit your local resource centre or link on to online sources such as http://www.people-searchpro.com/journalism/. Locate magazines or journals that are associated with your selected industry, that reach your potential customers, and that are directed at your suppliers. Spend some time on the Internet or at the library researching your list and delving more deeply into the information.

4. After completing your industry research, select at least one magazine or journal from each of the categories and request a media kit. The kits will help you fine-tune your research.

Business Plan Building Block

WHERE AM I NOW?

From the point of view of the potential readers of your business plan (bankers, loan officers, rich relatives, close friends with money, venture capital professionals), the most important part of the plan is you, the entrepreneur who wrote the plan.

Your goal, from the very first sentence on the very first page, is to inspire confidence. Before you write your business plan, study how you look from some of your old résumés. What picture do the résumés present? Who are you? Where have you been?

The résumé work is for your eyes only. Jot notes to yourself about strengths and weaknesses. To trigger your brain to perform this task, review the eight Action Steps in this chapter as you search for ways to transfer your skills and aptitudes to an entrepreneurial situation. If you already have a business up and running, use this same start-up energy to improve it.

No one is perfect. Recognize your shortcomings and make a list of people who have talents that you might lack. It's never too early to think about team building. With hard work and an honest look at your personal skills picture, you'll be able to fine-tune this information when you showcase your founding team in your final business plan.

WHERE AM I GOING?

Now that you've looked at the past and the present, think about where you are going. How do you see yourself in the future? How do you want to be known? Take a closer look at your personal goals. What are your likes and dislikes? Are you passionate about what you want to do? Are you ready to put in the long hours?

Checklist Questions and Actions to Develop Your Business Plan

Your Great Adventure—Exploring Your Options
Ask yourself ...

❏ Am I organized? Do I have a central deposit for all my ideas?

❏ Do I have what it takes to be an entrepreneur?

❏ Have I assessed my interests, abilities, and weaknesses as they relate to owning a business?

❏ Have I assessed my past accomplishments and shortcomings?

❏ Do I have a list and a plan of new skills that I will have to work on?

❏ Is my family or those I live with "on board"?

❏ Am I prepared to take the time and do the necessary research before writing a business plan?

❏ Have I interviewed entrepreneurs to see what it is really like to be in business for myself?

❏ Do I have any business ideas that I am passionate about?

Case Study: Mechanic To You®

We want you to go back and reread the Mechanic to You® story in the opening vignette. Matt Turner is a successful entrepreneur with POP—he is passionate, opportunity seeking, and persistent. Turner recognized a market need, satisfied it, and translated it into a financial benefit.

We can all learn from Turner's successful entrepreneurial experience. Take time to check out his website: http://www.mechanictoyou.ca.

Case Study Questions and Activities

1. Mind mapping

    Mind mapping is a great way to get and record ideas. Many entrepreneurs, such as Adrienne Armstrong of Arbour Environmental (Figure 1.2), mind map naturally. They are visionaries, and they think in pictures. But mind mapping is an entrepreneurial skill that can also be learned. In Action Step 5, we encouraged you to do a mind map of your future, or "what you want to become." We now want you to hone this skill further. Reread the opening vignette and review the Mechanic To You® website. Now, answer this question: Why do you think Matt Turner was so successful? Mind map your reasons.

2. Entrepreneurial skills

    Many people want to start a business, but to do so successfully, they require skills and characteristics discussed in this chapter.

    What entrepreneurial skills and character traits helped Matt Turner launch his successful business? To refresh your memory about entrepreneurial skills and characteristics, you might want to go back to "The Age of the Entrepreneur" on page 6 or link on to the CFIB report *Do You Have What It Takes?* at http://www.cfib.ca/research/reports/rr3000.pdf.

3. Roadblocks

    Along the way to success, Turner was challenged with barriers. Briefly describe how he overcame these major roadblocks.

4. Entrepreneurs as networkers

    As we learned in this chapter, entrepreneurs are not loners. They constantly learn and get help from others. Briefly explain the help that Turner received.

5. Innovation

    Innovation is often the result of asking questions of "what if" scenarios. Matt Turner and Chris Castillo asked, "What if we go to people's homes instead of them coming to an automotive shop?" Why was a mobile automotive shop such a brilliant innovation? What other services or products can Mechanic To You® offer? What other businesses do you think can also go mobile?

6. Business plan

    In this case study, start-up financing required a comprehensive business plan.
    a. What is a business plan?
    b. What is the purpose of a business plan?
    c. On which areas did Turner focus in his business plan?

Notes

1. Source: http://www.mechanictoyou.ca.
2. According to Statistics Canada's April 2009 *Labour Force Survey*, there are about 2.6 million self-employed persons in Canada, of whom about 35 percent are female and 65 percent male (see Table 1.1). See, for example, Industry Canada, *Key Small Business Statistics—July 2012*, http://www.ic.gc.ca/eic/site/061.nsf/eng/02715.html.
3. "The World Competitiveness Scoreboard 2012," *IMD World Competitiveness Yearbook 2012*, http://www.imd.org/research/publications/wcy/upload/scoreboard.pdf. See, for example, Industry Canada, *Key Small Business Statistics—July 2012*, http://www.ic.gc.ca/eic/site/061.nsf/eng/02715.html.
4. "Survey Reveals Post-recession Entrepreneurship Surge," *Globe and Mail.* http://m.theglobeandmail.com/report-on-business/small-business/sb-tools/sb-how-to/start-or-buy-a-business/survey-reveals-post-recession-entrepreneurship-surge/article642007/?service=mobile.

5. Business Development Bank of Canada, *Canadian Entrepreneurship Status 2010*, http://www.bdc.ca/Resources%20Manager/misc/CES_2010_EN%20Final.pdf.

6. http://www.enterprisetoronto.com/files/content/EA45B89F-1803-830F-D28FC2A784273467.pdf.

7. Ibid.

8. Ibid.

9. http://www.ic.gc.ca/eic/site/061.nsf/eng/02722.html.

10. Peter Drucker is quoted in Louis E. Boone, David L. Kurtz, and Ronald A. Knowles, *Business*, 1st Cdn. ed. (Toronto: Dryden, 1998), 113.

11. Canadian Federation of Independent Business (CFIB), *Do You Have What It Takes?* http://www.cfib.ca/research/reports/rr3000.pdf; Rick Spence, *Secrets of Success from Canada's Fastest-Growing Companies* (Toronto: John Wiley & Sons Canada, 1997), 228; and Human Resources Development Canada, *Entrepreneurial FAQ*, http://www.jobsetc.gc.ca/pieces.jsp%3bjsessionid= 151E8490E00EB696327E55363E41E29D.jvm7?category_id=372&lang=e.

12. Rick Spence, *Secrets of Success*.

13. CFIB, *Do You Have What It Takes?*

14. Networking interviews with Adrienne Armstrong, Arbour Environmental Shoppe, (http://www.arbourshop.com). Reprinted with permission of Adrienne Armstrong.

15. Louis Garneau Sports Inc.,http://www.louisgarneau.com/lang_select.php (accessed January 17, 2013).

16. CIBC World Markets, *For Love or Money? A Study of Entrepreneurship in Canada*, https://www.cibc.com/ca/pdf/entrepreneurship-study.pdf (accessed January 17, 2013).

17. Industry Canada, *How Many Businesses Are There in Canada?* http://www.ic.gc.ca/eic/site/061.nsf/eng/02715.html.

18. Industry Canada, "Table 2: Number of Business Establishments by Sector and Firm Size (Number of Employees), December 2011," *Key Small Business Statistics—July 2012*, http://www.ic.gc.ca/eic/site/061.nsf/eng/02715.html.

19. Industry Canada, "When Is a Business Small?," *Key Small Business Statistics—January 2009*, http://www.ic.gc.ca/eic/site/061.nsf/eng/02714.html.

20. http://www.cba.ca/en/media-room/50-backgrounders-on-banking-issues/124-small-and-medium-sized-enterprises#.

21. Industry Canada, "Small Business Financing Program," http://www.ic.gc.ca/eic/site/csbfp-pfpec.nsf/eng/Home.

22. Industry Canada, "When Is a Business Small?," *Key Small Business Statistics—January 2009*, http://www.ic.gc.ca/eic/site/061.nsf/eng/02714.html.

23. BC Chamber of Commerce, "Advocacy and Policy," http://www.bcce.bc.ca/myfiles/Policy_Development_Process.pdf.

24. Industry Canada, "Table 2: Number of Business Establishments by Sector and Firm Size (Number of Employees), July 2012," *Key Small Business Statistics—July 2012*, http://www.ic.gc.ca/eic/site/061.nsf/eng/02719.html.

25. CFIB, *Do You Have What It Takes?*, http://www.cfib.ca/research/reports/rr3000.pdf; Rick Spence, *Secrets of Success from Canada's Fastest-Growing Companies* (Toronto: John Wiley & Sons Canada, 1997), 228; and Human Resources Development Canada, *Entrepreneurial FAQ*, http://www.jobsetc.gc.ca/pieces.jsp%3bjsessionid= 151E8490E00EB696327E55363E41E29D.jvm7?category_id=372&lang=e.

26. Amelia DeMarco and Bradley George, "The Future of Atlantic Canada: Dealing with Demographic Drought," *CFIB Research*, October 2009, http://www.cfib-fcei.ca/cfib-documents/rr3092.pdf.

27. Industry Canada, *Key Small Business Statistics—July 2012*; see especially "How Long Do Small Businesses Survive?" and "How Many Businesses Appear and Disappear Each Year?" http://www.ic.gc.ca/eic/site/061.nsf/eng/02715.html.

28. Industry Canada, "How Long Do Small Businesses Survive?" *Key Small Business Statistics—July 2012*, http://www.ic.gc.ca/eic/site/061.nsf/eng/02717.html.

2 Spotting Trends and Opportunities

This chapter will help you prepare part A of your business plan, The Product or Service.

Minerva Studio/Shutterstock.com

LEARNING OPPORTUNITIES

After studying this chapter, you should be able to

- use mind mapping and brainstorming to discover business opportunities;
- identify trends and market signals that will create opportunities;
- discover market forces that underlie the trends;
- understand how to analyze the potential for small business success by applying the life-cycle yardstick to industries, products, services, and locations;
- use diagrams and mind maps to explore market segmentation;
- determine what business you're really in;
- begin describing your business.

ACTION STEP PREVIEW

9. Travel back in time and observe a marketplace of the past.
10. Explore the new technologies.
11. Discover how changes = trends = opportunities.
12. Compile a list of trends and opportunities.
13. Match trends with life-cycle stages.
14. Have some fun with segmentation and gap analysis.
15. Define your business, and begin to develop your "pitch."

SHOPIFY

Back in 2004, Tobias Lütke, a young entrepreneur from Ottawa, Ontario, had a problem. He was having trouble finding suitable e-commerce software to sell his snowboarding products. So Lütke decided to design a software product that would solve his problem and that he would like and want to use.

His product proved to be an improvement over e-commerce platforms available at that time. When other people saw his e-commerce software, they asked for permission to use it to sell their products online, too. Since people were asking him to use his software, Lütke figured that there might be a market for it. He decided to launch a company, Shopify, in 2006.

And now, Shopify is a Canadian tech success story.

Shopify Inc. provides an online e-commerce platform to individuals and companies that want to sell their products online but lack the technical expertise to design an e-commerce platform or are not satisfied with other e-commerce solutions in the marketplace.[1]

The creation of Shopify was a natural progression from trying to solve a problem. A firm believer in having a few advantages, Lütke understood technology and was able to solve a technical problem by including these advantages in order for him to improve something.

"Successful entrepreneurs are product-centric," says Lütke. "They have an innate distaste for products that offer poor solutions." Lütke attributes his success with Shopify to this characteristic. "Be always trying to find a better solution," he advises.

Lütke believes that "good companies begin and end with good products." "Just look at Jeff Bezos, who started Amazon, or Reed Hastings, co-founder of Netflix," Lütke says. "These guys created amazing businesses and understand how to make a company reinvent itself." He notes that they also had great product knowledge and strong leadership qualities.

Lütke's favourite quotation comes from George Bernard Shaw: "The reasonable man adapts himself to the world; the unreasonable one persists in trying to adapt the world to himself. Therefore all progress depends on the unreasonable man."

And because Tobias Lütke was "unreasonable," he developed an e-commerce solution that customers across the world are adopting. Given that Shopify has more than 150 employees serving over 40,000 customers in more than 90 countries, as well as having raised over $22 million in venture capital, the company Lütke founded is sure to expand further throughout the world.

Shopify exemplifies a good Canadian company that begins and ends with good products.

PACIFIC WESTERN

Back in the early 1990s, the Pacific Western Brewing Company closed its doors. This small brewery, located in Prince George, British Columbia, could not compete with the likes of Labatt and Molson. That's when Kazuko Komatsu, a seasoned businesswoman with 20 years of successful marketing, brewing, and exporting experience, came to the rescue. Komatsu bought the company and began by retraining the staff and improving the quality of the beer. By the mid-1990s, Pacific Western became the first brewery to achieve ISO 9002 certification from the International Organization for Standardization, the most respected quality assurance program in the world. Then, in the late 1990s, Pacific Western became the first Canadian brewery to produce a 100 percent–certified organic beer.

Today, Pacific Western (http://www.pwbrewing.net) produces 13 different types of beers to satisfy a diverse range of tastes and exports to markets, including China, Taiwan, Argentina, Brazil, Russia, France, and the United States; its beer is the third most popular imported beer in Japan, behind the giant Budweiser and Heineken brands. Pacific Western adheres to a few carefully chosen guiding principles: quality of ownership, quality of product, and quality of service.[2]

Successful entrepreneurs recognize market trends and resulting opportunities. Tobias Lütke saw the market opportunity for an e-commerce solution for online retailers. Kazuko Komatsu found a way to capitalize on the market need for quality beer. But remember: Tobias Lütke, for one, not only recognized an opportunity but also responded to it with passion and persistence. As we learned in Chapter 1, successful entrepreneurs have POP: they're **P**assionate, **O**pportunity seeking, and **P**ersistent.

Chapter 2 is designed to help you recognize emerging business trends and opportunities, so you can put your passion and persistence to work. We'll help you to brainstorm and to keep mind mapping and researching your ideas. We'll encourage you always to be on the lookout for emerging trends in exporting, technology, the Internet, changing demographics, and consumer values. After we have persuaded you to be a trend spotter, we'll introduce you to the life-cycle concept, segmentation, and gap analysis, all of which will help you to focus on specific industry opportunities. Then we'll encourage you to step back and refine your business idea.

RECOGNIZING OPPORTUNITIES

What are the best business ventures to pursue today? Where can you find a business that will really pay off? One that will make you rich? One that you will enjoy?

Only you can answer the question because the best business for you is one that you enjoy. The best business for you uses those experiences, skills, and aptitudes that are unique to you—as we learned from Matt Turner's experience in the opening vignette of Chapter 1 and Tobias Lütke's new venture at the beginning of this chapter. The early Action Steps in this book are designed to help you discover what is unique about you. Who are you? What are your skills? What excites you? What do you already know that distinguishes you from others?

Let's back up and see the big picture. Before the Industrial Revolution, most people were self-employed. In this agricultural, or first, wave, farmers and shepherds were risk takers, because they had to be. There were few other options. The second wave, or the industrial age, began with the Industrial Revolution and was characterized by machine power and mass production.

We are now firmly entrenched in the information wave. Some have termed these times the knowledge-based era. Others have even called this the mass customization era. We like to think about it as "the entrepreneurial age." These times, to a large extent, are marked by the growth of a new craft economy distinguished by quality; small, customized quantities; technology; and service. As in the first wave, working from home has again become both popular and common, as we will see in the Tanya Shaw Weeks story, below, and again in Chapter 7.

The existence of the mega corporation in the new millennium should be considered not a threat to the small entrepreneur but an opportunity. Many large corporations outsource many of their products and services to small businesses. **Outsourcing** refers to the contracting of outside specialists to perform functions that are or could be performed by company employees. This outsourcing trend will continue in the years ahead. Large companies know that outsourcing is a more efficient and effective way to do business. Therein lies opportunity for enterprising small business entrepreneurs who can aid companies in fulfilling key functions.

Let's pause for a moment and see how Tanya Shaw Weeks, of Halifax, Nova Scotia, took advantage of the outsourcing trend.[3] Shaw Weeks is a classic serial entrepreneur with POP who always knew that she wanted to start her own fashion business. At age 14, she was already sewing for her friends and earning a little spare cash. After graduating, she founded her first business, XZEL Designs, first sewing clothes in the basement of her parents' home and then moving the business into her own home. Eventually, Shaw Weeks moved XZEL Designs out of her house and into an industrial park. Today she is owner/partner in at least three interrelated businesses. Today, Unique Solutions (http://corporate.uniqueltd.com/about) is the parent company employing many employees—about half of whom work out of their homes across Canada. Some work on a contract basis; others are full-time employees. In recent years, Shaw Weeks's business has gone high-tech. The flagship product is the Me-Ality™ which takes an accurate set of body measurements in fewer than 10 minutes. It's like a dressing room in a store. The customer walks into a portable kiosk, and the scanner takes 40 body measurements using patented laser technology.

When one of the largest sewing pattern companies in the world—Butterick® and McCall's®—wanted customized patterns for each customer, it partnered with Unique Solutions. Unique Solutions became the customer service arm of Butterick® and McCall's®. It was a winning solution for everyone. In a single move, Shaw Weeks tapped heavily into the outsourcing trend and the massive U.S. market. With moves like this, it's no wonder that Tanya Shaw Weeks has won several national awards and become almost a legend in parts of Nova Scotia.

The exploding need for specialized products and services—from customized sewing patterns to flowers and beer—is mind boggling. You'll probably see as much change in the next 10 years as your parents have seen in their lifetime. Such change creates opportunities for fast, flexible, and focused firms such as Unique Solutions. If you stay in touch with change and the exploding market niches that change creates, you will always see more opportunities than you can pursue.

To help jump-start your mind, we want you to have fun and begin with some new-eyes research. It's a great way to find opportunities. Action Step 9 will help you get some new perspectives on change. As you work through this, and all our other Action Steps, allow yourself to dream. After reading this text or taking this class, you might not open a business immediately, but don't let this discourage you. By keeping an open mind and exercising your research skills, you will likely seize an incredible opportunity—just as Tobias Lütke (in the opening vignette) did and as the many students who have worked through this text over the past dozen years have done.

Now we want to introduce you to brainstorming—a powerful entrepreneurial technique for discovering opportunities that are right for you.

OUTSOURCING

Contracting outside specialists to perform functions that are or could be performed by company employees

---

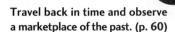

ACTION STEP 9

Travel back in time and observe a marketplace of the past. (p. 60)

BRAINSTORM YOUR WAY INTO SMALL BUSINESS

Pete and Geoff loved to snowboard. For seven years, they looked for opportunities to make a living from doing what they loved.

At a local college, Pete and Geoff discovered the technique of mind mapping—a method of note taking that involves using clusters and bubbles, letting the information float along its own course (see Chapter 1). They also learned a technique called "brainstorming"—an open exchange of ideas. The goal of brainstorming is to come up with as many ideas as possible related to a specific topic.

Now it was time for them to put their brainstorming skills into practice and record their ideas in a mind map. They just knew they could brainstorm and mind map their way into the snowboarding business!

Pete and Geoff gathered a few friends together, found a comfortable spot, and ordered some pizza. Soon, ideas began to flow. In the centre of a large sheet of paper, they wrote "snowboarding." In a bubble next to "snowboarding," they wrote "segments," which led to bubbles with the words "skateboarders," "teens," "families," and "adults."

"This is fun," Pete said, as the momentum built. "This smells like money and fun," Geoff added.

Pete, Geoff, and their friends kept on brainstorming, mind mapping, and eating pizza until they developed an idea for their business: Snowboard Express, which would provide roundtrip weekend bus transportation to various mountain ski resorts from five local pickup points. Pete and Geoff's completed mind map is shown in Figure 2.1.

The point of this example is to show what can result from **brainstorming**—a free and open exchange of ideas. If you gather people with wit, spark, creativity, positive attitudes, and good business sense, the synergy will almost always surprise you and could lead to new ideas, company growth, expanded profits, or perhaps the information for a new industry. The possibilities are limitless, but the trick is to structure brainstorming sessions in a way that maximizes creativity. A few suggestions follow.

BRAINSTORMING

A free and open exchange of ideas

1. Pick a Saturday, Sunday, or other day when everyone has some free time.
2. Find a site where you'll have few interruptions.
3. Invite 10 to 15 people (some will drop out, and you want to allow for no-shows).
4. Schedule the starting time at 9:00 a.m., serve coffee and doughnuts, and really begin at 9:30.
5. Allow time for self-introduction. Tell participants not to be modest. They're getting together with winners. Have them talk in terms of accomplishments.

Here are some tips.

- Have everyone arrive with a potential business idea.
- Before the close of the first meeting, select one or two hot ideas (take a vote), and ask participants to prepare a one-page checklist summary and analysis of the ideas.
- Get together again and brainstorm the hot ideas. Make it clear that the basic purpose is to spin ideas off one another, not to form a huge partnership.
- The best brainstorming sessions occur when you come brain-to-brain with other creative, positive people. Brain energy is real, and you need to keep tapping it.

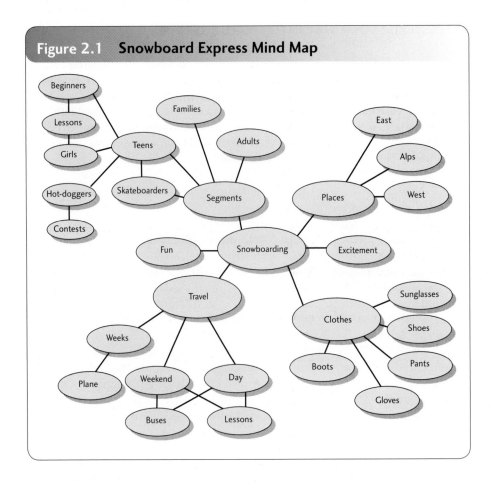

Figure 2.1   Snowboard Express Mind Map

Here are some things to remember when gathering participants and planning your meeting:

- Try to find imaginative people who can stretch their minds and who can set their competitive instincts aside for a while.
- Remember that in brainstorming sessions, there's a no-no on no's. You're not implementing yet, so don't let skepticism kill an idea.
- Find a neutral location.
- Try to focus on one problem or opportunity.
- Encourage the members of a group to reinforce and believe in one another.
- Use helpful equipment, such as an audio recorder and a flip chart. Don't forget to bring a supply of paper and pencils.

BE A TREND WATCHER

Industry or market trends reflect our economy's response to change. And change creates entrepreneurial opportunities. As an entrepreneur, you will want to make sure that your business serves a need. Knowledge of market trends will help you identify growth opportunities.

Major trends creating opportunities for enterprising entrepreneurs are shown in Box 2.1. Even more trends are provided in the E-Exercise, Box 2.2. Five of the most pervasive macro trends that Canadian small businesses must embrace are globalization, technology, the Internet and e-commerce, the boomer trend, and the splintering of the mass market. These trends deserve more attention—and that's where we're going next.

Box 2.1 Major Trends in the New Millennium

1. **The need to protect our environment.** Adrienne Armstrong, owner of Arbour Environmental Shoppe (Chapter 1), took advantage of this trend.
2. **Downsizing, de-layering, and outsourcing.** Large corporations will continue to shed their corporate fat. A "free agent" movement toward just-in-time employment will grow as large corporations subcontract and contract out everything they can.
3. **Alternative energy sources.** Solar power and fuel cells are two well-known examples.
4. **Media change.** The digital shift from broadcast (e.g., television) to interactive media (e.g., the Internet) will continue.
5. **Demographic changes.** As they prepare for retirement, those in the over-50 age group will assume a growing importance as they do everything in their power to push back the aging process.
6. **Democratization of information.** The Internet will gradually give both small businesses and individuals access to the same information available to large firms.
7. **Telecommuting and home-based business.** The number of people working out of their homes will continue to grow, increasing the presence of electronic cottages and freelancers.
8. **Cocooning.** Outside stresses will be reduced as people spend more leisure and work time at home.
9. **Poverty of time.** People will find it increasingly difficult to do it all.
10. **Home and Internet security.** There will be increased interest in home and Internet security.
11. **Globalization.** The world is becoming more connected through technology and the Internet.
12. **Dynamic partnering.** These partnerships extend up and down the supply chain. Some enterprising businesses are even partnering with their potential competition, as we will learn in Chapter 5.
13. **Increased interest in entrepreneurship.** According to a CIBC World Markets *In Focus* article, as of June 2012, more than half a million Canadians had started their own businesses. New businesses were mostly started in British Columbia, followed by Alberta and Saskatchewan. The fastest growth segment of the start-up market is the 50+ age group. Self-employment among immigrants has risen radically over the past two decades, with almost 20 percent of self-employed now being immigrants.[4]

Box 2.2 E-Exercise

Market Trends Create Opportunities

Interested in becoming more involved with our entrepreneurial community? Link to some of our favourite sites, and get started.

- Entrepreneurship (Atlantic Canada Opportunities Agency [ACOA]): http://www.acoa-apeca.gc.ca/Pages/welcome-bienvenue.aspx
- Looking for a business opportunity? Check out *From Ideas to Business Opportunities*, a workbook produced by Business Development Bank of Canada (BDC) and Atlantic Canada Opportunities Agency (ACOA): http://publications.gc.ca/collections/Collection/C89-4-25-1995E.pdf. Read Section IV, "The Big Picture, Part A: Some Market Trends to Watch." Complete this exercise by listing an opportunity for each of the 14 trends identified. What is the difference between a trend and a fad? What is meant by the term *trend tracking*?

GLOBALIZATION

Globalization is the process of international integration. Now, more than ever, we are becoming more integrated with, connected with, and interested in current events, products, and services from around the world.

Globalization is a macro trend that affects everyone. Why? Because we can see the effects of globalization in our local communities. We can now purchase products and services from around the world. Shipping companies such as FedEx and UPS deliver products around the world within days. What's more, we are becoming more interested in products and services from around the world. For example, we can see movies produced in India and China on our Netflix® accounts; or, we can stream the movies from our computers and connect them to our smart TVs.

Travel companies now offer vacation packages to exotic areas. As an example, the Adventure Travel Company, a Canadian company, works with travel partners from around the world to offer Canadians a choice of more than 12,000 tours in over 100 countries (http://www.atcadventure.com). It offers adventure travel because consumers now seek such experiences and the ability to discover and explore other cultures and ways of life.

Beyond more Canadians purchasing products and services from around the world, consumers in many other countries are demanding Canadian-made products and services. This demand has created a tremendous opportunity for Canadian entrepreneurs to export their products and services. Furthermore, with technology, being an international entrepreneur has become much easier.

In recent years, the export market accounted for about 40 percent of Canada's Gross Domestic Product (GDP).[5] Increasingly, "new breed" Canadian small businesses are seeking to participate in and benefit from this export trend (see Box 2.3).

Exporting was a key factor contributing to the success of Pacific Western Brewing Company, which found a way to capitalize on the fast-growing exporting trend. According to a 2009 *PROFIT* guide article, foreign markets accounted for an additional $13 billion in revenue for Canadian companies in 2009. On average, 73 of the 100 companies listed received 53 percent of their 2008 sales from outside Canada, up from 27 percent in 2003.[6] This finding is proof that foreign markets represent big opportunities for global-minded entrepreneurs! For winning companies, exporting is a growing trend.[7] We caution you, however, that competing in another country can be a lengthy challenge, as attested by most PROFIT 100 business owners. Maybe that's why only about 15 percent of all small businesses have been able to export their product or service. But those who persist and succeed are reaping rewards—Tanya Shaw Weeks of Unique Solutions Design among them. Exports to the United States now account for more than 90 percent of her sales.

Box 2.3 Exporting: Another Adventure Beckons

Get ready for opportunities in the global marketplace. We encourage you to think about exporting your product or service. Click on the book's website at http://www. www.nelson.com/knowlescastillo7e.

Learn how to choose an export strategy, develop an export plan, and sell your product across the world.

TECHNOLOGY

Technology is growing at a phenomenal rate and at mind-boggling speed.

What has been the core lead in this technological revolution has been the microchip. The microchip is empowering technology in every field from science to medicine to agriculture. Microchips are now common in veterinary medicine, and pacemaker implants are almost an everyday occurrence. In just a few short years, we've seen the development of powerful personal digital assistants, such as the iPhone™ or the BlackBerry®, e-books, and toxin testers. Many of us hardly know where our local bank is anymore. We bank online or at an ATM (automatic teller machine). And with many people using an iPhone™, connectivity to online banking and other services such as GPS—Global Positioning System—is now within touch.

These examples continually remind us that we remain deeply embedded in the technology revolution—one that will continue to change the way we live and work. Many of today's successful entrepreneurs are profiting from this trend. For Tanya Shaw Weeks of Unique Solutions Design, the creation of the Me-Ality™ was key to her success. But you don't necessarily have to invent a new product or technology. Many creative entrepreneurs have found a proven technology in one industry and put it to a different use in another industry. That's what Paul Schmitt did!

While touring a trade show in Las Vegas, Paul Schmitt discovered that the insurance industry was successfully using 360-degree digital imaging technology, and this ignited his passion.

What if this technology could be used in the real estate business to help people search for and view real estate properties? he thought. His new-eyes research paid off, and he launched his Manitoba-based Webview 360 (http://www.webview360.com/wv/). Webview 360 provides prospective purchasers with a virtual tour of real estate properties. With passion and persistence, Schmitt has grown Webview into a successful small business.

How will technology give you a competitive edge in your new business? Your new-eyes and primary research will help. We also suggest that you begin by locating "industry gurus." Read everything that they've written. These people make a business out of trend watching. Here's a short list to get you going:

- Don Tapscott: international authority, consultant, and speaker on business strategy and organizational transformation
- Nuala Beck: influential economist, researcher, author, and columnist
- Faith Popcorn: renowned consumer trend expert, industry advisor, and author
- Dr. David Foot: world-renowned demographics expert and professor of economics at the University of Toronto
- Martha Barletta: internationally recognized expert and consultant on successful marketing to women
- Watts Wacker: lecturer, bestselling author, political commentator, and social critic
- P.J. Wade: leading authority on retirement, housing, boomers, and the maturing marketplace

Action Step 10 asks you to do a Google™ search and explore new technologies in more depth.

ACTION STEP 10

Explore the new technologies.
(p. 60)

INTERNET AND E-COMMERCE

Matthew von Teichman is a shrewd entrepreneur who knows that market trends create opportunities. Having successfully owned and operated several small businesses in the food service and home decor industries, in addition to working as a marketing consultant for a major Canadian winery, von Teichman, along with other visionary partners, turned his attention to the Internet and the online recruiting trend. His company, JobShark Corporation (http://www.jobshark.ca/caeng/index.cfm), was recognized by *PROFIT* guide as one of the 50 fastest-growing Canadian companies. Furthermore, JobShark has pursued the lucrative international market by expanding its operations to England, Ireland, Mexico, Chile, Argentina, Brazil, Peru, Colombia, Mexico, and Venezuela.

The Internet is a ubiquitous part of Canadian life, business, and culture. Most Canadian households and businesses are connected to the Internet, and with the growing popularity of such social media sites as Twitter and Facebook, we are becoming more and more connected through technology and the Internet. As shown in Table 2.1, individuals using the Internet from any location were highest in British Columbia, followed by Alberta and Saskatchewan.

The question now facing the business community is how to profit from this connectivity. Tobias Lütke, for one, met this challenge. He knew that the number of transactions was increasing so he launched Shopify. Many people had asked him if they could use his unique e-commerce platform to sell their products online. Most Canadian businesses, especially small enterprises, have been slow to use the Internet for online sales, however.

The Internet can provide many more benefits than just online selling. It's more than a sales tool. Successful companies such as JobShark and Webview 360

Table 2.1 Individuals Using the Internet from Any Location, 2010

Location	% of Individuals
Canada	**80**
Newfoundland and Labrador	73
Prince Edward Island	75
Nova Scotia	79
New Brunswick	70
Quebec	76
Ontario	81
Manitoba	79
Saskatchewan	80
Alberta	84
British Columbia	86

Source: Statistics Canada, *The Daily*, October 12, 2011. Individual Internet use and E-Commerce, Table 1: Individuals using the Internet from any location, http://www.statcan.gc.ca/daily-quotidien/111012/t111012a1-eng.htm

Table 2.2 Electronic Commerce, Number and Value of Orders, 2010

	Value of Orders
Number of orders	
Total number (millions)	113.8
Average number per person	10.2
Value of orders	
Total value ($ billions)	15.3
Average value per person ($)	1,362

Source: Statistics Canada, *The Daily*, October 12, 2011. Individual Internet use and E-commerce, Table 2: Electronic commerce, number and value of orders, http://www.statcan.gc.ca/daily-quotidien/111012/t111012a2-eng.htm

are using **e-commerce** (or e-business) strategies. E-commerce is a catchall term that includes any business function or business process performed over electronic networks. In other words, suppliers, distributors, and customers use the Internet as the basis for their operations. E-commerce business functions include

- advertising, customer relationships, and after-sales service;
- management of supplies and internal operations;
- communication;
- payments and financial services;
- online collaboration;
- order management, distribution, and delivery.

In 2010, 80 percent of individuals who were at least 16 years old used the Internet for personal purposes. Residents of British Columbia and residents of Alberta accounted for the highest use rates at 86 percent and 84 percent, respectively. In the same year, 51 percent of Internet users ordered goods or services for personal or household use. Canadians placed 114 million orders for goods and services, valued at $15.3 billion[8] (see Table 2.2). This figure represents an increase from 2007's figure of $12.8 billion.[9] What were these Canadians ordering? According to Table 2.3, they were buying

- travel services;
- entertainment products such as concert tickets;
- books and magazines;
- clothing;
- jewellery and accessories.

If you want your new business to be successful, start thinking about your e-commerce strategy. According to Industry Canada, your plan should be composed of five stages.

Stage 1: Communicating—use email and Internet access
Even if your firm never goes any further than hooking up to the Internet, the effort would be worthwhile. Your staff will be able to communicate inexpensively and precisely with suppliers, customers, and others by email while creating instant records of the exchanges.

Stage 2: Promoting—create your own website
Even at its most basic, the Web is like a 21st-century Yellow Pages, used regularly by growing numbers of well-informed browsers with money to spend. Even if you

E-COMMERCE

Any business function or business process performed over electronic networks

Table 2.3 Electronic Commerce, Type of Products Ordered (% of Online Shoppers), 2010

Products Ordered	% of Online Shoppers
Travel arrangements (e.g., hotel reservations, travel tickets, rental cars)	55
Tickets for entertainment events (e.g., concerts, movies, sports)	48
Books, magazines, online newspapers	40
Clothing, jewellery, or accessories	36
Memberships or registration fees (e.g., health clubs, tuition, online television subscriptions)	32
Music (e.g., CDs, MP3)	30
Software	23
Consumer electronics (e.g., cameras, stereos, TVs, DVD players)	22
Videos or DVDs	20
Toys and games	19
Photographic services	16
Computer hardware	15
Gift certificates or gift cards	15
Other health or beauty products (e.g., vitamins, cosmetics)	12
Housewares (e.g., large appliances, furniture)	12
Sports equipment	11
Food or beverages (e.g., specialty foods or wine, pizza delivery)	11
Home improvement or gardening supplies (including tools)	7
Prescription drugs or products (e.g., glasses)	3
Other	13

Source: Statistics Canada, *The Daily*, October 12, 2011. Individual Internet use and E-Commerce, Table 4: Electronic commerce, types of products ordered (% of online shoppers), http://www.statcan.gc.ca/daily-quotidien/111012/t111012a1-eng.htm

don't take the next step and turn your website into an interactive forum or an order site, at the very least it can serve as a great place to show what you do.

Stage 3: Linking internally—communicate better within your firm

Using an intranet, you can improve company processes such as project management, payroll, human resources, purchase orders, and inventory. By sharing information, your team members can leverage one another's insights and efforts.

| Box 2.4 | **E-Commerce Revolution** |

Begin learning more about e-commerce by checking out these sites.

1. Planning for e-business: http://www.canadabusiness.ca/eng/145/148/4327/
2. Tips on Building an Effective Website: http://website-creation-software-review.toptenreviews.com/tips-on-building-an-effective-website.html
3. E-commerce—Exporting Your Options: http://www.canadabusiness.ab.ca/index.php/e-business/253-e-commerce-exploring-your-options
4. Federal E-Forms and E-Services: http://canada.gc.ca/forms-formulaires/e-services-eng.html

Doing Business on the Internet: http://www.canadabusiness.ab.ca/index.php/component/content/article/11-operations/92-doing-business-on-the-internet

Stage 4: Linking externally—bring in suppliers and customers
The really exciting payoff comes when a business uses the Internet to link with suppliers and customers (extranet). The Internet can serve both as an inexpensive way to increase sales and as a cost-effective way to link with suppliers. Firms that introduce internal systems that are open to suppliers and/or customers can orchestrate production and delivery to minimize delays, shrink inventories, and eliminate mistakes.

Stage 5: Creating new business models—share resources and risk with virtual business partners
The Internet has the potential to act as a central nervous system coordinating the business activities of new types of corporate organisms. Imagine setting up an arrangement whereby sales information is shared instantaneously with wholesalers, shippers, manufacturers, designers, and even suppliers of raw material. Suddenly you have an integrated supply chain. Administrative responsibilities and even marketplace risks can be shared.

Box 2.4 will help you learn more about e-commerce. At the very least, you'll need an e-mail account and Internet access (Stage 1) before you start your business. But we also want you to begin thinking about building a website (Stage 2), which will allow you to sell your products over the Internet. Fortunately, most college and university business programs include website development courses, so many of you have a head start.

THE BOOMER TREND

As of 2011, the **baby boomers** (those born between 1947 and 1966) accounted for 42.4 percent of the nation's working-age population which is the highest proportion of working people ever observed.[10] An excellent animated graphic of Canada's changing population structure can be found at Statistics Canada's website: http://www12.statcan.ca/census-recensement/2006/index-eng.cfm. The boomer trend is not unique to Canada, as boomers are getting set to retire in major countries across the world. We caution you, however, that each country has its own distinct boomer patterns. If your business plan is depending on American boomer information, we strongly suggest you back it up with Canadian demographic statistics (see Table 2.4).

The boomer trend is one that no self-respecting, opportunity-minded entrepreneur can ignore. Soon the front end of the boomer generation will be looking for things to do in their "new job": retirement. A **wave** of retirement will sweep

BABY BOOMERS

Those born between 1947 and 1966 (about 10 million Canadians, or about 30 percent of the total population)

Table 2.4 Canada's Changing Population Profile (Millions)

Age	2001	2011
0–4	1,924.3	1,980.1
5–9	2,082.2	2,016.6
10–14	2,124.8	2,104.8
15–19	2,124.5	2,259.2
20–24	2,115.2	2,332.3
25–29	2,177.7	2,392.8
30–34	2,366.4	2,416.1
35–39	2,723.4	2,443.0
40–44	2,716.3	2,544.5
45–49	2,399.6	2,801.9
50–54	2,140.1	2,722.0
55–59	1,651.4	2,362.2
60–64	1,300.9	2,063.6
65–69	1,154.0	1,544.5
70–74	1,027.1	1,142.5
75–79	831.9	906.1
80+	1,017.7	1,398.1
Total	31,877.3	35,420.3

Source: Statistics Canada, *Population Projections for Canada, Provinces and Territories, 1993–2016* (Catalogue 91-520, January 23, 1995).

across Canada and other major countries. Boomer retirement needs—many of which might not be obvious—will create all kinds of opportunities for enterprising entrepreneurs.

Real opportunities will be found by those who dig more deeply into this retirement wave. Tanya Shaw Weeks of Unique Solutions knew that home sewing was a fast-growing North American leisure activity of the aging female boomer market. When we did some of our own secondary research, we found out that education and healthcare will likely be two of the first industries to feel the retirement crunch and provide business opportunities. If you are looking for a new business idea, education and healthcare industry segments may be good places to start.

Catering to the needs of retiring boomers is only one opportunity. There are all kinds of opportunities resulting from this trend. As this segment ages, not only in Canada but also around the world, boomer needs will have a profound impact on sectors such as real estate, when boomers begin selling their homes; finance, as they begin cashing in their RRSPs; and healthcare, as boomers live longer and healthier lives. We encourage you to do your research. How can the boomer needs help you find a new profitable business?[11] How about considering the needs of the boomer children—the **echo boomers**, whom we describe next.

ECHO BOOMERS (MILLENNIALS, OR Y GENERATION)

Those born between 1980 and 1995 (about 6 million Canadians, or about 20 percent of the total population)

THE SPLINTERING OF THE MASS MARKET

Today's consumers are informed, individualistic, and demanding. Their buying habits are often difficult to isolate, because they tend to buy at several levels of the market. For instance, a materials management person might buy the office copier from Xerox but the paper from a discount office supply warehouse. Some high-fashion, high-income consumers patronize upscale boutiques yet buy their household appliances at discount outlets. They may even buy some clothing or accessories at the "GT" (Giant Tiger) boutique.

Understanding how the mass market is splintering is a key for the entrepreneur. Now more than ever, entrepreneurs need to be attuned to what consumers want. What are their buying habits and why do they make certain purchases? Knowing the answers will help us understand potential customers and thereby help them make purchases.

For the consumer, five key factors have splintered the mass market.

1. **A shrinking middle class.** There are more high-end, affluent consumers and an increasing number of consumers (for example, part-time workers, single parents, and contract workers) who live at or near the poverty level.

2. **Shifting sizes of age groups.** Each group has particular, well-defined needs. How about the echo boomers (or Y generation)—about 6 million Canadians born between 1980 and 1995 (approximately 20 percent of the total population)? They have been given many names: the Nintendo Generation, Generation Y, the Millennial or Digital Generation, and the one we like best: the Sunshine Generation. They smile on their cell phones and happily cruise and buy on the Internet with the same ease that their boomer parents accessed "dead wood" information such as magazines and newspapers. And what about the tweens—8- to 14-year-olds—or affluent over-80-year-olds? All of these changing segments have specific needs.

3. **Changing and evolving living arrangements.** These include stepfamilies, dual-career families, single parents, grandparents raising grandchildren, three-generation households, more adult children returning to the nest, and empty nesters. Each of these groups has different needs for such things as furniture, housing, transportation, and food preparation.

4. **Shifting and growing ethnic groups.** Our visible-minority population has tripled since 1981. More facts on this growing trend are provided in Box 2.5. Furthermore, ethnic diversity will continue to increase, leading to more opportunities for those who can cater to this trend.[12]

Box 2.5   Our Growing Ethnocultural Profile

Over the next decade, Canada's minorities will continue to grow in size and in the share of the population. Successful companies such as Kumon (http://www.kumon.com)—a Japan-based franchise operation that offers after-school help in math and language arts for children—has taken advantage of this changing and growing Canadian ethnocultural trend. And so can you!

Here are a few facts about our changing mosaic.

- In 2006, about 5 million individuals (16.2 percent of the total population) identified themselves as visible-minority persons (other than Aboriginal peoples) who are not white. This proportion has increased steadily over the past 20 years from 11.2 percent of the total population in 1996.

- South Asians, Chinese, and Blacks are the three largest visible minority groups, accounting for two-thirds of the visible-minority population. The populations of both South Asians and Chinese are well over 1 million.

(continued)

- Visible minorities have a strong presence in census metropolitan areas. About 96 percent of Canada's visible-minority population lives in a census metropolitan area, compared with 68.1 percent of the population.

- Six in 10 visible-minority people reside in just two census metropolitan areas: Toronto and Vancouver. The visible-minority population makes up a large proportion of the population in these two census metropolitan areas, 42.9 percent and 41.7 percent, respectively. Abbotsford, British Columbia, has the third largest proportion (22.8%) of visible minorities among all census metropolitan areas in the country, after Toronto and Vancouver.

- Between 2001 and 2006, the visible-minority population increased at a much faster pace than the total population with a 27.2 percent growth rate—five times faster than the 5.4 percent increase for the population as a whole.

- In 2006, the median age of the visible-minority population, or the point where exactly one-half of the population is older and the other half is younger, was 33 years, compared with 39 years for the total population in Canada.

Many of our new young entrepreneurs will be coming from this growing segment and new product and services will be required to satisfy ethnic needs. How about after-school language training especially targeted to the fast-growing Asian segment? What about new food opportunities? Some food companies are already taking advantage of these trends by introducing new products such as wasabi-flavoured potato chips and sour cream. If you would like to start a restaurant, consider having an ethnic theme. What city would you want to be located in? (Remember what we said about Toronto, Vancouver, and Abbotsford.)

Source: Statistics Canada, 2006 Census: Analysis Series, Canada's Ethnocultural Portrait: The Changing Mosaic (Catalogue no. 97-562-X, Census year 2006, *Canada's Ethnocultural Mosaic, 2006 Census*): http://www12.statcan.ca/census-recensement/2006/as-sa/97-562/pdf/97-562-XIE2006001.pdf.

5. **Improved information access.** The new electronic, digital economy means that Canadians are far better informed than they once were. They can search the Internet, get product and company information from around the world, and make purchases with the click of a button. The mass production era is on the decline. We have now entered into what some experts have called the **mass customization** era. Successful companies customize their products and services efficiently and cost-effectively and then sell in large quantities. This is another trend that Tanya Shaw Weeks of Unique Solutions took advantage of. She found a way to provide individualized sewing patterns for the mass market of women who wanted to customize their sewing creations.

MASS CUSTOMIZATION

The ability of companies to customize products and services efficiently and cost-effectively in large quantities

SOCIAL MEDIA TRENDS

Social media, which allow us to be connected through technology and the Internet in order to communicate, are having a huge impact on society and business. Furthermore, social media trends will continue to affect entrepreneurs. If we know the mega trends, we can use social media in business proactively, communicating with others and ensuring that we stay connected.

What are some of the trends in social media? Here a few key ones:

- **Connected society.** Growing connectivity to social media ecosystems will continue. With such thriving media tools as Facebook, Twitter, Google, and Pinterest, people will continue to get connected and engage in conversations and content creation.

- **Global awareness.** The trend toward being connected to global events and happenings will strengthen. Social media tools will continue to grow and allow people to chat, discuss, and debate on a variety of topics ranging from soccer matches to political grassroots movements.
- **Growth in vertical and local markets.** As more and more people connect, there is a growth in social media connectivity in vertical markets, such as music and fashion. Businesses, on local and even rural levels, are also connecting and joining conversations and content creation. These businesses are leveraging social media to connect, engage, and ultimately sell to their customers.
- **Brand-driven social media.** When people have a bad experience with a company, they tend to tell their friends and family about that experience. The growing trend will be to go to their social media circles and let the world know about their bad experience. Businesses can't hide anymore. People will share their interactions, good or bad, with people online through social media. Businesses need to understand how their customers are emotionally connected with their brand and how they can better serve their customers through social media.

TRENDS CREATE OPPORTUNITIES

Change creates market trends that lead to opportunities for innovative entrepreneurs. We want to encourage you to become a "trend tracker" and take advantage of the resulting business opportunities. So, let's dig more deeply. How can all these trends help you find a profitable business?

Industry or market trends reflect our economy's response to change, and these changes create entrepreneurial opportunities. Take a minute, and return to the opening vignettes of this chapter to confirm this. The e-commerce strategy of Tobias Lütke allowed him to expand his local market and offer his unique solutions to other entrepreneurs wanting to sell online. Kazuko Komatsu of Pacific Western Brewing Company found a way to capitalize on the fast-growing exporting trend.

Changes within the business and social worlds can be grouped into six major environmental categories:

1. **Social/Cultural**—immigration, single parents, religion, ethnic shifts, and aging population;
2. **Economic**—recessions, inflation, changing income levels, cost of housing, food, and energy;
3. **People (demographics)**—the boomers, the echo boomers, and changing ethnic and multicultural patterns;
4. **Technology**—biotechnology, the Internet, nanotechnology, personal genomics, and universal translation;
5. **International (legal/political)**—who is in power and changing rules locally, provincially, and nationally; tax laws; and where the growing export markets are;
6. **Competition**—deregulation, the impact of big-box stores, and foreign companies.

Each change within these six environmental categories, as well as the subsequent market trends, signals possible opportunities that will need further research. Your research for opportunities should begin with an environmental scan of the big picture. Action Step 11 will help you get started on the process of identifying change, subsequent trends, and market opportunities.

We encourage you to scrutinize boomers carefully. Determine if you can develop products or services that will make money. The following list of opportunities should help you get started.

ACTION STEP 11

Discover how changes = trends = opportunities. (p. 60)

- **Technology coach.** The boomers need help understanding and making use of new technologies. How about helping them find "e-friends" over the Internet? How many older people are familiar with MSN? the iPad? What about helping them access electronic libraries? How about e-shopping? Or helping them create digital photo albums? The list goes on.
- **Upmarket travel advisor/agent.** Boomers will be travelling and looking for unique travel experiences—for example, trips that focus on world sporting events, native culture, or spirituality. How about ecotourism? This is a combination of nature appreciation and cultural exploration in wild settings—bird watching and whale watching, to name a few obvious examples.
- **Lifestyle coach.** Boomers are looking for help and advice to improve their lifestyle and well-being. There may be need of spiritual advisors, diet coaches, and personal trainers, for example.
- **Financial advisor/Retirement planner.** Boomers will need help managing their wealth.
- **Concierge service agent.** Help boomers to take care of all the little things they don't have time or desire to do, for example, fixing the stove, cleaning the windows, and picking up the dry cleaning. The list goes on.
- **In-home service provider.** Help the parents of boomers to remain living in their homes and maintain their independence—through shopping, going to the doctor, cleaning, food preparation, animal care, and so on—by providing a concierge service for boomer parents. Many boomers will not have (or be willing to make) the time they need to help their aging parents—but they will have the money.

The needs of the aging boomers will create many opportunities for enterprising entrepreneurs. But that's not the only demographic trend creating business opportunities. Think about where some other openings might exist. Obvious business opportunities to meet the needs of dual-income families and single parents include child care, home security systems, and home pet care, to name a few. Those caught up in the "poverty of time" trend are also likely to be favourably disposed toward easy-to-fix meals, fast food, teleconferences, feel-good products for stressful times, and in-home services. Here are other trends and corresponding business opportunities:

- **Ethnic trend.** Canadian society will evidence a growing ethnic diversity. *Opportunity:* Help schools and business integrate by providing cultural-sensitivity workshops for businesses and schools.
- **Fitness trend.** More and more people are concerned about their fitness. *Opportunity:* For those who want to look good while sweating, sell attractive sports clothes. How about e-shopping services for those who have little time?
- **The health-consciousness trend.** *Opportunity:* For those who care about what they eat, how about selling or growing organic foods? *Other opportunities:* These include homeopathy, naturopathy, chiropractic, and herbal medicine.
- **Employment trends.** Jobs are changing more quickly than they used to. As a result, there is a growing need for retraining. *Opportunity:* Businesses related to education, training, and career planning have potential.
- **Environmental trend.** People are becoming more concerned about the environment. *Opportunity:* As previously noted, there may be demand for ecotourism agents; there is also *ecoretailing*—selling planet-friendly products that do not contain materials harmful to the body or environment.
- **Energy conservation trend.** Most Canadians have become very concerned about the high cost of energy. *Opportunity:* There is a need for energy-efficiency businesses that do caulking and insulation, replace windows, and upgrade furnaces.

Many more ideas and opportunities are contained in Box 2.6 and the E-Exercise in Box 2.7.

Box 2.6   *The Futurist's* **Top Ten Forecasts for 2013 and Beyond**

Each year since 1985, the editors of *The Futurist* have selected the most thought-provoking ideas and forecasts appearing in the magazine to go into their annual Outlook report. Over the years, Outlook has spotlighted the emergence of such epochal developments as the Internet, virtual reality, and the end of the Cold War. Here are the editors' top 10 forecasts from Outlook 2013 and beyond:

1. **Neuroscientists may soon be able to predict what you'll do before you do it.** The intention to do something, such as grasp a cup, produces blood flow to specific areas of the brain, so studying blood-flow patterns through neuroimaging could give researchers a better idea of what people have in mind. One potential application is improved prosthetic devices that respond to signals from the brain more like actual limbs do, according to researchers at the University of Western Ontario.
   World Trends & Forecasts, Jan–Feb 2012, p. 10.

2. **Future cars will become producers of power rather than merely consumers.** A scheme envisioned at the Technology University of Delft would use fuel cells of parked electric vehicles to convert biogas or hydrogen into more electricity. And the owners would be paid for the energy their vehicles produce.
   Tomorrow in Brief, Mar–Apr 2012, p. 2.

3. **An aquaponic recycling system in every kitchen.** Future "farmers" may consist of householders recycling their food waste in their own aquariums. An aquaponic system being developed by SUNY ecological engineers would use leftover foods to feed a tank of tilapia or other fish, and then the fish waste would be used for growing vegetables. The goal is to reduce food waste and lower the cost of raising fish.
   Tomorrow in Brief, Nov–Dec 2011, p. 2.

4. **The economy may become increasingly jobless, but there will be plenty of work.** Many recently lost jobs may never come back. Rather than worry about unemployment, however, tomorrow's workers will focus on developing a variety of skills that could keep them working productively and continuously, whether they have jobs or not. It'll be about finding out what work needs to be done, and doing it, suggests financial advisor James H. Lee.
   "Hard at Work in the Jobless Future," Mar–Apr 2012, pp. 32-33.

5. **The next space age will launch after 2020, driven by competition and "adventure capitalists."** While the U.S. space shuttle program is put to rest, entrepreneurs such as Paul Allen, Elon Musk, Richard Branson, and Jeff Bezos are planning commercial launches to access low-Earth orbit and to ferry passengers to transcontinental destinations within hours. Challenges include perfecting new technologies, developing global operations, building new infrastructure, and gaining regulatory approval.
   "The New Age of Space Business," Sep–Oct 2012, p. 17.

6. **The "cloud" will become more intelligent, not just a place to store data.** Cloud intelligence will evolve into becoming an active resource in our daily lives, providing analysis and contextual advice. Virtual agents could, for example, design your family's weekly menu based on everyone's health profiles, fitness goals, and taste preferences, predict futurist consultants Chris Carbone and Kristin Nauth.
   "From Smart House to Networked Home," July–Aug 2012, p. 30.

7. **Corporate reputations will be even more important to maintain, due to the transparency that will come with augmented reality.** In a "Rateocracy," as envisioned by management consultant Robert Moran, organizations' reputations are quantified, and data could be included in geographically based information

(continued)

systems. You might choose one restaurant over another when your mobile augmented–reality app flashes warnings about health-department citations or poor customer reviews.

"'Rateocracy' and Corporate Reputation," World Trends & Forecasts, May–June 2012, p. 12.

8. **Robots will become gentler caregivers in the next 10 years.** Lifting and transferring frail patients may be easier for robots than for human caregivers, but their strong arms typically lack sensitivity. Japanese researchers are improving the functionality of the RIBA II (Robot for Interactive Body Assistance), lining its arms and chest with sensors so it can lift its patients more gently.

Tomorrow in Brief, Nov-Dec 2011, p. 2.

9. **We'll harness noise vibrations and other "junk" energy from the environment to power our gadgets.** Researchers at Georgia Tech are developing techniques for converting ambient microwave energy into DC power, which could be used for small devices such as wireless sensors. And University of Buffalo physicist Surajit Sen is studying ways to use vibrations produced on roads and airport runways as energy sources.

World Trends & Forecasts, Nov–Dec 2011, p. 9.

10. **A handheld "breathalyzer" will offer early detection of infections, microbes, and even chemical attacks.** The Single Breath Disease Diagnostics Breathalyzer, under development at Stony Brook University, would use sensor chips coated with nanowires to detect chemical compounds that may indicate the presence of diseases or infectious microbes. In the future, a handheld device could let you detect a range of risks, from lung cancer to anthrax exposure.

Tomorrow in Brief, Sep–Oct 2012, p. 2.

Source: Originally published in THE FUTURIST. Used with permission from the World Future Society (www.wfs.org).

Box 2.7   E-Exercise

Link onto Small Business BC's Web resource, *Forty Concepts for a Small Business*: http://www.smallbusinessbc.ca.previewmysite.com/workshop/concepts.php.

Here you'll find 13 ways to take advantage of the market. Do a mind map of these ideas and opportunities. The ideas will help you complete Action Step 12. Make sure you put this in your 24/7 Adventure Notebook.

ACTION STEP 12

Compile a list of trends and opportunities. (p. 61)

Now it's your turn. Action Step 12 will help you come up with your own list of trends and opportunities. But we want to caution you: Once you figure out an opportunity, you will have to make sure that you have the talent, skills, and interest to take advantage of it.

THE LIFE-CYCLE STAGES

LIFE CYCLE

Four stages, from birth to death, of a product, business, service, industry, or location

When you've produced a long list of trends, divide them into four groups according to the stage of their **life cycle** (see Figure 2.2). If a trend is just beginning, label it an *embryo*. If it's exploding, label it *growth*. If it's no longer growing and beginning to cool, label it *mature*. If it's beyond maturity and is feeling chilly,

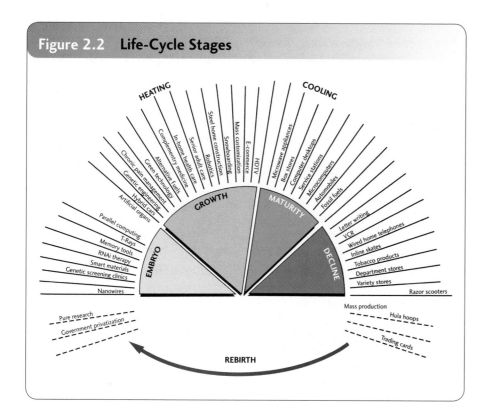

Figure 2.2 Life-Cycle Stages

label it *decline*. You don't necessarily have to create a new life-cycle chart with a new set of trends. You might choose to start with Figure 2.2 and add new products or services within each of the four stages. Perhaps you could open a new section of your 24/7 Adventure Notebook. Keep adding new products or services into your life-cycle chart.

The point is everything changes—products, needs, technology, neighbourhoods—so we want you constantly to be thinking about categorizing these changes in life-cycle stages. Looking at the life-cycle diagram, you can see, for example, that the auto industry, as a whole, is very mature. Nonetheless, some of its segments are promising—for example, minivans, sports models, and upscale imports. Convertibles are back, and in the suburbs, you see young mothers driving around in Jeep® four-by-fours. Despite traffic jams, people are still driving. But the cars they drive reflect changing lifestyles. What you have with this example is a growth segment in a mature industry.

How do consumer habits determine trends? Well, people are keeping their cars longer, so one growth segment in the auto industry would be the **aftermarket**. Examples of business in that segment would be paint, detailing, electronic accessories, and engine rebuilding. If you're interested in the auto industry, consider the aftermarket.

Where can you find gaps in the life-cycle diagram? If you have a business, where is it in the four-stage cycle? Action Step 13 will prompt you to match life-cycle stages with trends you have discovered.

WATCH FOR MARKET SIGNALS

Market signals are everywhere: on the Internet, in electronic display bulletin boards, in the newspaper (classified ads, bankruptcy notices, display ads), in the lines at the theatre, in the price slashing after Christmas, and in discount

AFTERMARKET

The marketplace where replacement items, such as auto tires and sewing machine belts, can be purchased

ACTION STEP 13

Match trends with life-cycle stages. (p. 61)

coupons, rebates, store closings, and grand openings. With practice, you can follow a product in the market right through its life cycle.

For example, consider designer jeans. In the early 1980s, massive ad campaigns convinced otherwise-sane Canadians that they should pay $40 and up for jeans carrying designer labels. These jeans were available only in the posh stores. A year later, designer jeans had reached the discount stores. Jeans that had sold for $55 were now going for $19.99. A bargain? Yes, and also a trend. But what has now replaced that trend? Custom-fit jeans with more than 440 combinations to ensure the exact fit.

What items have you seen go through their life cycle, from upscale to deep discount?

Now go back to the life cycle, and see if you can add some products and industries to it.

Next, try to discover opportunities that exist within the relevant stages. If you're entering the embryo stage, be prepared to "beat the pavement" for new business. If you're entering the maturity or decline stage, you must be ready to meet—and beat—the competition head on!

HOW DEEP IS DEEP?

GROWTH SEGMENT
An identifiable slice of an industry that is expanding more rapidly than the industry as a whole

GROWTH INDUSTRY
An industry whose annual sales increase is well above average

When merchandise slides into deep discount, the profit party is over. The market is flooded, sinking is likely, and drowning is possible. The product is at the end of its life cycle. If that's happened to your job—or to your business—it's time for you to find a **growth segment** of a **growth industry**.

Experts tell us that the average worker will have at least seven kinds of jobs in his or her lifetime and several careers. No one's job is completely secure. Rhonda Van Warden thought hers was until the school system eliminated her position. When that happened, she began to look at the trends in her community and in the country. Rhonda has some great assets, including intelligence and good listening skills, and she has the flexibility to see herself in a totally new role when opportunity knocks.

After being downsized from her job as a school counsellor, Rhonda began to attend seminars, read books about job hunting, surf the Internet, and network with her friends for leads. One day she was talking to two friends, and their conversation turned to lingerie.

"What I wish," said Kary, "is that I could buy some of that semi-sexy stuff without having to go into Le Sex Shoppe to buy it."

"There are always the catalogues," Marsha pointed out, "and there are ads in the back of every magazine I subscribe to."

"I don't trust those catalogues," Kary replied. "When I pay that much money for something that small, I want to see what I'm getting!"

Marsha turned to Rhonda. "You're sitting there not saying a word, Rhonda. What're you thinking about?"

"I think," Rhonda said, "I've just discovered the business I want to be in."

Rhonda's idea was to tap her women friends for potential target customers who would like to come to her home for a private showing of women's intimate undergarments. Rhonda named her business Private Screenings (fictitious name) and had letterhead stationery printed. Then she began to contact suppliers and manufacturers' reps. They were interested in her idea.

Her first "private screening" was well attended. Only women were present, and Rhonda sold almost a thousand dollars worth of merchandise.

The women loved what they saw, and they had fun. Ten years earlier, they probably wouldn't have considered buying the things they bought that night, but times and people change.

Rhonda went on from her success in selling to develop a line of products that she markets through her own catalogue and on her Web page. Her husband has joined her in the business, and she has hired a woman to present her intimate merchandise through seminars. (The seminars also are held in private homes.) Rhonda spends most of her time recruiting personnel and developing new products.

"When I started in this business," Rhonda admits, "I thought it might help to supplement my husband's income. But it's expanded so much that we have to scramble to keep up with orders. We travel a lot, talking to manufacturers about trends, picking up ideas. This business is a full-time job for both of us."

Rhonda was a sharp reader of market signals—the trends that reflect changes in how people think. What trends helped to make Rhonda's business successful?

1. **Specialized consumer tastes.** Rhonda's target customers are discreet middle-class women in their 40s and 50s, many of whom would be uncomfortable walking into a specialty shop to see intimate apparel. When Rhonda brings the merchandise to them, they feel comfortable, special, and adventurous.
2. **High-tech/High-touch.** We can't stop the entry into our lives of computers and the information age. But we all try to balance the electronic effects of whirring machinery with human responses—just look at dance, the arts, and anything feeding our fantasies. Private Screenings capitalizes on the desire for softness in these high-tech times.
3. **Relaxing attitudes about sex.** Private Screenings was founded in the 1990s, a time when attitudes toward sex were becoming much more relaxed.

What other trends do you see contributing to the success of Private Screenings?

SEGMENTATION AND GAP ANALYSIS

The idea of **market segmentation** is to keep breaking down potential markets into as many similar subsegments as possible. The more you learn about an industry, the better informed you will be to write your business plan.

This procedure will help you identify opportunity gaps and see combinations of gaps that might constitute markets. Segmenting the consumer market can be done geographically (e.g., by province), demographically (e.g., by age under 20, 20–30, and so on), psychographically (e.g., concern for safety), by benefits sought (e.g., sports utility in cars), and by the rate of product/service usage (e.g., one-time purchase for a number of years of a vacuum cleaner or weekly purchase of dry cleaning service). Figure 2.3 illustrates a mind map that dissects one segment of the healthcare industry into subsegments. It reflects the kind of thinking we want you to do in Action Step 14. It's another brainstorming activity, so have fun with it.

MARKET SEGMENTATION
Breaking down potential markets into homogeneous groups with similar characteristics and qualities

ACTION STEP 14

Have some fun with segmentation and gap analysis. (p. 62)

KNOW YOUR REAL BUSINESS

Watch a carpenter framing a new house, working close to the wood, nailing with quick hammer strokes. But to get a view of the total house—the structure that

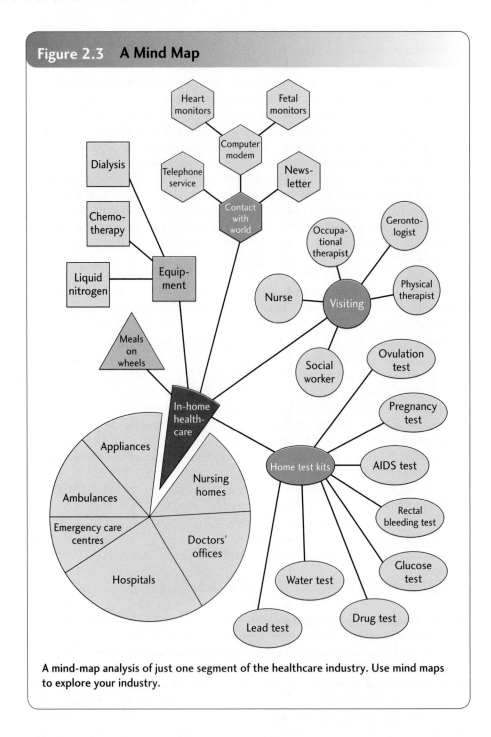

Figure 2.3   A Mind Map

A mind-map analysis of just one segment of the healthcare industry. Use mind maps to explore your industry.

will become someone's home—the carpenter must step back from the detailed work, cross the street, and examine the shape of the whole.

What business is the carpenter in? The nail-driving business? The framing business? The home-building business? Or the business of satisfying the age-old "nesting" need?

Only by stepping back can you answer the question of what business you are in. Once you know who your customers are and what satisfies their internal and external needs, you can move forward. Mary Clark's experience illustrates the importance of understanding what business you are really in.

Mary Clark was a 40-year-old teacher who had always been more interested in riding her prize-winning saddle horses than in teaching school. When her grandmother died and left her $200,000, Clark made a down payment on a boarding stable and left teaching forever, or so she thought.

The boarding stable was run down. It had stalls for 100 horses, but only 40 were occupied. Clark did everything she could think of to make the place better for horses. The $57,000 she spent on rebuilding, painting, and grading made Clark's Stables a very attractive place. She bought the highest quality of feed and gave the horses the best care money could buy.

So, when owners began to move their horses to other stables, Clark couldn't understand. She hadn't increased her fees, and she treated the horses like friends. Six months later, only three customers remained. In nine months, she was behind on her mortgage payments. In her 10th month, Clark had to sell the stables. What went wrong?

Mary Clark had made the simple mistake of thinking that horses were her target customers. She thought she was in the business of stabling horses. In fact, the business she was in was providing service for girls between the ages of 7 and 14 who rode horses. The girls wanted recreation, training, and social activities. Clark's customers left because other stables were providing lessons, trail rides, barbecues, and a fun experience. Today, Clark is back in the classroom, wondering why people don't care more about their horses—and why they didn't care about the quality of her stables.

DEFINE YOUR BUSINESS

Having defined a specific industry segment, you're ready to define what you do. Naming anything is a game of words, and a small business is no exception. If you're hesitant about defining it at this early stage, remember what happened to Mary Clark's stable.

When defining your business, keep in mind that people don't buy products or services—they buy what the product or service will do for them (for example, make their lives easier, safer, or more fun). Cosmetics firms frequently say they are in the business of selling "hope in a jar." The examples in Table 2.5 can help you define your business.

Now complete this sentence:

I'm in the business of ____.

Explain why you chose this definition and how it relates to your target customer. Include benefits.

Keep honing your definition of your business. Once a month is not too often to redefine it, especially before the start-up. Check your definition against the signals you get from your potential target customers, as they might perceive your business differently. You might have to print new letterhead stationery after you talk to them, but as business expenses go, that's a small price to pay to prevent customer confusion. By developing a questionnaire about your business idea and getting feedback from a number of potential customers, you'll be able to redefine the business you are in.

Table 2.5 Defining Your Business

If you're in	Try saying:
software sales	"I'm in the problem-solving business."
small business teaching	"I'm in the dream-to-reality business."
personal financial planning	"I'm in the peace-of-mind business."
personal fitness training	"I keep you feeling young and buff."
auto manufacturing	"I'm in the ego-gratification business."
mattress sales	"I'm in the sound sleep business."
cameras/camcorders	"I'm in the happy memory business."
gourmet cookware	"I bring fun back into the kitchen."
locksmithing	"I'm in the security business."
badge manufacturing	"I'm in the recognition business."
coffeehouse ownership	"I provide a place to see and be seen."
cosmetic surgery	"I'm in the don't-grow-old business."

DEVELOP YOUR PITCH

In addition to looking at what business you are really in, you should also consider how your business definition can impress not only your prospective customers but also your suppliers and potential investors. We suggest that you begin to formulate your "**elevator pitch**," or speech that can hook your listener into responding, "Tell me more." It's a clear, concise description of your business idea, the market need, how your business will satisfy that need, and how your business, your customers, and your investors will benefit. It should last only a few minutes—some say the time it takes to ride up in an elevator. This short description or pitch should answer three major questions.

ELEVATOR PITCH

A clear, concise description of your business idea that can hook your listener into responding, "Tell me more"

1. What is the market?
   What is your product or service?
   What are the features and benefits?
   What are the driving trends? Why does your target market need that product or service?
2. How does your business satisfy this market need?
   What is your competitive advantage?
   Who is your competition, and why will your customer buy from you?
3. How do you, the business, and the target market benefit from this venture?
   How will your business satisfy its financial objectives—in other words, how will it make money?
   Why will your customer be happy to buy your product or service? (Price? Service? Convenience?)

At this point, it might be a little too early for you to develop a finely tuned elevator pitch. But we want you to start thinking about this. While you are developing your business plan, keep in mind that you should be working on your pitch all the time. Don't be afraid to write and rewrite it. Remember: it should be no more than two minutes.[13]

Now you're ready for Action Step 15. Take a moment to define your business and develop your elevator pitch.

ACTION STEP 15

Define your business, and begin to develop your "pitch." (p. 62)

In a Nutshell

A trend is a direction of movement. For example, the trend of our present civilization is away from the smokestacks of the industrial age and toward the computers and the Internet of the entrepreneurial age. An easy way to start studying trends is to step back in time and observe a marketplace of the past. Then, move on to your own arena—the neighbourhood, nearby shopping malls, Main Street, your trade association, and your supermarket.

Two tools will help you chart trends: (1) looking around with new eyes, as you play marketplace detective, and (2) applying the life-cycle yardstick to products, industries, and so on. As you learned earlier in this chapter, a life cycle has four phases: embryo, growth, maturity, and decline. Before you open the doors of your small business, you need to be aware of what phase your product is in. For example, if you think there's easy money in selling microcomputers, you need to know that this industry is now maturing. If you want to install security products, you need to know that this industry is in the growth stage. If you're thinking about opening a toy store, you need to know that the toy industry is mature and may be on the decline, and that you might be forced to steal customers from other people.

Just for fun, select three to six businesses at random—for example, a foreign auto repair business, a restaurant/bar, a flower shop, a bedding manufacturer, a travel agent, and a computer school—and determine their life-cycle stages. While you're doing that, remember how the old post office had to adjust. Is the same thing happening to some of the smaller firms you know because they're failing to see what business they're really in?

Information on trends is all around you: on the highways, in the stores in mid-December and after the holidays, in the headlines and classifieds, at government agencies, and in the many trade associations. This information can give you the big picture if you know how to seek it out.

Key Terms

aftermarket	growth industry
baby boomers	growth segment
brainstorming	life cycle
e-commerce	market segmentation
echo boomers	mass customization
elevator pitch	outsourcing

Think Points for Success

✓ A valuable tool you can use for charting trends is the four-stage life-cycle yardstick.
✓ The life-cycle yardstick helps you find a growth industry, decide what business you're really in, and discover gaps and segments that are promising.
✓ Once you know what segment you're in, you can focus on market research with new eyes.
✓ Try to latch onto a trend that will help you survive (in style) for the next 10 to 15 years.
✓ Trends don't develop overnight. The signs are out for all to read months—even years—in advance.
✓ Develop a list of trends and opportunities. Keep this in your 24/7 Adventure Notebook.

Action Steps

ACTION STEP 9

Travel back in time and observe a marketplace of the past.

Place yourself in a time warp, and take a look at a marketplace of the past. What was selling 25 years ago? 50 years ago? 100 years ago?

To get this picture, look at old magazines, catalogues, movies, TV shows, high-school yearbooks, and family photographs. What do you see? Are all of the people dressed alike? Does everyone have the same smile, the same frown, the same serious look? How small is their world? How small is their horizon?

Study the advertisements in old magazines and newspapers, and then do the following:
1. List the products that are still around today.
2. List the products that are no longer on the market.

ACTION STEP 10

Explore new technologies.

If you're a tech expert, share your insights with others. Bring them up to speed! Technology affects every aspect of small business today—distribution, marketing, products, and so on. If you're not tech savvy, it's time to shift gears.

- **Do a Google™ search.** Start by entering the names of the industry gurus listed. See what they have to say about technology and the new economy.
- **Read magazines.** *Wired* (http://www.wired.com/), either online or in hard copy, would be a good place to start. Read several copies of *The Futurist*, *Science*, or high-tech magazines in your selected industry. List all of the new, developing technologies. Can you spot any trends or opportunities?
- **Surf the Internet.** You might want to start with some of the secondary sources of information listed in the last section of Chapter 1. Visit your local resource centre or library, and find five articles on new technologies. Can you discover any trends developing? future opportunities? Share your findings with others. A technological breakthrough in one industry will often lead to breakthroughs in other industries.
- **Link to the CATA*Alliance* website** (http://www.cata.ca). What does the Canadian Advanced Technology Alliance, "Canada's high-tech voice," have to say about emerging technologies and resulting opportunities?

With this information in hand, you will be better prepared to focus on the opportunities within these changing technologies.

ACTION STEP 11

Discover how changes = trends = opportunities.

Get started on your industry secondary research. Pick up the six most recent issues of magazines such as *Maclean's*, *Canadian Business*, or *Time* (your local resource centre should have copies) and your notes from Action Steps 9 and 10, and begin reading. What's happening in the world? Fill in the chart below with the areas that are changing within each environmental variable. If you are fortunate and have done your research, you'll spot the changes before trends begin to develop. Being at the forefront of trends has made business-savvy people rich. Remember when the biotechnology industry began? How about the cell phone industry? Or digital photography? If you had spotted the changes within these technologies, hopped onto one of the trucks, and ridden the opportunities to success, where would you be today?

The six "S E P T I C" environmental variables:

Social/Cultural
    Change:
    Trends:
    Opportunities:

Economic
    Changes:
    Trends:
    Opportunities:
People (Demographics)
    Changes:
    Trends:
    Opportunities:
Technology
    Changes:
    Trends:
    Opportunities:
International (Legal/Political)
    Changes:
    Trends:
    Opportunities:
Competition
    Changes:
    Trends:
    Opportunities:

Let's look at the well-known boomers trend, which you could have identified in this Action Step. We know that the baby boomers represent a large segment of the population. Chances are, many of these boomers will have lots of money to buy your product or service. Therefore, knowing the needs of this growing demographic force can result in huge benefits for the imaginative entrepreneur.

ACTION STEP 12

Compile a list of trends and opportunities.

It's time for you to start developing a list of trends. Review this section (including Boxes 2.1, 2.2, and 2.5). Brainstorm with your friends. Form a focus group of your friends or colleagues, and ask them about their wants or needs. Do some electronic research. Visit your local malls.

Write down five or six trends that appeal to you and then list a few opportunities arising from those trends. Here are a few examples to get you started.

TREND	OPPORTUNITY
Information	Information broker
Cocooning	Home security
Home-based	Networking business home computers
Internet	Online shopping
Downsizing	Downsizing consultant
Dual-income	Pet-sitting earner services

Now it's your turn!

	TREND	OPPORTUNITY
1.	_____	_____
2.	_____	_____
3.	_____	_____
4.	_____	_____
5.	_____	_____
6.	_____	_____

Add your list of trends and opportunities to your 24/7 Adventure Notebook.

ACTION STEP 13

Match trends with life-cycle stages.

By now, you will have identified a number of emerging market trends. Review Figure 2.2 and determine where the trends you've discovered belong on the life cycle. How many of your listed trends belong in the embryo stage? the growth stage? the maturity stage? the decline stage?

ACTION STEP 14

Have some fun with segmentation and gap analysis.

Form some of your friends into a focus group and poll them about gaps in the marketplace. Ask them to respond to the following questions:

- What frustrates you most about your daily life? Shopping? Banking? Dating? Living? Buying a car? Grocery shopping? Other kinds of shopping?
- What products do you need that you can't get?
- What products or service would enhance your quality of life?
- How could you increase your productivity without working more hours?

Make a list of the gaps that the group identifies. Then project the list out as far as you can, and follow the wants and frustrations of your friends into the marketplace. Are any of the needs they mentioned national in scope? Global?

ACTION STEP 15

Define your business, and begin to develop your "pitch"

Brainstorm what business you're really in. Let your mind play at this. Remember your customers' comments when you were probing their psyches. You should be able to summarize your business in one or two sentences.

Next think of yourself riding up fifty floors in an express elevator. You have thirty seconds to explain to a stranger what your business is. What will you say? Can you dazzle this stranger, so that he or she will ask for more? Questions you should answer include the following: What is the market and who is the customer? How does your business satisfy this market or customer need? How do you, the business, and the target market or customer benefit from this venture?

Keep working and refining your "elevator speech" throughout the semester. This Action Step will also help you draft your mission statement (Chapter 3, Action Step 23).

Business Plan Building Block

INDUSTRY OVERVIEW

You need to demonstrate your knowledge and understanding of the business opportunity you want to pursue. How big is the total industry? How old is it? Is it growing and, if so, in what direction?

What segment have you chosen? It is vital that you present a comprehensive understanding of who your customers are and why they will buy from you. Get on the Internet. Use some of the secondary sources provided in this chapter, or you might have to get your own supporting evidence. The point is, your secondary research should be supported with facts, data, and sources. Be sure to do your primary research and show your results.

_____

_____

_____

_____

_____

CURRENT POSITION AND FUTURE OUTLOOK

Example:

This is what you learn about Big Wheels, a growing bike shop in your town. The two owners are well-known trail bike riders who, for the past two years, have been repairing and servicing all kinds of bicycles out of the oversized garage of one of their partners. In the past 12 months, this part-time venture grossed $161,000 without the benefit of advertising or a retail location.

The market for high-quality and custom-made bicycles has grown by more than 10 percent per year over the past 10 years, and industry observers expect the trend to continue. The new retail store will have 465 square metres in showroom space and another 280 square metres for doing repairs and stocking goods. Big Wheels will also have a website, where customers will be able to purchase customized bikes and have them delivered within two weeks.

The bicycle industry in North America sells two dollars' worth of accessories and clothing for every dollar spent on bicycles. Between the store and the website, Big Wheels expects sales to at least double in the first year (the company previously had not sold clothing) and to reach $1 million in three years.

It's your turn again. Develop your section on the current situation and future outlook. It's important to demonstrate an understanding of growth problems (such as choosing the right location and attracting customers), as well as cash management, gross margins, inventory control, and vendor sources. Ready or not, start writing down what you already know and what you need to know. You will have many opportunities to upgrade this section as you gather data. Your primary research, when complete, will help you understand what your potential customers want.

_____

_____

_____

_____

_____

MANAGEMENT AND OWNERSHIP

Needed now is a mini-résumé of the key player (or players) you'd like to have on your founding team. Lenders, capital firms, and vendors consider the founding team to be the most important factor in a business plan.

At this point, keep the résumés brief, focusing on the past experience that will give this start-up a competitive edge. (Save the full-blown résumés of the management team for the appendix at the back of the plan.) Explain your business form (that is, corporation, partnership, or sole proprietorship) and, if you have more than two people on the team, include an organizational chart.

Your turn again. Who are the players?

_____

_____

_____

_____

_____

DESCRIPTION OF YOUR BUSINESS

Think of yourself riding up 50 floors in an express elevator. You have 30 seconds to explain to a stranger what your business is about.

Example:

My partner and I retail high-end bicycles from our store in Halifax. We repair, service, and modify off-road bikes for the serious trail rider. Ninety percent of our customers are from Halifax, and they see us as a valuable resource in helping them to achieve a healthy and enjoyable exercise lifestyle.

Note that this description is short and to the point, but it also includes important customer benefits.

Now it's your turn.
My business is

_____

_____

_____

_____

_____

Checklist Questions and Actions to Develop Your Business Plan

Spotting Trends and Opportunities

❑ What trends will influence your small business?

❑ What business are you really in?

❑ What segment of the market will be your niche?

❑ Is it a growth segment in a growth market?

❑ Initially define your target market, and determine how large that customer base is.

❑ Identify the secondary sources you will use as part of your market research.

❑ Does this business fit your vision and values?

❑ Other than making money, what are the goals of your proposed venture? (You should be able to establish four to six over the next three years.)

❑ For your business, what objectives do you wish to achieve this time next year?

Case Study: Trends and Opportunities

Case Background

As profiled in the chapter opening vignette, Shopify has become an inspiring success story. We can all learn from Tobias Lütke's experience and advice. So, we want you to dig a little deeper, go back, and link to the following sites:

* Shopify's website: http://www.shopify.com
* Canadian Intellectual Property Office: http://www.cipo.ic.gc.ca/eic/site/cipointernet-internetopic.nsf/eng/Home
* Tim Ferriss—The 4 Hour Work Week: http://www.fourhourworkweek.com/blog/2011/09/12/engineering-a-%E2%80%9Cmuse%E2%80%9D-%E2%80%93-volume-4-case-studies-of-successful-cash-flow-businesses/

Case Study Questions and Activities

1. Entrepreneurial skills (e-skills)
   We introduced you to an e-skill called "mind mapping" in Chapter 1. In this chapter, we learned about brainstorming as an entrepreneurial skill that will help you discover trends and business opportunities.
   a. Briefly, what is brainstorming?
   b. Brainstorming is a skill that can be learned with practice. Get together with a group of friends or classmates. Because trends create opportunities, brainstorm the possible trends that would help Tobias Lütke in growing Shopify. Record your results in the form of a mind map.

2. Trends creating opportunities
   Industry or market trends reflect our economy's response to change, and change creates entrepreneurial opportunities. A knowledge of market trends will help you identify growth opportunities.

    a. Briefly, what is a trend? And what is the difference between a trend and a fad? Explore dictionary and Internet resources.

    b. Faith Popcorn is the author of *The Popcorn Report*, a bestselling book on market trends. She tells us that ideally, a winning business idea should include or encompass at least three major trends. On page 38, five pervasive macro trends that Canadian small business must embrace were listed. Briefly describe these five trends. Which of these trends did Tobias Lütke take advantage of?

3. Mass customization

The new electronic era means that Canadians are becoming far better informed, with a resulting trend toward individualism. Many Canadians search the Internet, get product and company information from around the world, and buy what they want at the click of a button. Electronic access to information is a key factor in the splintering of the mass market. We have now entered a growing trend called "mass customization."

In this chapter, we learned how Tanya Shaw Weeks took advantage of mass customization (page 36). Show how Tobias Lütke has now begun taking advantage of this trend, as well.

4. Outsourcing and contracting out

    a. Click onto "What Is Outsourcing?" (http://www.outsourcing-center.com) and watch the video. According to Peter Bendor-Samuel, a top authority on outsourcing, what is the distinction between outsourcing and contracting out?

    b. What are the possible major benefits of outsourcing?

5. Tips for building an effective website

Go to http://website-creation-software-review.toptenreviews.com/tips-on-building-an-effective-website.html. How does shopify.com compare against these tips?

6. What business are you really in?

In this chapter, we have encouraged you to begin thinking about customer needs. We have also urged you to think about defining your business in terms of the benefits to your target customer.

    a. Who is Shopify's target, or major, customer?

    b. What business is Shopify really in?

7. Pitching your product

Tobias Lütke raised $22 million dollars in venture capital by pitching his business, Shopify. Assume for a moment you are Tobias Lütke and you need an additional $5 million. You have to satisfy the needs of potential venture capitalists, and you don't have much time to convince them. You need an elevator pitch.

    a. What is an elevator pitch?

    b. What are the basic needs of venture capital investors?

    c. What key issues would you address in your elevator pitch?

Notes

1. Shopify.com, http://www.shopify.com.
2. Pacific Western Brewing Company, "About Us," http://www.pwbrewing.net.
3. Unique Solutions Design Ltd., http://www.uniqueltd.com/about.
4. Benjamin Tal, "Start-ups—Present and Future, " *In Focus*, http://research.cibcwm.com/economic_public/download/if_2012-0925.pdf.
5. http://www.ic.gc.ca/eic/site/061.nsf/eng/02728.html.
6. Profit.guide, PROFIT 100 Overview, http://www.profitguide.com/manage-grow/success-stories/profit-100-overview-29574
7. Ibid.
8. Statistics Canada, "Individual Internet Use and E-commerce," http://www.statcan.gc.ca/daily-quotidien/111012/dq111012a-eng.htm.
9. Ibid.

10. Statistics Canada, *The Canadian Population in 2011: Age and Sex*, http://www12.statcan.gc.ca/census-recensement/2011/as-sa/98-311-x/98-311-x2011001-eng.cfm.

11. Statistics Canada, *The Aging Workforce*, http://www12.statcan.ca/english/census01/products/analytic/companion/paid/canada.cfm#5.

12. Statistics Canada, *Canada's Ethnocultural Portrait: The Changing Mosaic, 2001 Census*, http://www12.statcan.ca/english/census01/products/analytic/companion/etoimm/canada.cfm/three_largest_urban_centres.

13. Business Know-How, "How to Write an Elevator Speech," http://www.businessknowhow.com/money/elevator.htm; and The Social Software Weblog, "Pinpoint Connections," http://www.switched.com/category/@socialnetworking.

Chapter 3

Positioning Yourself as an Entrepreneur for Market Opportunities

This chapter will help you prepare part B of your business plan, The Market and the Target Customer.

Pixland/Thinkstock

LEARNING OPPORTUNITIES

After reading this chapter, you should be able to

- connect your personal vision and values with market opportunities;
- mesh your personal business objectives with one of the many opportunities in the marketplace;
- narrow your industry research until viable gaps appear;
- gain insight into hidden pockets of the life cycle by using an industry chronology;
- understand how problems can be turned into opportunities;
- combine demographic (population) data with psychographic (picture of a lifestyle) data to produce a customer profile;
- identify heavy users of your product or service;
- create a business mission statement for your business;
- develop a strategy for your business using a SWOT analysis;
- use a matrix grid for blending your objectives with your research findings to produce a portrait of a business.

ACTION STEP PREVIEW

16. Clarify your values.
17. List your business goals for the next three years.
18. Collect secondary data on your favourite industry segment.
19. Identify three or four market gaps that look promising.
20. List problems that need solutions.
21. Brainstorm for solutions.
22. Mesh possible solutions with your goals and objectives, using a matrix grid.
23. Begin drafting your mission statement.

PASSION AND VISION: FROGBOX.COM

Doug Burgoyne always wanted to be an entrepreneur, but he had no idea of what type of business to get into. So, Burgoyne and his partner would often meet over a beer to discuss different business ideas they could develop.

"We discussed many business ideas," says Burgoyne, "but we really wanted a business idea that was based on passion ... service, ... environmental yet profitable." Burgoyne also noted that he and his partner preferred a business based on cash and with a short sales cycle.

Their focus turned to the moving business. Together, they brainstormed and developed an idea based on an environmental solution called "FROGBOX." They came up with a way "to make moving more sustainable," says Burgoyne, "by reusing plastic boxes hundreds of times, instead of using cardboard boxes that are sent to the landfill or recycled after only a few uses." The experience of using cardboard boxes had led to the idea of reusable moving containers and the launch of Frogbox.

Frogbox, an eco-friendly supply company, provides reusable plastic moving boxes to people who are moving from one place to another, as well as a rental service that delivers and picks up the reusable containers when customers are finished with them. Boxes can be ordered from the company website: www.frogbox.com.

"It was a risky business idea since the business model was new," says Burgoyne. But he and his partner took a chance and started Frogbox in Vancouver, British Collumbia, in 2008. The business model proved to be a winner, and within one year, Frogbox expanded to Seattle, Washington.

"It was at this point that we knew we had something great in our hands," says Burgoyne. He quit his original job and began to work full time with the business.

What key characteristics are important to have in order to be a successful entrepreneur? "Passion and persistence!" says Burgoyne.

Passion and persistence have helped Burgoyne grow Frogbox to 17 locations in Canada and three in the United States with a planned growth strategy of 30 Canadian and 100 U.S. locations by 2014.

Burgoyne attributes much of his success to his team. On the advisory board alone, he counts on successful entrepreneurs to help him: these include W. Brett Wilson and Jim Treliving from the CBC show *Dragons' Den*. Who gave him the best advice? "It came from Steve Rogers, from College Pro Painters," says Burgoyne. Rogers advised him not to grow "until you've figured out the business model."

This advice from an experienced entrepreneur is certainly sound. As a result, Burgoyne has taken the time with his business partner to figure out the business model and how to scale it.

Burgoyne will face many ups and downs on the road to franchising. But one thought helps him to get through the tough times: "This too shall pass."

Burgoyne knew he wanted to start a business, but he and his partner were unsure of what type of business. His experience is true of many entrepreneurs. They want to start a business but are not sure what type of business to start.

STRONG MISSION AT KINNIKINNICK FOODS

Edmonton-based Kinnikinnick Foods Incorporated is an award-winning bakery that specializes in gluten-free foods. Its target customers are people who are allergic to wheat, barley, rye, or oats; people who are dairy or lactose intolerant; people who are on a special diet for the biological treatment of autism; or people who simply want to expand, balance, or rotate their diet.

Founding partner Ted Wolff von Selzam had a background in environmental education and teaching programs when he started the company as a home-based business in 1991, selling his homemade products at a local farmer's market. A specialized bakery was a natural extension of his love for food and his personal vision of helping people live in harmony with their environment.

The first retail location of 46 square metres opened in February 1992. In the space of 10 years, the company grew from a mom-and-pop operation to a corporate structure that meets the demands of a growing North American market. Kinnikinnick now offers more than 120 brand products, including a wide variety of breads, buns, bagels, donuts, cookies, muffins, cereals, easy-to-use mixes, soups, sauces, and snack foods.

Kinnikinnick owes its success to the following:

- **a compelling vision:** to be a leading producer of alternative foods;
- **a focused mission:** Kinnikinnick's mission statement reads: "To provide people with celiac disease, people with autism, and people with special dietary requirements with an uncontaminated, risk-free source of food products. And to provide our customers with food that actually looks and tastes good."

An e-commerce–enabled website (http://consumer.kinnikinnick .com/index.cfm/fuseaction/consumer.home.html) is the third key to Kinnikinnick's success. Since the site was launched in 1998, sales have grown by nearly 500 percent. Much of this growth is attributable to online sales. "Our U.S. sales account for at least 50 percent of our business," says Marketing and IT Manager Jay Bigam, "and a very large portion of that 50 percent is driven by the Internet."[1]

In Chapter 1, we asked you to step back, take a good hard look at your strengths and weaknesses, and think about your personal vision, values, and goals. In Chapter 2, we encouraged you to be on the lookout for industry trends that signal entrepreneurial opportunities.

Now we want to help you align your personal vision and values with the market opportunities. Think for a minute: This "alignment" was a major factor contributing to the success of Doug Burgoyne of Frogbox and Ted Wolff von Selzam of Kinnikinnick Foods. Burgoyne loved the environment, and his goal was to start a business that cared for the environment. He wanted to ensure that his personal vision and values were aligned with the market opportunities. In the same fashion, Wolff von Selzam's personal vision—"to help people live in harmony with their environment"—was in keeping with the healthy-eating trend and his resulting business mission.

As you work your way through this self-assessment chapter, you will better understand what type of business best suits you. The sky is the limit on ideas for your small business. On the other hand, you may already have firm ideas about what type of business you plan to start. If you aren't sure, keep your options open as you assess your vision and values; establish your mission, goals, and objectives; and let your ideas percolate. You will want to match your business idea with your interests. Box 3.1 diagrams the flow of the thought process from your vision to your strategy. As was the case for Doug Burgoyne and Ted Wolff von Selzam, your best business opportunity will be where your personal vision and values meet your business mission.

YOUR VISION AND VALUES

VISION

A mental picture of yourself or an event at some time in the future

The ability to visualize is a key skill that all entrepreneurs should develop. If you can visualize yourself at some point in the future, then you have a **vision**. A vision is a mental picture of yourself or an event at some time in the future.

Knowing where you want to be at some point in the future helps you to identify business opportunities that will be more aligned to who you are. Having a clear vision of the future is a key success ingredient for entrepreneurs as author David Chilton, also now a Dragon on CBC's *Dragons' Den*, points out in Box 3.1.

The clarity of this vision will help you as an entrepreneur. You will need some time to think about your future and the future of your business. Even when you are operating your business, you will need to take time to think about your future again and ensure that you are on track.[2]

The culture of a company and the way its employees behave is a reflection of the owner's personality and values. The owner's personal style of doing business and treating others is disseminated through the rest of the organization.

Box 3.1   The Power of Vision

Why would David Chilton pack up his lucrative speaking career, invest more than a million dollars, and partner with two business neophytes in a new venture called "Crazy Plates"? After all, he's the author of *The Wealthy Barber*, Canada's all-time bestselling book. It's not as if he needs to lose a million dollars. But Chilton has always had a knack for recognizing great ventures from the get-go.

Crazy Plates sells frozen, ready-to-assemble meals designed for small families that want fresh, healthy food that they can prepare themselves from pre-cut ingredients. The product line was developed by sisters Greta and Janet Podleski. To a large degree, success of this new venture and Chilton's million-dollar investment depend on these two sisters and their popular cookbooks, *Looneyspoons: Low-Fat Food Made Fun*; *Crazy Plates: Low-Fat Food So Good, You'll Swear It's Bad for You*; and their most recent book, *Eat, Shrink & Be Merry*. Janet and Greta's bestselling cookbooks have helped more than a million Canadians combine great taste with good health.

According to Chilton, many ingredients lead to the success of a new venture, especially hard work and clever marketing. But a clear vision is critical to the success of a business. Janet and Greta Podleski are passionate about healthy food and good eating. From Day 1, their compelling vision for Crazy Plates has been to help time-strapped adults prepare and eat healthy meals. Now that Crazy Plates has snagged an exclusive distributorship with the giant Loblaws chain of stores across Ontario, it seems as though Chilton's recipe for success has led to another winner.

According to Chilton, Crazy Plates is not done yet. There's much more to come—and it all started with a passionate vision.

Sources: Jack Kohane, "Cookbook Authors Enjoy Rags-to-Ricotta Ride," *Business Edge*, http://www.businessedge.ca/archives/article.cfm/cookbook-authors-enjoy-rags-to-ricottaride-11623; Canadian Business Online, Professional Speakers' Bureau Inc., http://www.prospeakers.com/speakers/David-Chilton.

The business that you start must embody values that you strongly believe in. For example, one of your values may be a concern for the environment. Let's say that you are presented with a profitable business opportunity for a chemical-based solution to eliminate weeds. You wouldn't be happy with this opportunity and would feel at odds with a business based on it. Likely poor business performance would result.

So you need to ask yourself what intrinsic **values** guide your day-to-day activities, behaviour, and decision making. Think about what things in life are really important to you. You may not be ready to die for them, but they are principles that mean a great deal to you. Now make a list. Use the values as a guide, but don't incorporate them as yours unless you firmly believe that they are important to you. The following is a cross-section of both personal and business values that a person may have:

VALUES

The things in life that are important to you

- achievement
- concern for others (e.g., customers, teamwork)
- concern for society (e.g., environment, heath)
- creativity
- desire to make continuous improvement
- family
- friends
- hobbies
- honour
- independence
- loyalty
- material items
- money
- ownership and control
- play
- quality
- security
- simplicity
- trust
- work ethic

Values serve as guideposts for your actions. They help you deal with problems you have never seen before. As successful business leaders, including Alex Tilley, owner and chairman of Tilley Endurables, constantly remind us, a business reflects the values and personalities of the people who own and operate it. Box 3.2 spells out the relationship between vision and values.

Values, once crystallized, become the basis of your mission statement and goals (Figure 3.1). Action Step 16 will help you to begin clarifying your values. After you have had a chance to think about your values, it's time to focus on market opportunities that support these values.

ACTION STEP 16

Clarify your values. (p. 86)

Box 3.2 It's All Connected

YOUR VISION
is
Based on YOUR VALUES and beliefs.
It is spelled out in
YOUR BUSINESS MISSION statement
fleshed out in
YOUR GOALS and OBJECTIVES
and accomplished through
YOUR STRATEGY.
What does your list look like? Which are business values,
and which are personal values?

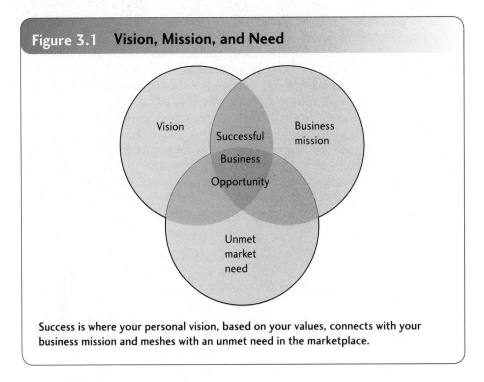

Figure 3.1   Vision, Mission, and Need

Vision

Business mission

Successful Business Opportunity

Unmet market need

Success is where your personal vision, based on your values, connects with your business mission and meshes with an unmet need in the marketplace.

WELCOME TO OPPORTUNITY SELECTION

Think of the process for selecting the right opportunity for you as a huge funnel equipped with a series of idea filters. You pour everything into this funnel—your visions, values, and long-term goals; solutions to problems; personality; short-term business objectives; industry data; industry problems; your hopes and fears; and primary, secondary, and new-eyes research—and a valuable business idea drains out at the bottom. This opportunity selection process contains seven steps that will help you find market segments that match your personal vision and goals (see Boxes 3.1 and 3.2). The process connects your skills to your research and shows you the skills you need to develop. It aims the power of your mind at the particular segment of small business that suits you (see Figure 3.2).

Here's a quick preview of the seven steps to opportunity selection.

1. Identify your business goals.
2. Learn more about your favourite industry.
3. Identify promising industry segments.
4. Identify problems that need solutions.
5. Brainstorm for solutions.
6. Mesh possible solutions with opportunities in the marketplace.
7. Take stock of, and focus on, the most promising opportunities.

To understand how this process works, let's see how Steve and Anne found their business opportunity. Steve, a graduate from a technical school, had been bounced from job to job over a few years. Anne had graduated with a major in marketing but still hadn't found a real job—but then, she had not been looking that hard. The couple weren't too sure about whether they wanted to start a business together, so they took a night course in small business to help sort things out. Both could articulate their personal visions and goals, and now it was time to see if they could come up with a good business idea.

We'll show you how they worked through their idea using the seven steps of opportunity selection. This case study also introduces another important concept: teamwork. Let's begin with Steve and Anne's business goals.

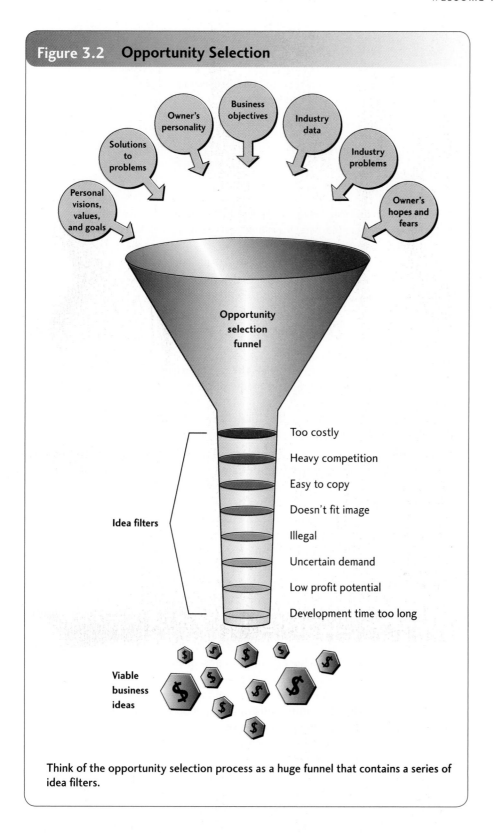

Figure 3.2   Opportunity Selection

Think of the opportunity selection process as a huge funnel that contains a series of idea filters.

STEP 1: IDENTIFY YOUR BUSINESS GOALS

Anne and Steve's first step was to develop a list of business goals. Their small business professor had asked, "If you were to start a business, what would your goals—in relation to your values—be? Security? Money? Independence?

Box 3.3 Small Business Tips

Ultimately, each of your broad goals will boil down to a set of specific business objectives. These objectives should be S M A R T:

- **Specific,**
- **Measurable,**
- **Action based,**
- **Realistic,**
- **Time framed.**

SMART objectives can be applied to your personal life as well as your business planning. For example, here is a simple example of a possible SMART personal objective for a student:

- I [name] will graduate from this course [specific name] on [provide exact date] with a grade of [provide grade level] as determined by [name of professor].

We encourage you to get started using SMART goals. What is your goal for this course?

Control?" She added that eventually these general goals would have to be refined as short-term objectives and made much more specific and measurable (see Box 3.3).

It took a few days—more time than they thought—but Steve and Anne finally came up with a list of broad goals that sounded like heaven.

1. **Psychological rewards.** They wanted to plant a seed and watch it grow into a business that they and their future family would be proud of.
2. **Teamwork.** Throughout their married life, they had planned to work together to build a strong family unit. Now they wanted to practise these teamwork skills in business. They wanted their business to be something bigger than they could accomplish as individuals—the value of synergy. As individuals, both Anne and Steve had listed their strengths and weaknesses. As a team, they wanted to build on their strengths.
3. **Money.** They wanted to earn a respectable family income—a minimum of $50,000 a year.
4. **Safety.** There was no way they wanted to lose money now. They had a family to think about.
5. **Growth industry.** They wanted to find a booming segment of a growth industry (an industry whose annual sales growth is considerably above average).
6. **Time.** They knew that getting a business up and running could take a year at the very least. They wanted to define and develop their business so that they could make a little money in the first year, get a bit of experience, and then go bigger in the next two to four years, once they knew what they were doing and what the market really wanted.
7. **Key people.** They wanted to operate the business themselves for the first year. But as the business grew over the next four years, they wanted to be able to attract the best people to work with them.
8. **Fun, adventure, and excitement.** They knew that starting a small business, even in a growth or glamour industry, would involve hassles, problems, and surprises. So they decided to make sure their business would be one that they would enjoy.

Now it's your turn. Why do you want to start your own business? What are your goals? Action Step 17 will help you work through this.

ACTION STEP 17

List your business goals for the next three years. (p. 87)

STEP 2: LEARN MORE ABOUT YOUR FAVOURITE INDUSTRY

As you searched for trends in Chapter 2, you probably found a dozen industries that seemed interesting. Now it's time to explore one of them in more depth. Choose the industry that interests you most and about which you have at least some knowledge, whether it's genetics, robotics, entertainment, food service, travel, education, publishing, retailing, construction, manufacturing, information, or whatever. Here, trade associations can be a valuable source of information. For example, if you plan to be in the gift business, you will want to check out the Canadian Gift & Tableware Association (http://www.cgta.org). If you're planning to start a restaurant business, you would certainly connect with the Canadian Restaurant and Foodservices Association (http://www.crfa.ca). As we note in Chapter 5, Associations Canada (http://circ.greyhouse.ca) would be a good starting point if you're looking for an association related to your particular industry.

As you move into your selected industry, collect information from previous Action Steps. For secondary data, the Internet is probably the best place to start, but you need to sift through a lot of information. Visit a resource centre or library; study periodicals such as *The Globe and Mail*, *Canadian Business*, the *National Post*, *PROFIT* guide, and other general business or news sources. Most libraries have computer databases to help you search. In addition, the Canadian Business Index (http://www.canadianbusinessindex.com) and other such sources will point you to dozens of articles in your field. Is there a trade show you can attend? What you're looking for is an accurate picture of trends in the industry that interests you. You need to learn what's breaking, what's cresting, and what's cooling down.

In focusing on your industry, break down your search into categories such as life cycles, speed of change, history, competition, recent industry breakthroughs, costs of positioning yourself, target customers, and so on. Later, after you've gathered the data, you can use these categories as idea filters for sifting information through the power marketing funnel.

For example, using the life-cycle concept discussed in Chapter 2 will sharpen a first look at any industry. When you're reading a newspaper and you see the headline "CBC Tries to Shed Stodgy Image in Prime Time—But Can It Be Hip?" you make three fast-reflex judgments. First, the industry is entertainment. Second, the segment is network television. Third, the shows are in the mature phase, on their way to decline.

And when you're driving down the street and see a shopping mall being renovated, you know that the facelift is an effort to move the mall back from a mature or decline phase into a growth phase.

The point of all this is to find an industry segment where there is room for growth.

After market and target customer, a second helpful category is competition, which we'll be analyzing in detail in Chapter 5. Competition, which varies with each stage of the life cycle, is an idea filter that can save you years of grief.

A third helpful category is the concept of industry breakthroughs, or hot buttons. What really hums in your industry or segment? Consider that the first computers filled large rooms and ran on punch cards. The first industry breakthrough was the printed circuit, the second was the microchip processor, and the third was the Internet. What is the fourth? What breakthroughs are now occurring in your selected industry? Does your business idea capitalize on the latest advances in technology and imagination?

Let's return to Anne and Steve. They had a firm idea of their favourite industry. After doing much primary and secondary research, they decided to focus on the information industry. All the numbers told them this was still a growth market. On a personal level, Steve loved the technical world, whereas Anne knew there was a real need for marketers in the technology sector, and she

ACTION STEP 18

Collect secondary data on your favourite industry segment. (p. 87)

MARKET GAP

An area of the market where needs are not being met

liked working with techies. They had chosen a growth industry that meshed with their personal visions and goals.

Now it is your turn. Research your favourite industry. Is it in a growth phase? What breakthroughs are occurring? Does your business capitalize on the latest advances in technology and imagination? Put this kind of thinking into Action Step 18.

STEPS 3 AND 4: IDENTIFY PROMISING INDUSTRY SEGMENTS AND PROBLEMS THAT NEED SOLUTIONS

When you write your business plan, you'll need to explain why you've chosen a particular **market gap** and what you believe the resulting business opportunity is. If you have selected a promising opportunity and have communicated your excitement about it, you'll have developed a "hook" for the banker or investor who will read your plan. As we discussed in Chapter 2, e-commerce is one example of an industry where market gaps will abound. More evidence of this trend is provided in Box 3.4. As related in the opening vignettes, Doug Burgoyne found his niche with eco-friendly moving boxes whereas Ted Wolff von Selzam of Kinnikinnick Foods found his in the e-retailing of alternative food products.

Box 3.4   Internet Commerce in Canada—10 Key Metrics

1. Value of online sales (private and public) in 2007 = $62.7 billion
2. Value of online sales (private only) in 2007 = $58.2 billion
3. Value of online sales (public only) in 2007 = $4.5 billion
4. Percentage of business-to-consumer (B2C) sales climbed to 32% in 2007
5. Percentage of business-to-business (B2B) sales reached 62% of online sales in 2007
6. Percentage of firms purchasing goods and services online in 2007 = 48%
7. Percentage of private sector firms using wireless communication in 2007 = 77%
8. Percentage of private sector firms using the Internet in 2007 = 87%
9. Percentage of private sector firms using email in 2007 = 41%
10. Percentage of private sector firms using Internet-based systems in 2007 = 36%

Use of Information and Communications Technologies (ICTs)

	2006	2007
Email		
Private sector	78	81
Public sector	100	100
Wireless communications		
Private sector	74	77
Public sector	91	91
Internet		
Private sector	83	87
Public sector	100	100
Having a website		
Private sector	40	41
Public sector	94	93

Source: Statistics Canada, http://www.statcan.gc.ca/daily-quotidien/080424/dq080424a-eng.htm.

The secret to focusing on market gaps is to find a target customer—a person or business that needs a particular product or service that you could provide. You then profile your target customer (we do this in detail in the next chapter), and that profile becomes one of your idea filters.

Let us return to Anne and Steve. The couple had done a lot of primary and secondary research. They knew that computers and the Internet were explosive market segments (see Figure 3.3). They also learned that there was a growth

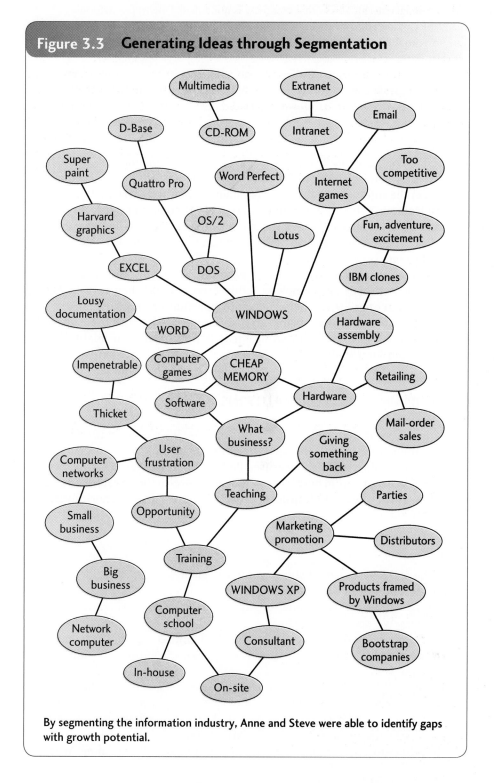

Figure 3.3 Generating Ideas through Segmentation

By segmenting the information industry, Anne and Steve were able to identify gaps with growth potential.

> ## Box 3.5 Brainstorming—The Rules
>
> Brainstorming requires an environment and attitude in which innovative thinking can occur. In a brainstorming session, everyone is encouraged to contribute ideas. Stimulation is provided by the ideas of others. The goal is to come up with lots of ideas, some of which might seem far-fetched or even erroneous, and then, as momentum grows, to see where concepts develop. A key to brainstorming is to reserve judgment initially so that creativity is not stifled. Finally, brainstorming must be conducted in an environment in which "anything goes." People must not be made to think that their ideas are silly or stupid. Negative statements or actions, reservations, or criticisms are not allowed.
>
> Now that you understand what brainstorming is and what it can accomplish for a business, give it a try with your own business. Assemble your partners or friends and go for it. Action Step 21 provides some directions.

market for computer networks—especially for small businesses. From their research, they had isolated four breakthrough segments: (1) the home computer market, (2) the Internet, (3) intranets (communication networks that companies build to maintain internal communication), and (4) computer networks. Wisely, Anne and Steve also listed some of the major problems in the industry: consumer distrust of products and services, speed change, information overload, security, cost, and so on.

ACTION STEP 19

Identify three or four market gaps that look promising. (p. 87)

ACTION STEP 20

List problems that need solutions. (p. 88)

Now it's your turn to focus on the segments within your industry and spot some that look promising. Complete Action Step 19, and then turn to Action Step 20. Action Step 20 will help you spot opportunities in your industry segment. If this exercise draws a blank, go back and do some more brainstorming. Remember, the process of generating ideas is not linear. You might have to bounce around for a while.

STEP 5: BRAINSTORM FOR SOLUTIONS

In Chapter 2, we introduced you to brainstorming. It's a process used by many groups—think tanks, middle managers, major corporations, and, especially, small businesses—to generate fresh ideas (see Box 3.5 on this page). What follows is a short recap of a brainstorm held by Anne and Steve—with their best friends, Carol and Rick—as they began to transform problems into business opportunities.

"Anne and I have invited you over for a pizza and to get some ideas on business opportunities," Steve began.

"As you know," said Anne, "we are thinking about starting our own business. We have done all kinds of research and have decided to focus on the information industry. We have even identified a few hot segments. We want to brainstorm for more ideas and some solutions to industry problems."

The four spent the first hour tossing around ideas. Some of these did not appear to be going anywhere. Rick, for example, thought the company should design computer games and go head-to-head with Sega® and Sony. Ideas kept coming out—virtual training, leveraged buyouts, virtual games, software manufacture, hardware assembly, retailing, Web design, and on and on. Anne wrote them all down on a flip chart. Finally, she said: "I'm exhausted. Time for a break."

When they came back, it was Steve's turn to keep track of the ideas. He flipped to a clean sheet on the chart. Over the next hour, the four friends created a mind map loaded with ideas for a business (see, for example, Figure 3.3).

By the time the brainstorm session wound down, they had identified two areas to explore. The first area was the installation of and training for network computing systems. Their target market would be small business. Steve had just finished reading about a Statistics Canada survey that said computer networks (especially LANs) were now being installed in small businesses at a record pace. Their second option was intranet design and installation for small and medium-sized businesses.

"Well, this about wraps it up for tonight. Anne and I have a lot of ideas to mull over," concluded Steve. "We're going to have to think about these two options."

"Wait a minute," said Carol. "How will you decide?"

"We'll have to do more research, then use a matrix grid. We learned about the matrix grid in class last week," Anne responded.

It's helpful—and, in most cases, necessary—to summarize after a brainstorming session so that you can identify the useful ideas. Let's review what happened in this session.

1. Using brainstorming, the team identified problems and possible solutions.
2. Most ideas were good ideas.
3. The two ideas that looked best involved computer networks and intranet systems.
4. It did not seem that Anne and Steve could pursue both ideas at once. They had identified two different target customers. They would likely have to hold one idea in reserve (not a bad thing given that every product or service has a life cycle—they might be able to use the budding idea later).

ACTION STEP 21

Brainstorm for solutions. (p. 88)

STEP 6: MESH POSSIBLE SOLUTIONS WITH OPPORTUNITIES IN THE MARKETPLACE

Some people like to use lists or mind maps for arriving at opportunities, but others prefer a more systematic method. A **matrix grid** can provide the desired structure for decision making. After you have brainstormed some possible solutions, you need to improve your focus on them and evaluate them. The matrix grid shown in Figure 3.4 helped Steve and Anne do this. The day after their brainstorm with Carol and Rick, they reviewed the various criteria on the list. They then ranked the top three in order of greatest importance and the bottom three in order of least importance. The top 3 were then assigned a value of 3, and the bottom 3 were given a value of 1. This way, each criterion did not receive the same value.

Steve, Anne, Carol, and Rick voted on several of the possible solutions they brainstormed. When the numbers were tallied, the group decided the network computer business was the preferred option. They liked the idea of working with small businesses. This segment was starting to heat up. They would provide advice and consulting in computer networks. Their target market would be smaller, independent business that wanted growth. If they succeeded, the intranet would be the next focus.

MATRIX GRID

A screen through which ideas are passed in order to find solutions

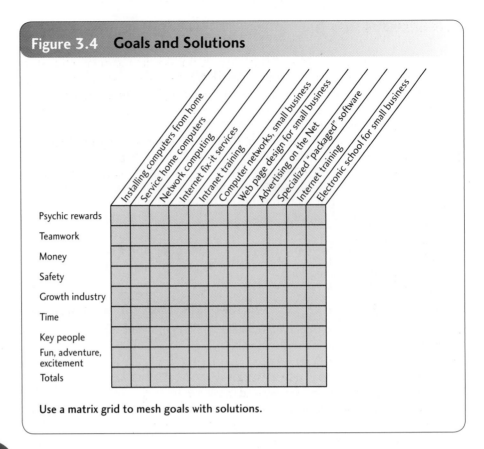

Figure 3.4   Goals and Solutions

Use a matrix grid to mesh goals with solutions.

ACTION STEP 22

Mesh possible solutions with your goals and objectives, using a matrix grid. (p. 88)

Now prepare a matrix grid, and weigh your criteria to help you focus on the best course of action. Action Step 22 tells you how to do it.

STEP 7: TAKE STOCK OF, AND FOCUS ON, THE MOST PROMISING OPPORTUNITIES

What have you learned about the opportunity selection process? Before you answer this, take some time to rethink what you want to achieve in your small business. If you feel a little uneasy about how fast you've run the last couple of laps, perhaps it's because you haven't yet identified your industry. It's time to take stock.

What is your industry? What is your market gap? What are some opportunities for you?

BUSINESS MISSION STATEMENT

Now that you have identified your market opportunity—one that reflects your values and is aligned to your personal vision—you need to think about a business mission.

Your personal vision and values give you guidance and direction in the conduct of your life. In much the same way, a business mission—the **business mission statement**—is a statement of your company's purpose and aims. Business mission statements are normally connected to the values and vision of the business owner. In small business, a business mission statement is concise (about 25 words or fewer) and briefly describes the product or service, who the target customer is, and what niche or segment is the focus.

BUSINESS MISSION STATEMENT

A statement of your company's purpose and aims

YOUR BUSINESS MISSION

Your business mission is your road map. First, it states what you believe in—the difference that the organization makes. Second, it becomes a way of measuring your success as you evaluate your results over time against what you stated you wanted to do. Third, it becomes your promotional message, as you incorporate it as part of your printed material.

A business mission statement expresses the nature and raison d'être, or purpose, of the business. According to Industry Canada, it usually covers the major functions and operations of the organization and answers the following questions:

- What are the products and services?
- Who is the expected or target customer?
- What industry is it in?
- Which markets does it serve?
- What is its major driving force?
- Why will this business be successful?

In his book *The Practice of Management*, Peter Drucker[3] notes that we should think about a number of factors in developing a mission statement.

1. **Customers.** Who is your target customer?
2. **Product or service.** What is your business all about—in a sentence or two?
3. **Geographic market.** Are you serving your local city, the province, Canada, or—if you are exporting—even world markets?
4. **Concern for financial contribution and growth.** What returns do you expect on your investment, and what growth pattern do you expect to achieve (e.g., growth of 5 percent per year)?
5. **Core values and beliefs.** Look back at the list of values you created earlier in this chapter. Are these values consistent with what you want to do?
6. **Self-concept.** Because of knowledge and expertise, you may bring to the business a special skill that will give you a unique niche.
7. **Concern for public image and stakeholders.** Are you an environmentally friendly business? Will you be contributing a percentage of all sales to charity? Are you actively involved in your community?
8. **Concern for employees.** Are you planning to run your business on a team basis? Or will you alone be it?
9. **Technology and systems.** Does your business offer a value-added benefit by using technology or a particular system?

Your business mission statement is unique. Some people capture their thoughts in a few words; others take pages. Some people express them in poems, some in music, and some in art. Some experts advise that an empowering mission statement

- represents the deepest and best within you,
- fulfills the contribution your business will make,
- deals with your vision and principle-based values.[4]

For example, Anne and Steve's mission statement for their business might read like this:

To help growing small businesses improve their profitability, effectiveness, and long-term growth through the implementation of, and training in, computer networks.

Here are a few other examples of business mission statements:

To own a flower and gift shop that specializes in highly stylized floral arrangements for "special occasions," and that services the local community.

To be a proud and profitable home-based business providing responsive and efficient word-processing services and laser-quality correspondence to local small businesses.

To sell environmentally friendly cleaning products to convenience stores in our city in order to reduce our growing dependence on chemicals.

In some cases, the business mission statement is embedded in or followed up with a set of guiding principles or personal beliefs of the company/owner. For example, Vivienne Jones operates a by-appointment jewellery studio out of her Victorian home in downtown Toronto.[5] Her mission—to create a very personal form of expression through her jewellery—is rooted in her statement of personal beliefs about the way she does business:

Jewellery to me is much more than "decoration." I see it as a very personal form of expression, both for the maker and for the wearer. I make jewellery for personal creative expression, and my work is an expressive and versatile medium into which I can put my thoughts and ideas and aesthetics. Intrinsic to the way I work is my imagining that the pieces I make will be worn and valued and hopefully will become a meaningful object in someone's life. It is perhaps because of the very personal attributes of jewellery that, when asked, I will enjoy working with a client to create a piece for them.

Vivienne Jones's beliefs help her stay true to herself and to her vision of providing individualized jewellery that is both wearable and meaningful.

If you have been able to isolate an opportunity gap in your industry, it is now time to begin drafting your mission statement. Complete Action Step 23.

YOUR BUSINESS STRATEGY

A **business strategy** is a broad program for achieving an organization's objectives and thus implementing its vision. It creates a unified direction for the organization in terms of its many objectives. It also guides those choices that determine the nature and direction of an organization.

Before you start developing the strategy for your business, it's helpful to have a context or framework in which competitive strategy is formulated. A number of business models can help you begin to formulate your business strategy. An excellent positioning tool is the **SWOT** approach. SWOT is an abbreviation that refers to an analysis of internal **S**trengths and **W**eaknesses; and external **O**pportunities and **T**hreats.

The strengths and weaknesses are factors that are internal to the business. Here, you would be evaluating the strengths and weaknesses of both owner(s) and the business itself. Doing a strengths and weaknesses evaluation of yourself is an important piece of advice provided by successful entrepreneurs, such as Mike McCarron of MSM Transportation Incorporated (see, for example, E-Exercise, Box 3.6).

Let's say that you want to open a new restaurant. If you have extensive experience in the food business (product knowledge), this would be an internal strength. If you have no demonstrated teamwork (managing skills) abilities, then this would be an internal weakness. As for the business, it might be short on cash. This lack would be an internal weakness of the business. On the other hand, if you found a wonderful location, it would be an internal strength of the business.

Now let's go to the external aspects of a SWOT. External opportunities are those factors that are outside the control of the owner and the business. These include aspects such as new distribution channels, changing tastes, or technology

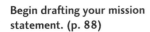

ACTION STEP 23

Begin drafting your mission statement. (p. 88)

BUSINESS STRATEGY

The broad program for achieving an organization's objectives and implementing its vision

SWOT

An abbreviation that refers to an analysis of internal strengths and weaknesses, and external opportunities and threats

Box 3.6　E-Exercise

Test Your Business Idea

Atlantic Canada Opportunities Agency (ACOA): http://www.acoa-apeca.gc.ca/eng/publications/FactSheetsAndBrochures/Pages/DevelopingyourInnovativeideas.aspx—Visit the "Developing Your Innovative Ideas" page on the ACOA website. Test your business idea by exploring these four themes.

1. **Personal considerations.** Does your business idea satisfy your personal goals and objectives?
2. **Marketing considerations.** Is there a market need for your product or service?
3. **Production considerations.** Will you be able to produce the required volume and quality of products and services?
4. **Financial considerations.** Can your operation satisfy the required financial goals?

SWOT Yourself and Others

To understand your competitors, you're going to have to snoop. As we will learn in our Chapter 12 case study, Mike McCarron is a founding partner of MSM Transportation, an award-winning trucking company. Link onto his Streets Smarts article "I've Got a Secret": http://www.todaystrucking.com/ive-got-a-secret-getting-the-dirt-on-your-rivals-isnt-as-hard-as-you-think. What advice does he give on how to learn more about the competition?

improvements. As a new restaurant owner, for example, an external opportunity might be a growing demand for ethnic foods or healthy eating. External threats relate to outside forces such as competition or a declining trend for restaurant patrons to consume alcohol.

An underlying weakness of the SWOT approach is its subjectivity. There is a tendency for an enthusiastic entrepreneur to overvalue the strengths and opportunities and undervalue the weaknesses and threats. To reduce this evaluative risk, you might want to get a "reality check" by asking knowledgeable people to do a SWOT on both you and your business idea. Another suggestion is to apply a particular weighting factor (say 1 to 10) to each of your SWOT elements. Nevertheless, SWOT is an excellent way to position your business idea and begin your strategic thinking process. We will return to this SWOT framework when it comes time to talk about the competition, in Chapter 5, and your human resource requirements, in Chapter 12. In the meantime, if you want additional information on SWOT, a good website is Tutor2u (http://www.tutor2u.net/business/strategy/SWOT_analysis.htm).

Now is a good time to test your business idea. We encourage you to do the "Test Your Business Idea" E-Exercise in Box 3.6.

To help you understand the context from which your business strategy is formulated, it is useful to look at *Competitive Advantage: Creating and Sustaining Superior Performance*, by Michael E. Porter.[6] In his book, Porter describes the internal and external factors that will affect a business's competitive strategy.

1. Internal Factors
   - *Company strengths and weaknesses*—Strengths could be such things as financial assets and technical assets. Weaknesses might be lack of brand awareness and lack of intellectual property.
   - *Personal values of key implementers*—Values held by the key people who will be implementing the strategy of the business range from focus on customers to competitive drive.

2. External Factors
   - *Industry opportunities and threats*—These factors include the current opportunities and potential threats that a company might face in the industry. Opportunities include a growing market; threats include a declining customer base.
   - *Broader societal expectations*—This factor relates to things such as social concerns, evolving mores, and government policy and how they will have an impact on the business. For example, society expects that a business will not dump toxic chemicals into lakes and rivers, and a business must be aware of government policy pertaining to this.

THINKING ABOUT YOUR BUSINESS MODEL

So far, we've been looking at developing a business mission statement, a business strategy, and a SWOT analysis tool. We have also looked at a model developed by Michael E. Porter to help us understand the context in which a competitive strategy is formulated.

> **BUSINESS MODEL**
> A framework of how all the different, interrelated parts of a business work together to create value in the marketplace

To further understand how all these topics can help you to formulate your business idea, it is useful to discuss business models. A **business model** is a framework of how all the different, interrelated parts of a business work together to create value in the marketplace.

A business model helps you to think about all of the different, interrelated functions of a business and how they work together to bring products and service to markets. Interrelated functions encompass products, services, image, distribution, and delivery. They also pertain to how many people you will need to work for you and how you will operate your business to deliver products and services to customers at the right time, right place, and right price.

To help you think about your business model, take a look at the Business Model Canvas (http://www.businessmodelgeneration.com/canvas), developed by Alexander Osterwalder.[7] (See Figure 3.5.)

The Business Model Canvas has nine basic building blocks, outlined below:

1. **Customer segments.** What are the target markets you are going to sell to? (See Chapter 4.)
2. **Value propositions.** What benefit or value will customers receive when they do business with you? What is unique about your business? What is your competitive advantage? (See Chapter 5 and Chapter 6, page 164.)
3. **Channels.** What are the different distribution channels you will use to deliver your product or service? (See Chapter 7.)
4. **Customer relationships.** What kind of relationship do you want to have with your customers? How will you relate to these customers? For example, will you just have an online store with no live person or have an operator to answer questions online for people? (See Chapter 6.)
5. **Revenue streams.** What are the different ways you will make money? (See Chapter 7, on pricing; and Chapter 10.)
6. **Key resources.** This aspect refers to operational infrastructure. What are the key resources you will need to perform the key activities? What type and size of location and what human resources are needed? (See Chapter 7, on location; and Chapter 12.)
7. **Key activities.** What are the key activities you need to perform well to create value? (See Chapter 3.)
8. **Key partners.** Who are the key partners, and why do you need them to create value?
9. **Cost structure.** What are your major costs for the resources, location, and activities? (See Chapter 7, on pricing and location; and Chapter 10.)

Figure 3.5   The Business Model Canvas

Key Partners

Who are our
Key Partners?
Who are our
Key Suppliers?
Which Key
Resources are we
acquiring from partners?
Which Key Activities do
partners perform?

MOTIVATIONS FOR
PARTNERSHIPS:
Optimization and economy
Reduction of risk and uncertainty
*Acquisition of particular resources
and activities*

Key Activities

What Key Activities
do our Value
Propositions require?
Our Distribution Channels?
Customer Relationships?
Revenue Streams?

CATEGORIES
Production
Problem Solving
Platform/Network

Key Resources

What Key Resources do
our Value Propositions
require?
Our Distribution Channels?
Customer Relationships?
Revenue Streams?

TYPES OF RESOURCES
Physical
*Intellectual (brand patents,
copyrights, data)*
Human
Financial

Value Propositions

What value do we
deliver to the customer?
Which one of our customer's
problems are we
helping to solve?
What bundles of products and
services are we offering to each
Customer Segment?
Which customer needs are we
satisfying?

CHARACTERISTICS
Newness
Performance
Customization
"Getting the Job Done"
Design
Brand/Status
Price
Cost Reduction
Risk Reduction
Accessibility
Convenience/Usability

Customer Relationships

What type of relationship
does each of our Customer
Segments expect us to
establish and maintain with them?
Which ones have we established?
How are they integrated with
the rest of our business model?
How costly are they?

EXAMPLES
Personal Assistance
Dedicated Personal Assistance
Self-Service
Automated Services
Communities
Co-creation

Channels

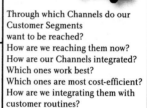

Through which Channels do our
Customer Segments
want to be reached?
How are we reaching them now?
How are our Channels integrated?
Which ones work best?
Which ones are most cost-efficient?
How are we integrating them with
customer routines?

CHANNEL PHASES:
1. *Awareness*
   *How do we raise awareness
   about our company's products and
   services?*
2. *Evaluation*
   *How do we help customers
   evaluate our organization's Value
   Proposition?*
3. *Purchase*
   *How do we allow customers to
   purchase specific products and
   services?*
4. *Delivery*
   *How do we deliver a Value
   Proposition to customers?*
5. *After sales*
   *How do we provide post-purchase
   customer support?*

Customer Segments

For whom are we
creating value?
Who are our most
important customers?

Mass Market
Niche Market
Segmented
Diversified
Multi-sided Platform

Cost Structure

What are the most important costs inherent in
our business model?
Which Key Resources are most expensive?
Which Key Activities are most expensive?

IS YOUR BUSINESS MORE:
*Cost Driven (leanest cost structure, low price value proposition, maximum
automation, extensive outsourcing)*
Value Driven (focused on value creation, premium value proposition)

SAMPLE CHARACTERISTICS:
Fixed Costs (salaries, rents, utilities)
Variable Costs
Economies of Scale
Economies of Scope

Revenue Streams

For what value are our customers really willing to pay?
For what do they currently pay?
How are they currently paying?
How would they prefer to pay?
How much does each Revenue Stream contribute to
overall revenues?

TYPES:	FIXED PRICING	DYNAMIC PRICING
Asset sale	*List Price*	*Negotiation (bargaining)*
Usage fee	*Product feature dependent*	*Yield Management*
Subscription Fee	*Customer segment dependent*	*Real-time-Market*
Lending/Renting/Leasing	*Volume dependent*	
Licensing		
Brokerage fees		
Advertisings		

Source: The Business Model Canvas, BusinessModelGeneration.com

Use these nine building blocks to build your own business model. Having a business model really makes you think about the different parts of a business and how you can create value for your customers. As we discussed in Chapter 1, innovation is a key tool of the entrepreneur. Use innovation to develop a unique business model like Michael Dell did when he developed a new way to make and deliver personal computers. To help you think of innovative business models, ask yourself "What if" questions. "What if customers purchased a different way? What if delivery of the product or service was done this way?"

In Chapter 1's opening vignette, Matt Turner and Chris Castillo asked "what if" to develop an innovative business model for fixing vehicles. Now, it's your turn to ask "what if" and think about a unique business model for yourself.

In a Nutshell

In the first few chapters, we encouraged you to come to grips with your personal vision and goals, and to look at the industry trends with new eyes. In this third chapter, we want you to begin to match your personal vision, values, and goals with market needs. Here, we provide you with a seven-step opportunity selection process and encourage you to brainstorm and complete a matrix grid to help you get your personal vision in sync with your business mission. To illustrate how this process works, we followed the progress of Steve and Anne, who ended up deciding to start their business in the field of network computers. Next, we wanted you to begin thinking about your mission statement. We hope that we have helped you connect your personal vision to a mission statement for a new business opportunity and that you are on the way to establishing your strategy for achieving your vision.

Key Terms

business mission statement	matrix grid
business model	SWOT
business strategy	values
market gap	vision

Think Points for Success

✓ Your business must reflect your personal values. These values provide you with guidance and direction in the conduct of your business and life.
✓ Select an opportunity by using the seven-step opportunity selection process as a guide.
✓ Align your mission statement with your personal values. The statement must include the purpose and aim of your firm.
✓ Establish a strategy that supports your vision.

Action Steps

ACTION STEP 16

Clarify your values.

Okay, you've listed your values. Now we want you to list five of your most important personal values and five of your most important business values. Next, we want you to think about and describe each value in more detail. Are your personal values consistent with your business values? These values are the basis for your actions—the way you conduct your personal life and your business. Now we want you to get started. Jot down at least two ways you could implement these values into your day-to-day life or your prospective business. Here's one example to help you get started:

Personal Value: Simplicity
 Short description: Simplifying a task will make the results more efficient and effective, reduce my stress level, and give me more time to play.
 Action: Take any small task and come up with at least two ways to simplify it.
 Develop two ways in which I can simplify my life.

Feeling a little overwhelmed? Link to the Values Center: http://www.gurusoftware.com/GuruNet/ValuesCenter.htm. It's a great source to get you started. It helped us craft the above example.

ACTION STEP 17

List your business goals for the next three years.

What do you want from small business? Money? Fame? Job security? To be your own boss? Freedom to explore the marketplace? Control of your own destiny? Just want to be a president?

Think back to the forces that first made you interested in small business. What were those forces? Where were you when you first thought about owning the store? How have circumstances changed your goals?

List everything you want, even if it seems unreasonable or embarrassing to you. This is your personal list, after all, and you will sift through the ideas later.

ACTION STEP 18

Collect secondary data on your favourite industry segment.

What industry segment really attracts you? What's out there that has a magnetic pull you can't resist? To help you get started, recall what you discovered in Action Steps 9 through 15.

Start with a wide-angle view by looking at two or three segments that interest you. After you've decided on "your" segment, research it in depth. It might help to organize your research into categories such as life cycle, speed of change, history, competition, recent industry breakthroughs, costs of positioning yourself, and customer base.

If you're working alone, it will help to write your industry overview. If you're working with a team, you'll save yourself some confusion if each team member writes an overview and later shares his or her perspective with the others.

This is a never-ending action step. Once you are in business, you will have to be as diligent in keeping up with the industry segment as you were in your initial research.

ACTION STEP 19

Identify three or four market gaps that look promising.

Now that you're hip-deep in your industry, scrutinize segments where you think you could survive and prosper. It's time to begin to profile your target customer.

Prepare a combination demographic–psychographic checklist to help you explore target markets. Include items for evaluating

- demographic data—age, sex, income, family size, education, socioeconomic status, place of residence, religion, and political affiliation among them;
- psychographic data—occupation, lifestyle, buying habits, dreams, interest and leisure activities, ambitions, and the like.

Or, if you're going after a commercial/industrial market, use company size, type of industry, number of employees, location, departments of large companies, and so on.

Tailor your checklist so that it provides a thorough profile of your target customer.

ACTION STEP 20

List problems that need solutions.

When you surveyed your friends in Action Step 12, you were approaching the list of problems you need to develop now. The difference is that the problems you are seeking now are those that are unique to the industry you've been exploring.

Get together with people who know something about your industry. Ask them for input and write down everything. Use this input to develop your list.

Each problem you identify multiplies your opportunities to prosper in your segment.

ACTION STEP 21

Brainstorm for solutions.

Now you need to get really creative. Dig out the list of problems in your industry that you made in Action Step 20. Every problem can be turned into an opportunity.

You'll generate better ideas in the long run if you just let your imagination roll. Don't be concerned with a lot of logic and reason—not at this stage. You might begin with a quick overview of what you know so far and then slide into possible (and impossible?) solutions. An audio recorder can be useful.

Have fun.

ACTION STEP 22

Mesh possible solutions with your goals and objectives, using a matrix grid.

A matrix analysis will help you focus, especially if you're working with a group and have diverse objectives to satisfy. If you prepare a large grid and put it on the wall, all members of the team can participate.

1. Down the left side, list the goals you brainstormed in Action Step 17.
2. Along the top, list the possible solutions you came up with in Action Step 21.
3. Select a rating system to use for evaluating the match of each possible solution with each of your goals. It could be a 10-point scale or a plus-zero-minus system:
   Plus (+) = 3
   Zero (0) = 2
   Minus (−) = 1
4. When you've rated all of the combinations, find the total for each column. The totals will indicate your best prospects. The rest is up to you.

ACTION STEP 23

Begin drafting your mission statement.

In Chapter 2, Action Step 15, we asked you to define your business and begin to develop your "pitch." Now you are ready to begin drafting your mission statement. We will help you to refine this statement over the course of the next few chapters. In Chapter 4, Action Step 27, and in Chapter 5 when we discuss competition, we'll encourage you to go back and refine this statement.

In a short paragraph, describe the nature and purpose of your business. Try to address the following:

- What are your products and services?
- Who is your expected or target customer?
- What industry is your business in?
- Which markets does the business serve?
- What is the major driving force of the business? Why will this business be successful?

You might also want to expand your statement by including your core set of values and beliefs, concern for stakeholders and the environment, or concern for employee well-being.

Now go back and revisit your personal vision. Does your personal vision connect with your business mission? It should. If you're having trouble, here is one example that might help.

Beatrice had two visions. Her personal vision was "to live a life in which others would remember her with dignity and respect." Her business mission was "to be a respected flower and gift shop owner specializing in highly stylized floral arrangements for 'special occasions' and catering to her local community needs." In real terms, Beatrice's business mission was that she wanted to be remembered with respect and dignity through her flowers.

Business Plan Building Block

CURRENT POSITION AND FUTURE OUTLOOK

You will need to explain your current position and future outlook for this business projected out three to five years. You will also have to back up your explanation with industry research.

What does your secondary research say about your industry and industry segment? Go back to Action Step 18, page 76, and review your results. Consult with industry associations or experts. Review trade magazines.

If you're planning for an existing business, you must perform a critical analysis of your current situation and how you will grow the business over the next few years.

Focus on how you are unique and how to build on your strengths. If this is a start-up venture, base your forecast on industry research and your plans to exploit your market niche.

You began this process of defining your business in Chapter 2. Now it's time to build, correct, and polish your first attempt.

What industry are you in? What is your industry segment? How do you plan to grow your business over the next few years?

UNIQUENESS AND DIFFERENTIATION

It is important that you demonstrate that you are addressing an unfilled need. You are different and unique, and you understand the meaning of pricing and value from your potential customers' perspective.

YOUR BUSINESS IS UNIQUE BECAUSE ...

Your product is smaller, faster, neater, more flexible, lighter, more attractive, or stronger. Or your service is quicker, more reliable, and mobile. Your people are better trained. Your location is more convenient. Your prices are competitive, and your business has many advantages over the existing competition.

Nobody wants to hear about a "me too" business. Stress the ways in which your company is different—then translate these features into benefits for a hungry market. It's important to show how you have an edge over the competition. Try to think in terms of a "personal niche monopoly."

MARKET OPPORTUNITIES

Based on your research, arrange the most promising opportunities in the marketplace according to the following categories:

1. new or emerging markets—gaps and niches,
2. neglected customer needs,

3. failing competitors,

4. complementary product mix,

5. expanded use of existing facilities,

6. new geographical and international opportunities,

7. potential for profits.

Rank by priority order those that are most attractive now and up to five years forward.

Checklist Questions and Actions to Develop Your Business Plan

Positioning Yourself as an Entrepreneur for Market Opportunities

❏ How is your product or service addressing the needs of the target market and offering benefits ?

❏ What are your business and personal values?

❏ Define your market niche.

❏ Define the idea filters you used to establish the business viability for your product or service.

❏ Complete your business mission statement.

❏ Revisit and update your business goals and objectives under Chapter 2's Checklist Questions and Actions.

❏ Identify market segments that have potential.

❏ List industry problems that your business might face, and describe how you would address them.

Case Study: Shopify— An E-Commerce Alternative

Case Background

Tobias Lütke, profiled in Chapter 2's opening vignette, was newly arrived from Germany. The vignette on him shows the importance of positioning yourself as an entrepreneur for market opportunities. Throughout this chapter, we have considered topics such as market opportunities, uniqueness and differentiation, business strategy, vision, mission, and values. Now, for this case, please respond to the questions and do the activities outlined below to help you apply these concepts.

Case Resources

The following are useful websites to further understand this case:

- http://www.shopify.com/
- http://www.profitguide.com/industry-focus/technology/canadas-smartest-company-44283
- http://www.theglobeandmail.com/report-on-business/small-business/sb-growth/success-stories/fluke-and-luck-shopifys-co-founder-profited-from-both/article4575360/?page=all

Case Study Questions and Activities

1. Values

In this chapter, you learned the importance of aligning your personal vision and values with the market opportunities. This "alignment" was a major factor contributing to the success for Tobias Lütke, featured in the opening vignette in Chapter 2.

  a. Briefly describe what is meant by the term *values*.
  b. In the section "Your Values" (page 71), we provided you with a possible list of personal and business values. Based on this list, state three key values that Lütke exhibited. For each value, explain how these values have assisted Lütke in becoming a successful entrepreneur.

2. Passion and vision
Passion and vision are key characteristics of a successful entrepreneur. How did Lütke display these two characteristics as he launched Shopify?

3. Market segmentation
Lütke found a market segment, or niche, that was consistent with his vision and values. What was Shopify's market segment or niche?

4. Mission statements
Mission statements help successful entrepreneurs focus on their market niche.
  a. What is a mission statement?
  b. Draft a mission statement for Shopify.

5. Trends creating opportunities
In both this chapter and Chapter 2, we learned that trends can create business opportunities.
  a. Briefly explain how market trends have contributed, so far, to the success of Shopify? (To refresh your memory on trends, you might want to link onto http://www.acoa-apeca.gc.ca/eng/publications/FactSheetsAndBrochures/Pages/DevelopingyourInnovativeideas.aspx.)
  b. What is a SWOT? If you were to do a SWOT analysis of Shopify, in what sections of your SWOT would you be discussing trends?

6. Problems creating opportunities
Lütke had a problem, but he developed a solution to that problem.
  a. Clearly describe Lütke's problem.
  b. Clearly describe the solution that Lütke came up with.
  c. Briefly describe the market opportunity that Lütke saw.
  d. Why is identifying problems so important for creating opportunities?

7. Find a competitor to Shopify and answer this question: What features, advantages, and benefits does Shopify offer that this competitor does not?

Notes

1. Kinnikinnick Foods website: http://consumer.kinnikinnick.com/index.cfm/fuseaction/consumer.home.html; and Industry Canada, "Electronic Commerce in Canada, Success Stories," http://www.ic.gc.ca/eic/site/ecic-ceac.nsf/eng/home.

2. http://www.ascd.org/publications/books/107042/chapters/developing-a-vision-and-a-mission.aspx.

3. Adapted from Peter F. Drucker, *The Practice of Management* (New York: Harper and Row, 1954).

4. Stephen R. Covey, A. Roger Merrill, and Rebecca R. Merrill, *First Things First* (New York: Simon and Schuster, 1994).

5. Vivienne Jones website: http://www.viviennejones.com; and Janice Lindsay, "Jewel in Parkdale," *The Globe and Mail*, July 13, 2002, p. L7.

6. Michael E. Porter, *Competitive Advantage: Creating and Sustaining Superior Performance* (New York: Free Press, 1985).

7. Alexander Osterwalder and Yves Pigneur, *Business Model Generation: A Handbook for Visionaries, Game Changers, and Challengers* (Hobokan, NJ: John Wiley & Sons, 2010).

Profiling Your Target Customer

Chapter 4 will help you prepare part B of your business plan, The Market and the Target Customer.

Lisa A/Shutterstock.com

LEARNING OPPORTUNITIES

After reading this chapter, you should be able to

- understand that your key to survival in small business is the target customer;
- recognize three kinds of customer groups;
- use primary and secondary research to profile your target customer;
- match your target customer with what he or she reads, watches, and listens to;
- become more aware of, and start being on the lookout for, potential partnerships, alliances, and associations;
- recognize the market and the target customers who are about to surface;
- research your prospective target customers and refine your mission statement;
- visualize your business and target customers.

ACTION STEP PREVIEW

24. Develop your own psychographic profile.
25. Research specific magazines in your business area.
26. Profile three firms using the Canadian Company Capabilities database.
27. Research your prospective target customers, and refine your mission statement.

LANDS' END

DIRECT MERCHANT (INTERMEDIARY)

Business that works directly with manufacturers in an attempt to eliminate the markups of middlemen

Lands' End is a successful multinational retailer that sells clothes, luggage, and household products worldwide through outlet stores, catalogues, and the Internet. It's a **direct merchant (intermediary)**, meaning it works directly with mills and manufacturers in an attempt to eliminate the markups of intermediaries. In the mid-1990s, Lands' End recognized the power of the Internet and became an "early adopter." Landsend.com was launched and, since then, it has grown to become one of the world's largest (in business volume) apparel websites.

What does this successful multinational company have to do with Canadian small business? Much of the Lands' End's dot-com success has to do with the vision, passion, and persistence of two Canadian entrepreneurs—Louise Guay and Jean-François St-Arnaud. Their company, My Virtual Model Incorporated (MVM), which began operation in the late 1990s, now provides much of the technology for Lands' End to sell its apparel online.

At Lands' End, here is how the My Virtual Model works. You log on and fill in a customer-friendly questionnaire. If it's your first time, the idea is to get quick feedback and to understand that the online system is easy, user friendly, and efficient. When you are finished, your silhouette appears on the screen. You can then go shopping. You click on the garments you want and put them on the model. The virtual model allows you to mix and match different colours, styles, and sizes, and even turn a full circle. It's quite real, and it's fun. You can also add accessories.

MY VIRTUAL MODEL

Since the early 2000s, MVM has grown into a multimillion-dollar company. Its major clients, beginning with Lands' End, now include retail heavyweights such as Sears, L.L. Bean, and Adidas. The technology has fitted more than 4 million virtual models with 100 million garments, and the garments are increasing by 300,000 per month. My Virtual Model improves the profitability of e-retailers in three ways. First, it increases the online "conversion rate"—the percentage of website visits that are converted into purchases.

"Customers who use My Virtual Model have a 34 percent higher conversion rate," said Sam Taylor, vice-president (in 2002) of e-commerce for Lands' End. In addition, the average order value is increased by as much as 15 percent, and the return rate can be reduced by up to 50 percent.

In the early years, a critical factor contributing to the success of MVM was the ability of the founding partners to identify a champion client, or primary customer. According to Louise Guay,

> We decided to hire a consultant … and he said, let's go to Lands' End. And we were very lucky because Lands' End was very advanced with e-commerce, and the moment we came there, I swear, they said, we were waiting for you. I said, what do you mean? Because they had so many problems with returns, with the fact that people cannot see themselves online … And once you have one or two, then it grows for sure and people are followers—very rare are the ones that want to be the first.

MVM found a customer—Lands' End—with a market need and the money to buy and support its product. MVM's technology was created to help solve the needs of a specific customer. Once the company found a leading customer, Guay and St-Arnaud knew investment money and other customers would follow.

Of course, many other factors that are almost as diverse as the entrepreneurial personalities of the founding partners contribute to the MVM success story. In Chapter 4 and 5 case studies, we will encourage you to return to this example, and analyze and reflect on some of these entrepreneurial success factors. For now, you might want to learn a little more about e-retailing. Click onto the My Virtual Model website (http://www. myvirtualmodel.com) and explore.[1]

ONE-TO-ONE CUSTOMER RELATIONSHIPS

When Mercedes-Benz, Procter & Gamble, Nike, and Philips Electronics decided they wanted to establish a compelling presence on the Internet, they turned to website developer Critical Mass. This Canadian business-to-business company has earned a reputation for innovative Web personalization. Critical Mass is an interactive services firm that provides solutions to help the world's leading companies increase their revenues, reduce costs, and deepen customer relationships. It's a Canadian small business success story with a host of international awards.

Critical Mass began operation in 1995. At that time, cofounder Ted Hellard offered to develop the Mercedes-Benz website in three months—no money upfront, no strings attached. "If you like it, then you can pay us for it," he told the luxury car manufacturer. "If you don't like it, you've risked nothing." Mercedes-Benz liked it, and Critical Mass has never looked back.

Today, Critical Mass has more than 300 employees serving Fortune 500 companies, with offices in Calgary; Toronto; Chicago; New York; and Austin, Texas. According to Dan Evans, former president and managing director of Critical Mass, "People expect to go on the Net and be treated as individuals. The concept of mass marketing has kind of disappeared. What the Internet has allowed marketers to do is to actually deliver on the promises of one-to-one relationship marketing."

Take a look at Box 4.1, and see how Critical Mass helped Nike build its one-to-one relationship with its customers.[2]

In Chapter 3, we asked you to focus on your product or service. Your prime concerns were the following: "Do I have a product or service that is in a growth segment or a growth market?" "Are my business goals consistent with my personal values, goals, and long-term vision?" By now, we hope you have some pretty solid ideas as to what products or services are right for you. In the old way of thinking, entrepreneurs would have next focused their attention on the basic features of the product, such as size, colour, or price. We call this old view a "product-push" mentality, and it goes like this: "I think that there's a market there somewhere, and all I have to do is to produce what I think to be a quality product at a competitive price, and the market will respond with a sale."

Most marketers tell us that a product-push strategy doesn't work well in today's marketplace. More promising is an important trend called **customer relationship marketing (CRM)**—the development of long-term, mutually

CUSTOMER RELATIONSHIP MARKETING (CRM)

The development of long-term, mutually beneficial, and cost-effective relationships with your customers

Box 4.1 The One-to-One Marketing Challenge

Critical Mass, which is based in Calgary, Alberta, was approved by Nike to enhance NIKEiD, an online interactive portion of nike.com. Through NIKEiD, Nike customers can customize and purchase athletic shoes (http://nikeid.nike.com/nikeid/index.jsp).

A PR Newswire article quotes Mark Allen, general manager of NIKEiD, as saying, "Nike's roots are in working one-on-one with athletes, learning what they need and building them the best possible shoes."

The key technology behind NIKEiD is the NIKE iD Shoe Configurator, a fast-loading and user-friendly online tool that lets visitors design their own shoes. Customers interact with the software and experiment with hundreds of different color combinations, getting the results in real time and from any angle.

Critical Mass helped Nike develop an e-commerce initiative that puts personalization at the forefront. The centrepiece is the iD Configurator, which allows visitors to customize their Nike gear by choosing from hundreds of possible colour combinations and adding 3- to 16-character personal iDs. Products change in real time with each design decision a customer makes. The site continues to be built largely on visitor feedback, a clear reflection of NIKEiD's responsiveness to the needs of its customers.

Critical Mass focused on enabling Nike to meet the needs of its customers. Nike wanted to keep it simple—plug-ins, applets, Flash, heavy page size, and other usability barriers were not options for Nike. Critical Mass recognized that the company's prime requirements were performance and accessibility.

Source: http://www.prnewswire.com/news-releases/nike-selects-critical-mass-to-bring-nike-id-to-the-next-level-of-online-personalization-73284962.html. Reprinted by permission of Critical Mass.

MARKET-PULL APPROACH

Determining what the customer wants through a customer profile, and then adapting or creating a product or service to satisfy this want or need

ONE-TO-ONE (ONE-2-ONE) MARKETING

The process of identifying the specific needs of each customer, repeatedly satisfying those needs, and creating a long-term value-added relationship

beneficial, and cost-effective relationships with your customers. Relationship marketing emphasizes a **market-pull approach**. You determine what the customer wants through a customer profile and then adapt or create a product or service to satisfy this want or need. In other words, you design your business around what the customer wants rather than trying to make the customer purchase what you want to produce. The market-pull approach explained, to a large degree, the success of My Virtual Model and Critical Mass in the opening vignettes. These thriving companies knew who their target customers were and what they wanted. They were also prepared to work with their customers over the long haul. Their goal has been to help other businesses implement a **one-to-one (one-2-one) marketing** strategy. They have jumped onto the mass customization trend we talked about in Chapter 2 by helping their clients identify the specific needs of each customer (consumer), repeatedly satisfying those needs, and creating a long-term relationship.

MOBILE APPS: THE ULTIMATE ONE-ON-ONE MARKETING

The ultimate one-on-one marketing strategy is getting customers to download an app (an application, basically a software) and claiming a piece of real estate on their mobile phones.

Mobile apps have become a huge business for which people are developing everything from games to how-to tips to a mobile version of their websites.

Box 4.2   E-Exercise

Mobile Apps

Learn how to create your own mobile app. Click onto one of these sites and explore:

- http://ibuildapp.com/
- http://www.theappbuilder.com/
- http://www.buildanapp.com/
- http://www.appmakr.com/
- https://www.snappii.com/

Furthermore, many entrepreneurs are jumping on the mobile app development bandwagon by developing apps for their businesses … or developing apps for other businesses! Many have developed apps for the Android, iPhone, and BlackBerry. Opportunities exist to use apps to deliver content and brand messages that can lead to customer satisfaction and ultimately sales.

Businesses are looking at how to take advantage of mobile apps to further engage with customers and provide them with information on what they do, contact information such as phone numbers and email capabilities, and finally real-time information for people seeking more information before making purchases.

Mobile phones, and the ability to get into people's phones by developing mobile apps, is now touted to be a bigger revolution than the Internet. Here is one wave that entrepreneurs can't miss.

Now, go to Box 4.2 and click on some of the app development sites provided. How easy is it to develop your own mobile app? Which platform is better? Is it Android, iPhone, or BlackBerry? Is there a site that creates one mobile app for *all* platforms?

In this chapter, we want you to start thinking about how you can develop a market-pull one-to-one marketing strategy. This means that you'll have to begin with a customer profile. We'll also show you how to use key secondary and primary research and resources to your advantage.

THE POWER OF PROFILING

An understanding of the needs of your customer is your key to survival in small business. For that reason, you will have to do a profile of your customer. **Profiling** is about describing both needs and behaviour. In this chapter, we'll focus on specific profiling techniques and sources to help you understand that elusive customer. But first, let's take a look at the different kinds of customers. Entrepreneurs we have known tell us you should be watching for at least three typesof customers.

PROFILING

Describing the needs and behaviour of your customer

PRIMARY CUSTOMER

Your **primary**, or **target**, **customer** is the person, type of person, or business that has the highest probability of buying your product or service. This target customer is perfect for your business and could be a heavy user. For example, during their start-up phases, Lands' End was MVM's target customer, and Mercedes-Benz was Critical Mass's target customer.

PRIMARY, OR TARGET, CUSTOMER

A person, type of person, or business that has the highest probability of buying your product or service

SECONDARY CUSTOMER

SECONDARY CUSTOMER

A person, type of person, or business that needs to be convinced to buy your product or service

The **secondary customer** is the customer who needs convincing, one who almost slips away before you can focus the camera. Louise Guay of MVM calls this kind of customer the "follower." Once MVM had found Lands' End, their target customer, then secondary customers, such as Sears, L.L. Bean, and Adidas, followed. In the Critical Mass case, once cofounder Ted Hellard signed on its primary customer, Mercedes-Benz, other companies such as Procter & Gamble, Nike, and Philips Electronics turned to it, as well.

Sometimes your secondary customer will lead you to the third customer, who is invisible at first.

INVISIBLE CUSTOMER

Many entrepreneurs set their focus and base their whole business plan on a specific target market, such as primary and secondary customers. This decision reflects the logical side of entrepreneurs who make the decision to go after obvious customers based on research for the selling of their product or service. But smart entrepreneurs know that things are not so logical, especially when it comes to customers. We may think people buy for a specific reason, but in reality, they buy for a totally different reason than what our logic would suggest. Smart entrepreneurs, therefore, try not to be so smart and, instead, work on developing a keen sense of awareness for opportunities.

INVISIBLE CUSTOMER

A person, type of person, or business you don't anticipate but has a need for your product or service

Enter the invisible customer. The **invisible customer** is the one you don't anticipate but emerges due to a need for your product or service. This customer appears after you open the doors, after you have the courage to go ahead and start your business. Although you can't anticipate this customer, you must always be ready to change so that you can take advantage of new market opportunities. This is what Ross Angus did.

Ross Angus's entrepreneurial career began while he was watching a minor league hockey game. There was a near-fatal accident when a young player was cut by an errant blade. Angus left the game that night determined to find a way to prevent this kind of accident. He persisted and eventually invented and sold his hockey Body Armour—a high-tech, cut-resistant body undershirt. Along the road, an invisible customer showed up. A local police force was looking for a product to protect officers handling glass. This need led to a new customer and product. Angus developed the Breacher—a special glove that protects an officer's arm and hands during breaching, or forced entry, operations.[3]

The invisible customer becomes particularly important now that we are well entrenched in the Internet age. If you create an exciting, informative, and active website, many invisible customers from around the world will link on. They will be demanding, well informed, and somewhat impatient. Your website must find a way to "listen to" and respond to these new customers. They can lead your company into an entirely new direction.

In this chapter, we focus on your primary and secondary customers, because they are the ones you can see right now. But remember the experience of Ross Angus and the potential of the invisible customer. Keep on the lookout for these elusive "invisible" customers.

You will have to think about two basic customer types:

- consumers (or end users) and
- business-to-business (or supply chain) customers.

Most retail business, for example, deal directly with the consumer, or end user (also called the "final customer"). Consumers are the final customers who buy and use the products or services sold. A company that deals with the consumer is called a **business-to-consumer (B2C) business**. If you are planning a B2C business, you will have to think about doing a consumer, or end-user, profile.

CONSUMER, OR END-USER, PROFILE

Normally, when we think of a target customer, we picture the consumer, or end user. This is the case for most of our retail businesses. In Chapter 3 opening vignette, Doug Burgoyne began his entrepreneurial adventure by focusing on consumers who wanted an eco-friendly solution to moving while Tobias Lütke, in Chapter 2, looked at himself as the customer first. He wanted a better e-commerce shopping solution so he built himself one and others then enquired about his solution. These examples are typical of B2C companies, because their "heavy" target customer is the consumer, or end user.

If you're planning to start a B2C company, your customer profile will require **demographics**—the segmenting and statistical analysis of your target customer by age, sex, income, education, location, and the like. You'll also need a new tool called **psychographics**—first-hand intuitive insight into lifestyle, buying habits, patterns of consumption, and attitudes.

DEMOGRAPHIC PROFILE

If you are targeting your product or service to an end user, you will have to arm yourself with a demographic profile of your target customer. Major demographic variables that you should be concerned with are

- age,
- sex,
- marital status,
- ethnicity,
- education,
- earnings,
- work status,
- family status,
- religion.

Where do you obtain demographic information? You might choose to rely on your primary research, such as surveying and interviewing—as we discuss later on in this chapter. There are a number of possible sources for your secondary research.

The Census of Population is one of the major Statistics Canada sources of information. Census data are gathered every five years (e.g., 2006, 2011, and so on) through a massive survey of the Canadian population. The data are organized into a number of categories (e.g., age, sex, and household income) that are then described and published by Statistics Canada. Census data are produced for a number of standard geographic areas.

The major advantages of the census are twofold:

1. **It is comprehensive.** Data can be tabulated by age, sex, employment status, sex, income, and so on.
2. **It is detailed.** Data can be tabulated for small geographic areas, the smallest of which is the enumeration area (about 300 dwellings).

The major disadvantage of the census is its lack of timeliness. A census is conducted once every five years. By the time the data are published, it could be

BUSINESS-TO-CONSUMER (B2C) COMPANY

A firm whose "heavy" target customer is the consumer, or end user

DEMOGRAPHICS

Key characteristics of a group of people, such as age, sex, income, and where they live

PSYCHOGRAPHICS

Segmenting of the population by lifestyle behaviour, buying habits, patterns of consumption, and attitudes

Box 4.3 2011 Census Information—Getting Started

To begin learning about the census and your community, visit Statistics Canada, Census of Canada: http://www12.statcan.gc.ca/census-recensement/2011/dp-pd/index-eng.cfm, and click on "Geography."

Here you will find community information on

- population (e.g., age, sex, and marital status),
- education,
- earnings,
- work status,
- income,
- families and dwellings,
- religion.

More free information can be obtained by clicking on the "Summary Tables": http://www.statcan.gc.ca/tables-tableaux/sum-som/index-eng.htm. Customized census information is also available for a fee. See, for example, Custom Services.

To learn more about the kinds of census information available, we suggest that you click onto Statistics Canada's *Labour Market and Income Data Guide*: http://www.library.mcgill.ca/edrs/data/dli/statcan/LFHR99/Doc/LMIDGE.PDF.

several years out of date. However, in many cases, census data can provide much-needed historical trend information.

Finding the right census information can be time consuming and sometimes frustrating. To get started, go to the "Geography" link provided in Box 4.3. Once you've become familiar with census terms and information, we suggest that you visit a main library that carries Statistics Canada information. You should find the information clearly indexed, but don't be afraid to ask the librarian for help.

Although the census can be a powerful tool for demographically profiling your target customer, it's not the only source. You should not stop here. Another good source of Statistics Canada information is the Statistics Canada *Market Research Handbook, 2008 Edition*. This annual publication has all kinds of consumer information. Statistics Canada's *Spending Patterns in Canada* (Catalogue No. 62-202-X, http://www.statcan.gc.ca/pub/62-202-x/62-202-x2008000-eng.pdf) is another useful source that normally can be found at your resource centre or public library.

Detailed information by postal code is available from Canada Post but at a fee. The price you pay will depend on the size of the area and the information you request.

The Software School Inc.: B2C Target Customer Example

The example business plan in Chapter 15 is based on a fictional school called The Software School Inc. In this example, The Software School Inc. used the following variables to describe its secondary B2C Target Customers:

Our B2C Target Customer

Our secondary target is the home user with these characteristics:

- sex—50 percent male, 50 percent female;
- age—18–45;

- education—some college;
- owns PC—30 percent;
- has access to a computer at work—52 percent;
- lives near a computer store—73 percent;
- household income—$55,000+;
- occupation—professional, managerial, executive, or entrepreneurial.

PSYCHOGRAPHIC PROFILING

In Chapter 2, we talked about the importance of demographics and how the boomers, in particular, have affected and will continue to affect market trends. In a strange way, this "bulging" phenomenon (social change), combined with our knowledge-based/change economy (economic change), has forced marketers to ask why people purchase products or services, not simply who is buying. Although the demographics of the population are still predictable, the lifestyle and buying habits are no longer tied to demographics. Today, we have to know *why* people are buying. For example, two adults with a combined income of $85,000 but with no children (**D**ouble-**I**ncome-**N**o-**K**ids— DINKs) have different spending patterns than two adults earning $75,000 to $125,000 but with four children. Why? Because these two groups have completely different wants and values. People now buy products and services that reflect the needs of their lifestyles, not necessarily those of their sex, age, or income group.

Psychographics explore the whys and wants of consumer purchases. It is a process of segmenting the population by lifestyles and values, recognizing that people in each segment or slice have different reasons for making a purchase. Psychographic analysis groups (or segments) individuals into specific categories based on attitudes, needs, values, and "mental postures." It helps marketers, researchers, and business owners understand why people buy specific products and services. What are their motivators? Why does one product appeal more than another?

There are a number of "proprietary" psychographic models in use in North America. Two of the most prominent are the VALS (value and lifestyle model), from SRI International, and the Goldfarb model. In Action Step 24, we encourage you to become more comfortable with psychographics by profiling yourself using the VALS psychographic model.

Several for-profit companies can provide you with a psychographic or lifestyle profile for a specific area. For example, Compusearch or Generation 5 (see Action Step 24) can provide lifestyles data by postal code. The *Financial Post's FP Markets, Canadian Demographics* is another good source of psychographic data as well as demographic information. These kinds of data can be obtained in published form for large areas, but when it comes to a specific neighbourhood, you will most likely have to pay for the data. The cost can range from hundreds of dollars to hundreds of thousands of dollars, depending on the level of detail you need.

You will probably have to do most, if not all of your own research to get a psychographic handle on your target customer—mainly because of cost factors; however, this is your opportunity to practise your new-eyes and primary research, and learn why people buy things. In addition, this might be your opportunity to piggyback all of the information gathered for use by media sources. Check out Box 4.4 to see how one entrepreneurial firm, Decode, Inc., profiles its target customer—the Nexus generation. Then use Action Step 24 to begin developing your own psychographic profile.

ACTION STEP 24

Develop your own psychographic profile. (p. 113)

Box 4.4 Target Market—The Nexus Generation

Businesses, governments, or other organizations trying to reach Generation X soon come up against a major roadblock: no one knows exactly who or what Generation X is!

According to some, Generation X is all about the year you were born: 1963, 1969, or (depending on who's talking) 1976. On the one hand, Generation Xers have been described as wanderers, slackers, and couch potatoes interested only in watching *Simpsons* reruns. On the other hand, they have been portrayed as the most conservative, hardworking generation since those born during the Great Depression. Similarly, some experts say Xers are serious about marriage, whereas others see the X generation as a group reluctant to make commitments.

Robert Barnard feels the term *Generation X*, as a label, is widely overused, ambiguous, and a cliché. "It means too many things to too many different people," says Barnard, a thirty-something Xer from Toronto. Barnard founded Decode, a small consulting firm that helps companies and government departments better understand what makes this group tick. In place of the term *Generation X*, Decode uses the phrase *Nexus generation* to characterize this target group—those born in the early '60s to late '70s. *Nexus* means a bridge, or connection; in this case, the connection is between the industrial age and the birth of the information age.

Decode helps its private and public sector clients decipher the aspirations, preferences, and unique features of the age group born at this critical nexus. It works with them to design marketing, human resources, or public policy strategies that connect with Nexus-generation consumers, employees, and citizens. In the process, Decode strives to build bridges across generations.

The Nexus group is a powerful demographic making up about one-third of the Canadian population. According to Decode, the generation has a number of key psychographic likes and dislikes:

- For Nexus, financial compensation is less important than it is to the preceding generations. Nexus ranks quality of life (e.g., longer vacations) and opportunities for on-the-job training ahead of a huge paycheque.
- Nexus is more skeptical about and has less confidence in traditional institutions, such as the church, the university, the nuclear family, the state, and the corporation.
- Nexus is more media savvy, techno literate, educated, and worldly than any previous generation.
- Nexus is composed of "experience seekers" who put off marrying, having children, and making house payments longer than members of previous generations.
- Nexus is more comfortable—and less anxious—about change.
- Nexus uses the Internet more than other demographic groups do.
- For Nexus, small business ownership is the most desirable occupation.

Sources: Personal correspondence with DECODE Inc. and DECODE's website at http://www.d-code.com.

WHAT WE CAN LEARN FROM MEDIA SOURCES

Mina Cohen was an archaeologist and teacher by training. She had worked on numerous excavations and had been a pedagogic advisor for the Department of Foreign Affairs and a teacher at a local high school. But despite her talents and extensive training, it seemed that she was always worried about her next job. The market just wasn't there for her talents. She even had to take a few secretarial jobs to supplement her income.

One day in late summer, she decided to take control of her life and entered a small business program at a local college. At first, the course seemed incomprehensible. Techniques such as brainstorming and mind-mapping were foreign to her; up to this point, she had been taught, in a "right-brained" manner, to be logical. In the end, however, she decided to persist and stay in the course. Finally, after a few group brainstorming sessions and extensive primary and secondary research, she had an idea: why not offer archaeological excursions? She would be in the holidays-with-a-purpose business.

But who were her target customers?

One fall evening, she was curled up, browsing her favourite magazine, *National Geographic Traveler*. She had been noticing a lot of ads by travel agencies and airlines. For these major advertisers, readers of *National Geographic Traveler* were their target market. It suddenly occurred to her that these readers might be her target market as well. After all, this was *her* favourite magazine. She began flipping through past issues and then reached for her laptop. With a Google search and the click of a few buttons, she had the preliminary confirmation information she needed from Bonnier Publications:[4]

Reader Profile:

- slightly more men (54 percent),
- between 25 and 54 years of age (median age 44),
- high level of education (70 percent of the readership had attended or graduated from college or better),
- high level of income (average individual income of $50,000),
- travelled often,
- interested in technology,
- quality conscious.

Advertising profile:

- watches;
- cars;
- travel agents and airlines;
- technological products, such as mobile phones, cameras, and information technology;
- fashion and personal care;
- financing;
- beverages;
- pharmaceuticals;
- information sources, such as daily newspapers, magazines, cinemas, and television.

"I just might be on the right track," she mused. Her primary target market would be well-off people—especially knowledge workers—who wanted to travel and learn.

The next day she sent away for the publisher's reader profile. Within a few weeks, she received the data, which confirmed her new-eyes research. Now she was sure that she had a growing market for her services. Her target customers were affluent (they could pay for her services), influential (they would tell and influence others about them), active (they liked travelling and learning), and increasing in number (a large segment would be boomers). It didn't take her long to summarize the demographic and psychographic information from the publisher, which would become an important part of the marketing section of her business plan.

As we can learn from Mina Cohen, a fun and easy way to understand the power of profiling is to analyze media sources that are aimed at different target markets.

What's more important is that most, if not all, of the major media sources have conducted extensive research on the demographic and psychographic profiles of their target customers. In many cases, these profiles are available through media kits from the advertising departments of the media sources. For example, if your target customers were sports oriented, you could ask a sports-related magazine for its readership profile. If you know which media sources your target customers read, listen to, or watch, you can get in-depth profiles from these media companies, because they need to know this information for their advertising. Dun and Bradstreet Research can provide the reverse information: the publications your target customers are likely to read.

In this section, we focus on magazines (don't forget the online magazines). However, you can take advantage of almost any of the media—especially commercial ones—because of the useful information contained in ads. We could just as easily expand our discussion to include TV programs, radio stations, and, to a lesser extent, books and movies.

What can you learn about target markets, consumption patterns, and buying power from the advertisements in a magazine? Put yourself in an analytical frame of mind. Link to the magazine index Magazines: Canada (http://www.people-searchpro.com/journalism). Begin by counting the ads. Then, notice the types of products that dominate the ads; these ads are probably aimed at the heavy users of those products. Next, study the models, fantasy images that the target customer is expected to identify with, connect to, and remember. The activities pictured in the ads enlarge the fantasy, and the words link it to real life. A good ad becomes a slice of life, a picture that beckons the customer inside, toward the product.

In addition to magazines, customer profiles are also available from newspapers and radio and TV stations. Media advertisers spend lots of money seeking the attention of their prospective target customers. We can benefit from this big-business advertising.

Trade media and trade associations also have resources you can use to learn about your target market. Some of these include

- *Restaurant Business*
- *Photography World*
- *Guide to the Financial Services Industry*
- *Retails Chains in Canada*
- *Builders' Digest* and *The Construction Book* (Toronto Construction Association)
- Canadian Cosmetic, Toiletry, and Fragrance Association

Your local library is an excellent source for trade journals and magazines.

Now it's time to focus your attention on some specific media sources. Action Step 25 will get you started on conducting research on your target customer at little or no cost to you.

BUSINESS-TO-BUSINESS PROFILE

Many businesses today—small and large—don't deal directly with the final consumer. Instead, they are subcontractors, part of the supply chain. Critical Mass, profiled near the start of the chapter, is one example of a **business-to-business (B2B) company** whose target market is other businesses such as Mercedes Benz, Procter & Gamble, and Nike, which, in turn, deal with the end user. My Virtual Model is another B2B player whose major business clients include Lands' End, Sears, and L.L. Bean. B2B niche players such as Critical Mass and My Virtual Model are, to a large extent, by-products of the outsourcing trend (introduced in Chapter 2), something that has given birth to thousands of companies or proprietorships whose sole purpose is providing services or products, on a contract basis, to other businesses.

According to *PROFIT* guide, even small B2C businesses are turning to outsourcing. Potentially, small business owners get more time to focus on the target customer, can reduce cost, and gain access to specialized knowledge only when they need it. What this means is that, even if you plan to be a B2C business, you might still have to learn how to do a B2B profile—as Trevor Lewington and Craig Milner did.

BUSINESS-TO-BUSINESS (B2B) COMPANY

A firm whose target market is other businesses

When Trevor and Craig opened their B2C—an East Side Mario's franchise—in Lethbridge, Alberta, customer service was their primary concern. Payroll was something they did not want to do. As a result, they profiled local payroll firms and outsourced this function to a B2B—Ceridian Canada Limited—that offered a cost-effective online payroll service. They got professional service, and the cost was much less than if they had hired a part-time accountant.[5]

Factors you should consider when developing your B2B profile are listed in Box 4.5.

ACTION STEP 25

Research specific magazines in your business area. (p. 113)

Box 4.5 Profiling Other Businesses

Your B2B profile should include the following information.

Company Profile

- size of business (sales revenue, number of employees, etc.)
- type of business (e.g., consumer or industrial products)
- type of ownership (e.g., public, federal, private, provincial, cooperative, nonprofit)
- account size
- number of years in business
- location
- credit risk

End-User Profile

- end-use application
- ability to reach decision maker
- purchase decision (group or individual)

Industry Profile

- economic and technological trends affecting various industries
- competing firms
- international versus Canadian sales
- barriers to entry

As a member of the B2B supply chain, you will find it important to create partnerships, joint ventures, alliances, or associations with your target customer. In his analysis of Canada's fastest-growing PROFIT 100 companies, Rick Spence concluded that these types of associations were a key component of fast-growth companies, helping them to

- develop better products,
- stretch their marketing dollars,
- reach more customers,
- obtain more feedback on their products or services,
- provide better customer service,
- extend their operations around the block or around the world.[6]

Ten tips for developing and nurturing a successful alliance are shown in Box 4.6. You'll want to keep these in mind, but first, you should start a list of possible target customers. You'll need to conduct business profiles of potential partners or business associates. There are many kinds of secondary information you can draw on. In the next few chapters, you'll learn about a number of hard-copy sources, such as *Fraser's Canadian Trade Directory* (http://www.frasers.com/public/home.jsf). For now, to get you started, we want to introduce you to what we think is the key source of business information, Canadian Company Capabilities, which can be found on the Industry Canada website (http://www.ic.gc.ca/eic/site/ccc-rec.nsf/eng/Home). Connecting to Canadian Company Capabilities will help you

- locate a list of your potential target customers,
- promote your new business venture,

Box 4.6 Ten Tips for Joint Ventures and Strategic Alliances

Successful business alliances are like standing on one foot: easier to start than to maintain. Here are 10 tips on developing and nurturing the most productive joint ventures and strategic alliances possible.

1. **Have a common purpose.** Articulate shared interests and objectives early in the process.
2. **Conduct research.** Assess your organization's strengths and weaknesses. Know where you want to go, and then identify the areas where you need help. Research the market to learn who can help you reach your goals.
3. **Consider mutual benefits.** Before you propose an alliance or joint project to another organization, ask yourself, "What's in it for them?"
4. **Provide a structure.** Having some kind of structure (e.g., which partner does what, and when) in place at the outset can be a useful safeguard against problems.
5. **Consider potential disadvantages.** Identify and address any factors that might undermine the project.
6. **Invest in human resources.** Put the best available person(s) on the project. Your associates and partners deserve quick access to the relevant decision makers.
7. **Put it in writing.** Spell out your mutual expectations and responsibilities in a contract. Determine allocation of costs. Both sides should obtain legal advice.
8. **Stay in touch.** Maintain open lines of communication with your partners. They can be formal (regular reports) or informal ("let's meet for coffee").
9. **Keep tabs.** Use regular feedback sessions to review the project's progress. Is it meeting the goals of both parties? If not, how can you fix things?
10. **Exit stage left.** Before forming an alliance, determine how either side can get out.

Source: Rick Spence, *Secrets of Success from Canada's Fastest-Growing Companies* (Toronto: John Wiley & Sons Canada, 1997) pp.117-118. Reproduced by permission of the author.

- provide market research,
- locate Canadian suppliers,
- discover potential partnerships and associations,
- research your competition,
- uncover export opportunities.

Canadian Company Capabilities is a database that contains more than 40,000 company profiles and over 200,000 products, services, and technologies. This free Industry Canada online service allows you to search for and profile your potential target customer by product, location, or activity. When you are ready to start your business, you will want to register your company in the Canadian Company Capabilities database and promote your products or services worldwide. For now, we want you to learn about this amazing website, get some practice in profiling potential target companies, and learn more about the power of the Internet. You will even need this source when time comes to research your competition. Complete Action Step 26.

ACTION STEP 26

Profile three firms using the Canadian Company Capabilities database. (p. 114)

THE SOFTWARE SCHOOL INC.: B2B TARGET CUSTOMER EXAMPLE

In Chapter 15, the fictional school called The Software School Inc. uses the following variables to describe its primary B2B Target Customers:

Our B2B Target Customer

Our primary target consists of small and medium-sized businesses with these characteristics:

- size—1–30 employees,
- annual sales—$250,000 to $500,000,
- type of business—light manufacturing/retail,
- major output—paper (reports, letters, documents, etc.).

B2B OR B2C: WHICH ONE WILL IT "B"?

Adrienne Armstrong, owner of Arbour Environmental Shoppe (Chapter 1), was in the "respect the earth with planet-friendly products business." In the early years, she set up her retail outlet—a small store—in a "planet-friendly" neighbourhood. Her target customers were B2C. Her husband, Sean Twomey, was often called on to staff the store. He had a financial and entrepreneurial background and often found himself designing environmentally safe products. Sometimes, the product would work, and the store would sell them. But Twomey knew one thing for sure: retailing was not his forte. He would much rather be in his workshop creating products, and Armstrong knew that.

One evening, Armstrong dragged her husband out to a local business seminar. At a coffee break, they found themselves networking with a local business man who was in B2B work. Later that night—actually, well into the night—Armstrong had another one of her business visions and woke up wondering, "Why can't we have a B2B division? We don't have to be strictly a B2C." The nightlight went on, and her 24/7 Adventure Notebook gained a new section containing a huge B2B mind map.

This was the start of the rain barrel division. Twomey had designed an environmentally friendly rain barrel that sold well in the store. Why not sell rain barrels to garden centres, landscape companies, and independent retailers? It took a lot of networking and planning, but Twomey and Armstrong persisted. Today, Twomey spends most of his time in the community, and he is much happier attending trade fairs and selling to businesses. The Arbour Environmental Rain Barrel can be found at Home Hardware, in dozens of municipalities, and in health food and environmental companies, eavestrough repair companies, seasonal landscape businesses, and more! Arbour Environmental is now both a B2B *and* a B2C.

We want to encourage you to think about the opportunity to sell your product or service to businesses as well as to consumers. As we can learn from the experience of the Arbour Environmental Shoppe,[7] you can benefit from both worlds. For example, if you start a small gift store, why not prepare corporate gift packages? Those busy executives with oodles of money and poverty of time can have their special gifts sent to their loved ones or business associates with a quick telephone call or at the click of a button—if you have a website, that is.

PRIMARY RESEARCH CAN HELP TOO

Secondary sources of demographic, psychographic, or business profiling information might be enough to target customers. Chances are, though, that you'll need to test your profile against reality. Field interviewing and surveying are two important primary research tools that can help you develop a more accurate profile of your target customer.

FIELD-INTERVIEWING TARGET CUSTOMERS

A lot of people go into small business because they don't have much choice. Many of them have to learn new skills and learn them quickly. Fortunately, entrepreneurs tend to be bright, creative, and hardworking. Julia Gonzales is a good example.

"It's no secret that I was distressed when my husband was transferred. I didn't blame him wanting the transfer; I would have wanted it, too. But I had a terrific job as manager of a full-line baby furniture and bedding store, and to keep both job and husband I'd have had to commute over 160 kilometres daily, five days a week. So, I quit my job.

"But I missed the store, and it was hard living on one salary when we'd gotten used to two. When I started to look for work, I found that my reputation had preceded me. Store owners knew of the place where I'd worked, and they were pretty sure that all I wanted was to work for them to get a feel for the area so that I could open a store of my own and compete with them.

"This gave me an idea. I hadn't *considered* doing that. So when I couldn't find work, I decided to go for it: to go ahead and compete with them. Their fear gave me confidence!

"One thing I learned on my way up from stock clerk to store manager was that it pays to know your customer. So, in the mornings I'd get the kids off to school, do a few chores, and drive to a baby store. I'd park my car a block away, and when customers came out of the store, I'd strike up conversations with them.

"'Hi!' I'd say. 'My name's Julia Gonzales, and I'm doing market research for a major manufacturer who's interested in this area. I'm wondering if you might have a minute to answer a few questions about babies.'

"My enthusiasm must have helped. I like people and babies, and I guess it shows. Being a mother helps me understand other mothers, too. I always dressed up a little bit and carried a clipboard. I'd ask the obvious questions like

- What do you like about this store?
- What things did you buy?
- Were the people helpful and courteous?

"Sometimes, I parked in the alley to research the delivery trucks. At the beach and the shopping malls, I would stop every pregnant woman I saw. I developed a separate list of questions for pregnant women:

- Have you had a baby shower?
- Which gifts did you like best?
- Which gifts seemed most useful?
- What things are you buying before your baby comes?
- What things are you waiting to buy?
- How are you going to decorate the baby's room?
- What do you really need the most?

"The research was time consuming, but after 30 interviews, I had enough information to make some very sound decisions. I also knew the weaknesses of my competition."[8]

One way to get primary data is to interview or conduct focus group discussions among potential target customers. In some cases, this might be the way to go. You could also interview other businesses if your target customer is the consumer or end user.

We saw how Julia Gonzales used interviewing, something that helped her locate her new store. In the next chapter, when we discuss researching the competition, we'll come back to interviewing again. In the meantime, we'll move on and use another skill: surveying to get a more refined picture of our target customer.

ACTION STEP 27

Research your prospective target customers, and refine your mission statement. (p. 115)

SURVEYING TARGET CUSTOMERS

Let's see how one woman used the survey technique to get her started on her own business.

Elizabeth Wood was a supervisor at a local textile plant. Over the past few years, things had been tough. It seemed that she was always hearing about someone being laid off. She wondered when it would be her turn but, as time rolled on, she was becoming less and less concerned. She loved to be creative with food, and she had set her goal: opening a small neighbourhood restaurant.

For some time now, she had been developing her skills in business. She had taken several courses in restaurant and bar management. Next, she took a small business course at a local university. In an attempt to understand her target customer, she read many studies on the eating-out habits of Canadians. She knew that there was a trend to eating outside the home, but what did this mean for her local market? This secondary research was very revealing, but she just couldn't risk her future on someone else's research.

Wood decided to do her own survey. She studied survey design and got plenty of advice from her professor, who had lots of experience in surveying. Crazy's Roadhouse was one of the most popular eating spots in town. Often, Wood would have a bite to eat there, and she got to know Crazy's owner, Max, quite well. She told Max about her dream to open a small restaurant some day, and about how much she was learning in her small business course. They got to talking, and at last Max agreed to let Wood do her survey of his customers. After all, the price was right. She would do the survey free of charge and would give Max her results—a classic win-win proposition.

Wood spent the next few weeks designing her survey. How many customers should she survey? When should she survey? How should she conduct herself? There was so much to do. Fortunately, with the help of her small business teacher, Max, and the team she had been working with in school, she launched a week-long survey of Max's customers. To Max's surprise, customers wanted to fill out the questionnaire. To Wood's surprise, she heard Max explaining to someone that he thought it was about time he learned more about what the customer wanted.

Stay tuned. We'll hear more about the results of Elizabeth Wood's survey later on. But for now, here are three of the major findings related to Max's target customer:

1. The lunch trade (Monday to Friday) customers were older than expected: almost 40 percent were aged 35 to 44. In contrast, the weekend customers were younger: 52 percent were 25 to 44 years old. As for the "after five" crowd, the average customer was even younger—almost 33 percent were under 25.
2. Regarding income, Wood found that the major customer base was the affluent (those with $48,900+ in total family income). As a matter of fact, almost 50 percent of the customers had a professional as the head of the family, and 87 percent had two or more wage earners in the family unit.
3. From a psychographic perspective, Wood found that at lunch, Max was getting the business crowd, who were eating salads and sipping Perrier. More than 60 percent ate at a restaurant at least once a week. In the evening, Max's restaurant attracted the bar crowd.

Wood tried to answer a number of questions regarding the customer base: Why did the customer come to Max's? Where did his customer live and work? Who did the customer think the competition was? When her work was completed and she handed Max her results, she got a pleasant surprise. She received a cheque from Max. "A small token of my appreciation," Max said. "It's not a lot, but I really did learn something. I thought I knew my customer before you came along."

Wood didn't earn enough to quit her real job, but it was nice to get paid for developing a customer profile, one she could use to help her start her own restaurant. In the next chapter, we'll come back to Elizabeth Wood and find out what her survey said about Max's competition.

When Julia Gonzales and Elizabeth Wood discovered that they would have to work for themselves, they quickly began to research their target customers.

The method Gonzales chose was interviewing, and the method Wood chose was surveying.

Understanding the needs of the target customer is critical to your business success. You have to do your research. Action Step 27 tells you how to do this. It will also help you refine your mission statement.

VISUALIZE YOUR NEW BUSINESS AND TARGET CUSTOMER

A **business vision** is a mental picture of your business, product, or service at some time in the future. You might not get there, but this vision provides you with guidance and direction, and, in many cases, it's the raison d'être for your persistence and passion. It's the driving force.

Let's return to the My Virtual Model case. To a large degree, the success of this business was the compelling vision of its cofounders Louise Guay and Jean-François St-Arnaud. A local merchant with deep pockets had challenged Guay to "come up with an idea that will prove that technology will help women buy, and then I'll create a virtual store." She responded with a visual picture of her new business product—the Virtual Model.

BUSINESS VISION

A mental picture of your business, product, or service at some time in the future

I thought, wow, I can come back to my passion because I love fashion, art and creativity, stage, to invent things, and I thought, isn't it the right time to start, to come with a neat idea, to solve these problems? So I thought, I have seen this little CD-ROM called Barbie Fashion Designer. [Mattel's] Barbie was walking in 3-D on the runway and that was very well done. Very impressive. So I thought, it would be fantastic if we could create an experience where the user would fill a questionnaire about her measurements, the shape of her face, the colour of her eyes, her hair, and suddenly, a 3-D silhouette would appear and say: "Hi! I'm your virtual model, and I was born to look like you."[9]

Many e-type, or entrepreneurial type, people such as Louise Guay and Jean-François St-Arnaud of My Virtual Model and Adrienne Armstrong of Arbour Environmental Shoppe are dreamers. Their best ideas come in the form of visions. If you can identify with this e-type, then we encourage you to have the courage to follow your dreams. But make sure you record them in your 24/7 Adventure Notebook. Visualize your customers—primary, secondary, and even invisible customers, and the type of business you want. It will give you the passion and persistence to succeed. It will help you not only start but also grow your business. Remember, for example, Adrienne Armstrong had a new vision that helped her grow into a B2B rain barrel business.

Now, let's return to Louis Guay and Jean-François St-Arnaud's business vision for My Virtual Model. It's inspiring and a good way to end this chapter.

"In the next five years I really see that we will open new areas. Right now we are in the garment industry but I can see that we will be in beauty products. Imagine you will be in a video game playing with other people in the world and they will be in the game as you! In movies … we already have demands to be part of many trailers. So it will diversify the use of the model in other areas and, geographically speaking, we start to work in the Netherlands and in France and the UK and Germany. We are already with Lands' End in the UK, Germany, and Japan. The Japanese people love fashion, they love technology, and I know they will love us."[10]

In a Nutshell

Your target customer is the key to your survival in small business. Constructing a customer profile is like drawing a circle around that customer to turn the circle into a target at which you can aim your product or service. Before you open your doors, you should profile your target customer at least five times. Try to visualize your new target customer and business. After your doors are open, it's a good idea to gather data through surveys, interviews, and so on, and to refine the profile monthly.

An end-user profile combines demographic data (age, sex, income, education, residence, cultural roots) with psychographic insight (observation of lifestyle, buying habits, consumption patterns, attitudes). The magazines read by your target customer will reveal a well-drawn profile, because the chasers of this expensive advertising have already researched their customer thoroughly. What other media sources are important to your target customer? Can these media sources help you with your profile? The Internet is another useful secondary profiling tool, especially if your target customers are other businesses. Surveying and field interviewing are primary research tools that will also help you find your target customers. You might want to go back and revisit Action Step 27 and the online workshop of field interviewing.

Profiling your target customer is important because it shows you the following:

1. how to communicate your message with a minimum of confusion;
2. what additional service your target customer wants, such as delivery, credit, gift wrapping, installation, post-sales service;
3. how much the target customer can pay;
4. what quality the target customer wants;
5. where large groups of target customers are located;
6. who else is after your target customer.

If you like to dream, remember Adrienne Armstrong and visualize your business and target customer. Keep your 24/7 Adventure Notebook close by, and mind map your ideas.

Key Terms

business vision
business-to-business (B2B) company
business-to-consumer (B2C) company
customer relationship marketing (CRM)
demographics
direct merchant (intermediary)

invisible customer
market-pull approach
one-to-one (one-2-one) marketing
primary, or target, customer
profiling
psychographics
secondary customer

Think Points for Success

✓ Psychographics is derived from *psyche* and *graphos*, Greek words for "life" or "soul" and for "written," respectively. Thus, psychographics is the charting of your customer's life, mind, soul, or spirit.
✓ Profiling draws a "magic" circle around your target customer. Placing the customer in the centre of that circle transforms the whole arena into a bull's-eye.
✓ Segmenting is like slicing pie; it allows you to help yourself to a piece of the pie.

✓ You can be both a B2C and a B2B business.
✓ You can save a lot of steps by using market research that has been done by others.
✓ Contact major media sources such as magazines and newspapers. They employ market researchers.
✓ Visualize your new business and target customer.
✓ Be sure to use the Internet.

Action Steps

ACTION STEP 24

Develop your own psychographic profile.

1. **Profile yourself.** Eventually, you're going to have to do a profile of your target customer. To get some practice—and have a little fun in the process—we want you to profile yourself as a target customer.

   The VALS model places adult consumers into one of eight segments: Innovators, Thinkers, Achievers, Experiencers, Believers, Strivers, Makers, or Survivors. We encourage you to learn more about your own needs and attitudes by taking the following VALS psychographic test. Click on to SRI Consulting Business Intelligence (http://www.strategicbusinessinsights.com/vals/presurvey.shtml). What is your VALS type?

2. **Profile your target customer, using postal codes.** You can get a psychographic (and demographic) profile by postal code. Link onto Generation 5 (http://www.generation5.ca/trial.asp), then type in your postal code or the postal code of one of your customers. Generation 5 will provide you with a psychographic profile of this group of homeowners. If you know where your prospective customers live, this method is a great way to learn all about them.

3. **Do your own psychographic profiling.** You may even want to invite a few friends to a "psychographic" party, or get together with a group of classmates. Ask questions: What are their motivators? Why does one brand appeal more than another? Is price important? What do they buy most? Do they prefer to buy online? Why? What products do they buy online? This informal primary research will help you understand why people buy specific products and services.

ACTION STEP 25

Research specific magazines in your business area.

Go online, head out to a magazine shop, or click onto Magazines: Canada (http:// http://www.peoplesearchpro.com/journalism/mags/canada.htm). You might also want to check out trade magazines. As we suggested in Chapter 3, and will discuss later in Chapter 5, Associations Canada (http://circ.greyhouse.ca) is also a good starting point.

Choose at least two magazines that you think your target customer would read. Begin by conducting some new-eyes research, following the example of our analysis of *National Geographic Traveler*. What strikes your eye? Are the ads aimed at men? at women? at teens or seniors? What appears to be the age range of the target customer? What's the income range? What VALS psychographic group is the magazine targeting? What message is it trying to convey?

Next, turn your attention to primary research. Interview magazine buyers. Ask them why they buy the magazine. Use what they say to add to your reader profile. Without being too obvious, collect as much demographic and psychographic data as you can on these shoppers. Could any of them be your target customer?

Now we want you to do some secondary research. Email, fax, or, using your business letterhead, write to the magazines' display advertising departments. Ask for media kits and reader profiles. (If you don't have stationery yet, or if you are in a hurry, see if you can contact them over the Internet or give them a call.)

When the profiles arrive, check them out. How close were your new-eyes and primary research profiles? Are you developing a clearer picture of your target customer and what she or he wants?

ACTION STEP 26

Profile three firms using the Canadian Company Capabilities database.

The Canadian Company Capabilities database on the Industry Canada website (http://www.ic.gc.ca/eic/site/ccc-rec.nsf/eng/home) helps businesses find competitors or organizations that can supply them with products or services they need. The database offers two types of searches: a quick search and a refined search that allows you to search by product, city sales, and so on.

Go to the Canadian Company Capabilities database. Select three firms that could be your target customer and carry out a "complete profile" of each of these firms. Just follow the instructions on the site.

If your target customer is not another business, or you're still not sure exactly who your target customer is, we suggest you use this Action Step to practise your profiling skills. It is a great resource to learn about potential suppliers or your potential competition. Select any three companies to profile, and learn more about the power of the Internet.

If you don't find what you need, you might want to click on "List of Various Other Directories of Canadian Companies." There, you will find links to sites that will help you expand your B2B profile.

ACTION STEP 27

Research your prospective target customers, and refine your mission statement.

Now that you've profiled several target customers, it's time for you to take a big step. It's time to move from the tidy world inside your head to the arena of the marketplace. It's time to come into contact with people who'll be buying your product or service.

You know your target customer's habits, income, sex, personality, and buying patterns, and can guess at his or her dreams and aspirations. You've identified the heavy users of your product or service. Now you're going to check these things out by interviewing these potential customers.

If you need help in preparing your field interview, you might want to click onto "Field Research: Conducting an Interview": http://owl.english.purdue.edu/media/ppt/20071030120349_708.ppt. Make up some questions in advance. Some of them should be open ended—that is, calling for more than just a simple yes or no. Here are some questions to help get you started:

- Do you like to shop at this store? Why?
- Why do you shop at this location?
- What need is this store satisfying?
- What products did you buy today?
- Are the salespeople helpful and courteous?
- How did you learn about this store?
- Is this your first visit? If not, how often do you shop here?
- What are you looking for that you didn't find in the store today?
- Where do you live?
- What do you read?
- Which websites do you visit?

Now, we encourage you to return to your draft mission statement (Chapter 3, Action Step 23). Refine your discussion on the target customer. What are the needs of your target customer, and how will your business satisfy these needs?

Business Plan Building Block

CUSTOMER PROFILE

Describe your potential customers and why they will want to do business with you. If your target customers are end users, or consumers, segment them by demographics (age, sex, income, etc.) Refresh your memory: go back to our section on demographic profiling (page 99). Back up your profile with secondary and primary research. Now think about your customers' psychographic profile. What are the lifestyle and behaviour of your target customers? Why would they buy your product or service? Action Step 24 will help you do this. Remember, we want you to describe your consumer using both demographic and psychographic characteristics. For example (as we suggested in the text), link onto Generation 5 (http://www.generation5.ca/trial.asp) and type in your postal code or the postal code of one of your customers.

If your target customers are businesses, profile them using the categories provided in our business-to-business profile subsection. We suggest you refer to the information provided in Box 4.5, page 105.

Now here is a challenge for you. If your primary customer is a B2C, we want you to look for some B2B customers. Alternatively, if you are planning a B2B, then we want you to look for some B2C customers. As we noted in the text, we want to encourage you to think about the opportunity to sell your product or service to businesses as well as consumers. You are demonstrating that you know your market, and your research shows that there are enough customers to support your business idea.

Go back and review the material you have developed in the first three chapters of this text. You are now ready to explain your customer profile.

It's your turn. Explain your customer's profile: you will need 1 to 3 pages to elaborate. This exercise will take you more than a few lines of explanation.

BUILDING ASSOCIATIONS/PARTNERSHIPS

Creating associations or partnerships is a key marketing strategy. Try to list some businesses or associations with which you can create an alliance. For example, if you want to retail second-hand books, can you associate with a business that is in the coffee business? You could complement each other. While your customers are browsing, for example, they could have a cup of coffee. Make a list of some of the businesses or firms with whom you could strike up an association. Don't forget the nonprofit sector. What associations could you create with the Boy Scouts or the Cancer Society?

It's your turn. List potential associations or partnerships, then rank them by priority: take at least a page.

Checklist Questions and Actions to Develop Your Business Plan

Profiling Your Target Customer

❏ Profile your target market in terms of primary, secondary, and invisible customers.

❏ What do the results of your primary research questionnaire tell you about your target market?

❏ What information have you developed about your target customer from your secondary research?

❏ What characteristics are unique or clearly definable about your target customer?

❏ What is the best way to reach your target market?

Case Study: Customer Profiling

Case Background
In the opening vignette, we highlighted My Virtual Model Inc. (MVM), a successful company headed up by two Canadian entrepreneurs, Louise Guay and Jean-François St-Arnaud. Now we want you to link the sites provided below and learn more about this innovative company. Our case study questions will help you put into practice what you have learned from this chapter and improve your customer-profiling skills.

Case Resources
The following sites will help you answer the case study questions.
- Innovation in Canada, "The Practice of Innovation, My Virtual Model, Case Profile" (text version): http://www.collectionscanada.gc.ca/webarchives/20071115075409/http://www.innovation.gc.ca/gol/innovation/site.nsf/vdownload/pra_innov/$file/f694_ic_case_studies_e.pdf
- My Virtual Model, home page: http://www.myvirtualmodel.com/
- Lands' End, About Lands' End: http://www.landsend.com, then click on "About Us"
- "Lands' End First with New 'My Virtual Model™' Technology: Takes Guesswork out of Web Shopping for Clothes That Fit": http://multivu.prnewswire.com/mnr/landsend/11847/

Case Study Questions and Activities

1. Customer relationship marketing
   In this chapter, we discussed an important marketing strategy called "customer relationship marketing," which emphasizes a market-pull approach and one-to-one marketing.
   a. What is customer relationship marketing? Briefly explain how My Virtual Model (MVM) made use of this strategy.
   b. Briefly explain the market-pull approach to marketing. How did MVM use this approach to get its first customer, Lands' End?
   c. Explain the term *one-to-one marketing*. How did MVM help Lands' End take advantage of this strategy?

2. Three types of customer groups
   We discussed three types of customer groups. Briefly describe these three groups, and give an example of each based on the My Virtual Model case.

3. Profiling your target customer
   In this chapter, we broadly distinguished between two types of companies—business-to-business (B2B) and business-to-consumer (B2C).
   a. What type of company is MVM? If you were asked to profile MVM's target customer, what major variables or factors would you consider?
   b. What type of company is Lands' End? If you were asked to profile Lands' End's target customer, what major variables or factors would you consider?

4. Visualizing and researching your business and target customer
   A major reason for the success of MVM was the compelling vision of its cofounders Louise Guay and Jean-François St-Arnaud.
   a. What was Louise Guay and Jean-François St-Arnaud's visualization of their business and target customer?
   b. What is a business vision? What was MVM's business vision?
   c. You'll need to test your idea against reality. Field interviewing and surveying are two important primary research tools. Louise Guay and Jean-François St-Arnaud not only had a vision for their new business and target customer, but also knew they had to do some primary research. What is primary research and what primary research did they do before starting MVM?

5. Key success factors
   Market trends and partnerships were two key factors contributing to the success of MVM.

a. List five market trends contributing to the success of MVM.
b. As we explained in this chapter, alliances and partnerships are key success factors of fast-growth companies. Give two examples of how partnerships contributed to the success of MVM.

Notes

1. Innovation Canada, "Case 6, My Virtual Model Inc.," http://www.collectionscanada.gc.ca/webarchives/20071115075409/http://www.innovation.gc.ca/gol/innovation/site.nsf/vdownload/pra_innov/$file/f694_ic_case_studies_e.pdf; "Lands' End First with New 'My Virtual Model' Technology: Takes Guesswork out of Web Shopping for Clothes That Fit": http://multivu.prnewswire.com/mnr/landsend/11847/; Lands' End, "About Lands' End": http://www.landsend.com, click on About Us; and My Virtual Model, http://www.myvirtualmodel.com/.
2. Critical Mass, http://www.criticalmass.com/; http://www.prnewswire.com/news-releases/nike-selects-critical-mass-to-bring-nike-id-to-the-next-level-of-online-personalization-73284962.html.
3. Janet Eastman, "From Rinks to Riots," *Ottawa Citizen*, August 31, 2005, p. D1.
4. *National Geographic*, Bonnier Publications: http://en.bonnierpublications.com/national-geographic-0.
5. Ron Truman, "Take It Outside," *Canadian Business* Online, August 4, 2005, http://www.profitguide.com/manage-grow/human-resources/take-it-outside-28672.
6. Rick Spence, *Secrets of Success from Canada's Fastest Growing Companies* (Toronto: John Wiley and Sons, 1997), p. 103.
7. Primary research, "Networking and Brainstorming with Adrienne Armstrong, Arbour Environmental Shoppe," February 2006.
8. Interview with Ron Knowles, n.d.
9. Innovation in Canada, "The Practice of Innovation, My Virtual Model," http://publications.gc.ca/site/eng/242626/publication.html.
10. Ibid.

5 Learning from the Competition: Your Competitive Intelligence

This chapter will help you prepare part C of your business plan, The Competition.

Purestock/Getty Images

LEARNING OPPORTUNITIES

After reading this chapter, you should be able to

- use competitive intelligence to collect and use information about your competition for the purpose of growing your business;
- discover how to create and grow your market with the help of your customers and competition;
- define your real competition through competitive touchpoint analysis;
- scout the competitive landscape to research your competition;
- evaluate your potential competitors using a competitive test matrix or SWOT analysis;
- begin your pricing strategy by completing a competitor pricing review sheet;
- define the unique benefits offered by your product or service;
- use the four-phase life cycle to change the arena and establish your competitive positioning strategy;
- discover ways to create uniqueness through service and product change;
- benefit from partnerships and associations with your potential competitors;
- draft your competitive strategy.

ACTION STEP PREVIEW

28. Conduct a competitive touchpoint analysis.
29. Create a competitor review sheet.
30. Construct a competitive test matrix and competitor pricing review sheet.
31. Develop your competitive positioning strategy.

RESEARCHING YOUR COMPETITORS

Ron Taylor's family had been in the business of building new homes until the early 1990s, when there was a recession in the housing market. When the bottom fell out of new-home construction, the family business closed, and Taylor was left with the opportunity to find another business. It wasn't easy. It took healing time, a lot of soul searching, and a new skill—competitive intelligence.

In time, his new-eyes research led Taylor into the business of renovating basements. People couldn't afford high-priced new homes or high interest rates, so they renovated. Secondary research from Statistics Canada and CMHC (Canada Mortgage and Housing Corporation) told him that this was a growth segment. His psychographic research led him to conclude that his primary target customers would be those who couldn't afford to build new homes but who wanted to build a sanctuary for their teenage offspring. He would be in the business of cocooning for teens.

It then came time for him to research his potential competitors. At first, he thought they were obvious. His major competitors were other contractors and builders—after all, if you could build a house, doing a basement renovation would be no problem. But he soon realized that this same type of logic had gotten his family into trouble in the early 1990s. His new business couldn't survive with a market sharing/price-cutting mentality. He could no longer afford to share a market. So, using primary research—interviewing, conducting focus group discussions, and listening—as well as a new technique called "touchpoint analysis," he began to build a list of the benefits that his target customers were looking for, and a list of who, in the eyes of the customers, were the best companies or individuals to satisfy their wants. His first list included benefits such as

- electrical outlets—lots of them for teen toys;
- soundproofing;
- an area equipped for dancing;
- a bathroom with a full-length mirror.

One night, after a long session with his mentor and some close friends, Taylor realized that his competition wasn't other contractors at all. His competition was almost invisible. It was anyone who could provide the same benefits. He began to realize that, in a strange way, even his customers could be major competitors.

GOODBYE GRAFFITI

Back in the late 1990s, while living in a downtown Vancouver condo, Perri Domm was asked by his condo board to look into getting the graffiti removed from the building but could find no one to do the job. That's what gave him an idea. He formed Goodbye Graffiti Incorporated, a community-minded company whose vision was to "clean the world one wall at a time."

Like most start-ups, Goodbye Graffiti had a humble beginning. Domm began with a used truck, a power washer, and a variety of "so-called" graffiti removal products. In the early years, business was brisk. There was little competition, so Domm didn't give much thought to his competitive strategy. "We created an industry when we started our company," he recalls. "We never really had to test our ability to compete."

But by the early 2000s, unexpected and fierce competition moved in. The result: A hefty slump in sales. Because he had no competitive plan, Domm had to take swift, unplanned action, and he could only hope to survive. He needed his B2B customers to know the benefits of his service—and fast. Domm launched an expensive name and product recognition campaign. His goal was "to distinguish his company against the low price guy who drives up in the rusty pickup truck with no logo and no insurance." His brand recognition campaign included both proactive and reactive benefits:

- A graffiti removal program would provide ongoing services, such as patrolling a customer's entire property at least once a week (proactive benefit).
- His company would repair windows damaged through scratching and acid etching (reactive benefit).
- He made available a proprietary product, which he developed, called Scratchiti, to protect windows against scratching and graffiti (proactive benefit).
- He launched an online graffiti removal program. With the click of a button, building owners could have their buildings inspected and cleaned. Goodbye Graffiti would inspect the building, send (electronically) a detailed estimate (including photos), and, if approved by the owner, do the necessary work. Under this one-to-one marketing program, building owners would never have to leave their offices (proactive benefit).

Fortunately for Perri Domm, the benefits strategy worked. Today Goodbye Graffiti (http://www.goodbyegraffiti.com/index.htm) has at least 14 locations throughout Canada and the United States servicing some 3,000 properties. Major B2B customers include building owners, property managers, cities, municipalities, street equipment owners, parks superintendents, and vehicle fleets. But Domm had learned his competitive lesson. He now arms himself with competitive intelligence, has a competitive plan, and keeps a sharp lookout for competition—spending some $150,000 to maintain and build his unique brand. By the end of his company's ninth year, Goodbye Graffiti had removed 6.5 million pieces of graffiti across North America.[1]

Only a few years ago, the subject of competition conjured up warlike terms such as "beat the competition," "disarm your competitor," "take a piece of their market," and so on. This market-sharing mentality assumed that when you went into business, you would take a piece of the action away from someone else. In a steady-state environment in which industries changed at a slow and predictable pace, the focus was on attacking the competition. Because little change was occurring, this strategy seemed to be the only way to drum up new business.

The knowledge-based economy, technology, and the informed customer have changed the way businesses view competition. Competitive strategy is now about creating your own market niche or brand, and continually changing and improving your product or service as the customer dictates. Competition is healthy, but it's not easy to deal with new competitors. You must be prepared. Competition can come quickly, and it can threaten a business's life—as Perri Domm learned. In some cases, it might even be difficult to determine who the real competition is, as Ron Taylor learned from his experience in the construction business.

Brian Scudamore is founder and CEO of 1-800-GOT-JUNK?, North America's largest junk-removal service. His first competitive challenge taught him to be prepared to learn from competitors. A "learning" competitive strategy will help you grow your business. Brian and GOT-JUNK are highlighted in the opening vignette and case study in Chapter 6.

In this chapter, we will help you understand and learn from your competitor, develop your competitive intelligence, and further define your specific product or service through competitive analysis.

WHO IS YOUR COMPETITION?

Recall that in Chapter 2 we talked about defining your business not in terms of a product or service but in terms of the benefits that your product or service provides to the potential customer. For example, you don't sell a book per se. You are really selling the benefits of information, enjoyment, or pleasant memories. In the same vein, your competition is not necessarily other businesses that provide a similar product or service. So we now want you to think of your competitor in a broader context. Your **competition** includes those companies or individuals that provide products, services, or benefits similar to yours, as perceived by your target customer. **Direct (first-level) competitors** are those companies or individuals that offer the same types of products or services as yours, as perceived by your target customer. These are the most obvious types of competitors. They offer a product or service that is potentially interchangeable with yours in the eyes of the consumer. For example, if your business is selling ice cream, your direct competitors would be other ice cream and yogurt stores in your area. In the case of Ron Taylor, in the opening vignette, his direct competitor might be other local building contractors.

When thinking about your competition, you must also consider **indirect (second-level) competitors**. Indirect competitors are individuals and companies that provide the same benefit as your company does, as perceived by your target customer. Indirect competitors compete with your business for "same occasion" dollars. If you sell ice cream, for example, and the benefit for your target customer is an afternoon treat, then your indirect competitor is anyone who provides those treats. Your customer could stop and buy flowers, specialty coffee drinks, yogurt, muffins, low-carb bars, or cookies. The sellers of these products might not provide the same product or service, but they are providing a competing benefit. As for Ron Taylor in the opening vignette, his indirect competitor might very well be a big-box store like Home Depot, which offers all kinds of home improvement services—mainly through outsourcing to its list of local contractors.

Now we want to introduce you to a third kind of competitive threat called the **invisible competition**—that is, any business that has the *capacity* and *desire* to provide similar products, services, or benefits to your customer. In a borderless, virtual environment where you can order goods from as near as your next-door neighbour or from a place whose name you can't even pronounce, this type of invisible competition has become a real threat. It is definitely not virtual! Suppose that "Ted," for example, operates "Ted's Maintenance"—a successful building maintenance company in Halifax. He's feeling quite secure. His equipment is paid for, and he has some healthy corporate clients. He thinks it would be difficult for a new company to invade his turf quickly. Then, almost overnight, a Goodbye Graffiti franchisee enters Halifax with a strong corporate partner, high-tech, efficient cleaning processes, and an online service program. That's right: Goodbye Graffiti, with its head office in Vancouver, is in the franchise business. It has some 14 franchise outlets and an aggressive program to grow its domestic and U.S. market. If Ted cannot offer at least equivalent services at comparable prices, he is likely to begin losing some of his best corporate customers.

Your invisible competitor does not necessarily have to live on the Internet. For example, imagine that you are in the fast-food business in a small town that doesn't have a McDonald's. Then Walmart comes to town. Your invisible competition has just arrived with a McDonald's within its store. In the chapter's

COMPETITION

Those companies or individuals that provide similar products, services, or benefits, as perceived by your target customer

DIRECT (FIRST-LEVEL) COMPETITORS

Those companies or individuals that offer the same types of products or services, as perceived by your target customer

INDIRECT (SECOND-LEVEL) COMPETITORS

Those companies or individuals that provide the same benefit, as perceived by your target customer

INVISIBLE COMPETITION

People or businesses that have the capacity or desire to provide the same products, services, or benefits that you do opening vignette, we also learned that Ron Taylor's business had somewhat invisible competition—his customer might be able to do the job and not need his services.

We encourage you to define your competition as broadly as possible at the beginning and then work through your industry to identify both direct and indirect competitors—and always be on the lookout for invisible customers. Remember, as well, that your competition is not necessarily who *you* think it is (although your views are important). Your customers define the competition in terms of those who can best satisfy their needs.

COMPETITIVE INTELLIGENCE

To identify your direct, indirect, and invisible competitors, you will need to conduct **competitive intelligence (CI)**. There is a myriad of definitions for the term *competitive intelligence*. A simplified definition is the process of learning, collecting, and using information about your competitors for the purpose of growing your business.[2] Competitive intelligence is proactive, not reactive. Your major objective is to find new customer needs and opportunities as a result of your analysis of the competition. The objective is not to eliminate your competitors but to learn and benefit from them. CI is future oriented. You are looking to develop and improve your specific niche or position in the marketplace.

Ten common goals of competitive intelligence are to

1. improve your product features (especially price) and customer benefits,
2. improve your customer service,
3. find new ways to distribute your product/service,
4. improve your advertising and promotions,
5. develop more efficient production processes,
6. reduce your reaction and delivery time,
7. add value to your product or service,
8. find new alliances and strategic partners,
9. find new ways to grow your current product/service,
10. develop new product/service opportunities.

Your competitive intelligence will require a well-researched understanding of

- your target customers,
- your current competition,
- your future competition.

How and where do you find information to conduct your competitive intelligence? Your target customer should be your major focus, so we will start with your customer research and the resulting competitive touchpoint analysis.

COMPETITIVE TOUCHPOINT ANALYSIS

People don't just purchase products or services—they also buy what the products and services do for them. The customer wants to know: "What's in it for me? How does it make my life better, easier, more effective, and fun?" **Competitive touchpoint analysis** is a way to begin learning about your competition. It involves analyzing customers' perceptions of the competition to find out what benefits and features are important to them. A touchpoint represents an instance when the customer has contact with anything affiliated with a firm: advertising, products, packaging, public relations, receptionists, salespeople, or the building or store. Provided below are a few examples of customer touchpoints that you might look for in your competitive analysis. (Of course, many more possible touchpoints could be added to this list.)

COMPETITIVE INTELLIGENCE (CI)
The process of learning, collecting, and using information about your competitors for the purpose of growing your business

COMPETITIVE TOUCHPOINT ANALYSIS
Analyzing customers' perceptions of the competition to find out what benefits and features are important to them

Possible competitor touchpoints include the following:

- **Receiving advertising in the mail.** What is the quality of the advertisement? Is it mailed first class? Is it addressed to the right person? How many mailings does the customer receive before he or she responds?
- **Making inquiries.** How quickly is the phone answered? What is the process for responding to a telephone inquiry? How long is the customer put on hold before being directed to a salesperson? Is there an online help service? Are the salespersons knowledgeable, articulate, and able to answer the customer's questions? Is the receptionist polite and pleasant?
- **Placing orders.** Is the order form easy to fill out and understand? Is the pricing clear? Are alternatives spelled out clearly? Is ordering online straightforward and quick?
- **Receiving orders.** Does the customer receive the right order at the right time and at the right place? Is there any follow-up?
- **Calling to complain or change an order.** Are the customer's complaints or requests to change an order addressed in a timely and considerate fashion? Are follow-up calls made to ensure that the customer's problem has been solved?
- **Balancing price and value.** Are customers looking for a sale, or are they looking for value? How important is the quality factor?

Competitive touchpoint analysis is a primary research tool. You have to talk to customers directly, and there are numerous ways to do this. Here are four possible methods.

1. Gather together a small group of your potential target customers to confer about your competitors. Some would call this a focus group. Walk together through the entire experience your customers encounter with your competition. Make a list of all the customer touchpoints, and rank their importance as perceived by your target customers.

2. A second method of getting touchpoint information is to be a customer yourself. Go to competing establishments, and ask a lot of questions. Make sure that you bring a pad of paper and a pencil. You don't have to pretend to shop from your competitors. It's okay to buy something. Make a small investment. Not only will you gain first-hand experience of the company's products and services, but you will also understand how the company services the customer. Remember that many businesses are now selling over the Internet. If that's the case, you might want to "Net" buy a competing product. What was your experience? How did the company deliver the product? How long did it take you to receive it? What did the company charge? Was the website customer friendly?

3. A third approach is to go out and talk to your competitors' customers one on one. This approach could be useful for retail businesses such as hardware outlets, clothing stores, and restaurants. Normally, it involves talking to a customer soon after he or she has made a purchase. Here, you have to be careful and use your discretion. Be truthful. If the customers want to know why you are asking these questions, tell them that you sell similar products and want to improve your business by finding out what your competitors are doing right and doing wrong. We caution you. Be respectful of your competitors, as well. For example, you should not interfere with a competitor's business. You should not be seen as trying to steal business away. Above all, you should not "badmouth" your competitor. If you feel uncomfortable about talking to your competitor's customers, do a site visit. Walk around the competitor's place of business. Use your new-eyes research. Observe the corporate image, product displays, level of service, and corporate ambiance.

4. A final approach is to talk to or survey your own customers. Who do they think your competition is? Where do they shop, eat, or purchase services similar to yours? Now, this technique might not be useful if you are just starting a business since you don't have a real customer, but there are still

creative opportunities. Let's return to Elizabeth Wood (from Chapter 4) and see how she uncovered the real competitor for Max, the owner of Crazy's Roadhouse, by using a survey questionnaire. Remember, Wood's business was not yet off the ground. She was doing free research for Max to learn more about her favourite industry.

Max, the owner of Crazy's Roadhouse, didn't think he needed to know what the customer thought. He knew who the competition was: that other roadhouse down the street. Fortunately, Elizabeth Wood knew better. In her restaurant questionnaire, she asked the customers who the competition was: "If you did not eat here today, what restaurant would you have chosen?"

The results gave Max a new perspective on his business. He learned that his competition depended on the dining-out time. At noon, his competition was any restaurant within a two-kilometre radius that could serve the customer quickly. The noon-hour trade was more concerned with "getting in and out" than with the quality of the food.

Weekdays from 6 to 9 p.m. and weekends, his competition was any restaurant within an 18-kilometre radius of his roadhouse that provided great food and a fun atmosphere. During this period, Crazy's was perceived as a "destination" restaurant. In contrast to the noon-hour trade, these customers did not value quick service as much as quality food and dining atmosphere.

The crowd after 9 p.m. on both weekdays and weekends had a different need: fun time. Max's competition was not the great eateries but establishments that catered to the entertainment side of the business. Customers were prepared to drive as much as 50 kilometres to enjoy a good evening out.

Max was taken aback by the survey results. He didn't have a specific competitor at all. He had several potential competitors, depending on the dining-out period. With Elizabeth Wood's help, not only did Max gain a much clearer picture of his somewhat elusive competitors, but also began to get some new ideas about how to promote and grow his business.

To compete effectively, you need to stand out! Develop a **distinctive competency**—unique features and benefits that attract customers and encourage customer loyalty. Success in business is not based merely on obtaining customers; true success is achieved by retaining them. So, as you do your competitive touchpoint analysis, seek out your competitors' strengths and weaknesses. Look for those features and benefits that encourage customer loyalty by continually reviewing your touchpoints. Remember to keep focusing on the benefits your customers receive.

We encourage you to do your own competitive touchpoint analysis by completing Action Step 28.

DISTINCTIVE COMPETENCY
Unique features and benefits that attract customers and encourage customer loyalty

ACTION STEP 28

Conduct a competitive touchpoint analysis. (p. 137)

SCOUTING THE COMPETITIVE LANDSCAPE

Competitive touchpoints, where you get your target customers to help develop your competitive strategy, are a primary source of competitive intelligence.

Now we will ask you to research your direct, indirect, and even invisible competitors—to scout the competitive landscape—to further hone your strategy.

There are all kinds of primary and secondary sources that will help you learn more about your competitors. We have listed a number of key other sources below. To gain the most benefit from these information sources, you will need both your primary and your secondary research skills. The particular source(s) that will be most useful to you will depend on the type of business you are starting, your resources, time factors, and so on.

- **Suppliers.** Suppliers can provide great insight about your competitors and the big picture. Obtain a list of your major suppliers, maybe even your competitors' suppliers, if you can. Go out and talk to them. Ask questions such as these: Who else do you supply? How much do you supply? What are your pricing policies? Beware of and remember those suppliers who provide you with "confidential" information—they are likely to provide the same information about you to your competitors in the future!

- **Trade shows and conferences.** Attending trade shows and conferences, and asking questions, provides excellent market information, and if you go with a friend or partner, you can split up so that you can cover the entire show, compare insights, and return to ask more detailed questions. No one knows an industry better than the salespeople. The more of your competitors' salespeople you encounter, the more you will learn.

- **Competitors' literature.** Request, as a potential customer, product brochures and price lists from existing competitors. These will give insight into the product concepts, promotion, and corporate image.

- **Industry/Association journals.** Read industry journals. What are they saying about your potential competitors? Learn about the publicity competitors are receiving on new products and services.

- **Industry Internet analysis.** Start with one of the more common search engines: AlltheWeb, AltaVista, Excite, Gigablast, or Google. Do a search on your favourite industry. You might even find specific information on your competitors.

- **Company website analysis.** Many businesses, of course, have their own site. Visit the websites of your major competitors. In some cases, doing this can provide a gold mine of information. What you learn will depend on the company, the type of business, and your information needs. But you should be on the lookout for information on company structure, history, location, product prices, mission, and future plans. Who are the owners and major players? What is their experience? Sometimes, in B2B companies, you might even be able to get a list of your competitors' major customers. Do your competitors e-retail? If so, you might want to become a Net customer. Buy a product. Evaluate the e-retailing process. If you're satisfied with the process, how can you improve your process to connect with the customer over the Internet? Make a list of those competitors who don't have websites. If they don't sell online, you might have an opportunity to "fill the gap."

- **Franchise information.** Franchises are a fact of business life in Canada. Start with the Canadian Franchise Association (http://www.cfa.ca). Do you have any potential competitors in the franchise business? Do any franchises provide the same benefits? Is an invisible competitor looming?

- **Resource centres.** Community resource centres and public libraries are a very good source of commercial and government publications, and the information is usually free. Here, you'll find competitive information from industry reports, newspapers, trade journals, and company information and databases. A college or university resource centre can provide you with an even broader collection of competitive intelligence resources, such as *Financial Post—Industry Reports*; Dominion Bond Rating Service; Industry Studies Association and resources; Financial Post 500; *Report on Business* magazine: the top 1000; and Standard & Poor's *Industry Surveys* (a U.S. source that contains some Canadian information). You might want to check out Canadian business directories such as *Blue Book of Canadian Business, Scott's Industrial Directory*, and *Fraser's Canadian Trade Directory*.

- **Trade magazines.** Learn about competitors' new products and services. What publicity are they receiving? If you don't know your industry trade magazines, Canada's Information Resource Centre (http://circ.greyhouse.ca/page/association) would be a good start.

We hope we have encouraged you to start with some rich sources of competitor information. A more comprehensive list and discussion of on- and off-line sources of competitive intelligence can be found by linking onto Industry Canada's SME Benchmarking Tool (http://www.ic.gc.ca/eic/site/pp-pp.nsf/eng/Home).

Next we want you to think about how you can position yourself and your business.

ACTION STEP 29

Create a competitor review sheet. (p. 137)

DEVELOPING YOUR COMPETITIVE STRATEGY

Now that you have studied the competition and prepared your competitive review sheet(s), it's time to begin thinking about your competitive positioning strategy. **Positioning** is the process of establishing in the mind of the consumer a unique image or perception of a company, product, or service. Competitive positioning is the process of establishing unique benefits and features that the target customer values relative to the competition. What is it that makes your company unique? What is your distinctive competency? What key component will give you the competitive edge? We want you to think of yourself as building a moat around your castle, so that your competitors will find it difficult to enter. The key component you are looking for is what some have termed your company's driving force.[3] All decisions, including those about what products to develop, which customers to target, and which markets to enter, should be based on your driving force (also called "a value discipline" or "distinctive competency"). For most small businesses, there are three broad competitive strategies that provide a framework for homing in on your particular driving force.[4]

POSITIONING

The process of establishing in the mind of the consumer a unique image or perception of a company, product, or service

NICHE, OR FOCUS, STRATEGY

A company carves out a specific or narrow segment of a market. A firm is pursuing a focus strategy if it targets one or more narrow market segments, or "niches," which are segments within segments. This strategy is particularly popular among smaller businesses. Some specialist roles open to niche competitors include the following:

- End-user specialists serve one type of end-use customer (consumer).
- Vertical-level specialists limit themselves to one level of the production-distribution chain (e.g., producing raw material but not components).
- Customer-size specialists concentrate on small, medium, or large customers.
- Specific-customer specialists sell to only a few major customers.
- Geographic specialists sell only in a particular area or region.
- Product or product-line specialists produce a single product or line of products.
- Product-feature specialists produce only a certain type of product or product feature.
- Custom specialists create custom products to order.
- Quality/price specialists concentrate on the low or high end of the market.
- Service specialists offer one or more services not available from other firms.
- Channel specialists serve only one channel of distribution (e.g., airline food).

DIFFERENTIATION STRATEGY

A differentiation strategy helps a firm to compete by successfully developing and maintaining a unique perception of its product or service that is valued by the customer. This uniqueness may be physical, technological, or psychological. Here are four ways in which a firm can differentiate its offerings from those of competitors:

1. product design/quality differentiation,
2. services/support differentiation,
3. technology differentiation,
4. image differentiation.

COST LEADERSHIP STRATEGY

A company successfully competes on price by being a low-cost producer or service provider. Firms pursuing this strategy must be effective in engineering, purchasing, manufacturing, and physical distribution. Marketing is less important. Low costs enable the leader to price its products lower than its competitors in order to win a large market share. Firms with a large share of the market are usually able to achieve lower costs through economies of scale.

Normally, this strategy is not recommended for small businesses; however, there are creative exceptions, such as PropertyGuys.com. Ken LeBlanc and three other young Moncton, New Brunswick, entrepreneurs did their research and found a solid market need: consumers resented paying realtors high commissions. House sellers were looking for an alternative, so LeBlanc and his partners launched a "commission free" real estate company—totally undercutting the high costs of traditional real estate fees. (We'll discuss PropertyGuys.com in more detail in Chapter 14.)

Cost leadership can result from a variety of sources, including

- larger plants,
- reduced transportation costs,
- improved technology,
- labour efficiency,
- work specialization,
- new production processes,
- changes in the resource mix,
- product standardization,
- product design.

The better you understand your competition, the easier it will be for you to formulate your driving force and competitive strategy. But which strategy is right for you? Few businesses can excel in all three strategies, so most likely, you're going to have to focus on one strategy that distinguishes you from your competitors.

COMPETITOR ANALYSIS STRATEGY

COMPETITIVE TEST MATRIX

A grid that allows you to evaluate the strengths and weaknesses of your competitors' products, services, and benefits

COMPETITIVE SWOT

An analysis of the internal strengths and weaknesses, and external opportunities and threats for perceived competitors

A **competitive test matrix** is a method that can help you to evaluate your potential competitors and establish your unique, distinctive competency, or driving force. As shown in Figure 5.1, a competitive test matrix is a grid that allows you to evaluate the strengths and weaknesses of your competitors' products, services, and benefits.

Another approach to developing your unique product or services relative to your competition is the more traditional **competitive SWOT**, an analysis of the internal strengths and weaknesses and external opportunities and threats for perceived competitors. Recall that in Chapter 3, we introduced a SWOT analysis to help develop a strategy for your business idea. Now you can use this same SWOT framework as you analyze your competitors. You can develop a different type of competitor analysis by

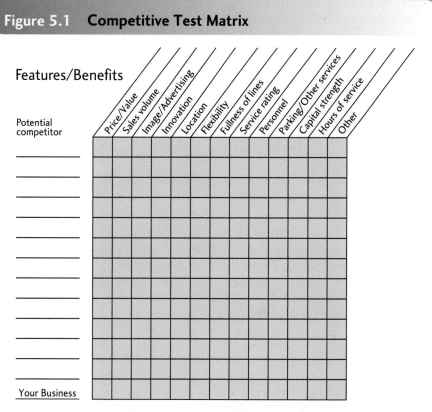

Figure 5.1 Competitive Test Matrix

Features/Benefits

Potential competitor

Columns: Price/Value, Sales volume, Image/Advertising, Innovation, Location, Flexibility, Fullness of lines, Service rating, Personnel, Parking/Other services, Capital strength, Hours of service, Other

Your Business

The competitive test matrix can help you evaluate your potential competitors. Use the features/benefits list as a guideline or checklist. Select or add those features/benefits that make sense for your particular business, industry, or competitive situation.

focusing in on each of the four SWOT factors, evaluating each major competitor's internal strengths and weaknesses (here you could draw on the results from your competitive test matrix). Next, consider the external opportunities and threats for each competitor. For example, an external opportunity might be the fact that your competitors have not taken advantage of the growth in online retailing. An external threat might be a cash-rich competitor ready to launch a price war.

The first section of Action Step 30 will assist you in developing your own competitive test matrix. If you think a competitive SWOT analysis would be more helpful, we encourage you to use this particular approach as you work through the first part of Action Step 30.

Now we want you to start thinking about your competitive pricing strategy.

COMPETITIVE PRICING STRATEGY

Note that the first column in your competitive test matrix asks you to evaluate, in general terms, the prices charged by your competitors for their products and services. In the next chapter, we'll introduce you to three broad strategies for setting the price of your products and/or services. Many new business owners with little real-life experience have little to go on when trying to set their opening price structures, so the market prices or the prices your competitors are charging will be an important consideration. In preparation for our discussion on pricing, we want you to begin thinking about the price to charge for your product or service given your competitor touchpoint and SWOT analyses.

Begin thinking about what price is acceptable to the market by completing the competitor pricing review sheet shown in Box 5.1. If you have several products or services, you might have to think about completing more than one review sheet. Completion of this exercise will help you prepare to address the issues related to pricing and promotion in Chapter 6. You're going to have to decide if this level of research is necessary given your competition and your product or service.

We have added your business to this list of competitors to help you clarify the comparative products and services.

After you've thought about the kinds of competitive pricing questions provided in Box 5.1, do Action Step 30. It will encourage you to think about your competitive pricing statement.

Up until now, we've talked about positioning your business idea in the mind of the customer. Now we're going to turn our attention to your product or service. We want you to start thinking about your competition in terms of product life cycles.

ACTION STEP 30

Construct a competitive test matrix and competitor pricing review sheet. (p. 138)

Box 5.1 Competitor Pricing Review Sheet—For Similar Products or Services

List your major competitors. For each competitor, we want you to consider the following pricing questions.

1. What price range is acceptable according to your customers' perceptions?

2. According to your touchpoint analysis, is the product or service sensitive to price?

3. Does good service affect the price? Will the customer pay more for good service?

4. Does quality affect the price? Will the customer pay more for quality? If yes, state the approximate increase in price.

5. Are there any other factors that affect the price?

6. For each major product or service, what prices are your three major competitors charging?

	Product and Price ($)	Comments
Competitor 1		
Competitor 2		
Competitor 3		

7. If prices differ, state possible reasons for price variations.

_____

_____

_____

8. What is your competitors' apparent strategy for pricing (low price, value price, market price)?

_____

_____

_____

9. What price will you charge based on your competitive analysis? What are your reasons?

_____

_____

_____

10. How will your competitors react (vis-à-vis their prices) when you enter the market?

_____

_____

_____

THE COMPETITION LIFE CYCLE

Like everything else in life and business, competition has a life cycle that can be divided into four broad stages: embryo, growth, maturity, and decline. These stages are, for the most part, determined by the product life cycle (see Figure 5.2). Briefly, we can describe the four stages of the competition life cycle as follows.

1. In the *embryonic* stage, the arena is empty except for you, your idea for a product or service, and a tiny core market.
2. As your industry *grows*, competitors smell money and attempt to penetrate the arena to take up positions they hope will turn into profit. Curious target customers come from all directions. You have visions of great success.

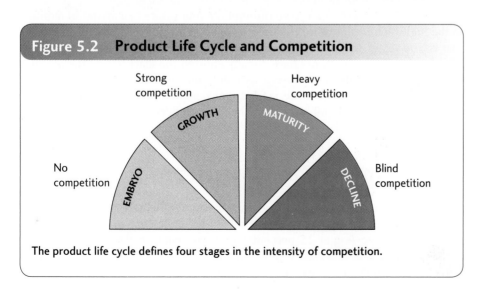

Figure 5.2 Product Life Cycle and Competition

Strong competition

Heavy competition

GROWTH

MATURITY

No competition

Blind competition

EMBRYO

DECLINE

The product life cycle defines four stages in the intensity of competition.

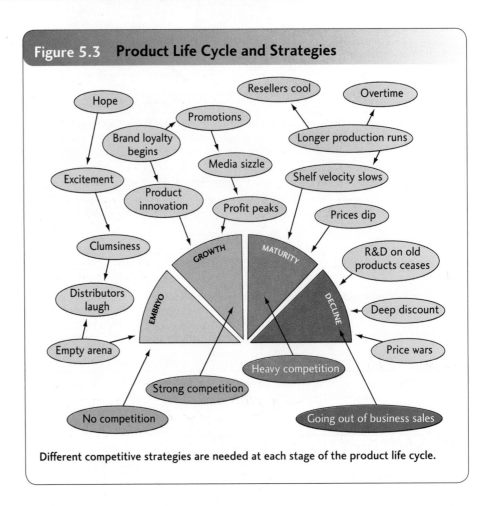

Figure 5.3 Product Life Cycle and Strategies

Different competitive strategies are needed at each stage of the product life cycle.

3. As the industry *matures*, competition gets fierce, and you quite probably steal customers to survive. Shelf velocity slows, production runs get longer, and prices begin to slide.

4. As the industry *declines*, competition becomes desperate. Many businesses fail, and weary competitors leave the arena, now silent but for the echoes of battle.

Today, movement from one phase to another can be at lightning speed. It's not unheard of for a product to go through the four cycles in a matter of months. In the high-tech business, for example, a common rule of thumb is six months—that is, you've got six months from the birth of an idea to **product penetration**. After six months, competitors have already entered the market, and the product begins to enter the decline phase. This reality means that, to survive, you must constantly be in touch with the market and compete with the right strategies accordingly. Figure 5.3 and Box 5.2 will help you understand the life-cycle stages more clearly.

PRODUCT PENETRATION

A calculated thrust into the market

YOUR COMPETITIVE POSITIONING STRATEGY

In previous chapters, we've learned that a major objective when starting or owning a business is to position your product or service in a growth segment. If your market is growing at 25 percent a year, you might make a lot of mistakes and still succeed. If, however, you're competing in the mature or decline stage, one mistake can spell disaster. In these stages, you'll be forced to lower prices,

Box 5.2   The Competition Life Cycle

The Embryonic Stage

The embryonic stage is marked by excitement, naïve euphoric thrust, clumsiness, a high failure rate, and much brainstorming. Competition has not yet appeared. Pricing is experimental. Sales volume is low, because the market is tiny, and production and marketing costs are high. It's difficult to find distributors, and resellers demand huge gross margins. Profit is chancy and speculative. Shrewd entrepreneurs, however, can close their eyes and divide the presence of a core market. And persistence can pay off. The authors of the bestselling Chicken Soup for the Soul series went to more than 30 publishers before finding the one that launched their multimillion-dollar empire.

The Growth Stage

The growth stage is marked by product innovation, strong product acceptance, the beginnings of brand loyalty, promotion by media sizzle, and ballpark pricing. Product innovation occurs. Distribution becomes all important. Resellers who laughed during the embryonic stage now clamour to distribute the product. Strong competitors, excited by the smell of money, enter the arena of the marketplace, as do new target customer groups. Profit shows signs of peaking.

The Mature Stage

The mature stage is marked by peak customer numbers and zero product modifications. Design concentrates on product differentiation rather than product improvement. Competitors are going at it blindly now, running on momentum even as shelf velocity slows. Production runs get longer, so firms can take full advantage of capital equipment and experienced management. Resellers, sensing doom, are cool on the product. Advertising investments increase, in step with competition. Prices are on a swift slide. Competitors entering the market now won't survive unless they offer a unique product or service and effectively convey the benefits of that product/service to the target consumer.

The Decline Stage

The decline stage is marked by extreme depression in the marketplace. Competition becomes desperate. A few firms still hang on, but research and development cease. Promotion vanishes, and price wars continue. Opportunities emerge for entrepreneurs in service and repair. Diehards fight for what remains of the core market. Resellers can't be found—they've moved on.

take business away from others, or invest lots of advertising money. These are market-sharing conditions, and you don't want to—or shouldn't plan to—share a market.

Positioning yourself in an embryonic competitive stage isn't desirable either. In this initial stage, you'll be all alone with virtually no proven market. We know that if you expect to make it, you'll need customers—a receptive market. But this means that you will need some competition, something virtually nonexistent in the embryonic stage.

In today's changing economy, there are no choices: your strategy must be a constant "war of movement" (if you think that your competitive strategy should be warlike) or a constant process of positioning and moving your product or service toward a growth market. In other words, competing is all about change and creating uniqueness as dictated, first and foremost, by your customers and, second, by your potential competitors. Figure 5.4 depicts this new **competitive positioning** strategy. Yes, you will always have competition, because you need their advice. The secret is to learn continually from your competitors and

COMPETITIVE POSITIONING

The process of establishing unique benefits and features that the target customer values relative to the competition

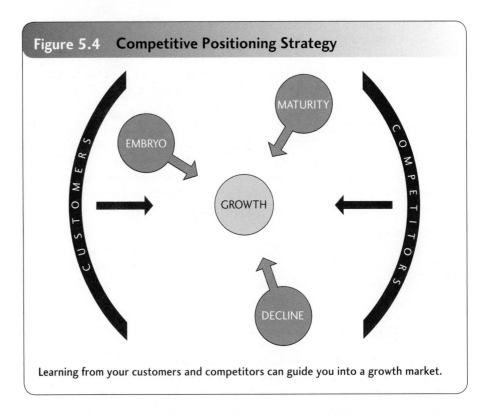

Figure 5.4 **Competitive Positioning Strategy**

Learning from your customers and competitors can guide you into a growth market.

customers, so that you can adjust your product or service to meet the needs and wants of the market. Your competitive strategy is all about changing the arena. By constantly adding benefits to your product or service, you will guide your business into growth segments. Another way to achieve this objective is to strike up partnerships with the competition.

FORMING STRATEGIC ALLIANCES WITH COMPETITORS

You'll recall Mina Cohen from Chapter 4. She decided she wanted to be in the "travel-with-a-purpose" business. Her product was archaeological excursions. The bad news was that she had created an embryonic product. No one else was offering this kind of service, so she was faced with questions like these: What price do I charge? How can I attract customers without massive advertising? To complicate things even more, her competitive analysis told her that her target customers valued their time and would likely get travel agencies to help them plan their vacation experiences. Her competition would be travel agencies that could easily enter her market if they wanted to, and they would have a strong customer base to draw from. Here, she was with an embryonic product, trying to position herself and do business in the fiercely competitive travel industry. What a challenge!

As Cohen sifted through the ideas she had recorded in her 24/7 Adventure Notebook, a creative solution gradually took shape. Why not partner with a travel agency interested in the ecotourism market? She would locate the best travel agency in town and offer her excursions as an add-on service. The agents would handle the advertising, pricing, and booking, as this was their strength—organizing and planning. Cohen could then focus on her strengths—teaching and archaeology—and get paid from the travel package for her knowledge and expertise.

The lesson from Mina Cohen's experience is clear. She moved her embryonic service into a competitive market by creating an association with her potential competitor. This arrangement is sometimes referred to as *co-opetition*. By understanding the needs and strengths of her competitors, Cohen was able to create a win-win situation by creating a **strategic alliance** with her potential competitors. A strategic alliance is a partnership between one or more organizations that is formed to create a competitive advantage. Partnership between competitors is a growing trend—one that should not be overlooked by small businesses, especially if they find themselves positioned in the embryonic stage.

STRATEGIC ALLIANCE

A partnership between one or more organizations that is formed to create a competitive advantage

CREATING UNIQUENESS THROUGH CHANGE

In today's competitive landscape, "If it ain't broke, don't fix it" has given way to "If it ain't broke, improve or change it, or it *will* be broke." Let's see how James Grenchik, owner of a retail tire company called Tire Pro, used this strategy to revive his flagging business.

It was painfully obvious to James Grenchik that Tire Pro, a family business serving a large farming community, was in trouble. Every time he turned around, there seemed to be a new competitor setting up shop in his backyard. Canadian Tire, a recent arrival, was starting to cut into his business, and there were rumours that Costco was thinking of moving in. Grenchik fought back with price promotions and distress sales, but these traditional strategies just didn't seem to work anymore. Profits were dwindling.

Grenchik realized he had two choices—get out of business or change. Before he could make that choice, however, he needed to evaluate his competitors. To get a clear picture of their strengths and weaknesses, he talked to employees and customers, and began to construct a competitive test matrix (see Action Step 30). After months of soul searching, networking, brainstorming, and reviewing his competitive test matrix, Grenchik decided to stay in business. To keep Tire Pro viable, he introduced the following unique benefits:

- **An installment plan for farmers.** This add-on service is a major benefit to Tire Pro's target customers—farmers—who need tires early in the growing season, just when they are experiencing cash flow problems.
- **Tires with free rotation and inspection.** Tire Pro's customers now receive a free six-month tire rotation. In addition to the inspection, they get a free report card on potential trouble spots. Every six months, reminder postcards are mailed to customers, something that keeps Tire Pro's name and image fresh in the minds of its customers.
- **A revamped waiting room.** Tire Pro has added some amenities to its shop. While they wait to have their tires serviced, customers can sip free coffee while reading *AgriFamily Business Magazine* or using one of the recently installed computers to search the Internet for the latest commodities report. The waiting room also has a bulletin board on which notices (ads for used farm equipment, for example) can be posted.

Tire Pro's competitive strategy is not restricted to add-on services and customer service improvements: James Grenchik is developing a website that will allow Tire Pro to build an online relationship with its target customers.

Throughout this chapter, we've encouraged you to learn from your competition to help you develop your unique product or service. We've provided you with techniques such as competitive touchpoint analysis and frameworks such as the competitive test matrix. Armed with your new competitive intelligence, it's now time to begin drafting your competitive strategy. Action Step 31 will help, as your strategy should answer the six basic questions asked in this Action Step.

ACTION STEP 31

Develop your competitive positioning strategy. (p. 138)

YOU CAN DO IT

We've told you about a number of entrepreneurs who have worked with and learned from competitors and brought about big changes in the marketplace. It's altogether possible that someday we will be telling such a story about *you*. Yes, you too can do it. You just need to

- know what business you're in,
- know your target customer,
- know your competition,
- develop a distinctive competency,
- express your creativity and your entrepreneurial spirit.

In a Nutshell

Your key source for learning about and defining your competition is your customer. Customers help us determine who our competitors are. Competition is a mind game, because buying decisions are made in the customers' minds. We have introduced you to three kinds of competitors—direct, indirect, and invisible—and have shown you how to use competitive intelligence to find your competitors and grow your business. We encourage you to conduct a competitor touchpoint analysis and to find your position on the competitive ladder. Evaluate your competition and work to define your distinctive competency by developing a competitive test matrix, a competitor review sheet, a competitor pricing review sheet, and a competitive positioning statement.

The competitive life cycle has four stages—embryo, growth, mature, and decline—and we've discussed the implications of this process for the enterprising entrepreneur. Your competitive positioning strategy should be to create uniqueness by continually adding benefits to your product or service. Listening to customer needs is the best way to guide your business into growth segments.

Case studies in the chapter showed how successful entrepreneurs work with and learn from their competition. These examples emphasized the key strategies of creating uniqueness through continuous change and establishing special partnerships or associations—even with your competitors.

Key Terms

competition	distinctive competency
competitive intelligence (CI)	indirect (second-level) competitors
competitive positioning	invisible competition
competitive SWOT	positioning
competitive test matrix	product penetration
competitive touchpoint analysis	strategic alliance
direct (first-level) competitors	

Think Points for Success

✓ Customers help you determine who your competitors are.
✓ There are three basic types of competitors—direct, indirect, and invisible.
✓ A competitive touchpoint analysis can be conducted by using primary research techniques such as questionnaires, interviewing, and surveying.
✓ Learning from the competition will help you formulate your competitive positioning strategy and position your business.
✓ Knowing your driving force and distinctive competency will help you make better decisions.
✓ Your competitive positioning creates uniqueness by continually adding benefits to your product or service, and it guides your business into growth segments.
✓ Establishing strategic alliances with your competitors also gives you a competitive edge.

Action Steps

ACTION STEP 28

Conduct a competitive touchpoint analysis.

Investigate your customers' perceptions of the competition and what benefits are important to them. As you look for a niche in the marketplace, you must review your competitors' actions and products.

Work with a group of your potential target customers; be a customer, talk to your competitors' customers directly, or do a survey. What is the customer experience of purchasing your competitors' products? Make a long list (as many as 60 items) of touchpoints—each time the customer comes in contact with any facet of the competitors' business. Each facet makes up the entire product: the jewel. The more you know about the jewel, the more you can make it shine!

Make a list of your customers' touchpoints, and rank their importance as perceived by your target customers. You need to consider which facets are worth going head-to-head with, which are not worth dealing with, and in which areas you can outperform your competition. Keep your touchpoints handy, because you will return to them in Chapter 6. When writing your Business Plan, capitalize on the touchpoints that make you stand out in the crowd!

ACTION STEP 29

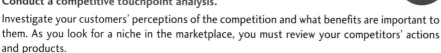

Create a competitor review sheet.

Using sources of competitor information such as those detailed in the section "Scouting the Competitive Landscape," compile a list of your competitors. Don't worry if your list of competitors gets too long. The more competitors you detect, the more you can learn.

- Using your list of touchpoints from Action Step 28 and past research, create a review sheet for each competitor. It should answer questions such as these:
- What is unique about this firm?
- Who are its target customers?
- What are its strengths and weaknesses?
- What needs aren't being met?
- What area could you capitalize on?
- Where do you see yourself being strong or weak?
- What images are your competitors projecting?
- What image will you project?
- What price(s) does the firm charge, and does the consumer feel he or she is getting fair value?

Keep this Action Step on hand, because you will need it to complete Action Step 30.

ACTION STEP 30

Construct a competitive test matrix and competitor pricing review sheet.

Now that you have a good idea of who your major competitors are, it's time to construct a competitive test matrix (see Figure 5.1 on page 129).

1. List all of your competitors or potential competitors in the rows. (Note that we have inserted your business in the last row of the list: this will help you clarify the comparative products and services.)

2. List the major benefits and features resulting from Action Step 29. Remember, your competitor might not be providing the same products, so you should be looking for benefits as well. If you want to sell healthy water, for example, your potential competitors are in the health business. The purpose of this Action Step is to learn from your competitors' strengths as well as weaknesses, so that you can borrow from their experience and create a better, more specialized product or service.

3. Rank each benefit and feature category for each competitor on a scale from 1 to 10 (10 being a high competitive strength and 1 being a clear weakness). By the time you're finished, you will have an overview of the strengths and weaknesses of your major competitors. You will want to focus on the column(s) with the lowest scores (weaknesses). They represent where you have the best competitive advantage in products or services. However, we also want you to be aware of your competitors' strengths. How can you learn from them, improve your idea, and differentiate your product or service? We don't want you to forget about your invisible competition either, so go back and review your competitive touchpoint analysis.

4. Name and briefly describe two invisible competitors. What two companies do not service your target customer but have the potential to do so?

   Invisible Competitor #1. Name/briefly describe:

   _____

   Invisible Competitor #2. Name/briefly describe:

   _____

   Finally, complete the competitor pricing review sheet provided in Box 5.1. You might want to consider this a first draft. In the pricing section of Chapter 6, we'll ask you to return to this analysis and review and refine your results.

   Now you're ready to draft the following competitor pricing statement.

   The price(s) of my products or services relative to my competitors' will be

   _____

   _____

   My justification is

   _____

   _____

ACTION STEP 31

Develop your competitive positioning strategy.

Take a look at your competitive touchpoint analysis and the competitive test matrix you created in Action Step 30. Who are your potential competitors? What do you think about joining forces with a potential competitor? What are their strengths, and how could you benefit from them? Review Box 4.6 ("Ten Tips for Joint Ventures and Strategic Alliances"), on page 106, and reflect on the experience of Mina Cohen, described in this chapter. Doing this will help you decide how you can join forces with a competitor who might even be a customer and create a win-win situation.

Now you're ready. To determine your competitive strategy, try to answer these six basic questions:

1. What is unique about your product or service relative to your competitors?
2. Why will the customer want to buy from you?
3. What is your driving force, or distinctive competency?
4. How is your business positioned in the competitive life cycle?
5. What other benefits and features can you add to your product or service?
6. How will you grow your business relative to your competitive landscape?

Business Plan Building Block

MARKET OPPORTUNITIES

Based on your research, identify the most promising opportunities in the marketplace according to the following categories:

- new or emerging markets—gaps and opportunities,
- neglected customer needs,
- failing competitors,
- complementary product mixes,
- expanded use of existing facilities,
- new geographical and international opportunities.

Now rank those that are most attractive now and up to five years forward.

_____
_____
_____
_____
_____
_____
_____

COMPETITIVE ANALYSIS

Summarize the material you have developed in this chapter to demonstrate that you haven't underestimated your competitors. A brief competitive overview could be sufficient for a small firm serving a local geographic area, a specialty distributor, a short-run manufacturer, or a professional service (1–2 pages).

A detailed competitive analysis is needed for larger firms ($2 million to $200 million in projected sales). Write a comprehensive analysis of their market share, marketing strategies, pricing, positioning, promotion, distribution, finances, and customers' perceptions (3–10 pages).

Make sure that you formulate your competitive positioning strategy. Answer the six basic questions provided in Action Step 31.

Checklist Questions and Actions to Develop Your Business Plan

Learning from the Competition

❏ Define and analyze your real competition through competitive touchpoint analysis.

❏ Construct a competitive test matrix or competitive SWOT analysis.

❏ Draft a competitive pricing strategy. Are your prices competitive?

❏ What is your major competitive positioning strategy?

❏ What is unique about your product or service?

❏ Are any invisible competitors ready to invade your territory?

❏ What is the size of the total market? What share do you expect to achieve in the first, second, and third years, and why?

❏ Are there any competitors you can approach for a mutual, win-win strategic alliance?

Case Study: My Virtual Model

Case Background

In the opening vignette of Chapter 4, we highlighted My Virtual Model (MVM), a successful company headed up by two Canadian entrepreneurs, Louise Guay and Jean-François St-Arnaud. MVM's major B2B clients include Lands' End, Sears, L.L. Bean, and Adidas.

In our case study for Chapter 4, we encouraged you to do further research into this winning company. Now we want you to dig even deeper and consider the competitive environment for MVM. Our Chapter 5 case study questions will help you put into practice what you have learned from this chapter and improve your competitive intelligence skills.

Case Resources

The following sites will help you answer the case study questions.

- Innovation in Canada, *The Practice of Innovation, My Virtual Model: Case Profile* (text version): http://www.collectionscanada.gc.ca/webarchives/20071115075409/; http://www.innovation.gc.ca/gol/innovation/site.nsf/vdownload/pra_innov/$file/f694_ic_case_studies_e.pdf
- My Virtual Model home page: http://www.myvirtualmodel.com/en/index.htm
- Lands' End: http://www.landsend.com, then click on "About Us"
- "Lands' End First with New 'My Virtual Model™' Technology: Takes Guesswork out of Web Shopping for Clothes That Fit": http://multivu.prnewswire.com/mnr/landsend/11847/

Case Study Questions and Activities

1. Types of competitors
   a. On page 122, we encouraged you to think about your competition in a broader sense. Briefly define MVM's competition in terms of this expanded definition.
   b. Briefly describe the difference between a direct and an indirect competitor.
   c. According to St-Arnaud of MVM, "We have the technological base to do everything more cheaply and more quickly than our competitors. It'll take them a long time to catch up."[5] In Chapter 2 we highlighted Unique Solutions onto The Virtual You (http://uniqueltd.com). Is Me-Ality™ a possible MVM competitor?
   d. In Box 4.1 we highlighted Critical Mass, a Canadian company that helped Nike build an online one-to-one relationship with its customers. Is Critical Mass a possible MVM competitor? Briefly explain the reason for your answer.
   e. Is it possible that Walmart or IBM could be an invisible competitor of MVM? Briefly explain your reasons.

2. Touchpoint analysis
   a. Briefly describe the objective of a competitive touchpoint analysis.
   b. Suppose you are a potential MVM competitor. Get together with three or four of your friends or classmates (or perhaps on your own), and link onto the My Virtual Model home page (http://www.myvirtualmodel.com/). Choose an online MVM shopping site, and go shopping. Begin developing your competitor review sheet (Action Step 29). Evaluate (1 is poor, 10 is great) the following touchpoints: shopping experience, price/value, product availability, customer service, product delivery, and method of payment. What was your average group rating for each category? Would you shop again on this site? Why? Why not?

3. Competitive positioning
   a. What is meant by the term *competitive positioning*?
   b. Based on your analysis in question 2, above, and a review of MVM, formulate a possible competitive positioning statement for MVM.

4. Competitive strategy
   a. As we described in this chapter, for most small businesses, there are three broad competitive strategies. Briefly describe these three competitive approaches.
   b. What was MVM's major competitive strategy and driving force (or distinctive competency)?

5. SWOT analysis
   a. Briefly describe the components of and rationale for a competitive SWOT analysis.
   b. What are MVM's internal strengths and weaknesses, and external threats and opportunities? (To learn more about SWOT analysis, you might want to link onto Mind Tools, "SWOT Analysis" (http://www.mindtools.com/pages/article/newTMC_05.htm#business).)

Notes

1. *Canadian Business* Online, "When Competition Looms" (website); and Goodbye Graffiti: http://www.goodbyegraffiti.com/index.htm; http://www.franchising.com/goodbyegraffiti/.

2. A number of definitions of *competitive intelligence* can be found in Richard Combs Associates' *The Competitive Intelligence Handbook*, chapter 1 (http://www.combsinc.com/chapt1.htm).

3. See, for example, Michel Robert, *Strategy Pure and Simple*, 2nd ed. (New York: McGraw Hill, 1998).

4. See, for example, Marketing Teacher website, http://www.marketingteacher.com/lesson-store/lesson-generic-strategies.html.

5. Library and Archives Canada, http://www.collectionscanada.gc.ca/webarchives/20071115075409/; http://www.innovation.gc.ca/gol/innovation/site.nsf/vdownload/pra_innov/$file/f694_ic_case_studies_e.pdf.

Marketing: Pricing and Promoting Your Product or Service

This chapter will help you prepare Part D of your business plan, Marketing Strategy. You will learn how to price your product or service, refine your product features and benefits, and develop a cost-effective promotional strategy.

James Peragine/Shutterstock.com

LEARNING OPPORTUNITIES

After reading this chapter, you should be able to

- understand how to price your product or service;
- develop a pricing strategy;
- understand how to communicate with target customers, using both conventional and guerrilla marketing techniques;
- get free publicity;
- maximize economy in advertising and promotion;
- understand the value of personal selling;
- use creative techniques to arrive at the right promotional mix;
- promote through networking;
- build your own network;
- attach price tags to your promotional strategies.

ACTION STEP PREVIEW

32. Calculate and justify your product/service price.
33. Build your network.
34. Brainstorm a winning promotional campaign for your business.
35. Attach a price tag to each item in your promotion package.

1-800-GOT-JUNK?

Brian Scudamore, like many successful entrepreneurs, thinks in pictures. He's a dreamer. Just before his 19th birthday he was in line outside a McDonald's, dreaming away, waiting for his lunch. A pickup truck filled with trash was waiting in line in front of him at the drive-through. Hungry at the time, and thanks to McDonald's, Brian experienced a business vision—one that would change his life. Why not "do real junk"? he thought.

Scudamore moved quickly and bought a used pickup truck the very next day. "The Rubbish Boys" was hatched overnight—a junk removal service with the slogan, "We'll Stash Your Trash in a Flash!" Scudamore was a university student at that time. After three increasingly successful summers, he was ready to take his business to the next level, investing in more trucks, hiring student drivers, and setting out to make his company the "FedEx of Junk" throughout the Vancouver area.

In the mid-1990s, an employee and friend, Mike McKee, decided to leave The Rubbish Boys and set up his own trash removal service, called the Trashbusters. Brian's warlike competitive juices kicked in, and he spent two years trying to find ways to "take Trashbusters down." Competitive, reactive bashing became an obsession for Scudamore and his employees—one that, he recalls, caused him almost to lose his business.

One evening Scudamore had a business epiphany while at his parents' cottage, sketching out his future business dreams. He realized that his experience with Mike McKee, his first direct competitor, could be the start of a long line of direct competitors. Scudamore came to understand the importance of learning from the competition. He learned that he needed a different way to grow his business. Not long after this "magical" evening, he decided that franchising was the way to go. He changed the company name to 1-800-GOT-JUNK? and quickly turned to franchising. With a catchy name, a new distribution channel, and a renewed focus on the customer, Scudamore outgrew his competition in a short time.

The first GOT-JUNK franchise was sold in 1999, and since then the company has enjoyed exponential growth and widespread recognition for its business achievements. As of 2012, the company had some 175 franchise locations internationally.

"We're revolutionizing the way the business is done," says Scudamore, now with a corporate nickname, "Junkdog." "This has always been a very fragmented mom-and-pop industry. We're creating the FedEx of junk removal."

Since the early days, Junkdog and his team have been driven to success through their compelling "FedEx" vision to make the collection and disposal of junk a respectable business.

Scudamore has also taken the junk business online. "If you're not comfortable using the Internet, we don't want you as a franchisee," says Cameron Herold, chief executive officer. According to one source, their business model seems to have attracted the attention of more than a few dot-com refugees. The linchpin of the company's business model is an intranet Web-based system that handles all booking, accounting, and dispatching tasks. The software maps each franchise partner's territory. It is a sophisticated system in which all job orders for the company's franchise partners are booked and dispatched by 32 office employees in the Vancouver head office—known as the "Junktion."

"We've created a business model that allows franchise partners to work on the junk business, not in the booking and dispatching business," says Scudamore.

Guerrilla marketing is a key promotional strategy of Scudamore and his franchisees. The small business promotional strategy involves unconventional methods of getting the customer's attention at minimal cost. The idea is to expend energy and creativity rather than money. Scudamore says, "Rather than spend a ton of money on advertising, I believe it is better to get out there and promote." For example, franchisees are encouraged to be creative. Waves are a common guerrilla tactic. Franchisees can be seen wearing blue clown wigs, standing on busy roads, waving to motorists, and passing out free lollipops (junk food) or junk bucks. Junk motorcades are also a common practice. For example, the Toronto franchisee has 12 trucks that sometimes travel in a convoy down Yonge Street, in the heart of the city. When not on a job, some crew members go on junk patrol, scouring neighbourhoods for cluttered yards or driveways. The driver knocks or leaves an estimate on the front door.

Service and quality are also key factors to the GOT-JUNK franchise system. As a result, their business format is highly controlled. For example, all franchisees must wear clean apparel, and trucks are to be washed every day. One franchisee in Calgary even lost his franchise rights when he drove a muddy truck with a peeling 1-800-GOT-JUNK? label. Follow-up calls are made to ensure total customer satisfaction.[1] The main job of the franchisee is to staff and run the operation—with an emphasis on promoting their services.

In our case study at the end of this chapter, we'll ask you to return to this 1-800-GOT-JUNK? vignette, do some research, and learn from the pricing and promotional tactics of this great Canadian success story.

Your business plan **marketing strategy** will include an analysis of four major elements: (1) external market and trends, (2) your target market, (3) product uniqueness and competitive advantage, and (4) the marketing mix. We have addressed the first three elements in the first five chapters of this book. In Chapters 2 and 3, we stressed the importance of external market trends. Chapter 4 focused on your target customers. We encouraged you to analyze and learn from your competition to create a competitive advantage in Chapter 5. In Chapters 6 and 7, we turn our attention to the fourth element of your marketing strategy, traditionally called the **marketing mix**—a blend of **p**roduct offering, **p**ricing, **p**romotion, and **p**lace (location). Some refer to this marketing mix as the "Four Ps." Up to this point, we've helped you develop your product offering—your market niche and the product or services that are right for both you and the market. In this chapter, we'll get you thinking about the next two "Ps" of your marketing mix: price and promotion. Then, in Chapter 7, we will help you with your last "P"—your place, or location. We begin with pricing considerations and strategy—a topic we first addressed in relation to your competition (Chapter 5).

GUERRILLA MARKETING

Small business promotional strategy that involves unconventional methods of getting the customer's attention at minimal cost

MARKETING STRATEGY

An analysis of four major elements: external market and trends, target market, product/service uniqueness and competitive advantage, and the marketing mix

MARKETING MIX

A blend of product offering, pricing, promotion, and place (location)

PRICING YOUR PRODUCT OR SERVICE

In principle, the price(s) you charge for your product or service must be acceptable both to you, the seller, and to your customer. From your customer's perspective, an acceptable price depends on competitive alternatives for your product/service in addition to the perceived value. As for you, the supplier of a product/service, your price can be based on any number of pricing considerations. But it's fairly safe to say that, ultimately, you will be trying to maximize your sales revenue and profits.

New businesses often make the mistake of charging either too little or too much for their product or service. To help you avoid making one of these mistakes, we're going to outline four basic methods for determining your price. These are the most common methods for small businesses, but we caution you: the process of setting a price can become quite complicated and technical—especially if you are starting up a manufacturing business. Pricing depends on many internal and external factors, and you might have to get professional help. For example, the process of estimating the price of a product will include product costs as well as labour costs. In contrast, if you are offering a service, you might not have to deal with any product costing. Retail pricing for a storefront with rent considerations will be very different from pricing for a home-based e-retailing operation with little or no rent.

Below are four common small business methods of pricing a product or service. Depending on your business idea, you might need a lot more information and guidance.

FOUR COMMON METHODS OF PRICING FOR SMALL BUSINESS

1. COMPETITOR-BASED PRICING

Recall that in Action Step 30 in Chapter 5, we asked you to review your competitive touchpoint analysis and state the prices of your products or services relative to your customers' perception of the competition. In fact, we were asking you to calculate your price relative to the market. We wanted you to find out what prices were acceptable to your potential customers given their possible choices and competitive options. Many new business owners begin their pricing strategy by first determining what prices or price range the target market will accept, relative to the competition. This approach is often referred to as **competitor-based, or market-based, pricing**, or pricing to market.[2]

The price of your product or service depends on your competitors' prices, but you're also going to have to figure out your costs. If the market price cannot cover your costs, then your business will lose money. And naturally, you want to make sure that the price you charge is enough to yield a profit. This concern leads us to a second approach, called **profit-based, or cost plus, pricing**.

COMPETITOR-BASED, OR MARKET-BASED, PRICING

Setting a price range acceptable to your customer that takes into consideration your competitors' prices

PROFIT-BASED, OR COST PLUS, PRICING

Setting a price that covers all costs plus a profit

2. PROFIT-BASED, OR COST PLUS, PRICING

One of the most common errors new owners make is setting their prices of products based only on the costs to produce them.[3] If you set your price based solely on the cost, your business won't make any profit. The price you charge must also take into consideration your profit expectations. After all, you don't just want to sell your service or product at the price you pay for it. There are different methods for calculating price to take account of profit. Here is a simple and common formula for estimating price (per unit):

Selling price = total costs per unit + estimated dollar profit per unit

Your costs for producing a particular product (or supplying a service) will include three broad costing groups: (1) direct material costs (or your cost of supplies), (2) direct cost of labour for producing your product or service, and (3) overhead, or fixed expenses (indirect costs), such as rent and advertising.

Your estimated profit will depend on a number of factors, such as the type of product or service, the market demand, and your costs. If possible, you're going to have to rely on your primary or secondary research, such as industry averages, for your type of business (see "SME Benchmarking Tool," http://www.ic.gc.ca/eic/site/pp-pp.nsf/eng/Home). Some businesses might even set profit targets for each of the three broad costing groups.

According to many industry analysts, pricing based on costs and profit establishes an estimate of the lowest price, or floor price, for your product or service,[4] in other words, the minimum price that you can accept to meet your profit targets. Second, the price you can charge will be determined by the demand for your product or service as well as by your competition.

3. INDUSTRY NORM, OR KEYSTONE, PRICING

Some businesses charge prices according to certain generally accepted or industry standards. This approach is called **industry norm, or keystone, pricing**. Two examples might be setting the price at triple the cost of goods sold or two times the labour costs.

The marketing concept of **markups** might also help you determine your price. A markup is a percentage of your cost of sales (sometimes the selling price is used) that you add to the cost to determine your selling price. Note that you don't include overhead costs in your markup calculation. Include only your costs for materials and supplies.

For example, if the selling price is $3 and the cost is $2, the markup is calculated as follows:

$$\text{Markup} = (\text{price} - \text{cost}) / \text{cost}$$
$$= (\$3 - \$2) / \$2$$
$$= 1/2$$
$$= .50 \text{ (or 50\%)}$$

When it comes to concept markups, you have to be a little cautious. Markups are calculated in some cases as a percentage of costs and in others as a percentage of the selling price. In the above example, the 50 percent markup was calculated as a percentage of cost. If we had calculated the markup as a percentage of selling price, then the markup would be 33 percent, or $(\$3 - \$2)/\$3$. It is common in the retail industry to calculate markups based on selling price.

If you know what the standard or industry markup is for your product or service, then you can estimate a selling price. For example, if you are selling greeting cards and you know that the industry markup (on the selling price) is 50 percent, then you can determine your selling price. You can use the SME Benchmarking Tool (http://www.ic.gc.ca/eic/site/pp-pp.nsf/eng/home) to compare your margins, or markups, with the industry averages. Your final price will ultimately depend on all of your costs (not just the material cost), the competition, and the market demand.

Here's another example of how to calculate markup:

1. Determine your product/service cost. For example, you plan to sell a product that cost you $2 to buy.
2. Next, determine the percentage markup you want to add to your product/service cost. Research your industry to determine the industry norm. You could use Statistics Canada's SME Benchmarking Tool. Let's say that, after you did your research, you discovered that the industry norm is a 40 percent markup.
3. Then, convert the percentage markup to a decimal. You can do this by dividing 40 by 100 to get 0.40.
4. Multiply your cost ($2) by your markup decimal (0.40) to get your markup amount. In this example, the markup is 0.80.

INDUSTRY NORM, OR KEYSTONE, PRICING

Setting a price that depends on generally accepted industry standards

MARKUPS

A percentage of your cost of sales (sometimes the selling price) that is added to the cost to determine your selling price

5. Now, add your markup (0.80) to the cost of your product/service ($2). In this example, the total selling price would be $2.80.

4. CEILING, OR PREMIUM, PRICING

CEILING, OR PREMIUM, PRICING

Setting the highest price target consumers will pay for a product or service, given their needs and values and the competitive options

Ceiling, or premium, pricing means setting the highest price target consumers will pay for a product or service, given their needs and values and the competitive options. This pricing strategy is recommended for most small business start-ups.[5] Your ultimate goal or strategy is to focus on a specific market segment, create uniqueness, and differentiate your product or service as perceived by the customer. Some pricing analysts refer to this ceiling price as the "highest price the market will bear." This differentiation strategy will make your product or service more inelastic, or less sensitive to price changes. If your product or service is inelastic, it means that your customers, on average, will be willing to buy your product or service even if your prices are on the high side relative to those of your competitors—because your customers value the fact that your product is different. But remember, you must also be able to justify that this ceiling or premium price more than covers your costs and yields the desired profit.

OTHER PRICING STRATEGIES

The four broad strategies just discussed are not the only options available. For example, common pricing strategies used mainly by larger firms include the following:

PENETRATION PRICING

Setting the initial or introductory price artificially low to increase sales volume

ECONOMY (LIMIT) PRICING

Setting "no-frills" low prices to increase volume and discourage competition

PRICE SKIMMING

Setting prices high initially to appeal to consumers who are not price sensitive, then lowering prices as competitors enter the market

- **penetration pricing**—setting the initial or introductory price artificially low to increase sales volume with the intent of raising prices after the introductory period;
- **economy, or limit, pricing**—setting "no-frills" low prices to increase volume and discourage competition;
- **price skimming**—setting prices high initially to appeal to consumers who are not price sensitive, then lowering prices as competitors enter the market.

YOUR PRICING STRATEGY

The price you will charge for your product or service will depend on a number of factors, including costs of production, market considerations, competitive forces, geography, size of business, the product, and service distribution channel. You are also going to have to think about your pricing strategy in relation to promotional factors (described in the next section), including sales promotions and quantity discounts.

We suggest that you begin your pricing analysis by considering the ceiling price strategy, then follow up by making sure that this price will cover your costs and lead to a profit. This approach is used by most successful small businesses such as 1-800-GOT-JUNK? Many small business owners think they should start out with low prices to attract customers, but, in most cases, this would be a mistake. In general, small businesses should not aim to sell products or services at the lowest market price. Strategies such as penetration pricing, economy pricing, and price skimming are approaches that should be reserved for large firms, such as Coca-Cola and Walmart, that want to increase their market share and dominate the market.

It is about time to introduce you to promotion, the next element in our marketing mix. Before we do, however, we want you to complete Action Step 32—calculate and justify your product/service price.

ACTION STEP 32

Calculate and justify your product/service price. (p. 167)

PROMOTION—YOUR WAY OF CONNECTING WITH THE CUSTOMER

Promotion is the art and science of moving the image of your business to the forefront of a customer's mind. Recall that in Chapter 4, we discussed three kinds of customers: target customers, secondary customers, and invisible customers. When promoting your business, you need to consider all three types.

Each business is unique, and you don't want to waste money on promotional schemes that won't work. For example, if your target customer is a university-educated, suburban woman aged 45 to 55 who earns more than $100,000, owns three cars, rides horseback 10 hours a week, and reads *Practical Horseman* and *Performance Horse*, your best chance of reaching her is through direct mail. If, on the other hand, your target customers are male and female university students aged 18 to 25 with limited incomes, you'll probably achieve better results by promoting at local colleges.

Developing a promotional plan requires meeting five steps:

1. Determine your sales and marketing goals (e.g., sales of $350,000 for the year).
2. Develop strategies to achieve a goal (e.g., increase repeat business of best customers by 10 percent).
3. Create specific promotional methods for carrying out one or several of the strategies, and having measurable objectives (e.g., a mailer for a special Christmas shopping night with a goal of selling $20,000 worth of merchandise during the evening).
4. Detail and enact a program involving the specific promotion(s) chosen following a predetermined budget (e.g., a gold-embossed mailer sent to 300 best customers in November for a special Christmas shopping night with free cookies, pastries, cider, and gift wrapping, at a cost of $1,750).
5. Evaluate the cost and effectiveness of your promotional vehicles and adjust as needed (e.g., expected return of $20 in increased sales for every dollar spent on advertising and promotion).

Your promotional efforts should be consistent with your overall image, target market, and business mission. The quality and professionalism of your promotional package is important. Remember to stress customer benefits and your "distinctive competency." Much of your marketing and promotion should be partially developed by now through past Action Steps, especially your "customer touchpoints" (Chapter 5). At this point, you know the areas in which you can and must shine. The next step is to begin the promotion selection and process to showcase your strengths.

Any promotion or **promotional mix** that advances the image of your business is worth considering. Survey some of the more common and traditional means of promotion before you decide on your promotional strategy, and be sure you remain open to all options. It is essential to keep an open mind as you brainstorm for strategies, examine promotional campaigns, and come to understand

PROMOTION

The art or science of moving the image of your business into the forefront of a prospective customer's mind

PROMOTIONAL MIX

All the elements that you blend to maximize communication with your customer the importance of planning ahead. You will then be able to make wiser decisions on how to connect with the customer.

Several considerations are critical to your campaign: these include what is appropriate for your customer, what you can afford to spend (your budget), and your own prior experience. Most important, though, is what is *most likely* to give you "the biggest bang for your buck." Here, creativity, consistency, and repetition are key elements for achieving a successful result.

THE PROMOTIONAL MIX

The key to connecting with customers is considering a wide variety of promotional strategies, selecting several, and working diligently to integrate them to put forth a consistent message to your target customer (Figure 6.1). There are times when a firm will select one or more elements to reach one target market and other variables to reach another target market. A closer look at many of these strategies follows. As you review the elements, please keep in mind the touchpoints from Chapter 5 and the gaps in the marketplace that you are trying to exploit. Remember for each touchpoint, you have the opportunities to connect with your customer; many times, this will not be through traditional advertising but through building a relationship with your customer, which is the key to your success.

Figure 6.1   Connecting with Your Target Customer

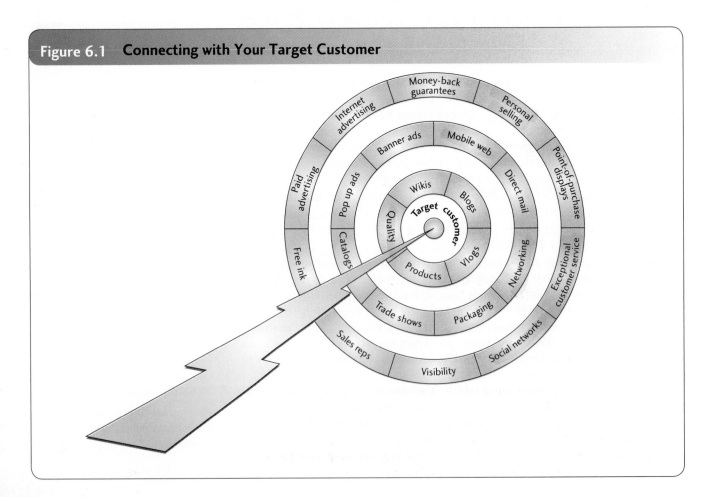

YOUR PROMOTIONAL CORNERSTONES: CUSTOMER SERVICE AND QUALITY

According to Jim Clemmer, author of the classic book *Firing on All Cylinders*, "Customer service and quality are back in vogue." Each year *PROFIT Magazine* announces its PROFIT 100 and PROFIT Hot 50. Winning companies such as Blueprint Public Relations (http://www.blueprintpr.ca) and Virtual Causeway (http://www.v-causeway.com) consistently remind us that the key to their success is pleasing the customer with exceptional service and quality.[6]

Time and again, surveys have shown that improved customer service and quality are key factors contributing to business profit and growth. Why is delighting the customer with service and quality so important? Here are a few market facts:

- You can charge up to 10 percent more if the customer perceives quality service.
- Firms with high service records are 12 percent more profitable than firms without, and their yearly sales growth is 12 percent higher.
- About 68 percent of customers stop doing business with a particular establishment because the employees appear indifferent toward customers.
- It costs five times as much to gain a new customer than to keep your present customer satisfied.
- A happy customer will tell 5 new people, but an unhappy customer will complain to 10 people.
- Only 1 dissatisfied customer out of 26 will bother to tell the owner. Consider that if only 1 customer complains, 25 others also have complaints, and each one is telling 10 people.
- Remember, the 80–20 rule: Eighty percent of the world is influenced by the other 20 percent. Word of mouth by the customer is a major way to get your message out once you are established. A customer who is happy because of quality service is the way to make word of mouth work for you.

OTHER MARKETING STRATEGIES

PAID MEDIA ADVERTISING

A sure-fire way to reach out is through advertisements on radio, television, display boards (written or electronic), newspapers, magazines, and trade journals. For some businesses, the Yellow Pages (paper and electronic) can be an effective promotional vehicle. Advertising tickles the customer's mind. With a good ad, you can reach right into your target customer and create the desire to buy from you.

Advertising has some obvious drawbacks: (1) it can be expensive to create; (2) if you don't spend a lot of money, your ad will lack wide exposure; and (3) major advertisers get preferred placements (the best locations within a publication, store, or business area; or the best time slots on TV or radio).

Advice

- Make sure that a large percentage of the listeners, viewers, or readers are in one of your target customer groups. Otherwise, your message is wasted.
- Your best ad is often yourself. Stay visible, and remember the importance of personal selling.
- Check with vendors. Ask for tearsheets, copy, and cooperative advertising money, and help on advertising design and layout.

- Explore creative co-op advertising, in which suppliers share a portion of the cost.
- Check with marketing departments of newspapers. Ask for help, advice, and information.
- Newspapers sometimes offer advertising in special supplements, such as a small business section, at reduced cost. The offer includes free editorial copy.
- Start small, and test and analyze the results of each promotional campaign.

BUSINESS CARDS

One restaurant owner we know gave individualized businesses cards to all employees. These employee business cards entitled the recipients to a 10 percent discount on meals. He encouraged the staff to hand them out, and they were rewarded for their promotional efforts. The restaurant would keep track of each card that was redeemed. Every month, the employee who generated the most business through businesses card handouts would receive a special reward, such as free tickets to a National Hockey League game. This strategy worked, generating 10 percent of all new customers.

Business cards are a marketing necessity. At the very least, they are an inexpensive way of improving the effectiveness of your networking and word-of-mouth campaign. Even if you haven't started your business, a business card will help you get the word out. These days, a box of well-designed business cards is very cost effective and quick to have printed. Just Google "business cards Canada" and a number of sites will pop up. Order your cards online or from your local business store, and in no time you'll be ready to market yourself and your business.

Advice

- **Provide basic information.** Make sure your business card contains such basic information as your name, business website, email and street addresses, fax number (if you have one), mailing address, and telephone number.
- **Project a professional image.** Make sure there aren't any typos or bad grammar.
- **Keep track.** When you hand out your cards, get the recipients' information. If someone doesn't have a card, write down the name and contact information. Keep a list of all contacts with their email address, telephone numbers, and location.
- **Incorporate a logo.** Think about designing a logo to go on the card.
- **Use both sides of the card.** Consider including the major benefits you are offering. How about your mission statement?
- **Consider a picture.** If you want a picture of yourself on the card, make sure it's not *your* ego needs you are trying to satisfy. Does your photo sell your business? If so, include it. If not, find some image that will. How about using your company logo instead?
- **Promote.** Use your business cards to attract customers and actively promote your word-of-mouth campaign.
- **Be creative.** 1-800-GOT-JUNK?, in the opening vignette, gives away refrigerator magnets. It's a business card their customers see every day. (http://www.1800gotjunk.com).
- **Remember your website.** Use your website to promote your cards. For example, if you order the 1-800-GOT-JUNK? fridge magnet online, you have to complete all kinds of information about yourself. The GOT-JUNK people promote these business card magnets to learn about their target customers.

POINT-OF-PURCHASE DISPLAYS

A **point-of-purchase (P-O-P) display** acts as a silent salesperson for a specific product. In the retail businesses, an estimated 70 percent of sales are impulse buys. Entrepreneurs Geoff Moss and David Minister are the owners of Poptech, a Toronto-based company that makes P-O-P displays. They took advantage of this market niche, added new technology and fresh ideas, and launched their business into a PROFIT Hot 50.[7]

Point-of-purchase displays, situated usually at or near the checkout counter or front desk, encourage impulse purchases of last-minute items such as paperbacks, pantyhose, candy, magazines, and gum. A sharp P-O-P display can also improve your image, and it serves as a tireless, silent salesperson, always on duty. A good P-O-P can be used for customer education. If it's hard to understand how to use your product or its benefits aren't clear to the target customer, your silent salespeople can deliver the message.

There are, at the same time, a few problems with these displays: (1) you can't sell large items, because they crowd customers at the cash register; and (2) the display must sell itself as well as the product. (A tacky P-O-P will turn prospective customers *off* instead of *on*.)

Advice

- Do weekly evaluations of all P-O-Ps. Make certain your silent salespeople are doing their work.
- Ask your suppliers for help. Many suppliers can assist with in-store promotion, signage, and P-O-P displays.
- Some wholesalers will carry racks and displays for their retail partners. Don't be afraid to ask.

PACKAGING

Don't forget the importance of product packaging. Review your competitors' packaging by purchasing their products and checking out the cost and effectiveness of their product packaging. What can you do better? What can you do more efficiently? What can you do more cost effectively? How could the packaging be made more attractive? Professionals in the packaging and distribution fields will be able to work with you on the proper sizing of packages and provide you with the benefits of their years of experience. One entrepreneur we know tried to sell her homemade sauces in two-litre jars until one of her retail accounts suggested she sell them in more "shelf friendly" one-litre jars and include her start-up story on the label to distinguish herself in the marketplace. Sales of her gourmet sauces tripled, as more accounts were willing to stock the smaller jars, which fit on the shelves much more easily.

Advice

- Consider environmental, safety, hygiene, and legal issues as well as customer requirements.

CATALOGUES

This sales tool is just right for isolated shoppers and shoppers in a hurry. Because we are becoming so "time poor," even general items are now being purchased

POINT-OF-PURCHASE (P-O-P) DISPLAY

A display that acts as a silent salesperson for a specific product via catalogues. Customers can shop at their convenience and not have to worry about store hours, parking, or traffic. Catalogue houses such as Lands' End don't usually manufacture anything, so they are always looking for good products. Use catalogues as another kind of silent salesperson to reach customers if your target customer tends to be a catalogue shopper.

If you try printing your own catalogues, you'll run into at least three problems: (1) cost (they are expensive to print and to mail), (2) size limitations (it's tough to sell anything by catalogue that's big, bulky, or inconvenient to ship), and (3) the challenge of establishing and maintaining a reliable mailing list.

Advice

- Be prepared to take advantage of online catalogues. They are growing in number, especially in business-to-business transactions.
- Let major catalogue houses do your promotion, but make sure you can deliver if your product takes off.
- Before you get in too deep, approach a few major houses with a product description plus photographs. If they don't like your product, they might help you locate a catalogue house that will. The feedback will be invaluable.

DIRECT MAIL

DIRECT MAIL
Advertisement or sales pitch that is mailed directly to target customers

This promotional tool lets you aim your brochures and fliers where they will do the most good. **Direct mail** is very important for small business, because it can go to the heart of your target market.

Direct mail reflects the importance of customer relationship marketing, which we discussed in Chapter 4, page 95. The success of direct mail will depend on your ability to focus on the needs of your target market. For example, a financial advisor might send one type of brochure to clients who have younger children and a slightly different pamphlet to clients who have grandchildren. If you don't know exactly what the needs of your target customers are—that is, your market is fragmented—the direct mail approach might not be appropriate.

Advice

- Know the needs of your target customers.
- Develop customer lists based on customer needs.
- Follow up your direct mail with a short telephone call.

MONEY-BACK GUARANTEES

You might not have thought of a guarantee as a form of promotion, but it is. You can reach security-minded customers by emphasizing the no-risk features of your product.

You must back up your guarantee with time and money. Therefore, if you have a guarantee, don't overlook the cost implications in your income and expense statements.

Advice

- Allow an extra 3 to 5 percent into your pricing to cover returned goods. If the product is fragile or easily misused—and people have been known to misuse just about everything—build in a higher figure.

FREE INK AND FREE AIR

Constantly ask yourself, "How can I get my company free publicity?" Brian Scudamore at 1-800-GOT-JUNK? is a master at using guerrilla marketing skills for getting free ink. GOT-JUNK was even able to get Dr. Phil, Oprah, CBS, and CBC to promote their company—all free of charge.

According to Scudamore, getting free press is a three-step process:

- **Step 1.** Clearly identify your target audience. In the franchise business, it might be franchise business reporters, for example.
- **Step 2.** Develop a hook or angle. Give them the right angle that's news-worthy—a high-profile sporting event or court case, for example.
- **Step 3.** Make calls. Call target reporters and make your pitch. Save your best prospects until the end. By this time, you will have honed your pitch.[8]

Free publicity through reviews, features, interview shows, press releases, and newspaper columns costs you nothing and can be effective. Think about sending out free samples of your product to news outlets. How about delivering free snacks to the media? Then listen to them rave about your treats. **Free ink and free air** are excellent ways to promote, because they establish your company in a believable way. The target customer is likely to attach more credence to words that are not paid advertising. The obstacle here is getting media people to see how your business is unique and noteworthy.

FREE INK AND FREE AIR
Information about a business that is published or broadcast free of charge

Advice

- Be prepared to spend significant time and effort to achieve full impact.
- *Every* business is newsworthy in some way. Dig until you find a different twist. Know the media people. Aim your release at *their* target readers, viewers, or listeners.
- Make your press kit visually appealing, include your story, and send accompanying photos of your principals, your facility, and your product being used or your service being performed.
- Caution is advised. Free ink/free air can also have a negative impact. If you are not careful, the "story angle" might not be the one you are hoping for. So, take the time, do your homework, and make sure that your promotional strategy reflects positively on the business.

FREEBIES

The GOT-JUNK franchisees are constantly looking to help at community events. Sometimes, they even pick up junk for community associations. A giveaway, or "freebie," can attract your target customer's attention, get you in the news, stimulate interest in a new product, or help you gather market research. Remember the free fridge magnets. They not only serve as a business card but also help provide customer information and research.

PERSONAL SELLING

It doesn't matter if you've never sold before: if you believe in your product or service, no one is a better salesperson than you are. You *are* the business. If you listen carefully, your target customers will *tell* you how to sell them your product or service. That's why a good salesperson is a creative listener, not a fast talker. Most customers like to talk with the owner of the business. Use that to your advantage (see Box 6.1).

DIRECT SELLING

The sale of a consumer product or service by an independent sales contractor in a face-to-face manner away from a fixed retail location

Box 6.1 Direct Sales Are Alive and Thriving

The Direct Sellers Association of Canada (DSA) defines **direct selling** as "the sale of a consumer product or service by an independent sales contractor in a face-to-face manner away from a fixed retail location." Direct sales are still alive and thriving, but few firms make house calls like the Fuller Brush salesman or Avon lady did in the 1950s and '60s. Direct selling mainstays such as Avon Canada and Quixtar Canada, or Canadian upstarts like Weekenders have adjusted to the "ding dong" tactics of the past. House parties, offices, and technology are their new stomping grounds—and, in many cases, their roads are electronic, and their doors are on computer screens. Here are some facts.

Direct Selling—Retail Sales in Canada (2008): $2.18 Billion

Location of Sales:	Percentage of Sales:
In the home	61.9%
In a workplace	6.7%
Over the phone (in a follow-up to a face-to-face meeting)	15.6%
Via the Internet	10.8%
At a fair, exhibition, shopping mall, etc.	3.9%
Other locations	1.1%

Industry Stats

Major Product Groups:	
Home/Family Care Products (cleaning products, cookware, cutlery)	30.4%
Personal Care Products (cosmetics, jewellery, skin care, etc.)	39.9%
Services/Miscellaneous/Other	5.5%
Nutritional/Vitamins/Wellness	17.9%
Leisure/Educational Products (books, encyclopedias, toys/games)	6.3%

Compensation Structure:	
Multi-level 81% of member companies	
Single-level 19% of member companies	

Sales Methods:	
Individual/Person-to-Person Selling	69.0%
Party Plan/Group Selling	28.5%
Customer placing order directly with firm (in follow-up to a face-to-face meeting)	1.7%
Other	0.8%

Estimated Total Retail Sales (2008): $2.18 billion

Source: DSA, "Location of Sales": http://www.dsa.ca/content/industry/stats.php (accessed January 2013) and http://www.dsa.ca/fileBin/mediaLibrary/SEIS_Executive_Summary.pdf. Reprinted by permission of the Direct Sellers Association of Canada.

Unfortunately, **personal selling** is expensive, especially if you have to pay others to do it, and it will boost your overhead unless you pay your salesperson only by earned commission. And if you try to do it all yourself, you won't have the time and energy for other things that only you can do. Still, for small businesses, the best form of promotion is personal selling.

PERSONAL SELLING

The selling and taking of orders by an individual salesperson

Advice

- Make everyone in your business a salesperson: delivery people, warehouse people, computer programmers, bookkeepers, clerical people, and switchboard operators. If nothing sells, they're out of a job. Remind everyone who works for you that your target customer needs a lot of TLC (tender loving care).
- Consider developing a network of sales reps who will work on a percentage of sales. Keep cheerleading. Reps need encouragement, too.
- Increase your personal visibility. Join a business or service club, as well as trade associations. Write a newspaper column. Be bold.
- Stay in touch with your customers, and listen to them. If you don't, you might lose your business.

TRADE SHOWS

These shows display your product or service in a high-intensity way. Trade shows focus on customers who have a keen interest in your business area. Your appearance at a trade show asserts your position in your industry. The local library or resource centre should have a copy of the publication *Canadian Industry Shows and Exhibitions*. This resource will help you learn where to display your products. You might also want to check the CARD (*Canadian Advertising Rates and Data*, available online at http://www.cardonline.ca/public/home.jsf), which lists many publications under various occupational and industrial classifications. Another option is to visit the Trade Show News Network (http://www.tsnn.com).

However, if the show is not in your area, you'll have transportation costs, as well as booths and space to rent. Furthermore, unless you're careful and make a study of the layout, you might end up with a space that is thin on traffic.

Advice

- Setting clear "show" objectives and having a training session with booth staff before the show can significantly improve effectiveness.
- Know beforehand what you want to achieve from each booth visitor.
- Have a plan in place for "after-show" follow-up—which relates to your show objectives.
- In the early years, at established shows, you might have to settle for low-traffic locations. If that's the case, try to get the show organizer to provide additional promotion in the show guide. Each year, try to obtain space in a higher traffic area.
- Always be on the lookout for cross-promotions. Try to arrange to hand out promotional items at the booth of a related non-competing company.
- Share a booth with another small business owner.
- Get your suppliers to help out—or share a booth with a supplier.
- Combine functions by doing some market research while you're promoting.

INDUSTRY LITERATURE

A good strategy to use is to become an industry expert. You can do this by writing a book on your experience, knowledge, and valuable wisdom! By writing a book, many people have promoted their businesses as industry leaders and attracted many new leads. You can also become an "expert" source of information for your industry by producing brochures, newsletters, handbooks, product documentation, annual reports, newspaper columns for the layperson, or even the "bible" for your industry. Your goal is to be recognized as an expert in your field.

We think trade literature is one of the best promotional devices around if your business lends itself to this kind of promotion. Remember that expertise is admired and sought out by others. As you grow in expertise, you'll also grow in confidence.

Advice

- If you're not a good writer, encourage a friend to help.
- Talk is cheap. If you get your thoughts down on paper, you're two steps ahead of the talkers.
- Sometimes, joint advertising with a manufacturer in a trade magazine is possible.
- Use your website to inform and help your customers.

WORKING VISIBLY

IMPACT MARKETING

Conducting special events designed to attract the attention of target customers

Working visibly is a major promotional strategy of the 1-800-GOT-JUNK? franchise team. Franchisees are encouraged to be creative, take initiative, and be visible. **Impact marketing** is a key strategy. Special events are designed to attract the attention of their target customers. As noted earlier, "junk motorcades" are a common practice for the Toronto franchise. GOT-JUNK encourages staff to wear blue clown wigs, stand on busy traffic islands, and wave to passing motorists. One franchisee reported a 20 percent increase in sales due to this high-impact marketing strategy. Most good service firms such as GOT-JUNK display their presence as they work: they put signs on everything—their business, their trucks, their work sites. Wherever they're busy, they let people know it. They make themselves visible.

The drawback here is similar to one of the drawbacks with point-of-purchase displays. If the presence you maintain doesn't sell itself—if it is unattractive or if it calls attention to an unappealing part of your business—you will lose potential customers rather than gain them.

Advice

- Exploit your public activities with signs that tell people who you are.
- Be unique and professional in your image and message.
- Make sure the message is working.
- Work visibly. Think about advertising on your car or truck, wearing a distinctive uniform, and placing signs where you work.

DISCOUNT COUPONS

If you book online at GOT-JUNK, you will likely get a $10 off coupon. In many businesses, a discount attracts a part of your market that likes a deal. Discount coupons are a special form of freebie, because they give you positive feedback on your promotion. They should have an expiration date and multiple-use disclaimers (as, for example, a disclaimer that the coupon cannot be used in conjunction with other promotions or discounts). They should also be coded to identify the source, so that you can find out where your advertising is paying off, and tested in small quantities before major use.

Everyone seems to like coupons. Even if your product or service is upscale, consider trying coupons as an introduction or at your slow times of the year. Another twist on the coupon is the entitlement card: "Buy five cups of coffee and get the sixth cup free." There are numerous variations on this theme.

Advice

- Consider giving away freebies that will catch customer attention.

BRANDING

The coffee mug you carry often has its own identity—maybe telling everyone, for example, that you're a Tim Hortons customer. Maybe it's the same with the baseball cap you wear: the "swoosh" tells everyone who's got you branded. A **brand** is a name, sign, symbol, design, or combination of these used to identify the products of one firm and to differentiate them from competitive offerings. 1-800-GOT-JUNK? is quickly becoming a brand name. Smart entrepreneurs figure out ways to make themselves—and thus their business—distinctive.[9]

BRAND

A name, sign, symbol, design, or combination of these used to identify the products of a firm

Advice

Start with answering the following questions:
- What makes you and your business unique?
- How does your customer benefit from your product or service?
- What would your customers say is your greatest strength?
- What is your most noteworthy personal trait? How is this trait tied to your business?
- Why should your customers buy from you instead of from your competitors?

ONLINE MARKETING

Online marketing is a powerful way to connect and promote your business. With millions of people online, now is the perfect time to consider an online marketing strategy.

Why are people surfing the Web? To get instant information on products, services, and businesses. And now people go to the Web to connect, learn, and share. It is open 24/7, is available to most parts of the world, and continues to expand. Here are some tools that you should consider for your online marketing strategy.

Website

Every business should have a website. It's your electronic telephone number and a valuable key to success. If you want to see a website that generates business, take a look at the 1-800-GOT-JUNK? site (http://www.1800gotjunk.com). Today, anyone can have a website, and almost everyone does. But a site with no visitors is of little benefit to you. You need to consider how to make your site worth bookmarking: of having visitors go through the process of tagging your website on an Internet browser so it is easy for them to click and go to it again at a later time.

Advice

- Promote your website offline. Offline promotion of a website can account for a major portion of first-time buyers. Include, for example, your website address on your letterhead and business cards. Be innovative; use every opportunity you have to promote your website with your company name.
- Get your website listed with search engines and directories. Doing this will help your customer find you.
- The title of your Web page should clearly indicate the contents or purpose of the site.
- Design your message so that it is simple and easy to update.
- The Web is good for selective reading. Help your customers select what they want quickly.
- Remember that your customers might not have the most recent Internet technology. If you design a site that requires the latest technology, you will lose some customers—how many will depend on your target market.
- Make your Web page action oriented. Show your customer the benefits of purchasing from you.
- In the interactive world, the ad is there only if the person finds it. Therefore, promoting on the Internet must give the customer a compelling reason to search out the site. Make your website rich and integrated with respect to content, but also make it entertaining.
- Make your website Google friendly. Ensure that your website uses search engine optimization (SEO) tools to make your site rank high on Google searches.

Social Media and Social Networks: Promoting Online

Social media and social networks provide savvy entrepreneurs with the ability to promote, converse, and otherwise let people build and shape their brand. Internet social tools, which provide the ability to interact with Web content, can help us start our businesses and connect with customers (see, for example, Box 6.2). With these tools, we can connect with other people and use those connections to make a business successful. Social media and networking tools evolve constantly. Some of the current social and technology tools available for entrepreneurs include these:

- Facebook.com
- Pinterest.com
- Twitter.com
- Youtube.com
- Linkedin.com
- Eventful.com
- Instagram.com
- Google Plus
- foursquare.com

According to co-author Shane Gibson in his book *Sociable!*, "social networks and social media sites have provided the masses with tools to communicate and

> ### Box 6.2　CampusCrow.com: Free Student Classifieds
>
> CampusCrow.com, a student site for classifieds and an auction site, uses Twitter and Facebook to let students know about deals regarding books and other items students have for sale. In addition to its website, it seeks to create friends through a Facebook page by using "Jake Crow" as a mascot to post information on people's Facebook walls; it also uses Youtube.com videos and other viral marketing techniques to promote its service on a very low marketing budget.[12]

propagate messages rapidly, in a viral way, that at times can even overpower traditional media."[10]

As discussed in Chapter 2, social media trends will continue to provide opportunities for proactive entrepreneurs. Smart entrepreneurs view social media as more than just "likes" or "fans." Social media allow entrepreneurs to engage more with clients than they could in the past.

These social media tactics are a must for entrepreneurs:

- Create a social media policy. It is important for entrepreneurs to take the time to write a social media policy for their business. The policy should outline acceptable topics and language, note such ideas as "no online bashing of the competition," identify who owns accounts and who can monitor accounts, and include a privacy policy.
- Engage. Build relationships and have conversations with your customers. Social media provide an excellent opportunity to engage with customers on a deeper level.
- Schedule. Take the time to post regularly. You'll need to set aside some time to write and connect with your customers using tools such as TweetDeck by Twitter.
- Listen. It is important to listen. Listen to what customers are saying to you and about you. Then, see how you can make changes as suggested by your customers.

Viral Marketing

Used effectively with social networks, **viral marketing** can be a great way to spread word of your products or services by letting people pass along your message like a virus. A classic example of this is Hotmail.com. Hotmail.com's viral marketing strategy was to attach a simple tag at the bottom of every free message sent out: "Get your private, free email at http://www.hotmail.com." According to a *Squidoo* article, this viral strategy allowed Hotmail.com to grow its subscriber base from zero to 12 million users in just 18 months.[11]

VIRAL MARKETING

A marketing technique that uses social networks to produce increases in brand awareness

Benefits of Viral Marketing

Viral marketing strategies are effective ways for entrepreneurs to promote their business. Here are a few key viral marketing strategies:

1. **Quick diffusion.** Viral marketing is a way to use the Internet effects of quickly spreading information to as many people as possible in the shortest time.
2. **Relevance.** If your content or information is worth telling others, then it will spread quickly. Make sure you have relevant information worth passing on.
3. **Social media.** Social media tools such as YouTube, Facebook, LinkedIn, and Twitter allow you to spread your message or information quickly to many people.

4. **Traffic direction.** Viral marketing strategies help to drive traffic to your website, profile page, or blog. Then, once people come to your site, your job is to ensure that you can engage them to take action. Actions include buying, joining, and engaging.

SALES REPS AS CONNECTORS

Suppose you have a new product that has immediate sales potential across the country. How can you connect with the whole country? Should you hire your younger brother to take care of it for you, or should you seek out a professional sales representative, who will act as a commissioned sales agent for you?

An army of sales reps awaits your call. Make your selection carefully. Exercise caution, because the reputation of your sales reps will become *your* reputation.

The best way to find good reps is to interview potential buyers of your goods. Ask them to recommend reps who have impressed them. When the same name surfaces several times, you will know where to start your contacts. Also, look carefully at who calls most frequently on your target customer.

Aggressive reps might contact you. Prepare yourself to ask them the right kinds of questions:

- Who are your customers?
- How many salespeople do you have?
- What geographic areas do you cover?
- What lines have you carried?
- What help can you offer in collecting overdue accounts?
- What ideas do you have for trade show presentations?
- Do you have a showroom?
- Could you work with us on a regional analysis while we get ready for national coverage?
- Do you promote over the Internet?
- What percentage commission do you expect?
- Can I participate in your sales meetings?
- Do you handle competing lines?
- What kind of reports on your sales calls can I expect?
- What kind of performance guarantees do you offer?
- How can the agreement be terminated?
- Can I pay out after I have collected from customers?

Provide all the encouragement and support to your reps that you can, and never stop being a cheerleader. At the same time, insist on sales call reports that will keep you informed on what is going on in the field, and pack your bags and make some calls with your reps. Write monthly sales letters, and encourage feedback from both your reps and their customers. You *could* learn the worst—that a new line has taken your place or that the reps have been sleeping. This feedback will help you evaluate your product line and your reps.

COURTESY AS PROMOTION

A dealer in luxury imported autos mailed 5,000 postcards to high-income prospects. The postcard message read something like, "Come in and test-drive this road warrior and receive a nice gift."

One potential customer travelled 65 kilometres for his test drive. The gift was a good incentive, but he'd been looking at cars for a year and was about to make a decision, so he wanted the test drive. That morning he had transferred funds to his chequing account. "Honey," he said to his wife as he left the house, "I'll be home with a car." His pink slip on his trade-in smouldered in the glove compartment.

Mr. Serious Prospect entered the dealer's showroom wearing old clothes and clutching his postcard. Four dapper salesmen in three-piece suits had seen him coming and had left the showroom quickly.

Without a salesperson in sight, the prospect spent 10 minutes waiting, reading the literature. The demos were locked, so he couldn't even sit behind the wheel for a fantasy drive. At last, a secretary entered the showroom, asked him for his postcard, and gave him the premium gift. About this time, one salesman returned, hands in his pockets, looking bored. The prospect took the opportunity to ask some questions about the car, to which the salesman responded without enthusiasm in monosyllables—and with a yawn.

Mr. Prospect took his business elsewhere that morning. He found the car he wanted and wrote a cheque for $45,000.

The promotion objective was to bring in customers for a test drive, not to give away premiums. Everything worked except the last person in the chain. How many other deals did that dealer lose during the promotion?

Be dramatic. Impress your employees with the fact that you mean business about customer courtesy. Close down your business for a day, and have all employees attend a sales retreat that stresses the importance of potential customers to your remaining in business. Follow up the retreat with incentive programs that reward employees for acts of exceptional courtesy to customers.

NETWORKING

Another source of promotional power is the technique of **networking**. Almost 40 percent of HOT 50 CEOs report that they belong to peer groups of entrepreneurs, and this percentage is growing.[13] Networking carries the image of your business to a support group of non-competitive helpers. Gena D'Angelo speaks for many when she gives this testimonial for networking.

NETWORKING

Communicating through person-to-person channels in an attempt to sell or gain information; talking to people with the purpose of doing business

When Rob and I decided to go into business for ourselves, we looked around for more than a year. I had some training in graphics and Rob is good with numbers, so what we finally decided on was a franchised mail-box operation. We paid the franchiser a flat fee and agreed to pay a percentage of our gross as well. In turn, we received assistance and a well-developed business plan.

What they didn't tell us about was networking.

When you're in the mail-box business, giving good service is how you forge ahead. We knew we had to promote our image, and we tried everything—brochures, leaflets, fliers, and full-page display ads in the local newspapers. But the business didn't start rolling in until I joined my first network.

It's a sales lead club, and the membership is varied. We have a real estate broker, an insurance agent, the president of a small bank, the owner of a coffee service, a printer, a sign manufacturer, the owner of a chain of service stations, a sporting goods store owner, a travel agent, two small manufacturers, and a contractor. We meet once a week for breakfast. If you don't bring at least one sales lead for another club member, you have to put a dollar in the kitty. I've gotten more business from that club than from all my other promotional efforts combined.

I then decided to join another club, and I used the contacts I made to build my own network. Business has been good ever since. We opened our second shop last April, put in a computer to keep track of our customers, and added an answering service. That first year, we networked our way to even more business, and we're planning to open a third shop 10 kilometres south of here by this time next year.

Networking gives you confidence, and it allows you to pass on helpful information to people who aren't competing with you—and to receive that kind of information too.

ACTION STEP 33

Build your network. (p. 167)

As a small business entrepreneur, you can network your way to a surprising number of new customer connections, which can spell success in big letters. If you don't have a network, use Action Step 33 to build one. Develop your network and build core groups of people within it. Because a network grows naturally from the loose association of people you already know, and because you are at the centre of the net, it has to help you. In Chapter 12, we will ask you to return to these networking sources when we encourage you to look for a mentor.

PLANNING AHEAD

You need to make a lot of intelligent noise before you open your doors for business. When you open, open with a bang. Start-ups are ironic: you often need to spend a large sum of money to overcome buyer inertia, yet you don't have those dollars to spend. What are you to do? Use your head instead of your chequebook.

Plan for your opening now. Few businesses are profitable at first, so yours probably won't be either. Many of the promotional tools we've just discussed cost very little, but you'll need to use them to lure customers and build confidence that you are in this game to win. Keep your target customers clearly in mind, so that you'll be able to tell them how your product or service will benefit them.

DON'T KEEP YOUR BUSINESS A SECRET

PROMOTIONAL CAMPAIGN

A sales program designed to sell a specific product or service or to establish an image, benefit, or point

When it comes to promotion, if you fail to plan, you're planning to keep your business a secret. One way to avoid keeping your business a secret is to brainstorm an ideal **promotional campaign** with no holds barred and no worries about costs. Action Step 34 makes sure you consider all of your creative ideas before you discard them as unrealistic. Save the ideas you come up with in this Action Step, because we'll use them later.

PROMOTION AND MARKET RESEARCH

ACTION STEP 34

Brainstorm a winning promotional campaign for your business. (p. 168)

CORE BENEFIT PROPOSITION

A statement about the benefits of your product or service to your target market

As you gain experience in promoting your small business, you'll see for yourself just how interlocked your promotional strategy and the target customer are. That's why you can't plan your promotional strategy without building on your market research. This research helps you develop your **core benefit proposition**. Your target customers are interested in what your product or service will do for them. You're selling benefits, not features. Your research will help you clarify the benefits of your product or service. That's why you can't plan your promotional mix without dipping back into market research. The pros do both at the same time.

ASK CUSTOMERS QUESTIONS TO HELP DEVELOP YOUR MARKETING STRATEGY

Review your customer touchpoints from Chapter 5 and your brainstorm from Action Step 34. Then ask your customers how they perceive your business. Ask them questions such as these:

- Is there anything you couldn't find?
- Is this your first visit to this store? (not "Can I help you?")
- What do you want and do we have it?
- How does our product or service fit your needs?
- How do we compare in price to the competition?
- Is there more value to you in shopping here than elsewhere?
- Where are you from?
- How did you find us?
- How else might our company be of service?

Listen to the answers your customers give you, and value the information for what it is: primary market research data. Write down each customer's exact words in your 24/7 Adventure Notebook.

ATTACH PRICE TAGS TO YOUR PROMOTIONAL STRATEGIES

A giveaway, like any other promotional strategy, costs money. Look at the ideal promotional strategies you came up with in Action Step 34, then determine the price of each. Action Step 35 walks you through the process.

Don't be discouraged if price knocks out part of your ideal promotional mix. Always evaluate whether there is a way to achieve the same result at less cost. That's why we've filled this chapter with so many inexpensive promotional ideas. Use the powers of your imagination to brainstorm the best possible promotional effort for your business.

When bankers review a business plan, they will want to know how and at what cost you will reach your target customers. You should also consider how much your industry spends, on average, for promotion. Here, trade associations can be very helpful. We also encourage you to check out Industry Canada's SME Benchmarking Tool (http://www.ic.gc.ca/eic/site/pp-pp.nsf/eng/Home). For example, if you were planning on starting a full-service restaurant, you can learn from the SME Benchmarking Tool that restaurants spend, on average, about 2 percent of their total revenue on advertising and promotion. Remember, however, that the SME Benchmarking Tool provides industry ratios for established businesses. You might have to spend a little more in the opening phase of your business.

A well-thought-out marketing promotion plan will demonstrate to your reader that you have done your homework and recognized the benefits and costs of promoting your product or service.

In a Nutshell

Your marketing strategy will consist of an analysis of your external market and trends, target market, product/service uniqueness and competitive advantage, and marketing mix. Within the marketing mix are pricing and promotion.

You'll have to think about the price(s) you will charge based on your target customer, competitive analysis, and costs of production. You then have to develop a pricing strategy. We encourage you to try to adopt a ceiling, or premium, price strategy.

Promotion is the art or science of moving the image of your business into the prospect's mind. Anything that will advance that image is a good to consider. The foundation of any promotional strategy is customer service and quality.

ACTION STEP 35

Attach a price tag to each item in your promotion package. (p. 168)

In this chapter, we recommended that you survey the whole range of promotional strategies available to you and then choose the promotional mix that would work best for your unique business. Two key potential strategies are customer service and quality. Others include paid media advertising, business cards, point-of-purchase displays, catalogues, direct mail, money-back guarantees, free ink and free air, freebies, personal selling, trade shows, industry literature, discount coupons, branding, online promotion, sales representatives, courtesy, and networking.

We also recommended that you seek creative "guerrilla marketing" solutions to the problem of promoting within a small budget, and we gave examples of how other entrepreneurs have responded to that challenge.

Throughout the chapter, we stressed the relationship between market research (your strategy for locating target customers and learning their needs) and promotion (letting your customers know your business can serve their needs and making them happy in the process). The overall message of the chapter is to use your head as well as your chequebook in connecting with the customer.

Key Terms

brand	marketing strategy
ceiling, or premium, pricing	markup
competitor-based pricing	networking
core benefit proposition	penetration pricing
direct mail	personal selling
direct selling	point-of-purchase (P-O-P) display
economy, or limit, pricing	price skimming
free ink and free air	profit-based, or cost plus, pricing
guerrilla marketing	promotion
impact marketing	promotional campaign
industry norm, or "keystone," pricing	promotional mix
marketing mix	viral marketing

Think Points for Success

✓ Be distinctive, and you can charge a ceiling or premium price.
✓ Be unique with your promotions. Instead of Christmas cards, send Thanks giving or April Fool's Day cards.
✓ Stand in your target customer's shoes. Think like your target customer. Find the need. Find the "ladder" in the target customer's mind.
✓ Maintain a visual presence.
✓ A world in transition means opportunities for entrepreneurship. Fast footwork can keep you in the game.
✓ To start your mailing list, give away something for free. In return, potential customers will give you their names.
✓ Rent a Santa. Rent a robot. Rent a hot-air balloon. Rent a talking dolphin.
✓ Brand yourself. Create some excitement, because excitement sells.
✓ When you think you have it made, keep connecting with that customer. You will never be so big that you can afford to disconnect. Remember this, and it may make you rich.
✓ Remember to promote the benefits and value of your product or service.
✓ Use the Internet to promote your business.

Action Steps

ACTION STEP 32

Calculate and justify your product/service price.

The marketing section of your business plan should tell the reader (1) what price(s) you are charging, (2) what your pricing strategy is, and (3) why you chose this pricing strategy. This three-step exercise will help you establish and justify a price for your product or service.

Step 1: Estimate your price based on market considerations.

In Action Step 30, Chapter 5, we asked you to review your competitive touchpoint analysis and state the prices of your products or services relative to your competitors. We were asking you to calculate your prices relative to the market. Now we want you to go back and review your results from Box 5.1. Ask yourself again: Is my product unique or distinctive relative to my competitors'? Is my product inelastic? If not, how can I make it unique and thus more inelastic? Can I charge higher prices relative to my competitors? This process will provide you with a product/service price estimate based on market considerations.

Step 2: Estimate your price based on cost considerations.

Now we want you to list all the costs associated with your product or service. Remember, you may have a network of suppliers. Can you find any costing estimates online? This particular exercise might involve plenty of primary and secondary research, but take some time with it. Determine the most realistic costs possible.

Once you have the costing numbers, calculate your product/service price based on the profit-based, cost plus, approach explained above. As long as it is right for your business, we suggest you try this costing method.

Step 3: Determine and justify your pricing strategy.

In Steps 1 and 2, you calculated one price based on market considerations and one based on cost considerations. What final price will you charge? This figure will depend on your choice of pricing strategy. Most successful small businesses use a ceiling, or premium, price strategy. They charge the highest price the market will bear and one that yields an acceptable profit given cost considerations. To complete the pricing section of your marketing plan, answer the following questions:

- What price(s) will you charge?
- What is your pricing strategy?
- Why have you chosen this strategy?

Keep these pricing results handy. You'll need them when it comes time to forecast your sales (Chapter 10).

ACTION STEP 33

Build your network.

Visualize yourself as being at the centre of a web of interpersonal contacts and associations. This web connects you with your family, friends, neighbours, acquaintances, business associates—everyone you know—and is your potential network.

To develop a functioning network for yourself, write down what you know about each person in your web: business, hobbies, residence, children, interests, and people he or she might know. Recall where you met the person. Does the meeting place tell you anything helpful? Are you members of the same group or club? What interests do you share? What is the connection between you and the person?

Now from all these people, build a couple of core groups. Start with two or three people. Are they interested in networking? Are they diverse enough? (You'll need doers, stars, leaders, technicians, an organizer or two—people who will tend to "balance out" your talents. See Chapter 12 on team building.) Make sure that the people you contact are not competing for the same target customers. The members of a core group must *not* be competitors; if they are, the group won't function as it should.

Set up a meeting. If you are working, breakfast usually works best. If the core group catches on, you can share phone duties and arrange further meetings.

Before you know it, you'll be networking your way through the channels of your community, business to business.

ACTION STEP 34

Brainstorm a winning promotional campaign for your business.

Disregard all budgetary restraints. Pretend that money is no object. Close your eyes, sit back, and develop the ideal campaign for connecting with your target customers. It's okay to "get crazy" with this, because excellent workable solutions often develop out of such unleashed mental activity!

- If your product or service needs a multimillion-dollar advertising promotion with endorsements by your favourite movie star, fantasize that it's happening now.
- If you need a customer list created in marketing heaven, specify exactly what you need, and it is yours.
- If you are looking for the services of a first-class catalogue house, just whisper the name three times, and you're in business.
- If your business at its peak could use 1,000 delivery trucks with smiling drivers who make your target customers feel terrific, write down "1,000 smiling delivery people."
- If your product is small, brainstorm the perfect point-of-purchase device, perhaps one that has slot machines with money-tubes connected to your private bank vault.
- How would you promote your product or service over the Internet? Design the perfect website. Watch the money roll in!

This chance to ignore cost won't come around again (reality is right around the corner). But for now, have fun.

ACTION STEP 35

Attach a price tag to each item in your promotion package.

What will your customer connection cost? Review Action Steps 32 and 33, and list the top five connections you want with your customers. Then find their cost.

Let's imagine that you've chosen this promotional mix.

1. **Magazine ads.** This choice assumes you know what your target customer reads. Contact the display ad departments of the magazines. Ask for their media kits, reader profiles, and the rates for their mailing lists for the geographic areas you want to reach. Many magazines will sell lists by a code.
2. **Direct mail.** Look up mailing list brokers in the Yellow Pages under Direct Mail. Ask for information, strategy tips, and sample names to check for mailing list accuracy against your target customer profiles. Compare the costs of buying the lists from brokers and from magazines.
3. **Press releases.** Visit the marketing department of your local newspaper for information on targeting its readers. Use this information to angle your release. Catch the reader's attention, but keep the message simple. Be sure to wield the five Ws (who, what, where, when, and why) and the noble H (how) of journalism.
4. **Personal selling.** If you can't reach customers this way yourself, you will need to budget for someone who can. If you plan to do the selling yourself, locate lead clubs in your area and build a network of contacts. Figure your salary and expenses as a promotional cost. (For tips on how to profile your personality and how it can be balanced by others, see Chapter 12.)

Once you know what each item of your promotional package will cost, you can decide which ones you can afford.

Business Plan Building Block

Before you begin these building block exercises, you might want to look ahead to the 1-800-GOT-JUNK? case and resources provided at the end of this chapter. The GOT-JUNK marketing, pricing, and promotional strategies might help you develop, refine, and clarify your plan.

PRICING YOUR PRODUCT

Describe what prices you will charge, and why, in relation to your customers, potential competitors, costs of production, and expected profit. Describe your pricing strategy and why you have chosen it.

ADVERTISING AND PROMOTION

Describe your advertising and public relations plan. What are the most cost-effective ways to reach your customers? Use the data you have developed from the text.

PUBLIC RELATIONS—UNPAID ADVERTISING

- Sample news releases (attach)
- Research articles or contributions to trade or technical journals
- Participation in or sponsorship of events
- Contributions to local media (air, press, and others)
- Community charities and/or networking activities

MEDIA ADVERTISING AND DIRECT MAIL

- Mail list applications
- Advertising space purchases
- Yellow Pages listings
- Computer bulletin boards and websites
- TV and radio commercials
- Point-of-purchase displays, signs, and billboards
- Brochures and selling sheets
- Business cards and ad specials
- Trade shows and informational seminars

Don't be afraid to be different and unique. Your message has to penetrate a lot of clutter.

Now it's your turn: take a page or more.

SERVICE AND SUPPLY

Once the sale is consummated, explain delivery of the product. Take-out? Will call? UPS? Purolator? FedEx? And so on. Follow up with sales support. What will your customer need from you once the product or service has been delivered? Look for techniques to turn your service into more sales opportunities.

Now it's your turn.

MARKET STRATEGY PHILOSOPHY

This general statement demonstrates that your business is customer driven. Use the information in Chapters 4 and 5 and in this chapter to develop a one-page marketing strategy philosophy.

SERVICES AFTER THE SALE

Once you have a customer, what will you do to keep that customer? Phone call follow-up? Correcting shipping or product mistakes? List ideas.

_____

_____

_____

_____

_____

Checklist Questions and Actions to Develop Your Business Plan

Marketing Strategies and Promotion: Connecting with the Customer

❑ What is your marketing strategy?

❑ What prices will you charge?

❑ What is your pricing strategy?

❑ What are the goals, objectives, and promotional mix?

❑ What stimulates your target market to buy or use your product or service?

❑ What has the primary and secondary market research told you about promoting your business?

❑ Develop a promotional strategy for your business.

❑ What percentage and what amount of your promotional budget will be spent on each of the components of a promotional mix, and why?

❑ Does your business have a unique twist for a possible publicity story?

❑ Why did you select the business name you are using?

Case Study: 1-800-Got-Junk?

Case Background

At the beginning of this chapter we highlighted 1-800-GOT-JUNK?—a Canadian franchise organization that has experienced meteoric growth. To a large degree, the success of this company can be attributed to its marketing and promotion strategies. GOT-JUNK has put in place a successful pricing and promotions strategy, leading to healthy profits for the franchise system.

Below are additional sources of information and case study questions to help you understand why GOT-JUNK has been so successful and to reinforce the major marketing, pricing, and promotional themes of this chapter.

Case Resources

Refresh your memory and reread the GOT-JUNK vignette at the beginning of this chapter. We also want you to link on to the sites listed below:

- 1-800-GOT-JUNK? home page: http://www.1800gotjunk.com
- "Cash for Trash," *Fortune Magazine*: http://money.cnn.com/magazines/ fortune/fortune_archive/2003/10/27/351639/index.htm; Franchise Zone, "1-800-GOT-JUNK, Company Background": http://www.entrepreneur.com/ franchises/1800gotjunk/293278-0.html
- "1-800-Got-Junk? Company Background," Entrepreneur.com: http://www. entrepreneur.com/franchises/1800gotjunk/293278-0.html
- "One Deadly Obsession," Profit website: http://profitguide.com/manage-grow/ strategy-operations/one-deadly-obsession-28818

Case Study Questions and Activities

1. Marketing strategies
   a. At the beginning of this chapter, we discussed the four key elements of the marketing strategy. What are these four elements?
   b. In Chapter 2 we explained how market trends create opportunities. The 1-800-GOT-JUNK? franchise system has linked on to a number of market trends. List five major trends that 1-800-GOT-JUNK? has taken advantage of.
   c. In Chapter 5, we explained the purpose and importance of competitive intelligence. According to Brian Scudamore, the war on Trashbusters—his first direct competitor—represented "an important chapter in the history of 1-800-GOT-JUNK?" Return to the opening vignette or link onto *Canadian Business* Online, "One Deadly Obsession" at http://profitguide.com/manage-grow/strategy-operations/one-deadly-obsession-28818. Explain what happened in the case of Scudamore's first direct competitor. What did Brian learn about the purpose of competitive intelligence from this experience?

2. Guerrilla marketing
   a. As we explained in the text, guerrilla marketing is a key promotional strategy of 1-800-GOT-JUNK?. Define the term *guerrilla marketing*, and give three examples of how GOT-JUNK uses this strategy.
   b. GOT-JUNK spent only $1,800 in advertising (in 2004) to reach potential franchisees. Free ink and free press comprise a key guerrilla marketing strategy for the company. Scudamore, the founder, recommends a three-step process to maximize this strategy. Briefly explain Scudamore's process.

3. Pricing
   a. In this chapter, we described four of the more common small business approaches to pricing: competitor-based pricing; profit-based pricing; industry norm, or "keystone," pricing; and ceiling, or premium, pricing. Briefly explain each of these strategies.
   b. Which of the four strategies in question 3(a) do you think is being used by 1-800-GOT-JUNK? Briefly explain why.
   c. A major marketing strategy of 1-800-GOT-JUNK? is to focus on a specific market segment, create uniqueness, and differentiate its service as perceived by the customer. Does this strategy lead to a more elastic or inelastic demand for company services? How does this marketing strategy affect GOT-JUNK's pricing policy?

4. Promotional strategies
   A number of promotional strategies were discussed in this chapter. Many of these strategies are being successfully used by GOT-JUNK. For each of the promotional strategies listed below, give one example showing how GOT-JUNK used it.

Strategy	Provide a 1-800-Got Junk Example
Freebies	
Free ink	
Free air	
Personal selling	
Working visibly/Impact marketing	
Discount coupons	
Branding	
Networking	
Word of mouth	
Recycling and charity	
Community involvement	
Contests	

5. Online promotion

The 1-800-GOT-JUNK? franchisor made heavy use of online promotion.
a. Evaluate the 1-800-GOT-JUNK? home page based on the criteria provided.
b. Do you think this website is an effective promotional tool? Give four reasons.

Notes

1. "Cash for Trash," *Fortune Magazine*, http://money.cnn.com/magazines/ fortune/fortune_archive/2003/10/27/351639/index.htm; Franchise Zone, "1-800-GOT-JUNK, Company Background": http://www.entrepreneur.com/ franchises/1800gotjunk/293278-0.html.

2. See "Marketing and Sales," Canada Business, http://www.canadabusiness.ca/eng/ page/2863//; and CCH, "Pricing Your Product," *Business Owner's Toolkit*, http:// www.bizfilings.com/toolkit/sbg/marketing/packaging-pricing/pricing-is-difference- between-success-failure.aspx.

3. See CCH, "Analyzing Your Costs and Overhead," *Business Owner's Toolkit*, http:// www.bizfilings.com/toolkit/index.aspx; and "Marketing and Sales," Canada Business, http://www.canadabusiness.ca/eng/page/2863/.

4. See Enterprise Saskatchewan, "Profit Pricing for a Manufacturer," http://www. enterprisesaskatchewan.ca/profitman; see, for example, Mark Deo, "Pricing Strategies," SBA, http://www.sbanetwork.org/company/solutions/market_ segmentation.htm.

5. "Six Secrets of Super Startups," *Profit Magazine*, http://profitguide.com/startup/ best-practices/six-secrets-of-super-startups-28717.

6. "Go Big or Go Home," *Canadian Business*, www.profitguide.com/manage-grow/ success-stories/go-big-or-go-home-28709.

7. "Six Secrets of Super Startups," *Profit Magazine*, http://profitguide.com/startup/ best-practices/six-secrets-of-super-startups-28717.

8. "Three Steps for Getting Free Publicity," *Investor's Business Daily*, http://news. investors.com/management-managing-for-success/112904-403340-three-steps- for-getting-free-publicity.htm.

9. See, for example, Industry Canada, "SME Direct," *Competitive Intelligence Printable PDF*, http://biblioteca.fstandardbank.edu.ar/images/8/8d/Competitiveness_ Intelligence.pdf.

10. Gibson, Shane, and Stephen Jagger, *Sociable!* (self-published, 2009).

11. "Viral Marketing—Why Is It So Powerful?" *Squidoo*, http://www.squidoo.com/ powerful.

12. Campus Crow (http://www.campuscrow.com).

13. "Tough Love," *Profit*, http://www.profitguide.com/manage-grow/leadership/tough- love-28325; and "Six Secrets of Super Startups," *Profit Magazine*, http://profitguide. com/startup/best-practices/six-secrets-of-super-startups-28717.

Chapter 7

Marketing: Distribution and Location

Chapter 7 will help you prepare part E, the location section, of your Business Plan.

iStockphoto/Thinkstock

LEARNING OPPORTUNITIES

After reading this chapter, you should be able to

- understand the contribution of location to small business success;
- begin to develop a multiple distribution strategy;
- understand the uniqueness of your business location needs;
- focus on customer needs when evaluating a location;
- develop a checklist for evaluating potential sites for your business;
- think about if and when you should locate your business out of the home;
- use both secondary and primary sources of information in locating your business; and
- understand and negotiate a lease contract.

ACTION STEP PREVIEW

36. Use your new eyes to evaluate business locations.
37. Fantasize your perfect location.
38. Decide whether a home-based business is in your future.

QUESTVEST

Gloria Brookstone's business idea struck when her handbag was stolen in Venice, Italy, where Brookstone was travelling with her husband, Jim. They were crossing a quaint arched bridge on their way to breakfast when two motorcyclists zoomed by. Brookstone felt a slight tug at her shoulder, and then all she could remember was seeing her handbag clutched in a biker's fist. The strap had been cut and was swinging free in her hand.

The ensuing paperwork "stole" the entire morning. "Have you ever thought of a money belt?" the policeman asked. "So many purses are stolen here."

Brookstone had tried a money belt, but it didn't feel right. Later that day, she borrowed Jim's safari vest. It was handy, with all those pockets, but it didn't look like Brookstone.

"I'm not on a safari," she told him. "And this vest swallows me up. It's too big. There has got to be a better way to protect my money."

When Brookstone returned home to Vancouver and her job, she talked to her friends and read a number of travel reports on the Internet. She learned that purse thefts were a common problem for travellers—especially female boomers. That's when her idea began to take shape.

"Why don't I create the perfect travel vest—one with panache, style, and rich colours," she mused. "It would come with secret inside pockets to place money and valuables safely. The need for safety and travel are growing trends—especially as we begin to enter our silver years."

Brookstone brainstormed with Jim and their friends, and sat up many nights designing Travel Vests. Her 24/7 Adventure Notebook gradually began to fill up with different designs and mind maps. Eventually, she decided on one basic design to test her idea, selected a garment maker in Montréal, and paid $5,000 (up front) for 200 vests—the minimum order. But the first vests looked shabby and cheap. When Brookstone complained, the garment maker responded: "Business is business. We produced exactly what you designed, Madame." Brookstone threatened to sue, but the money was gone. She eventually disposed of most of the vests at local craft fairs, but working with a large manufacturer taught her a valuable lesson. She needed far more control and would have to obtain it a different way.

After more brainstorming and mind mapping, and plenty of sleepless nights, Brookstone discovered what she really wanted to do: to work with cloth. Over the years, she had gathered cloth from Bhutan, the Kashmir, China, Turkistan, Tajikistan, Kenya, and Madagascar. Working with cloth had become her passion. She was tired of her job and yearned for independence. Brookstone desperately wanted to control her destiny and be her own boss.

But one thing she did not want to do was to finance her dream venture by putting in overtime. Instead of producing thousands of vests for a faceless mass market, she determined that her vision was to create one vest at a time while picturing a woman travelling the world wearing it. With the help of her husband and a local college professor, she created a detailed business plan. Now she was ready to make her dream come alive.

Brookstone used the Internet to locate her seamstresses. She found an artists' newsgroup, from which she learned of a sewing cooperative—people who worked from their homes and who cared about their craft. Several women were interested in her project. Brookstone used a scanner and sent her designs directly to these women over the Internet. This time she was much more careful. Before giving up her precious and very expensive cloth, she paid each woman to create a test vest. When the test vests were accepted, she met with and interviewed each seamstress before she handed over the cloth, outsourcing or contracting out the work.

To test the market for her vests, Brookstone contacted friends who travelled extensively internationally. She invited each of them to bring two or three friends to her first pre-Christmas trunk show in a hotel suite in downtown Vancouver. French pastries and espresso were served as the women tried on the vests and discussed their travels. There were 50 vests, each unique, with special buttons, fabric, and pockets. Forty-five vests were sold for prices ranging from $150 to $500. Brookstone also took several special orders. And, just as important as sales, she learned a lot about her target market's needs through networking and primary research.

Six months later, Brookstone left her job and began working from her home. There she could balance her busy family and social schedule, and save money on rent and office charges. Besides that, she could now work late into the night, the time when creative juices flowed and she was most productive. The walls of her design room were already covered with drawings, photos, and bits of cloth. At work, in her design room, she came up with a company name: QuestVest. She purchased a computer-ized clothing design program, and a techie friend helped her retool the program for vests and build a website.

Today Gloria Brookstone runs a profitable home-based business. A growing 10 percent of her sales come from the Web; 60 percent from specialty Canadian retail outlets in Vancouver, Toronto, Ottawa, and Halifax, and two American outlets in Seattle; and 30 percent from home parties and trunk shows.

Networking has always been one of Brookstone's stronger skills. These skills helped her start thinking about the future. At a craft show in Calgary, she met Adrienne Armstrong of Arbour Environmental Shoppe, from Ottawa. Armstrong and her husband, Sean, were selling their rain barrels. It was Armstrong who prompted Brookstone to think about all kinds of future possibilities.

"Can you make a QuestVest out of hemp?" Armstrong asked.

"I don't see any reason why not. I'll check it out with my seam-stresses," Brookstone replied.

She realized that the environment represented another trend she could link in to. "I can sell QuestVests wholesale to Adrienne and other environmental retailers. I can also sell them at home parties and craft shows—that will be a real hit for my target group."

In a subsequent brainstorm over coffee, the pair came up with the idea of selling QuestVests over the home shopping channel—if the price was right, of course. Other brainstorming options included e-wholesaling, mail order, and cataloguing. Armstrong had even dreamed up a special event "office party" distribution strategy, in which Brookstone could sell her vests directly to teachers at elementary schools. "What a niche. The teachers I know love to travel and share their experiences with students," she said as she snapped up her coffee and rushed back to her booth.

One of the most important decisions an entrepreneur has to make relates to the **business location**—the place where you distribute the goods and services for your business. Marketing people often refer to this location decision as the "4th P" (place) in the marketing mix. In addition, however, location considerations are important in the development of your operational

BUSINESS LOCATION

The place where you distribute the goods and services for your business strategy—especially when it comes time to think about how you will distribute your product or service.

According to an old axiom, "location, location, location" are the three most important reasons for business success. To some extent, and especially in "store-front" retail operations, this philosophy has a great deal of merit. But what if you want to operate your business out of your home? First, congratulations! As you will learn in this chapter, you may be on the right track because we have entered the age of the "gold-collar," or home-based, worker. More and more of us are working out of our homes, Gloria Brookstone, who was profiled in the opening vignette, and Sheila Mather, who is profiled later in this chapter, among us. Many entrepreneurs start their business from the home and then move out as the business grows.

All kinds of services and products are now provided by home-based businesses. With the growth in services, technology, and the knowledge-based industries, chances are that you, too, might one day be operating some sort of business out of your home. That said, in planning to set up your business at home, your location analysis is still just as important as if you were to lease in a storefront or manufacturing operation. There are a number of critical location questions that you're still going to have to think about: Do the municipality by-laws allow me to operate a business at home? How do I balance my family and work life? How do I deal with my target customers from my home? And so on.

Chapter 7 will lead you through the steps involved in finding a good location for your business using primary and secondary research—and, if necessary, in negotiating a lease that will serve you well. We'll also encourage you to consider all the pros and cons of locating your business out of the home. At the outset, however, we do want to caution you. What you believe will be a good location is certainly relevant, but it is more important to understand what your *target customer* believes is a good location. You have to be able to understand your customer to answer this question: "What is the *best* location?" To a large extent, then, your location decision will depend on how you plan to distribute your product or service—given your product or service and your customers' needs. So we begin this chapter by prompting you to think about your various distribution choices or channels.

DISTRIBUTION CHANNELS

DISTRIBUTION CHANNEL

The method or way in which a producer makes a product or service available to the consumer

RETAILING

Selling goods and services directly to the consumer, or end user

A distribution channel is the method or way in which a producer makes a product or service available to the consumer. It is the route or path that a product or service follows as it makes its way from the producer to the consumer. Here you will have two broad channel options: either directly, through retailing, or indirectly, through wholesaling. **Retailing** is the selling of goods and services directly to the consumer, or end user. The retailing channel includes B2C businesses that are selling products—specialty retail outlets selling QuestVests to consumers, for example—or services—haircuts or food sold in restaurants, such as Close Connections, profiled later in this chapter. There are two basic types of retailing channels: store and non-store. The most common type, of course, is store retailing, which represents about 95 percent of all retail sales. The other retail type—non-store retailing—includes subdistribution channels such as direct selling, online sales through a website, television home shopping, vending machine retailing, mail order, catalogue sales, craft fairs, and trunk shows (for example, see Statistics Canada, "Non-Store Retailers": http://stds.statcan.gc.ca/naics-scian/2007/cs-rc-eng.asp?criteria=454).

The second broad channel option is indirect. Here, you have two major options.

1. **Wholesaling.** This is the selling of products to retailers for resale to the end user, or consumer. For example, in the opening vignette, Gloria Brookstone took on a wholesaler's role when she decided to sell her QuestVests to high-end women's retail outlets, which, in turn, sold them to their customers. As with retailing, you can even have subdistribution channels within **wholesaling**, such as business trade fairs, online wholesaling, or catalogue sales.

2. **Franchising. Franchising** is a special kind of distribution system in which one company (termed the *franchisor*) grants the right to sell its products or services to another company or individual (termed the *franchisee*). The franchisor is normally selling a format or business process to another individual or company, which, in turn, uses this format to satisfy the needs of the end user. One example of a successful franchise is 1-800-GOT-JUNK?—a company we described in the opening vignette in Chapter 6. GOT-JUNK sold the rights to its junk removal system to others, who thereby became franchisees dealing directly with the customer to remove the unwanted trash. Note, however, that the franchise distribution channel could also involve wholesaling. For example, if Tim Hortons sold a can of its delicious coffee (at wholesale prices) to a franchisee, which then sold it to the customer, then Tim Hortons would be using both the wholesale and franchise distribution networks.

The point here is that there is no reason why you should not think about being the franchisor and franchising out your business idea. Creative and bold entrepreneurs such as Brian Scudamore of 1-800-GOT-JUNK? and Ken LeBlanc of PropertyGuys.com franchised out their business idea—and so can you! We'll talk a lot more about franchises in Chapter 14. For now, we just want you to understand that franchising is a major distribution channel for many Canadian small businesses and one that you might want to think about.

What is your distribution strategy? Well, this will depend on a number of factors, such as your type of business (B2C or B2B), customer needs, the type of product/service, transportation costs, and your competition. The important point here is that successful entrepreneurs take advantage of more than one distribution channel. Go back to the opening vignette for an example. Brookstone's broad distribution channel for her QuestVests was wholesaling, which constituted about 60 percent of her business, but she didn't rely on this one broad distribution channel. She also developed three other retail (non-store) subdistribution channels—e-retailing, home parties, and trunk shows. These other subdistribution channels accounted for another 40 percent of her business. And she might even think about franchising someday. Now, return for a moment to Adrienne Armstrong and her business, Arbour Environmental Shoppe (Chapter 1, page 11). She made use of four distribution channels: traditional store retailing, e-retailing, trade fairs, and wholesaling. We end this section by encouraging you to follow the direction of successful entrepreneurs, such as Gloria Brookstone and Adrienne Armstrong, and begin thinking about a multiple distribution strategy. The physical location you choose will be largely dependent on your multiple distribution strategy, and this is where we are going next.

WHOLESALING

The selling of products to retailers for resale to the end user, or consumer

FRANCHISING

A special kind of distribution system in which one company (termed the *franchisor*) grants the right to sell its products or services to another company or individual (termed the *franchisee*)

WHAT IS YOUR BEST LOCATION?

"There's nothing really like us," Janice Richmond, co-owner of Close Connections, says of the Elgin Street bar. "We're a restaurant on one side, with computers on the other. People can sit here and have a beer and plate of fries while they surf the Net." The target customer is between the ages of 20 and 35. The lounge is particularly appealing to tourists and business travellers who can "return home" online.

As with most storefront operations, choosing the right location was a critical decision for Richmond and her partner, Francine Jacobs. They wanted to be close to the tourist trade and the downtown core, and within walking distance of a community college and university. As it turned out, their research has paid off. The restaurant is busy, and the cyber lounge is booming. "Once the computers caught on, the lounge became our main income here," says Richmond. Two very different menus—a food menu and a computer menu—are featured on the cyber café's website.

ACTION STEP 36

Use your new eyes to evaluate business locations. (p. 194)

To a large degree, Close Connections has been successful because its owners found the right location to satisfy their target customer needs. A good location can make everything easier for a new business—especially if you are relying on the store retail distribution channel. Close Connections found a highly visible building that was convenient for its customers to reach, and it saved the owners plenty of advertising dollars. Once you've been discovered and your customer base is well established, however, the physical location might become less important. Nonetheless, for most store retail firms, a good physical location is essential, especially in the beginning.

But the "perfect" location is different for every enterprise. It will depend largely on your primary or major distribution channel. Should you decide on store retailing, like Close Connections, for example, you will have to look for a location that is convenient for your retail customers. You will have to think about issues such as parking, local competition, and store design. On the other hand, you might choose a business in which your primary distribution channels are online or direct, through home parties. In this case, a home-based business might be a strength. If your customers are other retail businesses and you are manufacturing a product, then your wholesaling channel of distribution might dictate warehousing space and transportation costs. Nonetheless, as you plan the location for your business, we do want you to think of the concept of multiple distribution channels and how this will affect where you locate your business.

Now work through Action Step 36. Use your new eyes to examine your consumer's behaviour. Doing so will help you understand the importance of location in making a purchase or providing a service. Will your location be "customer friendly"? Once you are armed with your new-eyes research from Action Step 36, please complete Action Step 37 and brainstorm the perfect location for *your* business.

ACTION STEP 37

Fantasize your perfect location. (p. 194)

Next, we want you to consider a location filter or checklist.

A LOCATION FILTER

Before you charge out to scout possible locations for your business, you need to decide what you really want from the location. The checklist below will help you zero in on the criteria that are important to your business. Use a scale of 1 to 10 to rate the relative importance of each item in terms of your target customers. When you have finished, go back and note the high numbers, say, anything above 5. Then, after you've read the rest of the chapter, come back to this list to see whether your priorities have changed. We also suggest you take a moment and complete the "Which Location Would You Recommend?" E-Exercise in Box 7.1.

Box 7.1   E-Exercise

1. **Which Location Would You Recommend?**
   Visit Marketing Teacher's "Newtown" (http://www.marketingteacher.com/Lessons/exercise_place.htm). Floor-Mart is considering where to put its new store. You must recommend a location. Which one would you choose?
2. **Store Layout Quiz**
   Visit http://crimeprevention.rutgers.edu/crime/shoplifting/layoutquiz.htm. Many shop owners, eager to sell their wares, jam a lot of stuff into a small space. The store illustrated on this site sells fabric and sewing supplies. It has many problems with poor sight lines and hidden corners. Take the Store Layout Quiz. What are the problems? How would you correct them?

RATING IMPORTANCE (1–10)

- **Local/Municipal licensing.** A wide variety of trades and establishments require a licence fee that can range anywhere from five dollars to thousands of dollars. In many Canadian municipalities, for example, licences are required if you operate a limousine service, refreshment vehicles, an auctioneer service, a billiard and pool hall, and skateboarding facilities. You'll also want to find out about local regulations on the installation, alteration, and maintenance of exterior signs and parking. We encourage you to begin learning more about your licensing and other local requirements. One option is to link onto Canada Business Network (http://www.canadabusiness.ca/eng/126/155) and click on the name of your province or territory. Another option for municipal regulations is to link to Canadian municipalities (http://www.municipalworld.com/index.php). Here you can start researching your municipal requirements. For example, if you link onto the City of Hamilton, Ontario, at http://www.hpl.ca/, you'll find a list and description of the various licences required as well as licensing costs. This site also explains which types of health, police, or fire inspections are required. Zoning, building signage, and other issues are also explained fully.

- **Neighbour mix.** Who's next door? Who's down the street? Who's going to help pull your target customers into the area? Which nearby business pulls in the most customers? If you're considering a shopping centre, who's the **anchor tenant** (the big department store or supermarket that acts as a magnet for the centre)?

- **Competition.** Where are your competitors located? Mapping the location of your competitors can sometimes indicate location patterns or illustrate opportunities. Do you want competitors kilometres away, or does your business benefit from the clustering of competitors, as is the case with many "shopping goods" retailers?

- **Security and safety.** How safe is the neighbourhood? Is it as safe as a nursery at noon but an urban jungle at midnight? Is there anything you can do to increase the security? (To learn more about security, complete the Store Layout Quiz in Box 7.1.)

- **Labour pool.** Who's working for you, and how far will they have to commute? Does your business require more help at certain peak periods of the year? How easy will it be to find that kind of skilled or technical help you need? How far will they travel? Don't overlook the potential of part-timers, teens, seniors, and homemakers. Are there any zoning restrictions?

NEIGHBOUR MIX

The industrial or commercial makeup of nearby businesses

ANCHOR TENANT

A business in a commercial area that attracts customers

LABOUR POOL

Qualified people who are available for employment near one's business location

- **Services.** These include police and fire protection, security, trash pickup, sewage, and maintenance. What is included in the rent, and who pays for those services that are not? Is your location near a bus or subway stop?
- **Costs.** What is the purchase price if you're buying, or what are the rent or lease costs? (And what is the type of lease?) Insurance, improvements, association dues, and routine maintenance: Who pays for what? Can you negotiate a few months' free rent?
- **Ownership.** If you're planning to buy the property, who will you choose to advise you on real estate? Consider a lease with an option to buy, but have the contract reviewed by a real estate lawyer.
- **Property owner/Landlord.** Have you considered the reputation of the property owner? There is no "hotter hell" for some business owners than a landlord who is slow to return calls, make necessary repairs, respond to "common area" issues, and so on.
- **Past tenants.** What happened to the past tenants? What mistakes did they make, and how can you avoid those mistakes?
- **Space.** If you need to expand, can you do it there, or will you have to move to a new site?
- **Accessibility.** Is your business where your target customer might expect to find you? Does your business require the "cumulative drawing power" of a mall or power centre? Is driving time rather than distance more relevant to your customer as an indicator of accessibility? Have you considered a Business Improvement Area (available in some provinces)?
- **Professional advice.** Have you considered using a commercial real estate agent, advisor, or mentor for help with storefront location selection?
- **Parking.** Most people like to park for free and close to your door. Is that possible?
- **History of the property.** How long has the landlord owned this property? Is it likely to be sold while you're a tenant? If the property is sold, what will happen to your business? What will happen to your tax obligations? If the property goes on the market, do you want the first right to make an offer?
- **Physical visibility.** Does your business need to be seen? If so, is this location easily visible? Can you make alterations to increase its visibility? Can you install the type of sign you want?
- **Life-cycle stage of the area.** Is the site in an area that's embryonic (vacant lots, open space, emptiness), growing (high-rises, new schools, lots of construction), mature (building conversions, cracked street, sluggish traffic), or declining (vacant building, emptiness)? What will the area be like in five years? What effect would that have on your business? What do the municipal planners have in mind for the area? When will the highway or roads department tear up the street? (See Figure 7.1.)
- **Image.** Is the location consistent with your firm's image? How will nearby businesses affect your image? Is this an area where your customers would expect to find a business like yours? (Look for a place that reinforces your customers' perception of your business.) Remember, in the case of a home-based business, an important factor is the maintenance of a professional image.
- **Hours of operation.** Most municipalities have by-laws regarding the hours of operation. These hours might be different for various areas within a region. If you're planning a retail operation, be sure to look into this detail.
- **Utilities.** The high cost for water, sewage, gas, or other utilities might bring some unpleasant surprises. You should list all your utility requirements. Are they adequate? What would you require to upgrade them?
- **Local zoning by-laws.** Check out the present and future zoning. What restrictions might apply to your business?

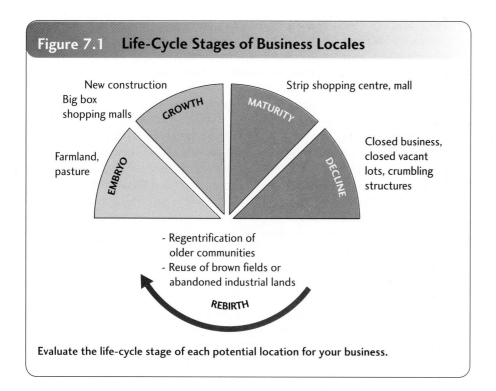

Figure 7.1   Life-Cycle Stages of Business Locales

New construction
Big box shopping malls

GROWTH

MATURITY

Strip shopping centre, mall

Farmland, pasture

EMBRYO

DECLINE

Closed business, closed vacant lots, crumbling structures

- Regentrification of older communities
- Reuse of brown fields or abandoned industrial lands

REBIRTH

Evaluate the life-cycle stage of each potential location for your business.

- **Taxes.** Property and business taxes can change from street to street. Try to find out if there are any plans for reassessment.
- **Approvals.** Have you considered necessary approvals, such as those required from health officials, the fire marshal, the city planning office, and the liquor licensing board?
- **Transportation.** How much will your business depend on trucks, rail, buses, airports, or shipping by water? If you're in manufacturing or distribution, you'll need to determine your major transportation channel. It's also a good idea to have a backup system. A good technique here is to make a diagram of the location and all the lines of transportation your business will use in both receiving goods and customers and shipping goods.
- **Your target customers.** This is the last but most important criterion. Will your customers—lured by your terrific promotions—find you easily but have no place to park? Consider highway access and potential obstacles that could make coming to your place of business inconvenient or unpleasant. What do your customers really want? Ease of parking? Convenience? Atmosphere? Proximity to work? Even the side of the street is important. (For example, a dry cleaner would want to be on the inbound side of the street, so customers can easily drop off their cleaning on their way into the city to work.) Your location must satisfy the needs of the customer, not your personal needs. This consideration is particularly important if you're planning to operate out of your home. Are you setting up a home-based business because it's convenient to you or your customer? Remember, you work from home, not at home!

HOME-BASED BUSINESSES

Exercise + people + fun + work + stress = start a physical fitness program in the workplace. Psychographic thinking and the guidance of visionaries such as Faith Popcorn have been put into practice successfully by

Sheila Mather. There she was, early on a Saturday morning, sharing her experience with an audience of soon-to-be businesspeople. She operates her business out of her home, but today this seminar was about her location, and she was marketing herself at a local small business seminar called "Look Before You Leap."

Mather began her talk with a few minutes of low-impact aerobics. When everyone was energized, she said: "You don't have to be a rocket scientist. I'm not in the high-tech business per se. But my job is to increase productivity in our growth high-tech sector. I'm in the 'feel good, energy, and people business.' These are the benefits that my customers want. You're also my potential customer, and after exercising, I hope you feel a little better now."

She explained that her home-based location strategy was not about finding a physical site. It was about finding ways to locate herself and her business in front of the customer. "My real location is where I meet and greet my customers. Yesterday, for example, my location was an empty office where I conducted my exercise program for one of my company clients. Today, my location is here at this seminar. Tomorrow, I am giving advice online to my virtual customers. In a home-based business, your location can be very fluid, and one thing is for sure: you should plan to be out meeting people, because it is people who will drive your business."

Working at home has become a major trend in the way Canadians do business. About two million Canadian households create jobs, stimulate local economies, and provide a growing commercial market. Most of these home businesses have been in operation for more than a year (44 percent, one to three years; 35 percent, more than three years). Almost half of the home workers are self-employed; 14 percent are substituters (employees who spend part of their day at home); and 39 percent are supplementers (employees who bring work home). According to these statistics, chances are that you will be working out of your home in the future—even if you have another job.

Home business is a growing trend with the annual growth rate expected to be in the 12 percent range. There are several major reasons for this trend.

- **Cocooning.** Many of us are striving to reduce outside stresses by spending more leisure and work time at home.
- **Computerization.** Technology, such as tablets, computers, laptops, and high-speed Internet connections, has made it easier and more convenient to operate out of the home.
- **Two-income families.** When both parents are trying to raise a family and make a living, working from home is far easier than working outside. The flexibility of working at home allows better sharing of chores and family responsibilities.
- **Growth of the service industry.** A service business generally has lower start-up costs, operational expenses, and equipment costs, making it much more sensible to run an operation out of the home.
- **Higher productivity.** Studies show that productivity increases by 20 to 60 percent when employees can work at their own pace during peak times. In fact, such statistics have influenced the new knowledge-based companies to encourage telecommuting.
- **Increased efficiency.** The home worker saves on transportation, rent, furniture, and equipment costs.
- **Improved service.** The new consumer demands more individual attention. Home-based businesses are well positioned to adapt to changing and individualized consumer needs.

- **Vigilant consumers.** The new customer is fragile and fickle, and craves superior service. This consumer doesn't tolerate the mediocrity of mass production and sameness.
- **Downsizing.** Today, companies are encouraged to go small and to contract out whenever possible.
- **Mobility.** With the growth in personal care and home care, more and more businesses are going to their customers, which means that a storefront isn't always necessary.

Starting your business out of your home does not mean that your plan is written on the back of an envelope. It takes just as much care to open and operate a home business as it does to establish a traditional retail business. Before you decide on a location, consider the advantages and disadvantages of operating out of your home. Box 7.2 will help you get started.

ACTION STEP 38

Decide whether a home-based business is in your future. (p. 195)

WHAT HOME-BASED BUSINESS IS BEST FOR ME?

We're often asked, "What is the best home-based business to go into?" Well, that will depend on your ability to connect your values, experience, and knowledge to current market trends—as we discussed in Chapter 2. You will have to figure out your skills and interests, determine what you are good at, and then look for a market opportunity that has confluence with your personal attributes. Here's a list of home-based opportunities based on growing market trends as outlined by industry leaders and business experts and our trend analysis in Chapter 2:

- technology coach;
- upmarket travel advisor;
- caterer for a healthy lifestyle;
- eco-friendly cleaning service provider;
- elder services provider;
- concierge service agent;
- personal health or fitness trainer;
- pet sitter/grooming provider;
- life balance, personal, or business coach;
- financial advisor;
- energy efficiency contractor/consultant; and
- home improvement advisor/décor contractor.

We hope you are ready to start thinking about a home-based business, and we suggest you begin by carefully weighing the pros and cons. Complete Action Step 38.

Box 7.2 Is Home the Best Place? A Location Checklist

The following checklist might help you determine if you should operate your business out of the home.

- **Target market.** How far will your customers be willing to travel to reach you? Can your business travel or deliver to the customer? How efficient is it for you to serve your customer from your home?
- **Neighbourhood mix.** Do you need other businesses to pull your customer to you?
- **Physical visibility.** Does your business need to be seen?
- **Competitors.** Why would your target customer deal with you out of your home-based business rather than with your competition? What advantages does your home business offer over that of your competitors? What are the drawbacks?

- **Life-cycle stage.** Is your area in an embryonic (e.g., vacant land), growing (e.g., plenty of construction, new schools), mature (e.g., cracked streets, sluggish traffic), or decline (e.g., vacant buildings) stage? Will you want to be doing business in the same location five years from now?
- **Image.** How would your target customers react if they learned that you were operating out of your home? For example, right or wrong, some customers might not take you seriously.
- **Local/Municipal regulations.** Do you require a licence to operate out of your home, and can you get one?
- **Local zoning by-laws.** Do local by-laws allow you to operate your business out of your home?
- **Space/Physical requirements.** Do you have enough space to serve the customer and your business needs effectively? What are your physical requirements? For example, do you need to add a washroom? Do you have a designated area to work? How will the customer enter your location? Do you need a separate entrance?
- **Approvals.** Have you considered the necessary approvals related to health, fire, transportation, environment, and labour?
- **Insurance.** Will your insurance company allow you to operate a business out of your home? How will this affect your insurance premiums?
- **Utilities.** Are there any extra utilities requirements (e.g., extra telephone lines)?
- **Work habits/Behaviour.** Do you need to "get away in the morning"? Many business people like to completely separate their business and personal lives. Do you have the discipline to work in your home?
- **Lifestyle.** Will your business disrupt your family and personal lifestyle? How will your neighbours feel about your running your business out of your home?

Source: Ron Knowles, *Writing a Small Business Plan: Course Guide* (Toronto, ON: Dryden, an imprint of Harcourt Brace, 1995), p. 44. Reprinted by permission of Elizabeth Knowles.

GETTING THE INFORMATION YOU NEED TO FIND THE RIGHT LOCATION

Businesspeople tend to stay in a location for a while because it is expensive to renovate and move. Thus, selection of your location will be one of your most important start-up decisions. You'll want to make sure that you are right in the heart of your target market. So, where do you go for information? We'll begin with secondary sources of location information—that is, published data that have been gathered and compiled by others.

LOCATION INFORMATION USING SECONDARY RESEARCH

Data collected by Statistics Canada—in particular, census information—could be one of your major sources of secondary information, especially if you are planning to rent, lease, or buy a retail or manufacturing business. We have already provided you with a number of possible Statistics Canada sources in the demographic profiling section of Chapter 4. You might want to go back and check these out again.

We also encourage you to get on the Net. Industry Canada (http://www.ic.gc. ca/eic/site/icgc.nsf/eng/home) is probably your best place to start. In Chapter 5, we asked you to use Industry Canada to seek out competitor information. Now we want you to go back to this research and see if you can discover some valuable information for locating your business.

As we know by now, Statistics Canada and Industry Canada are not our only sources of secondary information. Municipal and regional governments have all kinds of information, such as traffic counts, so a visit to your local planning office is a must. While you're there, check the zoning by-laws and future plans. For example, you might be awfully disappointed if you decide to locate your home-based business in a municipality that forbids home-operated enterprises. Or, locating your business on a road scheduled for sewer work might be your quick ticket to bankruptcy. If you are going into a mall, the mall owners should have a detailed location study. Get their analyses, or don't locate there. Consider potential suppliers. They should know which other businesses are doing the greatest business. If you approach suppliers in the right way, they might be pleased to help you. After all, they could gain more business because of this.

Private companies also will, for a price, get you some pretty detailed information. One such firm is MapInfo Professional® (http://www.pb.com/software/Data-Mining-and-Modeling/Geographic-Data-Mining-Tools/MapInfo-Professional. shtml), which maintains location databases that are highly targeted and include names of facilities and offices within a specific area. Commercial real estate agents can also be very helpful, particularly if you're thinking about a retail or manufacturing operation.

LOCATION INFORMATION USING PRIMARY RESEARCH

In the first six chapters of this book, we talked about your primary research techniques, such as brainstorming, interviewing, and mind mapping. As you know by now, we cannot rely strictly on secondary research because it is just that— secondary. For your location analysis, you are also going to have to do some of your own primary research. The hitch is that there is no formula or set framework to follow. Nevertheless, this is a real opportunity to practise your new-eyes research. To help, we will provide examples of how some enterprising entrepreneurs did their research. We then encourage you to find your own creative way.

Ben wanted to start a dry-cleaning business. He knew that the success of his business would depend on the number of cars that passed by a specific point during peak hours. Through experience in the business, he had found a direct relationship between the number of cars and the volume of dry cleaning. What did he do? He did not rely on the traffic counts from his local municipality, although this secondary information was useful in narrowing down possible sites. His answer was to sit in his car for several days and count the number of vehicles that went by his potential sites. After doing this a few times for various locations, he finally found the "perfect" spot. Today, Ben has 15 outlets, and we find him out counting cars, getting ready for his 16th store. He tells us that he is in the business of counting cars, because if he can get that right and competition is not a serious factor, then everything else should unfold nicely.

Now let's see how Lucy did her primary research by counting people.

Lucy wanted to start a gift store that her favourite grandmother would be proud of. The name of her new business would be Gramma's, so the location had to be right, for she wanted to keep this name for a long time. She also knew from working in gift stores that most of the business would come from the impulse buyer.

A new mall was opening down the street, and the manager, fresh from business school, had loaded her down with site plans, traffic studies, and potential store locations. "You had better hurry," he said. "The good spots are being snapped up awfully fast."

Fortunately, her small business teacher was close by and added a little sanity to her life. "It's easy," she said. "Just replicate, and you will know for sure. Find a mall that is under construction and tell me how much business the gift store is doing."

"That's crazy," exclaimed Lucy. "You can't possibly know how much a business is doing before the mall is built."

"That's true," said her professor. "Why don't you wait until you know what is going on."

"I'm going to miss this one," protested Lucy.

"Yes, you may, but when you find the right location, you will know it, because you will be able to back up the mall research with some of your own primary research."

About six months later, Lucy finished doing her pedestrian counts in front of an empty store at a more established mall on the other side of the city. Her own traffic counts and the mall studies convinced her that this was the location for her. Today, Lucy's gift store at the better established mall is doing well. She is not making a million, but she is making a good living, and her grandmother is proud of her.

Here is the lesson she learned: If your business relies on impulse buying, you had better know exactly how many people will go by your door and how many will enter and make a purchase—*before you open your doors.*

By the way, it took more than two years for the owners to fully lease the new mall that Lucy first looked at.

Specific primary research techniques worked for Ben and Lucy. The key to their success was knowing who their customers were and what they wanted. Their businesses were driven by the amount of traffic passing their doors—in one case, it was cars and in the other, people. Now let's return to Elizabeth Wood (remember Crazy's Roadhouse in Chapters 4 and 5?) and see how she helped Max, the owner, determine whether he had a good location.

"Of course I have a great location," said Max. "Just look at my sales."

"Just a minute," cautioned Wood. "Because you are fortunate enough to have customers does not mean you have the perfect location." Wood knew what she was talking about because she was standing in front of Max, a little smugly, with the results of her customer survey. "Let me ask you: Where do your customers live?"

That's easy," said Max. "They live in the neighbourhood. That's why I chose this location." Although Wood knew otherwise, she agreed he was partly right. "The fact is, your lunch trade lives at the workplace. That is, 'place of work' is the most important location criterion at lunch. As a matter of fact, the perfect luncheon location would be within walking distance of white-collar industry."

Then Wood explained to Max that most of his lunch customers were forced to drive to his restaurant, and that's why there were always a few empty seats at lunch during the first part of the week. "Now, as for your night and weekend trade," she continued, "most live at least 15 kilometres from your restaurant. Your target customers are 'grazers' who say that their household income is $50,000 plus per year and who come from all over the city. The most important thing to them is that they can get here within 20 minutes and there is adequate parking. Yes, parking is very important to them. You should begin thinking about the potholes in your parking lot before you start losing business."

Now that Wood knew where Max's customers lived and worked, there was a lot more they could talk about. For the next few hours, they brainstormed new ideas and approaches to making the location more accessible to the customer. For example, how could Max speed up the food service at lunch?

Now let's consider the importance of primary research for the home-based business. Remember Mina Cohen from Chapter 4? She was in the travel and learning business. She worked out of her home, but her location was at the dig site. For certain, the archaeologists at the site would demand that she and her customers "dig" with care. Much of her location analysis would concern itself with finding prime dig sites for her customers to visit.

For Ron Taylor (Chapter 5) and the business of cocooning for teens (basement recreation rooms), what is his location? His customer's house, of course. His location strategy is all about finding homes where teens live.

We can't stress it enough: If you operate a service business from home, your location analysis is just as important as if you are renting. After all, your location is at your *customer's* home or place of work. All of these cases point to the need for primary research before you determine your location. If you can support primary analysis with secondary data, so much the better.

Many of you will choose not to operate your business out of the home, although we encourage you to give serious thought to this strategy. For those who plan to rent a location, we'll enter the complex world of leases.

SOME THINGS YOU MUST KNOW ABOUT LEASES

A lease document is drawn up by the property owner's lawyer. A commercial lease is very different than a personal lease you would sign for renting a home. Although its language is very specific, the terms spelled out are provisional—that is, the terms are proposed as a starting point for negotiation. Nothing you see in the contract is unchangeable—unless you agree to it. Obviously, the terms proposed will probably favour the property owner. Consider the proposed lease seriously. Discuss it with your own lawyer and with others who have experience with leases, and determine how best to begin the negotiation. A sample Commercial Lease Agreement is available for download on the book website at http:// www. nelson.com/knowlescastillo7e. The following pages will guide you through this process.

ENTREPRENEUR, READ YOUR LEASE

Entrepreneur Mick Beatty failed to read the terms of his lease. He thought he had a "gentlemen's agreement" with his female building manager, but he was wrong. His story points out the importance of *assuming nothing* when it comes to leases.

"I was on vacation from the East when I discovered the perfect location. It was in the sleepy tourist town of White Rock, on the edge of the world in a fabulous part of British Columbia.

"It was late summer, I remember, and I'd just spent a week driving through the mountains from Calgary. When I reached White Rock, I thought I was home.

"I discovered Eddie's Pub my first evening in town. It faced the beach, and sitting there sipping a cool one, I could watch the sun reflect off the water. From time to time, people would drift in for a casual drink, and while sitting there, feeling like a million, I must have talked to 20 different folks.

"They loved the place, too. And most of them looked upscale.

"Vacations don't last forever, and when I got back home, I kept thinking about Eddie's in White Rock. I was working then for one of the giant mega corporations, making good money in a pressure cooker of a job, and even though I was enough of a culture freak to appreciate Toronto, I wanted more out of life. After one particularly hectic day at the office, I sat and stared out the window, thinking about those three days I'd spent in White Rock, on the beach.

"A business trip took me to Vancouver that next spring, and I managed to haggle for an extra day so that I could stay overnight in White Rock and stop in for a drink at Eddie's.

"Double surprise.

"The sun was shining—and Eddie's Pub was for sale.

"I called my banker back east. He said I was crazy. I phoned two buddies, one from college, one from the squash club. They thought it would be fun to be part of a new venture and were ready to invest. I talked to Eddie, the owner, made a deal to pay him so much down and the rest out of profits, and suddenly I owned a small business.

"When I phoned my boss in Toronto, he said I was crazy, too. 'Living somewhere on a beach is just a dream,' he said. But what he said next saved my life. 'Tell you what, Mick. Don't pull the plug until you're absolutely sure. We'll give you six months. If you're still out there dreaming, send in your resignation. Meanwhile, have fun. Every man needs a fling before he settles down.'

"I said okay, and thanks. And that was that.

"The location at Eddie's is only 200 square metres. The layout is long and narrow, and we used mirrors from the Gay Nineties to give the place atmosphere. The traffic is mostly walk-in—beach people, stray tourists—and the only promotion I had to do was to put up a sign that said "Happy Hour 4–6:30." I shook hands with my customers, passed out complimentary drinks, served the best espresso in the Vancouver area, and started making money my first day.

"Then trouble showed up.

"I hadn't been open a week when I got a call from my landlady. She was a crusty-voiced lady I'd barely talked to, and she said over the phone that there had been some complaints about the music.

"'Hey,' I said. 'I'm sorry. Who's complaining?'

"'Your neighbours,' she said. 'They have rights, too, you know.'

"'Is it too loud?'

"'No,' she said. 'It's not the volume. It's that rock stuff that's causing the trouble. It irritates the other customers.'

"'Rock?' I said. 'It's not rock, it's more like—'

"'I don't know what you call it,' my landlady said. 'But it's got to stop. And right now.'

"'My customers like it,' I argued. 'The music is part of my atmosphere.'

"'Young man,' she said, 'what your customers like is neither here nor there. I own that property, and I have other tenants to think about. And if you have any questions, I'd advise you to read your lease.' She hung up.

"Well, I read the lease, carefully. And then I saw a lawyer. He confirmed what I'd read—according to the terms of the lease, my landlady had the power to tell me what kind of music I could play in my own small business.

"Incredible, but true.

"I tried turning off the music. Right away, my customers missed it. Drink orders fell off. I surveyed my neighbours and made a list of songs they didn't find offensive, but when I played that junk in the bar, my steady customers (who were becoming less steady) asked me to turn it off. As a last resort, I even visited my landlady and tried to renegotiate the **lease**. But she wouldn't budge.

"There was only one thing to do. I sold the business. I went back to my job in Toronto. I still owe some money to my partners, and when the tension builds at work, I always think of the sun on the water at White Rock. I'll go back sometime. But right now I'm a little soured on the place. It's too bad. They've got a great beach. And a great little bar where you can sit and watch the sun go down.

"My advice? Have a plan, get some experience before you start, and last of all, read the small print in your lease."

LEASE

Obtain a new or modified contract for occupancy

ANTICIPATE THE UNEXPECTED

Bette Lindsay has always had a soft spot for books, and when she finally chose a business, it was a bookstore in a shopping centre. She had researched everything—trends, census data, newspapers, reports from real estate firms, and suppliers—but she failed to anticipate an important potential pitfall: dependency on an anchor tenant (a business in a commercial area that attracts customers).

Few small businesses are "destination locations." They must count on anchor tenants to draw traffic. Lindsay made an assumption that the anchor tenant in her centre would be there forever. This case study shows the importance of having Plan B ready.

"My husband and I researched the small business field for almost two years, and my heart kept bringing me back to books. I've read voraciously since I was seven years old, and I love a well-written story. So when a new shopping centre was opening 10 kilometres from our home, I told my husband, 'This is it.'

"Everything looked perfect. They had a great anchor tenant coming in—a supermarket that would draw lots of traffic. The real estate agent we'd been working with during most of our search showed us the demographics of the area, which documented that we were smack in the middle of a well-educated market. According to statistics put out by the federal government, a bookstore needs a population of 27,000 people to support it. Our area had 62,000 people, and the closest bookstore was more than eight kilometres away.

"Everything else looked good, too. We had lots of parking. The neighbours (three hardy pioneers like ourselves) were serious about their business and pleasant to work with.

"We wanted to be in for the Christmas season, because December is the peak season for bookstores. So we set a target date of mid-October. The contractor was still working when we opened a month later.

"We started off with an autograph party and we ran some bestseller specials. And even though construction work from our anchor tenant blocked our access, we had a very good Christmas that year. We started the New Year feeling very optimistic.

"One day in mid-January, construction work stopped on our anchor tenant's new building. The next day we read in the paper that the company had gone bankrupt.

"Well, the first thing I did was call the landlord. He was out of town, and his answering service referred me to a property management company. They said they knew nothing about what was happening and that all they did was collect the rent. January was slow. So was February, and March. In April, two of our neighbours closed up. The construction debris still blocked customer access. It was a mess.

"In May, I finally succeeded in getting in touch with the owner and tried to renegotiate the lease, but his story was sadder than mine.

"Fourteen months after we moved in, we finally got our anchor tenant. If I'd suspected it would take anything like that long, I could have built some provision for it into our lease."

Bette Lindsay and her husband learned the hard way.

HOW TO REWRITE A LEASE

You live with a lease (and a landlord) for a long time. If you're successful in a retail business, your landlord might want a percentage of your gross sales receipts. If you're not successful or if problems develop, you're going to want several Plan Bs and a **location escape hatch**—a way to cancel or modify your lease if your landlord fails to meet the specified terms. For example, your lease should protect your interest

LOCATION ESCAPE HATCH

A way to cancel or modify your lease if the landlord fails to meet the specified terms

- if the furnace or air conditioning system breaks down,
- if the parking lot needs sweeping or resurfacing,
- if the anchor tenant goes under,
- if the building is sold,
- if half of the other tenants move out.

The possibility of such grief-producing eventualities needs to be dealt with—with precise words and precise numbers in the lease.

Read the lease slowly and carefully (Boxes 7.3 and 7.4 will help you). When you see something you don't understand or don't like, draw a line through it. Feel free to rewrite the lease if you need to. It's *your* lease, too. If you need help from a lawyer, get it. And make sure that the owner (or the leasing agent) indicates his or her agreement with your changes by initialling each one.

Here's a checklist to start you on your rewrite.

1. **Escape clause.** If the building or area doesn't shape up, you will want to get out fast. Be specific. Write something like this into your lease: "If three or more vacancies occur in the centre, tenant may terminate lease."

2. **Option to renew.** Most businesses need at least six months to a year to get going. If your business does well, you will want to stay put. If it doesn't, you don't want to be saddled with a heavy lease payment every month. Get a lease for one year, with an option to renew for the next two or three.

3. **Right to transfer.** Circumstances might force you to sublet. In the trade, this is called "assigning." Make sure the lease allows you to transfer your lease without much hassle if such circumstances arise.

4. **Cost-of-living cap.** Most leases allow the owner to increase rents along with inflation according to the consumer price index (CPI). To protect yourself, insist on a cost-of-living cap so that your base rate won't increase faster than your landlord's costs. Try for half of the amount of the CPI increase, a standard measure. Thus, if the CPI rises 10 percent, your rate will go up only 5 percent. It's fair, because the owner's costs won't change much. Major tenants will insist on a cap, so you should be able to negotiate one also. Proceed with confidence.

5. **Percentage lease.** Common in larger retail centres, a **percentage lease** specifies that the tenant will pay a base rate plus a percentage of the gross sales. An example: $XX per square foot per month plus 5 percent of gross sales over $500,000 per year.

6. **Floating rent scale.** If you're a pioneer tenant of a shopping centre, negotiate a payment scale based on occupancy. For example, you might specify that you'll pay 50 percent of your lease payment when the centre is 50 percent occupied, 70 percent when it's 70 percent occupied, and 100 percent when it's full. You can't build traffic to the centre all by yourself, and motivation is healthy for everyone, including landlords.

7. **Start-up buffer.** There's a good chance you'll be on location fixing up, remodelling, and so on, long before you open your doors and make your first sale. Make your landlord aware of this problem and negotiate a long period of free rent. The argument: If your business is successful, the landlord—who's taking a percentage—will make more money. If your business doesn't do well or if it fails, the landlord will have to find a new tenant. You need breathing space. You've signed on for the long haul. By not squeezing you to death for cash, the landlord allows you to put more money into inventory, equipment, service, atmosphere—the things that make a business go.

8. **Improvement.** Unless you're a super fixer-upper, you don't want to lease a place equipped with nothing but a dirt floor and a capped-off cold water pipe. You need a proper atmosphere for your business, but you don't want to use all your cash to pay for it before you open. Negotiate with the landlord to make the needed improvements and spread the cost of them over the total time of the lease. Otherwise, find a space that doesn't require significant remodelling.

9. **Restrictive covenants.** If you are running a dance studio, and part of your income derives from holding yoga classes, you don't want a yoga studio moving into your centre. If you're selling hearing aids, you don't want a stereo store next door. Build **restrictive covenants** (things that your landlord cannot do) into your lease to protect yourself.

10. **Maintenance.** When the parking lot needs sweeping, who pays for it? If the air conditioner goes out, who pays? If the sewer stops up, who's responsible

PERCENTAGE LEASE

Lease that specifies that the tenant will pay a base rate plus a percentage of the gross sales

RESTRICTIVE COVENANTS

Things that your landlord cannot do that are written into your lease to protect you for the repairs? Get all of this written down in simple language. Your diligence with words and numbers will pay off.

Box 7.3 provides two online examples of leases and information on the language of leasing.

Box 7.3 The Language of Leases

Learn More About Commercial Leases

- Lease Tips and Checklist:

  Link on to The Real Estate Lease Advisor: http://www.the-real-estate-lease-advisor.com/. Click on "Free Articles."

- Office Lease:

  See Legaldocs: http://www.legaldocs.com/.

Here you will find an example of an office lease; however, be sure to obtain legal advice before committing to any lease.

Before Signing on the Dotted Line

Before signing on the dotted line, be certain you understand the language of the lease. These terms will get you started.

- **Building gross area.** The total square-foot area of the building when the enclosing walls are measured from outside wall to outside wall.
- **Usable building area.** The square-foot area within the building occupied by tenants, measured from centre partition to centre partition.
- **Common area.** The square-foot area of the building servicing all tenants in common, such as lobby, corridors, lavatories, elevators, stairs, and mechanical equipment rooms. The building common area is usually between 10 and 12 percent of the gross building area.
- **Rentable area.** A combination of the tenants' usable building area plus each tenant's pro rata share of the common area.
- **Gross rent.** Gross rent is a rental per square foot, multiplied by the rentable area, to determine the annual rent due on a lease, where the landlord provides all services and utilities, including tenant janitorial services.
- **Net rent.** Net rent is a rent per square foot multiplied by the rentable area to determine the annual rent due under a lease, whereby the tenant also pays, in addition to the rent, its pro rata of all utilities and services and real estate taxes.
- **Loss factor.** The proportion of usable building area to total rentable area. The usable area is that in which you may put furniture and equipment for actual office use. The rentable area often includes a proportionate share of ancillary building services. The lower the loss factor, the more usable space there is. Loss factors can vary from floor to floor in the same building. Rentable area may be calculated in a different manner for one building than it is for another, and this will affect your comparison of rental proposals.

Box 7.4 Ask These Questions

Before you sign a lease, ask these questions.

- Does the lease contain an escape clause?
- Does it have an option to renew?
- Can you "assign" the lease if you need to sublet?

GROSS RENT

A rental where the landlord provides all services and utilities, including tenant janitorial services

NET RENT

A rental whereby the tenant also pays, in addition to the rent, its pro rata of all utilities, services, and real estate taxes

- Do you have a ceiling on rent increases?
- Do you have a floating lease scale, according to how much of the centre is occupied?
- Have you tried to negotiate a period of free rent while you are preparing to open the doors?
- Have you negotiated to have the landlord make the needed improvements and charge you for them over the total time of the lease?

In a Nutshell

The main purpose of this chapter was to help guide you through the process of finding a location that is right for you, your business, and your customer. We have encouraged you to think about a multiple distribution strategy, to use your primary and new-eyes research as well as secondary sources, and to keep asking, "What is the best location according to my target customer?"

If you are planning to retail or manufacture your product or service, your choice of location is probably the most important decision you will make. You'll have to live with your selection for a long time. We encourage you to complete the location filter checklist and begin to understand the language and consequences of leases. Many of you will plan to start your business from your home. Doing so is fine, but don't think that your location analysis is not important. A location checklist for your home-based business was also presented. We wanted you to make sure that your home office will satisfy the needs of your customer and won't destroy your personal life. Finally, we discussed the need to understand the language and consequences of leases.

Key Terms

anchor tenant	location escape hatch
business location	neighbourhood mix
distribution channel	net rent
franchising	percentage lease
gross rent	restrictive covenants
labour pool	retailing
lease	wholesaling

Think Points for Success

✓ The irony of the search for a start-up location is that you need the best site when you can least afford it.
✓ Think about your distribution strategy and your customer's needs before searching for a location.
✓ Take your time selecting a location. If you lose out on a hot site, don't worry; another one will eventually turn up.
✓ Even if you start up your business at home, you will need a location analysis.
✓ A site analysis for a street-side location should include everything that is unique to a specific building or space. Many successful centres have some dead traffic areas.
✓ Who are your business neighbours? Are they attracting your type of customers or clients? What will happen if they move or go out of business?

✓ Know the terms and buzzwords—*net*, *gross*, and so on—and be aware that they might mean slightly different things in each contract or lease agreement.

✓ Everything is negotiable: free rent, signage, improvement allowances, rates, maintenance, and so on. Don't be afraid to ask.

✓ Talk to former tenants; you might be amazed at what you learn.

Action Steps

ACTION STEP 36

Use your new eyes to evaluate business locations.

Think about how location affects your spending habits. For example, where do you buy gas for your car? Do you buy it on your way to work or school, or on your way home? Why?

Now, with your 24/7 Adventure Notebook in hand, look through your home. How important was the location of the retailer when you bought the items you see? For example:

- candy or pop;
- prescription drugs;
- washing machine;
- designer clothes;
- paintings;
- wristwatch;
- wall hangings;
- jewellery;
- carpeting;
- paint;
- mail order items, such as books, DVDs, CDs, magazines, or clothing;
- power lawn and garden tools;
- collectibles;
- car, motorcycle, or bicycle;
- your home itself;
- custom-made golf clubs;
- eyeglasses.

A random look through your chequebook might trigger your memory. Feel free to add to this list.

How far did you travel, for example, for your last dinner out with a friend? for a carton of milk? a magazine? a lounge chair? How far would you travel to consult a brain surgeon?

What conclusion can you draw about the importance of location in making a purchase or providing a service?

Remember, also, that the cheapest location might not always be the best location.

You can expand on this Action Step by interviewing purchasing agents and buyers of commercial and industrial goods. Ask them what impact location has on their choice of vendors or on their recruitment of employees.

ACTION STEP 37

Fantasize your perfect location.

Sit down where you won't be disturbed, and brainstorm the ideal location for your small business. Get a pencil and paper, and let yourself dream. Draw a mind map, or use a list format; the idea is to record your thinking on paper.

Start with your target customer. How will you make it easy for him or her to meet and greet you? Why is your location "customer friendly"? For example, if you were going to open a candy-cigarette-cigar stand, you might want to locate in West Edmonton Mall, where people pass by every hour. Or, if you planned to open an extremely upscale boutique, you might visualize a location in Toronto's Yorkville. Do you really need a storefront operation, or can you meet potential customers online or at craft shows and trade fairs? If you plan to establish a home-based business, consider factors such as the availability of parking in your neighbourhood. What will your major distribution channel be? Remember, we want you to consider multiple distribution channels. How are you going to integrate other channels—especially the Internet? This is why we encouraged you to begin thinking about setting up a website in Chapter 3.

Once you have the general idea of the type of neighbourhood and location you have in mind, write down what else is terrific about this location. Writing everything down will give you a starting point as you move out to explore the world.

ACTION STEP 38

Decide whether a home-based business is in your future.

Before starting a business from your home, answer the following questions: What are the benefits? What are the negatives? What is your distribution strategy?

1. **List reasons to work at home.** Start with the obvious: low overhead, an easy commute, familiar surroundings. If you have children and want to be near them, working at home is one solution.
2. **List the problems with working at home.** How do you handle interruptions? How do you show that you are serious? How do you focus amid clutter? If you have clients, where do you see them? What's the zoning situation in your neighbourhood?
3. **List solutions to the problems raised in number 2.** If you're being interrupted, you need to get tough. Set up a schedule and post a notice: "Dad's working from 9 to 11. Lunch will be served at noon. If Dad does not work, there's no lunch!"
4. **Go technical.** What will it cost you? Consider expenses such as a computer, scanner, modem, printer, answering machine, and so on. Use email to connect with your customers.
5. **Where will your workspace be?** Garage? Basement? Bedroom? Den? How can you keep it yours? What will it cost to make it usable and productive space?
6. **Check out your home insurance.** What does it cover? What additional coverage do you need, and what will it cost?
7. **Review your extended health insurance, if needed.** Can you qualify? What will the cost be?
8. **Get advice.** Talk with your family and friends who own home-based businesses. What are their concerns? What are your concerns? Work out as many issues now as you can.

Business Plan Building Block

This section of your business plan explains why you have selected your location and how it satisfies the needs of your target customers and your business.

Your description should include the following key considerations.

- What is your distribution strategy?
- How close or accessible is your location to the target market?
- What distribution channels do you intend to use to reach the target customer if you do not have a storefront location?
- How does the location satisfy the exterior and interior requirements for the business? (If possible, include a floor plan or photos in an appendix.)
- How close is the competition to your location?

- What is the possibility of expansion?
- Is the building leased or owned? Has the lease been reviewed by a lawyer? (Include proof of ownership or a copy of the lease in an appendix.)
- Does the location conform to municipal bylaws and environmental regulations?
- Do you have a store layout plan?

Now it's your turn. Using materials from this chapter, describe your distribution strategy and why you have chosen your location.

Checklist Questions and Actions to Develop Your Business Plan

Location

❑ What is your distribution strategy?

❑ What criteria are important to your location?

❑ What secondary research do you need to make a decision about location?

❑ If you plan to operate a home-based business, be sure to answer all the questions in Box 7.2.

❑ Define the importance of location for your target customer.

❑ Do you have a plan for your store layout?

❑ If you are operating a home-based business, how have you separated work from home?

❑ Why have you chosen the site that you have selected?

❑ If you have a home-based business, identify any zoning issues you face.

Case Study: QuestVest

Case Background

Revisit the QuestVest case study in the opening vignette. Gloria Brookstone was in the "safety for travellers business." She established QuestVest—a business operating out of the home that designed and sold vests for women. These stylish vests came with secret inside pockets to place money and valuables safely.

Case Study Questions and Activities

1. Entrepreneurial skills
   In the first seven chapters, we have talked about and provided numerous examples of entrepreneurial personality traits and skills.
   a. List at least five entrepreneurial personality traits displayed by Gloria Brookstone.
   b. List five entrepreneurial skills that helped Gloria start and grow her QuestVest business.

2. Trends creating opportunities
   In Chapter 3, we learned that trends create market opportunities. Briefly describe four market trends that helped Gloria Brookstone grow her business.

3. Distribution channels
   a. What is a distribution channel?
   b. Briefly explain the difference between direct and indirect distribution.
   c. Within the two broad direct and indirect distribution channels, list five possible types of subdistribution channels or ways in which you could distribute your product or service.
   d. Gloria Brookstone's major distribution channel was wholesaling. She sold her QuestVests directly to high-end boutiques, but she also had three

subdistribution channels and had come up with five more possible subdistribution channels. List these eight different subdistribution channels.

e. What four distribution channels did Adrienne Armstrong, owner of Arbour Environmental Shoppe, use? (See page 177)

4. Home-based business
Gloria Brookstone chose to operate her business out of her home. She also chose to contract out her sewing to home-based seamstresses. What were the five advantages of this home-based strategy?

5. Business protection
Familiarize yourself with techniques to protect you and your business against common business crimes, such as break-ins, fraud, employee theft, shoplifting, and vandalism. Link onto http://crimeprevention.rutgers.edu/crimes.htm. List 10 ways you plan to protect your business.

6. Business plan location description
In your business plan, you will be required to write a section on your store location. We provide you with a "Sample Location Description" in Chapter 15, Box 15.8. On the book's website (http://www.nelson.com/knowlescastillo7e), we also provide you with a sample Store Overview for Annie's Business Plan Proposal. Using these examples as templates, briefly describe the location for your business.

This chapter will help you complete parts F and G of your Business Plan, Management and Human Resources.

ER_09/Shutterstock.com

LEARNING OPPORTUNITIES

After reading this chapter, you should be able to

- decide which legal form (sole proprietorship, partnership, corporation, or cooperative) is best for your business;
- anticipate potential surprises if you are going into business with someone else;
- explore the pros and cons of incorporating;
- conduct secondary research into corporations and incorporating;
- explore the various municipal, provincial, and federal legal regulations that might affect your business;
- understand the main characteristics of patents, copyrights, and trade-marks;
- develop tactics for finding the right lawyer and accountant;
- develop questions for probing the mind of a lawyer or accountant;
- understand the importance of having a will and succession planning; and
- describe and understand the bankruptcy process.

ACTION STEP PREVIEW

39. Do some secondary research on corporations.
40. Navigate an online tutorial on patent applications.
41. Take a lawyer and an accountant to lunch.

WHICH LEGAL FORM IS BEST?

Henry Bemis was doing really well with his coffee service until one of his onsite coffee dispensers spewed boiling water all over the hands of Jody Dawn, a professional model. Jody's hands earned her just over $200,000 a year. The day her hands were burned, she was at a branch of a major bank, doing a De Beers–sponsored commercial for diamond rings and safety deposit boxes.

The model's hands were her living and her future. On the advice of her lawyer, Jody sued Henry and his Easy-Cup Coffee Service.

Henry had insurance, and the courts ended up awarding Jody $1 million.

Here's the way the court figured it:

• She made $200,000 a year.
• She could expect an active career of at least five years.
• Five years × $200 000 = $1,000,000.

Luckily, Henry had had the good sense to incorporate and carried a lot of liability insurance. His personal assets were protected, and his business insurance paid the bill.

Although Henry Bemis's story is fictitious, the situation is possible and could happen to you. You might run your small business as a sole proprietorship or in partnership with another entrepreneur and be confident that it is in the best possible legal form. But are you sure? Or maybe you're in the planning stages of your new business, and you don't know what legal form (sole proprietorship, partnership, or corporation) is best. In this chapter, we will look at what kind of corporate structure might be best for you and your business. We'll also prepare you for some of the government red tape, help direct you toward legal advice, encourage you to have a will, and prompt you to think about bankruptcy.

LEGAL FORMS FOR SMALL BUSINESS

Generally, your small business can exist in one of three basic legal forms: a sole proprietorship, a partnership, or a corporation. For each of these standard forms of ownership (summarized in Table 8.1), we describe some of the important business realities—and paperwork—you should be aware of.

The cooperative is a fourth type of legal form to consider. Technically, it's a particular type or variant of the corporate structure. Highlights of this lesser-known form of ownership are presented in the final part of this section.[1] It is also important to note that other business agreements, such as joint ventures, exist.

SOLE PROPRIETORSHIP

SOLE PROPRIETORSHIP
A business that is owned by one person

Most small businesses start out as a **sole proprietorship**. If you start a business on your own—without partners—you are a sole proprietor. A sole proprietorship, in the eyes of the law, is not a separate entity from the person: The business and the individual are the same. For example, the assets of the business are

Table 8.1 Characteristics of the Four Main Legal Forms

Legal Form	Control	Need for Written Agreements	Raising Money	Taxes	Liability	Continuity
Sole proprietorship	absolute	may be needed for registration if own name not used	one-person show; save, save, save	profit or loss go with personal income	personally liable for everything	restricted—business ceases to exist when owner gets tired of business or dies
Partnership (limited)	total control by general partner	overwhelming	lots of laws	profit or loss passed onto ltd. partners	ltd. partners are liable only for $ invested	can be provided for in partnership agreement
Partnership (general)	divided	locate excellent lawyer	easier if more parties sign	profit or loss passed on to partners	personal liability for debts or misdeeds of partners	depends on buy-sell agreement
Corporation	shared (could be absolute)	locate excellent lawyer	market your "professional" appeal	some tax advantages to Canadian-controlled private corporations	limited to assets of incorporated entity; shareholders are usually not liable	perpetual existence

owned by the individual, and therefore the revenue and expenses are included in his or her personal income tax return.

The primary advantages of the sole proprietorship are that

- it is relatively easy and inexpensive to set up,
- it is directly controlled by the owner/operator,
- it is flexible and subject to little regulation,
- business losses can be deducted from other income,
- wages paid for work performed by a spouse are deductible from the income of the business,
- other investors may be added by written agreement, and
- it offers some tax advantages in certain situations (see Box 8.1).

The major disadvantages of a sole proprietorship are as follows:

- The owner can be held personally liable for all debts of the business. Personal assets, such as the house and automobile, can be seized for nonpayment of bills, provided the necessary legal steps have been taken to do so. To avoid such an unfortunate occurrence, some entrepreneurs register certain personal assets in the name of their spouse. This practice is allowed as long as it is done at least one year before financial problems are encountered; otherwise, the court may construe the action as a deliberate attempt to outmanoeuvre creditors and will not allow it.
- Opportunity for continuity is restricted. The sole proprietorship ceases to exist when the sole proprietor goes out of business or dies.
- To some extent, the owner's ability to raise capital is limited. Many small businesses encounter financial problems, as their owners are reluctant to share ownership with others who are able to contribute the needed funds.
- The sole proprietor might be required to pay taxes at a higher tax rate in certain situations. Depending on the income level of the owners, tax rates for a

> ### Box 8.1   Did You Know?
>
> Suppose you are a sole proprietor and your business suffers a loss. If you have income from other sources (a part-time job, for example), this business loss can be used to offset the other income. You can deduct your business losses as an expense on your personal income statement.
>
> If your business loss exceeds your other income in a particular year, the unused portion of that loss can be carried forward to offset income in future years. In this way, a sole proprietorship can offer its owner a "tax shelter." In contrast, losses sustained by a corporation can be used only to offset income earned by the corporation, not the owner, so there could be a decided tax advantage to a sole proprietorship especially during the formative years of operation. We caution you, however, to get professional accounting advice. It is important to note that you will require solid financial records. You must be able to justify your income and expenses accurately. For example, if you needed this book to start your business, you must keep the receipt to use it as a legitimate business expense.

sole proprietorship can be higher than those for a corporation. The sole proprietor includes the revenues and expenses from the business on his or her personal tax return, and the income is taxed at whatever his or her personal rate happens to be either in the three previous years and for the following seven years.

Sole proprietorships are regulated by the provincial/territorial governments and legal requirements vary from jurisdiction to jurisdiction.

PARTNERSHIP

PARTNERSHIP

An association of two or more individuals carrying on a business to earn income

GENERAL PARTNERSHIP

A partnership in which each partner has a hand in managing the business and assumes unlimited personal liability for any debts

LIMITED PARTNERSHIP

A partnership composed of at least one or more limited partners and at least one general partner

Many small businesses start as a partnership, and the arrangement works out well. A **partnership** is an association of two or more individuals carrying on a business to earn income. Legal requirements for forming a partnership vary from province to province, but generally a partnership can come into existence either through a written or oral agreement or, in some cases, even by implication. If you are considering a partnership, you must check out the specific regulations for the province in which you operate your business. For example, visit the Provincial Registrars website at http://www.canadabusiness.ca/eng/page/2730/. (You can also access additional resources at http://www.nelson.com/knowlescastillo7e.)

There are two types of partnerships: general and limited. In a **general partnership**, each partner has a hand in managing the business and assumes unlimited personal liability for any debts. In a **limited partnership**—composed of one or more limited partners and at least one general partner—the general partner assumes both management duties and the downside risk. A limited partner's liability is limited to the amount of his or her original investment as long as he or she has had no role in management decisions.

Note that all partnerships must have at least one general partner.

There are some advantages to a partnership.

- It is easy to set up.
- New partners can be added (some claim that this structure is more flexible and has a greater chance of continuity than a sole proprietorship).
- It involves few legal requirements. You can form a partnership with a handshake and dissolve it without one (though this is not a wise endeavour).
- Risk is generally shared equally among partners—except in the case of a limited partnership.

- Partners can provide mutual support and different skills. One of the best things about a partnership is psychological: It offers the moral support and contribution of teammates.
- It offers more potential sources of capital.
- Partners are taxed as individuals, and in some cases (as is with proprietorships), this can be advantageous (see Box 8.1).

There are some disadvantages, however.

- Tax and estate-planning options are more limited than for a corporate structure (as discussed below).
- Partners and all their assets—personal and business—are, to some extent, at risk for any losses suffered.
- Sometimes, business and personal liabilities of a particular partner aren't kept entirely separate; as a result, there may be potentially disastrous consequences to other partners whose shared business liability could result in unexpected personal losses.
- Decision making might be difficult if each partner expects to have equal rights.
- One partner can make decisions that bind all others.
- Dissolution can be ugly, sometimes resulting in the closing of the business or damaged feelings.

On the surface, partnerships can make a lot of sense. Two or more entrepreneurs face the unknown together and pool their skills. They might be able to raise more capital than one person could alone. But forming a good partnership can be as challenging as forming a good marriage. We strongly suggest that you get everything in writing before you start the business. Write out a partnership agreement with legal advice. Each partner should have his or her own lawyer.

At the very least, your written partnership agreement should include the following:

- rights and responsibilities of the partners;
- capital contributions of each partner;
- role and time that each partner will devote to the business;
- provisions for retirement, death, termination, and reorganization;
- how net income from business will be divided;
- means for settling disputes;
- a mechanism for dissolving the partnership or winding up the business.

While a partnership agreement might not be legally required, it is highly recommended. Furthermore, professional advice is strongly recommended. For example, any partner can enter into a contract on behalf of the partnership. By doing so, a partner can bind all partners in an unfavourable contract, as all partners are jointly and severally liable for the obligations of the partnership. An example of a partnership agreement is available on the book's website at http://www.nelson.com/knowlescastillo7e.

THE SHOTGUN

Partnerships, like marriages, do not always last. When a business partnership (or marriage for that matter) breaks up and the partners seek a divorce, one of the most disputed areas of contention is usually money or the value of the business. The sale price of a business, especially during an impending emotional breakup, is generally quite subjective. Often, it becomes extremely difficult to determine a fair price or market value for the business.

For this reason, a partnership agreement (and a shareholders agreement, as discussed below) must contain a clear process in which the partnership can be disbanded equitably. There are numerous methods of dispute resolution. Some partnership agreements, for example, contain an arbitration clause in which all partners would have to accept an arbitrator's decision.

In the case of an irreconcilable ownership dispute, many small businesses choose a "shotgun" method of resolution. The partnership agreement (or shareholders agreement) will contain a **shotgun clause** stating that one partner can make a buyout offer to the other partner for his or her share of the business. The receiving partner has the option (within a set time) of either accepting this offer or buying out the partner who proposed the offer under the exact same terms.

Some experts—such as Robert Berman, a business author, columnist, and expert specializing in strategic planning—claim that a shotgun clause is fair and efficient for most small businesses because it removes subjectivity and both parties should be satisfied with the outcome of the transaction.

A shotgun clause does not work in every case, however, as when the partner receiving the buyout offer does not have the available cash to purchase the business. But according to experts like Berman, this clause solves most problems associated with the dissolution of a business partnership on a fair and equitable basis. If you decide to go the partnership route, it is strongly advisable that you get professional help on the issue of partnership dissolution and conflict.[2]

> **SHOTGUN CLAUSE**
>
> A provision stating that one partner or shareholder can make a buyout offer to the other partner for her or his share of the business. The receiving partner has the option (within a set time) of either accepting this offer or buying out the partner who proposed the offer under the exact same terms

CORPORATION

> **CORPORATION**
>
> A legal entity with the authority to act and have liability separate and apart from its owners

A **corporation** is a legal entity that exists under authority granted by provincial or federal law. It stands legally separate from the owners, and it does business in the name of the corporation. It can sue and be sued.

Because a corporation is an artificial entity, a creation on paper, it needs more paperwork to justify its existence. There are fees required, as well as meetings of the board of directors. The secretary of the corporation must keep accurate, complete records of what transpires at meetings.

Nonetheless, for many businesses, it's worth forming a corporation as it creates a shield between the creditors and the owners' personal wealth. To keep the shield in place, active owners can become *employees* of the corporation; their business cards have the corporate name and logo and specify their job title. At the same time, owners sign contracts as *officers* of the corporations.

Following are some of the reasons that you should think about incorporating, or not incorporating, your business. In the end, your decision will depend on two key factors: your tax situation and your desire to limit your liability. However, we want to emphasize that becoming a corporation won't solve all your problems. In most cases, it won't immunize you against your creditors. The banks, for example, will still want a personal guarantee, which could mean your house. Taxes won't be eliminated, either. In fact, in the early years, the bank will treat a newly incorporated business as if it were a sole proprietorship. If you have losses, you are better off as a sole proprietor. Let's start with the major reasons for thinking about incorporating.

REASONS FOR INCORPORATING

Liability

A corporation acts as a shield between you and the world. If your business fails, your creditors cannot come after your house, your beach condo, your Porsche, or your hard-won collections—provided you've done it right.

To keep your corporate shield up, make sure you (1) hold scheduled meetings; (2) maintain the minute book; and (3) act as if you are an employee of the corporation. Here's an everyday example of the corporate shield at work: One of your employees gets into a car accident while driving on company business. If you're a corporation, the injured parties will come after your corporation and not you. Reducing your liability or risk of being sued is a major reason for incorporating. We should stress, however, if your employees use *their own* cars on company business, make sure they're insured for an absolute minimum of $1 million.

See how limited liability helped Henry Bemis in the opening vignette. Again, remember that banks and other creditors will want personal guarantees as well as business guarantees; thus, the limited liability advantage of the corporation may be somewhat reduced.

You Might Enjoy Some Tax Advantages

Taxation laws are complex, and a good accountant can dream up several ways to minimize taxes, regardless of what legal form you choose. However, a concept called "integration" attempts to ensure that income is taxed to the same degree whether it is held by an individual or channelled through a corporation. You won't get rich on your tax savings. Tax laws and rates vary slightly from province to province in Canada. We therefore strongly recommend that you see an accountant to help you determine the best organization form from a tax standpoint.

However, there are some tax advantages to being incorporated. The major ones are listed below.

1. In general, a special small business tax rate applies to active income that is under $500,000 (2012). This tax reduction is called the "Small Business Deduction." The general corporate income tax rate varies from approximately 25 percent to 31 percent, depending on the province (see, for example, Taxtips.ca: http://www.taxtips.ca/smallbusiness/corporatetax.htm).
2. Only incorporated companies are eligible for manufacturing and processing tax credits.
3. Certain tax-free benefits, such as some insurance premiums, are available only to employees of incorporated companies.
4. With regard to pensions, there are still greater options for tax deferral under the corporate form.
5. Owners of corporations can potentially enjoy personal tax savings. For example, once the income of a business reaches a certain level, the total tax paid by the corporation and the owner will be less than that which the owner of a sole proprietorship would pay. The exact level depends on the individual situation. As a ballpark figure, once you start earning $25,000 to $30,000 (income after expenses), consider incorporating to save you some personal tax.
6. Benefits can be paid to employees in different forms by a corporation, which could yield a tax saving. These forms include salaries, dividends, and profit-sharing plans. In the case of a deferred profit-sharing plan, for example, a corporation can make contributions on behalf of employees. The contributions are allowed as a current business tax deduction, but the employee pays no tax until withdrawals are made. This type of plan is not available to the sole proprietorship. Careful analysis needs to be made in each situation to determine the optimal structuring of an owner/manager's earnings. You should be aware of the different forms of compensation and, if necessary, consult an accountant for advice on those your business should use.

If you want to learn more about the tax benefits of incorporating, a good starting point is the Canada Revenue Agency (CRA) website (http://www.cra-arc.gc.ca/).

Obviously, the whole issue of corporate tax benefits is complicated. You should always seek the advice of a corporate tax accountant in these matters.

You Upgrade Your Image

What does the word *corporation* imply to you? IBM? Bell? GM? Heavy hitters, right? Let's look at the word with new eyes.

Corporation comes from the Latin, *corpus*, which means "body." To incorporate means to make or form a shape into a body. Looked at from that angle, incorporating starts to sound creative.

It will sound that way to lots of your target customers, too. As a corporation, you might be perceived as

- having more longevity and solidity in the world,
- attracting better employees,
- enjoying more prestige.

You Have the Opportunity of Channelling Some Heavy Expenses

For example, with some legal help, you can write a medical assistance clause into your by-laws. Here's the way it works:

1. Your corporation pays the insurance premium on your extended health insurance.
2. Your corporation reimburses you for the deductible.
3. Your corporation writes off the money paid to you as a business expense.
4. You aren't liable to pay taxes on the reimbursement.

You Simplify the Division of Multiple Ownership

For example, say you're going into the printing and graphic business with two very good friends.

- The business needs $110,000 to get started.
- You can contribute $60,000.
- Friend A delivers $25,000.
- Friend B delivers $15,000.

The business borrows the remaining $10,000 from your friendly banker. The way to handle the ownership is with stock. You get 60 percent, Friend A gets 25 percent, and Friend B gets 15 percent.

You Guarantee Continuity

If one of your shareholders or founders dies (or departs by other means), the corporation will likely keep chugging along. That's because you've gone through a lot of red tape and planning to set it up that way. (This continuity is one of the few justifications for red tape we know.) However, if you are an individual incorporated and you die, the business will likely die with you anyway.

You Can Offer Internal Incentives

When you want to reward a special employee, you can offer stock options or a promotion (for example, a vice-presidential title) in addition to (and sometimes in place of) pay raises. Becoming a corporation officer might carry its own special excitement, which gives you flexibility. An ownership position (shares) can also motivate an employee to keep the company's best interest in mind.

You Are in a Good Position for Estate Planning

As your company grows, you might want to set up other companies and include members of your family in your organization. At this point, you can engage in complicated share exchange and asset transfers. If you find yourself in this situation, you should consult a knowledgeable corporate estate lawyer.

There are also some potential disadvantages of incorporating. These are identified below.

POTENTIAL DISADVANTAGES OF INCORPORATING

Potentially Fewer Tax Writeoffs at the Beginning

Business losses incurred by a corporation can be used for taxation purposes only to offset income of the preceding three years and the seven successive years. If your business suffers losses in its first few years of operation, the losses of the early years could conceivably never be used to reduce tax liability. In the case of a sole proprietorship, however, losses from the business can be used to offset income from other sources in the year in which they are incurred. Thus, if losses are projected in the beginning years of the business and you have income from other sources, it may well be advantageous not to incorporate your business.

Higher Start-up Costs

Start-up costs are higher if you choose to incorporate rather than carry on business as a sole proprietorship or partnership. For example, federal incorporation costs $200 if done electronically (without a lawyer). Provincial incorporation varies from province to province. Although it is not necessary to obtain legal and accounting advice to incorporate, we strongly advise you to do so, particularly if you are considering setting up with a complex share structure. If you decide to use a lawyer and professional accounting services, the cost could easily be $2,000 to $3,000. Of course, legal advice means legal fees.

Increased Paperwork

Carrying on business as a corporation might increase the number of tax filings you are required to make. For instance, the *Canada Business Corporations Act* requires that you file an annual return (Form 22) each year and inform the Corporations Directorate of any changes in your board of directors or the location of your registered head office. You have to file separate income tax returns for yourself, which might lead to an increase in your ongoing professional costs. Your company is also required to maintain certain corporate records. Furthermore, you will likely be asked to register your company in any province or territory where you carry on business. Registration is different from incorporation. Although a company may be incorporated only once, it may be registered in any number of jurisdictions to carry on business. You should contact the local corporate law administration office in each province or territory in which you plan to carry on business to determine what filing requirements you will have to fulfill.

THE PROCESS OF INCORPORATION

Obviously, the issue of incorporation is somewhat complicated. Some of the most frequently asked questions, and their answers, are summarized below.

Who Can Form a Corporation?

Under most circumstances, one or more individuals who are 18 years of age or older can form a corporation. Similarly, one or more companies or "bodies corporate" may incorporate an additional company. These persons or companies are called "incorporators." An incorporator may form a corporation whose shareholders, officers, and directors are other persons, or may serve as the sole director, officer, and shareholder of the company. An incorporator is also responsible for organizational procedures, such as filing the articles of incorporation and designating the first directors.

Do I Incorporate Federally or Provincially?

A company can incorporate either federally (under the *Canada Business Corporations Act*) or provincially, under the laws of a province or territory. Whether you incorporate federally or provincially, you will be required to register your business in the province or territory where you carry on business.

A major advantage of incorporating federally is that the head office can be located in any Canadian province, and it can be relocated if circumstances dictate. If you have the intention (either now or sometime in the future) of operating in more than one jurisdiction, you should probably choose to incorporate federally in order to simplify your business relations later. Still, the federal corporation must register in each province in which it is doing business.

Another reason given for choosing federal incorporation is the heightened name protection provided to federal corporations. While every incorporating jurisdiction in Canada screens potential corporations, the level of scrutiny varies. At the federal level, stringent tests are applied before the right to use a particular name is granted.

A final major advantage of federal incorporation is limited liability. A federally incorporated company is considered a legal entity anywhere in Canada. Therefore, its shareholders are protected by limited liability anywhere in the country. In contrast, a provincially incorporated company is a legal entity only in the province or territory in which it is incorporated. Thus, its shareholders are not protected by limited liability if it does business outside its own jurisdiction.

What Kinds of Businesses Can Incorporate?

Almost any type of business may incorporate. However, banking, insurance, loan and trust companies, and nonprofit corporations are incorporated under different statutes. There are no restrictions such as minimum company size on the businesses.

Do I Need to Hire a Lawyer to Incorporate?

No, though we recommend you do. A lawyer can provide valuable advice, but that is not required for incorporation. If you want to incorporate without a lawyer, get ready for a lot of paperwork.

Do I Need a Board of Directors?

Yes. Your company must have at least one director. In your articles of incorporation, you are required to specify the number of directors. At each annual general meeting, shareholders elect directors (depending on the length or term of office the shareholders choose).

Shareholders may decide that, for various reasons, they want to remove a director they had previously elected. The procedure is simple. It generally needs the approval of a majority of the votes represented at a meeting of shareholders called for the purpose of removing the director.

WHO CAN BE A DIRECTOR?

A director must

- be at least 18 years old,
- be of sound mind (mentally competent),
- be an individual (a corporation cannot be a director).

He or she must also not be an undischarged bankrupt.

In addition, a majority of the directors of a corporation must be individuals who are ordinarily resident in Canada. You should keep this in mind when electing directors and filling vacancies. There is no requirement for directors to hold shares in the corporation, nor is there any restriction against their holding shares.

What Are the Responsibilities of the Board of Directors?

The company's directors are responsible for the overall supervision of the affairs of the corporation. They approve the company's financial statements; make, amend, and repeal by-laws; authorize the issuance of shares; and call and conduct directors' and shareholders' meetings. The directors, in turn, usually appoint officers, who are responsible for day-to-day operations. In a small, private corporation, one individual may act as sole shareholder, director, and officer.[3]

MUST A COMPANY HAVE SHAREHOLDERS?

Yes. An active company must have at least one class of shares (ownership) and at least one shareholder (owner). A person or company who owns shares in a corporation is called a shareholder. Generally speaking, and unless the articles of incorporation provide otherwise, each share in the corporation entitles the holder to one vote. A person becomes a shareholder by acquiring shares from the company (buying shares from the treasury) or from an existing shareholder. The larger the number of shares held, the larger the number of votes (and, in most cases, control) a shareholder can generally exercise.

Shareholders have limited liability in the corporation and usually are not liable for the company's debts unless, as noted earlier, the bank requires the owner/shareholders to pledge personal and company assets. On the other hand, shareholders generally do not actively run the corporation. Shareholders also have legal access to certain information about the corporation. For example, shareholders are entitled to inspect (and copy) the corporate records, and are entitled to receive the company's financial statements. Furthermore, shareholders also elect directors, approve by-laws and by-law changes, appoint the auditor of the corporation (or waive the audit requirement), and approve certain major or fundamental changes to the corporation. These changes could include matters such as a sale of assets of the business, a change of name, and articles of amendment altering share rights or creating new classes of shares.

Do I Need a Shareholders Agreement?

SHAREHOLDERS AGREEMENT

A legal document that establishes the rights of shareholders (owners) and the duties and powers of the board of directors and management

A **shareholders agreement** establishes the rights of shareholders (owners) and the duties and powers of the board of directors and management. A shareholders agreement is not necessary, but we strongly advise that you have one, except, of course, if you are a one-person corporation. It is an agreement entered into usually by all shareholders. The written agreement must be signed by the shareholders who are party to it. While shareholders agreements are specific to each company and its shareholders, most of these documents deal with the same basic issues. (An example of a shareholders agreement can be found by linking on to http://www.sfu.ca/~mvolker/biz/agreesmp.htm, which shows "The Shareholders Agreement—a Sample Agreement," prepared by Mike Volker.)

A typical shareholders agreement includes the following clauses.

Article 1: Definitions
Article 2: Conduct of Affairs of the Corporation
Article 3: Transfers of Shares
Article 4: Real Property
Article 5: Death of a Shareholder
Article 6: Bankruptcy, etc.
Article 7: Powers of Attorney
Article 8: General Sale Provisions
Article 9: Arbitration
Article 10: General Provisions

The relationship among shareholders in a small company tends to be very much like a partnership agreement, with each person having a say in the significant business decisions the company will be making.

Here are some of the major provisions of a shareholders agreement.

- **Who sits on the board of directors.** A very common shareholders agreement provision for a small company gives all the shareholders the right to sit on the board of directors or to nominate a representative for that purpose.
- **How the future obligations of the company will be shared or divided.** The shareholders may agree, for example, that when other means of raising funds are not available, each shareholder will contribute more funds to the company on a pro rata basis.
- **How future shares are purchased.** For example, three equal partners could agree that no shares in the corporation will be issued without the consent of all shareholders/directors. In the absence of such a provision, two shareholders/directors could issue shares to themselves by an ordinary or special resolution (because they control two-thirds of the votes) without including or requiring the permission of the third shareholder/director.

- **The right of first refusal.** This provision states that any shareholder who wants to sell shares must first offer them to the other shareholders of the company before selling them to an outside party.
- **Rules for the transfer of shares.** This provision is often termed the **buy-sell option**—a statement in a shareholders agreement that spells out how the shares will be transferred in an event such as the death, resignation, dismissal, personal bankruptcy, or divorce of a shareholder. (More information on this important clause is provided in a separate section below.)
- **Other shareholders agreement provisions.** These may include non-competition clauses, confidentiality agreements, dispute-resolution mechanisms, and details about how the shareholders agreement is to be amended or terminated.

Shareholders agreements are voluntary. If you choose to have one—and, as you now know, we recommend you do—it should reflect the particular needs of your company and its shareholders. While undoubtedly the best advice is to keep your agreement as simple as possible, we strongly suggest that you consult your professional advisors before signing any shareholders agreement.

Will I Need a Buy-Sell Option?

As we noted above, a shareholders agreement should (although it is not legally required) include a *buy-sell option* that clearly states what happens if one partner should die, become disabled, or want to sell her or his interest in the business. Restrictions can be detailed in plans governing, for instance, when a shareholder can or must sell shares, or what happens to those shares after the individual shareholder has left.

When business owners split up, and most eventually do for one reason or another, a shareholders agreement—and partnership agreement, for that matter—with a buy-sell formula will very likely save the business and keep you out of court. Think of it as a prenuptial agreement.

Often, these buy-sell agreements are funded by joint life insurance on the owners (partners), so that if you die, the business or the other owners will collect the life insurance proceeds and use those funds to buy out the interest in the business. Otherwise, your surviving family members might find it very difficult to sell the interest in the business they inherit from you, except at a giveaway price. In many instances, financial institutions will make a buy-sell agreement a condition of the loan. As with partnership agreements, many small businesses' shareholder agreements will contain a "shotgun" provision in case of irreconcilable shareholder disputes.

Do I Have to Get a Corporate Seal?

Not necessarily. A corporation under the federal *Canada Business Corporations Act*, for example, is not required to have a seal. If you wish to have a corporate seal for your corporation, you may purchase one from a legal stationery store or commercial supplier.

If I Decide to Incorporate, What's Next?

Our advice: See a lawyer—despite the cost savings of doing the work yourself. For example, if proper legal formalities are not followed, the shareholders can be liable for the corporation's debts. However, should you want to do it yourself,

BUY-SELL OPTION

A statement in a shareholders agreement that spells out how the shares will be transferred in an event such as the death, resignation, dismissal, personal bankruptcy, or divorce of a shareholder contact your provincial authority if you want to incorporate locally or the Corporations Directorate of Industry Canada should you decide to incorporate federally. If you plan to do it on your own, get ready for lots of paperwork. Check out the "Industry Canada's Create a Business Incorporation" page at http://www. ic.gc.ca/eic/site/cd-dgc.nsf/eng/cs02717.html.

COOPERATIVE

COOPERATIVE

An organization owned by the members who use its services

A **cooperative** is an organization owned by the members who use its services.[4] Cooperatives can provide virtually any product or service, and can be either nonprofit or for-profit. Cooperatives exist in every sector of our economy and can touch every aspect of our lives. You can be born in a healthcare co-op and buried by a funeral co-op. In between you can work in a workers' co-op; live in a housing co-op; buy your groceries, clothing, and other items from retail co-ops; send your children to a childcare co-op; do all your banking at a credit union; and purchase your insurance from an insurance co-op.

Unlike the private, public, or voluntary sectors, all cooperatives in Canada and around the world are guided by the same seven principles:

1. voluntary and open membership;
2. democratic member control;
3. member economic participation;
4. autonomy and independence;
5. education, training, and information;
6. cooperation among cooperatives;
7. concern for the community.

Perhaps the best-known example of a successful Canadian cooperative is Mountain Equipment Co-op, but there are many other examples of successful co-op ventures. See, for example, the numerous case studies and examples provided on the site of B.C.'s Centre for Co-operative and Community-Based Economy (http://www.uvic.ca/research/centres/cccbe/). Here you will find many community-based enterprises that are taking advantage of a growing trend often referred to as **social entrepreneurship**—not-for-profit businesses that are adapting creative "profit" approaches to satisfy social and community needs.

SOCIAL ENTREPRENEURSHIP

Not-for-profit businesses that are adapting creative "profit" approaches to satisfy social and community needs

Although relatively little has been written about cooperatives, give some consideration to this form, particularly if you are considering a home-based business that can benefit from a group pooling of talents and the trend toward social entrepreneurship.

A cooperative is a special form of corporate structure, often formed by a number of small producers who want to be more competitive in the marketplace. As such, it can be somewhat complicated. Here a few distinct features are outlined.

Incorporation

Generally, at least three people are needed to incorporate a cooperative. You can incorporate provincially (each province has its own legislation) or federally under the *Canada Cooperatives Act*. Each government has its own legal wrinkles, so you will need to get some legal advice or do a lot of research.

Organization

A cooperative is organized and operated for the purpose of providing its members with goods or services. There are various types and structures. Traditional co-ops, such as co-op retail stores, farming co-ops, or housing co-ops, supply service to their members. In worker co-ops, everyone is expected to work in the corporation, and all members are employed in this one business. Worker co-ops can be a useful format for home-based craft or consulting businesses, where members can pool their talents and benefit from one another's skills. Another format is the marketing co-op, whereby members have their own business (product or service). The purpose of this cooperative organization is to market and sell the different products or services.

Capital

Start-up funds for a cooperative are raised by member shares. The return on capital investment to the members is limited by federal or provincial/territorial legislation. For example, the cooperative surplus is normally returned to the members in the form of patronage refunds—sometimes called "patronage dividends"—and each member receives a share of that surplus proportionate to the business done or work carried out by the member with or through the cooperative.

Voting

Each member can have only one vote, regardless of the number of shares he or she possesses.

Liability

The cooperative is an entity distinct from its members, who thus benefit from the standard limited liability protection of a standard corporate structure.

Shares

Shares cannot be transferred. They must be sold to members of the cooperative.

Priorities

Employment security is usually more important than capital, especially in worker co-ops.

Advantages of Cooperatives

Here are a few of the major advantages of a cooperative:
- Given the number of members, there are potentially more sources of capital than in other business forms. In addition, government regulations for raising start-up capital generally favour co-ops.
- Members are owners and are therefore more motivated to produce and be successful.
- Cooperatives offer members plenty of opportunity to network and share ideas and expertise.
- Generally, cooperatives are entitled to receive the standard corporate protection such as limited liability.
- In most cases, it is relatively easy for members to sell their shares to other members.

Disadvantages of Cooperatives

A few disadvantages of cooperatives are as follows:

- With large member groups, it is sometimes difficult to get agreement. Conflict resolution becomes an issue.
- Management is supposed to be a cooperative (shared) responsibility. In some cases, management becomes unwieldy because of differing goals and objectives or, in other cases, lack of experience.
- Some members find it difficult to work cooperatively or in teams.
- Some major institutions are not familiar or comfortable with how cooperatives work, making financing relatively more difficult to obtain.

Establishing a cooperative is tricky. We strongly advise you to consult with provincial or federal authorities and a lawyer. We also encourage you to network with co-ops in your area to understand how they are managed, and to learn first-hand the advantages and disadvantages of the co-op form of business. For more information, you might also want to visit websites such as that of Corporations Canada at http://www.ic.gc.ca/eic/site/cd-dgc.nsf/eng/cs03954. html or Canadian Co-operative Association at http://www.coopscanada.coop/ en/coopdev/Incorporating-your-Co-op.

ADDITIONAL LEGAL STRUCTURES FOR SOCIAL ENTREPRENEURS

Have you had an idea to help people in need? Or maybe you've thought of organizing a group of people who enjoy a particular sport? If you seek to be an agent of social change, then you want to be a social entrepreneur. Social entrepreneurs desire to make changes in their community or in other countries that provide a benefit to society or the environment. Social entrepreneurs can create nonprofit organizations (NPOs) or charities from which to do their good work.

Commander David J. Newing, LVO, Royal Navy (retired), knows a lot about charities and nonprofit organizations. As a social entrepreneur, he has been involved in founding several nonprofit organizations and charities. He is the founder of the highly successful Canadian Youth Business Foundation; cofounder of Digital Opportunity Trust, an international charity; cofounder of Net Corps Canada; and the former secretary general of the Duke of Edinburgh's Award International Association. He has carefully chosen either a nonprofit organization or a charity from which to implement social change.

What is the difference between a charity and a nonprofit? According to Canada Revenue Agency,[5] "[a] **non-profit organization (NPO)** is a club, society, or association that's organized and operated solely for

- social welfare,
- civic improvement,
- pleasure or recreation,
- any other purpose except profit."

Commander Newing further makes a distinction between charities and NPOs. "A charity is an organization that is designed and [has] gone through the process of Canada's system of charity law. In this regard a charity has to follow strictly laid down legal rules concerning its legal charitable objects and associated activities to support and achieve those objects whereas nonprofit organizations are free to carry out any activity that is legal and would be allowed under normal for-profit activity."[6]

Canada Revenue Agency provides the following table (Table 8.2) to further explain the differences between a charity and a nonprofit organization.

NONPROFIT ORGANIZATION (NPO)

Club, society, or association that's organized and operated solely for social welfare, civic improvement, pleasure or recreation, or any other purpose except profit

Table 8.2   Registered Charity versus Non-profit Organization (NPO)[7]

Topics	Registered Charity	NPO
Purpose	Must be established and operate exclusively for charitable purposes.[8]	Can operate for social welfare, pleasure, sport, recreation, civic improvement, or any other purpose except profit. Cannot operate exclusively for charitable purposes.[9]
Registration	Must apply to the Canada Revenue Agency (CRA) and be approved for registration as a charity.	No registration process for income tax purposes.
Charitable Registration Number	Is issued a charitable registration number upon approval by the CRA.	Is not issued a charitable registration number.
Tax Receipts	Can issue official donation receipts for income tax purposes.	Cannot issue official donation receipts for income tax purposes.
Spending Requirements (Disbursement Quota)	Must spend a minimum amount on its own charitable activities or as gifts to qualified donees.[10]	Not applicable.
Designation	Is designated by the CRA as a charitable organization, a public foundation, or a private foundation.	Does not receive a designation.
Returns	Must file annual information return (Form T3010) within six months of its fiscal period end.	May have to file a T2 return (if incorporated) and/or an information return (Form T1044) within six months of its fiscal period end.[11]
Personal Benefits	Cannot use its income to personally benefit its members.	Cannot use its income to personally benefit its members.
Tax-Exempt Status	Is exempt from paying income tax.	Is generally exempt from paying income tax. May be taxed on property income or on capital gains.

Source: Canada Revenue Agency, Registered charity vs. non-profit organization: http://www.cra-arc.gc.ca/chrts-gvng/chrts/pplyng/rgstrtn/rght-eng.html. Reproduced with permission of the Minister of Public Works and Government Services Canada, 2012.

Commander Newing says that there are significant restrictions for a charity compared to a nonprofit organization. In addition, the only advantages for registering as a charity are as follows:

1. A charity that is registered by Canada Revenue Agency can issue charitable tax receipts whereas an NPO cannot.
2. A charity can access funds from charitable foundations whereas an NPO cannot.
3. The general public is more empathic to a charity and more likely to make donations—as indeed are other sources of private sector and government funding agencies—though government agencies don't differentiate between giving funds to charities and NPOs as they don't need tax receipts.

Kimberley Cunnington-Taylor, a lawyer specializing in not-for-profit and charity law, agrees with Commander Newing's description of nonprofit organizations and charities. Cunnington-Taylor adds that while all charities are nonprofit organizations, not all nonprofit organizations are charities. This distinction, while important, is commonly misunderstood.

What is needed to register a charity? Cunnington-Taylor says that registering a charity is a two-step process. "First there must be an organization of some sort (i.e., a corporation, a trust, or an unincorporated association), and second, that organization must apply to CRA for registration as a charity, and must meet the criteria to qualify as a charity (as established in the *Income Tax Act* and through the courts)."[12] This process usually takes between four and nine months to complete. However, the cost and length of time it takes to incorporate a not-for-profit corporation and register a charity can vary greatly. Cunnington-Taylor recommends that social entrepreneurs first talk to a lawyer specializing in not-for-profit and charity law. Why?

- Many organizations first need (or prefer) to incorporate in order to carry on their activities. Then once the corporation is in place, the corporation applies to CRA for charitable registration.
- The corporate legislation applicable to Ontario and federal not-for-profit corporations has changed.[13] The federal government enacted the *Corporate Not-for-profit Corporations Act* on June 23, 2009, and that is affecting all not-for-profit corporations originally governed by the *Canada Corporations Act*.
- A charity is a bundle of legal rights and restrictions. The *Income Tax Act* outlines the rights, obligations, and privileges afforded to organizations that qualify as charities and CRA regulates charities through administration of the *Income Tax Act*. Unfortunately, many organizations do not meet the criteria for registration due to numerous issues, including simple misunderstandings about what the permitted objects and activities of a charity include.

Cunnington-Taylor notes that many individuals and groups rush into trying to set up a nonprofit organization or charity without first fully understanding the costs, implications, and ongoing compliance issues involved in such a venture. She suggests that you do your homework so that you can determine which business structure is right for you.[14] For more information about nonprofit organizations, you may visit http://www.cunnington-taylor.ca.

It is wise for future social entrepreneurs to seek the proper advice from professionals when deciding on whether to start a nonprofit organization or charity. Now do a little research on your own. Complete Action Step 39.

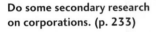

ACTION STEP 39

Do some secondary research on corporations. (p. 233)

YOUR BUSINESS NAME

So you now have a business idea you think will fly. You've spent a lot of time on your business plan and are beginning to think that it just might work. You've come up with a name for your business that makes you feel proud. Where do you go from here?

We suggest you next think about some legal protection for your name. After all, you don't want someone else to start a business using your name. The process of protecting your business name will depend, in part, on the province where you want to conduct business and your legal form (which is one of the reasons we wanted you to consider your legal framework in the first part of this chapter).

According to provincial authority, a sole proprietorship or partnership does not necessarily have to register its name. Normally, if your business name is exactly the same as your own name, registration is not needed. For example, Mary Smith could operate a business as Mary Smith without registration. However, she would have to register the name of her business if the business name differed—even slightly—from her name. If she called her business Mary Smith *Consulting*, then she would have to register that name with the province where she is conducting her business.

Provincial registration does not require the business name to be unique. Thus, in some cases, you can register your business name without a search, but we advise that you do one, as you might later discover that there are other businesses with similar names. If your registered name causes confusion with another business, you might be subject to penalties and might even have to change the name of your business. In other words, provincial registration does not necessarily protect your business name.

In searching a name you have two choices: doing a provincial search or doing a federal search. All incorporated businesses must register their corporate name with any province in which they do business. Although provinces will do a name search for you, your best bet is to ask for a federal name search report. If you incorporate federally, and we suggest you do, you will need a NUANS (Newly Upgraded Automated Name Search) report. A NUANS report is a five-page document that includes a list of business names and trade-marks that sound similar to the name you are proposing. The list is drawn from the national data bank of existing and reserved business names, as well as trade-marks applied for and registered in Canada.

A NUANS report will make you aware of any existing businesses that could prevent you from using your business name. It also lets you know whether your proposed trade-mark is already in use by another business. This knowledge saves you from having to change the name of your business later when you find out you have been infringing on a trade-mark.

A NUANS report is obtained from private businesses known as Search Houses, which are listed under Incorporating Companies, Incorporation: Name Search, Searchers of Records, or Trade-mark Agents in the Yellow Pages.

Generally, when you register a name in federal incorporation, you must submit the NUANS report along with your proposed business name. The request for a numbered company is the same with one exception. You may request the federal government to grant your corporation a designating number, followed by the word "Canada" and a legal element, to serve as your corporate name. For this specific case, a NUANS report is not required. Any other kind of proposed name must be supported by a NUANS report. If there is another name that is similar to your name, you will be asked to make a new choice for your incorporated company.[15]

PATENTS, COPYRIGHTS, AND TRADE-MARKS

Patents, copyrights, and trade-marks are the three major forms of intellectual property that can be protected through federal legislation. These are important elements of your business. If you fail to protect them, (1) you might lose your business, (2) your ideas might be stolen, or (3) your products might be copied. In Canada, intellectual property is largely the responsibility of the Canadian Intellectual Property Office (CIPO).[16] (See http://strategis.ic.gc.ca/sc_mrksv/cipo/welcome/welcom-e.html.) Because intellectual property laws are complex and subject to change, you should consult with a lawyer who has experience in this area.

TEN THINGS YOU SHOULD KNOW ABOUT PATENTS

1. What Is a Patent?

A **patent** is a federal government grant that gives an inventor exclusive rights to his or her invention. Patents cover new inventions (process, machine, manufacture, composition of matter) or any new and useful improvement of an existing invention. Patent protection applies in the country that issues the patent. In Canada, this protection extends for 20 years from the date of filing. Patents are granted for products or processes that are new, workable, and ingenious (novel, useful, and inventive). In this way, patents serve as a reward for ingenuity.

Patenting your invention can take several years. The process usually begins with an initial patent search to compare your invention with current patent and technical literature. Then you assemble a patent application, which includes a detailed description of your invention and the claims that are the basis for your patent protection. In Canada, a patent is given to the inventor who first files an

PATENT

A federal government grant that gives an inventor exclusive rights to his or her invention application. It's therefore wise to file as soon as possible after completing your invention, because someone else might be on the same track.

2. Why Obtain a Patent?

Without a patent, you will be able to protect your invention only as a trade secret. Your secret will be out the moment you publish or begin to sell your invention, and anyone will be able to exploit your invention. Even if you can maintain your secret, if someone else independently makes the invention, that person might be able to obtain a patent and prevent you from exploiting the invention.

3. Is a Patent Application Mandatory?

To have patent protection, you must apply for and receive a patent. Application fees range from about $350 to $500. Because patent laws are national, you must obtain patent protection in each country in which you want protection.

4. Who Can Apply for a Patent?

The legal owner of an invention can obtain the patent. Typically, the owner is the inventor or inventors. However, if an inventor sells his or her rights, then a second party will own the invention and be able to obtain a patent. If the inventor makes the invention as part of an employment contract, the employer might own the invention and have the right to the patent.

5. How Long Is a Patent Effective?

The life of a patent in Canada is 20 years from the date the application was first filed. Payment of maintenance fees throughout the life of the patent is also required to keep it in force.

6. How Do I Obtain a Patent?

You can obtain a patent in Canada by submitting a patent application, with the appropriate fee, to

The Commissioner of Patents
The Canadian Intellectual Property Office
Place du Portage Phase I
50 Victoria Street,
Gatineau, Quebec
K1A 0C9

The *Guide to Patents* (http://www.cipo.ic.gc.ca/eic/site/cipointernet-interne-topic.nsf/eng/wr00102.html) gives additional information on the requirements for obtaining a patent. You can consult the tutorial on how to write a patent application.

7. Do I Need to Hire a Patent Agent?

You can do it yourself, but the Canadian Intellectual Property Office strongly advises that you employ the services of a patent agent. Patent agents are professionals with experience in drafting applications and navigating the patent process. They will be able to help you ensure that you get all of the rights to which you are entitled. A list of registered patent agents is available from the Patent Office.

8. Does a Patent in Canada Protect My Rights in Other Countries?

No. Patent laws are national, so you must obtain a patent in each country in which you want protection.

ACTION STEP 40

Navigate an online tutorial on patent applications. (p. 233)

9. What Are the Steps for Obtaining a Patent?

To get a patent, there are many steps and some complexities along the way. To help you understand the process, the Patent Office has prepared a summary entitled "How Your Patent Application Is Processed." A patent application must include a petition, a description of the invention, an abstract, a claim or claim(s), any drawing referred to in the description, and the filing fee. Consult the *Guide to Patents* to determine what information must be included for each of the above requirements, or go to the tutorial on how to write a patent application.

10. Will the Patent Office Ensure That My Patent Is Not Infringed?

No. Enforcement of patents is the responsibility of the patentee. Patents can be enforced through the judicial system.

Now is a good time to try your hand at Action Step 40.

TEN THINGS YOU SHOULD KNOW ABOUT COPYRIGHTS

1. What Is a Copyright?

Copyright is the exclusive right to copy a creative work or allow someone else to do so. Copyrights provide protection for artistic, dramatic, musical, or literary works (including computer programs), as well as for performance, sound recording, and communication signals. This protection includes the sole right to publish, produce or reproduce, perform in public, communicate a work to the public by telecommunication, translate a work, and, in some cases, rent the work. The copyright of a Canadian author is valid in foreign countries—as long as the country in question belongs to one or more of the international copyright treaties, conventions, or organizations. In a similar fashion, the copyright of a foreign author is valid in Canada.

Generally, copyright in Canada exists for the life of the author plus 50 years following his or her death. There are some exceptions. Copyright protection always expires December 31 of the last calendar year of protection.

COPYRIGHT

The exclusive right to copy a creative work or allow someone else to do so

2. To What Does Copyright Apply? Not Apply?

Copyright applies to all original literary, dramatic, musical, and artistic works: these include books, other writings, music, sculptures, paintings, photographs, films, plays, television and radio programs, and computer programs. Copyright also applies to sound recordings (such as CDs), performers' performances, and communication signals. A copyright *does not* apply to themes, ideas, most titles, names, catch phrases, and other short-word combinations of no real substance.

3. Who Owns the Copyright?

Generally, the owner of the copyright is
- the creator of the work;
- the employer, if the work was created in the course of employment, unless there is an agreement to the contrary;
- the person who commissions a photograph, portrait, engraving, or print for valuable consideration (which has been paid), unless there is an agreement to the contrary;
- some other party, if the original owner has transferred his or her rights.

4. How Do I Obtain Copyright?

You acquire copyright automatically when you create an original work or other subject matter.

5. Do I Have to Do Anything to Be Protected?

No. Because you obtain copyright automatically, you are automatically protected by law. However, it is still a good idea to register your copyright and to mark your works with a notice of copyright.

6. What Are the Benefits of Copyright Registration?

Registration gives you a certificate stating that you are the copyright owner. You can use this certificate in court to establish ownership. (The onus is on your opponent to prove that you do not own the copyright.)

7. How Do I Register a Copyright?

You must file an application with the Copyright Office and pay a prescribed fee. An application form and instructions can be downloaded from the main page of the Copyright Office (http://www.cipo.ic.gc.ca/eic/site/cipointernet-interne-topic.nsf/eng/h_wr00003.html?OpenDocument). You may file electronically. The registration process normally takes three and a half weeks. The fee covers review of your application ($65), registration ($65), and your official certificate ($35). The registration fee is a one-time expense. Once you have registered, you do not have to pay further fees to maintain your copyright.

8. Do I Need to Mark My Work with a Notice of Copyright?

Doing this isn't necessary for protection in Canada; however, you must mark your work with a small "©," the name of the copyright owner, and the year of first publication to be protected in some other countries. Even though it is not always required, marking is useful, because it serves as a general reminder to everyone that the work is protected by copyright.

9. What Is Copyright Infringement?

Copyright infringement is the unlawful use of copyright material. Plagiarism—passing off someone else's work as your own—is a form of copyright infringement. The Copyright Office will not prevent others from infringing your rights, however; the responsibility for policing your copyright rests with you.

10. Can Libraries or Educational Institutions Make Multiple Copies of Parts of Books or Articles for Student Use?

No. The making of multiple copies requires the consent of the copyright owner. This consent may be obtained through a licensing agreement with a photocopying collective. However, the *Copyright Act* does allow the copying by individuals of parts of works for private study or research. Such copying should be minimal. This exception falls within the "fair dealing" section of the act.

TEN THINGS YOU SHOULD KNOW ABOUT TRADE-MARKS

1. What Is a Trade-Mark?

A **trade-mark** is a word, symbol, or design, or a combination of these, used to distinguish the goods or services of one person or organization from those of others in the marketplace. There are three basic types. *Ordinary marks* are words and/or symbols that distinguish the goods or services of a specific firm. *Certification marks* identify goods or services that meet a standard set by a governing organization. *Distinguishing guise* identifies the unique shape of a product or its package.

> **TRADE-MARK**
> A word, symbol, or design, or a combination of these, used to distinguish the goods or services of one person or organization from those of others in the marketplace

The Trade-marks Office does not act as an enforcement agency. You are responsible for monitoring the marketplace for cases of infringement and taking legal action, if necessary.

Companies, individuals, partnerships, trade unions, or lawful associations, provided they meet the requirements of the *Trade-marks Act*, can register a trade-mark.

A registration is valid for 15 years and is renewable every 15 years thereafter on payment of a fee.

2. What Is the Difference Between a Registered and an Unregistered Trade-Mark?

A registered trade-mark has been approved and entered on the Trade-mark Register held by the Canadian Trade-marks Office. Registration is proof of ownership. An unregistered trade-mark might also be recognized through common law as the property of the owner, depending on the circumstances.

3. Why Register a Trade-Mark?

Registration is direct (prima facie) evidence of exclusive ownership across Canada and helps ward off potential infringers. It enables you to protect your rights more easily should someone challenge them, as the onus is on the challenger to prove rights in any dispute. The process of registration, with its thorough checks for conflicting trade-marks, will ensure that you are claiming a unique mark and help you avoid infringement of other parties' rights. A registered trade-mark is a prerequisite for franchising a business. Registration isn't mandatory, but it is advisable.

4. Do I Need to Hire a Trade-Mark Agent?

You can do it yourself, but the Canadian Intellectual Property Office strongly advises that you employ the services of a trade-mark agent. Trade-mark registration can be a complex process; an experienced agent can save you time and money by avoiding pitfalls such as poorly prepared applications and incomplete research.

5. How Do I Register a Trade-Mark?

You must file an application with the Trade-marks Office, or Branch, of CIPO in Gatineau, Quebec. The application undergoes stringent examination to ensure it meets the requirements of the *Trade-marks Act*.

6. Does Registration in Canada Protect My Rights in Other Countries?

No. If your products are sold in other countries, you should consider applying for foreign registration. Contact a trade-mark agent or the embassy of the country in question to find out about procedures.

7. What Is the Difference Between a Trade-Mark and a Trade Name?

A trade name is the name under which you conduct your business. It can be registered as a trade-mark, but only if it is used as such—that is, used to identify wares or services.

8. May I Register My Own Name as a Trade-Mark?

Normally, you may not register a proper name—neither yours nor anyone else's—as a trade-mark. An exception might be made if you can demonstrate that the name has become identified in the public mind with certain wares or services.

9. What Are the Steps of Trade-Mark Registration?

Trade-mark registration usually involves
- a preliminary search (done by you or your agent) of existing trade-marks,
- an application,
- examination of your application by the Trade-marks Branch of CIPO,
- publishing of the application in the *Trade-marks Journal*,
- time for opposition (challenges) to the application,
- allowance and registration (if there is no opposition).

10. May I Allow Other Parties to Use My Registered Trade-Mark?

Yes. You may sell, bequeath, or otherwise transfer your rights to a trade-mark through a process called "assignment." You may also license rights to your trade-mark.

PROTECTION STRATEGY FOR SOCIAL MEDIA IP

It is also important to discuss how social media are becoming a key concern for entrepreneurs as they look at protecting their intellectual property (IP).

If you can protect your business name online or be aware of how sharing information and content can affect you legally, then you will be prepared for the legal issues in social media. If you are thinking about a business name or want to find out if others have a similar name, then you will need to do some research on social media sites. Here are a few examples of social media sites to go to and register your intellectual property:

- GoDaddy.com (http://www.godaddy.com/) allows you to register your domain name.
- Twubs (http://twubs.com/) allows you to register your hashtags (labelling words preceded by a hash symbol (#) and used for identification on Twitter).
- Facebook (http://www.facebook.com/pages/create.php) allows you to create a fanpage and capture your business name.
- Knowem (http://knowem.com/) allows you to check for the use of your business name, brand, personal name, or even username on more than 550 social media websites.

MORE RED TAPE

When you start your business, you will become subject to all kinds of federal, provincial, and municipal red tape. Box 8.2 provides a checklist of some of the requirements your business may be confronted with. One thing is for certain: You will have to deal with the Canada Revenue Agency (CRA). Thus, we focus here on the major CRA start-up requirements because these will be common for everyone. We will also get you started on finding out your responsibilities regarding retail sales taxes—which, of course differ, according to the province you do business in.

THE BUSINESS NUMBER (BN)

Your first step in doing business with the Canada Revenue Agency is to obtain a business number (BN). The BN is the federal government's numbering system that helps to streamline the way it deals with businesses. It is based on the idea of "one business, one number."

You will need a BN if you require one of the four CRA business accounts: corporate income tax, import/export, payroll deductions, or Goods and Services Tax (GST) or Harmonized Sales Tax (HST). According to government, businesses will eventually be able to use their BN for other CRA accounts and other government programs. For instance, you will be asked to state the name of the business, its location, and its legal structure. You will also be required to outline what your business's sales will be. Without this type of information, you won't be able to complete the BN registration form.

Box 8.2 Checklist of Requirements That Might Affect Your Business

Have you considered the following?

Municipal

- Building permits (Failure to obtain proper municipal permits is one of the most common and costly mistakes by new business owners. Do not lease a new location until these permits have been approved.)
- Regulations regarding home-based or home-occupation business
- Zoning, rezoning, and obtaining of a minor variance
- Subdivision approval and consent to severance
- Demolition control and permits
- Site plan control approval
- Licensing of business and trades
- Compliance with municipal by-laws, such as signage and nonsmoking regulations
- Hours of operation
- Inspections—such as fire, health, traffic, and building
- Municipal tax (e.g., realty tax, business tax)
- Any more?

Provincial

- Health and safety regulations (Strict adherence to health and safety regulations is an important legal issue—one to which we will return in Chapter 9.)
- Workers' Compensation Board or Workplace Safety Insurance Board (WSIB)
- Provincial/territorial employment standards (e.g., hours of work, minimum wage, vacation pay, overtime pay, equal pay for equal work)
- Health insurance
- Environmental control regulations
- Provincial tax (e.g., corporate, retail sales, tobacco, gasoline, land transfer)
- Any more?

Federal

- Business Number (BN)
- GST/HST
- Payroll deductions (e.g., Canada Pension Plan, insurance, income tax)
- Food and drug regulations and inspection
- Patents, trade-marks, copyrights, and industrial designs
- Federal corporation tax
- Any more?

If you decide you need a BN, you will have to complete Form RC1, Request for a Business Number. For more information, contact your local CRA office. A good source of information is the CRA publication RC2, *The Business Number and Your Canada Revenue Agency Program Accounts* (available at http://www.cra-arc.gc.ca).

PAYROLL DEDUCTIONS

According to the CRA, you are an employer if you pay salaries, wages, bonuses, vacation pay, or tips to people working for you; or if you provide benefits such as lodging or room and board to the people working for you. If you are an employer, you will be responsible for deducting the following from your employees' pay-cheques:

- income tax,
- Canada Pension Plan (CPP) contributions,
- Employment Insurance (EI) premiums.

You might also be required to make payments and be subject to certain regulations under the workers' compensation legislation.

Payroll deductions can be complicated. So before you start your business, we strongly advise you to visit or call your local CRA office. An advisor might even come to your business and help you get started with all the forms you need. A good source of information on payroll deductions is the CRA publication *Employers' Guide to Payroll Deductions and Remittances* (http://www.cra-arc.gc.ca/E/pub/tg/t4001). You might want to consider outsourcing your payroll functions to a payroll service provider. For many business owners, the "small cost" of using a payroll service provider can be a wise investment, not only creating time for concentrating on other matters, but also getting expert advice when dealing with any disputes with CRA or provincial regulators.

FEDERAL INCOME TAXES

Generally, business income includes any money you earn with the reasonable expectation of making a profit.

If you are not incorporated, that is, you are a sole proprietor or in a partner-ship, business income (or loss) forms part of your overall personal income for the year. You will be taxed on your net earnings from the business, which you will include on your personal tax return as self-employment income. As a sole propri-etor, you must file financial statements with your personal income tax return. It is most likely (if you are not in farming and fishing) that you will be required to submit Form T2125, Statement of Business or Professional Activities, along with your T1.

As a sole proprietor, you are now eligible to be covered by Employment Insurance, and you will have to pay income tax and Canada Pension Plan (CPP) premiums on the self-employment income reported on your personal tax return. Depending on the province in which you operate, Workers' Compensation pre-miums may be payable. Self-employed people and their spouses or common-law partners have until June 15 each year to file their tax returns. However, any tax owing must still be paid by April 30.

A partnership by itself does not file an annual income tax return. Each partner must include a share of the partnership income or loss on a personal, corporate, or trust income tax return. As such, partners must file either financial statements or one of the two proprietorship forms referred to above along with their personal tax forms. Partnership taxes can get a little complicated, so you should get some accounting advice or, at the very least, consult with the Canada Revenue Agency.

A corporation must file a corporation income tax return (T2) within six months of the end of every taxation year, even if it doesn't owe taxes. Corporations report on an annual basis and are normally free to choose their year-end date. Corporations are also required to attach completed financial statements and the necessary schedules to the T2 return and, as the owner, you must also complete a separate personal (T1) tax return.

If your small business is incorporated, whether or not you pay yourself a salary is a tax-planning decision. Another option is to pay yourself (and other shareholders, depending on share structure) a **dividend**—an amount distributed out of a cor-poration's retained earnings (accumulated profits) to shareholders—which is not deductible for the corporation. There are many factors to consider, and professional

DIVIDEND

An amount distributed out of a cor-poration's retained earnings (accumu-lated profits) to shareholders

advice in this area is recommended. If you decide to pay yourself a salary, you will be required to deduct income tax and CPP premiums from your salary, and as the owner of the business, you will be eligible to be covered by Employment Insurance. Depending on the province in which you operate, Workers' Compensation premiums may be payable, even if you do not pay yourself a salary. See, for example, Taxtips.ca (http://www.taxtips.ca/contact.htm#repro).

Corporate tax is complicated, and you definitely should get professional help. But if you really do want to deal with it yourself, the best place to start is the "Setting Up Your Business" chapter of *Guide for Canadian Small Businesses* on the CRA website and Taxtips.ca (see Box 8.3).

GST/HST

Nova Scotia, New Brunswick, and Newfoundland and Labrador combined their respective provincial sales taxes with the GST (goods and services tax) to

Box 8.3   Tax and Legal Information

Guide for Canadian Small Businesses (Canada Revenue Agency): http://www.cra-arc.gc.ca/E/pub/tg/rc4070/—"Setting up Your Business" is the first chapter of the CRA's *Guide for Canadian Small Businesses*. Topics include these:

- How does a sole proprietorship pay taxes?
- How does a partnership pay taxes?
- How does a corporation pay taxes?
- Meeting legal requirements for keeping records
- Retaining and destroying records
- Bringing assets into a business

Canadian Tax and Financial Information: http://www.taxtips.ca—This is a great site to answer many of your tax and legal questions. Taxtips.ca is owned by a small private company located in Nanaimo, British Columbia. It is prepared by a husband and wife team who are retired from owning and operating a small business, with one being a retired professional accountant. Their goal is to provide a reference site for easy-to-understand tax, financial, and related information. Their information is timely.

Here is just a limited selection of questions you can get answered:

1. What books and records must be kept for a business?
2. How does a self-employed person choose a year-end when starting a business?
3. What is the deadline for filing a tax return for a self-employed person?
4. Where can I get the forms to file a corporate tax return?
5. If I have a small business, do I have to file both a personal and a business tax return?
6. Do my small business financial statements have to be audited?
7. As the owner of a small business, should I pay myself a salary? What deductions would apply?
8. Can I write off my business losses against my other income?
9. Should I incorporate my small business?

Provincial sales tax (PST): "Provincial Sales Taxes," Taxtips.ca: http://www.taxtips.ca/provincial_sales_tax.htm—Here you will find the general rates of provincial sales taxes for most purchases and links to the provincial (or federal) websites regarding provincial sales taxes.

Getting started: Canada Business: http://www.canadabusiness.ca/eng/page/2867/.

create a harmonized sales tax (HST) in each province. The HST rate in New Brunswick and Newfoundland and Labrador is 13 percent (5 percent federal part, equal to the 5 percent GST; and an 8 percent provincial part). On July 1, 2010, Nova Scotia increased its HST rate from 13 percent to 15 percent. Since July 1, 2010, Ontario and British Columbia have combined their respective provincial sales taxes with the GST to implement an HST. The HST rate for Ontario is 13 percent (a 5 percent federal part and an 8 percent provincial part). The HST rate for British Columbia is 12 percent (a 5 percent federal part and a 7 percent provincial part). More information is available from the CRA's website: http://www.cra-arc.gc.ca/tx/bsnss/tpcs/gst-tps/menu-eng.html.

If your taxable revenues do not exceed $30,000, you do not have to register for the GST or HST. However, you can register voluntarily and, in general, we suggest you do, for three major reasons.

1. **Business image.** Charging GST (which will require you to file for a Business Number) gives you a professional image. It gives the customer the impression that you are financially respectable (earn more than $30,000) and intend to stay in business for the "long haul."

2. **Customer relations.** At the point when you begin making in excess of $30,000 (say two years down the road), you will have to begin charging an additional 5 percent. Your returning customers might not be pleased with this, and might very likely see it as a price increase.

3. **Financial.** As we describe below, businesses that sell GST-taxable goods and services and are "small suppliers" are able to recover the GST that they have paid on their purchases. If you are not GST registered, you cannot collect the GST you pay on your purchases. See, for example, Taxtips.ca (http://www.taxtips.ca/gst.htm#WhatIsGST).

Although the consumer ultimately pays the GST/HST, businesses are normally responsible for collecting and remitting it to the government. Businesses that must register or that register voluntarily for the GST/HST are called registrants. Registrants can claim a credit—an input tax credit—to recover the GST/HST they paid or owe on their business purchases. If they pay more than they collect, they can claim a refund. Since there are goods and services that are tax exempt (most medical and dental services and daycare services provided for less than 24 hours a day, for example), it is important that you check with the CRA before you start your business.

To register for the GST or HST, contact your nearest tax services office. You will be asked to fill out Form RC1, *Request for a Business Number,* as we discussed earlier. You can get more information from the CRA publication *General Information for GST/HST Registrants* (http://www.cra-arc.gc.ca/E/pub/gp/rc4022/) or from the CRA's website (http://www.cra-arc.gc.ca/).

PROVINCIAL SALES TAXES

Provincial sales taxes (PST) are charged in many provinces on retail sales of many goods and services. A business that sells taxable goods and/or services in a province is required to register as a vendor to collect the provincial retail sales tax.

In all provinces except Quebec and Prince Edward Island, GST is charged on the selling price of the item before PST is applied, thus avoiding GST being charged on PST. In Quebec and Prince Edward Island, the reverse is the case. Each province has its own regulations and rates. As we have noted above, Newfoundland and Labrador, Nova Scotia, New Brunswick, Ontario, and British

Columbia charge a harmonized sales tax, or HST—a tax rate that includes both PST and GST.

GET A LAWYER AND AN ACCOUNTANT

The business world has become something of a legal jungle. As an entrepreneur, you can't possibly be expected to know and understand all the laws and their tax implications. So take the time to find a lawyer and an accountant who can help you with your specific needs.

A good small business lawyer and an accountant can help you create the right business and tax structure for a partnership or a corporation—a structure that gives you the flexibility and tax advantages you'll need. Some small business owners we know have invited their lawyer and accountant to sit on their board of directors or board of advisors. If you're incorporated, you might even want to think about inviting your lawyer and/or accountant to sit on your board of directors and provide "no-cost" advice in exchange for shares in the business. Remember, however, you might have to pay for directors' liability insurance.

Now let's learn from the experience of Paul Webber. If he had had sound professional advice, his story might have turned out differently.

A PARTNER'S UNFORESEEN DEATH

Paul Webber was a software game developer when he met MaryAnn Dominic. Dominic, a likable woman, had four years' experience designing game software and was a dynamite salesperson. They got together and formed Gamestar.

Their first year was okay—they netted more than $50,000 apiece— and their second year was looking even better. By May of their second year, their projections told them they could make $75,000 each before the end of the summer. They thought it felt great to have cash, and to celebrate, they went out to dinner.

At dinner, Dominic passed out and was pronounced dead by the paramedics on their arrival. At 32 years of age, MaryAnn Dominic was dead of a heart attack. Two weeks after the funeral, Webber was on the phone with a customer when Dominic's widower, Jason, walked in. Jason had inherited his wife's half of the business.

Webber didn't like Jason as his partner, but there was nothing he could do. He and Dominic had no succession plan for their business. They were young. What were the chances of either one dying? Webber knew he would have to break his back to teach Jason the business. Game software was a competitive field—it changed before you could take a breath—and Jason would have to learn an awful lot in a short time.

Webber was a good guy, so he tried. The first month, he was extra tired because he was handling his own customers while also spending long hours trying to teach Jason the business. The second month, two clients who were ignored defected to a competitor. Webber heard about it through the grapevine. The third month, the company almost ran out of cash, and Webber had to dump in $5,000 from his personal account to keep suppliers happy.

And Jason wasn't learning the business. Instead, he was distracting Paul and spending money. He wasn't able to hold up his end, and no improvement was in sight.

Webber hung on for another week. Then he did the only thing he could do for his own survival. He took what customers he had left and rented an office six blocks away in an attempt to keep going. He figured he had paid his dues to MaryAnn Dominic.

It wasn't long before Jason's lawyer came calling, though, making Webber nervous and unsure of the consequences and the future.

As we learn from Paul Webber, you will also need professional advice to help you draft a will, and a succession plan to handle unforeseen events that may cost you dearly.

GET A WILL

The importance of an up-to-date will cannot be overstated. Contrary to what most people believe, if you die without a will, things will not automatically work out as you would have wished. Disaster can result.

—David Chilton, author of *The Wealthy Barber*[17]

If you die without a will, all your assets will be frozen. The courts will then pay off all debts and divide up your business assets according to a set of rigid rules. If you want your property, business, or shares transferred a certain way after your death, you must say so in a will. If you have partners or other owners, make sure they have a will and that you all understand what is going to happen if someone dies. Here are a few rules, drawn from *The Wealthy Barber*:[18]

1. Get a lawyer. Don't make a will yourself. There are many issues to consider, both from a business and from a personal perspective.
2. Make your lawyer aware of your business arrangements.
3. Before you see a lawyer, decide exactly what you want to happen with your business should you die. Make sure that you discuss this with your business partners or other owners. Remember, also, that you have the right to know what is going to happen to the business if one of your key shareholders or partners dies.
4. Choose an executor. This person will handle your affairs and carry out the will's instructions.
5. Make sure that your business is insured in the event of your death.
6. Make sure that you have a succession plan in the event of your death.
7. Don't procrastinate. Do it now!

SUCCESSION PLANNING—ESPECIALLY FOR THE FAMILY-OWNED BUSINESS

John R. Beever doesn't know how his business would function if he fell out of an airplane today, but he's prodding his family and key managers to discuss it.

Beever, 59, runs a family-owned custom woodwork manufacturing business that his great-grandfather started in 1876. But discussing the future ownership and management of the business raises thorny questions. Beever's two sons, Geoffrey and John C., are in their 30s and vice-presidents of the firm. Both are enthusiastic about the business, and both are bright. Both want to succeed their father. Which son, if any, does the senior Beever choose as successor? Will that son be able to steer the company through a new era? And will Beever be able to let go and watch others toil without him?

SUCCESSION PLANNING

The process of establishing the procedures to change or transfer ownership or control of a business.

In small business, **succession planning** refers to the process through which an owner establishes the procedures to change or transfer ownership or control of the business.[19] The succession process—especially with family-owned businesses—requires owner/managers like John R. Beever to deal proactively with a slew of sticky questions: How can they choose among several capable successors? What happens if no one in the family is really interested in taking over?

Here are some key succession issues that you must prepare to confront:

- Is continuing the business into the next generation in the best interest of family members?
- Can family members handle the stress that continuity planning will cause?
- Who should be included in the decision making?
- What is the vision for the family business?
- What qualities should the next company leader have?
- How can important contacts, along with the title of owner, be transferred?
- How can the owner make a graceful exit? Once owners decide to go, they should go quickly—and not look back.
- On the unexpected death of the owner, how should control and ownership be transferred?

If you want to learn more about succession issues and potential problems in family-owned business, go to http://www.canadabusiness.ca/eng/page/2819. Now you're ready to do Action Step 41.

ACTION STEP 41

Take a lawyer and an accountant to lunch. (p. 233)

BANKRUPTCY

Entrepreneurs are optimists by nature. As you prepare to open your doors, the last thing you want to think about is the prospect of being forced to close them. But business failures do happen, and it's not too early to learn about some of the legal concerns arising from them.

If nothing else, an understanding of the bankruptcy process should encourage you to be proactive and avoid debt problems. Boxes 8.4 and 8.5 will also help you do this. In Chapter 11 we will encourage you to seek out and get a copy of your credit rating. But, for many young entrepreneurs, an important issue is not only the maintenance of a good credit rate but also the creation of a credit rating. So, in Chapter 11, we will also help you develop a positive credit history.

Box 8.4 Dealing with Debt

Check out Industry Canada's *Dealing with Debt: A Consumer's Guide* (Office of the Superintendent of Bankruptcy): http://www.ic.gc.ca/eic/site/bsf-osb.nsf/eng/br01861.html. Many Canadians and Canadian companies will face a financial crisis at some time. Some debt problems are easy to solve, but others need professional assistance. The best way to deal with your financial problems is to get control before they get out of hand. This booklet might help you determine whether or not you have a serious debt problem. It also provides suggestions for solving your difficulties and avoiding them in the future.

Box 8.5 Ten Things You Should Know About Bankruptcy

1. What is bankruptcy, and what are the benefits to the debtor?
Bankruptcy is a legal process, regulated by the *Bankruptcy and Insolvency Act*, by which you may be discharged from most of your debts. The purpose of the act is to permit an honest, but unfortunate, debtor to obtain a discharge from his or her debts, subject to reasonable conditions. Once you are legally bankrupt, you are required to perform specific duties as outlined in the act.

2. How does one become bankrupt?
First, you meet with a trustee in bankruptcy, who will assess your financial situation and explain other options available to you. If you decide to become bankrupt, the trustee will help you complete several forms, which you will have to sign. You are considered a bankrupt only when the trustee files these forms with the Official Receiver.

3. What happens to my property?
When you declare bankruptcy, your property is given to a trustee in bankruptcy, who then sells it and distributes the money among your creditors. Your unsecured creditors will not be able to take legal steps to recover their debts from you (such as seizing property or garnisheeing wages).
You do not have to assign to the trustee exempt property such as basic furniture, tools of trade, and, under certain circumstances, the GST credit payments. Exempt properties will vary from province to province. Your trustee can tell you what these are.

4. What kinds of forms will I have to sign?
You will have to sign at least two forms. One is an assignment, and the other is your *statement of affairs*. In the assignment, you state that you are handing over all of your property to the trustee for the benefit of your creditors. In the statement of affairs, you list your assets, liabilities, income, and expenses. In addition, you will have to answer several questions about your family, employment, and disposition of assets.

5. Does the bankruptcy affect my co-signers?
Your bankruptcy does not cancel the responsibility of anyone who has guaranteed or co-signed a loan on your behalf. For example, if your parent co-signed a loan for you, that parent would be liable to pay the loan in full, even if you decide to file for bankruptcy.

6. When is a bankrupt discharged?
There will be an automatic discharge for first-time bankrupts nine months after they became bankrupt unless the trustee recommends a discharge with conditions or the discharge is opposed by a creditor, the trustee, or the Superintendent of Bankruptcy.

7. What is the effect of a bankruptcy discharge?
The bankrupt is released of most debts. However, some debts are not released, among them an award for damages in respect of an assault; a claim for alimony, spousal, or child support; a debt arising out of fraud; any court fine; or debts or obligations for student loans when the bankruptcy occurs while the debtor is still a student or within 10 years after the bankrupt has ceased to be a student.

8. How does bankruptcy affect employment?
For the most part, bankruptcy should not affect your employment. However, there are some special cases. For example, you might have difficulty being bonded. Your trustee will be able to give you more information on other possible restrictions or prohibitions.

9. Is there anything I can do to improve my credit record?
Should you wish to improve your credit record after obtaining your discharge from bankruptcy, you could, for instance, contact your banker and request a meeting. For this meeting, you could bring your paycheque stubs, your budget, and your discharge papers. You could explain that you have obtained your

BANKRUPTCY

A legal process, regulated by the *Bankruptcy and Insolvency Act*, by which you may be discharged from most of your debts discharge and ask the banker how you can earn your way back to a good credit record.

10. Does it cost anything to go bankrupt?

Yes. There is a filing fee to be paid to the Superintendent of Bankruptcy. In addition, the trustee is entitled to be paid. These fees are prescribed by the Bankruptcy and Insolvency Rules.

Source: Industry Canada, *Dealing with Debt: A Consumer's Guide*, 2009. Online: http://www.ic.gc.ca/eic/site/bsf-osb.nsf/eng/br01861.html. Reproduced with the permission of the Minister of Public Works and Government Services, 2013.

In a Nutshell

There are three basic legal forms for your small business: sole proprietorship, partnership, and corporation (limited company). You can run a business as a sole proprietorship with a minimum of difficulty. You might need only a city licence, a resale licence, and a business name. If you use a business name other than your own, you will probably need to register the name with your provincial government. Be careful, however—this might not give you exclusive rights to use the name.

The legal paperwork for a partnership is a little more involved. It might be possible to form a partnership with a handshake, but we wouldn't advise it. Get a lawyer, and have a partnership agreement drawn up before you start. There are good skill-related reasons for forming a partnership. Let's say you're an inventor; you need a partner who can manage and sell. Let's say you're good at marketing; you need a partner who can run the office and keep the books. You might also form a partnership because you need the financial capital. Remember, however, these are the only two good reasons for forming a partnership: to provide skills and money. At least one of these needs must be met, or you're asking for trouble. For example, friendship is not a good enough reason for a partnership arrangement.

Forming a limited company or corporation takes the most paperwork and costs the most money. However, it gives you the most flexibility, as well as a shield in case your business hurts someone.

In this chapter, we also discussed the government red tape that will confront you when you start your business. We recommended that you seek some legal protection for your business name. We also emphasized the importance of using a lawyer and an accountant to help structure your business, prepare your will, and begin drafting a succession plan. Finally, we asked you to start thinking about some of the legal concerns arising from bankruptcy.

Key Terms

bankruptcy	partnership
buy-sell option	patent
cooperative	shareholders agreement
copyright	shotgun clause
corporation	social entrepreneurship
dividend	sole proprietorship
general partnership	succession planning
limited partnership	trade-mark
nonprofit organization (NPO)	

Think Points for Success

✓ Know the advantages and disadvantages of the basic legal forms when you establish your business.
✓ Get a lawyer and a partnership agreement drawn up before you form a partnership.
✓ Incorporation can help limit your liability.
✓ Protect your business name, and do a NUANS search to make sure you have not infringed on another business's name or trade-mark.
✓ Get a will, and start thinking about a succession plan.

Action Steps

ACTION STEP 39

Do some secondary research on corporations.

Before you take any action with legal forms, you need a lot of information and professional advice.

We suggest you begin by logging onto the Internet. If you prefer hard copy, go to the library or the resource centre of a college or university. You can also check the bookstores; handbooks on incorporation are helpful.

Once you get familiar with the broad concepts, you might want to do some specific research of companies in your industry. Write to the companies, or check out their websites. Remember that a cooperative is an option. You might also want to talk to a few small business owners you know. Ask for their opinion. What kind of structure would they suggest, and why?

While you are doing this research, remember to keep looking around with new eyes.

ACTION STEP 40

Navigate an online tutorial on patent applications.

Suppose that you're an inventor and you want to protect your invention. Visit the following page on the CIPO website:

Your Patent Application: http://www.cipo.ic.gc.ca/eic/site/cipointernet-internetopic.nsf/eng/wr01398.html

This tutorial will help you learn how to prepare a patent application and give you general information about patents and the patent process in Canada. It also explains how you can apply for a patent in another country.

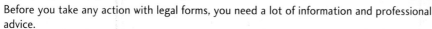

ACTION STEP 41

Take a lawyer and an accountant to lunch.

Canvass your business contacts for the names of three to five lawyers and accountants with experience in forming small business corporations and partnerships. If possible, concentrate on those who have worked in your industry.

The first thing you're looking for are professional advisors you can get along with. Then look for experience in the world of small business. For example, a hot trial lawyer might have a lot of charisma, and your personal lawyer might know a lot about buying a house or drafting wills, but you want a nuts-and-bolts small business specialist who can save you time, pain, and money.

Prepare a list of questions. Find out about fees and costs. Compare the cost, for example, of having your lawyer write up a complex partnership buyout agreement with the cost of setting up a corporation. In the event of your death, what will happen to your estate? Can the lawyer and accountant help you think about your succession plans? Use some questions presented in this chapter to start you off in your discussion.

A good lawyer or accountant will offer you perspectives that will be helpful in the formation of your business. You may have to look awhile, and it may cost you some dollars up front, but there's no substitute for sound professional help.

Business Plan Building Block

LEGAL STRUCTURE

State the type of legal structure—proprietorship, partnership, corporation, or cooperative—you intend to institute for your business. List the reasons you chose this structure.

_____

_____

_____

_____

RED TAPE FILE

Set up a red tape file. Make a list of all the municipal, provincial, and federal regulations with which you will have to comply. Beside each regulation, write the contact telephone number, address, and other pertinent information.

Checklist Questions and Actions to Develop Your Business Plan

Legal Concerns

❑ Explain why you selected your legal form of ownership.

❑ Do you plan to protect your idea, product, or service by obtaining a patent or copyright and/or by registering a trade-mark?

❑ What professionals have you referenced in your business plan, and did you allow for the appropriate cost?

❑ What are the major legal risks for your industry, and how will you address them?

❑ Are you prepared for the legal red tape?

❑ Do you have a will and a succession plan?

Case Study 1: Your Pal, Steve

Case Background

I have to admit, the motor-sailor was my idea. I persuaded my partner, Steve Savitch, to buy a boat—actually it was a fancy, 14-metre rig called *The Ninja*—for the partnership. We could write off some of the payments as an expense, and it would do our company image a world of good.

Steve and I had been friends for a dozen years and partners in Savitch and Johnson, Business Consultants, for the past three. We'd done quite well, and each of us would clear more than $50,000 this year. I persuaded him we could afford this perk. Besides, my marketing instinct told me it could really help close a few deals.

About two months after we bought the boat—and had a lot of fun—a fellow who sells radar equipment called me. Seems Steve had bought $2,000 worth of goods, and this chap was wondering when he'd get paid. After I hung up the phone, my secretary buzzed me with Mary, Steve's wife, on the line wanting to know where Steve was.

I thought he was on a business trip with a few of our best clients. As it turned out, Steve had disappeared with *The Ninja*, and no one knew where. In the end, I got stung for all his business debts, including the payments on *The Ninja*.

The problem was that Steve and I never saw the need for having anything in writing. We were both men of good faith (or so I had thought). We had each pulled our weight in business, and we had balanced each other's skills. For the first time in 12 years, I made an appointment to talk to a lawyer. He just shook his head. "You should have come to me a lot sooner, Phil," he said. "A *lot* sooner. And while I am at it, Phil, you should also have been in close touch with a professional accountant. These e-business writeoffs you're talking about might not be acceptable according to the CRA."

Last week, when I was closing the place down and getting ready to go back to work for my old boss, I got a postcard from Tahiti. "Sorry partner," Steve wrote. "Didn't mean to run out on you, but it was the only way I could handle the home front. These things happen…. Your pal, Steve."

Case Study Questions and Activities

1. Partnership agreements
   a. What is a partnership agreement?
   b. Briefly explain the two basic types of partnership agreements. Would a partnership agreement necessarily have protected Phil from Steve's actions?
   c. What are the advantages and disadvantages of a partnership agreement? What was Phil's major reason for wanting to establish an unwritten partnership agreement as opposed to a corporation?
   d. Suppose that Phil had approached his lawyer to draft a written partnership agreement. List the major items that should be included in this agreement that might have protected Phil.

2. Corporate structures
   a. What would be the major advantages and disadvantages for Phil to have established a corporate structure?
   b. If Phil had established a corporate structure, would a shareholders agreement have been required by law?
   c. Would you have advised Phil to have a shareholders agreement? Why or why not?
   d. List five key issues a shareholders agreement should address. (Here, in addition to the text, you might want to link to "Shareholder Agreements": https://www.ic.gc.ca/eic/site/cd-dgc.nsf/eng/cs04849.html).
   e. Briefly explain the type of legal structure—a partnership or corporation—that would have provided Phil with the most protection against Steve's actions.

3. Cooperatives
   a. What are the major reasons for considering a cooperative legal structure? Would this legal form have been of benefit to Phil?

Case Study 2: It Was a Fatal Accident*

Case Background

George Lopez's best friend died unexpectedly. Lopez was furious! His friend had been hospitalized for a minor surgical procedure, and a healthcare worker accidentally brushed against a poorly attached intravenous (IV) line, disconnecting it and subsequently causing Lopez's friend's death.

*Adapted from the Canadian Intellectual Property Office (CIPO) website (http://www.cipo.ic.gc.ca/eic/site/cipointernet-internetopic.nsf/eng/Home).

When Lopez heard the news by phone, he tried to throw the phone across the room, and it snapped back. Angrily, he inspected the cord and observed that a simple "click lock" attached it. If only his friend's IV tube had been attached by such a "click lock," his friend would still be alive. Within weeks, Lopez designed a workable prototype of an "IV click lock."

Today his IV click lock has become the world standard for IV delivery because George Lopez protected his idea.

More information on this invention and Lopez's successful business can be found by clicking onto the ICU Medical Incorporated home page (http://www.icumed.com/).

Case Study Questions and Activities

1. Patents, copyrights, and trade-marks are the three major forms of intellectual property that can be protected through federal legislation.
   a. Briefly explain each of these three legal forms of protection.
   b. If George Lopez wanted to sell his "IV click lock" in both Canada and the United States, which form of intellectual property would you advise George to use to help protect his inventive idea?
   c. Click on the Canadian Intellectual Property Office (CIPO) website. If you wanted to patent your idea, briefly describe the steps you would have to take to patent a new product or service.

Notes

1. Much of the research for this section was conducted on the Industry Canada website, http://www.ic.gc.ca/eic/site/icgc.nsf/eng/home?OpenDocument.
2. "The Value of Shotgun Clauses in Partnership Agreements!" Casual Articles website, http://www.casualarticles.com/article/17685/casualarticles-The-Value-of-Shotgun-Clauses-in-Partnership-Agreements.html.
3. Industry Canada, Corporations Canada, *Guide to Federal Incorporation*, http://www.ic.gc.ca/eic/site/cd-dgc.nsf/eng/h_cs04839.html.
4. See the Canadian Co-operative Association, http://www.coopscanada.coop/.
5. "Non-profit Organizations," Canada Revenue Agency, http://www.cra-arc.gc.ca/tx/nnprft/menu-eng.html.
6. Interview, November 2009.
7. "Non-profit Organizations," Canada Revenue Agency, http://www.cra-arc.gc.ca/chrts-gvng/chrts/pplyng/menu-eng.html.
8. Charitable purposes are relief of poverty, advancement of religion, advancement of education, and other purposes beneficial to the community not falling under any of the other three categories. These four "heads" of charity were first identified by Lord Macnaghten in the English House of Lords case of *Commissioners for Special Purposes of Income Tax v Pemsel* [1891] A.C. 531 (H.L.).
9. The definition of *nonprofit organization* in the *Income Tax Act* specifically states that a nonprofit organization cannot be a charity. See *Income Tax Act*, R.S.C. 1985, c. 1 (5th Supp.), ss. 149(1)(l).
10. The term *qualified donee* is defined in the *Income Tax Act*.
11. For more information about nonprofit organizations, including filing requirements, see Canada Revenue Agency's (CRA) website at http://www.cra-arc.gc.ca/formspubs/tpcs/nn_prft-eng.html.
12. Kimberley A. Cunnington-Taylor, *The Not-for-Profit Corporation: What Is It?* http://www.cunnington-taylor.ca/images/pdfs/nfp_corp_july_2008.pdf.
13. Some more important points regarding the changes represented by the *Corporate Not-for-profit Corporations Act* can be found at this site: http://www.cunnington-taylor.ca/images/pdfs/bill_c-4_july_2009.pdf.
14. For example, the CRA website includes all kinds of information about nonprofit organizations and charities. This website is a very useful resource tool that future social

entrepreneurs should take advantage of to help them understand the nonprofit and charitable sector, at least from the tax perspective.

15. Industry Canada, http://www.nuans.com/.

16. Adapted from the Canadian Intellectual Property Office (CIPO) website, http://www.cipo.ic.gc.ca/eic/site/cipointernet-internetopic.nsf/eng/Home.

17. David Chilton, *The Wealthy Barber* (Toronto: Stoddart Publishing, 1989), p. 67.

18. Ibid., pp. 69–71.

19. Adriane B. Miller, "Succession Planning," Fambiz.com, http://www.fambiz.com/template.cfm?Article=Succession/loyola-591.html&Keywords=succession%20planning&Button=fambiz (accessed May 4, 2010).

Risk Management Issues

Chapter 9 will help you manage risk and prepare parts H, I, and J of your Business Plan, the Financial Section.

Dwight Smith/Shutterstock.com

LEARNING OPPORTUNITIES

After reading this chapter, you should be able to

- develop a Plan B to minimize the ill effects of unfortunate surprises;
- determine your insurance needs and costs;
- draft a health and safety policy and action plan;
- develop a list of precautions that will help minimize the opportunities for employee dishonesty;
- prepare a 12-month start-up checklist.

ACTION STEP PREVIEW

42. Prepare your Plan B checklist.
43. Calculate your insurance needs and costs.
44. Draft a health and safety policy and action plan.

YOU NEED AT LEAST ONE PLAN B

Patty Fisher really liked kids, so she joined forces with her husband and made plans to open a daycare centre. They secured a bank loan and bought a property in a neighbourhood of young families with an average of 2.5 children. They spent weekends painting and fixing up the place. They worked hard, but it was fun, and it made them feel a part of something warm and cozy.

About three weeks before their opening, they called the light and power people to ask them to turn on the lights. "Sure thing," said sales manager Don Farthington. "Just send us a cheque for $700, and the lights will be on in a jiffy."

"What?" Fisher asked. "Did you say $700?" She and her husband had about $800 in reserve, but that was earmarked for emergencies.

"That's right. You're a new commercial customer with a good credit rating. That's the reason the figure's so low."

"You think $700 is low?" Fisher asked in disbelief.

"For your tonnage," he said, "it's right on the money."

"Tonnage? What tonnage?"

"Your air conditioner," Farthington said. "You have a five-ton unit on your roof."

"But we're not planning to run it!" Fisher said. "The breeze here is terrific. We don't need the air conditioner."

"Sorry, ma'am. Our policy is pretty clear. Sometimes we get three months' deposit, but for your business, we'll only require the two. Is there anything else I can help you with today?"

"No," Fisher said. "Absolutely nothing." As she hung up, she made a vow to take a good hard look at the daycare budget. They could not afford any more surprises like this.

Although a business plan is designed to demonstrate how the business will prosper, there is a need to demonstrate flexibility when things do not go exactly as planned. What can go wrong and what can be done to eliminate downside risk? When you interview successful entrepreneurs and ask them what surprises they had not anticipated when they started, they usually have quite a few. Almost always, you hear that it cost more and took longer than they had planned.

In the opening vignette, aspiring daycare operator Patty Fisher was badly shaken by an unexpected electricity charge. To protect yourself from such unpleasant surprises, you need at least one Plan B; we begin this chapter by showing you how to create one.

DEVELOPING A PLAN B

Reading the opening vignette, you might have wondered how Patty Fisher could have overlooked such an important detail. Remember that a budding entrepreneur is confronted with a formidable to-do list. That's why having at least one **Plan B**—an alternative strategy for bailing the business out of a tight spot created by some unforeseen or unfortunate situation—is a must before you open your doors. Box 9.1 presents a Plan B checklist that could help eliminate surprises, and Box 9.2, on page 243, provides some useful online resources.

PLAN B

An alternative strategy for bailing the business out of a tight spot created by some unforeseen or unfortunate situation

Box 9.1 Plan B Checklist

Here's a checklist of some obvious start-up concerns. Add to this list as you think of things.

1. **Advisors**
- Lawyer
- Banker
- Accountant/Bookkeeper
- Insurance agent
- Commercial real estate agent
- Mentor (advisory board)
- Consultants
- Suppliers
- Chamber of commerce
- Professional association
- Other organizations

2. **Organization**
- GST/HST registration (if necessary)
- PST registration
- DBA ("Doing business as" = business name)
- Partnership agreement
- Corporation
- Other

3. **Licences and Permits**
- Business licence
- Resale permit
- Department of health requirements
- Liquor licence
- Fire inspection permit
- Local building inspection
- Other

4. **Location**
- Lease review (lawyer)
- First and last months' rent (Rent might have to be paid while you are making improvements. Estimate time needed to do improvements.)
- Security deposit
- Leasehold improvements
- Insurance
- Security system
- Utilities, deposits, estimated monthly costs
- Electricity
- Gas
- Water
- Phone installation
- Other

(continued)

5. **Auto** (Consider new, used, leased.)
- Autos
  - New/Used
  - Lease/Purchase
- Trucks
  - New/Used
  - Lease/Purchase
- Insurance
- Maintenance, repairs

6. **Equipment**
- Computer
- Office
- Retail space
- Warehouse
- Manufacturing area
- Kitchen
- Dining area
- Communication
- Other

7. **Fixtures**
- Tables
- Chairs
- Desks
- File cabinets
- Workbenches
- Storage cabinets
- Display cases
- Lighting

8. **Supplies**
- Pencils and pens
- Notepaper and letterheads
- Tape
- Dictionary
- Calendar
- Appointment book
- Coffee, tea, soft drinks, bottled water
- And so on. Have you prepared a checklist of suppliers? (See Box 9.3.)

9. **Inventory**
- What are the minimum and maximum average inventory requirements you need on hand to do business on your first day?

10. **Advertising/Promotion**
- Signs
- Business cards
- Fliers/Brochures
- Displays
- Ad layouts and graphics

- Media (newspaper, radio, other) costs
- Trade show booths
- Other

11. **Banking**
- Chequing account
- Cheque charges
- Interest on account
- Chequing/Bookkeeping system
- Deposit box
- Savings/Chequing account
- Credit
- Credit cards
- Personal lines of credit or letter of credit
- Loans and interests
- Credit from suppliers or vendors

12. **Employees**
- Application/Employment forms completed (e.g., employer registration number from Canada Revenue Agency)
- Training program

Box 9.2 Online Resources

- **Checklists for Going into Business:** Canada Business (http://www.canadabusiness.ca/eng/) provides business support ranging from business information through advice, counselling, and workshops. The site provides questions and worksheets to help you think through what you'll need to know and do. Here are two examples:
- **Checklists and Guides for Starting a Business:** http://www.canadabusiness.ca/eng/page/2850/
- **Start-up Checklist:** http://www.canadabusiness.ca/eng/page/2749/
- *Guide for Canadian Small Businesses,* Canada Revenue Agency: http://www.cra-arc.gc.ca/E/pub/tg/rc4070/
- **Canadian Innovation Centre:** http://innovationcentre.ca/ Do you think you have an invention? You might want to check out this site. Ideas are evaluated, and advice is provided on costs, engineering, and the steps required to launch, position, and market a product. The Centre provides information for clients to help them manage the risks involved in bringing ideas to market.

Of course, we understand that there is a certain amount of risk in every decision that the owner of a small business makes. Risk is a fact of life. We encourage you to acknowledge risk and find ways to minimize its consequences. This is the key: While you cannot eliminate risk, you can take steps to minimize it. Here, we want you to be proactive and think about alternative strategies if your decisions don't pan out. For example, what happens if your computer crashes? What is your Plan B to back up important information? Too many small businesses suffer because they did not back up their data regularly. We might also add here that some entrepreneurs we know have benefited from

> ### Box 9.3   Checklist of Suppliers
>
> - Can you make a list of every item of inventory and all operating supplies needed?
> - Do you know the quantity, quality, technical specifications, and price ranges desired?
> - Do you know the name and location of each potential source of supply?
> - Do you know the price ranges available for each product from each supplier?
> - Do you know about the delivery schedules for each supplier?
> - Do you know the sales terms of each supplier?
> - Do you know the credit terms of each supplier?
> - Do you know the financial condition of each supplier?
> - Is there a risk of shortage for any critical materials or merchandise?
> - Are you aware of which suppliers have an advantage relative to transportation costs?
> - Will the price available allow you to achieve an adequate markup?
>
> Source: Business Infosource Canada—Saskatchewan Business Service Centre, "Feasibility Checklist for Starting a Small Business." http://www.enterprisesaskatchewan.ca/feasibility. Reproduced by permission of the Government of Saskatchewan.

the availability of "prepaid" legal services. They pay a certain monthly fee for legal advice and a select number of services (see, for example, LegalShield Legal Service: http://www.legalshield.com/corp/).

It is important for an entrepreneur to think in terms of Plan B. Just taking the time to think about the "what ifs" can help you be prepared for what comes.

If you get into the habit of making lists, doing mind maps, and writing everything down in your 24/7 Adventure Notebook, you'll improve your chances of surviving in small business. Action Step 42 will also help you anticipate potential surprises.

ACTION STEP 42

Prepare your Plan B checklist.
(p. 256)

INSURANCE PLANNING

If you plan on going into business for yourself, you will likely need some sort of insurance. (Types of business insurance are identified in Box 9.4.) If you operate a home-based business, you will probably need extra insurance as well; in most cases, basic homeowners' insurance will not cover your business needs (see Box 9.5, on page 246). You must make sure that all vehicles are insured for business purposes. In calculating your insurance needs, consider all the insurable risks faced by your business. We emphasize, however, you can never be insured for a bad management decision—and that's why you have to have your Plan B.

In general, the following risks can be covered by insurance if you have followed the law:

- Personal injury to employees and the general public. Some retail stores have become targets for "slip and fall" claims. Certain businesses have higher personal injury claims, and you need to protect accordingly.
- Employment practices such as hiring, firing, sexual discrimination, and libel.
- Loss to the business caused by the death or disability of key employees or the owner—an essential coverage needed to protect your business.
- Loss or damage of property—including merchandise, supplies, fixtures, and building. A standard fire insurance policy pays the policyholder only for those losses directly caused by fire. When dealing with your insurance agent, make sure that you understand your policy thoroughly. Keep asking until you do.

Box 9.4   Types of Business Insurance

As an entrepreneur, you can purchase insurance to cover almost any risk. Each of the following types of business insurance protects you from a different type of financial loss.

1. **Fire and general property insurance** protects against fire loss, vandalism, hail, and wind damage.
2. **Consequential loss insurance** covers loss of earnings or extra expenses when business is interrupted because of fire or other catastrophe.
3. **Public liability insurance** covers injury to the public, such as customer or pedestrian injury claims.
4. **Business interruption insurance** provides coverage in case the business is unable to continue as before.
5. **Crime insurance** protects against losses resulting from burglary, robbery, and so forth.
6. Two main kinds of bonds apply to small business owners: **fidelity bonds**, which provide insurance coverage from employee theft; and **completion bonds**, which provide insurance coverage to ensure that work on a contract is competed as agreed.
7. **Malpractice insurance** covers against claims from clients who suffer damages as a result of services that you perform.
8. **Errors and omissions insurance** covers against claims from clients who suffer from injury or loss because of errors you made, things you should have done but failed to do, or warnings you failed to supply.
9. **Employment practices liability insurance (EPLI)** covers against claims from employees for employment practices: sexual harassment, wrongful discharge, discrimination, breach of contract, libel, and so on.
10. **Key employee insurance** covers the life, death, dismemberment, or physical disability of owner(s) or key employee(s).
11. **Product liability insurance** covers injury to the public, such as customer use or misuse of products.
12. **Disability (long-term) and critical illness insurance** covers owners and employees against disability and serious illness and usually allows for payments to be continued during rehabilitation. Note that disability/critical illness for an owner is a much greater risk than death, and few owners insure themselves adequately.
13. **Life and supplemental health insurance** may be provided for employees.
14. **Extra equipment insurance** applies to specialized equipment not covered in standard policies.
15. **Directors' and officers' liability insurance** is desirable for protecting directors and officers when company stock is held by outside investors.
16. **Auto insurance** should be adequate. A business can be liable for injuries and property damage caused by employees operating their own or someone else's vehicle while on company business. The company might have some protection under the employees' liability policy, but the limits are probably inadequate. If employees use their vehicles while on company business, obtain non-ownership liability insurance.
17. **Life and disability insurance** provides coverage in the event of a serious disability or death. You will need "key employee" insurance to cover the financial obligations of the business. Note that many financial institutions will require you to have life and disability insurance as a condition of your loan.

FIDELITY BONDS

Insurance that protects an employer against employee dishonesty

COMPLETION BONDS

Insurance coverage to ensure that work on a contract is completed as agreed

Box 9.5 How Do I Insure My Home Business?

If you're running a business from your home, you might not have enough insurance to protect your business equipment. A typical homeowner's policy provides only $2,500 coverage for business equipment, which is usually not enough to cover all of your business property. You might also need coverage for liability and lost income. Insurance companies differ considerably in the types of business operations they will cover under the various options they offer. It's wise to shop around for coverage options as well as price.

When insuring your home business, consider

- business property (desks, computer, etc),
- theft,
- business continuation,
- liability (coverage for bodily injury arising from your home business),
- supplementary insurance,
- auto insurance.

If you are using your car for business activities—transporting supplies or products, or visiting customers—you need to make certain that your automobile insurance will protect you from accidents that might occur while you're on business.

In addition to your auto insurance, you have three basic types of home protection policies to choose from—depending on the nature of your business and the insurance company you buy it from.

1. Homeowner's Policy Endorsement

You might be able to add a simple endorsement to your existing homeowner's policy to double your standard coverage for business equipment such as computers. For as little as $25, you can raise the policy limits from $2,500 to $5,000. Some insurance companies will allow you to increase your coverage up to $10,000 in increments of $2,500.

We also strongly advise that you buy homeowner's liability endorsement. You need liability coverage in case clients or delivery people get hurt on your premises. They might trip and fall down your front steps, for example, and sue you for failure to keep the steps in a safe condition.

The homeowner's liability endorsement is typically available only to businesses that have few business-related visitors, such as writers. But some insurers will provide this kind of endorsement to piano teachers, for example, depending on the number of students. These types of endorsements are available, but they vary, so you should shop around.

2. In-Home Business Policy/Program

An in-home business policy provides more comprehensive coverage for business equipment and liability than a homeowner's policy endorsement. These policies, which may also be called "in-home business endorsements," vary significantly depending on the insurer.

In addition to protection for your business property, most policies will reimburse you for the loss of important papers and records, accounts receivable, and off-site business property. Some will pay for the income you lose (business interruption) in the event that your home is so badly damaged by a fire or other disaster that it can't be used for a while. They'll also pay for the extra expense of operating out of a temporary location.

Some in-home business policies allow a certain number of full-time employees, usually up to three. The policies also generally include broader liability insurance for higher amounts of coverage and may offer protection against lawsuits for injuries caused by the products or services you offer, for example.

In-home business policies are available from homeowners insurance companies and specialty insurers that sell stand-alone in-home business policies. In other words, you don't have to purchase your homeowners insurance from the latter.

3. Business Owners Policy (BOP)

Created specifically for small to-mid-size businesses, this policy is an excellent solution if your home-based business operates in more than one location. A BOP, like the in-home business policy, covers business property and equipment, loss of income, extra expense, and liability. However, these coverages are on a much broader scale than the in-home business policy.

A BOP doesn't include workers' compensation, health or disability insurance, or auto insurance.

- Loss of income resulting from interruption of business caused by damage to the firm's operating assets (through storms, natural disasters, electrical blackouts).

Other indirect losses, known as consequential losses, might be even more important to your company's welfare. They include

- extra expenses incurred when obtaining temporary quarters;
- loss of rental income on buildings damaged or destroyed by fire, if you are a landlord;
- loss of facility use;
- continuing expenses after a fire—for example, salaries, rents paid in advance, and interest obligations;
- loss of customer base.

You can protect yourself against consequential losses by obtaining business interruption insurance (see Box 9.4).

What type or types of insurance should you carry, and how much coverage should you have? To answer these questions, consider

- the size of any potential loss,
- the probability of loss,
- the resources available to meet a loss if one occurs,
- the probability of lawsuits (some industries and areas are heavily targeted).

If a particular loss would force you or your company into bankruptcy or cause serious financial damage, recognize the risk, and purchase insurance to help protect your assets. Losses that occur with predictable frequency, such as shoplifting and bad debts, can usually be absorbed by the business and are often budgeted as part of the normal cost of doing business; the cost of the loss should be incorporated into the price. Where probability of loss is high, a more effective method of controlling the loss is to adopt appropriate precautionary measures and purchase better-than-adequate insurance. The key to purchasing insurance (and all risk management issues) is simple: *Do not risk more than you can tolerate losing.*

Action Step 43 and the insurance planning worksheet in Table 9.1 and will help you calculate your insurance needs and costs.

In addition to business insurance, you will likely need the advice of a business insurance professional, who will probably not be the same person who brokered your homeowner and auto policies. We suggest you network your way to a good business insurance agent—the same way you select a lawyer. It is also a good idea to ask someone you know in your industry to recommend a broker. You will want an agent who understands your business, product liability, errors and omissions, bonding, and burglary coverage, as well as health, fire, life, and key employee insurance.

ACTION STEP 43

Calculate your insurance needs and costs. (p. 256)

Table 9.1   Insurance Planning Worksheet

Required Insurance

Types	Yes	No	Annual Cost ($)
1. Personal liability	❑	❑	—.——
2. General and public liability	❑	❑	—.——
3. Product liability	❑	❑	—.——
4. Vehicle	❑	❑	—.——
5. Errors and omissions liability	❑	❑	—.——
6. Malpractice liability	❑	❑	—.——
7. Key employee insurance	❑	❑	—.——
8. Directors and officers	❑	❑	—.——
9. Life insurance	❑	❑	—.——
10. Health	❑	❑	—.——
11. Crime insurance	❑	❑	—.——
12. Business interruption	❑	❑	—.——
13. Extra equipment	❑	❑	—.——
14. Consequential loss	❑	❑	—.——
15. Employment practices liability insurance (EPLI)	❑	❑	—.——
16. Fire and theft	❑	❑	—.——
17. Business loan	❑	❑	—.——
18. Personal disability and critical illness	❑	❑	—.——
19. Bonds (fidelity, surety)	❑	❑	—.——
20. Home	❑	❑	—.——
21. Other	❑	❑	—.——
Total Annual Cost			

Source: Reprinted by permission of the Insurance Information Institute (http://www.iii.org).

Insurance companies frequently put together packages for particular types of businesses, such as retail, wholesale, and service. Also explore group rates through your trade association or your local chamber of commerce. Most chambers of commerce offer a small business insurance package. Joining a group insurance program can save you a lot of money.

Remember that insurance is only one of the options to reduce risk—and in some cases, it should be considered the last resort. Insurance can reimburse you only for unintentional, unforeseen, and uncontrollable losses, not for everyday business risks. Other options include eliminating the risk with a Plan B (as we discussed above), assuming it, or transferring it to someone else.

As a final note, we want to emphasize that many small business owners ignore the need for a shareholders or partnership agreement with a buy-sell option (as we discussed in Chapter 8), or they put off having a will drawn up. The few hundred dollars you might spend on professional fees to draw up necessary protective legal agreements is probably one of the best investments you and your associates will ever make.

WORKPLACE HEALTH AND SAFETY

Why worry about safety? Simply because, besides the incalculable cost of pain and grief, there are high monetary costs attached to workplace accidents. These costs can include the inability to meet your obligations to customers, wages paid to sick and disabled workers, wages paid to substitute employees, damaged equipment repair costs, insurance claims, workers' compensation, and administrative and record-keeping costs. Both humanitarian desires and economic good sense have encouraged employers to create and maintain safer and healthier working conditions.

According to the Canadian Centre for Occupational Health and Safety (CCOHS), it is estimated that one worker out of 16 suffers an injury at the workplace. This statistic translates into one injury every nine seconds. In Canada, between 1998 and 2008, almost one million occupational injury claims were reported by provincial workers' compensation boards. In addition, 355,318 applications were accepted for compensation for loss of wages. In 2008, worker's compensation boards across Canada paid out approximately $7.7 billion in benefits for compensation. When you weigh in the indirect costs, the annual cost of occupational injuries to the Canadian economy is estimated to be close to $19 billion.[1]

Occupational health and safety (OH&S) legislation in Canada outlines the general rights and responsibilities of the employer, the supervisor, and the worker. As a general rule, the legislation applies to all workers performing work for an employer. Exactly who is responsible for what varies by jurisdiction and by workplace. However, the basic guiding principle is that, if a worker is injured in the course of performing work for the employer, the employer might be held liable.

There are two basic levels of OH&S legislation: federal and provincial. The federal government and the 10 provinces and three territories each have OH&S legislation—which makes this issue complicated and sometimes confusing. Federal OH&S legislation is governed by the *Canada Labour Code*, Part II. This legislation affects private and public sector workers in the federal jurisdiction, which includes the following businesses and enterprises:

- the public service;
- Crown corporations;
- international and interprovincial industries, including air, rail, roads, pipelines, banking, broadcasting, shipping and ports, and telecommunications.

If you think your business might be governed by federal legislation, visit the Occupational Health and Safety website of the Department of Human Resources and Social Development (http://www.hrsdc.gc.ca/eng/labour/employment_standards/regulated.shtml).

For the vast majority of small and medium-size businesses, OH&S is governed by provincial law. In each province or territory, an OH&S Act normally applies to all workplaces in that region (http://www.ccohs.ca/oshanswers/legisl/intro.html). Usually, a department of labour or ministry is responsible for OH&S; in some jurisdictions, however, occupational health and safety is the responsibility

> ### Box 9.6 Health and Safety Regulations
>
> - **Human Resources and Skills Development Canada (HRSDC):** http://www. hrsdc.gc.ca/eng/labour/health_safety/overview.shtml—Learn about occupational health and safety requirements for businesses that are set forth in Part II of the *Canada Labour Code*.
> - **Canadian Centre for Occupational Health and Safety (CCOHS):** http:// www.ccohs.ca—Learn about provincial/territorial OH&S legislative requirements, employer and employee responsibilities, joint health and safety committees, workplace hazardous materials, and due diligence.
> - **Workers' Compensation.** Don't start your business until you have checked out your health and safety responsibilities. For small business, laws relating to safety are mainly a responsibility of the provinces or territories. Learn about your safety rights and those of your employees'. Go to the Canada Business site at http://www.canadabusiness.ca/eng/page/3408/ and search for the Worker's Compensation and Workplace Safety site for your province or territory.

of the workers' compensation board or commission. To find out exactly what your responsibilities are, you should consult the relevant legislation and government department or agency. Information on OH&S legislative requirements for each province/territory, along with contact sources, is provided on the CCOHS website at http://www.ccohs.ca (see also Box 9.6). In this section, we will cover four basic elements of OH&S legislative responsibilities: government, employee, and employer responsibilities; joint health and safety committees; workplace hazardous materials; and due diligence.

OH&S GOVERNMENT, EMPLOYEE, AND EMPLOYER RESPONSIBILITIES

Workplace health and safety is everyone's responsibility. These basic responsibilities, rights, and conditions are well summarized at OH&S Legislation in Canada—Basic Responsibilities: http://www.ccohs.ca/oshanswers/legisl/responsi. html#_1_2.

Here you will find basic answers to the following questions:
- What are the general responsibilities of governments?
- What are the employees' rights and responsibilities?
- What are the supervisor's responsibilities?
- What are the employer's responsibilities?
- What does legislation say about forming health and safety committees?
- What is the role of joint health and safety committees?
- What happens when there is a refusal for unsafe work?

JOINT HEALTH AND SAFETY COMMITTEES

JOINT HEALTH AND SAFETY COMMITTEE (JHSC)

A group consisting of labour and management representatives who meet on a regular basis to deal with health and safety issues

A **joint health and safety committee (JHSC)** is a group consisting of labour and management representatives who meet on a regular basis to deal with health and safety issues. In all Canadian jurisdictions, a JHSC is either mandatory or subject to ministerial decision. There are some exceptions, however, depending on the size of workforce, industry, accident record, or some combination of these factors. In smaller companies, for example, a health and safety representative is all that may be required. In some cases, a representative might not even be needed. The best way to proceed on this issue is to contact your OH&S government authority and legislation to make sure you know your legal responsibilities. We also suggest that you visit the CCOHS's Health and Safety Committees Web page: http://www.ccohs.ca/oshanswers/hsprograms/hscommittees/whatisa.html.

Here you will find answers to these questions:

- What is a joint health and safety committee?
- Who is responsible for establishing a joint health and safety committee?
- What does a joint health and safety committee do?
- Is a committee or a representative required?
- What are the sources of legislation regarding joint health and safety committees?
- When is a health and safety committee required?
- How many people are on the committee?
- Who are the committee members?

WORKPLACE HAZARDOUS MATERIALS

An important part of complying with OH&S workplace safety legislation is making sure that you deal appropriately with hazardous materials. The **Workplace Hazardous Materials Information System (WHMIS)** is a comprehensive national plan for providing information on the safe use of hazardous materials used in Canadian workplaces. By law, you must provide information on hazardous material via product labels, material safety data sheets (MSDS), and worker education programs. Information on WHMIS is provided on the CCOHS website at http://www.ccohs.ca/oshanswers/legisl/intro_whmis.html.

WORKPLACE HAZARDOUS MATERIALS INFORMATION SYSTEM (WHMIS)

A comprehensive national plan for providing information on the safe use of hazardous materials used in Canadian workplaces

Here you will find answers to these questions:

- What are the main parts of WHMIS?
- Why was WHMIS created?
- How was WHMIS developed?
- Is WHMIS a law?
- What are the duties under WHMIS?
- What are controlled products?
- Who enforces WHMIS?
- How do I get more information?

DUE DILIGENCE

In the context of occupational health and safety, **due diligence** is the level of care, judgment, and caution that an employer would reasonably be expected to provide in order to prevent injuries or accidents in the workplace. As an employer, you might be legally responsible for situations that are not specifically addressed in the OH&S legislation. Due diligence requires you to implement a plan to identify possible workplace hazards. Find out more about due diligence by visiting the CCOHS OH&S Legislation in Canada—Due Diligence Web page: http://www.ccohs.ca/oshanswers/legisl/diligence.html.

DUE DILIGENCE

The level of care, judgment, and caution that an employer would reasonably be expected to provide in order to prevent injuries or accidents in the workplace

Here you will find answers to these questions:

- Why does due diligence have special significance?
- How does an employer establish a due diligence program?
- What is an example of a due diligence checklist?

It's time to apply your understanding of workplace health and safety to your own business. Complete Action Step 44.

ACTION STEP 44

Draft a health and safety policy and action plan. (p. 256)

THEFT AND FRAUD PREVENTION

One of the nastiest surprises for a budding entrepreneur is employee dishonesty. You might think that because you're small, employees won't steal from you, but you're wrong. Small firms get hit more often than big ones. Here are some examples of employee dishonesty:

- credit card fraud;
- cheque deception;
- shoplifting;
- cash register vulnerability (e.g., employees shortchanging customers);
- bookkeeping theft;
- fraudulent refunds;
- counterfeit money;
- fitting room theft;
- burglary;
- robbery;
- theft of items from stockroom, layaway, and displays;
- computer fraud;
- manipulation of timecard data;
- illegal use of company time;
- fraudulent trip expense reports;
- "sweethearting" (discounts for family and friends).

You will not be able to eliminate theft and fraud, but there are a number of things you can do to reduce the risk. You can begin by establishing a code of conduct that clearly communicates the legal—among other—consequences of employee dishonesty. First, have your employees sign the code of conduct, and review it regularly. Next, establish a set of anti-theft/fraud rules and procedures (Box 9.7 will help you get started). If you suspect employee dishonesty, take prompt action.

Box 9.7   Anti-Theft/Fraud Measures

Here's a list of precautions that will help minimize the opportunities for employee theft and fraud.

- Sign all cheques yourself.
- Don't let any one employee handle all the aspects of bookkeeping.
- Insist that all bookkeeping be up to date and clear.
- Insist that your bookkeeper take scheduled vacations.
- Do regular physical inventories.
- Open all mail containing payments yourself.
- Track all cash transactions, and maintain a rolling annual cash flow on a monthly basis.
- Use numbered order forms, and don't tolerate missing slips.
- Insist on fidelity bonds for every employee who handles cash.
- Triple-check references on résumés and employment applications.
- If your business is a cash business, be there. Absentee owners, beware!
- Try to eliminate cash by accepting debit, credit, and "smart cards."

Learn more about protecting your business against common business crimes such as break-ins, fraud, employee theft, shoplifting, and vandalism. Link onto "What Crime Concerns You?" (http://crimeprevention.rutgers.edu/crimes.htm).

GETTING ADVICE

Think for a moment about where you are right now on your road to the market-place. You're more than halfway through this book. You've analyzed your skills and needs. You've probed your past and surveyed your friends. You've discovered what success means to you, plotted trends, and found your industry segment. You've profiled your target customer, studied the demographics, and developed a marketing strategy, including your promotion campaign. You've examined the prime and indirect competition. You've used your new eyes to find a great location. Now you need to find a small business guru or establish an advisory board and get some advice.

Where might you find a business guru or someone who should be on your advisory board? Well, what about your banker? Many people come to her or him for money—some of them carrying business plans, others not knowing a spread-sheet from a bedsheet. What about your accountant? What about the real estate broker who helped you with your search for a location? What about your business insurance specialist or a retired person who is very knowledgeable about your industry? An advisory board should be no more than three to five people. Have you contacted your local Canada Business office? You can even get advice online.

You can use your network to find other people who can help you. Show them your goals, objectives, and list of potential surprises, and ask for their advice. Ask them for their ideas about what other surprises might be in store for you. If one of those people gives you wonderful advice, consider putting that person on your advisory board or, if you're incorporated, on your board of directors. Remember, you can make anyone part of your team—your lawyer, accountant, small business professor, even a customer.

PLANNING AHEAD: 12-MONTH START-UP CHECKLIST

Think about the things you need to start action on 12 months before you open your door for business. For example, if you want to place an advertisement in the Yellow Pages, you might need to plan for it 10 months before the business opens or wait until the next edition comes out. Refer to Box 9.8 for an example of a 12-month checklist.

Box 9.8 Complete Your Own Start-up Appendix for Your Business Plan

1 year before launch

- Research the demand for your product or service from both primary and secondary sources.
- Read an environmental scan that addresses your project.
- Prepare a test market analysis, including an analysis of competition, price, and market share.
- Register your product or service.
- Write out your mission and goals, and start your business plan.
- Establish your form of ownership.
- Set up a system to record all costs (with invoices) relating to your start-up expenses. Travel costs, for example, should be documented. These are start-up costs that you will be able to deduct from your income when the business is in operation.

(continued)

10 months Before Launch

- Establish the strength of your equity base and need for venture capital.
- Identify your potential fixed and variable costs.
- Investigate all channels of distribution.
- Identify potential suppliers and establish prices.
- Investigate packaging, design, and potential promotion approach.
- Start your search for site location, which will be established three months before opening.
- If necessary, place an advertisement in the Yellow Pages (might need to be sooner depending on your start date and the new phone book release).
- Establish a good relationship with a banker and a lawyer.

8 months before launch

- Evaluate the results of the field test, and establish prices and a promotion strategy.
- Confirm suppliers and prices.
- Start getting confirmed prices on promotion material.
- Prepare an overall capital and operating budget.
- Prepare position descriptions for staff.
- Complete competitive analysis.
- Establish an advisory board.
- Investigate all external funding sources.
- Complete your business name search.

6 months before launch

- Start listing potential locations.
- Meet with your board of advisors to assess progress and problems.
- Clearly identify the target market for your promotion strategy.
- Order any fixed assets that require long delivery time.
- Establish leases where appropriate.
- Gain approval from the appropriate government bodies if producing a product that requires it.
- Establish a bank line of credit.
- If a home business, verify the city/township by-laws.
- Establish your website

5 months

- Finalize location.
- Prepare a design and schedule for leasehold improvements.
- Order signs.
- Order inventory and supplies.
- Contact telephone company for information about home office service options.

4 months

- Contact the leasehold improvements.
- Finalize packaging (including design).
- Finalize your promotional approach.
- Complete details for GST/HST with the Canada Revenue Agency.

3 months

- Sign for all utilities and hookups.
- Develop job descriptions, and place ads for staff.
- Take possession of location.
- Start renovations and install fixed assets.
- Meet with board of advisors.

2 months

- Select staff to start.
- Start marketing approach depending on nature of business, and finalize renovations.
- Start receiving fixed assets.

1 month

- Shelve and price inventory.
- Start staff as required.
- Train new staff.
- Get marketing campaign under way.
- Etc., etc., etc.—all you forgot about!

Launch

- Hold grand opening.
- Offer opening specials.

Note that almost all the work takes place before the official opening.

In a Nutshell

Start-up needs to go smoothly. What you don't need are expensive surprises that seriously set you and your business back. Before you open your doors, you need to have anticipated as many potential unpleasant surprises as possible and have a plan of action for each one of them. For example, how would you turn the following unwanted surprises into opportunities?

- Your landlord decides to evict your business.
- Your Yellow Pages ad is terrible.
- The customer that accounts for 75 percent of your business declares bankruptcy.

Expecting and planning for the unexpected can make the difference between life and death in business. As you seek to manage risk by considering your insurance, health and safety, and other needs, just remember two things: No one can anticipate everything, and setting up will probably cost more and take longer than your planning indicates.

Key Terms

completion bonds

due diligence

fidelity bonds

joint health and safety committee (JHSC)

Plan B

Workplace Hazardous Materials Information System (WHMIS)

Think Points for Success

✓ Listen to your competition so that you can change and improve.

✓ Create partnerships and outsource what you can.

✓ Be aware of closing dates for Yellow Pages advertising and other key media.

✓ Keep a time log that tells everyone (you, your founders, your key employees) how you are progressing on the plan.

✓ Make sure that your partners are as committed to the business as you are, and have a shareholders or partnership agreement.

✓ Keep an ongoing list of unfortunate surprises that could hurt your business. Write down how you can turn these surprises into opportunities.

✓ Always have a Plan B. And a Plan C. And a Plan D.

✓ Let some key customers in on your planning; let them see it with their own eyes. Go one step further—create a customer board of directors.

Action Steps

ACTION STEP 42

Prepare your Plan B checklist.

Now that you've got your business in mind, take a few minutes to brainstorm a list of surprises that could cost you money or time, and, if possible, how you can turn these problems into opportunities. Use the checklist in Box 9.1 (page 241) to help you get started.

Next, conduct some primary research. Talk to business people in your industry. If you are intending a street-side location, ask the neighbours what has happened to them and how they're doing in this location. Talk to vendors, suppliers, customers, and insurance brokers. If you plan to operate out of your home, ask the opinion of other home entrepreneurs.

When you finish your list, put a checkmark beside each item that will cost money.

ACTION STEP 43

Calculate your insurance needs and costs.

Network your way to a business insurance salesperson. Discuss your business plan with that person, and complete the insurance planning worksheet in Table 9.1 (see page 248). Calculate the cost of insuring your business for the first year (include in your estimate any upfront deposit). Remember, if you operate your business out of the home, you will need business insurance.

Keep your completed insurance worksheet on hand. It will help you estimate your cash flow in the next chapter.

ACTION STEP 44

Draft a health and safety policy and action plan.

To complete this Action Step, you will need answers to these questions:

• How will you encourage a healthy and safe working environment?

• What will your responsibilities as an owner be?

• Who will be responsible for safety?

• What will be the responsibilities of your employees?

• What are the rules and regulations for your business regarding workers' compensation?

• Who is your government OH&S inspector? What are his or her expectations?

- For assistance in developing your occupational health and safety policy and action plan, visit the following Web pages:
  - Guide to Writing an OH&S Policy Statement: http://www.ccohs.ca/oshanswers/hsprograms/osh_policy.html
  - The Worker's Compensation and Workplace Safety site for your province or territory: http://www.ccohs.ca/oshlinks/subject/workerscompensation.html

Business Plan Building Block

Develop a list of issues that are unpredictable and difficult to control. Complete Table 9.2, or create your own list.

Problem   Opportunity

_____

_____

_____

_____

_____

_____

INSURANCE NEEDS AND COSTS

Make a list of your insurance needs and costs as recorded on your insurance planning worksheet. (See Action Step 42 and Table 9.1.)

_____

_____

_____

_____

_____

BEGIN THE FIRST DRAFT OF YOUR START-UP APPENDIX

What things do you need to start action on before you open you doors for business? Return to Box 9.8 for an example of a 12-month checklist.

Checklist Questions and Actions to Develop Your Business Plan

Protecting Your Business from Costly Surprises

❑ What operational goals and objectives do you want to achieve?

❑ What risks and challenges does your business face, and how will you address each one?

❑ Develop a start-up schedule beginning 12 months from the launch, indicating all the activities you must undertake, along with costs related to start-up.

❑ What are the major cash drains in your business?

❑ What types of insurance and employee bonding will you have for your business?

❑ Do you have a health and safety policy in place?

Case Study: Your Business Idea

Case Background

By now you should have a fairly good idea of the kind of business you want to start. This first case study is about you and your business. We want you to be proactive and begin thinking about possible risks and health safety issues for your business idea.

Case Study Questions and Activities

1. Plan B solutions
   a. When survivors from any field or profession get together, they often like to share horror stories. In Table 9.2, we collected a few of these small business "surprises" that we have encountered over the years. We want you to brainstorm with friends or classmates. Come up with some preventive measures to help avoid these costly surprises for your business—before you start your business. What are your Plan B solutions? Complete column 2 of Table 9.2 and add this information to your 24/7 Adventure Notebook.
   b. After brainstorming your Plan B solutions in question 1a, think about your business idea. Complete Table 9.3 by listing five costly surprises that might arise, and provide your Plan B solutions. Be sure to put this in your 24/7 Adventure Notebook.

2. Health and safety

   As we note in the text, you should be thinking about workplace health and safety issues before you start your business.
   a. In relation to occupational health and safety, what is meant by the term *due diligence*?
   b. Draft a health and safety policy statement for your business. Action Step 44 will provide you with some guidance.
   c. Before you start your business, familiarize yourself with the techniques to protect you and your business against common business crimes, such as break-ins, fraud, employee theft, shoplifting, and vandalism. Review the list of precautions in Box 9.7 (page 252). Link onto "What Crime Concerns You?" (http://crimeprevention.rutgers.edu/crimes.htm). List 10 ways you plan to protect your business.

Table 9.2 Your Plan B Solutions

Surprise	Plan B Solutions?
Your computer crashes.	
Your landlord decides to evict you and your business.	
The newspaper doesn't run the ad for your grand opening.	
A staff member borrows your car and gets in an accident.	
You're operating your business out of your house. Your house is robbed, and you lose your computer and $2,000 in cash.	
An hour after you sign your name to guarantee the lease, your best friend and partner gets cold feet and pulls out; you have nothing in writing to protect you against your partner's change of heart.	

(continued)

Table 9.2 Continued

Surprise	Plan B Solutions?
For eight weeks, during your peak season, the city has the sidewalk in front of your store torn up; the noise is deafening.	
Your general contractor goes bankrupt.	
Your bookkeeper disappears with $100,000, your books, two trade secrets from the company safe, and your spouse.	
Your best salesperson is hired away by the competition.	
Your largest customer declares bankruptcy; the money owed you in receivables is 50 percent of your gross annual sales.	
The bank where you have your chequing account refuses to extend you a $20,000 line of credit to buy more inventory to supply a new customer.	

Table 9.3 Plan B Solutions

Possible Costly Surprises	Your Plan B Solutions
1.	
2.	
3.	
4.	
5.	

Note

1. Jaclyn Gilks and Ron Logan, *Occupational Injuries and Diseases in Canada, 1996–2008*, Human Resources and Skills Development Canada, http://publications/gc.ca/collections/collection_2011/rhdcc-hrsdc/HS21-4-2008-eng.pdf.

Chapter 10

The Power of Numbers

Chapter 10 will help you prepare parts H, I, and J of your Business Plan, the Financial Section. Financial statements and ratios are important measures of the financial health of your start-up business. Cash is the lifeblood of your business, and cash flow is a key financial statement.

Pressmaster/Shutterstock.com

LEARNING OPPORTUNITIES

After reading this chapter, you should be able to

- formulate a personal financial vision;
- test your financial fitness;
- assemble a team of financial advisors;
- estimate your start-up costs;
- create your own balance sheet;
- project monthly sales and propose a sales forecast;
- understand that cash is the lifeblood of your business;
- understand that bills are paid with cash, not profit;
- create a cash flow projection and a pro forma income statement;
- use ratios to measure the financial health of your business.

ACTION STEP PREVIEW

45. Put your personal financial vision in writing.
46. Assemble a team of financial advisors.
47. Estimate your start-up costs.
48. Draft a projected cash flow.
49. Draft a projected income statement—a moving picture of your business.

YOUR PERSONAL FINANCIAL VISION

Ray and Joan Stewart were worried about their financial future. It seemed that every time the Canadian economy hiccupped, large corporations would respond with massive layoff notices. Ever since the early 2000s, forty-something Ray had known that his job with a large technology company was no longer secure. Some of his coworkers had already received their walking papers, and Ray was expecting his own golden handshake any day now. His cash-starved employer would be sorely tempted to replace him and his $75,000 salary with an eager twenty-something content to earn $35,000 a year.

The Stewarts' financial worries did not end there. They were supporting two teenagers, both of whom planned to attend college or university in a few short years. Would they be able to afford the ever-rising tuition fees? As well, a couple of disastrous investments in the stock market had left them wondering if there would be anything besides the Canada Pension Plan to support them in their golden years.

The Stewarts resolved to take control of their financial future by starting their own business. It was a formidable challenge, and they knew they needed help. Fortunately, Joan had done some networking in her small business class, which had led her to Patrick, a part-time college professor and small business consultant specializing in start-ups.

"No more procrastinating," Joan said to Ray one evening. "We'll call Patrick and get our thoughts and fears out in the open. Let's see what he has to say."

They met with Patrick the following week. He listened carefully as they explained their financial situation and voiced their concerns. At the end of the meeting, he said: "If you feel comfortable with me, I will help you. But remember, there'll be a few road bumps—especially when it comes to finance. And by the way, you have just travelled smoothly over the first money hurdle. This first session is free.

"The major source of funding for any new business almost always comes from the owner(s). So the two of you must begin by getting your personal financial house in order. To begin your journey, I want both of you to begin a review of your financial fitness and to draft your personal financial vision. Here are some online sites to help get your started …"

In this chapter and the next, we will encourage you to move out into the world of finance. These financial chapters will help you understand the fundamentals of small business financing and set you up to complete your financial plan. We'll help you ensure that your personal finances are in order, set financial goals, get your financial plan together, and find out how much money you'll need for your first year of operation and beyond.

Once you are ready with the knowledge and information to create your financial plan, we will encourage you to visit the sites provided in Box 10.3 on page 283. Before you create your financial plan, however, you should familiarize yourself with the financial basics contained in this chapter and in Chapter 11—unless, of course, you have a strong financial background.

As we learned from Patrick in the opening vignette, and as will be reinforced in Chapter 11, odds are that you will be the major banker for your start-up business. This reality means that your financial plan will begin with you and your financial fitness and vision. We encourage you to review your financial fitness and formulate a clear financial vision. We will introduce you to the basic financial statements and the financial indicators a business needs to survive and grow.

YOUR FINANCIAL FITNESS

We want you to begin your journey to finance your business by reviewing your personal financial situation. After all, if your personal finances are not in order, how can you expect to ask other people to invest in you and your business? The first step is to check out your financial fitness. The E-Exercises and sources provided in Box 10.1 will help you do that. These are the Internet sites that Patrick told Ray and Joan Stewart about in the opening vignette to help them get started. When it comes time for you to create your financial statements in Chapter 11, we will ask you to come back and review this information.

ACTION STEP 45

Put your personal financial vision in writing. (p. 300)

FORMULATING A PERSONAL FINANCIAL VISION

For many budding entrepreneurs, the world of finance is daunting. Ray and Joan Stewart are typical, in that they did not have a clear picture of their financial future. They lacked the guidance and direction of a personal financial vision.

Box 10.1	E-Exercise: Check Out Your Financial Fitness

How Do You Manage Your Money?

Do you think you're doing a good job of managing your money? Or do you feel your spending is out of sync with your income? To see what kind of shape you're in, take a few minutes to fill out the Canadian Bankers Association's financial fitness test (found within a 2003 *Globe* article by Suzanne Wintrob, "Conquering That Mountain of Debt Starts with a Pencil"): http://investdb.theglobeandmail.com/servlet/ArticleNews/story/GAM/20031129/STDEBT29

Test Your Financial IQ

What is your aptitude for and interest in personal financial planning? Take the "Can You Manage Your Money Test?": http://www.wisebread.com/financial-iq-test-how-healthy-is-your-financial-plan.

Take the Money Quiz

Take a few moments to answer the questions on the Credit Counselling Canada site: http://www.creditcounsellingcanada.ca/Consolidation-Credit-Card.aspx.

Getting Help

If, after taking these online tests, you discover that you need help with personal financial planning, we suggest that you seek help **now**. Here are some sources to get you started.

- **Credit Counselling Canada:** http://www.creditcounsellingcanada.ca—Here you will find help to solve debt problems and learn to manage money and credit wisely.
- **Your Money Network (YMN):** http://yourmoney.cba.ca/—This one-stop online resource offers non-commercial financial information for youth. YMN hosts 54 partners that provide information from all parts of the financial world on more than 800 resource areas.
- **Managing Money:** http://www.cba.ca/en/consumer-information/41-saving-investing/57-managing-money—Managing Money offers a step-by-step approach to budgeting, which is the first step in assessing and managing the flow of your money. The site also looks at borrowing and credit use.

We can't tell you what your financial vision should be. That's up to you to determine. But here are examples of a personal financial vision:

- to be financially independent,
- to be able to afford to travel to other countries,
- to be able to afford a new home and the furniture to fill it,
- to have the financial ability to retire and smell the roses before the big 5-0.

Having a financial vision will not, of course, guarantee the success of your business venture, but it will provide you with some all-important guidance and direction. Some entrepreneurs want to strike it rich. Others, like the Stewarts, seek financial security. Still others set for themselves the goal of earning enough money to support an early retirement.

We want you to begin thinking about your financial future. What is your financial vision? We encourage you to complete Action Step 45 and put your financial vision in writing.

GETTING FINANCIAL ADVICE

The first step for the Stewarts was to bring Patrick on board. His job would be to guide them through the maze of small business financing. In Chapter 9, we stressed the importance of making a small business guru or an **advisory board** part of your risk management strategy. Your business guru could be anyone from a banker to a real estate broker to a knowledgeable retired person. To help you with the financial section of your business plan—and perhaps with the formulation of your personal financial vision as well—you will need to find advisors with expertise in a wide range of financial matters (e.g., forecasting, taxes, retirement planning, and bookkeeping). Action Step 46 and Table 10.1 will assist you with the task of assembling an advisory financial team. Good advice in finding a financial advisor can be found by linking onto the Financial Planning Standards Council, "Find a CFP Professional" link (https://www.fpsc.ca/user/login).

ADVISORY BOARD

A group of individuals with expertise in various areas who provide advice but are not normally associated with the day-to-day operations of your business

Table 10.1 List of Financial and Business Advisors

1. Mentor
2. Banker
3. Accountant/Bookkeeper
4. Investment advisor/Broker
5. Insurance agent(s)
6. Lawyer
7. Tax consultant
8. Personal or entrepreneurial coach
9. Real estate agent (if you have a business with a high potential for multiple locations)
10. Business broker (recommended if you are buying a business)
11. Franchise consultant/Broker (if considering a franchise)
For each type of advisor, include contact information such as the individual's name, address, telephone number, and email address

ESTIMATING YOUR START-UP COSTS

In small business, you don't just rent a location, throw open the doors, and begin to show a profit. The reality is, it takes time and planning for a start-up to make money. In fact, you're likely to discover that you need a good deal more start-up capital than you ever expected.

To find out how much start-up money you'll need, you will have to complete an application of funds table. You will have to estimate all your expenses before starting your business, then organize this information into an application of funds table. To begin, we suggest that you divide your **application of funds**, or start-up expenses, into four categories:

1. **general start-up costs**—including organizational costs, prepaid expenses, and inventory and office supplies;
2. **leasehold improvements**—such as carpeting, mirrors, and light fixtures;
3. **equipment**—for example, tables, chairs, and computer;
4. **cash reserve fund**—cash on hand before you start your business (a pool of uncommitted cash).

Your cash reserve fund is your cash and bank account balances immediately before you start your business. There is no set formula for estimating how big this cash reserve should be. The amount will depend on your financial needs, tolerance for risk, and type of business, among other things. However, one rule of thumb for calculating cash reserve is to estimate your major operating disbursements for three months. These would be expenses such as rent, salaries, and utility bills, as shown in our cash flow in Table 10.6 on pages 276–277. You can refine your estimate for cash reserve using a method such as that shown in Table 10.2 on page 266.

Table 10.3 on pages 266–267 provides further examples of the types of start-up expenses in the first three categories. Now we want you to complete Action Step 47.

THE OPENING BALANCE SHEET

A **balance sheet** is a snapshot of the financial health of your business—what it owns and what it owes—at a given point in time. This key financial statement is required by all bankers; as well, you will need a balance sheet even if you decide to finance your own business. There are two common types of balance sheets: (1) the opening balance sheet and (2) the closing balance sheet. We will discuss the closing balance sheet later in the chapter. Here we focus on the opening balance sheet.

An opening balance sheet is a snapshot of the financial position of your business shortly before you open your doors. Table 10.4 on page 268 provides an example of a typical opening balance sheet. The upper section of the balance sheet shows **assets**—the dollar value of what the business owns (equipment or inventory, for example). The lower section shows what the business owes, in the form of liabilities and equity. **Liabilities** are the dollar value of what the business owes to parties other than the owner. **Equity** is the dollar value of what the business owes the owner. Sometimes a balance sheet is arranged with assets shown on the left-hand side of the page and liabilities plus equity provided on the right.

Why does a balance sheet balance? The answer is quite simple. By definition,

$$\text{Assets (what the business owns)} = \text{Liabilities (what the business owes others)} + \text{Equity (what the business owes the owner)}$$

Now let's examine each of these balance sheet components more closely.

ACTION STEP 46

Assemble a team of financial advisors. (p. 301)

APPLICATION OF FUNDS

Expenses you pay before starting your business

ACTION STEP 47

Estimate your start-up costs. (p. 301)

BALANCE SHEET

A financial snapshot of what the business owns and what it owes at a given point in time

ASSETS

The dollar value of what the business owns

LIABILITIES

The dollar value of what the business owes to parties other than the owner

EQUITY

The dollar value of what the business owes the owner

Table 10.2 Estimating Cash Reserve (Cash and Bank Account Balances at Start-up)

Item	Your estimate of monthly expenses based on sales of $	Your estimate of how much cash you need to start your business (See column 3.)	What to put in column 2 (These figures are typical for one kind of business. You will have to decide how many months to allow for your business.)
	Column 1 ($)	Column 2 ($)	Column 3 ($)
Salary of owner-manager			2 × column 1
All other salaries and wages			3 × column 1
Rent			3 × column 1
Advertising			2 × column 1
Auto/Truck/Delivery expenses			3 × column 1
Supplies			3 × column 1
Phone/Fax/Internet			3 × column 1
Other utilities (heat/electricity)			3 × column 1
Insurance			2 × column 1
Business taxes			2 × column 1
Bank payments			3 × column 1
Maintenance			3 × column 1
Legal/Other professional fees			2 × column 1
Miscellaneous/Unexpected expenses			2 × column 1
Total cash required to cover start-up operations—your cash reserve funds			Add the rows above. This amount will be recorded in the current assets of your opening balance sheet (see Table 10.4)

Table 10.3 Application of Funds

1. General Start-up Costs		
• Organizational Costs		
— Legal		
— Accounting		
— Government registration		
— Franchise fees	$ _____	
• Prepaid Expenses		
— Insurance		
— Licences and permits		
— First and last months' rent		
— Security deposits		
— Utility deposits		
— Opening advertising and promotion	$ _____	

• Opening Inventory		
— Total inventory on hand in order to do business the first day	$ _____	$ _____
• Office Supplies		
— Office supplies on hand to do business the first day	$ _____	
Total General Start-up		
2. Leasehold Improvements		
— Carpeting		
— Mirrors, light fixtures		
— Electrical, plumbing		
— Signage		
— Washrooms		
— Air conditioning		
— Wallpaper and painting		
Total Leasehold and Improvements		$ _____
3. Equipment Costs		
— Tables, chairs, desk, work benches		
— Filing cabinets		
— Storage cabinets		
— Cell phone		
— Computer		
— Copier		
— Fax machine		
— Auto		
Total Equipment Costs		$ _____
4. Cash Reserve Fund		
— Total cash on hand immediately before the business opens. This estimate must be justified (see, for example, Table 10.2).		$ _____
Total Application of Funds		$ _____

ASSETS—WHAT THE BUSINESS OWNS

Assets are generally divided into three major categories: current assets, fixed assets, and other assets.

CURRENT ASSETS

Current assets are assets or holdings of a business that can be converted into cash or consumed in the production of income in a short period of time. Under accounting rules, the period of time is almost always within one year. Current assets are recorded in order of liquidity. As Table 10.4 shows, they include the following.

- **Cash.** This is your cash reserve from your application of funds table (Table 10.3). It is the cash the business has available in the business account or on hand immediately before you start your business. This definition of cash could also include marketable securities, such as Canada Savings Bonds.

CURRENT ASSETS

Assets or holdings of a business that can be converted into cash or consumed in the production of income in a short period of time (usually one year)

Table 10.4 Opening Balance Sheet (Date of Opening)

Assets

Current assets

1. Cash and marketable securities

2. Accounts receivable

3. Inventory/Office supplies

4. Prepaid expenses

5. Other current assets

6. **Total current assets**

Fixed assets

7. Equipment/Furniture/Fixtures

8. Leasehold improvements

9. Land/Buildings

10. Auto/Truck

11. Other fixed assets

12. **Total fixed assets**

Other assets

13. Organizational fees (legal, accounting, etc.)

14. **Total other assets**

15. **(6 + 12 + 14) TOTAL ASSETS**

Liabilities

Current liabilities (due within the next 12 months)

16. Accounts payable

17. Short-term loans

18. Long-term loans (current portion)

19. Other current liabilities

20. **Total current liabilities**

Long-term liabilities

21. Long-term loans (minus current portion)

22. Mortgages and liens payable

23. Loans from shareholders (if applicable)

24. Other long-term debt obligations

25. **Total long-term liabilities**

26. **(20 + 25) TOTAL LIABILITIES**

Equity

27. Cash—Owner's capital (if a proprietorship or partnership)—shares outstanding (if a corporation)

28. General start-up (organizational costs, etc.)

29. Equipment/material/labour (provide details)

30. **TOTAL EQUITY**

31. **(26 + 30) TOTAL LIABILITIES AND EQUITY**

- **Accounts receivable.** This amount is the total money owed to the business by its customers who have purchased goods and services on credit. On an opening balance sheet, the dollar value of accounts receivable would normally be zero, because you have yet to start your business.
- **Inventory/Office supplies.** Inventory is recorded as the dollar value of all the physical items you have for sale in the course of doing business or as the dollar value of the items you use while making your product. Office supplies are items such as paper, pencils, and computer supplies. They are things you will use up over the current (one-year) period in the course of selling your products or services. Depending on your type of business, you might want to categorize your inventory and supplies separately. If you have difficulty deciding if an item is a piece of equipment or an inventory/supply item, think of the former as lasting more than a year (and thus retaining some sort of value) and inventory/office supplies as lasting one year or less (and thus having no appreciable value after that point).
- **Prepaid expenses.** Before you open your business, you'll likely have to prepay your insurance and your first month's rent. Prepaid expenses are classified as current assets because they are considered as being consumed in the production of income. Some banks do not classify prepaid expenses as current assets, however. Obviously, it would be difficult for them to "cash in" your prepaid insurance if your business were to fail.
- **Other current assets.** This category includes any remaining current assets you might have that can be translated into cash within a year. As an example, you could have a note payable or a security you don't want to cash in just yet.

FIXED ASSETS

Fixed assets are the longer-term (more than one year) holdings of a business that are used to earn revenue or produce products or services. Fixed assets are not for sale in the normal course of doing business. As Table 10.4 shows, fixed assets include items such as

- equipment, furniture, and fixtures,
- leasehold improvements,
- land and buildings,
- autos and trucks,
- other fixed assets.

FIXED ASSETS
Longer-term (more than one year) holdings or assets of a business that are used to earn revenue or produce products or services

OTHER ASSETS

These are intangible assets that cannot be assigned a fixed value. Items in this category include franchise fees; organizational fees, such as government registrations; consultant fees; and pre–start-up legal and accounting fees.

LIABILITIES—WHAT THE BUSINESS OWES OTHERS

Liabilities are normally divided into two major categories: current liabilities and long-term liabilities. In some cases, the liabilities section of the balance sheet includes a category called "other long-term debt."

CURRENT LIABILITIES

CURRENT LIABILITIES

Outstanding debts or obligations that are expected to come due within one year of the date of the balance sheet

Current liabilities are outstanding debts or obligations that are expected to come due within one year of the date of the balance sheet. They include

- accounts payable (such as money you owe to suppliers);
- short-term loans (such as contracts or notes payable);
- long-term loans (current portion only);
- other current liabilities, such as line of credit or demand loans.

Let's say that you have negotiated with your bank manager a long-term loan of $35,000. Let's also assume that you have agreed to repay the loan by paying $5,000 per year. Part of this yearly payment—let's say $3,000 for the purposes of this example—will go to repay the amount you borrowed—that is, the $35,000. This payment is called the principal portion of a loan. The other part of your loan repayment, in this case $2,000, will be used to pay interest charges. The current portion of your long-term debt is the principal payment on your loan for the 12 months following the date of your opening balance sheet: this is the amount due on your long-term debt within the next year. Remember, the current portion *does not* include your interest payments.

LONG-TERM LIABILITIES

LONG-TERM LIABILITIES (DEFERRED LIABILITIES)

Debts or financial obligations that are due after one year

Long-term liabilities (deferred liabilities) are debts or financial obligations that are due after one year. They include long-term loans, mortgages and liens payable, and loans from shareholders (if you are incorporated). They should not be confused with the current portion of the long-term debt. In the previous example of the $35,000 loan, we calculated the current principal portion (due over the next year) of this long-term loan to be $3,000. If we subtract the current portion ($3,000) from the total loan ($35,000), we arrive at a long-term portion of $32,000. This amount is what's due after the first year.

During negotiations for a long-term loan, a financial institution might ask you to sign a demand note that gives the lender permission to "demand on notice" the full amount of your loan. Technically, a demand note should be recorded as a short-term loan (current liability), because your lender can ask you to pay the full amount of the loan at any time. Thus, if our $35,000 loan were a demand loan, it would be recorded as a current liability.

OTHER LONG-TERM DEBT

This optional category includes any other long-term obligations, such as an equipment loan, a note payable, or a long-term loan to a relative.

EQUITY—WHAT THE BUSINESS OWES THE OWNER

Equity is the dollar value of what the business owes the owner. In start-up situations, it usually refers to what you, the owner, invest in the business. Often, it is defined as the residual of total assets minus total liabilities. Equity is not necessarily your cash investment, however. If, for example, you were to invest your own equipment or inventory, you would record the dollar value of this investment as equity. You might even decide to do the architectural plans, plumbing, or electrical work yourself. This kind of labour or knowledge investment is often called "sweat equity." Some banks and other lending institutions do not consider sweat equity a true equity investment.

All we can say is, stick to your guns. The value of your work must be considered as equity—otherwise, your balance sheet won't balance.

KEY BALANCE SHEET RATIOS

In reviewing your balance sheet, your banker will do a few calculations involving some important ratios to determine the financial health of your business. In this section, we focus on two key ratios: liquidity ratios and solvency ratios. Online calculators for these ratios are provided in Box 10.5 on page 297.

LIQUIDITY RATIOS

Liquidity ratios show the number of dollars of liquid assets available to cover each dollar of current debt (or the ability to pay your short-term obligations). Alternatively, they measure the ability of a company to honour its short-term or current financial commitments. The two basic liquidity indicators are the current (or working capital) ratio and the quick (or acid test) ratio.

Current Ratio

The current (or working capital) ratio is calculated by dividing current assets by current liabilities:

$$\text{Current ratio} = \text{Current assets} \div \text{Current liabilities}$$

The higher the ratio, the greater the liquidity. As a rule of thumb, the ratio should be greater than 2. That is to say, your current assets should be double your current liabilities. This ratio is also a measure of your relative working capital because, by definition,

$$\text{Working capital} = \text{Current assets} - \text{Current liabilities}$$

Working capital is not necessarily cash. For example, current assets include inventory and prepaid expenses in addition to cash, whereas current liabilities include accounts payable and the current portion of the long-term debt. In other words, a business could have a relatively strong working capital position (that is, a working capital ratio of greater than 2) but have no cash. For this reason, you should also consider the quick or acid test ratio (discussed below) when evaluating your liquidity position.

Now refer to Table 10.5 for a moment. Start-up Inc.'s current ratio is $20,370 \div 33,000 = .62$. This ratio tells us that Start-up Inc. has a working capital problem and might have trouble meeting its debt obligations in the short term (throughout the first year). A bank is not likely to lend Start-up Inc. money until the company increases its current assets and/or reduces its current debts.

Quick Ratio

The quick (or acid test) ratio measures a company's ability to pay current debts by taking into account only the most liquid assets:

$$\text{Quick ratio} = \text{Most liquid assets} \div \text{Current liabilities}$$

Most liquid assets are usually defined as cash and marketable securities (e.g., Canada Savings Bonds and treasury bills) and, in some cases, accounts receivable. However, we strongly recommend that you include only cash and marketable securities. There is never any guarantee that you will collect your accounts receivable.

Table 10.5 Start-up Inc.

Opening Balance Sheet (Date of opening)

Assets	$	$	$
Current assets			
1. Cash and marketable securities	8,195		
2. Accounts receivable			
3. Inventory/Office supplies	2,600		
4. Prepaid expenses	9,575		
5. Other current assets			
6. **Total current assets**		20,370	
Fixed assets			
7. Equipment/Furniture/Fixtures	53,030		
8. Leasehold improvements	38,800		
9. Land/Buildings			
10. Auto/Truck			
11. Other fixed assets			
12. **Total fixed assets**		91,830	
Other assets			
13. Organizational fees (legal, accounting, etc.)	2,800		
14. **Total other assets**		2,800	
15. **(6 + 12 + 14) TOTAL ASSETS**			115,000
Liabilities			
Current liabilities (due within the next 12 months)			
16. **Long-term loans (current portion)**	**3,000**		
17. **Short-term loans**	**30,000**		
18. **Accounts payable**			
19. **Other current liabilities**			
20. **Total current liabilities**		**33,000**	
Long-term liabilities			
21. Long-term loans (minus current portion)	32,000		
22. Mortgages and liens payable			
23. Loans from shareholders (if applicable)			
24. Other long-term debt obligations			
25. **Total long-term liabilities**		32,000	
26. **(20 + 25) TOTAL LIABILITIES**			65,000
Equity			
27. Cash—Owners capital (if a proprietorship or partnership)—shares outstanding (if a corporation)	40,000		
28. General start-up (organizational costs, etc.)			
29. Equipment/Material/Labour (provide details)	10,000		
30. **TOTAL EQUITY**			50,000
31. **(26 + 30) TOTAL LIABILITIES AND EQUITY**			115,000

As a rule of thumb, analysts and financial institutions like to see a quick ratio that is greater than 1. Your opening cash should be able to cover your expected current liabilities over the first year of operation. As Table 10.5 shows, Start-up Inc.'s quick ratio is $8,195 ÷ 33,000 = .25. This ratio suggests that the company might not have enough cash to cover short-term financial obligations, such as its monthly payments to the bank.

SOLVENCY RATIOS

Solvency ratios measure the ability of a company to meet its long-term debt obligations. The higher the ratio, the higher the risk to the creditor or lender. The two standard solvency ratios are the proprietorship ratio and the debt-to-equity ratio.

Proprietorship Ratio

This ratio is calculated as follows:

Proprietorship ratio = Owner's investment ÷ Total assets

Banks and other lending institutions like to see a proprietorship ratio that is greater than .50. In other words, if they see that you own at least half the assets, they know that you, the owner, are committed. Start-up Inc.'s proprietorship ratio is $50,000 ÷ $115,000 = .43. It's a little below the recommended .50, so Start-up Inc. might be asked to increase the owner's investment or reduce its assets.

Debt-to-Equity Ratio

This ratio is calculated as follows:

Debt-to-equity ratio = Total liabilities (debt) ÷ Owner's equity

As a rule of thumb, the debt-to-equity ratio should be less than 1. Lenders or creditors like to see that you have sufficient owner's equity to meet all debts. Start-up Inc.'s debt-to-equity ratio—$65,000 ÷ 50,000 = 1.3—is such that the company would likely be asked by its lenders to reduce its debt or increase its equity.

CASH FLOW AND INCOME STATEMENT: IMPORTANT PROJECTIONS

A projected (pro forma) income statement tells you when you're going to make a profit on paper. A cash flow projection tells you whether you can pay the bills and when you'll have to visit the banker. Both the income statement and the cash flow projection are necessary for the survival of your business. Many experts have told us that the projected cash flow statement is the most important statement in your financial plan, and this is where we will begin this section.

CASH FLOW PROJECTION

A **projected (pro forma) cash flow** is a financial statement that helps you control the money that comes into your business (receipts) and the money that is spent (disbursements). The cash flow statement is a tool to help you control this money flow and thus avoid running out of cash. Normally, you should prepare a monthly cash flow for the first year, then a quarterly cash flow for the next two years.

PROJECTED (PRO FORMA) CASH FLOW

A financial statement that helps you control the money that comes into your business (receipts) and the money that is spent (disbursements)

The monthly cash flow of a business, DISCovery Books and Magazines, is shown in Table 10.6 (see pages 276–277). The Business Planning and Financial Forecasting site in Box 10.3 on page 283 provides a detailed, step-by-step discussion on how to create a monthly cash flow.

It's nice to watch paper profits, but you must also be alert to what is happening to real cash. Figure 10.1 shows the typical pattern of cash flows.

WHY IS A CASH FLOW PROJECTION SO IMPORTANT?

First and foremost, a cash flow statement provides an estimate of the amount of money required to finance day-to-day operations of a business. This process relates to what is called the **current asset conversion cycle**—the time, in days, it takes to purchase a product or materials, produce and sell an item, and then finally collect on that item. For example, suppose a business purchases $1,000 worth of raw materials at the beginning of the month. It takes one month to produce the product, one month to sell the product for $2,000, and one month to collect its cash from its customer. It has to put out $1,000 at the beginning but doesn't collect $2,000 for three months. The owners still need to pay the overhead expenses, such wages and rent in the interim. Without cash or prearranged access to credit, this business could go bankrupt before collection.

A cash flow also provides

- an outline to show you and the lender that you have enough cash to make your loan payments on time,

CURRENT ASSET CONVERSION CYCLE

The time, in days, it takes to purchase a product or materials, produce and sell an item, and then collect on that item

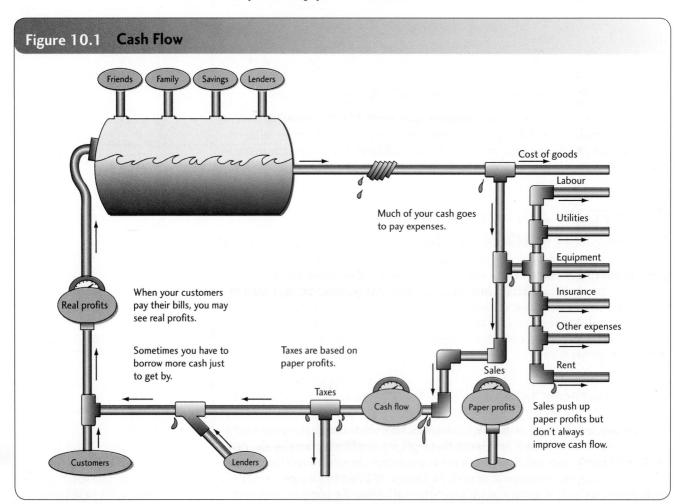

Figure 10.1 Cash Flow

- a format for planning the most effective use of your cash (cash management),
- a schedule of anticipated cash receipts,
- a schedule of priorities for the payment of accounts,
- a measure of the significance of unexpected changes in circumstances (e.g., reduction of sales and cost increases).

Make sure that you follow through on obtaining your cash receipts and paying accounts according to your schedule of priorities.

FIVE STEPS TO CREATING A START-UP CASH FLOW

STEP 1: CALCULATE YOUR OPENING BALANCE

In start-up situations, the first column of your cash flow should contain a record of all money invested and money spent before you begin operations. This first column (see Table 10.6, column 1) of your cash flow will contain the summary information based on the opening balance sheet and is used in start-up situations only. You will not require this column when it comes time to do a cash flow for your second year. You will notice, for example, for the start-up cash flow of DISCovery Books and Magazines, the total cash remaining at the end of the year (total column) is $27,395 (column 14, row 39). This number will become the "cash forward, previous month" (row 36) for the first month in the second year.

Here are some helpful hints for creating this first step in your cash flow statement.

Receipts

Equity ($80,000) is recorded in column 1, row (line) 10, and loans ($35,000) are recorded in row 11. The total cash in, or sources of funds ($115,000), is recorded in row 13. On your opening balance sheet, this would be the total of your equity and liabilities.

Disbursements

Total application of funds excluding cash reserve fund is recorded on line 32 ($105,000). If you have an opening balance sheet, this number would be the same as your total assets minus your cash and marketable securities. This "cash out" number, also recorded on line 34, represents everything you have paid for before you start your business.

Summary

Row 35 = row 13 ($115,000). Note as well that line 37 = line 35. There has been no money transferred from the previous month. Row 38 = row 34 ($105,000).

Line 39 ($10,000) is the cash your business has on hand immediately before starting your business. It is not the money or equity the owner invests into the business. It will be the cash reserve in the application of funds table or the cash (plus marketable securities) in your opening balance sheet. This number is now placed into the second column (month 1), line 36 ($10,000), of your cash flow. It becomes the cash you have to work with at the beginning of the first month.

Table 10.6 Monthly Cash Flow—DISCovery Books and Magazines Inc.

Step 1	Opening Balance	6% July	7% August	9% September	10% October	12% November	19% December	6.5% January	4.5% February	5% March	5% April	8% May	8% June	Total
Step 2														
1. SALES		9,000	10,500	13,500	15,000	18,000	28,500	9,750	6,750	7,500	7,500	12,000	12,000	150,000
2. —														
3. TOTAL SALES		9,000	10,500	13,500	15,000	18,000	28,500	9,750	6,750	7,500	7,500	12,000	12,000	150,000
Step 3: Receipts														
4. Cash In														
5. —Cash Sales		9,000	10,500	13,500	15,000	18,000	28,500	9,750	6,750	7,500	7,500	12,000	12,000	150,000
6. —Receivables Collected														
7. —Loan Proceeds														
8. —Personal Investment														
9. —Sale of Fixed Assets														
10. —Equity	80,000													80,000
11. —Loans	35,000													35,000
12. —														
13. Total Cash In (lines 5 through 12)	115,000	9,000	10,500	13,500	15,000	18,000	28,500	9,750	6,750	7,500	7,500	12,000	12,000	265,000
Step 4: Disbursements														
14. Cash Out														
15. —Purchases		5,255	9,880	9,305	8,030	8,720	6,575	5,080	3,760	3,045	6,545	7,440	8,420	82,055
16. —Advertising		200	200	200	200	400	400	100	100	200	100	100	200	2,400
17. —Auto and Truck														
18. —Bank Charges and Interest		300	300	300	300	300	300	300	300	300	300	300	300	3,600
19. —Insurance		450												450
20. —Professional Fees														
21. —Rent		1,200	1,200	1,200	1,200	1,200	1,200	1,200	1,200	1,200	1,200	1,200	1,200	14,400
22. —Business Taxes and Licences														

Line	Start-up	1	2	3	4	5	6	7	8	9	10	11	12	Total
23. —Telephone		50	50	50	50	50	50	50	50	50	50	50	50	600
24. —Utilities (Heat, Light, Water)		150	150	150	150	150	150	150	150	150	150	150	150	1,800
25. —Wages—Employees														
26. —Principal Draw or Management Salaries		1,600	1,600	1,600	1,600	1,600	1,600	1,600	1,600	1,600	1,600	1,600	1,600	19,200
27. —Term Debt (Principal Portion Only)		250	250	250	250	250	250	250	250	250	250	250	250	3,000
28. —Purchase of Fixed Assets (during operating period)					62,790 ↑									
29. —Taxes														
30. —Materials and Supplies (1%)		100	100	100	100	100	100	100	100	100	100	100	100	1,200 ↑
31. —Miscellaneous (3%)		325	325	325	325	325	325	325	325	325	325	325	325	3,900 ↑
32. —Start-up (Application of funds excluding cash reserve)	105,000													105,000
33. —														
34. Total Cash Out (lines 15 through 33)	105,000	9,880	14,055	13,480	12,205	13,095	10,950	9,155	7,835	7,220	10,620	11,515	12,595	237,605
Step 5: Summary														
35. Total Cash In (line 13)	115,000	9,000	10,500	13,500	15,000	18,000	28,500	9,750	6,750	7,500	7,500	12,000	12,000	265,000
36. Plus: Cash Forward Prev. Mon.—line 39	10,000	9,120	5,565	15,585	8,380	13,285	5	30,835	31,430	30,345	30,625	27,505	27,990	27,990 ↑
37. Equals: Total Cash Available	115,000	19,000	19,620	19,065	20,585	26,380	41,785	40,585	38,180	37,845	38,125	39,505	39,990	265,000
38. Less: Total Cash Out (line 34)	105,000	9,880	14,055	13,480	12,205	13,095	10,950	9,155	7,835	7,220	10,620	11,515	12,595	237,605
39. Equals: Closing Bank Balance	10,000	9,120	5,565	15,585	8,380	13,285	30,835	31,430	30,345	30,625	27,505	27,990	27,395	27,395

STEP 2: CALCULATE YOUR PROJECTED SALES FOR EACH MONTH— PROJECT MONTHLY SALES (LINE 3)

The most important, and often the most difficult, step is estimating sales for the first year of a new business. The 13th month becomes more manageable because you have a year of experience.

Forecasting sales is as much an art as it is a science. Marketing research is the key to preparing an accurate sales forecast. It involves conducting an industry overview, identifying total sales (internationally, nationally, province wide, and in your service area), and, in some cases, determining what part of the market you can reasonably expect to penetrate in the first few years. Trade magazines, census data, suppliers, and major newspapers often have already performed your secondary market research. Don't forget to do your e-research on the Internet.

If you're writing a business plan, attach appropriate printed data to your market research section in the appendix to substantiate your numbers. Fine-tune these numbers by showing your own research and notes from industry experts that support your assumptions about projected sales. A third party's estimate will have more value than yours, so quote as many sources as you can to support your sales forecast. When you list your competitors, don't forget to estimate their market share and the part of their market that you have targeted—if this is possible. The financial community wants to make sure that you have spent a lot of time and thought on your projection, because it drives everything else. You want to minimize surprises.

Even "good surprises" can play havoc with a well-considered plan. For example, imagine you receive 10 times the number of orders you expected, and you don't yet have the resources to fill them. Unanticipated sales could seriously damage your business if you lack sufficient cash to buy the needed inventory. When forecasting sales, then, you should consider including high, low, and medium sales projections. Doing so will allow you to prepare a Plan B for your cash-in and cash-out estimates.

There are numerous methods and techniques for forecasting yearly sales. Each one will depend on the kind of business and the amount and type of information available. Three of the most common general techniques are (1) the unit method, (2) the sales method, and (3) the break-even method. We briefly describe the first two of these approaches next.[1] Later in the chapter, we'll talk about the break-even approach.

1. **Forecasting using the unit method.** List all the products or services you plan to sell and forecast the number of units of each type you'll sell. Different businesses and industries use different unit measures (e.g., for a craftsperson, a unit might be one wooden item; for a researcher, a unit could be one hour of time). The number of units sold will depend on your estimate of the number of customers you expect to buy your product or service. Next, you will have to estimate the selling price for each unit. You might want to go back and review Action Step 32, Chapter 6 (page 149). Use the price(s) that you calculated in this Action Step. You can then develop a yearly sales forecast using the following equation:

   Price per unit × Number of units sold = Sales volume (revenue)

2. **Forecasting using the sales method.** Sometimes, a business cannot use unit sales, as it would be almost impossible to predict the unit sales for each of 5,000 items in a book and magazine store, for example. In this case, some business owners will go directly to revenue forecast. Major considerations are market size and the number of competitors in the market—based on your competitor analysis from Chapter 5. Total revenue or sales are estimated based on experience, and primary and secondary research. A key secondary resource of information on yearly sales of many small businesses is the SME Benchmarking

Tool site (Box 10.3). Sometimes, the break-even level of sales is used as a starting point. We will show you how to do this later on in this chapter.

Once you come to understand yearly revenue estimates—and this might take some time—you have to think about your monthly revenue. It is not sufficient to simply divide by 12 and forecast the same level of sales in each month; rather, you must base the monthly forecast on some sort of monthly growth factor and especially the seasonal nature of the business. Most businesses experience peaks and valleys. For example, if you're in the ice cream business, sales will "heat" up in the summer and drop off in the fall. The same is true of hardware (especially home improvement supplies) and auto parts, when everyone is getting the travel bug. If you run a ski shop, you might have to order your skis at a summer trade show, pay for them when they arrive in September, and wait until late February to make the final sale. For example, the owners of DISCovery Books and Magazines (see Table 10.6 on pages 276–277) knew from their market research that 50 percent of their sales would be made during the September-to-December period. Their understanding of the seasonality of their industry helped them determine how much inventory they would need to support sales over the peak period. (Service Sector Statistics at http://www.census.gov/econ/ provides monthly sales for a number of different types of businesses. It also provides a very good indicator, albeit for U.S. businesses, of seasonal trends for various industries.)

STEP 3: FORECASTING RECEIPTS

Receipts from Operations or Sales (Lines 5 and 6)

In your cash flow projection, you will have to figure out when you will actually collect your money. Cash receipts from the operations of your business can come from either cash sales (line 5) or receivables collected (line 6), if you offer credit. For example, if you're in the bed-and-breakfast business, you probably collect your money ahead of time (when the customer books the accommodation). A retailer normally gets paid when the product is sold. DISCovery Books and Magazines is a retail business whose monthly sales forecast (line 1) is the same as the revenue forecast (line 5). Other businesses must wait to be paid because they offer credit. There is a time delay between when the sale is made and when the cash is collected. For example, in a service trade, you might complete your work and bill for your service in July but not be paid for 30, 60, or even 90 days. On the cash flow, you would record this as a sale for July (lines 1 and 3). If you expect to be paid for this sale 30 days later (in August), then you would record it as cash in, receivables collected for August (line 6). Should your business fall into this category, you must have a policy in place for dealing with late payments; it will help you avoid a situation in which you are required to pay bills when no cash is coming in. Box 10.2 shows the typical payment and collection timelines for an electrical service company.

Other Cash in Receipts

When you are forecasting any cash that comes into the business, you will also have to think about any receipts (or cash in) from loans (line 7), investments (line 8), or the sale of fixed assets (line 9). Note that the initial investments or receipts of term loans (recorded in the opening balance sheet) will appear in the opening balance column. Any subsequent loan, investment, or asset sale will be recorded in the month it is received. For example, if DISCovery Books and Magazines planned on selling some of its fixed assets in February, then the expected cash received would be recorded on line 9 for February.

> ## Box 10.2   Electric Works—Payment and Collection Timelines
>
> **Payments**
> - Wages: weekly
> - CPP deductions: monthly
> - Income tax payments: quarterly
> - Raw materials: 30 days
> - Electricity inspector: 10 days
>
> **Collections (even though the terms might be net 30 days)**
> - Three or five contractors: 45 days
> - One contractor: 60–90 days
> - One contractor: 90–120 days

STEP 4: FORECASTING DISBURSEMENTS

Variable Disbursements

You must forecast your variable costs or purchases monthly (line 15). You will start with a certain amount of inventory, but as you begin to sell your product, you will have to replace that inventory. Purchases of supplies and material are called "variable costs," because they depend on the expected sales. You will have to preplan your purchases of inventory. Sometimes, you simply replace the inventory you have during the previous month. Sometimes, you will plan to build up your inventory prior to busy sales periods. Once this forecast has been made, forecast your cash disbursements in this area. If you pay cash for these purchases, the disbursement is equal to the purchase. If you have credit terms from the suppliers, then the purchase in one month becomes a disbursement from accounts payable the following month. (For example, a purchase in January becomes a disbursement in February.)[2]

Fixed Disbursements

You must project your fixed disbursements, or disbursements that don't change as sales go up or down, on a monthly basis. For example, your rent payments do not normally vary according to your sales. For DISCovery Books and Magazines, these fixed expenses are listed in lines 16 to 31. Normally, these expenses are projected evenly throughout the year. Note, for example, that rent for DISCovery Books and Magazines is fixed at $1,200 per month (line 21). In some cases, expenses such as advertising might change if the owner sees a need to increase (or decrease) advertising expenses for certain months. For example, in the case of DISCovery Books and Magazines, the advertising budget (line 16) was increased in anticipation of the December increase in sales. In forecasting these expenses, there are a few key points you should be aware of.

Loan Payments (Lines 18 and 27)

The principal payments (line 27) and interest payments (line 18) from any loan must be recorded as separate entries on the cash flow. Suppose, for example, that you borrow $5,000 for one year and pay an interest rate of, say, 6 percent. The total cost of the loan will be $5,164. Your total monthly loan payments ($430) will be blended to include both the payments on the principal you borrowed

($5,000) and the interest ($164). Your cash flow must show your monthly interest payments ($164 ÷ 12) and principal payments ($5,000 ÷ 12) separately. How do you separate principal and interest payments on a loan? The best way is to go to a loan calculator on the Internet (for example, http://www.bankrate.com/can/ or CIBC loan calculator, https://www.cibc.com/ca/loans/calculators/calculators. html). In addition, there are financial tables that provide this information.

ACTION STEP 48

Draft a projected cash flow. (p. 301)

Many entrepreneurs want to pay off their loans quickly to save on the interest charges. Here, the cash flow is an important determinant of how much a business can afford to pay off. For example, suppose that the owners of DISCovery wanted to pay off their $35,000 loan (line 11) in one year. Suppose, as well, the interest rate was 6 percent. The total cost of the loan, including principal and interest, would be about $36,150. DISCovery's original loan payments were $6,600 (line 18 + line 27). Payment for this new loan arrangement would increase cash disbursements by about $29,550 ($36,150 – $6,600). It would thus wipe out its original positive cash balance of $27,395. DISCovery Books and Magazines could find itself in a serious cash flow crunch. This example shows how your cash flow can tell you how much your business can afford to pay off in loans each month.

Purchase of Fixed Assets (Line 28)

In your monthly cash flow, you record only the cash outlays for those fixed assets you plan to buy throughout the year. If you purchase fixed assets to start your business, these purchases will already be accounted for in your opening balance column, line 32. Therefore, if DISCovery Books and Magazines planned to purchase more shelving in November, it would record a cash disbursement (line 28) only when it paid the invoice for this planned expense.

Principal Draw or Management Salaries (Lines 25 and 26)

If the business is not incorporated, the cash flow will record any money transferred to the owner operator (wages to owner) as a principal draw. On the income statement, these amounts will not show up as wages because, technically, they are not wages. They will be recorded as a reduction in equity on the ending or year-end balance sheet. If the company is incorporated, the owner can receive a wage, which is normally recorded as a management salary on the cash flow and ending balance sheet.

Dividends or Shareholder Loans

These should be recorded separately when the cash is withdrawn or injected.

Depreciation

Depreciation is not a cash item and as such is not recorded in a cash flow.

STEP 5: SUMMARY OF CASH FLOW (LINES 35 TO 39)

This is the final step in creating your cash flow. It tells you how much cash you have available at the end of each month (line 39). For example, DISCovery's opening balance was $10,000 (line 39), which is the cash available at the beginning of July for operations during this month (line 36). During July, its receipts (or cash in) were projected to be $9,000 (line 35). Thus, the total cash available for July

Table 10.7   Projected Cash Flow Statement—Worksheet

Step 1

Opening Balance	Month												Total
	1	2	3	4	5	6	7	8	9	10	11	12	

Step 2

	1	2	3	4	5	6	7	8	9	10	11	12	Total
1. Sales													
2. —													
3. Total Sales													

Step 3: Receipts

	1	2	3	4	5	6	7	8	9	10	11	12	Total
4. Cash In													
5. Cash Sales													
6. Receivables Collected													
7. Loan Proceeds													
8. Personal Investment													
9. Sales of Assets													
10. Equity													
11. Loans													
12. —													
13. Total Cash In (lines 5 through 12)													

Step 4: Disbursements

	1	2	3	4	5	6	7	8	9	10	11	12	Total
14. Cash Out													
15. Purchases													
16. Advertising													
17. Auto and Truck													
18. Bank Charges and Interest													
19. Insurance													
20. Professional Fees													
21. Rent													
22. Business Taxes and Licences													
23. Telephone													
24. Utilities (Heat/Light/Water)													
25. Wages: Employees													
26. Principal Draw or Management Salaries													
27. Term Debt (Principal Portion Only)													
28. Fixed Assets Purchase													
29. Taxes													
30. Materials and Supplies													
31. Miscellaneous													

Step 5: Opening Balance	Month												Total
	1	2	3	4	5	6	7	8	9	10	11	12	
32. Start-up Application of Funds (Excluding Cash Reserve)													
33. —													
34. Total Cash Out (lines 15–33)													
35. Total Cash In (line 13)													
36. Plus: Cash Forward (Previous Month, Line 39)													
37. Equals: Total Cash Available													
38. Less: Total Cash Out (line 34)													
39. Equals: Closing Bank Balance													

Box 10.3   Financial Planning Sites

- **E-Module 3, Business Plan Outline, Templates, and Examples:** http://www.nelson.com/knowlescastillo7e—Detailed, step-by-step instructions outline how to complete a financial plan to open and operate a business. The site includes a discussion of the importance of keeping financial records, financial templates, and worksheets to help you create and evaluate five basic financial statements:

  – sources and application of funds,
  – opening balance sheet,
  – cash flow,
  – income statement,
  – ending balance sheet.

- **Business Planning and Financial Forecasting: A Start-up Guide:** http://www.smallbusinessbc.ca/pdf/businessplanning.pdf—This online financial resource provides detailed instructions on how to create a financial plan. It is designed for the start-up business and contains a template with seven MS/Excel worksheets. This information is then assembled into the required financial statements. The model is interactive. Information can be changed, and the results of the change are immediately calculated for each of the financial statements. This site will guide you through a reasonable first draft of your financials. However, you will have to make some adjustments for your particular situation.

- **Business Owner's Toolkit (CCH):** http://www.bizfilings.com/toolkit/tools-forms.aspx—This site contains links to a downloadable balance sheet template, a cash flow budget worksheet, and an income statement template. The worksheets are easy to use and can be modified to suit your needs.

- **SME Benchmarking Tool (Industry Canada):** http://www.ic.gc.ca/eic/site/pp-pp.nsf/eng/home—Use this online performance-benchmarking tool to find out where your business stands as compared to a relevant industry average.

- **Sample Business Plans and Templates:** http://www.canadabusiness.ca/eng/page/2752/—Use this site to see other business plan templates and other sample business plans.

- **Zacks:** http://www.zacks.com—Although primarily American, this website provides valuable industry benchmarks and North American competitor financial information.

> ### Box 10.4 Cash Flow—Important Points to Consider
>
> The three most important ingredients in managing and operating a business? CA$H, CA$H, and more CA$H. And yet more than 80 percent of small businesses do not use a cash flow forecast.
>
> - Two factors ensure that you have sufficient cash to operate comfortably: (1) a 12-month forecast of sales and expenses, and (2) a workable and realistic policy stating when you pay your bills and when you can turn sales into cash.
> - Cash flow includes principal, bank payments, and interest—separately.
> - Cash flow includes only cash in and cash out, not depreciation.
> - Your year-end cash flow provides many of the estimates you'll need for your projected income statement.
> - Before offering credit, do a cash flow.

was $19,000 (Line 37). DISCovery's cash expenses (disbursements) in July were projected to be $9,880. We now subtract these July disbursements (line 38) from the cash available (line 37) to find out how much cash is available at the end of July, as shown in line 39 ($9,120). The owners of DISCovery make these summary calculations for each month. At the end of the year, they have a positive cash position of $27,395. DISCovery started out with $10,000 and ended up with $27,395. In other words, the business generated $17,395 in cash over the period: it had a positive cash flow over the period.

Note: You should have no negative numbers for line 39. If you do, it means that you have run out of cash. A negative cash flow means that you will be unable to pay your bills. If you do have a projected negative cash position, you have to go back and rethink your projections and plans. You can't run a business without cash. When there is a cash shortfall, it will normally require new equity, debt, or a bank line of credit.

Now it's your turn. Action Step 48 leads you through the mechanics of a monthly cash flow projection. Box 10.4 provides you with a reminder on some important points to consider. After you have completed Action Step 48, show the results to an expert. Does the picture look accurate? Does your business have a positive cash balance or a negative one? It's better to know the truth now, while you're working on paper. Paper truth is a lot easier on the wallet than real truth.

PRO FORMA INCOME STATEMENT

PRO FORMA (OR PROJECTED) INCOME STATEMENT

An itemized statement of sales (or revenues) and corresponding expenses

ACTION STEP 49

Draft a projected income statement—a moving picture of your business. (p. 302)

A **pro forma (or projected) income statement** is an itemized statement of sales (or revenues) and corresponding expenses. Like cash flow, it is an indicator of the financial health of your business. The major difference is that the income statement is not about cash; for example, as we explain below, an income statement records a sale even if you have not yet received the money. Normally an income statement is for a one-year period (sometimes on a quarterly basis). In a business plan, you might have to provide projected income statements for the first five years, depending on the size and complexity of your business.

We have constructed a typical projected year-end income statement for DISCovery Books and Magazines Inc. (see Table 10.8). Action Step 49 will help you project your own income statement. The major elements of an income statement are discussed next.

The figure at the bottom is net profit after taxes for the year. In Chapter 15, Action Step 73, we will ask you to refine these numbers.

Table 10.8 Pro Forma Income Statement—DISCovery Books and Magazines Inc.

Sales (revenue)	$150,000
Cost of goods sold	
Opening inventory	50,000
(plus) purchases	82,055
Subtotal	132,055
(minus) closing inventory	42,055
(equals) cost of materials	90,000
Total cost of goods sold	90,000
Gross profit	60,000
Operating expenses	
Rent	14,400
Utilities	1,800
Salaries—Employees	
Salaries—Principal draw (manager's salary)[a]	19,200
Advertising	2,400
Office supplies	1,200
Insurance	450
Maintenance and cleaning	
Legal and accounting	
Delivery expense	
Licences	
Boxes, paper, etc.	
Telephone	600
Depreciation	4,000
Miscellaneous	3,900
Total operating expenses	47,950
Other expenses	
Interest	3,600
Total: Other expenses	3,600
Total expenses	51,550
Net profit (loss) (pre-tax)[b]	8,450

[a] As we have said in the text, if a business is incorporated, then the owner'(s) salary will be recorded on the income statement. However, if this is a sole proprietorship, then the owner's salary will not be recorded on the income statement. In the case of a sole proprietorship, the owner's salary will be recorded as an owner's draw on the ending balance sheet.

[b] If DISCovery Books and Magazines were not incorporated, you would use the term *net income* rather than *profit*. The amount of this net income would then be recorded on the owner's personal tax form (T1) as self-employed income.

SALES

On the income statement, all revenues (sales) are recorded, even though you might not yet have received the cash. For example, in the case of DISCovery Books and Magazines Inc. (Table 10.8), the yearly sales or revenue is $150,000. This figure is the same as the yearly cash sales figure in the cash flow statement (Table 10.6, line 5), for the simple reason that DISCovery is a cash business—when it sells a book, it gets the money right away. However, many businesses operate differently. As we noted in our discussion of cash flow, many businesses, such as those in the service trades, can make a sale and not be paid until at least 30 days later.

COST OF GOODS SOLD

COST OF GOODS SOLD (CGS)

The cost of materials or inventory that you use up over a specified period (usually one year)

Cost of goods sold (CGS) is the cost of materials or the variable costs (those costs that depend on sales) that you use up over a specified period ($90,000, in the case of DISCovery Books and Magazines Inc.). CGS is calculated as follows:

1. Take the value of your opening inventory/office supplies from your opening balance sheet.
2. Add the value of your purchases over the income statement period.
3. Subtract the value of your closing inventory/office supplies. This will be the value of the inventory/office supplies from your closing inventory (usually after one year). If you were actually running a business, you would normally obtain this number by doing a physical inventory.

In the case the case of DISCovery, its cost of goods sold was calculated as follows:

$$\text{CGS } (\$90,000) = \text{opening inventory } (\$50,000) \\ + \text{ purchases } (\$82,055) - \text{closing inventory} \\ (\$42,055).$$

GROSS PROFIT

GROSS PROFIT

Total sales minus your cost of goods sold

Gross profit is your total sales minus your cost of goods sold. In the retail business, some refer to this as the contributions margin. As Table 10.8 shows, DISCovery's gross profit is $60,000 ($150,000 − $90,000).

OPERATING EXPENSES

These are the expenses you incur in the day-to-day operations of your business. Many of these items can be taken from the total disbursements column of your cash flow. These costs do not normally depend on the sales and as such are sometimes called "fixed costs." For example, the yearly rent recorded in DISCovery's income statement (Table 10.8) is $14,400, the same number that appears in the company's cash flow statement (see Table 10.6, line 21). Rent is considered a fixed cost, because you have to pay rent irrespective of your level of sales. When calculating your operating expenses, there are some important considerations.

- **Expenses.** Expenses are recorded in the income statement, even though you might not have paid for them yet. For example, if DISCovery had not paid for its rent in the past month, the total rent disbursements in the cash flow would have been reduced by $1,200, to $13,200. On the income statement, however, the rent costs would have remained unchanged at $14,400.
- **Principal payments and interest.** Principal payments on a bank loan are not an operating expense and thus are not recorded as an expense in the

income statement. Interest payments on a loan are recorded in the income statement as an interest expense ($3,600 in the case of DISCovery). Note that interest on a loan is not recorded as an operating expense.

- **Owner's draw.** If you are not incorporated and you pay yourself a salary, you should record this expense as an owner's draw in the closing balance sheet. You do not record this disbursement on your income statement. However, if your business is incorporated and you pay yourself a wage, you should record this expense as a management salary in your income statement.

Table 10.9   Projected Income Statement (Period Ending)

Sales (revenue)	
Cost of goods sold	
Opening inventory	
(plus) purchases	
Subtotal	
(minus) closing inventory	
(equals) cost of materials	
Total cost of goods sold	
Gross profit	
Operating expenses	
Rent	
Utilities	
Salaries—employees	
Salaries—principal draw (manager's salary)	
Advertising	
Office supplies	
Insurance	
Maintenance and cleaning	
Legal and accounting	
Delivery expense	
Licences	
Boxes, paper, etc.	
Telephone	
Depreciation	
Miscellaneous	
Total operating expenses	
Other expenses	
Interest	
Total: Other expenses	
Total expenses	
Net profit (loss) (pre-tax)	

OTHER EXPENSES

These expenses to the business do not relate to the operations. In the case of DISCovery, its other expense would be interest ($3,600) on its bank loan. The interest on a bank loan has nothing to with the operations costs of the business.

NET PROFIT (BEFORE TAXES)

NET PROFIT (BEFORE TAXES)

Gross profit minus total operating and other expenses

Net profit (before taxes) is defined as gross profit minus total operating and other expenses. In the case of DISCovery, its net profit is

$$\$60,000 - 51,550 = \$8,450$$

Profit Is Not Cash

A quick glance at DISCovery Books and Magazines's monthly cash flow (Table 10.6) and income statement (Table 10.8) makes it obvious that profit and cash are not the same thing. DISCovery's profit was $8,450, but its cash increase was $17,395 ($27,395 – $10,000). The cash increase might have given the bookstore's owners the illusion that they were doing better than they actually were. However, their cash flow did not reflect the fact that they were using up their equipment (depreciation). In addition, the cash flow did not take into account that DISCovery had a little more cash available because it used up some of its opening inventory and didn't replace it. (As the income statement shows, the opening inventory was $50,000, and the closing inventory $42,055.) By adjusting for changing inventory in the cost of goods sold entry, the income statement provides a dose of reality.

KEY INCOME STATEMENT RATIOS

Calculating income statement ratios will help you to determine how healthy your business is and how it compares to other businesses in your selected industry. You can learn more about your industry ratios at Industry Canada's SME Benchmarking Tool (http://www.ic.gc.ca/eic/site/pp-pp.nsf/eng/home) and your local resource centre. Also check out the Dun & Bradstreet *Industry Norms and Key Business Ratios*, or contact your industry association directly. If you have the numbers for your business, you can calculate your income statement ratios using the online calculators provided in Box 10.5, page 297.

Four key income statement ratios are listed next.

GROSS PROFIT MARGIN

GROSS PROFIT MARGIN (CONTRIBUTION MARGIN)

Gross profit divided by total sales

Gross profit margin equals gross profit (or contribution margin) divided by total sales.

Gross Profit Margin = Gross Profit (or Contribution Margin)/Total Sales

Sometimes, this ratio is multiplied by 100 to yield a percentage value. The higher this ratio or percentage is, the better. For example the DISCovery Bookstore (Table 10.8, page 285) has a gross profit margin of $60,000/$150,000 \times 100 = 40$ percent. Is this good? It's hard to know unless we can compare it to industry averages. One source might be Industry Canada, SME Benchmarking

Tool (http://www.ic.gc.ca/eic/site/pp-pp.nsf/eng/home). When we check out the financials for Bookstores and News Dealers (NAICS Number 45121 at http://www.statcan.gc.ca/concepts/industry-industrie-eng.htm), the gross profit margin for the industry as a whole (for 2006) was about 34 percent (incorporated businesses). But note that DISCovery had projected sales of $150,000. SME Benchmarking Tool provides income statement data for businesses with different sales volumes. For businesses with average sales of $147,000 (lower half of all incorporated businesses), the gross profit margin is 40 percent, which is the same as DISCovery's ratio. DISCovery's gross profit margin is in line with industry averages—according to this one source.

What would happen if the gross profit margin were 45 percent? DISCovery would be earning 5 percent more in gross profit for every dollar it sells. Its gross profit would now be $67,500 ($150,000 × .45), and its total profit would be increased by $7,500, from $8,450 to $15,950, so DISCovery—and all businesses—should always be looking at ways to improve the gross profit margin. DISCovery, for example, might want to try to reduce its cost of goods sold (through better buying). Another way might be to add or promote products of services with a higher gross profit margin. For example, if magazines had a 70 percent gross profit margin, then it would be in DISCovery's financial interest to promote its magazine business. Or, how about having a little lounge that sells hot coffee and tea? Coffee and tea have a very high gross profit margin—as most restaurant owners know. DISCovery customers would be able to browse books and magazines while sipping a tasty cup of coffee or tea. DISCovery would not only improve its service but also raise its average gross profit margin and net profit.

PROFIT MARGIN

Profit margin equals net profit (before taxes) divided by total sales.

Profit margin = net profit (before taxes)/total sales

In most cases, this ratio is multiplied by 100 to yield a percentage value. Again, the higher this ratio or percentage is, the better off the business. In the case of DISCovery (Table 10.8), the profit margin would be 5.6 percent ([$8,450 ÷ $150,000] × 100). DISCovery produces $.056 (5.6 cents) in profit for every dollar of sales. The owners of this business should check this ratio out with the average profit margin for their particular industry. When we check out the SME Benchmarking Tool financials for Bookstores and News Dealers (NAICS Number 45121, for the year 2010), the profit margin for the industry as a whole proves to be about 3.3 percent. In addition, according to the SME Benchmarking Tool, lower half column, incorporated businesses with average sales of about $121,000 showed a 9 percent profit margin. Bookstores with average sales of about $121,000 had a profit margin of 9 percent. This finding means that DISCovery had a profit margin below that of similar bookstores with similar sales ranges.

INVENTORY TURNOVER

If your inventory sits unsold on the shelf, you can't make money. You want to sell your stock on hand as quickly as possible. **Inventory turnover** normally refers to the number of times each year a company turns over or replaces its inventory. The higher this ratio is, the better. There are two standard ways of calculating this ratio. The simplest method is

INVENTORY TURNOVER

The number of times each year a company turns over or replaces its inventory

$$\text{Inventory turnover} = \frac{\text{Cost of goods sold}}{\text{Average inventory}}$$

Note: Average inventory is usually calculated by taking inventory at the beginning of the year and adding inventory at the end of the year and then dividing by 2. If you know what the monthly inventory is, you simply add the inventory for each month and divide by 12. If you know what your monthly turnover is, you simply add the turnover rate for each month to get your yearly rate.

Let's return to the DISCovery example in Table 10.8, page 285.

$$\text{Cost of sales} = \$90,000$$

$$\text{Average inventory} = \frac{\$50,000 + \$42,055}{2} = \$46,028$$

$$\text{Inventory turnover} = \frac{\$90,000}{\$46,028} = 2$$

Of course, not all items in the bookstore will turn over at this rate. Magazines will turn over much more quickly than, say, history books but, on average, all the items in the store will turn over twice in a year.

Is this ratio of 2 efficient? Is DISCovery Bookstore turning over its inventory fast enough? Are too many of its books just "sitting on the shelf"? One common way to find out how well you are doing is to compare your results with industry ratios. Commercial data banks, such as Dun & Bradstreet, can provide this information. As well, industry associations or suppliers might have the numbers. If we go to Industry Canada's SME Benchmarking Tool for incorporated businesses (NAICS Number 45121, Bookstores and News Dealers), we find that the inventory turnover ratio for the book-selling industry is 4 (368/94), and about 3 (87.7/31.6) for bookstores with average yearly sales of $147,000 (lower half of all businesses). So it seems that DISCovery's turnover rate is a little low relative to industry standards.

We must be careful when comparing ratios, however. Not all industries have similar inventory turnover ratios. For example, according to the SME Benchmarking Tool, grocery stores (NAICS: 4451, incorporated businesses, 2010) have an inventory turnover ratio of 14.2 and jewellery stores (NAICS: 44831) have an inventory turnover of only about 2. This makes sense, as grocery stores have a lot of perishable items such as milk and bread, which cannot sit on the shelf very long—they must turn over quickly. On the other hand, jewellery stores might have to wait a while to sell some of their more expensive items. DISCovery should know the industry standards and always be on the lookout for ways to improve its inventory turnover ratio. What would happen, for example, if DISCovery were able to operate effectively with an inventory turnover of, say, 3? How much inventory would it have to keep on hand? Here is the answer:

$$\text{Inventory turnover} = \frac{\text{Cost of goods sold}}{\text{Average inventory at cost}}$$

$$\text{Inventory turnover} = \frac{\text{Cost of goods sold}}{\text{Inventory turnover}}$$

$$= \frac{\$90,000}{3}$$

$$= \$30,000$$

With a new, more efficient turnover of 3, DISCovery would be able to reduce its yearly average inventory on hand by $16,028 ($46,028 − $30,000 = $16,028). It would have $16,028 more cash. This extra cash could be invested or used to buy more products.

GROSS MARGIN RETURN ON INVENTORY INVESTMENT

If you are in the manufacturing or retail business, you can increase your turnover but still not make more profit; a high turnover does not necessarily lead to higher profits. You could be selling more of a particular product and not be making any profit because your profit margin is so low. The idea in retail and manufacturing is to find products that have both a high profit margin and a high turnover.

The **gross margin return on inventory investment (GMROI)** helps us determine which products have the best chance of making the most profit given the turnover and gross profit or contributions margin. It measures the gross margin earned on the invested inventory. This ratio takes into consideration both gross profit and inventory turnover and is calculated as follows:

$$\text{GMROI} = \text{Gross profit margin (\%)} \times \text{Sales-to-stock ratio*}$$

$$\text{*The sales-to-stock ratio} = \frac{\text{*Total sales (revenue)}}{\text{Average cost of inventory}}$$

Always be on the lookout for products that have a high GMROI. These are the products you will want to promote. If you are planning a business and want to check your GMROI, you will have to rely on industry averages. For example, according to Industry Canada's SME Benchmarking Tool, the GMROI for Incorporated Bookstores and News Dealers (NAICS Number 45121, 2002) with sales averaging about $147,000 is about 185 (40.2 × 4.6). The GMROI for DISCovery is 130 (40 × 3.26), so DISCovery has a lower-than-average GMROI. It might now want to check out which products have the highest GMROI and promote these products.[3]

> **GROSS MARGIN RETURN ON INVENTORY INVESTMENT (GMROI)**
>
> An income statement ratio (gross profit margin X sales-to-stock ratio) that takes into consideration both gross profit and inventory turnover

THE CLOSING BALANCE SHEET

The closing balance sheet will give you a final indicator of the financial health of your business. A typical closing balance sheet is shown in Table 10.10, and its main elements are described next.

ASSETS

- **Cash**—your cash position, the final number in your projected cash flow statement.
- **Accounts receivable**—money owed to your business at the end of the financial period.
- **Inventory/Office supplies**—the closing inventory taken from your projected income statement.
- **Prepaid expenses**—non-organizational costs that you will incur before you open the doors: these include insurance, licences and permits, first and last month's rent, security deposits, utility deposits, business cards, and pre-opening advertising and promotion.
- **Other current assets**—any remaining current assets you might have that can be translated into cash within one year, for example, a note payable or maybe some securities you don't want to cash in yet.
- **Equipment, furniture, fixtures**—the equipment estimate taken from your opening balance sheet.
- **Leasehold improvements**—the leasehold improvements estimate taken from your opening balance sheet.

Table 10.10   Closing Balance Sheet (Period Ending)

Assets			
Current Assets			
Cash			
Accounts receivable	_____		
Inventory/Office supplies	_____		
Prepaid expenses	_____		
Other current assets			
Total current assets		_____	
Fixed Assets			
Equipment, furniture, fixtures	_____		
Leasehold improvements	_____		
—Depreciation	_____		
Land/Buildings	_____		
Auto/Truck	_____		
Other fixed assets	_____		
Total fixed assets		_____	
Other Assets			
Organizational costs			
Total other assets			
Total assets			_____
Liabilities and equity			
Liabilities			
Current debt (due within the next 12 months)			
Bank loans—current portion			
Loans—other			
Accounts payable			
Other current liabilities			
Total current liabilities		_____	
Long-term Debt			
Long-term (minus current portion)			
Mortgage and liens payable			
Loans from shareholders			
Other long-term debts			
Total long-term liabilities		_____	
Total liabilities			_____
Owner's Equity			
Equity at start of period			
(plus) profit over period			
(minus) owner's draw			
Total equity			_____
Total liabilities and owner's equity			_____

- **Depreciation**—your estimate of depreciation taken from your projected income statement.
- **Land/Buildings**—the land or building that you will use for your business.
- **Auto/Truck**—any automobile or truck you will use for your business.
- **Other fixed assets**—your estimate of "other assets" taken from your opening balance sheet.

Other Assets

- **Organizational costs**—legal fees, franchise, accounting, business advisor, this course and associated costs. (If you can prove you took this course with the express intent of forming the business, get a note from your banker saying you require training to start a business.)

LIABILITIES

- **Current debt**—your estimate of the principal due over the next year.
- **Bank loans: current portion**—the principal payment on your loan for the 12 months following the date of your opening balance sheet; the amount due on your long-term debt within the next year.
- **Loans: other**—loans such as contracts or notes payable, lines of credits, or demand loans.
- **Accounts payable**—money for such things as rent and inventory that your business owes to others.
- **Other current liabilities**—current liabilities that are grouped together, such as other debt obligations.
- **Long-term debt or liabilities**—your total principal due for all long-term loans minus the current portion.
- **Mortgage and liens payable**—debt instruments giving conditional ownership of an asset, secured by the asset being financed.
- **Loans from shareholders**—debts owed to the shareholders of the company.
- **Other long-term debts**—other long-term debts that are grouped together as debt obligations.

OWNER'S EQUITY

Owner's equity—what the business owes the owner—is calculated as follows.

Equity at start of period (total equity from your opening balance sheet)

+

Profit over the period (net profit from income statement)

—

Owner's draw

=

Total equity at the end of the period.

As we noted earlier, the owner's draw is recorded in the closing balance sheet only if the business is unincorporated. If you pay yourself a wage and your business is incorporated, you record this expense as a management salary in your income statement.

KEY RATIOS BASED ON THE BALANCE SHEET AND THE INCOME STATEMENT

Given that you have an income statement and an ending balance sheet, there are a number of important ratios you could calculate based on both of these two statements. Two of the most important ratios are the return on investment and the return on owner investment.

1. **Return on investment (ROI)** equals the net profit (before taxes) divided by total assets.

   ROI = net profit (before taxes)/total assets

   This is usually multiplied by 100 to give a percentage. It is a measure of effectiveness. How well are your assets generating profit? Let's say your total assets were $100,000 and your net profit was $10,000. Then your ROI would be $(10{,}000 \div 100{,}000) \times 100 = 10$ percent. Now let's assume that you have some assets that are not contributing to profit—say, a car that you are not using very much for business. You could reduce your assets by selling the car for $20,000. Your ROI would then be 12.5 percent, so you would be making more effective use of your assets. The higher the ROI, the better.

2. **Return on owner investment** equals net profit (before taxes) divided by the owners' equity (investment).

   Return on owner investment = net profit (before taxes)/owner's equity (investment)

   This is usually multiplied by 100 to give a percentage. This ratio helps the owner decide if her or his investment is effective. The higher the ratio, the better. Suppose profit was $10,000 and the owners' equity was $50,000. The return on owner investment (equity) would be $(10{,}000 \div 50{,}000) \times 100 = 20$ percent. The owner is getting a 20 percent rate of return from the business. In this case, it seems as though the owner has made a good business investment. On the other hand, if the return on owner investment was 2 percent, the owner would not be getting a "good" return and should consider getting out of the business. Owner's equity could be invested somewhere else and make a "better" return. Online calculators for these ratios are provided in Box 10.5.

BREAK-EVEN ANALYSIS

The break-even point is the point at which your sales revenue equals your total expenses (costs). At this point, you neither make money nor lose any. The break-even lets you know what it will take to survive and thus provides a good indication of the financial viability of a business idea. The break-even can also be used to evaluate a business expansion or any other business expenditure. You are simply asking how much more revenue will be required to cover the additional costs. Many new business owners use the break-even level of sales as a starting point for forecasting their yearly cash flow and income.

To calculate break-even, you will need to know the value of your fixed costs and the value of your variable costs and your output capacity.

Total costs equal fixed costs plus variable costs.

Fixed costs (sometimes referred to as "indirect expenses") are those expenses that do not depend on sales, for example, rent, heat, and hydro.

Generally, these are your operating expenses based on your income statement. It is common practice (for planning purposes) to include bank interest and principal payments. Remember, the income statement does not include principal bank payments. You will have to get this number from your cash flow.

Variable costs (cost of goods) are those costs that depend on the level of sales—materials and shipping costs, for example. Sometimes these are referred to as indirect expenses. In some cases, these indirect expenses may also include costs such as contract labour hired during peak sales periods.

Capacity governs your output. It can be measured in units of production, billable hours, or sales volume.

There are two basic ways to calculate your break-even—the unit method and the revenue method.

1. UNIT METHOD

To calculate the break-even in units, we use the following formula:

$$\text{Break-even in units} = \frac{\text{Fixed costs}}{(\text{Unit price} - \text{unit cost})}$$

The example below shows you how to calculate break-even using the unit method.

Jan is a home-based potter who makes custom mugs by the case. Her maximum capacity is 15 cases of mugs per week. She has calculated the variable cost (cost of materials) for each case, including clay, glaze, and packaging, to be $50 per case. It costs Jan $3,000 per week in fixed costs to run her business. This figure includes her wages and bank payments (both principal and interest).

Jan can now calculate her break-even sales level and corresponding price per case depending on the number of units she can produce, as shown in Table 10.11. For example, if she produces five cases, her total costs would be her fixed costs plus her variable costs [($3,000) + (5 × $50)] = $3,250. She knows that her break-even level of sales occurs where total costs = total revenue = $3,250. If she is producing five cases, the price she must charge to break even is her total revenue ($3,250) divided by the number of units or cases (5), which equals $650 per case. If she sells five cases at $650 per case, her total revenue will equal her total costs and she will break even. She now prepares a break-even table showing the number of cases produced and the corresponding price per case that she would have to charge (See Table 10.11 and Figure 10.1). Her capacity is 15 cases so that is where it will end. Note that Jan's break-even is not a point; it varies for each different price point ranging from $250 to $650.

For many start-ups, the projected break-even is the first step in establishing the viability of the business idea. For example, suppose that, after Jan does her competitive and market research, she estimates that she could sell 12 cases of her custom mugs at $425. This sale would generate revenue of $5,100 ($425 × 312). Her total cost would be $3,600 ($3,000 + [$12 × 50]). Her weekly profit would be $1,500. She is projecting sales of 12 cases per week, and she now knows that as long as she can sell at least 8 cases, she will turn a profit.

Now suppose that her market research told her that she could get only $200 per case. She would have to produce 20 cases per week to break even, but her capacity is only 15. Therefore, given her cost structure and market research, her business would not be financially viable.

Table 10.11	Jan's Pottery: Break-Even per Week Based on the Number of Units Produced		
Units Produced	Fixed Costs	Variable Costs	Price per Unit
5	$3,000	$250	$650
6	$3,000	$300	$550
7	$3,000	$350	$479
8	$3,000	$400	$425
9	$3,000	$450	$383
10	$3,000	$500	$350
11	$3,000	$550	$323
12	$3,000	$600	$300
13	$3,000	$650	$281
14	$3,000	$700	$264
15	$3,000	$750	$250

2. BREAK-EVEN USING GROSS PROFIT MARGIN (REVENUE METHOD)

Sometimes, a company doesn't sell products, or it sells so many different products that doing a break-even for each unit doesn't make sense. In this case, such as in retail businesses, we calculate the break-even in revenue rather than in units. Break-even is normally calculated by the following formula:

$$\text{Break-even} = \frac{\text{Fixed costs}}{\text{Gross profit margin}}$$

Fixed costs will normally include both operating expenses and other expenses. These numbers will come from your income statement. In most cases, you will want to add in your principal payment on your loan. Remember, principal payments are not recorded on your income statement. You will get this number from your cash flow.

Let's return to DISCovery Books and Magazines. Based on its income statement (Table 10.8), its fixed cost is $51,550 (total operating expenses [$47,950] + other expenses [$3,600]). Based on the cash flow, we add in the principal payments for its loan (Table 10.6, line 27) ($3,000). The total adjusted fixed cost is $54,550 ($51,550 + 3,000). Its gross profit margin is .4 (60,000 ÷ 150,000). DISCovery's break-even is $136,375 ($54,550 ÷ 4). The projected sales of $150,000 are only about 10 percent higher than its break-even level. With projected sales of only $150,000, it's unlikely that many lenders would lend DISCovery any money, unless the owners could provide a convincing argument that the $150,000 sales estimate was their worst-case scenario. In many cases, the break-even forecast provides owners and lenders with a worst-case sales estimate.

Ratio and Break-Even Calculators

- BDC, Ratio Calculators: http://www.bdc.ca/EN/advice_centre/tools/calculators/Pages/overview. aspx#.UMEKEYN_tLc
- Bankrate.com, Small Business Ratio Calculators: http://www.bankrate.com/brm/news/biz/bizcalcs/ratiocalcs.asp
- CreditGuru.com, Ratio Calculators: http://www.creditguru.com/ratios/calculate.html
- Dinkytown.net, Financial Calculators: http://www.dinkytown.net/business.html
- Bplans.com, Break Even Analysis Calculator: http://www.bplans.com/business_calculators/break_even_calculator
- Fast4Cast Break Even Analysis Calculator: http://fast4cast.com/break-even-calculator.aspx
- Dinkytown.net's Breakeven Analysis Calculator: http://www.dinkytown.net/java/BreakEven.html#calc
- HBS Toolkit Break-Even Analysis: http://hbswk.hbs.edu/archive/1262.html
- TANRO, Breakeven Analysis: http://www.knowledgedynamics.com/demos/BreakevenFlash/
- ANZ, Breakeven Analyzer: http://www.anz.com.au/aus/Small-Business/Tools-Forms-And-Guides/Benchmark-Your-Business/Breakeven-Analyser/

A break-even analysis is also useful when considering the financial implications of launching a new product or service, as we show in the example below.

A small manufacturing company was completing a plan for its second year of operation. Its first-year sales were $177,000. Its fiscal year ended in December. A sales breakdown for the last three months of the first year looked like this:

October	$24,000
November	$29,000
December	$15,000
Total	$68,000

The owners took a look at the numbers and called in a consultant to help. The consultant gathered information from sales reps, owners, and customers, and projected sales for the second year at a whopping $562,000. The owners reacted with disbelief.

"You're crazy," they said. "That's over three times what we did last year."

The consultant smiled. "Didn't you tell me you were going to add three new products?"

"Yes."

"And new reps in March, June, and September?"

"Yes, but—"

"And what about those big promotions you've got planned?"

"Well, sure. We've planned some promotion. But that doesn't get us anywhere near three times last year."

"All right," the accountant said. "Can you do $275,000?"

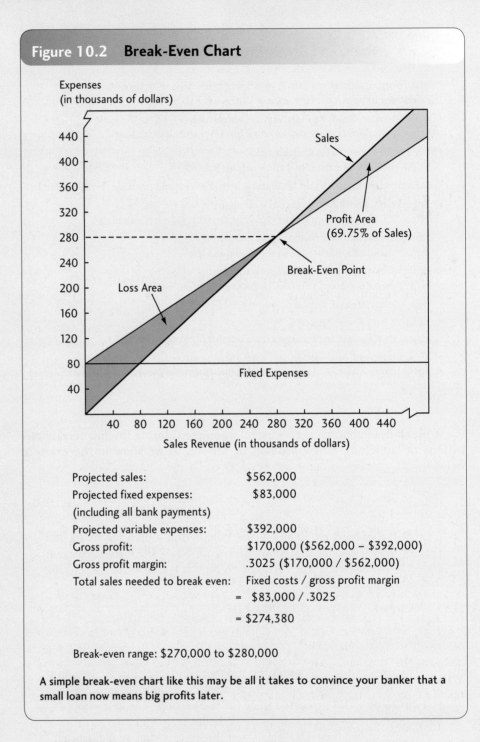

Figure 10.2   Break-Even Chart

Projected sales: $562,000
Projected fixed expenses: $83,000
(including all bank payments)
Projected variable expenses: $392,000
Gross profit: $170,000 ($562,000 – $392,000)
Gross profit margin: .3025 ($170,000 / $562,000)
Total sales needed to break even: Fixed costs / gross profit margin
                                                          = $83,000 / .3025
                                                          = $274,380

Break-even range: $270,000 to $280,000

A simple break-even chart like this may be all it takes to convince your banker that a small loan now means big profits later.

The owners got into a huddle. Recalling the fourth quarter, they were sure they could stay even, and 4 × $68,000 (fourth-quarter sales) was $272,000. They knew they had to do better than last year.

"Sure. No problem. We can do $272,000."

"All right," said the consultant, rolling out his break-even chart.

"I've just projected $562,000 in sales for the year. To break even, you need only $275,000."

"Hey," the owners said. "We're projecting $90,000 in the first quarter."

"I'm glad you're thinking my way," the consultant said. "Because if you don't believe you can reach a goal, you'll never get there." He paused, and then he said, "By the way, that $90,000 is three times what you did in your first quarter last year!"

"Just tell us what to do," the owners said.

Following a careful cash flow analysis, the consultant determined that the company would need to borrow money. The owners knew their business—industry trends, product line, competitors, sales, and promotion plans—but there was no way the bankers would believe a tripling of growth. The key to getting the loan was to convince the bankers the company could do better than the break-even, at $275,000. The break-even chart (see Figure 10.2) was built on the $562,000 sales figure. Note on the chart that after $280,000 in sales, the firm passed its break-even point and began making a profit.

The banker granted the loan, realizing that the company could pass the break-even point with room to spare. The key was a combination of numbers and confidence. And that is the final piece of advice we want to give you in this chapter: Whatever numbers you forecast for your new business, make sure that you can back them up with solid research. You will then have the confidence to find the money you'll need.

Now you are ready to move on to Chapter 11 and learn how to shake the money tree.

In a Nutshell

Not surprisingly, many entrepreneurs find it difficult to project numbers for their business. There are several reasons:

- They're action people who are in a hurry; they don't think they have time to sit down and think.
- They're creative; their strengths are greater in the innovation area than in the justification area.
- They tend to think in visual terms rather than in numbers or words.
- They don't know enough about the power of numbers.
- They think if they do what they love, money will follow—but money doesn't necessarily follow love.

Business is a numbers game, and you have to know the rules. In spite of the entrepreneur's feelings about numbers and projections, survival in the marketplace depends on having the right numbers in the right colour of ink. This chapter helps you formulate a financial vision, estimate your start-up costs, create a balance sheet, project your cash flow and pro forma income statement, use ratios to plan your business, and understand the value of break-even analysis.

When projecting numbers, make them as realistic as possible. Your numbers might seem reasonable to you, but they must seem reasonable to others, as well. Relate each projection to your specific business and to industry standards, and then *document* them (tell where they came from) in your business plan. This chapter will help you make your projections believable to your banker as well as to yourself.

Key Terms

advisory board	balance sheet
application of funds	cost of goods sold (CGS)
assets	current asset conversion cycle

current assets

current liabilities

equity

fixed assets

gross margin return on inventory investment (GMROI)

gross profit

gross profit margin (contribution margin)

inventory turnover

liabilities

long-term liabilities (deferred liabilities)

net profit (before taxes)

pro forma (or projected) income statement

projected (pro forma) cash flow

Think Points for Success

✓ Financial statements, such as balance sheets, cash flows, and income statements, bring the words of the business to life, and there must be a direct link between what is stated in the business plan and what appears in the financial statements.

✓ It's cheaper to make mistakes on a spreadsheet, before you go into business.

✓ When you work out numbers for a business plan, spend time completing your cash flow. Many businesspeople believe that cash flow is the most important statement, and we agree.

✓ If you have a negative cash position in any one period, be proactive and plan how you will pay your bills.

✓ When you visit your banker to ask for money, make sure you know how much you're going to need for the long run.

✓ Use balance sheet and income statement ratios to test the financial health of your business.

✓ Projecting will help you control the variables of your business: numbers, employees, promotion mix, product mix, and the peaks and valleys of seasonality.

✓ Do lots of "what if" scenarios. Be cautious. Most entrepreneurs tend to be overly optimistic on sales and underestimate expenses.

Action Steps

ACTION STEP 45

Put your personal financial vision in writing.

Sit back, close your eyes, and take a moment to dream. Where, financially speaking, do you want to see your business one year from now? How about five years from now? Ten years from now?

In the space provided below, write down your personal financial vision. Express it in terms of an objective—"to be financially independent," for example.

My personal financial vision is

_____

_____

Get in the habit of asking yourself every morning, "What am I going to do today that will bring my financial vision one step closer to reality?"

ACTION STEP 46

Assemble a team of financial advisors.

Use your networking skills to find people who can assist you in managing your financial affairs. Record the name of each person, along with other relevant information, in a chart like the one shown in Table 10.1.

Consider making one of your chosen financial advisors part of your advisory board. In many cases, this person will be your financial mentor. Don't be afraid to ask your mentor, or other financial advisors, to review your personal financial plan. Doing so will help keep you grounded in the financial realities of your business.

ACTION STEP 47

Estimate your start-up costs.

Now that you've got your business well in mind, take a few minutes to brainstorm a list of items you'll need to complete Table 10.2 (page 266)—your cash reserve fund. Then move on to Table 10.3 and begin listing and costing all your general start-up items, leasehold improvements, and equipment needs. Helpful worksheets can be found on the book's support website at http://www.nelson.com/knowlescastillo7e.

Don't rush this Action Step. Getting accurate numbers is critical to the survival of your business. Keep trying to uncover potential surprises and, if necessary, consult with vendors, suppliers, and other entrepreneurs. Write your estimates in your 24/7 Adventure Notebook.

ACTION STEP 48

Draft a projected cash flow.

Begin projecting your cash across the first year of your business. If you don't have an electronic spreadsheet program such as Microsoft Excel, you can download the cash flow budget worksheets from either of the two sites provided in Box 10.3. If you don't have access to a computer, use the blank cash flow worksheet provided in Table 10.7. Alternatively, major banks and most large accounting firms can supply you with worksheets for preparing your cash flow.

1. Calculate the cash you'll start the year with. In the case of DISCovery Books and Magazines, this was $10,000 (see Table 10.6, line 39).
2. For each month, enter the amount of cash you'll receive from sales or accounts receivable.
3. Enter any loans in the month you receive the cash from the lender.
4. Total the above, which will give you the cash available for each month.
5. Now list all disbursements (cash going out). Spread these out, too.
6. Then subtract disbursements from cash available, which gives you a monthly cash flow.
7. Examine your work. Have you explored the quirks of seasonality? Have you discovered the minimum and maximum time lags between when you make a sale and when the business gets paid in cash for the sale? Does the picture look accurate? Have you checked with an expert?

If your cash flow picture looks good, test your money management skills by dropping in a couple of "what ifs." What surprise expenses could upset your new business?

In Chapter 15, Action Step 72, we will ask you to refine these numbers.

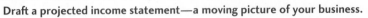

ACTION STEP 49

Draft a projected income statement—a moving picture of your business.

You can download income statement worksheets from any of the "Business Planning Tools" sites provided in Box 10.3 or you can use the blank income statement worksheet provided in Table 10.9 on page 287. Also, all major banks and most major accounting firms can supply you with worksheets for preparing your income statement.

Generate the numbers for the projected period as follows:

1. Using sales data from your cash flow, record the sales forecast for the year.
2. Calculate your cost of goods sold; subtract that from sales, and you have gross profit.
3. Add up all expenses, and subtract those from gross profit. That gives you the net before taxes.
4. Subtract taxes. (Governments will tax you on paper profit, so you have to build this figure in.)

Business Plan Building Block

NOW IT'S YOUR TURN

Explain how you developed your sales projections. Use hard data wherever you can. Summarize your research, and list people and firms that have influenced your conclusions. Include cost of goods sold, expenses, capital needs, and best- and worst-case scenarios. If you are using computer software or online templates to develop your plan, enter the information that you have developed in the text to fill in the cash flow and income statement.

Checklist Questions and Actions to Develop Your Business Plan

The Power of Numbers

- ❑ Do you have a financial vision?
- ❑ What are your estimated start-up costs?
- ❑ Validate your sales forecast based on your primary and secondary market research.
- ❑ Identify all your cost and pricing assumptions.
- ❑ Prepare an opening balance sheet.
- ❑ Prepare a monthly cash flow the first year and a quarterly cash flow for the next two years. Wherever there is a cash shortfall, it will require new equity, debt, or a bank line of credit.
- ❑ What is your fallback position if your sales forecast and cash flow don't reach expectations?
- ❑ Prepare an annual income statement for the first year.
- ❑ Prepare a closing balance sheet.
- ❑ What concerns might the banker have about your pro forma cash flow, income and expense statement, and balance sheet, and what is your response?
- ❑ Is your break-even within range of your minimum sales forecast?
- ❑ How do your financial ratios compare to industry averages obtained from sources such as the SME Benchmarking Tool?

Case Study 1: Financing Your Business—Getting Started

As we learned in this chapter, a financial plan to open a business should contain at least four basic financial statements for the first year of operation:

- an opening balance sheet based on your application and sources of funds,
- a projected monthly cash flow for the first year of operation,
- a projected income statement for the first year,
- an ending balance sheet after the first year of operation.

If you're now ready with the financial information for your business idea, we encourage you to create a first draft of your financial plan. Remember, even once it is completed, it is not crystallized. This plan, especially if you use the financial templates provided in Box 10.3, can be used to answer plenty of "what if" statements, such as "What if I want to pay off my business loan over a shorter time?"

Case Study 2: DISCovery Books and Magazines Inc.—Financial Statements

If you're not ready to do a financial plan for your business idea, answer the following case study questions based on the DISCovery example we have referred to throughout this chapter.

Case Study Questions

1. Application of funds

   Complete the following application of funds table for DISCovery using the cash flow statement (Table 10.6, page 276–277) and the income statement (Table 10.8, page 285) provided in the text.

2. Opening balance sheet
   a. Complete Table 10.13—Opening Balance Sheet for DISCovery—using the completed application of funds table (question 1 above), cash flow statement (Table 10.6), and the income statement (Table 10.8) provided in the text.
   b. Evaluate this opening balance sheet for DISCovery using the current ratio, quick ratio, and debt-to-equity ratio. Compare the current ratio and the debt-to-equity ratio with the industry averages based on those provided by Industry

Table 10.12 Application of Funds, DISCovery Books, and Magazines

General start-up costs		
Organizational costs	$?	
Prepaid expenses	$9,575	
Opening inventory/office supplies	$?	
Total general start-up costs		$62,375
Leasehold improvements		$19,800
Equipment costs		$?
Cash reserve fund		$?
Total Application of Funds		$?

Table 10.13   Opening Balance Sheet, DISCovery Books, and Magazines (Date of Opening)

Assets			
Current Assets	$	$	$
1. Cash	?		
2. Accounts receivable	0		
3. Inventory/Office supplies	?		
4. Prepaid expenses	?		
5. Other current assets	0		
6. Total current assets		?	
Fixed Assets			
7. Equipment/Furniture/Fixtures		?	
8. Leasehold improvements	?		
9. Land/Buildings	0		
10. Auto/Truck	0		
11. Other fixed assets	0		
12. Total fixed assets		?	
Other Assets			
13. Organizational fees (legal, accounting, etc.)	?		
14. Total other assets		?	
15. **TOTAL ASSETS (6 + 12 + 14)**			?
Liabilities			
Current Liabilities (due within the next 12 months)			
16. Long-term loans (current portion)	?		
17. Short-term loans		0	
18. Accounts payable	0		
19. **Other current liabilities**	0		
20. **Total current liabilities**		?	
Long-Term Liabilities			
21. Long-term loans (minus current portion)	?		
22. Mortgages and liens payable	0		
23. Loans from shareholders (if applicable)	0		
24. Other long-term debt obligations	0		
25. **Total long-term liabilities**	?		
26. **TOTAL LIABILITIES (20 + 25)**		?	
Equity			
27. Cash—owners capital (if a proprietorship or partnership)—shares outstanding (if a corporation)		?	
28. General start-up (organizational costs, etc.)	0		
29. Equipment/Material/Labour (provide details)	20,000		
30. **TOTAL EQUITY**			?
31. **TOTAL LIABILITIES AND EQUITY (26 + 30)**			?

Canada's SME Benchmarking Tool (http://www.ic.gc.ca/eic/site/pp-pp.nsf/eng/Home) for incorporated businesses (NAICS 45121), lower half category (average sales of $147,000).

3. Cash flow
    a. Review the DISCovery cash flow in the text (Table 10.6). Suppose the owners wanted to save on interest costs and decided that they wanted to pay off their loan of $35,000 in the first year. Calculate the revised total cash balance at the end of the first year. Would you advise the owners to pay off their loan over this one-year period?
    b. If the owners of DISCovery decided they wanted to pay off their entire loan in the first year, how would this decision affect the opening balance sheet and the first-year income statement?
    c. Suppose that DISCovery offered very liberal credit terms and received cash payments two months after they made a sale. Show how this would affect the closing bank balance. How would this decision affect the opening balance sheet?

4. Income statement
    a. Up until this point, the financials of DISCovery look fairly healthy. Evaluate DISCovery's projected income statement (Table 10.8) based on its gross profit margin, profit margin, turnover, and gross margin return on inventory investment (GMROI). One set of industry averages is provided by Industry Canada, SME Benchmarking Tool (http://www.ic.gc.ca/eic/site/pp-pp.nsf/eng/Home) for incorporated businesses (NAICS 45121), lower half category (average sales of $147,000).
    b. After doing your analysis in 4(a), what advice would you give to the owners of DISCovery?

5. Ending balance sheet
    a. Given the opening balance sheet (question 2), the cash flow (Table 10.6), and the income statement (Table 10.8), create an ending balance sheet for DISCovery. Remember, if you have made no arithmetic or accounting errors, your total assets will equal total liabilities plus equity—CONGRATULATIONS!
    b. Suppose that, at the end of the year, DISCovery decides to pay an extra $10,000 toward the principal payment (for its loan). How would this transaction affect the projected cash flow, income statement, and ending balance sheet?
    c. DISCovery was an incorporated business. On the income statement and cash flow, the owners of DISCovery paid themselves a wage ($19,200). Suppose DISCovery was not incorporated, and the owners paid themselves in terms of an owner's draw. How would this affect the projected cash flow, income statement, and ending balance sheet?
    d. Calculate DISCovery's return on investment (ROI) and return on owner investment.
    e. If you were advising the owners of DISCovery on the basis of the financial statements, would you advise them to go ahead and start their business? Why? Why not?

Notes

1. Western Economic Diversification Canada and Small Business BC, *Business Planning and Financial Forecasting: A Start-up Guide,* http://www.smallbusinessbc.ca/pdf/businessplanning.pdf, p. 21.
2. Ibid., p. 28.
3. A good discussion on the gross margin return on inventory (GMROI) can be found in Michael Levy, Barton A. Weitz, and Sheryn Beattie, *Retailing Management,* Canadian ed. (Toronto: McGraw-Hill Ryerson, 2005), pp. 238–40.

Chapter 11

Financing Your Business

Chapter 11 will help you prepare parts H, I, and J of your Business Plan, the Financial Section.

iStockphoto/Thinkstock

LEARNING OPPORTUNITIES

After reading this chapter, you should be able to

- understand that you, the owner, will be the major source of start-up capital for your business;
- determine your credit situation;
- find out how much unsecured credit you can draw on;
- create a personal balance sheet (or statement of net worth);
- chart your personal money future by preparing a monthly budget;
- discover your risk tolerance;
- understand the inherent risks in borrowing from friends and family;
- partner with, and gain the most support possible from, your banker;
- investigate the lending arena, including government and venture capitalists, for money to fund your new business;
- identify the pros and cons of debt versus equity financing;
- determine the types of financing options best suited for your business.

ACTION STEP PREVIEW

50. Find out what your credit rating is.
51. Prepare your personal balance sheet (net worth).
52. Prepare to meet your lenders.

FINANCING HELPED TURN DREAMS INTO REALITY*

Hugo Bosum, a Cree from Ouje-Bougoumou, Quebec, wanted to start a mobile business selling tires and accessories to Cree communities in the province.

"I saw a need to sell tires and accessories at a reasonable price that included delivery and mobile service," says Bosum. "And I also want the name of the business to be called H.M.A. Tires & Accessories* because the acronym, H.M.A., is made up of the first letters of my children's names and my first name, as well."

To start his mobile tire and accessories business, Bosum needed to purchase inventory, tire removal and balancing equipment, and marketing materials, and, of course, to obtain start-up cash. Although he had some savings, he knew that to make his business a success, he needed more funding. So, he spoke to many possible funding sources, and they all requested to see a business plan, which he subsequently prepared. Bosum then approached a variety of funding sources, including Eeyou Economic Group, Cree Regional Authority, and other local funding entities, plan in hand.

Hugo Bosum succeeded in securing funding for his business thanks to his business plan, his character, and the opportunity that he identified. Furthermore, H.M.A. Tires & Accessories has proven to be wildly successful—each month it outperforms the previous month.

"I knew I would be successful because of the need I saw," says Bosum, "but I also knew I needed funding to make this dream a reality."

Every business, regardless of its size or stage of development, will need some sort of financing. Where do successful entrepreneurs find money to start their businesses? The answer seems to be "almost everywhere," and persistence seems to be a key ingredient. Certainly, Hugo Bosum cobbled together the funding he needed from a number of sources. Entrepreneurs, such as Susan Squires-Hutchings, owner of The Potter's Wheel in St. John's, Newfoundland, have even been able to get some start-up money from their landlords.[1] But the key to success for many entrepreneurs, including Bosum and Squires-Hutchings, is perseverance. They believed in what they were doing, and eventually they found the money. So, if you don't succeed in getting financing the first time, we urge you to keep trying. After all, most entrepreneurs don't get what they want the first time.

A number of possible sources of financing are listed in Box 11.1. For a start-up business, it should come as no surprise, however, that the major source of financing will be you, the owner. Most start-ups rely heavily on informal or owner-based financing, such as personal savings and loans, personal lines of credit, and **love money** from family and friends. Start-ups are less likely to use formal types of financing, such as commercial loans and commercial credit cards, and leasing.

Therefore, you, the owner, likely will be the major source of financing. Thus, before you begin to shake the money tree, we encourage you to check out your credit rating, calculate your available credit, come to grips with your personal financial situation, budget for your future financial needs, and think about your risk tolerance. We'll also warn you to be very careful about asking for money from your friends and family.

LOVE MONEY
Investment from friends, relatives, and business associates

---

*Based on personal interview with Hugo Bosum

> ## Box 11.1   Types of Financial Instruments Used by All Start-up SMEs
>
> In 2011, 36 percent of small and medium-sized enterprises (SMEs) requested some type of external financing, with 26 percent requesting debt, 7 percent requesting leasing, 8 percent requesting trade credit, 4 percent requesting government financing, and 2 percent requesting equity financing.
>
> Chartered banks were the main suppliers of financing to SMEs in 2011, serving 55 percent of financing requests, followed by credit unions or caissespopulaires (16 percent), government institutions (7 percent), leasing companies (4 percent), family and friends (2 percent), venture capital funds or angel investors (1 percent), and foreign banks (0.4 percent).
>
> Source: Summary of the Survey on Financing and Growth of Small and Medium Enterprises, 2011, http://www.ic.gc.ca/eic/site/061.nsf/eng/02776.html, Industry Canada, 2013. Reproduced with the permission of the Minister of Public Works and Government Services Canada, 2013.

Next, we will help you understand and prepare to meet your banker. You will also be introduced to some of the other major sources of external capital, including the government. We want you to be aware of the pros and cons of debt versus equity financing. In case you want to do a detailed financial plan for your business, we have provided financial templates and instructions in the Student Resources section of the book's support website: http://www.knowlescastillo7e.nelson.com.

Throughout the chapter, we encourage you to have faith and persist in your search for money. As Rick Spence puts it in his insightful analysis of Canada's PROFIT 100 companies: "If your story truly has merit, there is a backer for your business somewhere."[2]

BEFORE YOU SHAKE THE MONEY TREE

As we have seen, most new ventures begin with the entrepreneur's own capital. Funds can usually be borrowed if you have other sources of income and collateral, such as sufficient equity in a home. So, before you can make any decisions about start-up financing for your business, you will have to review your own financial situation. We begin by asking you to check out your personal credit history.

WHAT IS YOUR CREDIT HISTORY?

Lenders, such as retailers and financial institutions, provide consumer reporting agencies with factual information about how their customers pay their bills. If you want to borrow money to buy a car, pay for furniture, or buy a house, the loan officer at your bank or financial institution will need to review your credit history and will probably request a credit report. Your credit report also becomes an important issue when you apply for any type of business loan. Unfortunately, lenders often request credit information without your authority, and only by obtaining a copy of your credit report will you discover these requests.

In Canada, there are three consumer credit reporting agencies—Equifax Canada, TransUnion, and Credit Bureau Services Canada—that keep track of all your financial moves: payment (or nonpayment) of bills, loans, liens, legal judgments, and so on. These consumer reporting agencies assemble financial information into a credit file on each consumer. The length of time the information is kept in your credit file varies by type of information. Most of your credit information remains in your file for up to seven years.[3]

Each lender has its own policies for making credit-granting decisions about customers, so your credit file will not tell you how an individual lender will rate you as a potential customer. The key factors[4] for making a decision about your credit are provided below.

1. **How you pay your bills** (35 percent of the score). The most important factor is how you've paid your bills in the past, placing the most emphasis on recent activity. Paying all your bills on time is good. Paying them late on a consistent basis is bad. Having accounts that were sent to collections is worse, but declaring bankruptcy is worst.

2. **The amount of money you owe and the amount of available credit** (30 percent). The second most important area is your outstanding debt—how much money you owe on credit cards, car loans, mortgages, home equity lines, and so on. Also considered is the total amount of credit you have available. If you have 10 credit cards, each having a $10,000 credit limit, that's $100,000 of available credit. But it depends on how you use this available credit. Statistically, people who have a lot of credit available use it to the maximum, making them a less attractive credit risk.

3. **Length of credit history** (15 percent). The third factor is the length of your credit history. The longer you've had credit—particularly if it's with the same credit issuers—the more points you get.

4. **Mix of credit** (10 percent). The best scores will have a mix of both revolving credit, such as credit cards; and installment credit, such as mortgages and car loans. Consumers with a wide range of experiences are potentially better credit risks.

5. **New credit applications** (10 percent). The final category is your interest in new credit—how many credit applications you're filling out. The analysis compensates for people who are rate-shopping for the best mortgage or car loan rates.

How do you find your credit rating? Under the *Consumer Reporting Act*, the three credit reporting agencies are required to provide you with a copy of your credit report on request. Getting this information is not that difficult. Action Step 50 will help you work through the process.

Now we want you to think about how much **unsecured credit** you have to draw on.

HOW MUCH UNSECURED CREDIT DO YOU HAVE?

CREDIT

Money loaned or the ability of an individual or company to borrow money

COLLATERAL

Something of value—such as property or assets—that is pledged as a guarantee to support the repayment of a loan or debt

UNSECURED CREDIT

Credit extended to a borrower on the promise to repay the debt with no collateral required

Credit usually refers to money loaned or the ability of an individual or company to borrow money. **Collateral** is something of value—such as property or assets—that is pledged as a guarantee to support the repayment of the loan or debt. **Unsecured credit** is credit extended to a borrower on the promise to repay the debt with no collateral required.

We encourage you to find out how much unsecured credit you have. Learning this will give you a very general picture of how the financial world rates you at this time. Once you've done this, you can determine whether there are any untapped sources of funds for your start-up, or fallbacks and emergency sources for your business or personal expenses. Use Table 11.1 or a blank sheet of paper. To learn your credit limits on your charge accounts, look at your most recent statements. If your credit cards have low limits, now might be the time to raise those limits before you open your business or quit your job. You might need to call or write to businesses for limit information if it is not clearly stated on your bills.

Table 11.1 Your Current Financial Credit Sources

Source	Limit	Available
Retail stores		
Sears	$ _____	$ _____
Home Depot	$ _____	$ _____
Others	$ _____	$ _____
Oil companies		
Esso	$ _____	$ _____
PetroCan	$ _____	$ _____
Shell	$ _____	$ _____
Others	$ _____	$ _____
Bank credit cards		
Visa	$ _____	$ _____
MasterCard	$ _____	$ _____
American Express	$ _____	$ _____
Discover Card	$ _____	$ _____
Others	$ _____	$ _____
Personal lines of credit		
Bank	$ _____	$ _____
Trust company	$ _____	$ _____
Credit union	$ _____	$ _____
Others	$ _____	$ _____
Any other unsecured credit		
Total credit available	$ _____	$ _____

When you've filled in the amounts for each account you have, add them up. Surprised? Few people are aware of how much credit they have. However, before you tell your boss what to do with your job, you might want to address a few more issues or concerns.

1. **Order complete medical checkups for your entire family.** You might also ask to read through your medical files to make sure there are no false statements which might preclude you from obtaining extended health or disability insurance. An example might be "possible problems with drinking or drugs." In addition, pre-existing conditions, such as uncontrolled high blood pressure, can be a major roadblock to securing extended health insurance.

2. **Check out the costs and possibility of extended or additional health and dental insurance.** Two frequently overlooked types of healthcare coverage are long-term disability and critical illness. If you are unable to qualify for a private insurance plan, a group plan might be available through a business trade association or possibly through a provincial program. Look into high-deductible plans. Many entrepreneurs find they need one member of their family to continue working for a company that provides family coverage. Consider going back and reviewing the insurance planning section in Chapter 8.

3. **Apply for additional credit cards or increased limits.** Check out Industry Canada's Cost of Borrowing Calculator (http://www.fcac-acfc.gc.ca/iTools-iOutils/creditcardselector/CreditCard-eng.aspx) for cards with the best terms. Use cards only for business expenses. Pay bills with a company cheque as they come due. Banks don't care who writes the cheque, as long as it clears. You will have documentation for your bookkeeper and the Canada Revenue Agency, as well as some additional credit for your business. You might need it! More information on credit cards can be found by linking to the Canadian Bankers Association's (CBA) website (http://www.cba.ca/en/media-room/50-backgrounders-on-banking-issues/123-credit-cards). Information and tips to building a good credit history are shown in Box 11.2.

Box 11.2   Your Credit History

Building a Good Credit Rating

Remember that your credit rating is your financial reputation, and you want to protect it. Your credit file shows your history of borrowing and repayment. Simply by paying your bills on time, you are building a good credit rating. Without a credit rating, few institutions will lend you money.

Tips for Building a Good Credit History

- Pay your bills promptly, especially credit cards.
- Borrow only what you need and what you can afford.
- Try to pay off loans on time and as quickly as possible. Doing this helps your credit rating and saves valuable interest costs.

Applying for Credit

Whether it's a credit card, a car loan, a mortgage, or a line of credit you're applying for, there are some basic guidelines you should follow:

- Know your income and expenses ahead of time, and have a detailed statement of your net worth.
- Make sure you have a good credit rating.
- Give yourself some time to apply before you need the credit. That way you can shop around for the best rates and conditions.
- Read and understand credit application forms before you sign them. Don't be afraid to ask questions if you don't understand something.
- Provide copies of your last T4 slip or a letter from your employer stating your annual earnings.
- Give details of any assets and their value (e.g., your home, vehicle, savings accounts, bonds, stocks, term deposits, and insurance policies).
- Give details of expenses and money owed. Provide a copy of your annual mortgage statement if you have a home, statements showing any outstanding balances on credit cards, and information on loan balances.
- Try to match your borrowing to your purpose. For example, use short-term credit for consumer goods, medium-term credit for vehicles, and long-term credit for homes. Don't use a more expensive form of credit than is necessary.
- Be realistic about the amount you want to borrow. Be willing to discuss alternatives if the lender can't totally accommodate you.

Source: Adapted from http://www.cba.ca/en/consumer-information/40-banking-basics/516-understanding-your-credit-report. July 8, 2010. Reprinted by permission of the Canadian Bankers Association.

4. **Consider applying for a personal line of credit.** Depending on the **four Cs of credit** (your capital, character, capacity, and collateral), you can obtain anywhere from $5,000 to $50,000 of unsecured credit at attractive rates. If you have a personal line of credit, you are in a much more flexible position for your new business. If you need it to finance the new business, it's available. If not, it can be your security blanket, to be available if unexpected expenses should pop up—and they will.

5. **Explore the possibility of a home equity loan or home equity line of credit.** A home equity loan is a type of loan for which the borrower uses the equity in his or her home as collateral. The amount of capital loaned depends on how much equity the borrower has in the home. A home equity line of credit is a loan for which the lender agrees to lend a maximum amount for a defined period. The collateral is the borrower's equity in his or her home. The major difference between these loans is that with a home equity loan, the borrower gets all the money upfront. With a home equity line of credit, the money is extracted when needed.

Bankers are much more relaxed about extending credit to a "steady citizen"— a person with steady employment income. By exploring the above options, you are making arrangements for the money when you don't need it, and bankers tend to like lending money to people who don't really need it.

A final word of caution. Don't quit your job until you've finished your Business Plan and checked with your banker. You need to have enough money to withstand setbacks. Don't be surprised when your business does not support you (right away) in the manner to which you've become accustomed or would like. It's to avoid such surprise that we will encourage you to chart your personal money future.

Now you'll develop your personal balance sheet or financial statement—a key indicator of your current financial health.

Don't forget, if you decide to go into business with a partner, the banks and other financial institutions will look at both the credit rating and the credit history of your partner. Your partner could sink you because he or she has a bad credit record. So, before you enter into a partnership, be sure to get a credit check on your partner—for your own protection, at the very least.

DEVELOP A PERSONAL BALANCE SHEET

In Chapter 10, you estimated your start-up costs. Do you have enough start-up money to be your own banker? Begin by getting a total for your personal assets. Personal assets are things you own that have a monetary value. The value of your assets is the market value. Market value means the selling price of a possession, not how much you paid for it. Next, tally up your personal liabilities. Liabilities are the debts you owe to other people or institutions. Find out your **net worth (personal equity)** by subtracting the market value of your assets (what you own) from the total value of what you owe. It will look something like the one in Table 11.2.

Pulling together a **personal balance sheet** or net worth statement is important because it tells you where you stand now, and it will indicate your borrowing capability. The higher your net worth, the more you will be able to borrow.

Now we want you to move on and chart your money future. How much do you need to live on? Can the business pay for your current lifestyle?

CHART YOUR PERSONAL MONEY FUTURE

Will your new business be able to support your current lifestyle? You won't know until you chart your personal money future. Look ahead into the next year. List your expenses, such as those for shelter, food, medical bills, transportation, insurance, phone, school, clothes, and utilities.

FOUR Cs OF CREDIT

Capital, character, capacity, and collateral

ACTION STEP 50

Find out what your credit rating is. (p. 334)

NET WORTH (PERSONAL EQUITY)

The market value of your personal assets minus your total personal liabilities

PERSONAL BALANCE SHEET

A list of the market value of assets (what you own) and liabilities (what you owe) that will show your net worth or personal equity

Table 11.2 Personal Balance Sheet (or Statement of Net Worth)

Assets (what you own)		
	Current Market Value ($)	Current Market Value ($)
1. Liquid assets		
Cash (chequing, savings, etc.)	$	
Stocks, bonds, etc.	$	
Cash surrender value of life insurance	$	
Other liquid assets	$	
Total liquid assets		$
2. Investment assets		
Mutual funds, real estate investments, etc.	$	
RRSPs/Pension fund	$	
Other investments	$	
Total investment assets		$
3. Personal (fixed) assets		
Furniture	$	
Residence	$	
Auto/Boat	$	
Jewellery/Art	$	
Other	$	
Total personal (fixed) assets		$
4. Total assets (1 + 2 + 3)	$	
Liabilities (what you owe)		
5. Short-term debt (liabilities)		
Credit cards owing	$	
Personal loans (amount outstanding)	$	
Income tax owed	$	
Other loans outstanding	$	
Total short-term debt		$
6. Long-term debt (liabilities)		
Mortgages (amount owing)	$	
Loans to purchase investment and other personal assets	$	
Other long-term debt	$	
Total long-term debt	$	
7. Total debt (5 + 6)	$	
Personal equity (4 − 7; Total assets − Total liabilities)	$	

Review your personal budget. How much extra in your budget can you commit to the venture? How much do you need to live on each month? Go back to the business cash flow and income statements that you created in Chapter 10. Have you budgeted enough to live on? Are you willing to change your lifestyle? Are you willing to rent? share an apartment? live in your parents' home? If you're planning on living at home, is your family prepared to support you? Are they willing to make sacrifices to help you realize your dream?

You've thought about your credit, reviewed your personal financial situation, and mapped out your financial needs. It's now time to go back and think again about your risk tolerance.

ASSESS YOUR RISK TOLERANCE

Ask yourself, "How much am I willing to risk? $10,000? $20,000? $200,000?" Are you willing to go deeply in debt for your venture? A sushi vendor we once knew worked for more than seven years and spent thousands of dollars before he hit on a successful way to flash-freeze his product. If additional capital is needed later down the road, will you and your partner(s) be able to provide equal shares? If not, will that be a problem, as the proportions of the amounts invested change? Go to Action Step 51 and do a reality check. Are you willing to give up a successful career with benefits for the unknown? If you lose your house, will you be devastated or will you pick yourself back up and start again?

You must also consider the risk tolerance level of your family members and partners. It might be time now to go back to Chapter 3 and revisit your values. What are your family values? Talk with your family about the time and money sacrifices that might be involved in developing your new venture. Is your family supportive? Are your loved ones ready to take the financial risk? For many, short-term financial pain is worth long-term gain; for others, it's not! Before leaping into the new venture, decide what you and your family are willing to sacrifice. Above all, do your best to listen to them. Sometimes, with the adrenalin of entrepreneurship, you can miss the message.

Now that you have reviewed your personal finances, you are a lot closer to finding out how much of your money you can put into the business. It's time to shake each branch of the money tree and look at your possible sources of financing. As we've already explained, the most fruitful money branches for start-ups will be informal—you, your family, and your friends—so that is where we'll begin.

INFORMAL SOURCES OF FINANCING— BOOTSTRAPPING

What do you do if you want to start a business but lack good credit and collateral, and don't know many people with money? You bootstrap the start-up of the business!

Bootstrapping describes the process of relying entirely on one's efforts and resources for starting a business. Bootstrapping is very important and often the only business strategy available to an entrepreneur who might not have good credit, a network of investors, or other access to various financial resources.

Bootstrapping allows an entrepreneur to use ingenuity, brainpower, and determination to fund the start-up of a business. Even when the business is operational, many entrepreneurs choose to not take on debt but rather rely on the positive cash flow of the business in order to continue to fund its operation.

ACTION STEP 51

Prepare your personal balance sheet (net worth). (p. 335)

BOOTSTRAPPING

Relying entirely on one's efforts and resources

Some bootstrapping strategies include these:

1. Self-financing—using your own money,
2. Family and friends—getting your family and friends to volunteer until you can pay them,
3. Preselling to customers—getting an order from a client,
4. Bartering—exchanging something of value between people,
5. Supplier financing—paying your suppliers when you get make a sale.

We'll address self-financing and family and friends here.

SELF-FINANCING

For start-ups, a key bootstrapping strategy is to self-finance the business. Self-financing is the most important source, and it might be your only one. New businesses have to rely on savings, personal loans, personal lines of credit, and credit cards. Review your personal balance sheet in Table 11.2. How much money can you draw on from your savings? Can you obtain a personal loan based on your equity? Go back to your current financial credit sources (Table 11.1). How much can you get from your personal line of credit? Can you finance your business from the judicious use of credit cards? Think about your monthly budget. How much do you need to live on?

Now we want you to look at look at other sources of informal financing—your family and friends.

FAMILY AND FRIENDS

For many entrepreneurs, heading to parents or guardians, or "Mom and Pop," is the second branch to shake after they've looked at their own financial contributions. If you plan on making it your next stop, think again! Having a banking relationship with your parents is fraught with potential problems. Before continuing further, ask yourself, "Is money for this venture worth damaging or losing my relationship with my parents?" At the moment, you might just be thinking about speeding ahead with your venture, and all you can see is success; the reality is, however, you could fail. You might not be able to pay back your parents in a timely fashion—or ever!

Consider your parents' emotional tie to money. Especially if your parents or grandparents lived through the Depression, money means security. If you borrow money, they might not feel secure until you have completely paid it back. Also, if you take a needed vacation while you still owe them money, will you feel guilty? Will you feel guilty if you purchase a new car? Will you truly be secure in expanding your business if you are not secure in your lending relationship? If you are borrowing money from friends or family, be sure that the loss of that money will not affect the lenders' future or lifestyle.

In addition to borrowing money directly from parents, you might consider asking them to co-sign loans. Remember: That legally obligates them to cover the debt and will affect their financial transactions and borrowing capabilities. Your parents, friends, or relatives might be more willing to lend you money if you put up your house, car, or jewellery as collateral.

Remain at your job, or get another job and save for another year before striking out on your own rather than risking the capital of those you love. Mixing money and personal relationships is never easy, and with family it tends to be even more emotional and volatile. Long-running family issues come into play, and sibling relationships might also be harmed if you borrow money. There are unseen and unknown issues for both parties. How will you deal with them? If your folks get sick, will you be able to pay back the loan? If your dad and mom want to be part of the business to oversee their investment, how will you feel? Do you want your parents only as lenders, or will you consider taking them on as partners and investors?

In all lending transactions, the lender wants to know what the money will be used for, what the chance of default is, what the interest rate will be, and how soon the loan will be repaid. If you are still willing to borrow from friends and family after reviewing potential issues and problems, here are a few ways to alleviate some of the difficulties.

- **Don't accept more money than a lender can afford to lose.** Borrowing Grandma's last $20,000 is not fair to you or to Grandma.
- **Put everything in writing.** Establish a partnership or shareholders agreement (discussed in Chapter 8) detailing the roles of all concerned.
- **Make it a business loan, not a personal loan.** Have loan papers drawn up. State the time period of the loan, interest rate, payment date, collateral, and late-payment penalties.
- **Include in the loan a provision for immediate repayment in case of emergencies.** This provision will alleviate a lot of stress and concern for both parties.
- **Discuss thoroughly with the lenders the company's goals and any potential problems.** Make sure they understand that the loan will be for a certain time. If the business starts to be profitable, it might still require their cash infusion. Cash is not profit—as we now know.
- **Obtain outside advice.** Don't finalize the deal until potential lenders have discussed it with an independent advisor.

One family we know lends to all their adult children in a bank-like fashion. To purchase a home, one son might receive a $50,000 loan at 7 percent interest. A daughter purchasing a franchise might receive a loan of $50,000 with an 11 percent interest rate. The youngest son, starting a high-tech business with two of his out-of-work and not-very-well-respected friends, will be required to pay 20 percent interest. All understand that the Bank of Mom and Dad operates on the basic investment principle of risk versus return, resulting in the various interest rates. If payments are late, a call goes out, and payment is expected immediately—just like a bank!

One son kept forgetting to pay on time. The Bank of Mom and Dad requested postdated cheques for the next six months to secure payments in a timely fashion. No comments about loans or the children's spending habits are made to the children. After 20 years, there are no hurt feelings, and strong, stable personal relationships remain. In addition, several flourishing entrepreneurial ventures continue to grow with the assistance of the Bank of Mom and Dad.

Borrowing from friends and family can be done successfully, but it's hard work and takes exceptional people with good relationships. *Tread lightly and carefully. Friends and family cannot be bought or replaced.*

We'll now move on and discuss more formal sources of financing, beginning with the most important source of outside funding—banks and financial institutions—which account for at least 50 percent of all SME funding.

FORMAL SOURCES OF FUNDING

BANKS AND FINANCIAL INSTITUTIONS

One way or another, you will probably have to deal with a major commercial bank, but we don't want you to forget about other financial institutions, such as trust companies, cooperatives, and credit unions (caissespopulaires). Although banks are in the business of lending money, they also have a responsibility to their depositors. Because of this, they have a major aversion to risk taking and tend to choose the safest deals. Hugo Bosum, introduced in the chapter opening vignette, addressed this tendency by preparing a business plan to show financial institutions how he could reduce their risk through careful planning, researching, and strategizing.

The main objective of a bank is to make profit for its shareholders, not to create opportunities for you, a new business owner, to make money. Banks can help businesses start up and expand, but they have to be careful. Their target for bad-debt losses ranges from 0.5 to 1 percent. In other words, they aim to get back their money in at least 99 out of every 100 loans.

In the case of an established small business, banks are much more cooperative because the venture is less risky—providing, of course, that the financing is backed up by plenty of collateral security. However, in a start-up situation, you will most likely deal with a bank or major financial institution because you will need a personal loan and will want to set up some sort of business-related account. It is advisable to deal with the bank's advisor on small business, although not all bank branches have such a position.

Here are some strategies for dealing with bankers.

Make Your Banker (or Any Lender) Part of Your Team

Take the time to visit your local banker before you apply for the loan. Find out what he or she wants, and be sure to deliver. Bring your banker into the information loop. Make sure that your banker understands your product or service before you apply for the loan. In fact, many advisors would welcome an opportunity to visit you at your business. Try to excite your banker about your idea. Yes, bankers are people, and they can get excited.

Befriend a Banker

Build a trusting relationship—even before you ask for the money. Underpromise, and overdeliver. Be clear, honest, and thorough.

Don't Surprise a Banker

Keep your banker informed. In many cases, keeping a banker informed might be a requirement of your loan. But even if it isn't, savvy entrepreneurs let their banks know about the good and the bad on a regular basis. Bankers are more willing to help if they understand your needs and know that you are trying to anticipate your expected financial needs. If you have a problem, don't procrastinate. Tell the banker right away what you will do about it. When you have a line of credit, banks will want to know the status of your accounts payable and receivable. We suggest you plan to send your banker regular updates, even if these are not requested.

Invite Your Banker to Your Business

On your own turf, you are less likely to feel intimidated, and the banker will better understand your business. Communications will flow more easily, and your enthusiasm might spark the same in your banker.

Have a Backup Banker

Shop around as you would for any major purpose. Make your banker aware—in a nonthreatening way—that you do have other options, but don't bluff. Seek out other options even after you get the loan. Bankers respect healthy competition for good clients.

Respect the Banker's Rules

Understand the banker's rules to have paperwork completed correctly and on time. Most account managers are overworked. Try to make their job easy.

Have an Up-to-Date Plan

Have a properly prepared financial plan, and be able to justify every number.

Get Professional Advice

Make sure that your banker is aware you are receiving professional advice. Have your loan agreement reviewed by an accountant, a lawyer, and, most important, an experienced businessperson—your financial mentor.

Be in Sync

Make sure that you and your banker see eye to eye before you apply for the money. If you foresee a personality conflict, look for another banker.

Ask for Enough

Show your banker that you can forecast and understand your situation. It helps the banker sleep at night, too.

Get Ready for Personal Guarantees

Many entrepreneurs say, "I incorporated so I won't have to sign my life away." From a banker's perspective, if you have a new corporation, few assets, and no track record, you'll probably have to personally guarantee your loan. It is very important to understand that the amount of a guarantee *might be negotiable*—and the amount of this guarantee should be one of your major concerns as you shop around for the banker who is right for you.

If you do have to sign personally for a loan, begin finding a way to get rid of personal guarantees right away. If your business is running smoothly after the first few years, be ready to switch your account to another bank if your bank doesn't want to lift or reduce the guarantees.

Negotiate the Best Deal You Can

The bank will respect you for being a good negotiator. If you still have a job, negotiate for a line of credit or loan while you are still employed. Personal lines of credit are reviewed each year, and chances are you can maintain this line if you keep up a good credit rating.

Understand the Banker's Discretionary Limits

Different managers have different maximum amounts they can lend, depending on their position and bank policy. Try to find out what the lending limit is for your prospective banker. If it is below the amount you are asking, he or she will need to get approval from a supervisor.

If you plan to take out a loan for your business, remember that banks and financial institutions are in the business of making money for their shareholders. Before you get a loan and "sign on the dotted line," *read the fine print* of your loan agreement. Remember the Buyer Beware rule, and be prepared for the following possible conditions.

Spousal Guarantee

In certain provinces, laws governing matrimonial assets might mean that your spouse's guarantee would be required. Needless to say, you should try to avoid spousal guarantees, but if you do have your spouse sign, your relationship had better be rock solid because your spouse will now be responsible for the debt.

Premium Rates

Be prepared to pay a premium interest rate. Banks consider small businesses high risk and charge accordingly. For the privilege of controlling your destiny, you can expect to pay as much as the prime rate plus 3 percent on unsecured loans, and usually prime plus 1 percent on secured loans. (The *prime rate*, set by each financial institution, is the interest rate the institution charges to its most creditworthy clients.)

Demand Loans

Most loans to small businesses, both operating and term, are demand loans. There will be a footnote on your financial agreement that says your financial institution can "demand" full payment at any time for virtually any reason. If, for example, your bank manager turns timid because of a faltering economy, he or she can call your loan and go after you personally if you have signed a guarantee. Try to avoid this type of demand loan arrangement, or, at the very least, try to limit the demand portion of the loan. Always have in place a backup plan, such as ensuring you have other cash sources available to meet this demand, in case the bank calls your loan.

Collateral

If you have no assets or security, you won't get a loan—period. Banks are not in the business of risking their shareholders' money. All banks will ask for business and (if they can get it) personal security or collateral for your loan. It is common practice to request a collateral amount that far exceeds the value of the loan. One Canadian study, for example, estimated that the average bank collateral requested by banks for start-ups was four times the value of the loan. Collateral for established businesses was at least double the amount of the loan. In effect, banks will ask you to guarantee personally an amount far in excess of what you are asking for—even if you are an existing business. The more collateral the banks have, the more secure they feel. We reiterate: You should negotiate to limit your collateral, especially if it is personal.

Insurance

Most banks and financial institutions will require you to have the standard personal and business insurance (e.g., fire, theft) to protect them should you have an unexpected problem. In many cases, a bank or financial institution will even require you to sign over your life insurance and disability policies to it. You should make absolutely sure that those close to you are also protected should you die or become incapacitated.

Covenants

There are dozens of covenants or legal conditions that could be built into your loan agreement to protect the lender. Some of these are likely to include

- an environmental assessment;
- the requirement to maintain a minimum level of cash;
- restrictions on certain financial activities, such as the payment of bonuses and dividends, without the lender's approval;
- a mandated time period (for example, 90 days after year-end) for providing financial statements to the bank (if this covenant is in your agreement, try not to agree to provide an audited statement—it could cost you thousands of dollars);
- the creation of a shareholders or partnership agreement;
- a limit on the dollar amount of capital purchases you can make without bank approval.

Fees

Banks might require you to pay a range of user and service fees for setting up your line of credit, requesting your loan balance, writing cheques, and using credit card facilities. Some of these fees are negotiable, and some are not. Here are the two major user fees that you should try to avoid or at least negotiate.

- **Application fee.** You might be asked to pay a loan application fee (usually ranging from $100 to $200), which is the bank's cost (including the cost associated with preparing a credit application form) for evaluating its opportunity to deal with you.
- **Loan management fees.** You might very well be subjected to additional fees if your bank is required to spend time on activities such as monitoring your accounts receivable or inventory, meeting with clients, and preparing statements.

Many owners of small businesses don't become aware of these extra charges until after the fact. Find out what your obligations are before you sign anything.

We also encourage you to keep a running list of questions to ask prospective bankers. These questions will get you started:

- What are your lending limits?
- Who makes the decisions on loans?

- What are your views on my industry?
- What experience do you have in working with businesses like mine?
- Could you recommend a qualified lawyer? a bookkeeper? an accountant? a computer consultant?
- Are you interested in writing equipment leases?
- What kinds of terms do you give on accounts receivable financing?
- What is the bank rate on Visa or MasterCard accounts? What credit limit could I expect for my business credit cards?
- What interest can I earn on my business chequing account?
- Do you have a merchants' or commercial window?
- Do you have a night depository?
- If you can't lend me money, can you direct me to people who might be interested in doing it?
- Do you make Canada Small Business Financing (CSBF) loans? (We'll discuss CSBF loans later in the chapter.)
- If I open up a business chequing account here, what else can you do for me?

OTHER SOURCES OF START-UP CAPITAL

James Brown knows the benefits of looking around. After his doctors told him he would never work again as a fisher in Nova Scotia, he was able to secure a small loan of $500 from Calmeadow, Nova Scotia, a nonprofit organization that provides micro financing to low-income individuals. He found a loan that was based on his character, "not on collateral." As the business grew, he borrowed a total of $16,000, including supplier credit. He now has two employees and operates year-round.[5]

By now, you should have improved your money skills and developed a firm grasp on your personal finances. Ideally, you have also befriended a banker. Now it's time to zero in on some other sources of start-up capital. For more information on other sources of financing, see Box 11.3.

ANGELS

ANGELS

Wealthy individuals from the informal venture capital market who are willing to risk their money in someone else's business

Angels are wealthy individuals from the informal venture capital market (e.g., retired small-business people) that are willing to risk their own money in someone else's business. In Canada, angels have financed approximately twice as many firms as have institutional venture capitalists. Angels tend to finance the early stages of the business with investments in the order of $100,000.[6] (Angel investor links are available on the NACO site; see Box 11.3.) Angels often require an active management or operations role. They are most active in smaller firms, where they might even take part in day-to-day operations. In larger firms, the role of the angel is more distant and usually takes the form of management advice and counsel through the board of directors.

Angel investors can be hard to find, but you can start with professional advisors (e.g., accountants and lawyers), your local chamber of commerce, and the local office of the Business Development Bank of Canada (http://www.bdc.ca). Or, you could visit the "Private Sector Sources of Assistance with Competitive Strategy" page on the Industry Canada website (see Box 11.3).

SUPPLIERS

Most suppliers will offer your small business at least 30 days to pay for their product once you are established. Suppliers might also allow you to defer your

> ### Box 11.3 Sources of Financing
>
> - **Government and Community-Based Financing Programs (Canada Business):** http://www.canadabusiness.ca/eng/page/2669/—Here you will find a long list of government and community-based financing programs, such as the Community Business Development Corporation (CBDC), Women Entrepreneurs' Fund, and the Canada–Alberta Western Economic Partnership Agreement (WEPA) funding.
> - **Centre for Small Business Financing:** http://www.grants-loans.org—This great site can lead you to all kinds of loan and granting programs. Depending on the size and nature of your business, you might be eligible for anywhere from $100 to $100,000.
> - **Sources of Private Sector Financing:** http://canadabusiness.ca/eng/page/2735/—Search this comprehensive database for financial providers that can meet your specific business needs. Browse a list of banks, credit unions, leasing companies, venture capital companies, and much more.
> - **Micro Credit (Canada Business):** http://www.canadabusiness.ca/eng/program/search/—Search through a wide array of micro credit providers to find financing of less than $25,000 to suit your particular business needs.
> - **Canada Small Business Financing Program (Industry Canada):** http://www.ic.gc.ca/csbfp—Access a wealth of information about government programs and services relevant to your business situation.
> - **Venture Capital**
>   a) **Canada's Venture Capital & Private Equity Association:** http://www.cvca.ca—Learn more about venture capital, and check the list of Canadian venture capitalists.
>   b) **National Angel Capital Organization (NACO):** http://www.nacocanada.com/—The NACO does not make angel investments, but the Links section contains the names and websites of angel investors whose members have participated in NACO initiatives.

payments over a longer period if you pay some sort of interest charges on the deferred payment. You might even want to negotiate a consignment arrangement with some hungry suppliers. In this case, the supplier owns the goods until you sell them. In Box 11.4, we describe one strategy that can help you negotiate more favourable terms with your suppliers.

CUSTOMERS

Customers, especially for home-based and service businesses, are a potential source of credit. Don't be shy about asking for a deposit before you provide a service or go out and purchase supplies and materials. For example, if you are in the "fix it" business, get your customers to pay for your materials before you start the job by asking them for a deposit. That way, you can be more confident you will get full payment, and you don't have to tie up your own money.

EMPLOYEES AND EMPLOYERS

If you have a good idea, a current or past employer might well be a possible source of start-up capital. When you hire employees, don't be afraid to offer them a part of the action in return for a small investment.

VENDOR STATEMENT

A personally designed form that allows you to negotiate with each vendor from a position of informed strength

Box 11.4 The Vendor Statement Form

An often overlooked technique for reducing your capital requirement is to probe your vendors (major suppliers) for the best prices and terms available. Professional buyers and purchasing agents ask their vendors to fill out an information sheet, writing down the terms and conditions of their sales plans. This practice is a good idea for you, as well.

As the owner of a small business, you must buy professionally, and a **vendor statement** will help you do just that. With this form, your vendors' verbal promises become written promises. How well you buy is as important as how well you sell, because every dollar you save by "buying right" drops directly to the bottom line. To compete in your arena, you need the best terms and prices you can get, and the statement will help you get the best.

Personalize your form by putting your business name at the top. Then list the information you need, leaving blanks to be written in. Some of the basics include

- the vendor's name;
- the vendor's address, phone number, fax number, email, and website, if applicable;
- the sales rep's name;
- the vendor's business phone number (Will the vendor accept collect calls?);
- the vendor's home phone number (for emergencies);
- the minimum purchase required;
- quantity discount size (How much?) and conditions (What must you do to earn it?);
- whether dating or extended payments terms are available;
- advertising/promotion allowances;
- policies on returns for defective goods (Who pays the freight?);
- delivery times;
- assistance (technical, sales, and so on);
- product literature available;
- point-of-purchase material provided;
- support for grand opening (Will the supplier donate a prize or other support?);
- the nearest other dealer handing this particular line;
- special services the sales rep can provide;
- the vendor's signature, the date, and some kind of agreement that you will be notified of any changes to terms.

Remember, the information the vendor writes on this statement is the starting point for negotiations. You should be able to negotiate more favourable terms with some vendors because these people want your business. Revise your application form as you learn from experience how vendors can help you.

Leasing

About one-third of all small businesses use leasing as a source of debt financing, amounting to about $3 billion in contracts annually. Commercial banks are now becoming more involved in the leasing business.

A leasing company (lessor) will purchase an asset such as equipment, computers, automobiles, or land. The small business (lessee) will then sign a legal agreement to pay the lessor a fixed amount over a specific period of time. There are several types of leasing arrangement, including a "walk-away lease," or "net lease," which entitles the lessee simply to return the asset at the end of the term.

A "capital," or "open-end," lease requires the lessee to buy back the asset at the end of the term. Most leases can be tailored to the lessee requirements, and the lease type will depend on the situation.

The obvious advantage is that a small business does not have to tie up its start-up or operating funds. Unlike loans, leases normally cover the total asset costs, including installation and transportation charges. Lease charges are usually fixed and are likely higher than a bank loan rate. They provide small businesses with a reliable payment schedule. A lease is likely one of the few options in hard economic times, when loans from financial institutions might not be available. As well, lease payments are a business expense.

Leasing also has its disadvantages, however. For example, chances are that the lease will cost you more over the long run. Leasing companies are in the business of making money, and they have to meet their profit margins. Unless you have a specific kind of lease, you will have no assets to show for it after the lease is over. In other words, leases do not improve the asset base of the business. A lease payment also commits the owner over a specific period of time and thus limits the flexibility the owner might otherwise have to sell the equipment for a more efficient factor of production. One other note of caution: Lease rates normally carry a high interest rate.

MICRO-LENDING PROGRAMS

Several non-government and community-based agencies have initiated innovative start-up programs to aid very small businesses, or micro businesses, for young entrepreneurs (see Box 11.5). According to the Department of Finance, "micro-credit refers to small loans made to low-income individuals to sustain self-employment or to start up very small businesses. Although there is no standard definition of micro-credit, in practice such loans are quite small, amounting to a few thousand dollars."[7]

One well-known micro-lending organization is the Canadian Youth Business Foundation (CYBF). PropertyGuys.com—a company that we highlight in Chapter 14—is a good example of a highly successful Canadian franchise organization that relied on the start-up and micro-lending assistance of the CYBF. According to Ken LeBlanc, a founding partner and president of PropertyGuys.com, "Without

Box 11.5   Canadian Youth Business Foundation: Community-Based Funding Program

Look into the Canadian Youth Business Foundation's (CYBF) community-based funding program. This business loan program provides essential start-up credit to youth (ages 18–34) who have good business ideas but not the resources to get up and running.

Loans are available only in locations where CYBF has set up a program in partnership with a local community organization. The pool of funds available in each community is limited. Therefore, loans (up to $15,000) are granted on a merit and need basis, similar to a scholarship, to young people most likely to succeed and where the money will make a critical difference to the individual's ability to begin the enterprise.

At the very least, you'll need a Business Plan to qualify. For more information, visit the CYBF website (http://www.cybf.ca).

the injection of capital from the CYBF loan, I would dare say we would not exist as we are today."[8]

Another good example of a micro-lending initiative is the Calmeadow program used by James Brown to start his business in Nova Scotia (profiled at the start of this section). Calmeadow (http://www.calmeadow.com) also operates in other centres across Canada.

There are basically two types of community-based models: the lending circle (also known as "peer lending"), and very small loans with no group affiliation but which require some sort of security. Because there is no central clearinghouse for these types of micro-borrowing opportunities, you will have to start by getting in touch with local economic development departments and chambers of commerce.

ACTION STEP 52

Prepare to meet your lenders. (p. 335)

GOVERNMENT PROGRAMS

A number of local, provincial, and federal programs are designed to assist small businesses. These plans change from time to time, however, so it is important to obtain the most recent information from the respective government. Governments know a growth market when they see one, and they do make an effort to help. In recent years, they have been moving away from helping finance small business to merely providing information and advice. However, a number of financial support programs for small business still exist—the sources of which are far too numerous to detail here. We encourage you to visit a government information office even before you begin putting the final touches on your plan. A good starting point would be a visit or call to the Canada Business Network for the location nearest you (http://canadabusiness.ca).

VENTURE CAPITALISTS

With venture capital firms, we enter the world of high rollers and high fliers. Unlike banks, which lend money that is secured usually by real estate or other "hard" assets, venture capitalists don't lend money. They are equity investors who buy a piece of the business with private or publicly sponsored pools of capital. Venture capitalists gamble on the business's rapid growth, hoping to reap a 300 to 500 percent return on their investment. They often expect at least 35 percent annual return on their investment.

According to Canada's Venture Capital & Private Equity Association (http://www.cvca.ca), venture capitalists prefer to enter the financial picture at the second stage of a firm's development, when the business has proven its potential and needs a large infusion of cash to support growth. In the late 1990s, the hungriest consumers of venture capital were technology companies with high-growth potential.

NONPROFIT FUNDING

There are also many funding progams for your nonprofit or charity organization. From funding sources such as corporations to government sources of funding, your nonprofit may benefit from these many sources. You will need to carefully read through some of these organizations' funding requirements in order to ensure that you qualify. Some of these agencies and funding sources are listed on CharityVillage's website: https://charityvillage.com/directories/funders.aspx.

COOPERATIVE PARTNERSHIP

More and more small businesses are beginning to recognize the financial benefits of combining resources in some kind of cooperative arrangement. These types of arrangements go under many names: joint venture, strategic partnering, strategic alliance, corporate partnering, and so on. No matter what business you are in or what business you want to start, you can benefit from establishing strong collaborative alliances. For example, if you are establishing a home office, why not consider entering into an agreement with major customers or clients who need your services? They will supply you with an office, and in return, you provide them with the services they require for a set number of hours per week. If you have a product you want to sell and need the distribution channel, why not enter into a marketing agreement with a larger, more experienced firm? It will market and sell the product that you supply. If you have a new idea and have built a prototype, you don't have to manufacture the product yourself: Strike up an arrangement with a manufacturing plant to build the product, and you simply sell it. The number of options available is limited only by your imagination.

In Action Step 52, we ask you to list potential lenders and investors and to develop your persuasive arguments. Without persuasive inducements, lenders have no reason to invest in your business. If you need help in listing your reasons, you might begin by profiling your target customer. List industry trends, and dovetail them with a scenario of where your product or service fits. Move from there to marketing strategy, selling, the profit picture, and return on investment.

In the final part of Action Step 52, you will test your tactics on friends. Ask your friends to respond as though they were potential investors. You will want to hear objections so that you can address them. When you have completed this Action Step, you will be well prepared to meet your lenders.

WILL THAT BE DEBT OR EQUITY?

If you or others invest money in a business and expect, in return, a portion of ownership, this is called an "equity, or ownership, investment." Equity investors, as owners, usually expect a say in the day-to-day operations of the business and how the profit or net income is to be distributed to the owners. When others, or even you, lend money to a business, it is called **debt financing**—an obligation of a business to repay a lender the full amount of a debt (loan) in addition to interest charges.

DEBT FINANCING

An obligation of a business to repay a lender the full amount of a debt (loan) in addition to interest charges

A lender does not usually have any ownership rights or say in the operations of the business. The type of debt instrument will depend on the particular business need. For example, you would obtain a mortgage for buying a building and use a credit card or operating loan for purchasing inventory.

How should you finance your business: debt or equity, or some combination of the two? The trick is to find the right balance between debt and equity—one that will satisfy the needs of you, the owner; the business; and the market. However, in looking for money to finance your business, remember that any "external" source of capital will always consider the extent of your financial commitment to the business. Normally, an investor will require at least a 50 percent investment by the owner. In terms of the solvency ratios discussed in Chapter 10, lenders like to see a debt-to-equity ratio that is less than 1.

If personal funds (equity) are not sufficient, you must decide on debt or selling a piece of the ownership (also equity), or some combination of the two. Generally, Canadian independent businesses rely far more on debt than on equity, with the banks playing a predominant role as sources of financing.

Listed below are some of the pros and cons of debt versus equity financing.

ADVANTAGES OF DEBT

Financing through debt, mainly by line of credit, is useful in meeting a short-term deficit in the cash flow or in financing lower-risk projects. For example, it would be appropriate where money is needed to fund inventory before it's sold. Some of the advantages of debt are these:

- The entrepreneur does not have to give up or share control of the company.
- The term of the debt (loan) is generally limited.
- Debt may be acquired from a variety of lenders.
- The kind of information needed to obtain the loan is generally straightforward and would normally be incorporated into the business plan.

DISADVANTAGES OF DEBT

Taking on debt can become problematic when a project is risky and the return is uncertain. For example, new product development is no guarantee of success in the marketplace. It would be more appropriate to find an investor to share the risk in this activity rather than going into debt. Debt can also become a problem if it isn't managed properly. The most frequent errors include

- taking on more debt than the company needs to fund expansion,
- adopting too restrictive a policy toward debt and thus not accessing funds that might be readily available,
- misapplying funds in ways that yield inadequate returns and make it difficult for the company to repay its loans,
- making mistakes in servicing the debt (accepting inappropriate repayment terms, encountering cash flow difficulties, or taking on too large a debt-service burden).

ADVANTAGES OF EQUITY

Many entrepreneurs associate finding an investor with giving up control of their company. An appropriate investor, however, can contribute expertise, contacts, and new business as well as money. If the result is substantial growth in profitability, the original owner's overall wealth will increase, even if his or her share in the company is somewhat smaller. Equity investment is especially appropriate for

- larger projects with longer time frames or additional skill requirements,
- high-risk ventures where the costs of debt would be prohibitive,
- rapidly growing ventures that might quickly exhaust available bank financing as they expand,
- situations in which debt financing is not available.

DISADVANTAGES OF EQUITY

Finding an investor brings another viewpoint to a company, and there is always the danger of incompatibility and disagreement. Because an equity owner is an integral part of the company, however, it becomes much more difficult to terminate the relationship if disagreements occur. With a partner, it is important to have a shareholders agreement.

There is another point to consider when deciding between debt and equity. Canada is a country with significant regional differences, and these might become apparent to entrepreneurs attempting to secure equity financing. In some parts of the country, businesses might not have the same access to equity capital as do their counterparts established closer to larger financial centres. Access will also be influenced by the availability of government funding through provincial programs and federal regional economic development agencies, such as the Atlantic Canada Opportunities Agency and Western Economic Diversification Canada. On the other hand, regionalism plays less of a role in securing business loans. For example, each of Canada's major chartered banks operates a nationwide system of branches, all of which offer the same access to loans on the same terms in any member branch.

Finally, equity investment should not normally be used for short-term obligations. For example, it would not make much sense to get a new partner to finance inventory fluctuations. Equity is usually thought of as a long-term financial instrument.

PRIMARY TYPES OF DEBT FINANCING

The major types of debt financing for start-up business are spelled out below. Other "secondary" types of financing are shown in Table 11.3.

SHAREHOLDER LOANS

Should you decide to incorporate your business—and there are a number of good reasons for doing so, as we will learn in the next chapter—you have the option of investing by means of a **shareholder loan**. Although many banks will not lend money to a business per se, they will provide a personal loan to the owner, who, in turn, lends the money to the business. There are a number of advantages to an owner to invest in the form of a loan as opposed to equity (through purchasing shares). First, you can deduct the interest payments as a company expense. If you buy shares (equity investment), however, you will receive payment in the form of dividends, and these dividend payments are not tax deductible by the company. Second, in most cases, it is easier to withdraw your money when it is in the form of a loan. Third, if your loan is properly secured, your investment will be safer in the event of a business failure. The main point here is that there are advantages to lending the company money, but you should ensure that you get sound professional advice.

SHAREHOLDER LOAN
Owner investment in the form of a loan

CANADA SMALL BUSINESS FINANCING (CSBF) LOANS

Under the *Canada Small Business Financing Act*, the federal government guarantees loans to small businesses through Canadian chartered banks and a few other Canadian financial institutions, such as Alberta Treasury branches, and credit unions/caisses populaires.

The CSBF program has become a major funding source for start-up business. Historically, of the total CSBF loans granted, about one-third have gone to firms less than a year old. These loans can be used to finance up to 90 percent of the cost of the purchase and improvement of three categories of fixed assets:

- the purchase of land required to operate the business;
- the renovation, improvement, modernization, extension, and/or purchase of premises;
- the purchase, installation, renovation, improvement, and/or modernization of new or used equipment.

CSBF loans are available to all businesses operating for profit in Canada—excluding farms and charitable or religious enterprises—that have annual gross

CANADA SMALL BUSINESS FINANCING (CSBF) LOAN
A loan guaranteed by the federal government under the *Canada Small Business Financing Act*

Table 11.3 Secondary Types of Loans and Credit Arrangements

Type of Loan	Explanation
Floor plan loan	These loans are provided mainly by manufacturers to stock up goods in the retailers' or distributors' premises. The retailer reimburses the manufacturer for the loan amount when the product is sold.
Bridge financing	This type of interim financing provides short-term funding to cover the cost of a start-up project until long-term funds become available.
Mezzanine financing	Mezzanine financing combines long-term lending with an equity position.
Factoring	This form of financing is available from specialized firms (and banks, to a limited extent). A business sells its accounts receivable to a factoring company at a discounted rate (as much as 85 percent of a "high-quality" account). This will reduce the risk of not receiving a payment and frees up needed cash.
Letter of credit	Letters of credit are widely used in exporting and importing businesses. One of the most common exporting problems, for example, is collecting the accounts receivable. A popular method—and the most secure one—is a letter of credit issued by the purchaser's bank. This is the purchaser's guarantee that the money has been set aside and will be paid to the supplier on satisfactory delivery. Most banks and major financial institutions can provide this letter, given proper security, of course.
Inventory financing	In some cases, banks and financial institutions will allow small businesses to borrow against a percentage value of their inventory. The business must have inventory that can be readily sold. Depending on the salability of the inventory, the owner could receive financing as high as 70 percent or as little as 30 percent of the market value.
Accounts receivable	In this type of financing, the money owed by customers of a business (accounts receivable) becomes the collateral for a loan. Banks and financial institutions have been known to provide as much as 75 percent of the value of the accounts receivable that are not more than 60 days old. Again, adequate security is an important consideration in determining the percentage value of the receivables.
Conditional sale	Some manufacturers will provide financing to small businesses for a particular product on a conditional basis. They will require a substantial down payment and then allow the business to pay for the remaining portion on an installment basis over time. This arrangement is termed a conditional sale because the business will own the product only on the condition that all the payments are made.

revenues of less than $5 million. These loans cannot be used to acquire shares or provide working capital and may not exceed $250,000. Borrowers must pay the federal government a one-time, upfront loan registration fee of 2 percent of the amount of each loan. This amount may be added to the loan. The maximum rate of interest charged by the lending institution cannot exceed the prime rate plus 3 percent for floating-rate loans or the residential mortgage rate plus 3 percent for fixed-rate loans. This interest rate includes an administration fee of 1.25 percent, which is paid annually to the government. Personal guarantees may not exceed 25 percent of the amount of the original loan. The maximum period over which a loan may be repaid is 10 years.

It is important to note that some of the terms and conditions, including the interest rates, are negotiable. In the past, at least one major bank has eliminated the requirement for personal guarantees under the CSBF program. Other banks have reduced the interest rate to prime and added automatic overdraft protection of up to 10 percent of the CSBF loan. Our advice: CSBF loans are a great opportunity, but shop around for the best deal. For more information, visit the Canada Small Business Financing Program's link on the Industry Canada's website (http://www.ic.gc.ca/eic/site/csbfp-pfpec.nsf/eng/h_la02855.html).

OPERATING LOANS (LINE OF CREDIT)

Operating loans (sometimes called "revolving loans") are used by more than 75 percent of small-business borrowers to finance their short-term business needs. Normally, these loans help finance inventory and accounts receivable—that is, money that has yet to be received from customers to whom a product has been sold. It is important to note that a line of credit or operating loan should not be used to finance the purchase of fixed assets. Generally, the line of credit is the largest part of the loans outstanding of a small business's debt obligations.

How much can you borrow? In the normal course of business, the amount will be determined by whichever is lower: your authorized borrowing limit or your margin requirement.

> **OPERATING LOAN (LINE OF CREDIT)**
> Money lent to help finance short-term business needs, such as inventory and accounts receivables

1. Your authorized borrowing limit is established by determining your projected maximum (peak) cash needs in any one month of the year. This is one of the main reasons that accurate projected cash flows are so important.

2. Your margin requirements are based on the fact that you can borrow only up to a specific percentage of accounts receivable outstanding and inventory on your books in any one month. Although you might have a predetermined operating line of, say, $50,000, this doesn't mean that you can go out and use all of it when the need arises. These margins, or limits, will vary depending on the policies of the bank or financial institution. For example, in the past, banks have been known to finance up to 66 percent (sometimes as high as 75 percent) of accounts receivable that are less than 60 days old. But this margin, or percentage, will vary depending on the quality of the receivable and the type of industry. As for inventory, the margin might be as high as 50 percent of the market value but is often lower, depending on how easy it is to sell your inventory. The bottom line here is that if you need an extra $50,000 in a given period to finance inventory and receivables, you will get only a portion of this, and the rest will come from your resources.

What interest rate will you pay? Depending on the financial institution and the business circumstances, you can normally expect to pay 1 to 3 percent above the **prime rate** for an operating loan. Expect to pay higher interest rates for smaller operating loans. For example, you might pay as much as 3 percent above prime for a $25,000 loan and only 1 percent above prime for a $2 million operating loan. The main point is that interest rates for operating loans can differ between financial institutions, so we encourage you to shop around. You can negotiate a rate closer to prime if you have good security.

> **PRIME RATE**
> The lowest rate of interest charged by banks on commercial loans to their most preferred customers

What security is required? An operating line of credit will be secured by the accounts receivable or inventory as well as a personal guarantee. Personal guarantees are required because financial institutions will never recover the full value of an asset should your business fail. Remember, the amount of your personal guarantee is negotiable. At the very least, you should try to limit your personal guarantee to the amount of the unsecured portion of the loan. So if you have an operating loan of, say, $25,000 that is secured by inventory for $12,000, then you should try to keep your personal guarantee below $13,000.

TERM LOANS

TERM LOAN

Loan used for medium- to long-term financing of fixed assets, such as equipment, furniture, expansion, or renovation

Term loans are used by close to one-half of small businesses and are the major source of medium-term (two to five years) and long-term (greater than five years) financing. In most cases, businesses use term loans to finance the purchase of fixed assets, such as equipment, a truck, or furniture. Term loans may also be used to finance expansion or renovation.

How much can you borrow? Under normal circumstances, you will be able to borrow up to 75 percent of the value of buildings or property. In the case of equipment, you should expect to get about 50 percent of the asset value. Normally, you will repay the loan through a fixed schedule of payments, which corresponds to the life of the asset. If you expect a piece of equipment to last five years, then the payments would be spread over five years.

FIXED RATE

Interest rate that remains the same over the period of a loan

FLOATING RATE

Interest rate that changes with changes in the prime rate

What interest rate will you pay? Term loans can be repaid at either a fixed or a floating interest rate. A **fixed rate** is one that remains the same over the period of a loan. A **floating rate** changes according to fluctuations in the prime rate. Many small businesses prefer a fixed interest rate because they know how much they have to pay and can budget accordingly. However, fixed rates are generally not available for loans of less than $25,000, and banks will normally charge higher interest for a fixed term. The reason is that a term loan usually commits the bank for several years, increasing the risk that a business might deteriorate. It should be noted that when short-term rates are low, financial institutions will be even more inclined to ask for a higher interest premium for a fixed term loan. Why? Because of the increased risk of rising interest rates. As with operating loans, the terms and conditions for term loans differ from bank to bank.

What security is required? Financial institutions will require you to secure a term loan with the asset being purchased and, in most cases, a guarantee backed by personal assets. If you default on the term loan, the institution will be able to liquidate the asset and hold you personally responsible for any outstanding balance. Again, you should always try to limit your personal guarantees to a specific amount.

PRIMARY TYPES OF EQUITY FINANCING

At some point, you will have to decide whether to incorporate your business. We covered the pros and cons of incorporating in Chapter 8. At this point, we want you just to understand that the type or form of equity that your business will require will depend, to some degree, on the legal structure of your business.

If you plan to run your business as a sole proprietorship or partnership, your investment in the business will be recorded as an owner's personal investment. You are the owner, and your equity is what you put into the business. The main point here is that if other partners are involved in your business, a handshake is not enough. You must have some sort of agreement outlining the terms and conditions of each equity investor's contribution. You will need a partnership shareholders agreement that details issues such as these: Who is investing what? How will the investment be paid back, and under what conditions? What happens if someone dies? What is the procedure for selling out? What happens if the business fails? You should draw up a formalized legal agreement, with each equity investor consulting his or her own legal and financial advisors beforehand. The legal cost of a straightforward shareholders agreement is approximately $300 to $500.

Should you decide to incorporate, we strongly recommend that you have a lawyer draw up a shareholders agreement to detail the rights and responsibilities of each equity investor. In the case of incorporation, you can structure an equity investment in a number of ways to benefit and protect both you and your potential shareholders. For small businesses, the three principal forms of equity financing are common shares, preferred shares, and convertible debentures. As any formalized equity arrangement can become quite complex, we strongly suggest that you get some expert advice before you sign any agreements.

COMMON SHARES

Common shares confer part ownership of the company and are frequently issued in exchange for a company's initial capital. As the company grows, the shares increase in value and provide dividend income. If the company fails, however, common shareholders risk losing their investment. As an incentive to investors to place capital in small businesses, some provinces have set up development corporations that will repay as much as 25 to 30 percent of a shareholder's investment in such enterprises.

COMMON SHARES
Equity investments that confer part ownership of the company but are not as safe as preferred shares should the company fail

PREFERRED SHARES

Preferred shares may also be offered to investors. Such shares also represent partial ownership of the company. Preferred shares, however, usually earn a dividend at a fixed rate and, in the event of business failure, they are better protected than common shares, although their claim is still junior to that of debt holders. A company derives several advantages from issuing preferred shares. Unlike debts, preferred shares have no maturity date, and dividend payments are not as binding as interest payments on debt.

PREFERRED SHARES
Equity investments that confer part ownership of the company, earn investors dividends at a fixed rate, and are safer than common shares

CONVERTIBLE DEBENTURES

Convertible debentures are loans that can be exchanged for common shares in a company at a predetermined price. Like other debentures and bonds, they carry a fixed interest rate and a specified date by which they must be paid. Like shareholders, the holders of convertible debentures have the opportunity to benefit if the company grows. They are also better protected than are holders of common or preferred shares in the event of a failure. And because the debenture is a type of loan, interest is tax deductible. As a result, larger companies might find it easier to sell convertible debentures than other types of equity. Issuing convertible debentures is therefore a way to raise equity more cheaply than by selling common shares.

CONVERTIBLE DEBENTURES
Loans that can be exchanged for common shares at a stated price and are better protected than common and preferred shares

In a Nutshell

Money creates its own world. It has its own customs, rituals, and rules. Before you start asking people for money for your business, spend the necessary time researching the world of money. Here are some things you can do to streamline your research.

1. Get your personal finances in order.
2. Take some time, prepare, and study the world of finance.
3. Find someone who knows more about money than you do, and keep asking questions.
4. Know that loans are made on the basis of the four Cs: cash, character, capacity (to repay), and collateral.
5. Start to develop the Financial Section of your Business Plan. You need to show your plan to bankers, vendors, and lenders. If you feel overwhelmed, start with an outline. (See Chapter 15 for a model plan.)
6. Begin thinking of a banker as your gateway to the world of money.
7. Search out potential lenders.
8. Establish your balance between equity and debt.

Key Terms

angels	four Cs of credit
bootstrapping	love money
Canada Small Business Financing (CSBF) loan	net worth (personal equity)
	operating loan (line of credit)
collateral	personal balance sheet
common shares	preferred shares
convertible debentures	prime rate
credit	shareholder loan
debt financing	term loan
fixed rate	unsecured credit
floating rate	vendor statement

Think Points for Success

✓ Your banker can provide a wealth of information. Maintain a good relationship with that person. If your banker ever turns you down, there is usually a very good reason. Correct it.
✓ How well you buy is as important as how well you sell.
✓ Partner with your vendors or customers. It's often the best way to get the best deals.
✓ In dealing with bankers, vendors, and lenders, use lots of open-ended questions, such as "What else can you do for me?"

Action Steps

ACTION STEP 50

Find out what your credit rating is.

It is a standard practice for most loan officers to review your credit report. If it doesn't pass, the bank will not loan you any money! However, approximately 40 percent of all credit reports have one or more problems, and it is your responsibility to clear these problems. So, we want you to obtain your credit report.

You can arrange to obtain the report for free by mailing or faxing a written request with copies of two pieces of identification to Equifax, TransUnion, or Credit Bureau Services Canada. Within a few weeks, your report will be mailed to you. You can also go to one of their offices and ask to see your report. Note that if you apply for your credit rating online, a service charge applies. The URLs are provided below.

A numerical score called the FICO (Fair Isaac & Co.), or Beacon score, is now used by many credit grantors. FICO scores range between 300 and 900. The lower your FICO score, the worse your credit rating. If, for example, you had a score below 600, you would be in the bottom 8 percent of all Canadians, and you probably would not get any type of loan. About 50 percent of Canadians have a FICO score over 760. So, if your score were, say, 780, most lenders (based solely on the FICO) would consider offering you very attractive and competitive rates and terms on loan products.

Please note: A FICO score is not usually included in the free credit report you order by writing the credit bureau. If you are serious about learning more about your credit rating, we encourage you to pay for your FICO. The cost is about $20, and you can get the information online. See, for example, Equifax (http://www.equifax.com/home/en_ca).

Your Credit Rating—Address Information
- Equifax Canada Inc.: http://www.consumer.equifax.ca/home/en_ca
- TransUnion consumer relations: (http://www.transunion.ca/)
- Credit Bureau Services Canada: (http://www.cbscanada.com)

ACTION STEP 51

Prepare your personal balance sheet (net worth).

Sit down with a pencil and paper and do some figuring. You might want to use Table 11.2 as a template.

1. List everything you own that has cash value, and estimate its worth. Include cash, securities, life insurance, accounts receivable, notes receivable, rebates/refunds, autos and other vehicles, real estate, pension, and so on. Don't stop now. Go on to list the market values of your home furnishings, household goods, major appliances, sound system, sports equipment, collectibles, jewellery, tools, computer, livestock, trusts, patents, memberships, interests, investment clubs, and so on.
   Add up the amounts you've written down. The total represents your assets.
2. List every dime you owe to someone or something: accounts payable, contracts payable, notes payable (such as car loans), taxes, insurance (life, health, car, liability, etc.), mortgage or real estate loans, and anything else you owe. These are your liabilities.
3. Subtract your liabilities from your assets to find your net worth. It's that simple.

Now you know how much you have. You need these figures to determine your financial needs and also to assess the financial contribution you will be able to make to your business.

ACTION STEP 52

Prepare to meet your lenders.

Know who your potential lenders are and why they should want to help you.

Part A

List potential lenders and investors. Begin with yourself, your family, and your friends, and then move on to business acquaintances and colleagues. Don't forget institutional lenders.

Part B

Now list some reasons that lenders should want to invest in your business. What inducements are you offering potential investors? If you're offering them a very small return on investment (ROI), what are you offering that will offset that?

Think about the legal form of your business. Would you attract more investors if you incorporated?

Part C

Test your tactics by talking to a few friends. Tell them, "This is just a test, and I'd like your reactions to my new business venture." Watch their reactions, and list the objections they give you: the reasons they cannot lend you money.

Using the list of your friends' objections, write down your answers to those objections. Are there any objections you cannot address? What does this mean for your business?

Business Plan Building Block

POTENTIAL SOURCES AND EQUITY AMOUNT

List your potential sources and amount of equity for your start-up business. Complete the table below.

Potential Lending Sources	Potential Amount ($) (Market Value*)
Personal equity	_____
Savings	_____
Borrow on your life insurance	_____
Mortgage your property	_____
Obtain a line of unsecured personal credit from your bank, credit union, or other financial institution	_____
Sell old stock you have been holding onto, even if it means taking a loss, or get a loan using the securities as collateral	_____
Get a part-time job; moonlight your way to more money	_____
Invest your own equipment (computer, furniture, tools)	_____
Automobile (Will the business own your vehicle?)	_____
Inventory (paper, books, software)	_____
Leaseholds (fixtures, plugs, paint)	_____
Organizational costs (Have you paid for training, or have you consulted a lawyer or accountant and paid for this out of your own money?)	_____
Sweat equity (the value of the time or labour you can invest in the start-up of your business)	_____
_____	_____
_____	_____
_____	_____
Total personal equity	_____
Other equity sources	_____
Friends and family	_____
Angels	_____
Venture capitalists	_____
Government programs	_____
Employer and employees	_____
_____	_____
_____	_____
_____	_____
Total other sources	_____
Total equity	_____

*Note: Market value is the price someone else (the market) is prepared to pay for this asset.

POTENTIAL LENDING SOURCES AND AMOUNT

List your potential lending sources and amounts. Complete the table below.

Potential Lending Sources	Potential Amount ($) (Market Value*)
Banks	
Other financial institutions (trust companies/ credit unions, etc.)	
Friends and relatives	
Cooperative partnerships	
Suppliers and customers	
Leasing	
Employers and employees	
Government programs	
Total	

*Note: Market value is the price someone else ("the market") is prepared to pay for this asset.

Checklist Questions and Actions to Develop Your Business Plan

Financing Your Business—Shaking the Money Tree

❏ What is the total amount of equity you need to establish and operate your business for the first year? Identify all sources of funds.

❏ Identify your funding shortfall each month from the cash flow, funding sources, and the expected rate of interest.

❏ Are there any sources of government, agency, or foundation funding (if you are a nonprofit organization) for your venture?

❏ How much, if anything, do you expect from a venture capitalist, and what ownership are you prepared to forego? (Note: If you are working with a venture capitalist or other partners, what do you expect in a shareholders agreement?)

❏ Who are your prime vendors? What type of purchase agreement do you have with them?

❏ What is your debt-to-equity ratio, and how does that compare to industry ratios?

Case Study: Financing Your Business—Getting Started

Case Background

A major part—if not all—of the funding for any new start-up will come from you, the owner. Answer the following case study questions to help you to get ready to finance your business.

Case Study Questions

1. What is your credit rating?
   If you want to borrow money for personal reasons, such as buying a car or furniture, the loan officer at your bank will need to review your credit history to determine your credit rating. Your credit rating is also an issue when you apply for any type of business loan. You determined your credit rating in Action Step 50.

2. How much unsecured credit do you have? List your current financial sources.
   Many start-ups have to rely heavily on unsecured credit, such as Visa, MasterCard, and personal lines of credit. Complete Table 11.1, page 311. If you have no credit, we suggest that you apply for at least two credit cards, but use them with care. Make sure to pay credit card bills before the due date. Doing this will help you improve your credit rating.

3. Chart your personal money future.
   Look ahead into the next year. List your expenses, such as shelter, food, medical bills, transportation, insurance, phone, school, clothes, and utilities.

4. Complete a personal balance sheet or financial statement.
   Complete Table 11.2. First, record everything you own. The things that you own, such as furniture, cars, registered retirement savings plans (RRSPs), and even cash in the bank, are called "personal assets." Next, list those things that you owe. These are your financial obligations, or personal liabilities, such as personal loans, credit card debts, and mortgages. Finally, subtract the total dollar amount of what you own from the dollar value of what you owe. This net value is your personal net worth, or personal equity. Your ability to finance a business or borrow money will depend, to a large degree, on your personal equity or personal net worth. If you need to borrow money—for whatever reason—your lender will want to know how much you are prepared to "guarantee" personally on your loan. To a large extent, this decision will depend on your personal equity.

Notes

1. Charise Clark, "The Fight for Funding: Try, Try Again," PROFITguide.com (November 1998), http://www.consumer.equifax.ca/home/en_ca.
2. Rick Spence, *Secrets of Success from Canada's Fastest-Growing Companies* (Toronto: John Wiley & Sons Canada, 1997), p. 160. Reprinted by permission of the author.
3. Canadian Bankers Association website, http://www.cba.ca/index.php?option=com_content&view=article&catid=50&id=123&Itemid=56&lang=en.
4. Equifax, http://www.consumer.equifax.ca/home/en_ca.
5. Adapted from "Growth in the Grassroots," *Profit Magazine* (October/November 1996), cited in Allan Riding and Barbara Orser, *Beyond the Banks: Creative Financing for Canadian Entrepreneurs* (Toronto: John Wiley & Sons Canada, 1997), p. 93.
6. Riding and Orser, *Beyond the Banks*, p. 15.
7. Canada Business Network, http://www.canadabusiness.ca/eng/page/2868//.
8. Canadian Youth Business Foundation, "Young Entrepreneurs Awarded for Their Innovative Approach to Real Estate," http://www.cybf.ca.

12

Building and Managing a Winning Team

Chapter 12 will help you prepare parts F and G of your Business Plan, Management and Human Resources.

Corepics VOF/Shutterstock.com

LEARNING OPPORTUNITIES

After reading this chapter, you should be able to

- understand the basic management functions of leading and organizing;
- chart your organizational structure;
- consider the benefits of a virtual or network organization;
- evaluate the skills that you and the members of your founding team possess;
- understand the value of an advisory board and external advisors;
- take another look at yourself and identify your strengths, weaknesses, and business needs;
- use the idea of balance to brainstorm your ideal team and scout potential team members;
- develop an action plan with your new team before you open the doors;
- consider the merits of the just-in-time team, partnerships, leased employees, and the independent contractor or associate;
- recognize the need for a mentor;
- learn how to hire your first employee.

ACTION STEP PREVIEW

53. Understand your personal strengths and weaknesses.
54. Consider a just-in-time team.
55. Find a mentor.
56. Decide who's in charge of what.

TEAMWORK SPELLS SUCCESS

Charlene Webb loved food. Baking was her passion. She began her career as a hotel assistant chef—armed with a two-year course in hotel management at a local college and a part-time course in management at a local university. But Webb had always had a streak of independence, and it wasn't long before she decided to open her own business—a gourmet cookware shop in a major mall.

She hired two assistant managers and three shift supervisors, thinking that good management would be the key to her success. She made one of her managers responsible for basic bookkeeping.

But just six months after opening day, Webb knew she was in trouble. Three cheques had been returned "NSF," and she did not understand why this had happened. Webb learned too late that her manager-bookkeeper had no skills in accounting. Apparently, Webb had been losing money every month, and because her books were a mess, she had no idea why. Sales seemed to be on target, so she assumed that her costs were too high.

Webb hired an accountant and learned that high labour costs were, indeed, the main problem. She had too many managers and not enough workers. By this time, though, it was too late. Creditors were knocking at the door. She scrambled for a buyer, took her losses in a "fire" sale, and found herself back in the kitchen working part-time at a local restaurant. She also worked two nights a week as a waitress at a local bar. This extra work helped pay off her outstanding business accounts.

After two years of hard work, she got herself out of debt and wanted her independence back. By this time, she had become very interested in the fashion industry, so she decided to open a women's specialty store. The shop was small—about 1,500 square feet—and was located in a neighbourhood centre in an upscale rural community of about 20,000 people.

This time she had a different management strategy. First, she hired Jill, a local accountant, on a contractual basis. Jill would do the books and provide her with monthly income and cash flow statements. At the first meeting, Jill told Webb that full-time employees would increase her labour costs by as much as 40 percent, so Webb decided to staff the business with part-time employees. She would be both the owner and the manager. Jill, who eventually became Webb's mentor, also showed her how to set up an advisory committee that would help guide the business. This committee consisted of Jill, two local business owners, and two community leaders. They would meet every two months and talk about her business over soup and sandwiches at a local restaurant.

Through networking, Webb discovered that her ideal employees were local women who were active in community life and who preferred to work only one day a week. Monday's help was a golfer whose country club friends came in to visit and buy from her on her day of work. Tuesday, the tennis player was on, and her friends also followed her to the store. Wednesday was staffed by the yacht club member; Thursday, by a leader of hospital volunteers; Friday, by a well-known club woman; and Saturday, by a lawyer's wife. All of the employees were friendly women who knew much about fashion and had energy to spare, because they never had a chance to tire from the routine.

Webb happily managed the store operations and began writing a society column (as free PR) in the community newspaper. Gradually, she became regarded as a local fashion expert, as many women began to view her shop as the one to buy from—especially for formal events.

From Day 1, Webb's business prospered. Each month, Jill showed her a growing profit and positive cash flow. A major reason for these positive financials was her attention to managing and the relatively lower labour costs due to her part-time employment strategy. Jill told her she was well below industry averages for labour costs, but Webb understood that there were other benefits associated with her part-time employees, too. Her team members were effective marketing and promotion agents, serving as local fashion consultants. They also helped Webb make wise purchasing decisions—since they knew their products and local trends.

Your chances of success? As we noted in Chapter 1, about 80 percent of new businesses survive their first year, but less than 50 percent survive their first five years; approximately 30 percent make it for 10 years. An important key to your small business's survival is how you build and manage your team.

The importance of having a team of people around you to help you with your business cannot be stressed enough. This strategy is also crucial in order to avoid "burnout" later on.

As we learned in the opening vignette, business success is all about working with people you trust and respect to accomplish your personal and business goals and objectives. In Chapter 1, we explained that success means different things to different people. Some say, for example, that success is the process of realizing goals that are driven by a compelling vision and committed people. We like this kind of definition: It stresses the importance of achieving results through people, and today we can no longer make it happen without others. Our changing economy has created the management need for people to work together to generate a constant flow of new ideas. Today more than ever, business success will depend on how well we manage and work with people. We begin with the basics of managing your team.

THE BASICS OF MANAGING YOUR TEAM

LEADING

In the old economy, you were the leader because you were the owner of the business. In the new economy, leadership has to be earned. You don't lead your employees because you own the company. You lead because your employees share your vision and want to follow you. **Leadership** is about creating the work climate that motivates people to do what is expected of them because they believe in what you are doing and share your vision.

Researchers have identified the key ingredients of successful leadership. Studies consistently show that the "transformational style" of leadership brings tremendous payoffs in company performance and innovation. The primary focus of this style is to make change happen in ourselves, in groups, and in organizations.[1] Because entrepreneurs are agents of change, it is important that they consider this particular type of leadership style.

The transformational style is based on five kinds of behaviour that inspire exceptional performance.

1. **Visioning.** The leader communicates a compelling vision of the future that is widely shared by the organization's members. The vision describes the ultimate outcome employees need to achieve. Transformational leaders lead by example and act in ways consistent with the vision.
2. **Inspiring.** The leader communicates the vision with passion, energy, and conviction; expresses optimism about the future; and shows enthusiasm about future possibilities. The leader generates excitement in the workplace

LEADERSHIP

The act of motivating others to do what is expected of them because they believe in what you are doing and share your vision and heightens others' expectations through symbols and images, which, in turn, build commitment to the vision.

3. **Stimulating.** The leader arouses interest in new ideas and approaches, and enables employees to think through problems in new ways. The leader who practises intellectual stimulation encourages the rethinking of ideas and the questioning of traditionally accepted ways of doing things. The leader considers "wild" ideas and supports divergent thinking. He or she uses reasoning and analytic thinking to problem-solve and select from the creative ideas generated.

4. **Coaching.** The leader coaches, advises, and provides hands-on help for employees to develop their capabilities and improve their performance. He or she listens attentively; understands individual needs, motivations, and aspirations; and expresses encouragement, support, and confidence in individuals' abilities to meet the expectations inherent in the vision. The leader gives constructive feedback, encourages people to take on greater responsibilities, and provides opportunities for development by delegating challenging and interesting tasks.

5. **Team building.** The leader builds effective teams by selecting team members with complementary skills and encouraging them to work together toward common goals. She or he increases team confidence and commitment by giving positive feedback, sharing information, using individuals' skills, and removing obstacles to team performance.[2]

In his classic book, *Leadership from Within*, Peter Urs Bender tells us that implementing this style of leadership requires fulfilling five key steps: (1) to know yourself, (2) to have vision and passion, (3) to take risks, (4) to communicate; and (5) to check progress and results.[3] To learn more about this qualities of leaders, see Box 12.1.

Box 12.1 Leadership Within

Leadership is not management; leadership is about inspiring people from within. While management is mainly about managing things, leadership is about leading people: about leading by example, by encouraging and inspiring people—by bringing out the best in them. Here are some of the top qualities of effective leaders.

1. **Visionary**—Leadership begins with having a vision. An envisioned future is one where the leader develops a vivid picture of some desired state in the future. This picture inspires the leader and, once it is shared, the team works toward making that vision reality.

2. **People-Centred**—Effective leadership is people centred. Business comes down to people. And people want to be recognized, appreciated, well compensated, inspired, and given a chance to realize their potential.

3. **Caring**—Good leaders care. They genuinely care about the best interest of their team members, their customers, and their other stakeholders. This caring attitude brings a whole new level of interaction with people.

4. **Focused**—Leaders are focused on achieving results but appreciate that they need a team to achieve great goals.

5. **Confident**—Leaders are confident in themselves and in the people they work with. This confidence inspires others to believe in the driving vision, as well.

6. **Full of Integrity**—Leaders have integrity; that is, they adhere to moral or ethical principles. They are honest and do what they know is right. They do the right things even when no one is looking. Their integrity and honesty build the foundation for all business success.

7. **Innovative**—Leaders think innovatively to bring about change in their organizations and encourage others to do the same. The basis of innovation is risk taking. Risk taking is doing something out of the ordinary. It can be as simple as risking money to start a business or risking beliefs in favour of a new way of looking at things.

What is your leadership strategy? How will you empower—give power to—your business? Be prepared to include a statement about how you will motivate your team to achieve the goals and objectives that will make you—and them—successful. Don't be afraid to show emotion. Emotion is a driving force, and, in fact, some experts say that leadership is the emotional part of managing.

ORGANIZING

In Chapter 8, we discussed ways in which you might want to organize your business—sole proprietorship, partnership, corporation, or cooperative. But you will have to come to grips with such organizing questions as these: What tasks are to be done? Who does them? How are the tasks to be grouped? Who reports to whom? Where are decisions made?

The key to developing an organizational structure or framework to accomplish your business goals is to remember that we are deeply entrenched in a business environment that demands innovation, proactivity, and risk taking. Businesses can no longer form bureaucratic structures that inhibit the transfer of information. Table 12.1 shows the basic differences between the new "organic" structures and the old mechanistic ones. Bureaucracies inhibit the flow of information. In the management section of your plan, you will have to explain

Table 12.1 Organic Versus Mechanistic Organizational Structure

Organic	Mechanistic
1. Channels of communication open with free flow of information throughout the organization	1. Channels of communication highly structured with restricted information flow
2. Operating styles allowed to vary freely	2. Operating styles must be uniform and restricted
3. Authority for decisions based on expertise of the individual	3. Authority decisions based on formal line management position
4. Free adaptation by the organization to changing circumstances	4. Reluctant adaptation, with insistence on holding fast to established management principles
5. Emphasis on getting things done unconstrained by formally laid-out procedures	5. Emphasis on formally laid-down procedures, with reliance on long-accepted management principles
6. Loose, informal control with emphasis on norm of cooperation	6. Tight control through sophisticated control systems
7. Flexible on-job behaviour permitted to be shaped by the requirements of the situation and personality of the individual	7. Constrained on-job behaviour required to conform to job description doing the job
8. Participation and group consensus used frequently	8. Decisions made by superiors, with minimum consultation and involvement of subordinates

Source: Adapted from Dr. Pradip N. Khandwalla, *The Design of Organization* (New York: Harcourt Brace Jovanovich, 1977), p. 411. Reprinted by permission of the author.

Figure 12.1   Charting Your Organizational Structure: Three Traditional Approaches

Functional

The functional approach to an organizational structure is one of the most widely used forms in small business. Teams are formed according to the duties or functions they perform, such as accounting, service, or sales. Shown below is a simple functional organizational chart for a restaurant.

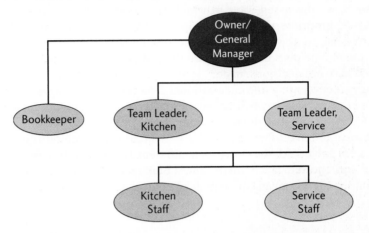

Geographic

Some types of independent business might decide to organize on the basis of geography. Provided below is an example of a "flat" service type of organizational chart that has a structure based on territory or geography.

Customer driven

Some independent businesses are starting to organize their company on the basis of type of customer. After all, it's the customer who drives the business. Here is one simple example of a small research and development organization that has a "customer-driven" organizational structure.

Source: Ronald Knowles, *Writing a Small Business Plan: TVO Course Guide* (Toronto: Dryden, an imprint of Harcourt Brace & Company, Canada, 1995), pp. 49, 50. Reprinted by permission of Elizabeth Knowles.

how you will organize your activities and structure your business to focus on your target customer and respond to a changing environment.

Traditionally, most small businesses have been organized on the basis of function, geography, or type of customer. Examples of these traditional types of structures are shown in Figure 12.1.

At this point, we want you to consider the benefits of the **virtual, or network, organization**. In this type of organizational structure, the core business functions (such as sales, accounting, retail, and manufacturing) are separated from the main business by small businesses or independent teams, often called **strategic business units**. In other words, a business no longer has to compete under one roof. Activities such as human resources, advertising, maintenance, and sales can be contracted out to small businesses on an as-needed basis or handled by remote employees.

Here's how the concept might work for an advertising agency. The entire agency might consist of only one person who presents the client with an idea. Once the idea is approved, the single person assembles "associates": graphic designers, copywriters, photographers, models, performers, and media experts to produce the package. The team is virtual—it is not housed in one central location. It might even have a "shamrock" structure, as shown in Figure 12.2. This virtual ad agency has little staffing overhead but can bring together the best talent to provide the client with a high-quality campaign at a reasonable cost. Once the project is completed, the team of associates disbands, with each member moving on to other projects.

For independent businesses, the virtual organization can allow the little guy to compete with the larger firm without sacrificing scale, speed, or agility. It is much like forming an all-star team to exploit a market opportunity. Here are some key characteristics of the virtual organizational structure.

- **It is customer driven.** It is created to take advantage of a specific, customer-driven, time-based opportunity.
- **It is flexible.** It is disbanded when the opportunity ceases to exist.
- **It relies on mutual trust and teamwork.**

VIRTUAL, OR NETWORK, ORGANIZATION

Organizational structure in which the major functions are broken up into strategic business units

STRATEGIC BUSINESS UNITS

Independent teams or small businesses that support the functional needs of the main organization

---

Figure 12.2   The Shamrock Model

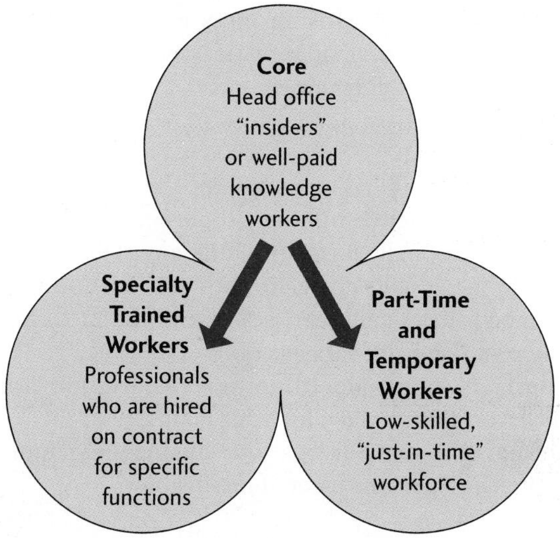

Core
Head office "insiders" or well-paid knowledge workers

Specialty Trained Workers
Professionals who are hired on contract for specific functions

Part-Time and Temporary Workers
Low-skilled, "just-in-time" workforce

The Shamrock Model is a type of virtual organization with strategic business units.

Source: Adapted from *The Age of Unreason* by Charles Handy, published by Arrow Books. Reprinted by permission of The Random House Group Limited.

- **It is based on outsourcing.** Requirements are met with outside resources, not those from inside the organization.
- **It promotes supplier competition.**
- **It delegates selling duties to selling agents, not staff.**
- **It offers a web of associates or partners.** The corporate structure is linked by a web of alliances such as partnerships, joint ventures, and associates. This web replaces the traditional core functions such as manufacturing, warehousing, and supply.
- **It relies on outside expertise.** Emphasis is shifted from in-house knowledge to outside expertise.[4]

TEAMWORK

THE FOUNDING TEAM

A business is only as strong as the people who breathe life into it.[5] Therefore, it is important to think about the skills that you and the members of your founding team possess and how these skills will help bring your product or service to market. There are three areas you should focus on: (1) management team profiles and ownership structure, (2) the board of directors or advisory board, and (3) human resources requirements.

MANAGEMENT TEAM PROFILES AND OWNERSHIP STRUCTURE

No matter how large or small your business is, good management is central to its success. It is important to think through and identify all management categories, necessary skill sets, and possible job titles. It isn't necessary to fill each position with a different person. You should, however, be able to identify the people who are capable of assuming roles when necessary, whether it be you or someone else. You should have a current copy of everyone's résumé in addition to a profile of each member of your management team (even if the team is just you), identifying his or her unique skills. You should be able to describe how each person will add to the team's success. You should also be able to answer these questions:

- What are the major categories of business management in your company (e.g., marketing, sales, research, administration)? Explain your function and the functions of the key team members.
- Who are the people who have agreed to work with your business? What are their job descriptions?
- What positions are still unfilled at your company?
- What skills and job experience will the people who fill these positions have?
- What skills do you personally have? (Include any skills from your last job or business.) How do these skills correlate with your business?
- What is the compensation package for you and the management team (e.g., salary, benefits, profit-sharing schemes)?
- What work contracts, noncompetition agreements, and other contractual agreements have you put in place for your management team?
- What is the ownership structure of your business (including percentages controlled by the management team, if applicable)?

BOARD OF DIRECTORS OR ADVISORY TEAM

In the case study at the end of this chapter, we highlight MSM—a recognized leader in the Canadian transportation industry. The company's success is largely due to its two founding partners—Mike McCarron and Robert Murray—who constantly seek out advice. They rely on a broad-based team of advisors ranging from lawyers and accountants to transportation specialists, and they even make a point of treating some of their senior managers as advisors.[6]

Creating a board or team of advisors for your company is an excellent way to benefit from the skills and expertise of people you might not yet be able to afford to employ. In addition, a board of directors or advisors provides networking opportunities and an introduction to key people within an industry. If you have decided to incorporate, now is the time to give some serious thought to your board of directors. In Chapter 8, you found out that, by law, you must have a board of directors. Many small companies take the easy route and simply elect key shareholders to the board. We want you to think about forming a board that will provide true guidance and advice to your company. It is your chance to make a lawyer or accountant part of your team. If you need marketing help, elect a marketer. As we learned, your company's board of directors can make some very important decisions in the guidance and direction of your company. You don't want to lose this important opportunity to obtain outside expertise and advice.

But what happens if you have decided not to incorporate? You can also draw on the power of teamwork and advisors. Forward-looking entrepreneurs, such as Charlene Webb in the opening story, have created what is termed an "advisory board" with a rather formalized structure. Mike McCarron and Robert Murray of MSM (see end-of-chapter case study) took a less-formalized advisory team approach. You can include professionals such as bankers, lawyers, and accountants—even your business professor. It is important to ensure that you look for board or advisory members who can supplement skills your business might be lacking; for example, if your business is technology based, try to include people with marketing and finance backgrounds. Colleagues, associates, and friends can also take on a semi-official responsibility for the company's welfare and meet with you four or five times a year to review your updated business plan or new objectives, or to discuss difficult problems. Some enterprising entrepreneurs we know have even created a customer board of advisors. Sound a little unusual? Not at all. Since customers drive a business, it makes sense to set up a formal mechanism like a focus group to listen to their concerns. Even if you are incorporated, an advisory board can be a big advantage. You will need as much help as you can get.

HUMAN RESOURCES REQUIREMENTS

Once you have defined your management and advisory team, you need to think about the other employees or independent associates your business might need and their function(s). In the beginning, it might be just you and a selection of freelance, contract, or part-time help. You will need to think ahead and consider all the options you might be faced with. Many small business owners make the mistake of hiring only for their immediate needs. If the administrative assistant you hire in year two, for example, is chosen for future potential, then a workable "hire/train from within" policy could be a company strength. This type of hiring foresight is a major strength of successful companies such as MSM. You will need to give some thought to the human resources checklist, shown in Box 12.2. These are the types of issues we will work through in the latter part of the chapter.

BUILDING BALANCE INTO YOUR TEAM

As we will learn in the MSM case study, balance, not sameness, is essential in a winning team. For many entrepreneurs who have taken ownership of their ideas, finding this new freedom to let go and share their vision can be excruciatingly difficult. Entrepreneurs most in need of help are the stereotypical visionaries who

> ### Box 12.2   Human Resources Checklist
>
> ❑ How long do you plan to own this business?
> ❑ What jobs need to be done? Who is the best person to clean the bathroom? do the books? prepare the tax forms?
> ❑ What are your staffing options (e.g., part-time, full-time, leasing, contracting out)?
> ❑ How many people do you require for your business?
> ❑ What are the real costs (both money and time) of recruitment, selection, orientation, training, evaluating, and so on?
> ❑ What specific skills do employees and associates need to possess?
> ❑ Will your new employees fit in with the culture of your organization? Do they share your vision and mission?
> ❑ Are your employees protected by workers' compensation coverage? Is your business registered with your provincial workers' compensation board/commission? Most businesses—by law—need to be.
> ❑ Is there sufficient local labour? How will you recruit people if there is not?
> ❑ How will you train your team?
> ❑ What is your policy for ongoing training for your team?
> ❑ Are you hiring for the future? What is your policy on hiring and promoting from within?

founded a company and set out to do everything themselves. The day of the lone-wolf operator is quickly coming to an end—business today is just too complex.

Realize that you cannot do everything yourself. You will need a team with different skills and personalities, depending on your strengths and the needs of the business. For example, we'll learn that MSM Transportation benefited from the differing personalities of the founding partners: they questioned each other's assumptions and strategies. "My partner has made me much more effective and, I believe, much better at what I do," said Robert Murray. The key here is to not clone yourself. Surround yourself with people whose skills can complement yours.

Now is a good time for a thorough self-assessment. Begin thinking about your strengths and weaknesses, and the kinds of people you will need to create your team. Complete Action Step 53. Then take one or more of the personality tests listed in Box 12.3. We also encourage you to revisit your entrepreneurial assessments (Chapter 1) and your values (Chapter 3).

ACTION STEP 53

Understand your personal strengths and weaknesses. (p. 360)

> ### Box 12.3   E-Exercise
>
>
>
> **Your Personality Profile**
>
> • **The Keirsey Temperament Sorter II (Advisor Team):** http://www.keirsey.com/sorter/register.aspx—This online personality inventory, which tells you if you're an Artisan, a Guardian, a Rational, or an Idealist, is used in career development programs at Fortune 500 companies and in counselling centres and career placement centres at major universities.
>
> • **The Big 5 Personality Test:** http://www.outofservice.com/bigfive—This test measures what many psychologists consider to be the five fundamental dimensions of personality.
>
> • **The Leadership Motivation Assessment, Mind Tools:** http://www.mindtools.com/pages/article/newLDR_01.htm—Are you motivated to lead? This assessment helps you find the answer.

NON-TRADITIONAL TEAMS

Be on the lookout for people who complement your personality and skills characteristics, as well as compensate for your weaknesses. Because you need to work with people who take ownership of your vision, the 9-to-5 employee mentality might no longer be in the equation. In the traditional team, business owners thought of their members as employees, but your new dream doesn't have to take the form of an employee–employer relationship.

THE "JUST-IN-TIME" TEAM

Think outside the box. Think about such relationships as joint ventures or strategic alliances with other companies, or formal associations/partnerships with individuals. How about subcontracting, or creating informal partnerships or associations?

Here are a few examples of how **just-in-time teams**, which are an alternative to traditional employment relationships, might work.

JUST-IN-TIME TEAM

A group of individuals who are hired on a contract basis to perform a specific function

A general contractor pulls together a team of subcontractors who can be trusted to build a high-quality building. If the job goes well, there will be other opportunities for this team of specialists, but they get paid only while they are on contract.

A local printer discovers that her sales ability exceeds her ability to produce. She redefines herself as a "printer's broker" and uses her knowledge to select the most appropriate product from a wide variety of printers. She then sells her own small shop to an employee and increases her income several times over by providing assistance to customers who know little about printing. Her virtual organization now has just-in-time access to hundreds of experienced printers.

With continued corporate downsizing come mushrooming opportunities for alert entrepreneurs to find just-in-time workers. The benefits include

- having access to the skills and experience of proven experts in their field,
- paying only for services rendered,
- reducing administrative and overhead costs,
- gaining higher reliability,
- achieving better quality and consistency,
- having lower internal development costs,
- getting a customer who is pre-sold,
- maintaining flexibility to address new market opportunities instantly.

ACTION STEP 54

Consider a just-in-time team. (p. 360)

The just-in-time team needs to be customer driven and opportunity focused. There must also be agreement and a shared vision among all participants. Partners and opportunities must be selected with care, as performance standards will be critical. Flexibility and adaptability are important. Your just-in-time team might exist for a few weeks or a year or more. Then, when the opportunity has been fully exploited, the team must be prepared to disband quickly and move on to the next opportunity.

Take a moment and consider a just-in-time team. Complete Action Step 54.

GOAL-ORIENTED PARTNERSHIPS

Consider as partners those firms with special capabilities that will share your risk in bringing a product or service to market. For example, if you have a new product, a team that includes retailers or end users could solve many of your marketing problems. Businesses usually form partnerships or associations in two fundamental ways: joint venture and strategic alliance.

A **joint venture** is usually a goal-oriented cooperation among two or more businesses. It involves the creation of a separate organization owned and controlled jointly by the parties.

JOINT VENTURE

Partnership formed for a specific undertaking, resulting in the formation of a new legal entity

The joint venture usually has its own management, employees, production systems, and so on. Cooperation is limited to defined areas and, often, a predetermined time frame.

A **strategic alliance**, sometimes called a "business network," is a goal-oriented cooperative effort among two or more businesses, based on formal agreements and a business plan. In contrast to a joint venture, however, it usually does not involve the establishment of a separate new organization. The objective is to improve the competitiveness and capabilities of the individual members by using the strengths of the team. Depending on the need, the network may be organized in a variety of forms with regard to function, structure, and organization.

STRATEGIC ALLIANCE

Goal-oriented partnership formed between companies to create a competitive advantage

THE INDEPENDENT CONTRACTOR OR ASSOCIATE

Although it is wise to build a web of complementary business associates to ensure success of your start-up, the reality is that you might need an employee, or several. Should this be the case, you should first consider the benefits of the "near employee," or the independent contractor.

Many people misunderstand government rules on independent contractors. If you tell the worker when to start and stop work, and if you supply the tools or office equipment, you have an employee. On the other hand, if the work assignment is task or project driven, if the worker sets his or her own hours, if you pay by the job and not by the hour, and if most of the work takes place away from your office using the worker's resources, then you may have an independent contractor or associate relationship. For example, many real estate agents who work on straight commission would qualify as independent contractors.

Think about using independent contractors or associates. If you pay by the job, on contract, you can save a lot of administrative costs. To start with, you pay only for work performed. You don't pay for coffee breaks. If the job isn't done, you don't pay. Consider the employee benefits that you, as an employer, would be expected to pay—these would take up a big chunk of your payroll. According to a KPMG survey, the wages and salaries that employers pay represent only about 58 percent of payroll costs; the remaining 42 percent are in benefits, such as sick leave, employer's contribution to CPP, Employment Insurance, health insurance, and workers' compensation. So, if you were paying an employee $172, you'd be paying about $100 in wages and $72 for benefits.[7]

A strong word of caution is in order, however. You need to be careful about the legal ins and outs of hiring on contract. We strongly recommend you check with both provincial/territorial and federal employment bodies, especially the Canada Revenue Agency (CRA), before you contract-out work. Make sure, in writing if you can, that they will accept the conditions you set out for your associates or independent contractors.

EMPLOYEE LEASING

Consider employee leasing as a way of reducing administrative costs, paperwork hassles, legal issues, and costly benefits. In an arrangement not unlike leasing physical property, you could lease people (employees) from a leasing organization that handles payroll and most, if not all, of the human resources functions.

The leasing firm will help you keep in compliance with the myriad of federal, provincial, and local employment laws. Labour codes and employment standards codes are complicated. Keeping in compliance, in some cases, can become fulltime job. For your protection, we suggest you use only a firm that has a strong track record and a sound financial background. Many new ventures are unable to offer employees health insurance benefits and retirement programs and thus lose out on top employees. Because of economies of scale, large leasing firms are able to provide these benefits to your leased employees.

Employee leasing might appear to cost more initially, but it allows for additional benefits, these among them:

- Background screening checks are completed by the leasing organization.
- Termination issues are eliminated—if the person doesn't fit the position, you can send that person back to the leasing organization.
- Turnover is reduced.
- Hiring costs (e.g., advertising, interviewing time, reference checks, turnover) are eliminated.

A list of employee leasing agencies can be found by linking onto the goodstaff.com website: http://www.goodstaff.com.

THE MENTORING RELATIONSHIP

James and Brenda found their business mentor when they took a two-day "Look before You Leap" small business seminar. In time, they were able to bounce ideas back and forth and obtain valuable feedback from a seminar guest speaker who had 25 years of sound experience.

"We couldn't have done it without her," says Brenda. "She gave us strength, direction, and confidence. She agreed to be our mentor on the condition that we become a mentor for a new business owner once we became successful. That made us feel good. For her, it was not a question of if we were going to be successful, it was a question of when. She believed in us—unconditionally."

For independent business, **mentoring** is a mutually beneficial partnership between a more experienced entrepreneur or businessperson, and an entrepreneur who is in the infant, or start-up, phase of a venture. The experienced partner is one who is reflective about his or her venture and is able to communicate and share an understanding and knowledge about what has made the venture grow. The inexperienced entrepreneur, or protégé, is receptive to the suggestions of the mentor and also willing to try to implement some of them in the new business.

Mentoring is an ongoing partnership that might last for a number of months before any benefits are realized by either partner. The partners need to commit themselves to regular meetings with a focused agenda. Usually, the mentor has more frequent and in-depth involvement than an advisory board member would.

MENTORING

A mutually beneficial partnership between a more experienced entrepreneur or businessperson, and an entrepreneur who is in the infant, or start-up, phase of a venture

Much of what is learned in small business comes from experience, as business, to a large extent, is an art. To be successful, we need to know how successful entrepreneurs think. We need help and direction, and in many cases, we will not be able to get what we need from a book. That's why we need a mentor, someone who can give us start-up advice and encouragement.

Essential characteristics of effective small business mentors include these:

- **a desire to help**—individuals who are interested in, and willing to help, others;
- **past positive experiences as emerging entrepreneurs**—individuals who have had positive formal or informal experiences with a mentor;
- **a good reputation for developing others**—individuals who have a good reputation for helping others develop their skills;
- **time and energy**—individuals who have the time and mental energy to devote to the relationship;
- **up-to-date knowledge in the related field**—individuals who have maintained current, up-to-date knowledge or skills;
- **a learning attitude**—individuals who are still willing and able to learn and who see the potential benefits of a mentoring relationship; and
- **demonstrated effective managerial and mentoring skills**—individuals who have demonstrated effective coaching, counselling, facilitating, and networking skills.

ACTION STEP 55

Find a mentor. (p. 361)

Although we strongly recommend that you get a mentor, we think that you should be aware that mentoring relationships don't always succeed the first time. Here are four of the most frequent problems with mentoring relationships.[8]

- **Personality mismatch.** One or both members of the relationship might feel uneasy with the other, or they might be unable to achieve the level of friendship necessary for rich communication.
- **Unrealistic expectations.** It is important that expectations be defined clearly from the beginning.
- **Breaches of confidentiality.** To develop the type of relationship in which the mentor can be effective, he or she must first be perceived as trustworthy and able to keep confidences, and vice versa.
- **Lack of commitment.** Both parties must do what they say and say what they do.

Table 12.2 provides some guidelines for choosing your mentor. Now it's your turn. Start looking for a mentor. Complete Action Step 55.

Once you have identified some candidates, develop a set of questions, and arrange for one-to-one meetings to explore the potential of each person as a mentor. Here are some things to consider when choosing a mentor:

- Do you feel comfortable with this person?
- Can you trust this person?
- Is he or she easy to communicate with?
- Does this person have experience and contacts that can help your new business?
- Is she or he willing to devote the time to help you?

After you have made your choice and the person has agreed to help you, keep in close contact. See the person at least once a month. Set up regular meetings with an agenda, and use the phone or email to smooth out rough spots.

HIRING YOUR FIRST EMPLOYEE

You have considered all your options and the kinds of questions provided in Box 12.2. Before you hire your first employee, we want you to take another look at your personal skills, values, and passion. We again encourage you to do some self-analysis. Complete the online self-evaluation tests (Box 12.3). Revisit Action Step 16

Table 12.2	Characteristics of Mentors
Mentors Are …	**Your Mentor Must …**
… winners	… have extensive business experience
… humble	… have at least one admitted failure
… caring	… truly care about you as a person
… believers	… truly believe you can move mountains
… guides	… be able to guide and direct without preaching
… encouragers	… be able to encourage the answer from within you
… honest	… have the strength and knowledge to be honest with you
… empathizers	… be able to empathize, not sympathize
… listeners	… want to spend time listening to you
… excited	… be excited about your ideas

Source: Ronald A. Knowles and Debbie White, *Issues in Canadian Small Business* (Toronto: Dryden, an imprint of Harcourt Brace & Company, Canada, 1995), p. 78. Reprinted by permission of Elizabeth Knowles.

(Chapter 3, page 71). Is the decision to hire staff consistent with your values? Do you have the demonstrated skills to manage people effectively? If you hire new employees, you will have to rely on new skills, such as administrating, delegating, organizing, communicating, and developing teamwork. As we learned in the opening story, this was a major downfall for Charlene Webb's first business. Many entrepreneurs discover that after they hire staff, they spend more time managing the staff than doing the business. They begin to lose their passion for the business. In fact, some business owners end up deciding not to grow their businesses, because they prefer not to manage staff and be responsible for all the administrative red tape.

If you decide that you need to hire employees and take on more of a managing role, then consider the following basic steps.

STEP 1: JOB ANALYSIS

First, you will have to determine the jobs or functions that need to be done to achieve your businesses goals. Many entrepreneurs—especially those operating out of the home—suffer from loneliness and boredom. They hire staff to satisfy their social needs, not the requirements of the business. This can't be your reason. You will need to determine what jobs are required and how new employees will contribute to the objectives of your business. Revisit your cash flow and income statements (Chapter 10). How will these new functions improve output and contribute to the cash flow and profit? How much can the business afford to pay?

STEP 2: JOB QUALIFICATIONS

You will need to consider the skills and knowledge required to do the job. What are the qualifications, traits, and characteristics essential for someone to satisfy the job requirements? These qualification issues may include education level, relevant experience, skill level, and physical characteristics.

STEP 3: JOB REQUIREMENTS

Once you determine what the jobs are and the corresponding skills required, then you have to figure out who will do the work. First, you should determine whether your current team is sufficient to fill future job requirements. Maybe you can solve the problem with overtime, for example. However, if you still anticipate a shortage, you will have to find new people or alternative ways to fill expected needs. Consider the pros and cons of the just-in-time team—strategic alliances, joint ventures, subcontractors, and employee leasing—as we discussed above.

If the just-in-time team is not an option, you will then have to consider the advantages and disadvantages of staffing—hiring employees on a part-time or full-time basis. Many small firms use part-time or temporary workers until the owners have a strong feel for what needs to be done and who is best suited to do the job. Today, more than one in five workers is a part-timer (working fewer than 30 hours per week). There are a number of advantages for firms in hiring part-time employees. First, as part-time wage rates are typically 60 percent of regular full-time wages, you can reduce your labour costs significantly. Part-time workers also usually receive fewer benefits, which reduces yet another company expense. Part-time employment can be an effective strategy for companies to benefit from the experience of the "retired" workforce, which, as we know, is a growth segment. Weigh these benefits against some of the negative long-term implications. For example, overreliance on part-timers might leave your company without any experience or continuity. This lack could stifle your growth potential, as part-time workers normally have less commitment and loyalty to their company.

STEP 4: STAFFING DECISIONS AND RECRUITMENT

Should you decide to hire your staff, either part- or full-time, you have to make four basic staffing decisions on

- recruitment,
- selection,
- training and development,
- compensation.

RECRUITMENT

In the process of finding the right staff, you will be confronted with two basic recruitment options: internal and external recruitment. Here are some pros and cons of each.

1. **Internal recruitment**—promotion from within the company.

Advantages include

- knowledge of the organizational culture,
- knowledge of the candidates' performance histories,
- lower recruiting costs.

Disadvantages include

- possible internal rivalry and competition ensuing,
- no "new blood" to enhance creativity and innovation,
- lower morale on the part of those who were passed over.

2. **External recruitment**—searching for employees from outside the company.

Advantages include

- new blood,
- new expertise,
- new energy.

Disadvantages include

- greater costs,
- the new employee not being known to the organization,
- a longer time to "socialize" the employee,
- lower morale from those in the organization who were passed over.

Some of the most common methods of finding new employees through external recruitment are as follows:

- the Internet (with one great source for job seekers and job posters being the Job Bank on the Service Canada website (http://www.jobbank.gc.ca)),
- company websites,
- employee referrals,
- word-of-mouth advertising,
- college/university placement offices,
- employment/temporary worker agencies,
- newspaper classified advertising,
- ads in trade and professional journals.

In Box 12.4, we have provided you with the most common recruitment methods for small business.

Box 12.4 Did You Know?

1. Recruitment

A study by Duxbury and Higgins surveyed 103 Canadian small businesses and found the following: "Small businesses recruit employees by

- taking referrals (75 percent),
- placing ads in the newspaper (56 percent),
- asking friends and relatives if they know someone (40 percent),
- walk-ins (37 percent),
- by going through private employment agencies (31 percent)."

2. Non-financial Compensation

In a survey of 300 small businesses in Canada, the Centre for Families, Work, and Well-Being asked, "What are the work–life strategies that make small companies successful in concurrently meeting their business objectives and being a good place for employees to work?" The survey found that

- more than 80 percent of companies offer at least one flexible work arrangement for employees, and flextime is the most common arrangement;
- 83 percent provide time off to care for sick family members;
- 80 percent provide extended healthcare benefits;
- 70 percent offer time off for "eldercare";
- 21 percent offer an EAP (employee assistance program).

Sources: Monica Beauregard and Maureen Fitzgerald. *Hiring, Managing and Keeping the Best: The Complete Canadian Guide for Employers* (Toronto: McGraw-Hill Ryerson, 2000), p. 27; cited in Service Canada, "Exploring Recruitment Options," http://www.jobsetc.gc.ca/eng/home-accueil.jsp; Canadian Plastics Sector Council, "Work-Life Balance," http://www.cpsc-ccsp.ca/Employee%20Retention/Work-Life_Balance.htm; Linda Duxbury and Chris Higgins, *Work-Life Balance in the New Millennium: Where Are We? Where Do We Need to Go?* CPRN Discussion Paper No. WI12, Canadian Policy Research Networks, October 2001, online at http://www.cprn.org/documents/7314_en.PDF.

SELECTION

EMPLOYEE SELECTION

The process of determining which persons in the applicant pool possess the qualifications necessary to be successful on the job

Should you decide to recruit for the position, you will have to follow an **employee selection** process involving

- initial screening (application and interview),
- employment testing (aptitude, personality, or skills),
- selection interviews,
- background and reference checks,
- requests for and evaluations of physical examinations,
- the decision to hire.

A critical stage in the selection process is the interview. About 86 percent of those hired by interview alone will not work out for the company, so you have to be very careful about hiring in this way. Should you decide to recruit a full-time employee, part-time employment is one of the least risky ways of "road testing" prospective employees. If you must select by the interview process, we suggest that you conduct at least two interviews in different venues or settings for your final candidates. Try to have existing employees, especially coworkers, involved in the hiring process. The attitude of prospective employees is a key factor. You must ensure that the new hire shares the values and beliefs of your company.

For more details on recruitment and selection, click on the "Guide to Screening and Selection in Employment" links of the Canadian Human Rights Commission at http://www.chrc-ccdp.gc.ca/sites/default/files/screen.pdf.

Issues related to human rights, employment standards, and hiring are complicated, so the government has created brochures to help explain various regulations. About 90 percent of employee rights legislation comes under provincial jurisdiction, and provincial laws can vary extensively. Failure to follow legal requirements can result in stiff penalties or even lawsuits from disgruntled employees. So be very careful about what you say and check with your provincial labour departments if you have any doubts. You might find it beneficial to use an employment agency to hire your first few employees.

At the interview, ask the right questions. Prepare a list of questions that solicit responses to applicants' skills, experiences, or knowledge needed in the job. Similar questions should be asked of each applicant, so that you can evaluate their responses and suitability. You might want to look over a few books that employees use to prepare for job interviews. These could give you ideas on questions to ask. To start, here are some questions that you could use:

1. How did you prepare for this meeting?
2. Why do you want to work for us?
3. How do your skills match the job description?
4. What would you do in the following situation? (Explain a problem the applicant might face on the job.)
5. What type of training will you need to perform this job?
6. What are some of the obstacles you have overcome?
7. What do you expect from a boss?
8. What gives you satisfaction in a job?
9. What do you think you will like most and least about this particular job?
10. What kinds of things disturb you on the job?
11. What have been your most pleasant work experiences?
12. What do you want to be doing in five years?
13. What would your references say about you?
14. What did you like or dislike about your last job?

In general, you can stay out of trouble if you refrain from asking job applicants questions about the following:

1. age or birth date,
2 place of birth,
3. a woman's maiden name,
4. racial or ethnic background,
5. religious affiliation,
6. marital status and sexual orientation,
7. number of children and ages,
8. medical condition or non-job-related physical data,
9. disabilities.

TRAINING AND DEVELOPMENT

Once you decide to hire staff, you have to put into place a program to train your new staff and then determine how much this will cost.

COMPENSATION

There are two general types of financial compensation—direct and indirect. However, consider nonfinancial compensation, as well.

Direct compensation is the wage or salary received by the employee. Examples include basic pay, which encompasses

- hourly wages,
- salaries,
- incentive (performance) pay, which includes

  – piecework,
  – commissions,
  – pay for knowledge,
  – bonus pay,
  – profit sharing.

DIRECT COMPENSATION

The wage or salary received by the employee

Indirect compensation (fringe benefits) refers to the employee benefits and services that are given entirely or partly at the expense of the company. Many benefits are governed by federal and provincial laws. Examples include these:

- pensions,
- provincial health insurance premiums,
- vacation pay,
- sick leave,
- child care.

INDIRECT COMPENSATION (FRINGE BENEFITS)

Employee benefits and services that are given entirely or partly at the expense of the company

Many small businesses informally offer some of these benefits—especially those related to time off and flexibility—to create a supportive work environment. Nonetheless, there are four major mandatory programs that require contributions by both employers and employees and which will increase your payroll by about 10 percent:

1. Canada and Quebec pension plans (CPP and QPP)—for retirement, disability, and survivors' and death benefits;
2. workers' compensation—for disability benefits and pensions for spouses and dependants;
3. vacation and holiday pay;
4. employment insurance.

Many small business owners have initiated nonfinancial compensation initiatives in their workplace and have done so out of a conviction that providing such benefits can substantially improve productivity, revenues, and employee retention and commitment. Some of these nonfinancial forms of compensation include

- challenging jobs,
- recognition,
- flexible work hours,
- compressed workweek (working 10 hours a day for four days, for example),
- job sharing,
- home-based work.

WHAT DO EMPLOYEES REALLY COST?

If you plan on hiring, consider all the costs associated with hiring, training, and retaining employees, including

- ad placements (very expensive);
- recruiting and staffing;
- training;
- direct compensation (salary/wages);
- indirect compensation (especially Canada and Quebec pension plans, workers' compensation, vacation and holiday pay, and employment insurance);
- space, furniture, and equipment;
- additional management time;
- any specific perks you might offer (e.g., car allowance).

Each employee can cost you his or her salary plus 60 percent of that salary or more. Employees in an entrepreneurial venture need to pull more than their own weight. So our best advice is to select wisely.

MANAGING AN AGING AND MULTICULTURAL WORKFORCE

The increase in employment and labour force participation of people aged 55 and over reflects a steady trend in Canada's population aging. In 2011, nearly one-third of the population aged 15 and over was at least 55 years old (up from 22 percent three decades ago).

The makeup of the Canadian workforce is also becoming increasingly multicultural. According to Statistics Canada, from 2010 to 2011, there was a 4.3 percent rise in employment among immigrants 25 to 54 years of age. The bulk of the employment increase in 2011 was accounted for by established immigrants (in the country for more than 10 years). This rise in employment among immigrants was much stronger than the 0.5 percent growth among their Canadian-born counterparts in the same age group. Most of the growth in immigrant employment during this period was in healthcare and social assistance, and in information, culture, and recreation services.[9]

As you look at managing your workforce, be sure to pay extra attention to certain workforce realities, including these:

- religious and cultural sensitiveness,
- work–life balance,
- shifting priorities among employees of different ages.

How can you, the entrepreneur, best prepare to deal with a changing workforce? By increasing your knowledge and obtaining information on how to address these challenges. Some approaches include becoming more knowledgeable about different cultures and their behaviours, and appreciating the differences. Smart entrepreneurs know that there are many opportunities available to them when they have a diverse workforce; according to some, a diverse workforce leads to increased profitability. More information on this topic can be found by going to http://www.gov.ns.ca/PSC/default.asp?mn1.162.295.

Now it's your turn again. Complete Action Step 56 once you have built your team.

ACTION STEP 56

Decide who's in charge of what. (p. 361)

HR BEST PRACTICES

What are some of the best practices in human resources (HR)? ECO Canada developed an HR Best Practices Report in 2009.[10] Some of those best practices are featured below:

- **Reinforcing company values and staff involvement:** Rescan Environmental Services Ltd.—Rescan's staffing and recruitment strategy is to hire individuals who share the same values as the company. These include the ability to demonstrate flexibility, resilience, and commitment to excellence and dedication. In addition, Rescan encourages staff involvement in the recruitment process by promoting an employee referral program. If an employee recommends a new candidate, and the new candidate completes the three-month probationary period, that employee receives $1,000.
- **University internships:** Stratos Inc.—Stratos uses its internship program to attract students who excel academically. The company then provides the interns with an opportunity to obtain practical work experience.
- **Orientation checklists:** Terrapex Environmental Ltd.—Terrapex uses a detailed new employee orientation checklist to help new employees learn basic workplace operations. New employees receive this checklist in their orientation packages.
- **Hands-on learning:** Ecometrix Incorporated—Ecometrix uses hands-on learning to encourage staff to develop professionally. Employees may have little work experience at the beginning, but this approach sets them on course to take initiative and advance in the company.
- **Transferring senior knowledge:** Ecometrix Incorporated—Each senior staff member is responsible for the professional and personal development of one or two junior or intermediate employees. This practice allows for the transfer of knowledge from senior to junior.

In a Nutshell

Leading is a key management function, and you'll have to learn how to inspire and empower your team. In addition, you will have to be able to justify and chart your organizational structure. We want you to consider the benefits of a virtual, or network, organization. We also want you to understand that you won't be able to do everything yourself. You will need a founding team with different skills and personalities, depending on your strengths and weaknesses and the needs of the business. We encourage you to consider less traditional team arrangements, such as subcontracting, joint ventures, strategic alliances, and mentoring. We also encourage you to take a proactive approach to human resources planning and recruitment. If you decide to hire employees, either full- or part-time, we strongly suggest that you follow the recruitment and selection process we've set out.

Key Terms

direct compensation

employee selection

indirect compensation

joint venture

just-in-time team

leadership

mentoring

strategic alliance

strategic business units

virtual organization (or network organization)

Think Points for Success

✓ You can't grow until you have the right people.
✓ People tend to "hire themselves." How many more people like you can the business take?
✓ Balance the people on your team.
✓ A winning team is lurking in your network.
✓ Look to your competitors and vendors for team members.
✓ How much of your team can be built from part-timers and moonlighters?
✓ How "virtual" can you make your business structure?
✓ Can you form a joint venture or a strategic alliance?
✓ Do you know what your legal responsibilities are?
✓ What is your job selection process?
✓ Have each team member write objectives for his or her responsibilities within the business.

Action Steps

ACTION STEP 53

Understand your personal strengths and weaknesses.

What do you need to be successful? Money, of course, and tremendous energy and leadership. You need a vision, a terrific idea, the ability to focus, a sense of industry and thrift, and the curiosity of Sherlock Holmes. Do you have all these qualities or personality traits? Of course not. That's why you need a team—people to support your effort and to take over tasks that you're weak in or that you don't understand.

So, we want you to analyze yourself. Doing this will help you know the kind of team you need. Take a few minutes, and complete the personality analysis created by Peter Urs Bender, reproduced in Appendix 12.1. Follow this up by asking yourself these questions: What do I like? What am I good at? What do I hate? What does my business need that I cannot provide myself? Who can fill this need for me?

These simple exercises will help you start building a winning team.

ACTION STEP 54

Consider a just-in-time team.

Make a list. Better still, create a mind map of the people or firms that might assist your efforts on an "as needed" basis—a just-in-time team. Think about a joint venture or strategic alliance with vendors, suppliers, coworkers, and even competitors. Look for those who share your vision. Keep on the lookout, and be prepared to expand this list or mind map as new ideas emerge.

ACTION STEP 55

Find a mentor.

First, develop a list of attributes you are looking for in a mentor and areas where you need help. Network with your friends, coworkers, and business associates. Tell them what you're looking for—that is, a successful business owner with a good track record. The perfect mentor would be one with experience in your particular industry. You can also contact your local chamber of commerce, alumni association, Rotary club, or one or more of your local business clubs/associations. You might want to see if your local small business centre can help, or you might want to return to the various networking sites provided in Chapter 6. Consider getting advice from a business coach (see, for example, the "My Story" link of Clive Prout: http://www.thesabbaticalcoach.com). You can even look for a virtual mentor on the Internet. Visit, for example, the "Mentor Programs" page on the Canadian Youth Business Foundation (http://www.cybf.ca/mentors)

ACTION STEP 56

Decide who's in charge of what.

It's time to impress your business plan reader. Investors or vendors are often more interested in the founders than in the Business Plan itself. Experience in the same type of business and former business experience and/or ownership are significant strengths. Focus on past responsibility and authority. Present the balance and diversity of your founding team.

A couple of paragraphs in the Business Plan might be sufficient for each key founder. If experience is lacking, discuss consultants or committed strategic partners who will bring balance to the management team and contribute experience and special skills. You might also want to include an organizational chart in your Business Plan's appendixes. You will need to complete full résumés later for the appendix of your Business Plan.

Business Plan Building Block

MANAGEMENT AND OWNERSHIP

Who's in charge? Investors or vendors are often more interested in the founders than in the Business Plan itself. Experience in the same type of business and past business successes are powerful positive components of the plan. Focus on responsibility and authority.

A paragraph or two might be sufficient for each key founder. If retail experience is lacking, list consultants or committed strategic partners who can balance the management team. Consider including an organizational chart.

Name the other key management team members, and include their résumés, focusing on their contribution to your business and how they will give you a competitive edge. Save the full-blown résumés of the management team members for an appendix at the back of the plan.

The lender, vendor, or venture capital firm weighs the founding team as one of the most important factors. Present balance and diversity with a history of past achievement. It is here that you should explain your business form (incorporation, partnership, sole proprietorship, or cooperative). If you have more than two people on the team, include an organizational chart.

Your turn again. Who are the players in your business, and what role will each play?

_____

_____

_____

_____

_____

List consultants, advisory board members, or strategic partners who can contribute experience or special skills.

_____

_____

_____

_____

_____

HUMAN RESOURCES PLAN

1. Types of workers needed (Include just-in-time, seasonal, and part-time workers.)

_____

_____

_____

2. Compensation, commissions, bonuses, and/or profit sharing

_____

_____

_____

3. Provincial and federal compliance requirements

_____

_____

_____

4. Performance standards, training, and retraining

_____

_____

_____

5. Workers' compensation and insurance costs

_____

_____

_____

6. Employee handbook (look for professional help)

_____

_____

_____

7. Union contracts

_____

_____

_____

8. Professional certifications

_____

_____

_____

Checklist Questions and Actions to Develop Your Business Plan

Building and Managing a Winning Team

❑ What major human resources issues does your business face, and how do you plan to address these issues?

❑ Have you included an employment schedule in your appendix and corresponding wage costs for your staff and yourself?

❑ Have you allowed for benefits? To comply with legal statutory requirements, you need to consider *at least* 20 percent of your wage and salary costs for benefits.

❑ Do you have job descriptions in place and plans to conduct an annual performance appraisal?

❑ Do your wage rates fit within the industry norm? Are you prepared to pay more than the industry to be a "top draw" company?

❑ Outline your leadership style, and your strengths and weaknesses as an entrepreneur.

❑ How might a "virtual organization" work for you?

❑ If you are starting out just by yourself, at what point in sales or other volume indicator will you add a second or a third person?

Case Study: Management and Teamwork at MSM Transportation

Case Background

Robert Murray and Mike McCarron are two of the founding partners of MSM Transportation Incorporated. When they started the company back in the late 1980s, they knew they were combining two different types of management expertise and two very different personalities. McCarron, the company's managing partner and primary marketer, was enthusiastic, outgoing, passionate, and—as he admits—impulsive. Murray, MSM's president, trained originally as a credit manager, came across as quiet, diplomatic, and thoughtful—more of a long-term thinker. Oil and water? Of course.

Murray recalled that the duo's strength lay in the fact that they could disagree, argue feverishly, work it out, and move on. Their vision was to become a dominant player in the Canadian transportation industry. Because the two partners shared a similar vision for the company, if not the same temperament, debate became a positive force that generated new ideas and better decisions. In an industry notorious for its lack of marketing and financial skills, MSM benefited from both personalities, because the men questioned each other's assumptions and strategies. Noted Murray, "My partner has made me much more effective and, I believe, much better at what I do."

Since its humble beginnings in the late 1980s, MSM has grown into a recognized leader in the Canadian transportation industry. In 2005, for example, MSM Transportation ranked highest in customer satisfaction among Canadian shippers, according to the readers of *Canadian Transportation & Logistics* magazine.[11] It has become a multimillion-dollar Canadian success story. MSM Transportation is now a group of six interrelated companies—MSM Group of Companies Incorporated—that employs close to 200 people, owns and operates over 300 pieces of equipment, and handles more than 50,000 shipments per year. MSM even owns a Junior A hockey team.

In 2006, MSM earned membership in the Platinum Club of Canada's 50 Best-Managed Companies (https://www.canadas50best.com/en/Pages/Home.aspx). To become a member of this elite group, MSM had to sustain consistent profitability and growth and maintain its designation as one of this country's best-managed companies for a minimum of six consecutive years. To a large extent, the day-in and day-out success of this company relates to the teamwork, leadership, and management skills of the two founding partners. At MSM, McCarron and Murray have established an enthusiastic workplace culture and have ensured that all employees believe in and strive toward the MSM mission:

Customer Satisfaction through On-Time-Delivery is our prime goal, and MSM customers are paramount in our daily decisions and successes.

Case Resources

- MSM Group of Companies home page: http://www.shipmsm.com/
- https://www.canadas50best.com/en/Pages/Home.aspx
- Legacee, "Types of Leadership Styles": http://www.legacee.com/Info/Leadership/LeadershipStyles.html
- Ray Jutkins, "The Situational Leader": http://www.rayjutkins.com/ezine/20030812.html
- Mike McCarron, "Why Partnerships Fail," *Today's Trucking*: http://www.todaystrucking.com/why-partnerships-fail
- Mike McCarron, "Personnel Best," *Today's Trucking*: http://www.todaystrucking.com/personnel-best

Case Study Questions

1. Personality types
   a. In Appendix 12.1, we describe four personality types—analytical, amiable, driver, and expressive. What were the dominant personality types of Robert Murray and Mike McCarron? According to Robert Murray, how did these two different personality types contribute to the success of the company?
   b. What is your personality type? Take a few minutes and conduct the personality analysis provided in Appendix 12.1.

2. Transformational leadership
   a. The primary focus of transformational leadership is to make change happen—or "transform," as the name implies. According to the text, people with this leadership style exhibit five basic types of behaviour. Briefly describe these five behavioural traits.
   b. Over the past several years, MSM has had a successful track record in managing a "remote" location in Los Angeles. McCarron's transformational leadership style has had much to do with this success. Link onto the *Today's Trucking* article at http://www.todaystrucking.com/personnel-best. List four ways in which McCarron inspires and stimulates his team.

3. Other leadership styles
   a. The transformational style of leadership is particularly appealing and effective for many entrepreneurs, as its major focus is to make change happen. However, there are other leadership styles. For example, three classical styles are laissez faire (free rein), autocratic, and participative.

   Link onto the Legacee "Types of Leadership Styles" site (http://www.legacee.com/Info/Leadership/LeadershipStyles.html). Briefly explain these three classic leadership styles as described there.
   b. Situational leadership is another style that has gained much popularity over the past 40 years. It's a "different stokes for different folks" approach. Because people and tasks are different, the leadership approach will depend on the situation. This approach involves a combination of four styles. Link onto "The Situational Leader" (http://www.rayjutkins.com/ezine/20030812.html). What are the four "S" styles or options available to the situational leader, as described on the site?

c. Given these various leadership styles, what type of leadership do you plan to use when you open your business? How will this style help you to achieve your goals and objectives? As noted in Box 12.3, you might want to begin by linking onto the Mind Tools site for "The Leadership Motivation Assessment" (http://www.mindtools.com/pages/article/newLDR_01.htm).

4. Organizational structures
   a. In this chapter, we described three types of traditional organizational structures used by small business. Briefly describe each of these types of classical organizational structures.
   b. In the early 2000s, MSM launched an aggressive expansion policy. It expanded its freight forwarding, logistics, and distribution services, and even bought a Junior A hockey team. What type of organizational structure did it create to handle this expansion? What are the five major benefits of this type of structure? (*Hint*: You might want to link onto MSM, "Our Services," http://www.shipmsm.com/.)

5. Strategic partnerships
   a. Strategic partnerships with customers, suppliers, and even employees have been critical to the success of MSM. Go to "Why Partnerships Fail" on the *Today's Trucking* site: http://www.todaystrucking.com/why-partnerships-fail. According to Mike McCarron, what are five ways in which you can improve your partnership relationships?

6. Human resources requirements
   a. In this chapter, we encouraged you to consider the "just-in-time" team and three specific human resources options before deciding to go out and hire full-time staff for your new business. Briefly describe these three alternatives to hiring staff.
   b. According to Mike McCarron at MSM, "the quality of service our people deliver is the only competitive advantage any of us has." What advice does he offer when it comes time to hire a new staff member? (See "Personnel Best," on the *Today's Trucking* site: http://www.todaystrucking.com/personnel-best.)
   c. After considering your alternatives, you decide to hire a new staff member on a full-time basis. According to the text, what are the basic steps you should follow to improve your chances of gaining the "right" person for your business?

Notes

1. See, for example, Legacee, "Types of Leadership Styles," http://www.legacee.com/Info/Leadership/LeadershipStyles.html.
2. Excerpted from J. Howell and B. Avolio, "The Leverage of Leadership," *The Globe and Mail*, May 15, 1998, p. C1. © 1998 Ivey Management Services. Used with permission from Ivey Management Services.
3. Peter Urs Bender, *Leadership from Within* (Toronto: Stoddart Publishing, 1997), p. 23. Reprinted by permission of Stoddart Publishing Co. Limited, Toronto, Ontario.
4. Adapted from Steven L. Goldman, Roger N. Nagel, and Kenneth Preiss, *Agile Competitors and Virtual Organizations* (New York: Van Nostrand Reinholdt, 1995).
5. Information for much of this section is excerpted or adapted from Royal Bank, "The Team," *Business Plans*, http://www.rbcroyalbank.com/sme/bigidea/team.html.
6. http://www.shipmsm.com.
7. Cited in Bruce Little, "Statistics Belie Perception of Less Help for the Needy, Part II," *The Globe and Mail*, January 20, 1994, pp. A1, A6.
8. Canadian Youth Business Foundation, http://www.cybf.ca/mentors.
9. Statistics Canada, *The Canadian Immigrant Labour Market, 2008–2011* by Lahouaria Yssaad, The Immigrant Labour Force Analysis Series, Catalogue no. 71-606-X, http://www.statcan.gc.ca/pub/71-606-x/71-606-x2012006-eng.pdf.
10. ECO Canada (Environmental Careers Organization), *ECO Canada's HR Best Practices Report, 2009*, http://www.eco.ca/pdf/ECO_HR_BestPractices_Report.pdf.
11. Canadian Transportation and Logistics, "Shippers Choice Awards," http://www.ctl.ca/issues/story.aspx?aid=1000197482.

Appendix 12.1
THE PERSONALITY ANALYSIS

Take a few minutes to do the following simple self-assessment. You will learn some fascinating things about yourself in the process. You might also want to compare yourself to others you know—a significant other, your children, or your coworkers.

In the following lists, underline those words (or phrases) that describe you best in a *business* or *work situation*. Total your score for each group of words.

GROUP

A Reserved, uncommunicative, cool, cautious, guarded, seems difficult to get to know, demanding of self, disciplined attitudes, formal speech, rational decision making, strict, impersonal, businesslike, disciplined about time, uses facts, formal dress, measured actions.
Total score: _____

B Take-charge attitude, directive, tends to use power, fast actions, risk taker, competitive, aggressive, strong opinions, excitable, takes social initiative, makes statements, loud voice, quick pace, expressive voice, firm handshake, clear idea of needs, initiator.
Total score: _____

C Communicative, open, warm, approachable, friendly, fluid attitudes, informal speech, undisciplined about time, easygoing with self, impulsive, informal dress, dramatic opinions, uses opinions, permissive, emotional decision making, seems easy to get to know, personal.
Total score: _____

D Slow pace, flat voice, soft-spoken, helper, unclear about what is needed, moderate opinions, calm, asks questions, tends to avoid use of power, indifferent handshake, deliberate actions, lets others take social initiative, risk avoider, quiet, go-along attitude, supportive, cooperative.
Total score: _____

Write your total scores below:

A = _____ C = _____

B = _____ D = _____

Next, determine which groups are larger and by how much:

A vs. C: Which is larger? _____

By how many points? _____

B vs. D: Which is larger? _____

By how many points? _____

FILLING IN THE PERSONALITY GRID

Now mark your results on the grid below:

To determine where you fit on the vertical axis, look at your A vs. C result. For example,

If A is larger than C by 6 points, put a dot (•) at A-6.
If C is larger than A by 5 points, put a dot (•) at C-5.
If A and C are equal, put a dot (•) at "0," in the centre of the grid.

To find your place on the horizontal axis, use your B vs. D result. For example,

If B is larger than D by 4 points, put a dot (•) at B-4.

If D is larger than B by 7 points, put a dot (•) at D-7.

If B and D are equal, put a dot (•) at "0," in the centre of the grid.

In the grid below, draw an X where lines extending from your two points meet (as shown in the sample). The quadrant you're in indicates your personality type.*

This sample grid shows the results for two different people: One is a driver; the other is amiable.

Sample Grid

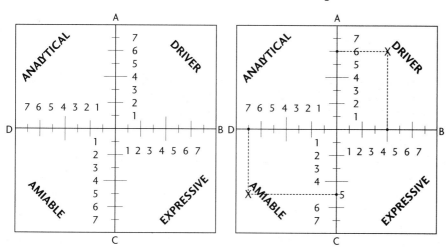

INTERPRETING YOUR RESULTS

Now that you know where you fit, let's find out what it means!

The words shown in the diagram below describe each of the personality types. Read those that apply to you, and see how these words fit your image of your own personality. Then ask others what they think. It helps to get different perspectives.

After considering your own personality, look at people around you. What personality types* do they exhibit?

ANALYTICAL	DRIVER
Logical	Efficient
Precise	Independent
Serious	Candid
Systematic	Decisive
Prudent	Pragmatic
AMIABLE	EXPRESSIVE
Loyal	Enthusiastic
Cooperative	Outgoing
Supportive	Persuasive
Diplomatic	Fun-loving
Patient	Spontaneous

Remember that there is no right or wrong personality type. People of different types simply think and act in different ways.

*These four personality types are adapted from Personality Styles and Effective Performance, by David W. Merrill and Roger H. Reid (American Management Association, 1996).

13

Buying a Business

This chapter will help you investigate the advantages and pitfalls of buying a business.

Monkey Business Images/Shutterstock.com

LEARNING OPPORTUNITIES

After reading this chapter, you should be able to

- evaluate objectively businesses that are for sale,
- understand the pros and cons of purchasing an ongoing business,
- assess the market value of an ongoing business,
- recognize when you need professional help,
- decide whether it is better for you to buy an ongoing business or to begin from scratch.

ACTION STEP PREVIEW

57. Prepare a letter of inquiry.
58. Study a business from the outside.
59. Study a business from the inside.
60. Probe the depths of ill will.

BEN AND SALLY RAYMUNDO

Ben and Sally Raymundo bought a women's sportswear store in a thriving community about two kilometres from a regional shopping mall. They learned too late that the seller had a more profitable store in another part of the county and that she had used that store's records to misrepresent the store they bought. Here are the particulars.

1. The seller moved the cash registers from the higher-volume store to the store she wanted to sell, so the store's sales were greatly inflated.
2. The price was fixed at inventory plus $10,000 for goodwill. This seemed a bargain for a store whose cash register records showed it was grossing $300,000 per year at a 40 percent average gross margin.
3. Ben and Sally paid full wholesale value ($60,000) for goods that had been shipped there from the other store, but the goods were already shopworn and out of date. Eventually, they had to be marked down to less than $20,000.
4. Ben and Sally assumed the remainder of an ironclad lease at $5,000 per month, and the landlord made them sign a personal guarantee by which they pledged their home as security on the lease.
5. The location proved to be a "dead" foot-traffic location in a marginally successful centre.

Fortunately, Ben had kept his regular job. Sally worked at selling off the unwanted inventory and replaced it with more salable stock. The Raymundos spent an additional $50,000 for advertising during the 12 months they stayed in business. It was another year before the landlord found a new tenant, and Ben and Sally could get out of the lease.

In this chapter, you'll learn some ways to evaluate businesses that are up for sale. Although we focus on ongoing, independent operations, many of the strategies are the same for evaluating franchise opportunities. We'll discuss franchising more specifically in Chapter 14.

When you buy an ongoing business, you're buying an income stream. You might also be buying inventory, location, goodwill, an agreement that the sellers will not compete with you, a training program, a business plan, advertising assistance, lease negotiation assistance, and purchasing advantages.

You should explore businesses for sale whether you're serious about buying or not. By now, you're far enough along in your quest to have a sense of the marketplace. Talking to sellers is just one more step in your education in entrepreneurship. Have fun, but leave your chequebook at home until you have done all your research.

Here are some tips to get you started on your exploration of the pros and cons of buying a business.

1. **Determine which type of entrepreneur you are before taking the plunge**. Some businesspeople are "serial entrepreneurs." They seek out and purchase a business with turnaround potential, work to restore it to financial health, and sell the revitalized business at a profit. Other entrepreneurs thrive on the start-up phase of the entrepreneurial journey and are not so interested in the day-to-day operations. A review of the self-assessment Action Steps you completed in Chapter 1 will provide valuable clues as to your entrepreneurial strengths and weaknesses.

2. **Fall in love with the business, not the deal**. As you conduct your search, make finding the "right opportunity"—as opposed to getting the "right price"—a priority. Ask yourself questions such as these: Do I have what it takes to manage this business day in and day out? Will I enjoy interacting with the customers? with the employees? Can I see myself working each day to improve this business? Am I passionate about the business?

3. **Obtain legal representation and financial advice before you sign the contract**. The importance of due diligence cannot be overstated.

WHY PURCHASE AN ONGOING BUSINESS?

The main reason for buying an ongoing business is *money*, primarily the income stream, which can make it a good deal. If you do your research and strike a good deal, you can start making money the day you take over an ongoing business. Because many start-ups must plug along for months (maybe even years) before showing a profit, it's smart to consider the business purchase option. But remember: The uncertainties of a start-up business are reduced but not eliminated. When you buy a business, it is a financial investment. Make sure you are getting the "highest" rate of return on your time and investment dollars.

Other things to consider when buying an existing business include the following.

1. If you find a "hungry seller," you should be able to negotiate good terms. You might be able to buy into a business for little up-front cash and might also negotiate seller financing.

2. Fixtures and equipment will be negotiable. Be sure the equipment is in good working condition and has been well maintained. Ask to see service records. What equipment is being leased? Are there any liens on the equipment?

3. Training and support might be available through the seller and can sometimes be negotiated. If the seller is financing, he or she will have a stake in your success. Many banks like to see some seller financing, because they believe it secures the seller's interest and thus the bank's interest. Request that the owner continue to work in the business for a short time to help you adjust and to serve as a bridge with the customers.

4. An established customer base should be in place. You will need to determine how loyal the customers are and whether there is goodwill or ill will. If the customer base is not strong or loyal, consider this fact appropriately in your price negotiations. If business has recently been souring, goodwill might be difficult to quantify. Assess both the cost and the possibility of rebuilding customer loyalty.

5. Make sure that relationships with suppliers and distributors are in place. Spend time talking to suppliers and distributors to determine the status of the relationship. They should provide great insight.

6. The location might be excellent and not easily duplicated. Determine whether the lease can be reassigned to you. Have your lawyer review the lease, and assess whether the owner of the building has other goals for the location.

7. Employees might possess specialized knowledge that can benefit your business immensely. In high-technology industries, purchasing businesses for brainpower is a common practice. You will have no guarantee, though, that the employees and their expertise will remain—you must consider the possibility that key employees will leave and compete.

8. Existing licences and permits might be difficult to replicate. Check with your lawyer or licensing agencies to determine the availability and process of transferring licences and permits before proceeding with any purchase.

9. Make sure that you can see actual financial data and tax-reporting forms. Investigate!

10. An inside look into the business operation will determine whether using advanced technology could increase operational effectiveness and thus profits.

HOW TO BUY AND HOW NOT TO BUY

Smart buyers scrutinize everything about a business with a microscope, computer analysis, a clipboard, and sage advice from business gurus. They don't plunge into a business for emotional reasons. The business has to make sense from a marketing and financial perspective. For example, you might have eaten lunch around the corner at Millie's Cafeteria with your pals for years, and when the place goes up for sale, nostalgia might prompt you to write out a cheque for it on the spot. Don't buy a business that way.

Rather, examine a business for sale from a business perspective. Can you recoup your investment? How much money will you make? What are the industry trends? Is the market growing? You will need to discuss the business for sale with a lawyer, including the legal consequences of buying this business. Treat your lawyer as a key team member in helping you do your due diligence. Meet with your accountant, as well, to see if there are any issues or warning signs from a financial perspective. The investment made in meeting with an accountant and a lawyer will help you avoid even bigger costs and possible surprises down the road.

Every business in the country is for sale at some time. Deals are like planes; if you miss one, another will be along soon. Seeking the right business to buy is much like an employment search: The best deals are seldom advertised. In contrast, the worst business opportunities are advertised widely, usually in the classified sections of newspapers. When you see several ads for a particular type of business, you know where the unhappy businesspeople are.

Running your own ad can be a good idea, however. A man ran this ad in the business section (not the classifieds) of a large-circulation Toronto newspaper:

> Sold out at 30. Now I'm tired of retirement and ready to start again.
> Want to buy a business with over $1 million in annual sales.
> Write me at Box XXXX. H.G.

H.G. received more than 100 replies, and he says that reading the proposals was one of the most educational and entertaining experiences he has ever had. Five of them looked like good deals, but only one fit his talents and interests. After three months of investigation, he decided he would rather start his next venture from scratch. (The firm he almost bought was a beer distributorship whose supplier went out of business the following year. Perhaps the seller knew something ...)

GETTING THE WORD OUT

Once you're ready to look for a business to buy, you'll need to find out what's for sale. These tips will help you.

1. Spread the word that you are a potential buyer.

2. Contact everyone you can in your chosen industry—manufacturers, resellers, agents, dealers, trade associations, and so on. Let them know you are looking.

3. Ask your network of bankers, lawyers, accountants, and community leaders to help you in your search.
4. Advertise your needs in trade journals and answer ads that have been posted.
5. Use Internet blogs and social networking sites to spread the word and look for opportunities.
6. Send letters of inquiry to potential sellers (see Action Step 57).
7. Knock on doors. You may be surprised!
8. Check with business brokers.
9. Talk with firms that deal in mergers and acquisitions.
10. Don't allow yourself to be rushed; time is your ally, and the deals will get better.

Action Step 57 will help you get the word out. It should be interesting to read the letters you receive in response to your form letter.

ACTION STEP 57

Prepare a letter of inquiry. (p. 393)

INVESTIGATE THE BUSINESS FROM THE OUTSIDE

Once you've found a business that looks promising, check it out in every detail. After analyzing it from the outside, you'll be ready to move inside to evaluate the financial records, talk to the owner, and try to learn the real reasons for wanting to sell. But the first step is to get your telescope and your telephoto camera and gather as much information as you can from the exterior. As outlined in the opening vignette of this chapter, Ben and Sally Raymundo didn't do this, and they learned about fraud the hard way.

LEARN FROM OTHERS' MISTAKES

What could the Raymundos have done to avoid their mistake? Many things. They could have asked the mall merchants how well the shopping centre was doing. They could have spent some time observing the store and the shopping mall before they committed. They could have insisted that Sally be allowed to work in the store before or during the sale, and included a clause in their agreement that would have allowed them to bail out. A talk with suppliers might have uncovered the seller's fraud.

Ben and Sally Raymundo were honest, hardworking people who took the seller at face value—a huge mistake. They are now suing, but the lawyer they have hired could have helped them before they purchased the business. The chance of their recovering their money is slim.

Some sellers don't count the value of their time as a cost of doing business. As a result, the firm will show an inflated return on investment (ROI). Let's say such a firm earns $60,000 per year and has an inventory of $100,000. It could be a bad buy if the seller, her spouse, and their two children work a total of 200 hours a week and if a $100,000 investment instead could earn 8 percent or more per year in high-yield bonds.

Look at each deal from the viewpoint of what it would cost to hire a competent manager and staff at market wage rates. In this case, let's suppose you had to pay $40,000 a year for a manager, $30,000 a year for an assistant, and $30,000 a year for two hourly employees. You would have spent $100,000 and lost the opportunity to earn an additional $8,000 on your investment. Yes, this would be a "no-brainer," but a lot of businesses are bought with even less going for them.

It's time now to go out and investigate a business on your own. Remember what you've learned from the Raymundos' bad experience, and take along your new eyes and your camera. You'll be surprised how much there is to see. Action Step 58 tells you how to do it.

ACTION STEP 58

Study a business from the outside. (p. 393)

KNOW WHEN YOU NEED OUTSIDE HELP

We've already discussed the need for a team of small-business gurus to help you realize your dream of ownership. When you evaluate small businesses for purchase, however, you might need a special kind of outside help. If you have any lingering doubts about the business you are researching, you may need the perspective of someone who is more objective than one of your team players. If you're not the Sherlock Holmes–type yourself, hire someone who is. Your dream might be shattered by this kind of investigation, but you'll save money in the long run.

Here is Georgia's story. It's well worth taking a lesson from it.

"My husband, Fred, and I wanted to have a business of our own. We both loved sports, so we decided to look around for a sporting goods store.

"We found the perfect store, The Sports Factory, by networking with our sports-minded friends. It was located a block from a complex of tennis courts, three blocks from a new racquetball club, and half a kilometre from a park where volleyball tournaments are held every other month.

"An accountant friend checked over the books and said they looked perfect. 'Great P and L,' he said, 'and excellent accounting ratios. If you get the right terms, you could clear 30 Gs every quarter, and that's only the beginning. This buy doesn't even advertise.'

"We learned that the owner wanted to sell the store because he was tired of it—the long hours, being tied down, and so on. He'd been doing that for a dozen years.

"But I wasn't so sure. I sensed we needed help—some sort of Sam Spade of the business world—but Fred was in a hurry to close the deal. I knew Fred was unhappy in his job, but half the money we were going to invest was mine, and I felt something was not quite right. Frankly, the owner of The Sports Factory didn't look all that tired to me.

"So I asked around—networking again—and I located a community college professor who knew a lot about small business and had written a book about going into small business. I called him, and he listened very patiently when I told him our story. He said he'd be glad to check things out for us for a small fee. I told him to go ahead, but I didn't tell Fred about it.

"Two days later, Harry, my marketplace detective, called and said he had some news.

"'Oh?' I said. 'So soon?'

"'Yes. Do you remember seeing a bulldozer working across the street from The Sports Factory?'

"'No, I don't. What bulldozer?'

"'It started grading last week. Right across the street. I talked to the driver on his lunch break. It seems a developer is putting in a seven-store complex, and one of the stores is going to be a discount sporting goods store.' Harry paused.

"'Oh, no,' I said. 'Are you sure?'

"'He explained that the store going in was part of a monster chain. I could see that we would have a hard time competing with them. I asked him if the owner knew, and if maybe that's why he was so 'tired.'

"'Yes,' Harry said, 'I double-checked at the city planning office where building permits are issued.' And he paused again.

"I was having trouble catching my breath. 'Could I get this in writing,' I asked, 'so that I can show my husband? He likes everything documented.'

"Harry chuckled. 'No problem,' he said. 'I'll email it to you tomorrow. Let me know what you decide, okay?'

"'Don't worry,' I said. 'And thank you very much.'

"This marketplace detective work cost us $475, but it saved us thousands of dollars and years of heartache. Armed with what we learned through that experience, we examined almost a hundred businesses before we found the right one for us. It pays to investigate."

Georgia and Fred came very close to buying the wrong business. The outsider's perspective helped them avoid making a terrible mistake. Now it's time to gain some inside perspectives.

INVESTIGATE THE BUSINESS FROM THE INSIDE

ACTION STEP 59

Study a business from the inside. (p. 394)

Once you've learned all you can from the outside, it's time to cross the threshold for a look at the interior, an important, time-consuming process and a milestone in your quest. Action Step 59 will help you.

There are two ways to get inside the business: You can either contact the owner directly or seek assistance from a **business broker**. We recommend that you use a reputable business broker (sometimes called a "business intermediary")— someone who sells a business on behalf of the owner or the seller. In almost all cases, a real estate licence is a requirement in this fast-growing profession. Business brokers have expertise in and detailed knowledge about business opportunities. A good way to find a broker is to seek a referral from a trusted source. Ask your accountant, lawyer, peers, and industry association for names of good business brokers. You can also check your local Yellow Pages and the newspaper classifieds under "Real Estate" or "Business Brokers." The Business Book Press is a good online source (http://www.businessbookpress.com/resources/brokers_can.htm).

BUSINESS BROKER (BUSINESS INTERMEDIARY)

Someone who sells a business on behalf of the owner

Ask your broker if there are listings in your area of interest. If so, check out the ones that appear interesting, but be prepared for disappointment. If you do find a business broker you like, we strongly recommend you check him or her out with your local Better Business Bureau (http://www.bbb.org).

You will probably look at several businesses before you find anything close to your requirements. Here are a few things to keep in mind when buying a business:

- Make sure that you're clear on your business vision before you start looking. It is all too easy to let emotions govern your decision.
- Consider buying a business you know how to operate. In that case, you'll find it easier to take over and run.
- Be prepared to work long hours.
- Be prepared to lead people.
- Look for a business in a growing industry.
- Look for a retiring entrepreneur; then, see whether that person can stay on to help you as you take over the reins of the business.

We want to emphasize that buying a business is an investment decision. If you're thinking about buying a business, make sure that you compare what your money can do elsewhere. You'll want to ensure that you earn a good return on your investment. Later on in this chapter, we'll return to this topic when we talk about business valuation.

DEALING WITH BROKERS

Reputable business brokers are active in most large cities, and they often play an important role in matching sellers with buyers. The level of competency of business brokers ranges from specialists who know as much about fast-food franchises such as McDonald's as there is to know, to real estate agents who know so little about business that they will only waste your time. But a good broker can save you time and play a helpful third-party role in negotiations. The International Business Brokers Association (IBBA) supports the granting of a certificate of competency, known as a CBI (Certified Business Intermediary). There are now more than 550 business brokers (over 100 in all of Canada) with their CBI designation. If looking for a broker, ask whether the candidate has this designation. There are also numerous business broker franchises. Two of the most notable are Sunbelt Business Brokers and VR Business Brokers. To learn more about the role of the business broker, go to the Robbinex site, the "Market and the Players" link at http://www.robbinex.com/articles_market_players.php.[1]

A broker has a responsibility to represent the seller and is not paid unless he or she sells something. Typically, the broker's commission ranges from 10 to 15 percent, but it is less on bigger deals. Everything is open to negotiation.

Some sellers list with brokers because they don't want it generally known (to their customers, employees, and competitors) that they want to sell their business. Most sellers who list with brokers, however, do so out of desperation, because they've already tried to sell their business to everyone they know.

Spending time with a skilled broker can be a fascinating educational experience. If you want a particular type of business and are able to examine a half-dozen that are on the market, you will probably end up with a better grasp of the business than the owners have. Network with your business contacts to locate a competent broker, and ask brokers for referrals from former clients. And, as we've said many times before, leave your chequebook at home. Don't let anyone rush you.

HOW TO LOOK AT THE INSIDE OF A BUSINESS

Once you have your foot in the door and have established yourself as a potential buyer, you will be able to study the inner workings of the business. Take full advantage of this opportunity. For general information on the business valuation process, visit the "Valuation of Small Businesses" website profiled in Box 13.1.

STUDY THE FINANCIAL HISTORY

You need to learn from the financial history where the money comes from and where it goes. Ask to see all financial records (balance sheet, income statement, and bank statement for at least five years back, if they're available), and take your time studying them. If you don't understand financial records, hire someone who does. Your aim in buying an ongoing business is to step into an income stream. The financial records provide a picture of that stream.

Look at the history of cash flow, profit and loss, and accounts receivable. If the seller has a stack of accounts receivable a foot high, remember that

- after three months, the value of a current-accounts dollar will have shrunk to 90 cents;
- after six months, it will be worth 50 cents;
- after a year, it will be worth 30 cents.

Like an auditor, review every receipt you can find. If a fast-food owner tells you she sells 900 hamburgers a week, ask to see the receipts from the suppliers. If none are offered, ask permission to contact the suppliers for records of shipment. Make her prove to you that she has bought from suppliers. You can then accurately measure sales. If the seller won't cooperate, walk away: she's hiding something.

Box 13.1   How Much Is a Business Worth?

1. Valuation of Small Businesses

Link to the Business Owner's Toolkit: http://www.bizfilings.com/toolkit/sbg/run-a-business/exiting/use-best-business-valuation-formula.aspx. This page discusses the role of the business appraiser and how, in placing a price tag on a business, you need to consider the following:

- **Key factors.** What factors are most important to buyers? What are secondary?
- **Addition of value.** How can the seller boost these important factors before the sale?
- **Recasting of financial statements.** How might the seller's accountant adjust the company's financial statements before showing them to potential buyers?
- **Valuation methods.** What are some of the methods and formulas commonly used to put a price tag on a business?
- **Partial interests.** If the owners are selling only part of the business, how does that affect the price?

2. Valuing Your Business

- Link to Biz Help 24: http://www.bizhelp24.com/?s=valuation. Here, you will find plenty of discussion on valuation methods, such as the multiplier valuation, asset value, owner benefit valuation, and the comparison valuation.
- Link to Canada Business Network, "Put a Price Tag on Your Business: A Guide to Business Valuation": http://www.canadabusiness.ca/eng/page/2725/.

Evaluate closely any personal expenses that are being charged to the business. (Your accountant can help you determine a course of action that will keep you out of trouble.) Doing this allows you to achieve a clearer picture of the firm's true profits. Compare the financial results to industry standards.

Take a look at cancelled cheques, income tax returns, and the salary the seller has been paying herself. If your seller was stingy with her own salary, decide whether you could live on that amount.

You can use the seller's accounts receivable as a point for negotiation, but don't take over the job of collecting them.

Find out if you have to pay GST/HST on the sale (see Box 13.2).

Box 13.2   Did You Know?

According to the Canada Revenue Agency, if you buy a business, you and the seller may be able to elect jointly to have no GST/HST payable, if

1. you and the seller agree that the sale will not be subject to GST/HST;
2. you complete Form GST44, *Election Concerning the Acquisition of a Business or Part of a Business*;
3. you buy all or substantially all of the property, not only individual assets.

Learn about the basic tax implications of buying an existing business at the Canada Revenue Agency, Guide for Canadian Small Businesses site (http://www.cra-arc.gc.ca/E/pub/tg/rc4070/).

COMPARE WHAT YOUR MONEY COULD DO ELSEWHERE

How much money will you be putting into the business? How long will it take you to make it back? Have you factored in your time?

Let's say that you would need to put $50,000 into this business and that the business will give you a 33.3 percent return, which is full payback in three years. Are there other investments with similar risk that would yield the same amount on your $50,000?

If you will be working in the business, you need to add in the cost of your time; let's say that's $25,000 per year (your present salary) over the three-year period, or $75,000 (assuming no raises). In three years, the business would need to return $125,000 after expenses and taxes to cover the risks involved with your $50,000 investment and to compensate you for the loss of $25,000 in annual salary.

EVALUATE THE TANGIBLE ASSETS

TANGIBLE ASSETS

Things your business owns that you can see and touch, such as real estate, equipment, and inventory

INVENTORY

Items carried in the normal course of doing business that are intended for sale

If the numbers look good, move on to assess the value of everything you can touch, specifically the real estate, the equipment and fixtures, and the inventory, which are **tangible assets**.

- **Real estate.** Get an outside, professional appraisal of the building and the land. It might be worth more as vacant land than as a business.
- **Equipment and fixtures.** You can obtain a good idea of current values by asking equipment dealers and reading the want ads. Scour your area for the best deals, because you don't want to tie up too much capital in equipment that's outmoded or about to come apart. Suppliers have lots of leads on used equipment, so check with them. If you're not an expert in the equipment field, get help from someone who is. Find out the maintenance costs in the past two years.
- **Inventory.** Count the **inventory** yourself, and make sure that the boxes are packed with what you think they should be. Make certain you specify the exact contents of shelves and cabinets in the purchase agreement. Don't get careless and write in something vague like "All shelves are to be filled." Specify what goes on the shelves. More important, find out if the inventory is salable, and if the styles and models of the stock are still valid. Don't accept old stock unless the discount is very low.

Once you've made your count, contact suppliers to learn the current prices.

If you find merchandise that is damaged, out of date, out of style, soiled, worn, or not ready to sell as is, don't pay full price for it. Negotiate. This is sacrifice merchandise, and it should have a sacrifice price tag.

In addition to doing all this, talk to insiders. There's no substitute for inside information. Every detective takes it seriously.

- **Bankers.** It is essential to discuss business with your banker and, ideally, with the current owner's banker. The latter will be limited with respect to what he or she can say, but your banker will be a good help in analyzing the financial statements.
- **Suppliers.** Will suppliers agree to keep supplying you? Are there past difficulties between seller and supplier that you as new owner would inherit? Remember, you're dependent on your suppliers. How do suppliers evaluate the business?
- **Employees.** Talk to the key employees early. In small business, success can rest on the shoulders of one or two people, and you don't want them to walk out the day you sign the papers.

- **Competitors.** Identify the major competitors, and interview them to learn what goes on from their perspective. You need to understand the industry fully. Expect some bias, but watch for a pattern to develop. (Chapter 5, you'll remember, tells how to identify the competitors.)

GET A NONCOMPETITION COVENANT

Once you buy a business, you don't want the seller to set up the same kind of business across the street. Customers are hard to come by, so you don't want to pay for them and then have them lured away by the seller as a rival. Get an agreement, in writing, that the seller will not set up in competition with you—or work for a competitor, or help a friend or relative set up a competitive business— for the next five years. You will need a lawyer to prepare such an agreement. Be sure to specify the exact amount you're paying for the noncompetition covenant. That way, the Canada Revenue Agency will allow you to deduct it against income over the life of the covenant.

ANALYZE THE SELLER'S MOTIVES

People have all kinds of reasons for selling their business. Some of these reasons favour the buyer, whereas others favour the seller.

Here are some reasons for selling that can favour the buyer:

1. retirement or ill health;
2. too little time to manage, as the seller has other investments;
3. divorce or other family problems;
4. disgruntled partners;
5. lack of cash due to too quick an expansion;
6. poor management;
7. seller burnout or loss of interest due to other reasons.

These reasons for selling may favour the seller (Buyer, beware!):

1. decline in the local economy,
2. decline in this specific industry,
3. intense competition,
4. high insurance costs,
5. increasing litigation,
6. skyrocketing rents,
7. technological obsolescence,
8. problems with suppliers,
9. high-crime location,
10. nonrenewal of lease,
11. the location in a decline.

EXAMINE THE ASKING PRICE

Many sellers view selling their firms as they would view selling their children; that is, they are emotionally attached to the business, and they overestimate its worth. Pride also plays a role; they might want to tell their friends that they started from scratch and sold out for a million. If you run into irrational and emotional obstacles, walk away or counter with reasonable terms—such as $100,000 down and 10 percent of the net profits for the next four years, up to $1 million.

Some industries have rule-of-thumb benchmarks for pricing. For example, a service firm might be priced at 6 to 12 months of its total revenue. Use of such pricing formulas is often unwise, however. The only formula that makes sense is the return on your investment minus the value of your management time, where

$$\text{Return on Investment (ROI)} = (\text{Hours spent} \times \text{Value of your time per hour}).$$

If you can earn 10 percent without sweating on high-grade bonds, you should earn at least a 30 percent return on a business that will make you sweat.

It can be useful to consult the newspaper financial pages to learn the **price/earnings (P/E) ratios** of publicly traded firms. Firms that have low P/E ratios (the stock price is less than 10 times its earnings) are not regarded as growth opportunities by sophisticated investors. Firms with above-average P/E ratios (price is more than 25 times its earnings) are regarded as having above-average growth potential. Thus, you should be willing to pay a higher price for a firm with above-average growth potential than for one that is declining. In fact, you should not buy a declining business unless you think you can either purchase it very inexpensively and turn it around, or dispose of its assets at a profit.

PRICE/EARNINGS (P/E) RATIO

The market price of a common stock divided by its annual earnings per share for the latest 12-month period

NEGOTIATE THE VALUE OF GOODWILL

If the firm has a strong customer base with deeply ingrained purchasing habits, this has value. It takes a while for any start-up to build a client base, and the wait for profitability can be costly.

Some firms have built up a great deal of *ill* will—customers who have vowed never to trade with them again. A large proportion of businesses on the market have this problem. If the amount of ill will is great, the business will have little value; it might be that *any* price would be too high.

A smart seller will ask you to pay something for **goodwill**. You'll therefore need to play detective and find out how much goodwill there is and where it is. For example, consider the seller who has extended credit loosely. Customers are responding, but there's no cash in the bank. If you were to continue that policy and keep granting easy credit, you could be in the red in a couple of months. Or maybe the seller is one of those very special people who is loved by everyone and will take the goodwill with him—like a halo—when he walks out the door.

Therefore, negotiate.

You can determine the value of a company's goodwill by subtracting the total value of the tangible assets from the purchase price. Let's say that the asking price for the business you'd like to buy is $145,000 and that the business's tangible assets (equipment, inventory, and so on) are worth $95,000. In other words, the seller is trying to charge you $50,000 for goodwill. Before you negotiate, do the following.

GOODWILL

The dollar value obtained when you subtract the total value of the tangible assets from the purchase price

1. Compare the goodwill you're being asked to buy to the goodwill of a similar business on the market.
2. Figure out how long it would take you to pay for that amount of goodwill. Remember, goodwill is tangible; you'll be unhappy if it takes you years to pay for it. Even the most cheerful goodwill comes out of profit.
3. Estimate how much you could make if you invested that $50,000 in a high-yield security.
4. Consider how long it would take you to reach the same level of profitability if you started the business from scratch instead.

This exercise gives you a context in which to judge the seller's assessment of the value of goodwill, and you can use the hard data you have generated to negotiate a realistic—and perhaps more favourable—price.

LEARN WHETHER BULK SALES ESCROW IS NEEDED

Bulk sales escrow, which is an examination process intended to protect buyers from unknown liabilities, might be needed when buying a business. For example, you need to know whether any inventory you would buy is tied up by creditors.

If it is, the instrument you'll use to cut those strings is a bulk sales transfer, a process that will transfer the goods from the seller to you through a qualified third party.

If there are no claims by creditors, the transfer of inventory should go smoothly. If there are claims, you'll want to be protected by law. Either consult a lawyer who has experience in making bulk sales transfers or get an **escrow company** to act as the neutral party in the transfer. Ask your banker or accountant to recommend one, preferably one that specializes in bulk sales escrow.

BULK SALES ESCROW

An examination process intended to protect buyers from unknown liabilities

ESCROW COMPANY

A neutral third party (usually a lawyer) that holds deposits and deeds until all agreed-on conditions are met

AN EARNOUT SUCCESS STORY

Sam Wilson had held several key executive positions in large manufacturing firms after receiving his master of business arts degree from Western University in the early 1990s. His last position was as vice-president of a medium-sized firm with branch offices throughout North America. Wilson was squeezed out when a large conglomerate purchased the firm and moved the headquarters to London.

After doing some freelance management consulting, Wilson arranged to purchase an executive search firm that specialized in finding engineering talent in the aerospace industry. Buying the business seemed like a good idea to him, because the business had been profitable for more than 20 years. The key personnel agreed to stay with the firm, and it had loyal customers and a solid reputation. Wilson knew it would take him years to build a similar business from scratch, even though he understood the business.

He purchased the business for no cash down and agreed to pay off the entire purchase price from the earnings over the next five years. (He made what is called an **earnout**—a contractual arrangement in which the purchase price is stated in terms of a minimum, and the buyer of the business agrees to make future payments to the seller after the closing based on the achievement of predefined financial goals.) The seller was an older man who knew Wilson's reputation as a winner. Wilson was one of the few prospective buyers who were willing to pay full price for the business and seemed qualified to continue the growth of the firm.

EARNOUT

A contractual arrangement in which the purchase price is stated in terms of a minimum, and the buyer of the business agrees to make future payments to the seller based on the achievement of predefined financial goals after the closing

Buying a business on an earnout basis is an option only if the seller has great confidence in the buyer's skills and knowledge of the business. Thus, the burden of persuading the seller to agree to such terms is on the buyer. It's necessary to show the seller that the business will continue to show a profit.

THE DECISION TO BUY

Even if you think you're ready to make your decision, don't do it—not yet. Look for the "red flags" in Box 13.3, and review the checklist in Box 13.4. It reminds you of important details you might have overlooked. Even if you know you've found your dream business, complete this checklist before you sign the papers.

Box 13.3   Ten Red Flags

We can't warn you often enough of the traps inherent in purchasing a business. Informed, experienced advisors familiar with your industry are essential, and you should undertake no purchase without extreme due diligence and legal representation.

Here are 10 common red flags. If you hear any of these statements from a prospective seller, you should do a thorough investigation.

1. "I've got two sets of books."
2. "I usually take a few dollars out every week. Save on the GST and sales taxes. So the *real* cash flow is much better than it looks."
3. "I have a couple of buyers interested. So the first one in gets the deal."
4. "Think of all the goodwill you're buying."
5. "If I had more time, I could do a lot better."
6. "My staff has been robbing me blind. So the numbers are much lower than they really are. With good management, a lot more money can be made."
7. "We don't need lawyers and accountants here. It's not that much money."
8. "Slip me a few dollars 'under the table,' and I can drop the price."
9. "I want all cash for the business."
10. "It's not a lot to pay for this business. You're not risking much money, but the payoff can be massive."

Box 13.4   The Before-You-Buy Checklist

❑ How long do you plan to own this business?

❑ How old is this business? Can you sketch its history?

❑ Is this business in the embryonic stage, the growth stage, the mature stage, or the decline stage?

❑ Has your accountant reviewed the books and made a sales projection for you?

❑ How long will it take for this business to show a complete recovery on your investment?

❑ What reasons does the owner give for selling?

❑ Will the owner let you see bank deposit records? (If not, why not?)

❑ Have you calculated utility costs for the first three to five years?

❑ What does a review of tax records tell you?

❑ How complete is the insurance coverage?

❑ How old are the receivables? (Remember that age decreases their value.)

❑ What is the seller paying him- or herself? Is it low or high?

❑ Have you interviewed your prospective landlord?

❑ What happens when a new tenant takes over the lease?

❑ Has your lawyer checked for any potential problems in the transfer of licences and permits?

❑ Who are the major competitors?

   • Do you want to be close to competitors, or do you want to be kilometres away?

   • Could a competitor move in next door the day after you move in?

   • Have you checked out future competition?

❑ What do the neighbours know about the business?

❑ Will the neighbours help draw target customers to your business?

❏ What is the life-cycle stage of the community?

❏ Where is the traffic flow?

❏ What's the location?

  • How does the area fit into the city/regional planning for the future?

  • Is there good access?

  • Is parking adequate?

  • Is the parking lot a drop-off point for car-poolers?

❏ Is the building in good repair?

❏ Have you interviewed the seller's customers?

  • What do they like about the store? Is the service good?

  • How far will your target customer have to walk?

  • What changes would they recommend?

  • What services or products would they like to see added?

  • Where else do they go for similar products or services?

❏ Have you checked that the customer lists are up to date?

❏ Who are the business's top 20 customers? its top 50?

❏ Is the seller locked into one to three major customers who control the business?

❏ How well is the business using technology, computerized systems, and business management?

❏ Are you buying inventory? What is the seller asking?

❏ Have you checked the value of the equipment against the price of used equipment from another source?

❏ To whom does your seller owe money?

❏ Has your lawyer checked for liens on the seller's equipment?

❏ Do you have maintenance contracts on the equipment you're buying?

❏ Has your lawyer or escrow company gone through bulk sales escrow?

❏ Have you made certain that

  • you're getting all brand names, logos, trade-marks, and so on that you need?

  • the seller has signed a noncompetition covenant?

  • the key lines of supply will stay intact when you take over?

  • the key employees will stay?

  • the seller isn't leaving because of stiff competition?

  • you aren't paying for goodwill but taking delivery on ill will?

  • you are getting the best terms possible?

  • you're buying an income stream?

PREPARE FOR THE NEGOTIATIONS

Let's say you know you're ready to buy. You've raised the money, and the numbers say you can't lose, so you're ready to start negotiating.

We suggest two things about negotiations.

First, when it comes time to talk meaningful numbers, the most important area to concentrate on is *terms*, not asking price. Favourable terms will give you the cash flow you need to survive the first year and then move from survival into success. Unfavourable terms can torpedo your chances for success, even when the total asking price is well below market value.

Second, when the seller brings up the subject of goodwill, be ready for it. Goodwill is a "slippery" commodity; it can make the asking price soar. It's only natural for the

ACTION STEP 60

Probe the depths of ill will.
(p. 394)

seller to try to get as much as possible for goodwill. Because you know this ahead of time, you can do your homework and go in primed to deal. Action Step 60 will help you with this. When the seller begins talking about goodwill, you can flip the coin over and discuss ill will—which hangs on longer, like a cloud above the business.

PROTECT YOURSELF

Evaluate each business opportunity by the criteria we present in this chapter. When you find one you think is right for you, start negotiating. Your goal is the lowest possible price with the best possible terms. Start low; you can then negotiate up if necessary.

If you are asked to put down a deposit, handle it in this way.

1. Deposit the money in an escrow account.
2. Include a stipulation in your offer that says the offer is *subject to your inspection and approval* of all financial records and all aspects of the business.

Doing this gives you an escape hatch, so that you can get your deposit returned—and back out of the deal—if things don't look good. Also, consider working in the business for a few weeks with the option to back out if you have a change of heart.

NEGOTIATING THE PRICE

What is a fair price? Obviously, the seller and the buyer have arrived at their values from widely separated viewpoints.

The seller has committed considerable time and money to the business, often for less return than could have been earned elsewhere, and sees the sale as the opportunity to make up for the years of "doing without." The buyer, on the other hand, is concerned only with the present state and future potential of the business and cares little for the time and effort invested by the vendor.

Valuing a business is not an exact science. The valuation process involves comparing several approaches and selecting the best method, or a combination of methods, based on the analyst's knowledge and experience. Practitioners may use several methods to value businesses, such as asset-based pricing, market-based valuations, future earnings–based valuations (such as net present values), and so on. The particular method chosen can become quite complex and will depend on one or more of the following factors:

- the nature of the business (retail, service, manufacturing, for example) and its operating history;
- the industry and economic outlook;
- the financial condition of the company;
- the company's earnings and debt-paying capacity;
- the level of interest rates, which will affect both the cost of borrowing money to buy the business and your return on investment.

We provide three useful methods of valuing a small business below, but we caution that these are only three of the many approaches and methods available. Should you find yourself wanting to buy a business, we strongly advise professional help in setting a fair price. You might also want to go back and check out the valuation methods suggested by the Business Owner's Toolkit and Biz Help 24, provided in Box 13.1.

ASSET-BASED VALUATION

The purchase price of a business determined, in large part, by the assets of the business

1. ASSET-BASED VALUATION

In an **asset-based valuation**, the purchase price of a business is determined, in large part, by the assets of the business. If you are purchasing assets, the seller will usually have a spec sheet prepared, listing the assets and offering an estimate of their value. The asset value can be calculated using various formulas, including

- fair market value: the price of similar assets on the open market;
- replacement value: what it would cost to replace the asset (from the original supplier);
- liquidation value: what the asset would bring if the business were liquidated (as in a bankruptcy);
- book value: a valuation based on the company's balance sheet.

In that list of assets, however, goodwill may be included, representing the value of intangibles, such as location, reputation, and the established customer base of the business. Goodwill is virtually impossible to value objectively; it depends more on instinct and gut feeling than on a strict accounting formula.

The most common method of asset valuation is the adjusted book value. The **book value** is the owner's equity, or total assets minus the total liabilities. The **adjusted book value** is the book value amended to reflect market values. For example, in the balance sheet shown for XYZ Company Limited on pages 388–390, you would appraise the equipment. What is the real market value? What would it cost to replace this equipment? You would want to look at the inventory and ask: Can it actually be sold, or has it been sitting on the back shelf for 10 years? You would examine the accounts receivable. Are there any accounts with no chance of collection?

An adjusted book value usually reflects a minimum valuation of a business. For example, suppose you wanted to buy XYZ Company. Examining the assets, you find $5,000 in assets that have no market value. Your adjusted book value, and thus the estimated value of the business, would be $33,890 ($38,890 – $5,000).

Furthermore, this valuation of individual assets tells only part of the story. The real value of the business depends to a large extent on the future income that it generates. This might not be directly related to the value of the assets, especially in service businesses. We therefore encourage you to look at the company's income history over a period of years (at least three is usual) to determine what its gross revenues, costs, cash flow, and profit were. You are really buying an income, and one way of looking at the purchase price is in terms of a return on your investment.

We now provide two other techniques for valuating a small business that take into consideration the revenue potential of the business.

BOOK VALUE

Owner's equity, or total assets minus total liabilities

ADJUSTED BOOK VALUE

The book value amended to reflect market values

2. ABILITY-TO-PAY VALUATION

Most new business owners cannot afford to buy a business without taking out a loan or getting some sort of earnout. So, before buying a business, they want to make sure that the business can pay off the loan or earnout and, at the same time, have enough cash to pay all the other expenses—which include, of course, a salary to the new owner. In the **ability-to-pay valuation**, a value of the business is thus determined by its ability to pay off the loan over a specified period and provide a reasonable return on the owner's investment.[2]

Provided below are the steps to determine this cash flow value.

ABILITY-TO-PAY VALUATION

A valuation approach based on the ability of a business to pay off its business loan and provide a reasonable return on the owner's investment over a specified period

Step 1: Estimate the Amount of Cash the Business Will Generate with No Debt and Reasonable Salary or Payment to the Owner

Start with the most recent cash flow of the business. Adjust this cash flow by adding back in any bank payments (both principal and interest) or payments to purchase fixed assets. Here, you are making the assumption that the business is debt free and can pay a reasonable salary to you, the owner. At this point, you are looking at this cash flow only in terms of whether it can pay normal monthly operational costs.

Example

The end-of-the-year cash flow of DISCovery Books (Table 10.6, pages 276–277) was $27,395. We know that it started with $10,000, so company operations generated $17,395 in excess cash over the first year. We will assume that these are actual and not projected numbers. To get the adjusted cash flow, we would *add* the bank payments—including both bank charges and interest ($3,600) and the principal portion of the term debt ($3,000)—for an adjusted cash flow of $23,995 ($17,395 + $6,600). Now you would check the salary paid to the owner DISCovery Books ($19,200). Suppose you felt that you needed to take home $3,600 more a year. Then the adjusted cash flow would be *reduced* by $3,600 and would be $20,395 ($23,995 – $3,600). You have now estimated the amount of yearly cash—$20,395—the business will generate with no debt and reasonable payment (salary) to you the owner.

Step 2: Calculate Your Return-to-Owners Investment

First, you must determine how much you are prepared to invest in the business and what rate of return you expect. Then calculate the amount of cash the business will need to generate to give you a reasonable return on your investment.

Subtract this amount from the available cash flow in Step 1. The cash remaining is the amount the business will generate that can support a rate of return on your investment. Note that this cash flow will still have to support loan payments—we'll address that in Steps 3 and 4.

Example

In the case of DISCovery Books, suppose you were prepared to invest $30,000. First, you will have to determine what interest rate return you want for your business investment—10, 15, or 20 percent, for example. Suppose you decided that 15 percent was reasonable. This means that DISCovery would have to pay you, from its available cash, $4,500 each year ($30,000 × .15 = $4,500 per year). We know from Step 1 that DISCovery has $20,395 available in its first year. From this amount, you subtract the $4,500 to get $15,895. This is the amount the business has available to pay the interest on your investment in the first year. Most business owners want to see a rate of return of anywhere between 15 and 30 percent, so the expected rate of return used in this example (15 percent) is on the low side.

Step 3: Estimate the Number of Years You Reasonably Expect It Will Take to Pay Off the Loan to Buy the Business

Example

Let's suppose you were thinking about buying DISCovery Books and found that there were three years left on the lease. You know that financial institutions are reluctant to provide loans that extend beyond the term of the lease. In this case, a three-year loan might be reasonable. Note that with this valuation method, the longer the time period you choose, the higher the value of the business. So, if you were selling DISCovery Books, you might want to get the lease extended to raise your asking price.

Step 4: Estimate the Size of Loan Needed to Support the Available Cash Flow (Step 2) to Be Paid Off in the Period Specified in Step 3

Example

Assume that you want to buy DISCovery Books and decide to pay off the loan over three years. You do research and decide that an estimated 8 percent interest rate would be reasonable. You know that you have $15,895 (Step 2) available in the first year. If you were to assume that this amount will also be generated in the next two years, then the total cash available to pay off a three-year loan will be $47,685 (3 × $15,895). So, over three years, the business will have $47,685 to pay for principal and interest on a loan.

But how do you find out the amount of the loan? You can obtain this estimate in a number of ways: financial calculators, special financial tables, and so on. An easy way is to use the Internet and click onto a loan calculator (http://www.calculatorplus.com). You will find out that a loan of $42,200 will cost about $47,600 over a three-year period at 8 percent. A loan of $42,200 will mean that every month for three years, the business will have to pay $1,322 in principal and interest. After three years of these monthly payments, the loan will be paid ($42,200 in principal and $5,400 in interest). The point is that your projected three-year cash flow can support a loan of about $42,200.

We should note that we have assumed that the first-year cash flow also applies in years 2 and 3. As we learned in Chapter 10, forecasting is an art. If you have only one year of cash flow, you might have to make the assumption of a constant cash flow over the loan period. But you should ask yourself whether this assumption is reasonable. For example, you might want to pay yourself a higher salary in the next few years. This increased expenditure would reduce your future cash flows. If you have historic cash flows for a particular business, you might find a trend (maybe, for example, a yearly increase or decrease of 10 percent). You might then want to adjust your projected cash flow according to this kind of thinking.

Step 5: Estimate the Value of the Business Based on Its Ability to Pay the Costs out of Its Cash Flow

In Step 4, we found out the total amount of money we could borrow. Add this to the owner's investment, and you get the total value of the businesses. The business would be able to support all the cash flow payments, if you were to pay this price—and if your assumptions are correct!

Example
In the case of DISCovery Books, we know from Step 4 that the business can afford a loan of $42,200. We also know that the owner has invested $30,000 in the business, so the value of the business is $72,200 ($42,200 + $30,000). This estimate is based on its cash flow and its ability to pay you a rate of return (15 percent, in this case), to pay off the loan (both principal and interest), and to cover all monthly operating costs.

3. EARNINGS-ASSETS VALUATION

In the first method—asset-based evaluation—no consideration was given to the earnings potential. In the second method—ability to pay—no consideration was given to the value of the assets. This third method—**earnings-assets valuation**—takes into consideration both earning potential and asset value. This valuation approach requires copies of the financial statements for the business, as it is only from these figures that a valid analysis can be made.

There are various methods for calculating an earning-assets evaluation. See, for example, the Business Owner's Toolkit "excess earnings" method provided on its website (http://www.bizfilings.com/toolkit/sbg/run-a-business/exiting/use-best-business-valuation-formula.aspx). Below is another method suggested by the Business Development Bank. We also encourage you to work through this approach in our end-of-chapter case study (question 4b).

EARNINGS-ASSETS VALUATION
A business valuation approach that takes into consideration both earning potential and asset value

Earnings-Assets Pricing Formula

Step 1. Calculate the tangible net worth of the business. This is, in its simplest form, the total tangible assets (excluding goodwill, franchise fees, etc.) less total liabilities (both current and long term).

Step 2. Estimate the current earning power of this tangible net worth if this amount was invested elsewhere (stocks, bonds, term deposits). This earning power will vary with economic trends and other factors but should be based on current interest rates.

Step 3. Determine a reasonable annual salary that the owner could earn if similarly employed elsewhere. Remember to take into consideration benefits paid by the business (automotive, insurance, pensions, etc.) in determining a comparable outside salary.

Step 4. Determine the total earning capacity of the owner that would result from the net worth invested plus employment sources by adding the results of Steps 2 and 3.

Step 5. Calculate the average annual net profit of the business. This average will be the total of profit from all financial statements available (before any management salaries or cash withdrawal for partners, proprietors, taxes, etc.) divided by the number of years used in the analysis. We suggest three years minimum but preferably five years for a more accurate result.

Step 6. Calculate the extra earning power of the business by subtracting the result of Step 4 from that of Step 5. This figure represents the additional money you can expect to earn if you buy the business rather than invest an amount equal to the net worth and obtain or retain outside employment.

Step 7. Calculate the value of intangibles by multiplying the extra earning power (Step 6) by a figure that we will refer to as the "development factor." This development factor is designed to weigh things such as uniqueness of the intangibles, time needed to establish a similar business from scratch, expenses and risk of a comparable start-up, price of goodwill in similar firms, and so on.

If the business is well established and successful, a suggested factor of 5 or more might be used; a more moderately seasoned firm might rate a factor of 3, and a young but profitable business might rate a factor of only 1.

Step 8. Calculate the final price. This is arrived at by adding the tangible net worth of the business (Step 1) to the value of intangibles (Step 7).

Here is one example of how this formula works. Assume you are interested in purchasing the XYZ Company, and the asking price is $200,000. At your request, the owners of XYZ have given you the following financial statement representing the last complete year of operation. (Note that we are using only one year's statement in this example. When using this formula for real, you should seek to obtain statements for at least three but preferably five years.)

XYZ Company Limited

Balance Sheet

As at December 31, 20XX

Assets	
Current	
Cash	$ 180
Accounts receivable	6,560
Inventory	13,150
Total current assets	19,890
Fixed assets	
Land	5,000
Buildings	35,000
Equipment	14,500
Furniture	1,800
Vehicles	11,500

Less: Accumulated depreciation	8,100	
Total fixed assets	59,700	
Total assets		$ 79,590
Liabilities		
Current liabilities		
Bank	$ 3,000	
Accounts payable	6,600	
Current portion—Long-term	1,100	
Total current liabilities	10,700	
Long-term liabilities		
Long-term mortgage loan	21,500	
Equipment loan	9,600	
Total long-term liabilities	31,100	
Less: Current portion	1,100	
Total long-term liabilities	30,000	
Total liabilities	40,700	
Shareholders' equity		
Share capital	$ 10,000	
Retained earning	28,890	
Total shareholders equity	38,890	
Total liabilities and shareholders' equity		$ 79,590
XYZ Company Limited		
Operating Statement		
For the 12 months		
ended December 31, 20XX		
Sales (revenue)		$250,000
Cost of goods sold		
Opening inventory	$ 12,000	
Purchases	151,150	
	163,150	
Closing inventory	13,150	
Total cost of goods sold		150,000
Gross profit		100,000
Operating expenses		
Advertising	1,500	
Automobile	2,400	
Bad debts	300	
Depreciation	3,700	
Equipment rental	400	
Insurance	1,200	
Interest and bank charges	4,000	
Management salaries	16,000	
Miscellaneous	400	
Office supplies	1,100	
Professional fees	800	
Taxes and licences (municipal)	300	
Telephone	800	

(continued)

Utilities	2,100	
Wages and benefits	40,000	
Total operating expenses		75,000
Operating profit		25,000
Less: Income taxes[a]	6,250	
Net profit		$ 18,750

[a] Arbitrarily set at 25 percent for demonstration purposes only. Rates can vary not only provincially but also within individual businesses.

Formula Calculation (figures have been rounded)

1. Tangible net worth	$39,000
2. Earning power (assume 10 percent)	3,900
3. Reasonable salary for owner	16,000
4. Earning capacity	19,900
5. Average annual net profit (operating profit before taxes, $25,000 + owner's salary, $16,000)	41,000
6. Extra earning power	21,100
7. Value of intangibles (development factor of 3)	63,300
8. Final price (63,300 + 39,000)	102,300

By applying the formula, you come up with a suggested final price of $102,300, compared to the asking price of $200,000.

Try out a net present value valuation by clicking on the interactive business valuation site in the E-Exercise in Box 13.5.

Any price negotiated must, of course, be related to the new financing of the business. Your combination of personal investment and borrowed money might be very different from the position of the vendor and as such will produce a very different operating result. Your negotiations will be strongly influenced by what you can afford.

Once you are satisfied that you have given full consideration to all factors affecting the proposed acquisition and you are ready to proceed, you should formalize your offer with a purchase agreement. Be sure to seek professional help and advice in the preparation of this agreement.

Box 13.5 E-Exercise

Net Present Value Valuation, KJE Computer Solutions:
http://www.dinkytown.com/java/BusinessValuation.html

A net present value (NPV) calculation of a company's worth takes into consideration future business earnings. It provides you with a cash value of the business in today's dollars. Make some assumptions about DISCovery Bookstore's future cash flows (Table 10.6, on pages 276–277) over the next four years, cost of capital, and expected growth rate. Using an NPV calculation, determine how these assumptions would affect the value of DISCovery.

THE CONTRACT

Ultimately, the sale of a business involves a combination of final price, other terms, and overall risk. You might be prepared to pay a higher price as long as other conditions (such as the seller's agreeing to take a mortgage on easy terms) are suitable, or you might opt for a lower price in which you assume more of the risks of the transaction. The precise mix will vary according to the nature of the business and the inclinations of the individuals involved.

Once you have arrived at the terms, the details should be spelled out in a contract that itemizes all aspects of the sale. The following is a summary of some standard items that are usually found in such a contract:

- a definition of what is being transferred, from whom to whom, and at what price, including an itemized breakdown of costs, so that you have a record of the value of each asset, both those you can claim for depreciation and those you cannot;
- details of any leases or liabilities that you are assuming in making the purchase;
- the method of payment (in cash, by cheque, in shares in another company, in bonds), on what date, and by what means;
- any adjustments to the price to cover financial transactions occurring between the moment the offer is signed and the closing date (perhaps sale of inventory, equipment purchases, and tax payments);
- guarantees by the seller of the truthfulness of information supplied and provisions for any penalties in the event that information is not accurate;
- a description of the seller's obligations in operating the business up to closing, implementing the transfer of ownership, and performing any post-sale duties or services;
- mechanisms for dealing with any losses or damages that might occur to the business between the signing of the agreement and the closing date;
- a clause restricting the ability of the seller to compete with the business once the sale is closed, or limiting the seller's freedom to start up similar ventures;
- any conditions that should be met prior to closing (such as validation of deeds, liabilities, or agreements entered into by the business);
- details of closing, including the date, time, place, and individuals effecting the transfer;
- compensation to be paid by the seller to the buyer as damages or compensation if information is found to be false;
- the amount of the security deposit the buyer put up and held in escrow for a period of time as a guarantee that all terms and conditions have been satisfied;
- identification of who would decide the case in the event of a dispute.

EXPECT SOME PLEASANT SURPRISES

Well, you've come a long way, and you've worked hard on your research. Was the digging worth it? Only you can answer that. But there are bargains to be found. Woolett's Hardware, described below, was one. For hunter-buyers with vision and persistence, beautiful opportunities are waiting behind ugly façades.

"I heard about Woolett's being up for sale more than a year ago. I'd just opened up my second store at the time—it's also in the hardware line—and it took me just about a year, April to April, to streamline the paperwork. Thanks to a computer and a good manager, my sanity remained intact.

"So, when I finally got over there to check things out, Woolett's had been on the market about a year and a half. One look from the street and I could see why.

"The store was a mess. The building was pre–World War II, and so was the paint. Out front, the sign was sagging. The parking lot needed lots of work; there were potholes 15 centimetres deep. The entryway was littered with scraps of paper.

"Inside, things weren't much better. The floor needed a good sweeping. The merchandise was covered with dust. And all around there was this feeling of mildew, age, and disuse. It was dark—like a cave. It was tough finding a salesperson, and when you did, you couldn't get much help. Yet, there were customers all over the place.

"After you've been in business a while, you develop a sort of sixth sense about things. And the minute I stepped into the store, I knew there was something special about it, something hidden, something the eye couldn't see right off. I knew I had to dig deeper.

"A visit to the listing real estate broker didn't help much. 'Make us an offer,' he said. 'We just dropped the price yesterday. To $400,000.'

"'What do the numbers look like?' I asked.

"He dug into a slim manila folder. 'Last year,' he said, 'they grossed just under $600,000. The net was around $200,000.'

"'What about inventory?' I asked. 'What about loans and **liens** and accounts receivable? When can I interview the manager? And why is the owner selling?'

"'Are you just asking that,' he said, 'or is this for real?'

"'This is for my son,' I said. 'He's new to the business, and we don't want a lot of surprises.'

"'Like I said, make us an offer.'

"'Let me check the books,' I said. I deposited $500 with an escrow company, making sure I got my usual escape clause—a deposit receipt saying my offer for the business was contingent on my inspection of all assets and my approval of all financial records. Doing this has saved me tons of heartburn medicine over the years.

"The minute they got wind of a buyer, the manager and two of the employees up and quit. The back office was a mess, and it took me three days of searching to find something that would tell me I was on the right track. I found a supply of rolled steel. It was on the books at $12,000, but I knew it was worth $150,000. I took that as a buy signal.

"The next day, I made an offer: $12,000 down, with the balance to be paid out of profits over the next five years. The owner accepted, and we cleared escrow in 30 days.

"The first thing we did was clean the place up. We surfaced the parking lot with asphalt, added a coat of paint, fixed the door, and added lighting.

"Business picked up right away. My son, newly married, was settling down and learning the business. He seemed to have managerial talents. Buying this business was a pleasant surprise."

LIEN

A legal obligation filed against a piece of property

In a Nutshell

There are two good reasons to explore businesses for sale: You'll learn a lot by exploring the marketplace, and you might find a gem like Woolett's Hardware—a business that will make money right from the start.

A final note of caution is in order. Buying a business can take time, and it certainly involves new risk. In making the purchase, you are assuming new responsibilities to those who helped you finance the deal, to any employees working for the business, to its suppliers, and to its clients. Before you buy, do your homework, complete the checklist provided in Box 13.4, and make sure you have a watertight contract in place.

Key Terms

ability-to-pay valuation	earnout
adjusted book value	escrow company
asset-based valuation	goodwill
book value	inventory
bulk sales escrow	lien
business broker (business intermediary)	price/earnings (P/E) ratio
earnings-assets valuation	tangible assets

Think Points for Success

✓ Stick to what you know. Don't buy a business you know nothing about.
✓ Compare the price to what your money could do elsewhere.
✓ Don't let a seller or a broker rush you. A business is not a used car.
✓ If your seller looks absolutely honest, check him or her out anyway.
✓ Worry less about price; work harder on terms.
✓ Consider that most good businesses are sold behind the scenes, before they reach the open market.
✓ Make sure you're there when the physical inventory takes place. Look in those boxes yourself.
✓ Get everything in writing. Be specific.
✓ Always go through bulk sales escrow.
✓ Buying a corporation is tricky. Have an experienced lawyer and accountant help you.

Action Steps

ACTION STEP 57

Prepare a letter of inquiry.

Write a form letter of inquiry, and send it to three to five firms that you might be interested in buying. Keep it open-ended; let them make the disclosures.

It's best to learn about businesses for sale by networking, but you can find some of the most eager sellers by their advertising in the newspaper's classified section.

For now, leave your chequebook where it is. This Action Step will cost you practically nothing. The goal is to learn what's out there and how sellers talk about their businesses.

ACTION STEP 58

Study a business from the outside.

Studying the business from the outside will tell you whether you should go inside and probe more deeply.

1. **Make sure the business fits into the framework of your industry overview.** You want a business that's in the sunrise, not the sunset, phase of the life cycle. Here, you might want to go back and review the location filter in Chapter 7 or the location life-cycle chart (Figure 7.1, page 181).

2. **Diagram the area.** What's the location, and how does the area fit into the city/regional planning for the future? What is the life-cycle stage of the community? Where is the traffic flow? Is there good access? How far will your target customer have to walk? Is parking adequate? Is the parking lot a drop-off point for car-poolers?

3. **Take photographs of the exterior.** Analyze them carefully. Is the building in good repair? What are the customers wearing, driving, and buying? What can you deduce about their lifestyle? Take photographs on different days and at different times of day.

4. **Ask around.** Interview the neighbours and the customers. What do the neighbours know about the business? Will the neighbours help draw target customers to your business? Be up front with the seller's customers, as they might soon be your customers. What do they like about the store? Is the service good? What changes would they recommend? What services or products would they like to see added? Where else do they go for similar products or services?

5. **Check out future competition.** Do you want to be close to competitors, or do you want to be kilometres away from them? Could a competitor move in next door the day after you move in?

6. **Check with the local authorities.** What are the plans for this location? What is the local municipality planning to do with the sewers or roads? Are all the local permits in order? Are there any new proposals for building permits?

ACTION STEP 59

Study a business from the inside.

Looking at a business from the inside enables you to determine its real worth and to see what it would be like to own it. Make an appointment (or have a business broker arrange it) to take a serious inside look at the business you think you want to buy. Before you go, review everything we've explained in this section, and write down a list of what you hope to learn while you're there. Don't let anyone rush you. Leave the chequebook at home; this fun is free.

ACTION STEP 60

Probe the depths of ill will.

How many products have you vowed never to use again? How many places of business have you vowed never to patronize again? Why?

Make a list of the products and services you won't buy or use again. Next to each item, write the reason. Does it make you sick? Does it offend your sensibilities? Was the service awful?

After you've completed your list, ask your friends what their negative feelings about particular businesses are. Take notes.

Study the two lists you've made. What are the common components of ill will? How long does ill will last? Is there a remedy for it, or is a business subject to ill will unlikely to ever get past it?

Now, turn your attention to the business you want to buy. Survey your target customers. How do they feel about the business? You need to learn as much as you can about any ill will that exists toward the business.

Have fun with this step, but take it seriously—and think about the nature of ill will when your seller starts asking you to pay for goodwill.

Checklist Questions and Actions to Develop Your Business Plan

BUYING A BUSINESS

❏ Why would you buy a business rather than start from scratch?

❏ What are the potential "icebergs" (unknowns or major risks) in buying a business?

❏ Establish the value of goodwill. Is the business worth this amount?

❏ What would be the cost involved in starting from scratch versus buying a business?

Case Study: A Passionate Leap

Case Background

"Come on. Let's be realistic. You're really risking only $10,000. It's just not that much money. We hardly even need a costly lawyer or accountant. I'll tell you what. If you move quickly, I'll even throw in the inventory I just bought. With all the goodwill you're buying, you can make your small investment back in no time. I want to see my baby prosper after I'm gone. I like you guys, and I think you will take care of my business and make me proud. I really want to go with you. But, to tell you the truth, I have a couple of other offers. If you want the deal, you'll have to get back to me in the next couple of days."

Frank, the current owner of The Copy Centre Store, had started the business 18 months earlier. Now he was ready to bail out. He'd been advertising in the Businesses for Sale section of the local newspaper. Carolyn and Mitch were hungry to get into business. They had been watching this section of their local paper, and it seemed as if they had found the perfect opportunity. Here was an owner who wanted out quickly at a "bargain-basement" price—or so he claimed.

They could take over Frank's business for just $10,000 cash plus $98,000 for equipment and inventory. Frank offered to finance the $98,000 and even throw in a few perks, if they would move quickly and offer their house as collateral.

That evening, they asked Uncle Jack, an experienced entrepreneur, what he thought. "You have to research the business from the inside—go through the books, interview the previous owner thoroughly, and talk to everybody in the centre and in the business. Then, complete a total evaluation of the business from the outside—the location and so on. I'm tied up right now, but give me a few days and I will prepare a list of 'inside' and 'outside' questions that need to be answered."

Mitch and Carolyn both wanted to get into an established business. They had been looking for more than six months. Entrepreneurs move fast and take risks, they reasoned. This opportunity seemed perfect. Not much downside. After all, as Frank the owner had said, the most they could lose was $10,000. Deep into the night, they brainstormed. They even had a few good ideas to improve the storefront and sales.

The next day, Carolyn and Mitch made the deal—and when they told Uncle Jack later on, he looked grim. The third day after they opened, a big truck backed up to their back door and removed all the copy machines. Apparently, the previous owner had leased them and hadn't made payments in three months. This unpleasant brush with reality was only the start. A year later, Mitch and Carolyn were broke, and their house was gone. They learned the hard way: Passionate leaps require due diligence.

Case Study Questions

1. Reasons for buying a business
   a. List five reasons an entrepreneur would buy a business rather than start one.
   b. If Mitch and Carolyn had reviewed this list, would they have bought the business?

2. Investigating the business
   As Uncle Jack advised, Mitch and Carolyn should have investigated the business from both the outside and the inside. Suppose you were Uncle Jack.
   a. Prepare a checklist of possible research questions for Mitch and Carolyn related to the outside of the business.
   b. Prepare a checklist of possible research questions for Mitch and Carolyn related to the inside of the business.

3. Red flags
   a. Carolyn and Mitch should have listened carefully to Frank, who raised a number of "red flags" that he was trying to sell his business quickly (see Box 13.3, page 382). What red flags did Frank raise?

b. For every red flag statement listed in Box 13.3, give one reason why prospective buyers should be careful when they hear it.

4. Business valuation

Suppose that Mitch and Carolyn had done their financial due diligence and had calculated the following financial information:

Total assets (market value): $50,000

Goodwill: $10,000

Total liabilities: $35,000

Average annual net profit before taxes: $25,000

Salary to owner: $22,000

Suppose, as well, that Carolyn and Mitch had also estimated that they would need a combined salary of $32,000 to pay their personal expenses. This means that the net profit given to them by Frank would be $25,000 − $10,000 = $15,000. Assume that they had worked out the earning power of Frank's assets to be 10 percent. As Frank had been in business only 18 months, they would decide to apply a developmental (or times earning) factor of 1.

a. One method of valuing a business is the adjusted book value. According to this method, what is the value of Frank's business?

b. Using the earnings-assets valuation method (page 387), how much is the business worth? Complete the following steps.

1. Tangible net worth: _____

2. Earning power (10 percent) _____

3. Reasonable salary for owner(s) $32,000

4. Earning capacity _____

5. Average annual net profit _____

6. Extra earning power _____

7. Value of intangibles (developmental factor of 1) _____

8. Final earnings-assets valuation price _____

c. Compare your results in (a) and (b) above. Which valuation estimate is lower? Why?

Notes

1. Robbinex Intermediaries, "The Market and the Players," http://www.robbinex.com/articles_market_players.php.
2. "Historical Earnings Evaluation," Business Owner's Toolkit, http://www.bizfilings.com/toolkit/sbg/run-a-business/exiting/use-best-business-valuation-formula.aspx.
3. "How to Evaluate a Proposed Business Acquisition," BDC.ca website, http://www.bdc.ca/EN/advice_centre/articles/Pages/acquisition_business_evaluate.aspx#.UME9OIN_tLc.

Chapter 14

Buying a Franchise or Franchising Your Business

This chapter will introduce you to the world of franchising and help you decide if buying a franchise or becoming a franchisor is right for you.

© Philip Bird/Alamy

LEARNING OPPORTUNITIES

After reading this chapter, you should be able to

- appreciate the vast world of franchising,
- understand key franchising terms and conditions in an agreement,
- understand the relationship between franchisor and franchisee,
- learn the benefits and liabilities of owning and operating a franchise,
- learn how to become a master franchisee,
- learn the process involved in purchasing a franchise,
- understand what it takes to become a franchisor,
- decide whether buying a franchise or becoming a franchisor is the right step for you,
- investigate a member-owned buying group as an alternative business model.

ACTION STEP PREVIEW

61. Conduct secondary research on franchising.
62. Investigate the franchise system by interviewing franchisors and franchisees.

FRANCHISE SHOWS*

Franchising provides many opportunities to entrepreneurs, and a variety of franchising opportunities can be found by attending a franchise show.

The Franchise Show, hosted by the Canadian Franchise Association (CFA), is a forum where franchisor companies offering franchise opportunities set up booths with information, and potential franchisees connect with them and talk face-to-face, receive general information on franchises, take part in seminars by industry leaders, and meet others interested in buying franchises. The franchisors who participate at the Franchise Show are all CFA members.

Lorraine McLachlan, CFA president and chief executive officer, says that the Franchise Show allows potential franchisees to talk with a number of franchisors so that they can compare the different opportunities and narrow down the choices to what is right for them all within a short time frame. She advises people to plan the day around seminars so that they can learn about the industry before speaking to some franchisors.

What makes a good franchisee? According to Peter Druxeman, vice-president of marketing and co-owner of Druxy's, the most important part about finding a franchisee is ensuring that the individual's personality matches well with the company's character. Druxeman has seen franchisees fail not because they lacked business wisdom but because they weren't honest with themselves about what they wanted out of the franchise system. They weren't sincere about their personal goals and didn't have the character needed to make the franchise a success.

In other words, they lacked passion for a particular type of business.

For people who are considering purchase of a franchise, attending a franchise show like the one put on by the Canadian Franchise Association is recommended; however, more than that, potential franchisees must be clear on their personal goals and passionate about the business they want to get into. They need to believe in the franchise opportunity and be willing to make it a success. (More information on the CFA Franchise Show is available at www.thefranchiseshow.ca.)

Our walk-through of opportunities in small business is almost finished. Decision time approaches. If you've followed the Action Steps, you've spent several months gathering data and talking to people in small business. In Chapter 13, we explored buying a business and talking to sellers. In this chapter, we look at another option: acquiring a franchised business.

Franchisees have found success through buying a franchise. In Chapter 6, we learned how 1-800-GOT-JUNK?, established by Brian Scudamore, succeeded as a franchisor by franchising out its business format. In this chapter, we'll introduce you to other Canadian entrepreneurs who are "riding high" on the franchising wave.

The franchising industry is enormous. Each year, Entrepreneur.com publishes a ranking for some 500 franchises. It also publishes a series of top 10 franchises in the following categories: home-based low-cost, top new, fastest growing, and

*Maria Tzavaras, "The Franchise Show coming to Toronto Feb. 23 and 24," *The Etobicoke Guardian*, February 12, 2013, http://www.insidetoronto.com/news-story/2074174-the-franchise-show-coming-to-toronto-feb-23-and-24/

top global. Some of the top global franchises include Subway (with over 2,800 Canadian and more than 9,000 international franchises) and McDonald's (with over 1,100 Canadian and more than 13,600 international franchises).[1] If you were to buy or rent a car tomorrow morning, put gas in it, buy a coffee and doughnut, purchase some paint, and then go to a fast-food restaurant for lunch, you would likely support a franchise at every stop. Here are some "fast facts" from the Canadian Franchise Association's website:[2]

- Franchised businesses account for 40% of all retail sales.[3]
- There are over 78,000 franchise units across Canada.[4]
- CFA members represent more than 40,000 business outlets across the country.[5]
- Franchising directly employs over 1,000,000 people.[6]
- Every year, thousands of Canadians are improving their lives by becoming franchisees.[7]
- Franchising accounts for 10% of Canada's Gross Domestic Product (GDP).[8]
- Franchising has been reported to account for one out of every five consumer dollars spent in Canada in goods and services.[9]
- Any business that can be exactly replicated can be a franchise.[10]

What is a franchise? Is a franchise for you? Should you franchise your own business? If so, when does it make business sense? Are you ready to surrender some of your independence? Is a franchise a good first business, a stepping-stone to the future entrepreneurship you seek? We'll try to help you answer these questions in this chapter.

WHAT IS A FRANCHISE?

As we discussed in Chapter 7, a franchise is a distribution system used by businesses to sell or market their products or services. It's a special kind of partnership in which one company (the **franchisor**) grants the right to sell its products or services to another company or individual (the **franchisee**).

FRANCHISE SYSTEMS

A variety of franchise business arrangements or systems exist. If you buy a dozen doughnuts at Tim Hortons or get your trash removed by 1-800-GOT-JUNK?, you have just experienced familiar examples of the **business format franchise** system. In this type of franchise, the product, method of distribution, and sales and management procedures—the business format—are highly controlled. The franchisor "blueprints" every aspect of the business and then sells this business format to a franchisee. The main job of the franchisee is to staff and run the operation. This type of franchise system is the most popular. It encompasses most businesses, from used clothing to coffee to the selling of mufflers.

A second type of popular franchise system is the **dealership relationship franchise** (also termed a "licensing or associate relationship"). Here, the dealer or associate (franchisee) buys the right to distribute a franchisor's product or service. These types of licensing arrangements are less restrictive than the business format arrangement, where the key is standardization. Dealership franchisees distribute and sell the product under the franchisor's conditions but are left relatively free from any other franchisee obligations. PropertyGuys.com and Home Hardware are good examples of this kind of arrangement. Another example would be Coca-Cola and Pepsi, which license or franchise out the right

FRANCHISOR

The firm that sells the rights to do business under its name and continues to control the business

FRANCHISEE

The individual operator who is licensed to operate under the franchisor's rules and directives

BUSINESS FORMAT FRANCHISE

A type of franchise in which the product, method of distribution, and sales and management procedures are highly controlled

DEALERSHIP RELATIONSHIP FRANCHISE

Also called a "licensing or associate relationship," a type of franchise in which the franchisee buys the right to distribute a franchisor's product or service to distribute their products to a local bottler but don't normally tell the licensees how to run their business operations.

FRANCHISE NETWORKS

A franchisor has two basic types of franchise networks available to distribute its products or services. When a franchisee deals directly with the franchisor one-to-one, this type of network is referred to as **direct franchising**. For example, if you want to buy rights from a franchise company, such as PropertyGuys.com, to operate a franchise in your area, then you will deal directly with PropertyGuys.com. For any questions or problems, you will also deal directly with a representative of the franchisor.

If a franchisor wants to grow quickly and still provide hands-on service, it might turn to the master franchise format. **Master franchising** is a business arrangement or network in which a franchisor sells the rights to an area or territory to a franchisee, who is usually required to sell (or establish) and service a specified number of franchises (often called "subfranchisees") in a specified time period within its area. The master franchisee pays the franchisor (franchise company) an initial territory fee for the rights to develop its area. Normally, in return, it retains at least a portion of the franchise fees and royalties fees paid over time by the subfranchisees. These area subfranchisees work with the master franchisee in the operations of their business.

To learn more about master franchising, click on the sites shown in Box 14.1 on page 402.

WHY BUY A FRANCHISE?

In theory, a successful franchise system can benefit the customer, the franchisee, and the franchisor—a win-win situation.

WHAT THE CUSTOMER GETS

Imagine that you're on a holiday. You have been driving for hours, and it's time for lunch. Do you have lunch at Wendy's or Boston Pizza, or do you take a chance and pull in at a flashing "Joe's Diner" sign? If you're like many Canadians, you'll choose a name that is familiar. Why? Because to some degree, you've been branded. You've become comfortable with a product and gained a certain attachment to it. You know what to expect, so, even if it isn't perfect, you keep returning. It's hard to get out of this comfort zone.

Customer satisfaction and brand loyalty are the key reasons for buying a franchise. Each franchise outlet is cloned to offer a consistent standard of service and product. If the franchise system runs as planned, customers will know what to expect and how much they will pay every time. Franchises give customers a sense of security. Should a dispute arise, customers know that they can appeal to a larger organization. Franchises give the appearance that they will be around for the long run. There is also a good chance that the "owner" will be around, and customers like to know that they can speak to the owner should the need arise.

WHAT THE FRANCHISEE RECEIVES

Let's examine what you can expect to receive when you buy a franchise. In principle, a franchise can provide the following:

1. **brand-name recognition**—if you pick the right franchise with a high, positive consumer profile, you will have a recognizable brand;

DIRECT FRANCHISING

A business arrangement in which a franchisee deals directly with the franchisor

MASTER FRANCHISING

A business arrangement in which a franchisor sells the rights to an area or territory to a franchisee, who is normally required to sell (or establish) and service a specified number of franchises in its area within a specified time period

2. **support from the corporation**—corporate services can include help with site selection, employee training, inventory control, vendor supplies and connections, a corporate-produced business plan, lease negotiations, layout assistance, and more;

3. **training**—the franchisor will teach you the business and provide ongoing training;

4. **financial support**—lenders often prefer to lend to new franchises over new start-ups;

5. **a template**—you are buying a proven business plan and strategy that work;

6. **purchasing power**—you may share in economies of scale in purchasing goods, services, and promotion;

7. **corporate monitoring and assistance**—you are likely to receive psychological hand holding and field visits from the franchisor;

8. **less risk of failure**—the failure rate of franchises is less than half of self-start-ups;

9. **national/regional promotion**—you will benefit from pretested promotion and marketing programs;

10. **additional units**—you will likely gain opportunities to buy another franchise in your area.

WHAT THE FRANCHISOR ASKS OF YOU

Franchisors earn money in several ways.

1. They collect a **franchise fee** for the rights to use their name and system. This fee can range anywhere from $3,000 for a small service firm to more than $100,000 for a well-established name, such as that of a hotel, auto dealership, or major restaurant. The franchise fee is usually paid by the franchisee on the day the franchise agreement is signed and applies for the term of the agreement (usually 5–10 years). The franchise agreement will state if an additional franchise fee is due for any subsequent renewal period.

2. They normally collect a **royalty fee**, which ranges from 2 to 15 percent of the annual gross sales. Some franchisors collect their royalties by charging a percentage on the purchase of supplies rather than on sales.

3. Some franchisors make a profit on the markup of items (such as store fixtures) that they sell directly to franchisees.

4. Some franchisors receive volume rebates or other benefits from suppliers that they don't pass on to the franchisees.

5. Some franchisors require franchisees to pay advertising and promotion fees. These generally range from 2 to 5 percent of the franchisee's gross sales. Some of these are directed toward local promotions, but most go into the national advertising fund. (In some cases, depending on the age of the franchise, it may be possible to ask for some concessions in the payment of these fees.)

In addition, growth and market penetration are key benefits. Franchisors can expand their business quickly with limited capital from the original owners. A number of growth options are available. Some franchisors, for example, provide incentives for their successful franchisees to own multiple units. Other aggressive franchisors have been known to sell geographic territories to master franchisors.

FRANCHISE FEE

Fee paid by a franchisee for the rights to represent the franchisor in a given geographic area for a specified time, commonly 5 to 10 years

ROYALTY FEE

Ongoing obligation to pay the franchisor a percentage of the gross sales

ACTION STEP 61

Conduct secondary research on franchising. (p. 415)

INVESTIGATING FRANCHISE OPPORTUNITIES

Mac Voisin is the founder of M&M Meat Shops, a highly successful franchise chain of more than 450 outlets, started in Kitchener, Ontario. According to Voisin, true entrepreneurs will become totally frustrated in a franchise system, because they want to do everything their way. As Voisin points out, many of you will not be comfortable operating by the franchisor's strict rules and regulations. Your entrepreneurial spirit might make it difficult for you to follow detailed rules and policies.

But that doesn't mean you shouldn't look at franchises. You can learn a lot by examining the way good franchises work. It makes sense to evaluate franchise opportunities (especially those in your industry), because, at the very least, doing so will give you a better picture of the marketplace. You first step might be to attend a franchise trade fair, a great way to find new opportunities. If you are interested, we suggest you get in touch with the Canadian Franchise Association (see Box 14.1). Check to see if it is holding an event near you. Action Steps 61 and 62, and the E-Exercise provided in Box 14.2 will also help.

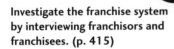

ACTION STEP 62

Investigate the franchise system by interviewing franchisors and franchisees. (p. 415)

Box 14.1 Franchise Information and Resources

- **Canadian Franchise Association (CFA):** http://www.cfa.ca/Look_for_Franchise/
- **Canada Business Network: Government Services for Entrepreneurs:** http://www.canadabusiness.ca/eng/page/2715/
- **Siskinds, Franchise Law Group:** http://www.franchiselaw.ca
- **Franchise Comparison Worksheet (Entrepreneur.com):** http://www.entrepreneur.com/formnet/downloads/frn1.doc—Use this form to help you determine the attractiveness of each prospective franchise you are considering.
- *The Franchise Magazine:* http://www.thefranchisemagazine.net
- **Canadian Business Franchise:** http://www.1minutefranchisefinder.com

Franchise Databases and Directories

Use the following sites to search for franchising opportunities.

- **Canadian Franchise Directory:** http://www.canadianfranchisedirectory.ca
- **Canadian Franchise Association:** http://www.cfa.ca
- **FranchiseOpportunities.com:** http://canada.franchiseopportunities.com/
- **Businessnation.com, Franchise Opportunity Listings:** http://www.businessnation.com/franchises/pages

Master Franchising

- **MegaDox.com, Canada Master Franchise Agreement:** http://www.megadox.com/docpreviews/4072.pdf
- **Canadian Business:** http://www.franchiseinfo.ca/franchisor/view.php?itm=24
- **Financial Post, Franchise Focus:** http://business.financialpost.com/2012/02/08/master-franchising-is-preferred-way-to-globalize-brands/

Box 14.2 E-Exercise

- "Is It Smart to Buy a Franchise Right out of College?" See what Jeff Elgin has to say in his franchise article at Entrepreneur.com (http://www.entrepreneur.com/article/75034).
- Find a franchise that suits you. Click onto the "2 Minute Franchise Matching Service" link of Selectyourfranchise.com (http://canada.selectyourfranchise.com/?src=adw) and find out about

  – free service—without obligation,

  – the five steps to finding your franchise matches,

- match criteria supplied by the franchisors themselves,
- franchise opportunities where you live and within your budget,
- franchise opportunities available from $15,000 to $750,000.
- Is franchising for you? Read some articles on this site: http://www.franchisehelp.com/.
- Check out FranNet's "Franchising Basics," at http://www.frannet.com/franchising-basics.
- Review Franchise Direct's "Franchisee Checklists—Evaluating Yourself" (http://www.franchisedirect.com/information/thefranchiseesperspective/checklistevaluatingyourself/9/99/).
- See what information on franchising Canada Business Network provides in "Franchising" (http://www.canadabusiness.ca/eng/page/2715/).

THE FRANCHISE AGREEMENT AND SYSTEM

When you purchase a franchise, you will be required to sign a contract that could be as long as 50 pages and with numerous appendixes attached. This contract is the franchise agreement, which lays out the system you will be working within, and the rules and policies that you are bound to operate by. It goes without saying that you need legal advice before you sign the agreement. The typical clauses in the contract include

- definitions,
- grant and term,
- franchise royalty fee and sales taxes,
- reports,
- general services of the franchisor,
- compliance with system,
- manual,
- training,
- advertising and promotions,
- leasing of the premises,
- improvements to the premises,
- engagement in similar business and nondisclosure of information,
- trade-mark,
- insurance,
- indemnification,
- events of default,
- effect of termination,
- assignment,
- general provisions,
- renovations,
- schedules related to the premises, trade-mark, sublease, and payments.

THE PROCESS INVOLVED IN PURCHASING A FRANCHISE

If you have explored and investigated franchising and believe it is the right fit for you, and if you have worked through the Action Steps, the process truly begins.

First, you must contact the franchise development office or the websites of the franchises you are exploring. They will ask you several questions to prequalify you. If the franchisors believe there might be a fit, they will send you a franchise packet. These packets are full of marketing pieces meant to sell you on the franchise. Try to read between the lines. Keep in mind that at this point you are reading advertising materials and that you are at the start of the process. Many of the packets will include an application for additional information (see sample Franchise Application on page 405). For example, if you go to the website of M&M Meat Shops (http://www.franchise.mmmeatshops.com/?lang=0), click on "How to Become a Franchisee" and then click on "Steps to Becoming a Franchisee" (http://www.franchise.mmmeatshops.com/franchise_application.pdf): you will gain a good idea of the kind of personal detailed information a reputable franchisor will require. Another option is to link onto the Subway "Application for Additional Franchise Information" site (https://www.subway.com/applications/AdditionalInfoApp/index.aspx).

If the franchise is large, a local sales manager or master franchisee will contact you after reviewing your application. Should there be a fit, you will meet and discuss capital requirements and possible locations in more detail. At this point, you should be exploring the franchisor and franchisees, current and past, in depth. Take your time, and ask the questions we have presented throughout the chapter. Within the franchisor's packet, you will find information on capital requirements.

You will want to know if the franchisor provides any financing or equipment leasing. In addition, if you are interested in an area or master franchise, now is the time to explore this option. Before going any further, ask if you can work within one of the franchises for two to four weeks to gain a feel for daily operations and responsibilities.

You may also want to find out from the Canadian Franchise Association whether there is a local association of franchisees for your selected franchise in your area. If so, contact the association, and delve as deeply as necessary and for as long as you need until your questions are answered. The more contact you have with franchisees, the better equipped you will be to make a final purchase decision.

If your experience working in the franchise confirms that you want to explore it further, you can work with the franchisor to determine the best site or area for you. The franchisor should provide you with the business information to support the numbers required for a successful franchise in the selected area. Deposits might be required before the site selection process begins. At this time, we strongly advise you to consult a lawyer. **Please, do not make a deposit or sign any agreement until you have had a chance to review the information with your lawyer.** You should have a lawyer who specializes in franchising to help you answer any questions you might have. Also, if you are beginning to look at offices or retail space, involve your lawyer immediately.

An accountant should also be called in to review material and point out financial issues that need to be discussed with the franchisor. Your accountant, if he or she has franchise experience, will help you assess the financial possibilities and feasibility of the venture, and perhaps help you compare it to other options. Use all the information you have gathered, and work through the Action Steps to develop your franchise business plan—yes, you still need a Business Plan.

With the advice of your accountant, lawyer, past and current franchisees, and banker, you are finally ready to negotiate with the franchisor to complete the sale. Be sure that you understand your role and the franchisor's responsibilities. Once you have negotiated your contract, you might be basically on your own, or

Figure 14.1   Sample Franchise Application

CONFIDENTIAL APPLICATION FORM
Cara's Coffee Ltd.

Please note:
1. **Please answer all items before submitting it.**
2. **This application must be completed by the intended café operator on their own.**
3. **Partner(s) must fill out a separate application form.**

Where did you learn about us?

Examples: Cara's Coffee Employee / Friend / Franchise Partner / Newspaper / Seminar / Existing Cara's Coffee Location / Trade Show / Internet / Magazines / Cara's Coffee Franchising at Home Office / If other, provide details:

This is my application to operate a Cara's Coffee café as a full-time operator. I understand that this application is intended to allow Cara's Coffee to consider my qualifications on a preliminary basis. The submission of this application form does not oblige Cara's Coffee or the applicant in any way or manner.

PERSONAL INFORMATION	
Name:	Date:
Day Phone:	Evening Phone:
Mobile:	Email:
Address:	

City:	Province:	Postal Code:

How long have you lived there? yrs. If less than 2 years give former address:		

Date of Birth: dd/mm/yy	Marital Status:	No. of Children:

Spouse's Name:		
Is Spouse Employed? If so, in what position:		
Citizenship: If new immigrant, date of Permanent Residency:		

REFERENCES	
Name:	Address:
Day Phone:	Email:

you might have a strong franchise organization behind you, helping you with site selection, store design, training, advertising, marketing, and possibly, a grand-opening celebration. The story doesn't end on opening—it has just begun! Good luck!

BUYER BEWARE: SOME PITFALLS OF FRANCHISING

Many franchise lawyers and desperate franchisees tell the same stories again and again. Investors are told a location makes $10,000 a week when it actually brings in $2,000; in some cases, refundable deposits are never returned; and some chains ask for deposits as high as $40,000 before giving the franchisee a contract to review.

Here are some of the more notable pitfalls that plague the franchising industry.

ENCROACHMENT

ENCROACHMENT

Situation in which franchisors compete with franchisees by putting an outlet nearby or setting up alternative distribution channels, such as mail order or Internet sales

Encroachment is a significant concern in the franchise industry. Encroachment is a situation in which franchisors compete with franchisees by putting a store nearby or operating through an alternative distribution channel, such as mail order or the Internet. For example, H&R Block now offers tax service on the Internet, you can buy a Tim Hortons coffee and doughnut at your local Esso station, and the Body Shop has online shopping as well as retail orders. Such developments mean that established franchisees are finding it more and more difficult to protect their territory.

GROUND-FLOOR OPPORTUNITIES

Beware of ground-floor ("grow with us") franchise opportunities. A franchisor offering such an "opportunity" is experimenting with your money. If you buy a franchise, you should be buying a recognized brand name, a proven business plan, excellent field support, and experience that demonstrates the particular franchise will work in your location. Otherwise, you are better off to start a business yourself. A franchise concept is not normally considered established until the business has lasted about five years.

RENEWAL PERIOD

Franchise agreements should stipulate the conditions for a renewal period after the contract agreement expires. For example, if you sign an agreement for five years, your franchise fee, royalty payments, and even your protected territory could change drastically when it comes time to renew—if you have not negotiated renewal conditions beforehand. Beware of contracts that do not provide for conditions of renewal *that are negotiable*. At the very least, try to negotiate an option to renew for a set period under the same terms and conditions as the original contract. One thing is certain: On renewal, you do not want to pay a second franchise fee. *Again, know that this can be negotiated.*

VERBAL AGREEMENTS

Beware of the franchisor who makes statements along these lines: "It's a two-way street. We have to trust each other. We'll make you a good deal if you want to renew. After all, who knows what will happen in the future? We don't need to put this in the franchise agreement." Most well-written agreements come with a "small-print" paragraph that says something to the effect that the franchisor or its representatives are not legally responsible for any promises made prior to the signing of the agreement. *Get everything in writing.*

MINIMUM FRANCHISE LEGISLATION

The federal government has developed franchise legislation in some provinces to protect franchisees. Alberta, Ontario, Manitoba, New Brunswick and Prince Edward Island are the only provinces that, as of 2013, have put in place any substantive franchise legislation (http://www.cfa.ca/Advocacy/Franchise _Legislation/). Outside these provinces, franchisors are not legally required to provide you with the following types of information about the company:

- balance sheet and income statement information,
- number of franchises,
- bankruptcy history,
- background of the owners and key officers,
- revenues and expenses of the franchisor,
- turnover rate of franchisees.

SIGNING PERSONALLY

If you are going into a partnership with a franchisor, we strongly advise you to keep your legal distance. You don't want to get your personal assets mixed up with a franchisor's business. Form a company, and sign the franchise agreement in the company name. If a franchisor wants personal guarantees, be prepared to say no.

AVAILABILITY OF INFORMATION AND FRANCHISING REALITIES

Are franchisees more successful and profitable than businesses that are not? It's hard to say. Most evidence is anecdotal and relies on information from franchise associations. For example, we told you at the beginning of this chapter that the average annual franchise sales growth during the past few years had exceeded 10 percent. Here, we relied on information provided by those in the franchise business, and we trusted that their sources were accurate. The fact is, there are no regular government surveys on franchising in Canada.

Having said that, a 2008 report by the Research Strategy Group (RSG) provides excellent insights into franchising. The following are some research findings from this report.[11]

1. Almost half (45 percent) of the franchisees interviewed considered starting up their own independent businesses.
2. The majority of franchisees surveyed were 35 years to 44 years old (38 percent), and 45 years to 54 years old (31 percent).
3. The number of women looking at franchising is rising.
4. A significant number of younger people are purchasing franchises.
5. The majority of franchisees surveyed (70 percent) are very satisfied with their decision to buy, 25 percent are somewhat satisfied, and 5 percent are not satisfied.
6. Name recognition or known business name was the number 1 choice (22 percent) given for choosing franchising instead of starting an independent business.
7. Twelve percent of those surveyed said they were not interested in starting their own businesses because the risks were too high.

The Canadian Franchise Association (CFA) is one of the few sources of franchise information. The organization has about 550 corporate members, and they are required to disclose certain types of information to prospective franchisees. Check the CFA Disclosure Document Guide on the CFA website (http://www.cfa.ca/About_Us/Disclosure_Documents/disclosureguide.aspx). Although this disclosure requirement is not backed by government legislation, a corporate member can be reported to the association. Note that even when a member provides you with information, "the Canadian Franchise Association has not checked the information and does not know if it is correct." Still, check the website for prospective franchisors, and see whether they are registered. If they are not members, find out why. If they are, you should be able to find some information. Keep in mind, though, that members are not required to file financial information about their operations. In other words, a franchisor could be close to bankruptcy, and you might not know it.

Here is a summary of other franchising realities to keep in mind:

- **Saturated markets.** Competition has become intense among competitive franchisors, which has led to a tendency for franchisors, especially fast-food outlets, quick-printing shops, and specialty retailers, to saturate market areas, thus resulting in many failures.
- **Poor training.** Some training programs are poor or nonexistent.
- **Supplies stipulation.** Some franchise agreements stipulate that you must buy your supplies from the franchisor. Problems emerge when franchisees are required to pay noncompetitive prices (that is, they are overcharged) for products supplied by the franchisor.
- **Insiders first.** Typically, current franchisees are offered prime locations before outsiders or first-time franchise buyers. Rarely is a new player offered a sure thing. Invariably, new players are offered franchises that have already been passed over.
- **Nonrefundable deposits.** Some franchisors ask for a nonrefundable deposit during the time the buyer is negotiating an agreement. Meeting the request is supposed to show the buyer's good faith. Be careful, even if you are presented with a request for a refundable deposit. Seek legal advice, and place the money in trust with your lawyer, not the franchisor's lawyer. Some refundable deposits are never returned.

EVALUATING A FRANCHISE

Evaluating a franchise opportunity is much like evaluating any other business that's up for sale, but because of the nature of franchisors, you need to ask some additional questions, these among them:

- How long has this franchise been in business?
- Who are the officers?
- Has the franchisor, or any of its officers, gone bankrupt or been convicted of any criminal offences?
- How many franchise outlets are operating right now?
- How well does this franchise compete with similar franchises?
- Where is this franchise in its life cycle?
- What will this franchise do for me?

In Chapter 13, we provided a checklist to use in evaluating an ongoing business you are considering buying. Most of that checklist applies to franchises as well. To supplement it, we're giving you a checklist prepared specifically for evaluating franchise opportunities (see Box 14.3). The questions will help you generate a profile of the franchise and make a wise decision.

Box 14.3 Franchise Evaluation Checklist

General

	Yes	No
1. Is the product or service		
a) considered reputable?	_____	_____
b) part of a growing market?	_____	_____
c) needed in your area?	_____	_____
d) of interest to you?	_____	_____
e) safe?	_____	_____
f) protected?	_____	_____
g) covered by guarantee?	_____	_____

2. What makes the franchisor's product or service distinctive or unique?

_____

3. How long has the product or service been on the market?

_____

4. What products must be purchased from the franchisor or designated supplier? Under what terms?

_____

5. Is the franchise

local?	_____
regional?	_____
national?	_____
international?	_____
Will the franchisee be working	_____
full time?	_____
part time?	_____
possibly full time in the future?	_____

6. Existing franchises

a) Date the company was founded
b) Date the first franchise was awarded
c) Number of franchises currently in operation or under construction
d) References
    Franchise 1: Owner
                Address
                Telephone
                Date started
    Franchise 2: Owner
                Address
                Telephone
                Date started
    Franchise 3: Owner
                Address
                Telephone
                Date started
e) Additional franchises planned for the next 12 months

7. Failed franchises

a) How many failed? How many in the past two years?
b) Why have they failed?

    Franchisor reasons:

    _____

    Better Business Bureau reasons:

    _____

8. Franchise in local market area

  a) Has a franchise ever been awarded in this area?

  b) If so, and if it is still in operation:
    Owner
    Address
    Telephone
    Date started

  c) If so, and if it is no longer in operation:
    Person involved
    Address
    Date started
    Date ended
    Reasons for failure

  d) How many inquiries have there been for the franchise from the area in the past six months?

9. What product or service will be added to the franchise package?

  a) Within 12 months?

  b) Within two years?

  c) Within two to five years?

10. Competition

  a) What is the direct competition?

  b) What is the indirect competition? Any invisible competition?

  c) What other outlets are planned to be opened near this territory?

  d) Is there any territorial protection or exclusivity?

  e) Does the franchisor sell its products through other channels such as the Internet? If so, what are these channels?

11. Are all franchises independently owned?

  a) Of the total outlets, how many are franchised, and how many are company owned?

  b) If some outlets are company owned, did they start out this way, or were they purchased from a franchisee?

12. Franchise operations

  a) What facilities are required, and do I lease or build?

	Build	*Lease*
Office	_____	_____
Building	_____	_____
Manufacturing facility	_____	_____
Warehouse	_____	_____

b) Getting started—
Who is responsible for the

	Franchisor	*Franchisee*
construction	_____	_____
design	_____	_____
employee training	_____	_____
feasibility study	_____	_____
financing	_____	_____
furnishings and equipment	_____	_____
lease negotiation	_____	_____

Franchise Company

1. The company

a) Name and address of the parent company, if different from the franchise company:

Name
Address

b) Is the parent company public or private?

c) If the company is public, where is the stock traded?

Toronto Stock Exchange _____
Over the counter _____

2. Is the franchisor a member of the Canadian Franchise Association? If not, why not?

_____

3. Does the franchisor have outlets in Ontario or Alberta? (*Note*: You want to know this, because franchisors in these provinces are subject to stricter legal conditions and must submit franchisor disclosure documents.)

_____

4. Forecast of income and expenses:

a) Is a forecast of income and expenses provided?

b) Is it
based on actual franchisee operations? _____
based on a franchisor outlet? _____
purely estimated? _____

c) Does it

	Yes	*No*
relate to your market area?	_____	_____
meet your personal goals?	_____	_____
provide adequate return on investment?	_____	_____
provide for adequate promotion and personnel?	_____	_____

5. What is the best legal structure for my company?
proprietorship _____
partnership _____
corporation _____

6. The franchise contract:

a) Is there a written contract? (Get a copy for lawyer and accountant to review.)

_____

b) Does it specify

	Yes	*No*
the franchise fee?	_____	_____
termination?	_____	_____
selling and renewal?	_____	_____
advertising and promotion?	_____	_____
patent and liability protection?	_____	_____
home office services?	_____	_____

	Yes	No
commissions and royalties?	_____	_____
training?	_____	_____
financing?	_____	_____
territory?	_____	_____
exclusivity?	_____	_____
supplier rebates?	_____	_____
record keeping?	_____	_____

c) Is there a dispute resolution mechanism?

_____

d) What are the terms and conditions relative to a master franchisor?

_____

CHOOSE YOUR PRODUCT OR SERVICE WITH CARE

As a potential franchisee, you should know everything about the product or service the franchise system delivers. Naturally, an exclusive product or service, or one that is of superior quality and value, is a good business bet, but these aren't the only criteria for judging the competitive strength of the product or service. There are good profits to be made or lost in products that are essentially not different from others in the market—except in how they are marketed. One franchise can be much the same as another, but if its marketing is superior, it can overpower the competition. So, when you assess the competitive strength of the product or service you're interested in, consider everything it takes to deliver that product or service to customers. Then ask yourself how well your prospective franchisor does all of these things.

REASONS FOR NOT BUYING A FRANCHISE

Many entrepreneurs have decided against buying franchises. Here are some of the reasons they have given.

- I know the business as well as they do.
- The franchise name is not all that important.
- Why pay a franchise fee?
- Why pay a royalty and advertising fee?
- My individuality would have been stifled.
- I don't want others to tell me how to run my business.
- I didn't want a ground-floor opportunity where I'd be the guinea pig.
- There were restrictions on selling out.
- If I didn't do as I was told, I would lose my franchise.
- The specified business hours didn't suit my location.
- The franchisor's promotions and products didn't fit my customers' needs or tastes.
- They offered no territory protection.

CAN YOU FRANCHISE YOUR IDEA AND BECOME THE FRANCHISOR?

"I wanted to be more than an employee," recalls Aileen Reid. "I worked hard and I wanted a piece of the business." But the insurance firm she worked for would not make her a partner. So after eight years of dedicated employment, she quit her job and started her own insurance company with a few credit cards and a lot of chutzpah.

Reid had always dreamed big but wanted to limit her financial risk. To grow the company fast without the financial risk of owning every office, she turned to franchising. Today her franchised company, A.P. Reid Insurance Stores Ltd., is Atlantic Canada's largest provider of group insurance, with revenues well over $12 million. "Don't let anyone tell you that you can't do it," she tells future business owners.[12]

Aileen Reid in Atlantic Canada franchised and grew her business. Remember Brian Scudamore (in Chapter 6) of 1-800-GOT-JUNK? He put his company into growth mode through franchising. These successful entrepreneurs are dreamers, and they dream big.

You, too, might be able to franchise your new business sometime in the future. Consider reading books by Fred DeLuca, the founder of Subway, and articles by other major franchisors. Learning from their experiences and losses can be an excellent first stepping-stone to becoming a franchisor. Take time to talk to others who have started franchises—both the successful and the unsuccessful!

We caution you, however, that it is not easy to build a successful franchise business. One former franchisor we know, for example, advises that franchising takes much money to start up, with no payoff guarantees, and recommends building a successful and profitable business model before attempting to sell any franchises. To franchise a business, you will have to ensure that it has a competitive advantage (as we learned in Chapter 6), has credibility, and is teachable. Can someone learn to operate your business in three months or less? Consider, too, the time and effort entailed in developing your franchisees, and be careful not to provide additional concessions and finances to help them financially beyond what is reasonable. Keep your idea simple, and make sure you can train franchisees within a short time. Depending on the type of business, franchisees might have only two or three days during training to learn the business. In addition, consider how much time will be expended to assist the franchisees, not only in their start-up phase but also in the first year of operation. Personnel, as well as personal and financial resources, can be drained by demanding and unsuitable franchisees, so selecting your franchisees becomes incredibly important for initial success.

Franchisors need to be aware that not all franchise ideas are transferable to other physical locations. You need to make sure that the concept can be replicated and is not dependent on the product or economic cycle. In addition, the success of many businesses is based on the personalities of the owners and employees. For a franchise, the success must be dependent not on the owner's personality but on the systems and the franchise's products or services.

Before becoming a franchisor, consider whether you are willing to fulfill primarily the needs of your franchisees rather than the needs of your customers directly. Being a franchisor means working with many different personalities and setting up systems, operations, and training. In addition, you must be willing to watch others grow your "baby." Be aware that many consultants are on the prowl for companies that think they can be the next Subway, and they will do their best to convince you that you are that next company.

A FINAL WORD ABOUT FRANCHISES

Buying a franchise or franchising your business can be a rewarding experience. But we want you to be very careful and do your homework. A franchise is a partnership, and you need to make sure that you or others can work under the controls of its system. We encourage you to look at franchising as an option—the E-Exercise in Box 14.2 will help you evaluate your suitability for becoming a franchisee, or a franchisor, for that matter. There is no reason that *you* cannot be the franchisor. If you can develop a winning formula, then with a little entrepreneurial flair, you can become a franchisor yourself. As we have learned, many entrepreneurs have done this, and it's another reason for learning all you can about franchising now.

MEMBER-OWNED BUYING GROUP: AN ALTERNATIVE

One of the main benefits to buying a franchise is increased purchasing power. Large corporate chains and franchises have the benefit of negotiating better pricing and terms that benefit their networks and franchisees. If you would still like to remain an independent business owner but have the benefit of increased purchasing power for your supplies, then an alternative business model called "Member-Owned Buying Group" might be for you. As an example, Source for Sports® (http://www.sourceforsports.com) is a national buying group of sporting goods stores across Canada. Each store is independently owned and operated and is a member of Sports Distributors of Canada Ltd. By joining this group, independent business owners can gain the benefit of increased buying power for their sports supplies, and everyone benefits from marketing under the name Source for Sports®.

There are many business opportunities related to member-owned buying groups within different industry sectors. As a starting point, contact the specific industry association for your business to get more information on member-owned buying groups within that sector.

In a Nutshell

There are many good reasons to consider buying a franchise. Notably, if the brand name is respected, you'll already be positioned in the marketplace, and if the franchisor is sharp, you'll inherit a business plan and a strong corporate partner that can work for you. It's important, however, to examine carefully the franchise's appeal with consumers—you want to get a marketing boost from the name. Depending on the franchise, you might also get other services for your money (e.g., help with site selection and interior layout, or vendor connections). The main thing you're buying, though, is brand-name recognition.

Just as if you were investigating an ongoing independent business, study the opportunity and franchisor thoroughly. Is a master franchise territory available? Examine the financial history, and compare what you'd make if you bought the business to what you'd make if you invested the same money elsewhere. Speak to other franchisees in the system. *If you are the first, be very careful.* Most of all, before you sign anything, obtain good legal and financial advice.

Finally, we want you to dream big. Consider franchising your idea or business.

Key Terms

business format franchise	franchisee
dealership relationship franchise	franchisor
direct franchising	master franchising
encroachment	royalty fee
franchise fee	

Think Points for Success

✓ Avoid ground-floor opportunities. "Grow with us" might really signal *"Caveat emptor"* ("Let the buyer beware").

✓ Talk to other franchisees.

✓ Consider becoming a master franchisee.

✓ If you plan to buy a franchise, obtain professional legal and financial help before you sign anything.

✓ Note that the franchisor receives a percentage of gross sales for advertising and royalty fees whether the franchisee enjoys a profit or not.

✓ Read the proposed agreements carefully.

✓ Do you really need the security blanket of a franchise?

✓ Think about franchising your business.

Action Steps

ACTION STEP 61

Conduct secondary research on franchising.

A great place to start exploring the world of franchising is the Internet. One option is to complete the E-Exercise provided in Box 14.2.

A second, more rigorous option would be to do a Web search on "buying a franchise." To narrow your search, check out the sites listed in Box 14.1. Begin with the information-related sites, then move on to the franchise databases and directories and do some comparison shopping. Which franchises are hot, and which ones are on their way out? As this is a learning exercise, record any franchising terms or good ideas you come across in the course of your search.

Next, visit the websites of two or three franchisors, and submit an email request for a franchise information packet. (Alternatively, use the information on their sites if it is comprehensive enough.) Write a one-page summary, identifying the advantages and disadvantages of each of your selected franchises. The Franchise Comparison Worksheet, which can be downloaded from Entrepreneur.com (see Box 14.1), will help you do a comparative analysis.

ACTION STEP 62

Investigate the franchise system by interviewing franchisors and franchisees.

Franchises are everywhere: Tim Hortons, Boston Pizza, Second Cup, RE/MAX, Dale Carnegie Training, Holiday Inn, Esso, Hertz, and many others. M&M Meat Shops and 1-800-GOT-JUNK? are two you might want to check out. To learn more about the system, interview people on both sides of the franchise agreement.

Part A: Franchisors

Leave your chequebook at home, and interview at least three franchisors. Here are some questions to start you off.

• What is the business experience of the franchisor's directors and managers?

• How many years has the franchise been operating?

• What are the start-up and ongoing royalty fees, and other fees and costs?

• What level of training and service could I expect before and after I open, and what support is given?

• What is the turnover rate of the franchisees?

• Is the territory well defined?

• What are the minimum volume requirements?

• Is the franchisor a member of the Canadian Franchise Association?

• Is the franchise registered in Alberta, Ontario, or Prince Edward Island, where there is greater regulation?

• How can the franchisor buy back or cancel the franchise?

Part B: Franchisees

Now interview at least three franchisees of the same companies. Ask them the same questions, with emphasis on the type of support they receive from the franchisors.

Checklist Questions and Actions to Develop Your Business Plan

The Franchise Option

❑ Why have you selected a franchise as your method of start-up?

❑ What were your lawyer's comments on the franchise agreement?

❑ Do your personal vision, goals, and personality match a franchise form of ownership?

❑ Have you considered a master franchise?

❑ Is there a possibility you can franchise your business in the future?

Case Study: Franchise Shows

Case Background

In the opening vignette, we discussed how The Franchise Show, hosted by the Canadian Franchise Association, provides a great venue for learning more about the different franchise opportunities available to entrepreneurs. Throughout this chapter, we discussed and examined various topics on buying a franchise and how they are organized. Now, let's look at franchising more closely.

Case Study Resources

Additional information can be found by linking to the following online sources:

- Franchise Show: www.thefranchiseshow.ca
- Canadian Franchise Association: http://www.cfa.ca
- Franchising Info (Canada Business): http://www.canadabusiness.ca/eng/page/2715/
- Entrepreneur.com—Mark Siebert's article, "How to Be a Successful Franchisor": http://www.entrepreneur.com/article/83230
- Tim Hortons: http://www.timhortons.com/ca/en/join/franchising-program-ca.html

Case Study Questions

1. Types of franchise systems
   a. What is a franchise?
   b. In this chapter, we discussed two basic types of franchise systems: business format franchise and dealership relationship franchise. Briefly describe the characteristics of these two systems.
   c. Which franchise system does M&M Meat Shops use?
   d. Return to the opening vignette of Chapter 6 on page 144. Which franchise system is used by 1-800-GOT-JUNK?

2. Franchise networks
   To distribute its products or services, a franchisor has the options to use a direct franchise or master franchise network—or a combination of both.
   a. Distinguish between a direct and master franchise network.
   b. In the Financial Post's article "Master Franchising Is Preferred Way to Globalize Brands" (go to http://business.financialpost.com/2012/02/08/master-franchising-is-preferred-way-to-globalize-brands/), author Chad Finkelstein suggests that master franchising is a preferred way to expand. Why does he recommend this? What are the pros and cons of expanding this way? Explain your answer.

c. Let's say you want to open up a Tim Hortons in your area. What type of franchise agreement would you need in your local area? Check out the Tim Hortons website.

3. Franchise checklist

Imagine that you are a franchise consultant, and a friend comes to you for advice on evaluating a franchise. Prepare a franchise checklist featuring what you consider to be the 10 most important franchise evaluation criteria. Based on these criteria, would you advise your friend to buy the franchise? (Hint: You might want to start by checking out Boxes 14.1 and 14.3.)

4. You, too, as a franchisor!

Bold entrepreneurs have chosen franchising as a distribution method to expand quickly at minimum cost. Link to Entrepreneur.com to see Mark Siebert's article "Are You Ready to Franchise?" (http://www.entrepreneur.com/article/82112). According to Siebert, what are the top 10 questions to ask yourself if you're thinking of franchising your business? Not that if you're not thinking of franchising, you can use these same questions to help you decide whether to start your own business.

Notes

1. Entrepreneur.com, 2012 Top Global Franchises, http://www.entrepreneur.com/franchises/topglobal/index.html.
2. Canadian Franchise Association, http://www.cfa.ca/Publications_Research/FastFacts.aspx.
3. Uniform Law Conference of Canada.
4. Canadian Franchise Association, http://www.cfa.ca/.
5. Ibid.
6. Manitoba Law Reform Commission, Franchise Law Consultation Paper, May 2007.
7. Ibid.
8. Ibid.
9. Ibid.
10. Canadian Franchise Association, http://www.cfa.ca/.
11. Research Strategy Group, *Franchising & Distribution: What Motivates a Franchisee to Invest?* (A Report for Gowlings' Franchise and Distribution National Practice Group), http://www.cfa.ca/files/PDF/PublicationsResearch/GowlingsReport7.pdf.
12. "The New Face of Franchising: Aileen Reid," *Profit*, http://portal.apreid.com/About/In%20the%20News/Profit%20oct%202002%20002.pdf.

15

Pulling the Plan Together

In Chapter 15, we tell you how to draw on all of the materials you have generated in the earlier chapters to create your finished Business Plan—a portable showcase for your small business, as well as a personal road map to success.

Peshkova/Shutterstock.com

LEARNING OPPORTUNITIES

After reading this chapter, you should be able to

- gather all the information you have together into one coherent unit, which becomes a working showcase for your business;
- study a sample business plan to see how one group of entrepreneurs defined and presented their business;
- match or surpass the sample business plan in value-added information, research, and effectiveness;
- complete a chart, called a "PERT," to organize the work ahead;
- put your finished business plan to work with passion.

ACTION STEP PREVIEW

63. Write a cover letter for your plan.
64. Write an executive summary.
65. Describe your product or service.
66. Describe the market and the target customer.
67. Describe your major competitors.
68. Describe your marketing strategy.
69. Show off your location.
70. Introduce your management team.
71. Describe your personnel.
72. Project your cash flow.
73. Project your income statement.
74. Project your balance sheet.
75. Construct a PERT chart, and go for it!

MECHANIC TO YOU®

As we read in the Chapter 1 opening vignette, Matt Turner knew he had a winning business idea. Nonetheless, he developed a business plan in order to map out how he was going to operate, market, and make money from his business.

In his business plan, Turner first outlined how he was going to get a van and outfit it with shelving, tools, and all the equipment needed to operate a mobile automotive repair shop. Early on, he also researched his target customers and in which part of Ottawa he would concentrate his efforts.

Next, he planned his target supplier network and determined who would have stock in hand while he was working on a customer's vehicle. He also worked out how to take calls from customers while on the road and how to schedule appointments in order to balance having enough work with ensuring that customers' vehicles would be serviced properly. Realizing he needed a mobile office in his van, he listed all the office equipment needed to operate the business with special attention to the mobile aspect.

Finally, Turner forecast his expected sales and expenses in order to determine how profitable his business would be.

Business planning helped Matt Turner figure out how to operate his business and make it successful—on paper. Then came the task of implementing all his ideas recorded in the business plan ...

You might be closer to completing your Business Plan than you think. If you have completed the Action Steps in the preceding chapters, you already have the major components of your plan. If you haven't completed them, return to Chapter 1 and work through the Action Steps. Throughout the preceding chapters, you have found gaps in the market, researched your target customer and your competition, defined your business, developed marketing and promotional ideas, and completed basic financial research and projections. As you develop your Business Plan using the Action Steps, you might recognize areas that need further attention and research. Chapter 15 provides you with the structure to put your facts, figures, ideas, dreams, passion, and intuition into a workable plan. Your Business Plan might be one of the most important documents you pull together.

We have provided you with a comprehensive online resource base, which can be found on the book's support website (http://www.nelson.com/knowlescastillo7e). The resource base includes another example of a completed business plan: the emphasis of the business proposal for Annie's Specialty Chocolates and Candy Concession is store operations. We also provide you with a detailed Business Plan template. Before writing your plan, you might want to review this material—especially the Business Plan template. Remember: A comprehensive list of Business Plan sites—sites that can help you create a winning plan—appears on the book's support website.

If you need to start your business immediately, consider using the fast-start business plan. This might be the alternative for you, particularly if your business is relatively simple and has low capital needs. Lots of examples and templates of fast-start business plans are contained on the book's support website.

Many entrepreneurs start a business that does not require extensive planning. An online business might be an example. Yet, even if your business idea fits this description, you are still wise to write down your plans, goals, market, and operations, and how you expect to make money.

If you are completing a Business Plan for a high-tech company and are seeking venture capital and angel investors, you may need access to additional business plans, as the specific requirements likely go beyond what is covered in the basic business plan presented in this text. For new high-tech products, lenders and investors are most interested in how you plan to introduce a new concept and where specifically you will find the early adopters for your product. For new ventures, the traditional channels of distribution might not work for your product, and you will therefore need to develop and substantiate your new distribution method. Again, the book's support site will help you prepare these kinds of plans.

Before you begin your Business Plan, think about your target audience. Are you presenting this plan to a banker, a panel of investors, or family members? What are their needs? What information do they require, and in what format? Will this plan satisfy the needs of your target market? For example, if you are presenting your plan to a financial institution or a panel of potential investors, your financial statements must satisfy their specific needs. Any grammatical errors will be frowned on. Major financial institutions, for example, are risk avoiders, so think about how you have reduced risks.

With a completed Business Plan in hand, you will also have something to present to the people who are important to your business: bankers, lenders, relatives, venture capitalists, vendors, suppliers, key employees, friends, and others. You must think about your presentation. In most cases, you will not have much time for presentation. Some investors will give you up to 10 minutes of their time. You might want to review your elevator pitch (see Chapter 2)—a clear, concise description of your business idea, the market need, how your business will satisfy that need, and how your business, the customer, and your investors will benefit. Most entrepreneurs will have to present their plans to someone.

The plan is portable, and you can make as many copies as needed to share with people who can help you succeed. You can either email it to contacts across the country or courier it to them. Be cautious, however. You might want to number every copy, keep a log of who has been given a copy, and make a note to retrieve your copies. You don't want them to be passed around without your permission. You might also want to put a note on your plan that it is not to be copied. Consider making a signed confidentiality agreement.

Planning is hard work. You will stay up nights, lose lots of sleep, and miss many meals, but in the end you will have saved time. Your plan should become a working, breathing, living document for your business dreams. Share your plan with others; they may have ideas, insights, and recommendations. In Chapter 6, we introduced you to networking, and in Chapter 12, we encouraged you to find a mentor and draw on the resources of an advisory team. Now is the time to seek their help. Have them read and evaluate your plan. Review their input, and revise your plan, if necessary. Business Plan reviewers sometimes ask for further details or backup data that, when added to your plan, will make it stronger and more effective. Sometimes, we become so close to a Business Plan that we omit important and relevant details and information. And, we remind you, keep looking for grammatical errors!

HOW TO START WRITING YOUR BUSINESS PLAN

It is now time for your passion to come to the forefront and to flow into every section of your Business Plan. If your Business Plan doesn't shout passion and confidence, you cannot expect your readers to go further than the executive summary. Before you begin, gather your completed Action Steps and backup data. Outline your plan, fill in the information from your Action Steps, refine your plan, proofread it, ask a knowledgeable person to review it, refine it further, proofread it, and prepare to present the plan to potential investors or lenders. If you are not seeking funding, now is the time to resolve this question: "Is it profitable to go forward with this plan?"

Remember that you and your readers should be looking at where you are now, where you are going, and how you will get there. Planning is ongoing. Your Business Plan is a road map, and it should represent a fast-growing industry sector where new roads, new opportunities, and new challenges constantly present themselves. If you're a creative thinker, your thought processes likely don't always follow a linear sequence. That's great—it will help you as an entrepreneur! Nonetheless, the Action Steps in this chapter do follow a linear sequence: the sequence of the parts of a completed business plan. This structure is a matter of convenience—you will see an example of each part as it would appear in the finished product. Bear in mind, however, that we don't expect you to write each part sequentially.

The best way to begin writing a Business Plan is to work with the material with which you feel most comfortable. For example, if you really enjoyed interviewing target customers, you might begin with The Market and the Target Customers. Sometimes, the best way is to simply think about your business and how you want it to be successful, and just start writing or keyboarding. Doing this will get your creative juices flowing.

In this chapter, the Action Steps will serve as a checklist for keeping track of which parts of the plan you have written. For example, in practice, you would probably write the cover letter last, but that is the first Action Step we present because we think writing this first cover letter is a valuable exercise. After completing Chapter 15 and your Business Plan, rewrite your cover letter. The more cover letters you write, the easier it becomes to write them effectively.

THREE-PART STRUCTURE: WORDS, NUMBERS, AND APPENDICES

Your Business Plan tells the world what kind of business you are in and where you are going. For ease of handling, divide your plan into two sections, and provide the needed documentation in appendices at the end.

In Section 1 use *words* to introduce your strategies for marketing and management. Strive to hook your reader with the excitement of creating a business, assessing the competition, designing a marketing plan, targeting customers, finding the right location, and building a team—all those human things that most people can relate to, even if they're not in business. Clearly point out your firm's uniqueness and ability to compete and handle change.

In Section 2 and the appendix, present *numbers*: projected income statements, cash flows, and balance sheets. This section is aimed primarily at bankers, credit managers, venture capitalists, vendors, small-business investment companies, and commercial credit lenders. Projected income statements for three to five years are usually included in an appendix. At the same time, you must also make it accessible to the casual reader who is searching for the bottom line.

Support Sections 1 and 2 with *appendices*, where you place résumés, maps, diagrams, photographs, tables, reprints from industry journals, letters from customers, letters from vendors, credit reports, personal financial statements, bids from contractors, and other documentation that demonstrates the viability of your plan.

Note that, in most cases, material in the appendices comes from existing sources. You are not stating anything new here; you are merely supporting what you have already said.

Appendices vary for each type of business; for that reason, sample appendices are not included in this book.

OUTSIDE ASSISTANCE IN WRITING A BUSINESS PLAN

Many people ask, "Should I hire a pro to write my business plan?" Our response is always, "*You* are the pro!" If you don't want to put the time and effort into writing your own Business Plan, you probably lack the energy and drive to develop a business. Also, only *you* can put the passion you feel into your plan. The information you have collected by completing the Action Steps now allows you to complete your Business Plan. We do suggest that on finishing your initial plan, you look for several business owners and possible investors to review it. In addition, attorneys, marketing specialists, accountants, and manufacturing experts might improve your plan with their review; they will show you what areas need further clarification or support data. Take all of their comments to heart, and rework your plan where necessary.

Hiring a business consultant to *refine* your plan is acceptable, but don't allow that professional to dream your dream! What's more, if you don't have total control over input to your plan, you might embarrass yourself by being unable to explain the details to investors and bankers.

REMINDERS

Completing a Business Plan helps reduce the risk of failure. No plan can guarantee success, but a well-researched plan will help acknowledge issues, anticipate problems, and determine the resources available to correct them.

The plan should be easy to read, with each number and figure well documented. Use bullets, graphs, and appendices to support the plan's strongest points. Be sure that the plan is well written and that there are no typographical or grammatical errors. If you are not comfortable with your writing skills, hire an editor to review your plan. Focus on the potential opportunities the business provides for investors. Tie together—with a clear, consistent message—all elements of the plan. Include possible risks as well; a business without risks does not exist.

The plan should consist of about 20 to 40 pages, with additional pages for appendices. Make the plan easy for your reader to write notes on, and include contact information so the reader can reach you—your email and street addresses, telephone and cell numbers, fax number, and so on.

In this chapter, we illustrate the steps involved in completing a business plan, along with providing you samples of each step, as completed by a hypothetical business, The Software School Inc. The Software School has been in operation for six months and has been self-financed by the owners, who are now seeking to expand and need more outside financing. Read through this chapter once and then reread it, completing the Action Steps. Although the Action Steps appear in the order they will be included in your Business Plan, you should complete Action Steps 65 to 75 first, then Action Step 64 (which focuses on the Executive Summary), and finally, Action Step 63, the cover letter.

ACTION STEP 63

Write a cover letter for your plan. (p. 445)

THE COVER LETTER

A cover letter aims your plan so that it will achieve the most good. Each time you send the plan to someone, write a special cover letter addressed to that specific reader. The cover letter introduces the excitement of your plan and tells the person why you are sending the proposal to him or her.

Read the sample cover letter in Box 15.1.

Box 15.1   Sample Cover Letter

In this sample cover letter, The Software School's CEO introduces his company's business plan to a potential lender.

November 24, 20XX

THE SOFTWARE SCHOOL
47 Turbo Drive
Suites 108–110
Toronto, Ontario

Mrs. Deborah Wallis
Manager, Royal Bank
1400 Market Circle
Anytown, Canada

Dear Mrs. Wallis:

We at The Software School Inc. want to extend our appreciation for the advice and guidance you have provided on revising and updating the enclosed Business Plan. Your input was helpful in the marketing area and invaluable for the financial section. Everyone here at The Software School Inc. appreciates the care you took reading over those early drafts.

We're now in the market for a loan of $50,000 (the figure you suggested) to be used for capital expenditures—computers, desks, chairs, and upgrading our curriculum—and we'd appreciate any guidance you could give us concerning sources of capital. (As I'm sure you'll recall, our venture was launched without any debt whatsoever, with each of our five principals putting up $20,000 apiece. And the present Turbo Drive location already has space available for the second classroom.)

We're planning to repay the loan out of new profit over the next three years. (For more information, please refer to the financial section of our plan, beginning on page 14.)

Again, thank you very much for your help and advice. We couldn't have done it without you.

Cordially,

Derek Campbell, CEO
Preliminaries

Let's summarize what's good about our sample cover letter.

1. The writer is making use of a previous contact.
2. The writer tells the reader—the manager of a bank—that he is in the market for a loan. He does not put the manager on the spot by asking for money.
3. Instead, the writer asks for advice on where to find sources of capital.
4. The writer strikes the right tone of enthusiasm and professionalism. (To do that, he rewrote the letter several times.)

You can do as well or better—and it's worth the effort! As you draft your cover letter, remember that the reader will pass judgment on your Business Plan (and on your business ability) on the basis of the letter. Do you want your small business to look bright, attractive, and welcoming? Your cover letter needs to give the same impression. A good cover letter will make its readers want to become involved in your venture.

Action Step 63 will help you write your cover letter.

THE TABLE OF CONTENTS

Box 15.2 provides a sample table of contents to give you a quick overview of a finished business plan. In practice, the table of contents is prepared last.

THE EXECUTIVE SUMMARY

The executive summary serves as an introduction to the business plan. In function, it is similar to the preface of this book: It is written to acquaint the reader with the nature of the business, to direct the reader's attention to

---

Box 15.2 Sample Table of Contents

The table of contents page of The Software School's Business Plan.

Table of Contents
Executive Summary 1

1. Description of the Business 1
   A. The Service We Provide 3
   B. The Market and Our Target Customer 4
   C. The Competition 6
   D. Marketing Strategy 8
   E. Our Location 10
   F. Management 11
   G. Human Resources 12

2. Financial Section
   A. Projected Cash Flow 16
   B. Projected Income Statement 18
   C. Projected Balance Sheet 19
   D. Other Financial Information 21

3. Conclusions*

Appendices**
   1. Customer Surveys, First Six Months of Operation
   2. Letters from Mass Merchandisers
   3. Quote from IBM Supplier
   4. Personal Résumés
   5. Personal Financial Statements
   6. Credit Reports
   7. Letters of Reference
   8. Bid from Contractor
   9. Diagram of the Turbo Drive Location and Associated Costs
   10. Industry Information and Trends
   11. Detailed Competitive Analysis
   12. Target Customer Profiles
   13. Promotion Plan, Budget, and Costs
   14. Legal Documents, Licensing, and Risk Management
   15. Sources of Information and Contacts

* You should not leave your reader "hanging on" at the end. Wrap up the plan, and "tie a bow around it" with a clear, concise conclusion.
** The need for specific appendices varies greatly from business plan to business plan. For that reason, this chapter does not include a sample of each of these appendices. As you draft your plan, you will need to document and substantiate your business strategies; this kind of documentation is best included as appendices.

whatever strengths the author (entrepreneur) wants to emphasize, and to make the reader want to turn the page and become involved. Because the executive summary gives perspective to the entire business plan, it needs to be written after the entire plan is completed. All the information should be condensed into one or two pages. Pay special attention to the *business description, current position and future outlook, management, uniqueness,* and—if funds are being sought—*funds sought, how they will be used,* and *when they will be repaid.* This summary will appear right after the table of contents (and the confidentiality statement, if one is used).

As you write your executive summary, remember that lenders prefer "hard" numerical data and facts; they cannot take speculations seriously. Therefore, phrases such as "50 percent return on our original $100,000 investment" and "secured agreements from 17 retail computer stores" make the example in Box 15.3 a strong executive summary. They help to paint a picture of good management and solid growth potential for The Software School.

You, too, can write an effective executive summary. Action Step 64 will help you to decide which facts and numbers will portray you and your business venture as credible and promising, and then to summarize them on paper.

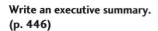

ACTION STEP 64

Write an executive summary.
(p. 446)

Box 15.3 Sample Executive Summary

The Software School Inc. provides numerical data and hard facts in its executive summary.

Executive Summary

The Software School Inc. is a user-friendly, state-of-the-art computer training centre. In our first six months of operation, we demonstrated our unique and profitable way of exploiting a strong and growing market within a fast-growing industry. The Software School's sophisticated electronic classroom provides "hands-on" education that teaches computer users how to use new software programs. By January 2, 20XX, we were operating at 92 percent capacity (50 percent is break-even) and had a waiting list of 168 students.

We plan to add a second classroom to double our capacity. This expansion will allow us to attain $400,000 in sales by the end of our 18th month. At that time, our pre-tax profits will have reached almost $50,000, representing a 50 percent return on our original $100,000 investment.

Our target customers seem to have insatiable appetites for software application knowledge, and The Software School Inc. anticipates an annual compound growth rate of 50 percent over the next five years. With respect to our business-to-business market, for example, we have secured training agreements with 17 retail computer stores in the area and firm contracts for more than 700 employees from eight industrial users.

Our competitors continue to train in the traditional style and currently show no sign of copying our unique instructional approach. Occasional price cutting by competitors has had no effect on our enrollment.

Management, led by Derek Campbell, has demonstrated how to offer superior training at competitive prices. Our plans for the future include developing more profit centres by providing on-site counselling and training for firms throughout Southern Ontario. Research and customer surveys indicate that we have just begun to satisfy the ever-increasing need for software education.

Extensive documentation is contained in the Appendices of our business plan. Note, for example, that our confidential legal documents, licensing our risk management analysis, are contained in Appendix 14.

SECTION 1: DESCRIPTION OF THE BUSINESS

You know your business, but you need to prove it with words and numbers. By the time your reader finishes your Business Plan, you should have a convert to your side. To give you examples to follow, we have reprinted key sections from the business plan (newly revised and updated) for The Software School, an ongoing business that is seeking financing for acquiring more equipment. Regardless of whether your business already exists or is just starting up, the goals of Section 1 are the same: to demonstrate that you know your business and that you are a winner.

Part A: The Service We Provide

Box 15.4 shows how The Software School Inc. tackled this part of Section 1.

The Software School Inc. will obtain its funding because the writer of the plan proves that the business is a winning concern. The writer has

1. let the facts speak for themselves,
2. supported all claims with numbers,
3. avoided hard-sell tactics,
4. refused to puff the product, and
5. projected a positive future.

Box 15.4   Sample Business Description

The Software School Inc. describes its business effectively in Section 1.

The Service We Provide

The Software School, a federal corporation, is a computer training facility located in Toronto, between Pearson International Airport and a high-density executive business complex. The area has a large number of computer users. Now in its seventh month of operation, the school has a waiting list of 168 students (67 percent of whom have paid a deposit).

We train people in computer software systems from the "Top 10" list of bestselling computer and Internet software packages. Because of their power, these systems are complex. They provide a learning hurdle, especially at first.

Students are drawn to our teaching method because it gives them hands-on experience and because we have a very knowledgeable staff. Our teaching works. Working people are busy, and a student can upgrade a given software skill by 80 percent in eight hours. (Slower learners are guaranteed a second try, and a third, at no additional cost.) Most of our courses can be completed in one day or two evenings. In contrast, the average college course (which emphasizes concepts rather than hands-on software systems) takes 12 to 18 weeks. Our price is $100 for most courses, and so far no one has complained about the cost.

The Software School Inc. achieves this learning speed with a sophisticated electronic teaching system adapted from flight simulation techniques used by airlines for training pilots. We are constantly streamlining and upgrading the system, using funds already allocated in our start-up budget.

One especially bright note: We have done far better than we had hoped. Our actual income figures average 24 percent above our original projections. Projected income for the first six months, with an assumed occupancy rate of 50 percent, was just over $10,000 a month. The actual occupancy has not peaked, and for the past two months we have operated at 92 percent capacity.

(continued)

As a service business, we sell seats as well as skills and information, and as Appendix 1 shows, our promotion has generated a heavy demand for present courses such as Computer Fundamentals, Excel, and Windows 2007. At the same time, customers are asking for courses to meet their needs—for example, courses in Adobe Dreamweaver.

Until the end of our fifth month, we were open six days a week from 8 a.m. to 10 p.m. To meet demand with our current classroom facilities, we are now also open on Sundays from 9 a.m. to 6 p.m., and the Sunday classes are full.

The demand increased dramatically when we contracted with some of Southern Ontario's large computer retailers to develop a training program. (See Appendix 2 for letters from specific sales managers.) These retailers sent us their salespeople for training; the salespeople, in turn, have referred their customers to us. Computer retailers quickly discovered they can sell better systems to buyers who are not afraid of computers, and they are in the business of selling, not training. We combat customers' fears in a logical way, with knowledge.

Our equipment (HP laptops) is top quality. Our staff combines excellent training skills and great practical experience with a focus on people and their needs. We have launched a solid start-up in a heated growth industry, and we plan to continue our growth and success.

The writer does a terrific selling job without appearing to be selling at all.

Matt Turner also developed a detailed list of services that Mechanic To You® was going to offer customers. The list of services included these:

- oil changes, tune-ups, and scheduled maintenance,
- diagnosis of electrical and drivability problems,
- drivetrain,
- brakes,
- suspension repairs,
- air conditioning diagnosis and repair,
- custom installs of aftermarket parts.

Now it's your turn. Do Action Step 65.

ACTION STEP 65

Describe your product or
service. (p. 446)

Part B: The Market and the Target Customer

Knowledge is power, especially in the information age. The Software School—an information business—capitalized on expert knowledge to define the marketplace. In the same way, if your research is sound, that knowledge will show up in your writing.

As you continue to read The Software School's business plan, remember that the reader of your Business Plan is a special kind of target customer. (How can you use your marketing abilities to look at this reader with new eyes? Have you developed a profile of this very special target customer?) Action Step 66 gives you a chance to show what you know about your market and target customer. If you need help getting started, review your work in Chapters 3 and 4. You can also review what the business plan for The Software School Inc. says about its market and target customers (see Box 15.5). Be sure to use secondary sources (such as documents, tables, and quotations) to lend credibility to this portion of your plan.

Matt Turner determined that the residential market would be his key market. The target market for Mechanic To You® became people who had vehicles, lived in residential areas, were mostly males, and were typically between the ages of 20 and 30 years.

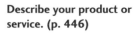

ACTION STEP 66

Describe the market and the
target customer. (p. 446)

Box 15.5   Sample Marketing Strategy Description

The Software School Inc. clearly describes its market and target customer.

The Market and Our Target Customer

Industry Overview

Fifteen years ago, the personal computer (PC) did not exist in the marketplace. There were mainframes, of course, and terminals linked to invisible data banks— but nothing you could carry home in a suitcase.

Things are different today. Approximately 200 firms are making PCs. The lion's share of the market goes to IBM, Dell Computers, and so forth, and yet someone brings out a new PC almost every day. The computer industry and the Internet are moving so quickly that statistics can hardly keep pace. According to a 2010 Canadian Internet Use Survey, 8 of every 10 Canadian households (79 percent) had access to the Internet. According to the same survey, more than one-half of households used more than one device to connect to the Internet. British Columbia and Alberta, at 84 percent and 83 percent respectively, followed by Ontario at 81 percent, had the highest rates of access.[1]

With all this sales flurry and emphasis on speed and the Internet, some people are being left behind because they don't know how to use computers. A computer can be your best friend, but only if you learn how to use it. This reality makes training people to use computers a booming industry, and The Software School Inc. is on the leading edge of a major growth segment.

Target Market

Our potential total market is Southern Ontario, with a logical concentration in the Toronto Census Metropolitan Area (CMA).

Geographically, our target market or industry segment includes Mississauga, Brampton, the area north to Barrie, and those areas east to Oshawa.

For now, our focus is the Greater Toronto Area. Within this highly concentrated population area, our target customer is the small-business person.

Given the success we have projected, we plan by the third year to service our clients in Brampton and Oshawa better by opening offices in these locations.

Our Target Customer

Our primary target consists of small and medium-sized businesses with these characteristics:

- size—1–30 employees;
- annual sales—$250,000 to $500,000;
- type of business—light manufacturing/retail;
- major output—paper (e.g., reports, letters, documents).

Our secondary target is the home user with these characteristics:

- sex—50 percent male, 50 percent female;
- age—18–45;
- education—some college/university;
- owns PC—30 percent;
- has access to a computer at work—52 percent;
- lives near a computer store—73 percent;
- household income—$55,000+;
- occupation—professional, managerial, executive, or entrepreneurial.

Company profiles on the primary, business-to-business segment and demographic/psychographic research on the secondary, business-to-consumer target market are contained in Appendix 12, "Target Customer Profiles."

Part C: The Competition

Obviously, if you know who your competitors are and how they fail to meet market needs, you are well on your way to strategic competition. You need to persuade your reader how great your competitive tactics are. (If you need a reminder, reread Chapters 4 and 5. Competition changes according to the life-cycle stage of the industry, so a good way to begin your section on competition is to place your industry in the proper life-cycle phase.)

How tough do your competitors look? As you read The Software School's assessment of its competition, note that the writer takes a cool, objective look. He doesn't belittle the competition, and he certainly doesn't underestimate them. (See Box 15.6.)

Matt Turner discovered that, because his idea was unique, he faced no major direct competition; however, he did discover that there were some "weekend

---

Box 15.6   Sample Competition Assessment

The Software School Inc. assesses its competition objectively.

The Competition

The Software School Inc. has four main competitors.

- **Traherne Schools.** Our oldest, most entrenched competitor. Three locations in the GTA: Etobicoke, North York, and Scarborough. Traherne conducts a six-hour course, Introduction to Microprocessors, for $95. It currently runs a course on desktop publishing for the Mac and has been planning to introduce an Internet course but to date has not done so. Traherne operates within our geographic market. Its Scarborough operation is closed on Saturdays.

- **Big Micro Computer Instruction.** Excellent classroom facilities, located in East York near the Don Valley Parkway. All instruction is tied to Mac machines and is free if you buy your hardware from Big Micro. Otherwise, courses usually cost around $95 and take six to eight hours. The instructors try hard, but Big Micro is really in the business of pushing hardware.

- **Micro Hut Computer Centre.** Friendly salespeople with teaching skills double as teachers. Courses at Micro Hut are Microsoft related. Prices range between $100 and $200 per student/day: VisiCalc, $89; Word Processing, $149.

- **Your Micro and You.** Local facility developed by professional educators. The atmosphere of YMAY is excellent. It offers a normal range of programs and a course in using the computer in a small business. Each course costs about $125. YMAY's market seems to be divided between adults with casual interest in computers and children aged 10 to 15. These people have done it right.

- **Other competitors.** Secondary competitors are colleges, which offer a range of 6- to 12-week courses. As well, more companies today are supplying in-house training for their employees. (More details on The Software School Inc.'s competitive analysis, including a SWOT analysis and competitive test matrix, are provided in Appendix 11.)

Meeting the Competition

The Software School Inc. is in the computer education business. We do not sell hardware or software.

Our program of instruction is relevant. We teach how to use software, and we are constantly on the lookout for trends that will lead us to new markets. For example, we have just added a course on how to create a home page. Furthermore, our prices are competitive, and we teach classes seven days a week.

Our price per hour might be higher than the college courses, but time and results are important to our students. Therefore, we are seen as price competitive.

---

warrior" mechanics working on cars for fun and for a little cash on the side. This knowledge gave Turner the confidence to move forward with his business idea.

How will you handle the competition in your Business Plan? Your readers will expect you to be cool and objective. Complete Action Step 67.

ACTION STEP 67

Describe your major competitors. (p. 446)

Part D: Marketing Strategy

Now it's time to describe your marketing strategy. Need a reminder? Look back at your work in Chapter 6.

The marketing strategy excerpt from The Software School's business plan (Box 15.7) demonstrates a carefully reasoned approach. The excerpt describes conscious marketing policies that will help this small business be competitive. If

---

Box 15.7 Sample Marketing Strategy Description

The Software School Inc. takes a carefully reasoned approach in its description of its marketing strategy.

Marketing Strategy

An analysis of our competitors indicates that our prices—$99 for a one-day course, $198 for a two-day course—are between two extremes. These prices are competitive but still maintain our image of quality.

We use a wide range of strategies to let our customers know where we are: mass media advertising (newspapers, television, and radio), special promotions (press releases, brochures, newsletter), and personal selling (commissioned salespeople, networking, corporate contracts, trade shows). (A promotion plan, promotion budget, and calendar of related costs are contained in Appendix 13.)

Mass Media Advertising

The Software School Inc. places ads in the *Toronto Star* and smaller area newspapers to keep a continuous presence in front of our target customers. In the beginning, we used inducement (e.g., two-for-one offers, 15 percent reductions), but that is no longer necessary, as our waiting lists grow. As we continue to expand, we will develop advertising on radio and TV.

Creative Promotions/Ink/Free Ink

In our first month of operation, we sponsored a scholarship contest in the local high schools, which resulted in very positive press. In addition, the school has been featured in several local newspapers.

We are in the information business, and toward that end we are developing three different publications: a computer handbook, a newsletter, and a brief history of the founding of The Software School. In time, we hope that this history (a how-to for computer educators) will become a guide for the industry.

Our mailing list grows daily. We log all incoming phone calls and email with information on the callers and how they found out about us. This information helps us define our target market.

Personal Selling

Personal contact has gained us our largest accounts so far. (Please refer to letters from computer retailers in Appendix 2.) We intend to intensify our efforts along these lines. Fortunately, our directors have experience and talent in the area of personal selling.

We maintain a booth at the major computer trade shows in the area. Approximately 17 percent of our hobbyist/home-user business has been generated this way.

you read a business plan in which the writer did not demonstrate this care and deliberation, how much faith would you have in the writer's business abilities?

Note that The Software School Inc. uses a three-pronged approach to reaching the public. This business understands the importance of finding a good promotional mix.

The entrepreneurs who run The Software School Inc. stay on top of the changing market picture. They have demonstrated this by

1. dropping discount inducements from their ongoing print campaign,
2. looking ahead to radio and TV exposure,
3. logging calls and gathering information on the callers to maintain a base of up-to-date information on their target market,
4. determining how they have gained their largest accounts and planning to intensify their efforts in those areas.

As a parallel, here is an outline of Matt Turner's marketing strategy:

- Promote the business to neighbours in Nepean, Ontario.
- Develop and hand out flyers.
- Develop a website.
- Use social media, such as a Facebook page and Twitter.
- Place free advertisements of service on classified websites, such as www.kijiji.ca.

ACTION STEP 68

Describe your marketing strategy. (p. 446)

Action Step 68 will help you to refine your marketing strategy. Note that you must continue to focus on the target customer.

Part E: Location

The next part of your Business Plan is the one on location. You might want to review your work in Chapter 7 now.

Read how The Software School Inc. shows off its location to its advantage (Box 15.8).

Box 15.8 Sample Location Description

The Software School Inc. paints an attractive picture of its location.

Our Location

The Software School Inc. is currently in the first year of a three-year lease at 47 Turbo Drive, Toronto, Ontario. The facility is on the ground floor and occupies 210 square metres.

The area, which is zoned for business use, is a hotbed of high-technology activity. Within the immediate area, there are two computer stores, one computer furniture store, one software dealer, an electronics store, and two printers. Within a 7-kilometre radius are 27 computer dealers.

During our lease negotiations, we persuaded the landlord to make extensive improvements to the interior and to spread the cost out over the three-year term of the lease. The decor—blue carpet, white walls, and orange furniture—gives the effect of a solid, logical, somewhat plush business environment in which our target customer will be comfortable and learn quickly.

The building is divided into four areas: a reception area (30 square metres), a director's office (10 square metres), a classroom (75 square metres), and a storage area (90 square metres).

The principals envision the storage area as a second classroom. See the diagram in Appendix 9. The costs associated with this site are also contained in Appendix 9.

The area is easily accessible by public transportation, and we offer free parking.

You need to paint an attractive picture of your business site and, at the same time, keep your reader interested by inspiring confidence in your choice. Location takes a tremendous amount of analysis. The Software School Inc. writer gives himself a subtle pat on the back by describing the lease arrangements and by identifying the need for a second classroom. The reader who wants more is referred to an appendix—this is smart writing.

As for Matt Turner, he figured that his location would be wherever his customers were: at their workplaces and homes. The location factor was extremely convenient for customers since they just had to call, and Turner would arrive to provide service.

Your plan will become very real when you showcase your physical facility. Complete Action Step 69.

ACTION STEP 69

Show off your location.
(p. 447)

Part F: Management

Management will make or break your small business. Writing this section will help you focus more closely on your management team members and inspire confidence in them. (If you need a refresher, review your work in Chapter 12.)

Nothing is more important than the people who will make your business work. Present their capabilities and focus on their track records and accomplishments as you complete Action Step 70. It is also essential to include résumés in an appendix.

Recall that Matt Turner decided that management of Mechanic To You® was going to be himself and Chris Castillo. A licensed automotive mechanic and an experienced business coach was definitely a winning team.

Now let's see how The Software School Inc. introduces its management (Box 15.9).

ACTION STEP 70

Introduce your management team. (p. 447)

Box 15.9 Sample Management Team Description

The Software School Inc. shows off its winning management team.

Management

• **Derek Campbell, CEO.** Mr. Campbell was born in Stratford, Ontario, in 19XX. He took a B.Sc. degree in Industrial Engineering from McGill University and then spent five years in the Canadian Forces, where he was a flight instructor, a check pilot, and a maintenance officer. While in the service, Mr. Campbell completed an M.A. degree in Marketing Management and Human Relations.

  Following military service, Mr. Campbell was employed as a pilot for Air Canada. He is currently the CEO of EuroSource, a software importing company. He is the author of several articles on computers and the information age.

• **Roberta Jericho, Vice-President.** Ms. Jericho was born in Lethbridge, Alberta, in 19XX. She has a B.Sc. degree in Geology and Physical Sciences from the University of Calgary. She has completed the Microsoft training program and has been the IT manager for EuroSource for the past five years.

Directors

• **C. Hughes Smith.** Mr. Smith was born in Halifax, Nova Scotia, in 19XX. He has a B.A. degree in Political Science and Philosophy from Dalhousie University, an M.B.A. from Stanford, and a law degree from the University of Toronto.

(continued)

Mr. Smith is a senior vice-president of Lowes and Lockwood, a residential home-building firm, and a partner in Graebner and Ashe, a Toronto law firm. He is the author of numerous articles in the field of corporate planning and taxes.

- **Philu Carpenter.** Ms. Carpenter was born in Winnipeg, Manitoba, in 19XX. Her B.A. degree is from the University of Manitoba, and her M.B.A., with a Marketing specialty, is from the University of Western Ontario.

  Ms. Carpenter spent 20 years in the corporate world (IBM, DEC, InterComp, etc.), where she worked in marketing and industrial sales. Currently a professor of Business at York University, Ms. Carpenter is the general partner in two businesses and a small-business consultant. She has written and lectured widely in the area of small business.

- **Dan Masters.** Mr. Masters was born in Mississauga, Ontario, in 19XX. His degrees (B.A., M.B.A.) are from the University of Western Ontario, where he specialized in Marketing and Finance. Mr. Masters has worked for Kodak and Nortel Networks (as senior account sales executive and sales manager, respectively) for a total of 25 years.

  Mr. Masters is currently a professor of Business at Seneca College. He is active in several small businesses, lectures widely, and has published numerous articles in the field of small business.

Personal résumés of all key personnel are provided in Appendix 4.

Other Available Resources

The Software School Inc. has retained the legal firm of Farney and Shields and the accounting firm of Hancock and Craig. Our insurance broker is Sharon Mandel of Fireman's Fund. Our advertising agency is George Friend and Associates.

Part G: Human Resources

Part G of your plan shows off your human resources. For a start-up business, you're peering into the future with confidence, conducting informal job analyses for key employees who will help you to succeed. For an ongoing business, you need to list your present employees and anticipate your future personnel needs. If you have five employees now and you want to indicate growth, try to project how many jobs you'll be creating in the next five years.

When you begin to think about tasks and people to do them, review your work in Chapter 12. Preparing a human resources plan is important, because it gives you one more chance to analyze job functions and develop job descriptions before you start interviewing, hiring, and paying benefits—all of which are expensive.

You'll notice that The Software School Inc. gives only a brief overview of its human resources situation (Box 15.10).

In describing their lean operation, the entrepreneurs who run The Software School Inc. keep their description brief, as well. They show good sense when they express a commitment to control operating costs. Their decision reflects business discipline and foresight. If you were a potential investor in this business, wouldn't you appreciate their control of the purse strings?

Every person on your team is important. Once again, consider Matt Turner's situation. Turner figured out that his human resources plan was going to be a challenge. Mostly he needed to be able to take calls, book clients, pick up parts, and service vehicles. Once he got busy enough, he hired another mechanic to help out with the overflow of customers. He also planned for the hiring of an administrative assistant. He worked with Chris Castillo to determine the scalability of his business.

Action Step 71 will help you describe the kinds of people you will need and how you will help them be productive.

ACTION STEP 71

Describe your personnel.
(p. 447)

Box 15.10   Sample Human Resources Description

The Software School Inc. provides a brief overview of its human resources.

Human Resources

At the end of six months of operation, The Software School Inc. has 3 full-time employees and 14 part-time employees. The full-time employees include

1. a manager, salaried at $3,000 per month;
2. a receptionist, salaried at $8 per hour;
3. a training director, salaried at $1,500 per month.

The part-time employees include three directors, who assist in the marketing function; three outside commissioned salespeople, and eight part-time instructors. According to our plan, one salesperson will become full time at the end of the seventh month.

We will continue to hold down overhead with qualified part-time employees as long as it is feasible. We believe that running a lean operation is important to our success.

SECTION 2: FINANCIAL SECTION

Good Numbers

The Financial Section is the heart of your business plan. It is aimed at lenders—bankers, credit managers, venture capitalists, vendors, and commercial credit lenders—people who think in numbers. Lenders are professional skeptics by trade; they will not be swayed by the enthusiasm of your writing in Section 1. Your job, therefore, is to make your numbers talk.

Given that you drafted your financial plan in Chapter 10 and investigated your financial options in Chapter 11, you are now ready to finalize your numbers into four standard categories:

1. the opening and projected balance sheets,
2. the cash flow projection (also called a pro forma),
3. the projected income statement,
4. other important financial information.

Examples from The Software School Inc. will serve as models for you. You can adapt them to fit your business.

You need to know where every dollar is going. You need to show when you'll make a profit, and you need to show that you are efficient, conservative, and in control. You'll know you've succeeded when a skeptical lender looks up from your Business Plan and says, "You know, these numbers look good." You might want to consider putting a financial summary right at the beginning of your Financial Section. You should not make the reader pore over all kinds of financials to get the necessary key information. Some plans even contain only a summary of the financial results and leave all the details for the appendices.

Provide Useful Notes

One way to spot a professional lender is to hand over your Business Plan and watch to see which section he or she reads first. Most lenders study the notes that accompany income and cash flow projections first. Knowing this allows you to be forewarned. Use these notes to list all assumptions, to tell potential lenders how you generated your numbers (e.g., "Advertising is projected at 5 percent of sales"), and to explain specific entries (e.g, "Leased equipment—Monthly lease costs on IBM computers").

Make these notes easy to read, with headings that start your readers off in the upper left-hand corner and march them down the page, step by step, to the bottom line. (Some sample projection charts use tiny footnotes on the same page. We prefer *large* notes on a separate page. Notes are important—no less important than the rest of the plan.)

Creating your Business Plan takes a lot of time. It's only natural for you to hope that lenders will read it, get excited, and ask questions. These notes can help you accomplish that, even if you haven't started up and the numbers and assumptions are only projections into the future.

Part H: Projected Cash Flow

Next, focus your attention on the projected cash flow, the lifeblood of your business. By projecting cash flow month by month, you obtain a picture of how healthy your business will be.

The Software School's cash flow projection is set out in Table 15.1. The notes for these numbers are reprinted in Box 15.11. If you compare the projected income statement (Table 15.2) with the cash flow projection, you will see that some items are treated differently in the tables. For example, expenses in the projected income statement are divided into monthly installments, whereas the same expenses in the cash flow projection are shown as bulk payment when due. Now look at insurance expense. In the projected income statement, we find a total expense of $960, shown as 12 monthly debits of $80 each. The same expense in the cash flow projection is shown as two payments of $480 each, falling due in the seventh and eighth months. If the entrepreneurs running the business had only $80 available to pay for insurance in the seventh month—that is what is shown in the income statement—they would be in trouble.

Profits don't pay the bills and the payroll; cash flow does. Potential lenders look at cash flow projections first. In Action Step 48, Chapter 10, you drafted your projected cash flow. Now it is time to revisit these estimates. Finalize your projected cash flow. Complete Action Step 72.

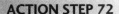

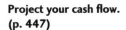

ACTION STEP 72

Project your cash flow.
(p. 447)

Part I: Projected Income Statement

Your next task is to put together your projected income statement (sometimes called a "profit and loss statement"). With the information you've gathered so far, it shouldn't be too hard. In fact, it will be enjoyable—if the numbers look good.

The Software School's projected income statement is shown in Table 15.2, and the careful documentation of each item is reprinted here. For instance, if a lender wanted to know how the figures for commissions were generated, Note 6 explains that they are estimated as 10 percent of sales (Box 15.12).

Refer to Table 15.2 as you predict your income.

Part J: Projected Balance Sheet

The professionals will look at your balance sheet (sometimes called a "statement of financial position") to analyze the state of your finances at a given point in time. They are looking at things such as liquidity (how easily your assets can be converted into cash) and capital structure (what sources of financing have been used, how much was borrowed, and so on). Professional lenders will use such factors to evaluate your ability to manage your business.

Table 15.3 shows two balance sheets for The Software School. Note that the first one shows its actual position at the end of its first 6 months and the second

Box 15.11 Sample Cash Flow Projection Notes

The Software School's notes for its cash flow projection are shown.

1. **Beginning of the month.** Cash available as the month begins.
2. **Sales.** Includes all sales by cash, cheque, or credit card at the time the class is taken. Does not include accounts receivable.
3. **Credit card expense.** Fees of 2.5 percent paid to credit card companies. Approximately 50 percent of customers use credit cards.
4. **Loans.** Loan for new course development and audiovisual equipment.
5. **Total sales.** Sum of all money available during the month.
6. **Books.** Books for sale are ordered and paid for one month in advance of projected sale.
7. **Instructional materials.** Covers course materials purchased from licenser.
8. **Salaries.** Net salaries paid employees approximate 80 percent of gross salaries paid.
9. **Payroll taxes.** Total of amount withheld from employees, plus income statement payroll tax item.
10. **Advertising.** Established as 30-day accounts with all media companies.
11. **Leased equipment.** Lease payments are due the first day of each month.
12. **Licences and fees.** Licence fees are due the 15th of the following month.
13. **Accounting/Legal.** Due 30 days after bill is received.
14. **Rent.** Due the first day of each month.
15. **Office supplies.** Paid at time of purchase or with subscription. No credit.
16. **Insurance.** Paid in month when expense occurs.
17. **Telephone.** Paid within 30 days of receipt of bill.
18. **Utilities.** Paid within 30 days of receipt of bill.
19. **Interest.** Interest only, paid each month.
20. **Loan payback.** $5,000 loan payment due every six months.
21. **Miscellaneous.** Paid in month when expense occurs.
22. **Income tax reserve.** Paid into a special tax account at the bank.
23. **Total disbursements.** Total cash expended during the month.
24. **Net cash before capital investment.** Cash balance before capital investment payments.
25. **Capital equipment.** Purchase of additional audiovisual equipment.
26. **Contracted course development.** Contract payment due for new course development.
27. **Monthly cash flow.** Cash balance after all payments at the end of the month.

is a projection of where it will be at the end of its first 18 months. If you're just starting up, *all* figures will be projections.

In Chapter 10, Action Step 49, you drafted a projected income statement. Now it is time to add the final touches. Complete Action Step 73.

Other Important Financial Information

The ratios, such as those calculated in Chapter 10, tell you a lot about the health of your business. They allow you to compare it with industry benchmarks and also to compare your results to your objectives.

Let's talk for a minute about **return on owner's investment**. It is a bottom-line figure that shows how much is earned on the total dollars invested in the business. You have this kind of information up-front if you invest money in bonds. The interest tells you your return on owner's investment. Imagine that you have two funds, Bond A and Bond B. Bond A pays you a 4 percent return, and Bond B pays you 25 percent. Which bond would have the better return on owner investment?

Compute return on owner investment for a business by dividing the net profit by investing dollars. For The Software School, the profit after taxes is $39,715 (from Table 15.2). Divide that by the owner's investment of $100,000 (from Table 15.3):

$$\$39,715 \div \$100,000 = 39.7 \text{ percent}$$

ACTION STEP 73

Project your income statement. (p. 447)

RETURN ON OWNER'S INVESTMENT

Net profit to owner's investment

Table 15.1   The Software School Inc. Cash Flow Projection

	7th Month	8th Month	9th Month	10th Month	11th Month	12th Month	13th Month	14th Month	15th Month	16th Month	17th Month	18th Month	Total
Cash Receipts													
Beginning of Month	$3,970	$7,365	$6,015	$51,575	$47,060	$35,275	$31,840	$28,645	$27,900	$33,115	$43,895	$47,800	$364,455
Sales	23,500	25,200	26,900	28,500	30,200	31,900	33,600	35,300	38,350	40,100	43,300	43,300	400,150
Less: Credit Card Expense	(295)	(315)	(335)	(355)	(380)	(400)	(420)	(440)	(480)	(500)	(540)	(540)	(5,000)
Loan			60,000										60,000
Total Sales	$27,175	$32,250	$92,580	$79,720	$76,880	$66,775	$65,020	$63,505	$65,770	$72,715	$86,655	$90,560	$81,9605
Disbursements													
Books	$175	$190	$200	$210	$225	$235	$250	$305	$350	$370	$370	$385	$3,265
Inst./Materials		6,000			7,500			9,000			9,000		31,500
Salaries													
Instruction	2,000	2,000	2,040	2,080	2,120	2,160	2,200	2,240	2,280	2,320	2,360	2,360	26,160
Administration	2,640	2,640	2,640	3,120	3,600	3,600	3,600	3,600	3,600	3,600	3,600	3,600	39,840
Commissions	1,730	1,865	1,995	2,130	2,255	2,390	2,530	2,660	2,795	3,030	3,170	3,420	29,970
Payroll Taxes	2,045	2,195	2,250	2,435	2,690	2,755	2,805	2,870	2,925	3,025	3,075	3,170	32,240
Advertising	1,080	1,175	1,250	1,335	1,410	1,495	1,580	1,660	1,750	1,895	1,980	2,135	18,745
Leased Equip.	1,270	1,270	1,270	1,270	1,270	1,270	1,270	1,270	1,270	1,270	1,270	1,270	15,240
Licences/Fees	2,160	2,330	2,495	2,665	2,820	2,990	3,160	3,325	3,495	3,790	3,960	4,275	37,465
Accounting/Legal	500	500	500	500	500	500	500	500	500	500	500	500	6,000
Rent	3,890	3,890	3,890	3,890	3,890	3,890	3,890	3,890	3,890	3,890	3,890	3,890	46,680
Office Supplies	60	65	65	70	75	80	85	90	95	100	110	110	1005
Dues/Subscript.	20	20	20	20	20	20	200	20	20	20	20	20	420
Repair/Maint.	235	250	265	285	300	320	335	355	385	395	435	435	3,995
Insurance	480						480						960
Telephone	325	355	380	405	430	455	480	505	530	575	600	650	5,690

	7th Month	8th Month	9th Month	10th Month	11th Month	12th Month	13th Month	14th Month	15th Month	16th Month	17th Month	18th Month	Total
Utilities	430	470	505	540	570	605	640	670	705	765	800	865	7,565
Interest				650	650	650	650	650	650	595	595	595	5685
Loan Payback									5,000				5,000
Miscellaneous	705	755	805	855	905	955	1,010	1,060	1,150	1,205	1,300	1,300	12,005
Income Tax Reserve	65	265	435	200	375	565	710	935	1,265	1,475	1,820	1,820	9,930
Total Disbursements	$19,810	$26,235	$21,005	$22,660	$31,605	$24,935	$26,375	$35,605	$32,655	$28,820	$38,855	$30,800	$339,360
Net Cash Before Capital Invest.	$7,365	$6,015	$71,575	$57,060	$45,275	$41,840	$38,645	$27,900	$33,115	$43,895	$47,800	$59,760	$480,245
Capital Equipment			10,000										10,000
Contracted Course Development			10,000	10,000	10,000	10,000	10,000						50,000
Monthly Cash Flow	$7,365	$6,015	$51,575	$47,060	$35,275	$31,840	$28,645	$27,900	$33,115	$43,895	$47,800	$59,760	$42,0245

Table 15.2 The Software School Inc. Projected Income Statement

	7th Month	8th Month	9th Month	10th Month	11th Month	12th Month	13th Month	14th Month	15th Month	16th Month	17th Month	18th Month	Total
Sales													
Instruction	$23,285	$24,950	$26,630	$28,215	$29,900	$31,580	$33,265	$34,945	$37,915	$39,600	$42,770	$42,770	$39,5825
Books	215	250	270	285	300	320	335	355	435	500	530	530	4,325
Total Sales	$23,500	$25,200	$26,900	$28,500	$30,200	$31,900	$33,600	$35,300	$38,350	$40,100	$43,300	$43,300	$40,0150
Cost of Instruction													
Clssrm. Matrls.	$1,765	$1,890	$2,020	$2,140	$2,265	$2,395	$2,520	$2,650	$2,875	$3,000	$3,240	$3,240	$30,000
Inst. Personnel	2,500	2,500	2,600	2,600	2,700	2,700	2,800	2,800	2,900	2,900	3,000	3,000	33,000
Books	150	175	190	200	210	225	235	250	305	350	370	370	3,030
Total Cost/Instr/ Books	4,415	4,565	4,810	4,940	5,175	5,320	5,555	5,700	6,080	6,250	6,610	6,610	66,030
Gross Profit	$19,085	$20,635	$22,090	$23,560	$25,025	$26,580	$28,045	$29,600	$32,270	$33,850	$36,690	$36,690	$33,4120
Expenses													
Sales													
Commissions	$2,330	$2,495	$2,665	$2,820	$2,990	$3,160	$3,325	$3,495	$3,790	$3,960	$4,275	$4,275	$39,580
Advertising	1,175	1,250	1,335	1,410	1,495	1,580	1,660	1,750	1,895	1,980	2,135	2,135	19,800
Credit Cards	295	315	335	355	380	400	420	440	480	500	540	540	5,000
Administrative													
Salaries	3,300	3,300	3,300	4,500	4,500	4,500	4,500	4,500	4,500	4,500	4,500	4,500	50,400
Payroll Taxes	570	580	600	695	715	725	745	755	785	795	825	825	8,615
Leased Equip.	1,270	1,270	1,270	1,270	1,270	1,270	1,270	1,270	1,270	1270	1,270	1,270	15,240
Licences/Fees	2,300	2,495	2,665	2,820	2,990	3,160	3,325	3,495	3,790	3,960	4,275	4,275	39,550
Accounting	500	500	500	500	500	500	500	500	500	500	500	500	6,000
Rent	3,890	3,890	3,890	3,890	3,890	3,890	3,890	3,890	3,890	3,890	3,890	3,890	46,680
Office Supplies	60	65	65	70	75	80	85	90	95	100	110	110	1,005
Dues/Subscript.	20	20	20	20	20	20	200	20	20	20	20	20	420
Repair/Maint.	235	250	265	285	300	320	335	355	385	395	435	435	3,995

	7th Month	8th Month	9th Month	10th Month	11th Month	12th Month	13th Month	14th Month	15th Month	16th Month	17th Month	18th Month	Total
Insurance	80	80	80	80	80	80	80	80	80	80	80	80	960
Telephone/Fax	355	380	405	430	455	480	505	530	575	600	650	650	6,015
Utilities	470	505	540	570	605	640	670	705	765	800	865	865	8,000
Depreciation	1,170	1,170	1,170	1,335	1,335	1,335	1,335	1,335	1,335	1,335	1,335	1,335	15,525
Interest				650	650	650	650	650	650	595	595	595	5,685
Miscellaneous	705	755	805	855	905	955	1,010	1,060	1,150	1,205	1,300	1,300	12,005
Total Expenses	$18,725	$19,320	$19,910	$22,555	$23,155	$23,745	$24,505	$24,920	$25,955	$26,485	$27,600	$27,600	$284,475
Net Profit	$360	$1,315	$2,180	$1,005	$1,870	$2,835	$3,540	$4,680	$6,315	$7,365	$9,090	$9,090	$49,645
Reserve for Taxes	65	265	435	200	375	565	710	935	1,265	1,475	1,820	1,820	9,930
Net Profit After Taxes	$295	$1,050	$1,745	$805	$1,495	$2,270	$2,830	$3,745	$5,050	$5,890	$7,270	$7,270	$39,715

Box 15.12 Sample Projected Income Statement Notes

Here are The Software School's notes for its projected income statement.

1. **Instruction.** Based on 2.5 percent occupancy growth per month, starting at 35 percent (235 students) and growing to 69 percent. Students pay $99 per course.
2. **Books.** Revenue from books sold averages approximately 1 percent of instructional sales, rounded to bring total sales to an even $100 figure.
3. **Classroom materials.** $7.50 per student.
4. **Instruction personnel.** Instructor cost is $100 per eight-hour class, starting with 25 classes and growing to 30 classes by the end of the year.
5. **Books.** Cost of books is 70 percent of selling price.
6. **Commissions.** Average 10 percent of instructional sales.
7. **Advertising.** Projected at 5 percent of sales.
8. **Credit cards.** Approximately 50 percent of sales are paid with credit cards. The cost is 2.5 percent of the sale.
9. **Salaries.** Start with three full-time employees. Bring on one additional person beginning the 10th month.
10. **Payroll taxes.** The company's share of employee taxes averages 7 percent of commissions and salaries.
11. **Leased equipment.** Monthly lease costs on IBM computers.
12. **Licences and fees.** Licence (right to use copyrighted material) costs 10 percent of instruction sales.
13. **Accounting.** Average accounting and bookkeeping costs for the area and size of the business.
14. **Rent.** Based on three-year lease.
15. **Office supplies.** Estimated at 0.25 percent of sales.
16. **Dues and subscriptions.** Estimated costs for magazines, newspapers, and membership in organizations.
17. **Repair and maintenance.** Projected to be 1 percent of sales.
18. **Insurance.** Based on current insurance contract for next 12 months, payable every 6 months.
19. **Telephone and fax.** Figured at 1.5 percent of sales.
20. **Utilities.** Figured at 2 percent of sales.
21. **Depreciation.** Schedule established by accounting firm.
22. **Interest.** Loan at 13 percent, with $5,000 payments due every 6 months until paid off.
23. **Miscellaneous.** Figured at 3 percent of sales.
24. **Reserve for taxes.** Local, provincial, and federal taxes estimated at 20 percent of net profit.

Could you get 39.7 percent from a savings account or a bond fund? No, so the company provides a good return on owner investment. It would dazzle lenders and probably draw the attention of a venture capitalist.

It is also helpful to include a comparison of your ratios to industry standards and your break-even analysis.

The Software School Inc. did not provide notes to its balance sheets because, in this case, no notes are needed. In conjunction with the income statement and the cash flow projection, all the entries in the balance sheet will make sense to your professional readers. Under some circumstances, you would want to note unusual features of a balance sheet for an actual fiscal year, but in most cases—and in most projections—this won't be necessary.

Now project a balance sheet for your business. Action Step 74 will help you.

ACTION STEP 74

Project your balance sheet. (p. 448)

Table 15.3 The Software School Inc. Balance Sheet

	Actual Balance Sheet as of September 30, 20XX (after first 6 months)		Projected Balance Sheet as of September 30, 20XX (after first 18 months)	
Assets				
Cash	$3,970		$59,670	
Instruction materials and books	2,500		4,495	
Total current assets		$6,470		$64,165
Leasehold improvements	$41,000		$41,000	
Furniture	15,100		15,100	
Audio/Visual	10,600		20,600	
Office equipment	3,600	$70,300	3,600	$80,300
Less depreciation		7,020	63,280	22,545	57,755
Licence agreement			25,000	$25,000	
New courses			–0–	50,000	75,000
Total assets		$94,750		$196,920
Liabilities				
Instructors' salaries	$1,250		$1,500	
Administrative salaries	1,650		2,250	
Commissions	2,165		4,275	
Accounts payable	4,495		9,020	
Current liabilities		$9,560		$17,045
Long-term debt		–0–		54,970
Total liabilities		$9,560		$72,015
Net worth (owner's equity)				
Capital stock	$100,000		$100,000	
Retained earnings	(14,810)	85,190	24,905	124,905
Total liabilities and net worth		$94,750		$196,920

EPILOGUE: ACT ON WHAT YOU KNOW

Well, do you feel like you're ready? You are. You have thoroughly researched your product or service, your market and target customer, your competition, your marketing strategy, and your location. You've discovered how to prepare for surprises you can't afford, how to handle numbers, how to pursue financing, when and why you should incorporate, how to build a winning team, and whether you should buy, franchise, or start on your own. And you've written it all up in a workable business plan that can be implemented.

Before you take off running, we want you to think about how you will implement your plan. A common and effective approach is to prepare a calendar showing week by week what has to be done and who is responsible for doing it. All too often, new entrepreneurs seriously underestimate the time it takes to

PERT

Program Evaluation and Review Technique

get their new business off the ground. So, spend the necessary time beforehand trying to make sure you minimize delays.

One management tool that can help you put your Business Plan to work is called **PERT** (Program Evaluation and Review Technique). It's often used to establish schedules for large projects, but small businesses can use it as well.

A PERT chart will help you overcome any feeling of being overwhelmed by the tasks of starting up and not knowing where to begin. If you're a person who sometimes tries to do everything at once, PERT is also recommended. It will help you focus your energy on the right job at the right time. A sample PERT chart is provided in Table 15.4. Yours will be bigger and more detailed. You can use days, weeks, or months to plot the tasks ahead. (If you think you should use years, reassess your industry and business idea.)

In constructing your PERT or "to do" calendar, be very careful. Time frames are often much longer than expected. The official time for obtaining a liquor licence, for example, is three months, but if you encounter any bureaucratic "glitch" or any opposition, it's easily double that. The search for a suitable storefront location usually takes months, and if Yellow Pages advertising is crucial to the business, then the actual start-up date might be planned to coincide with the distribution of the new Yellow Pages in December (with the insertion deadline in August also noted).

Note that development of the Business Plan could even be part of the PERT chart, especially in cases of complex business concepts for which plan development and implementation overlap—which they often do in practice. So you can even use a PERT chart to organize the writing of your Business Plan.

Action Step 75 symbolizes the first step that you will take on your own as an entrepreneur. It's the end, yes, but also the beginning. All our best wishes go with

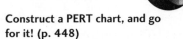

ACTION STEP 75

Construct a PERT chart, and go for it! (p. 448)

| Table 15.4 | A Sample PERT Chart |

Task	Week					
	1	2	3	4	5	6
Befriend banker	X	X	X	X	X	X
Order letterhead		X				
Select site	X					
Renovation		X	X			
Get business name approved	X					
Register company			X			
Select ad agency	X					
Lunch, lawyer			X			
Appointment, accountant				X		
Prepare vendor statement					X	
Make utilities deposit					X	
Review promotional material					X	
Survey phone system			X	X	X	
Order phone system						X
Hold open house						X

you as you embark on your great adventure. We hope that this book and its Action Steps have persuaded you that you can achieve success—whatever it means to *you*—and have fun at the same time. Good luck! Work smart, and enjoy your adventure!

In a Nutshell

It's been a long haul, and you're now ready to create your Business Plan. The Business Plan is a portable showcase for your business. When you visit vendors, bankers, and potential lenders, you can take along a copy of your Business Plan to speak for you, to show them you've got a blueprint for success.

Begin writing by focusing on the material you feel most comfortable with. Once you have finished one part of the plan, the other parts will fall into place more easily. Fortunately, your work in earlier chapters has prepared you for each section. Write the executive summary last.

You'll need to write a cover letter for each copy of the plan you send out. The cover letter will personalize the plan and target the prime interests of each reader.

Key Terms

PERT

return on owner's investment

Think Points for Success

✓ Who is your target audience?
✓ Who can provide you with advice and guidance on writing your plan?
✓ Section 1 of your Business Plan should generate excitement for your business. Section 2 should substantiate the excitement with numbers.
✓ Be sure to use sufficient footnotes to explain the numbers in your financial statements—Parts H, I, and J.
✓ The executive summary should read like ad copy. Hone it till it's tight and convincing.
✓ Now that you have Plan A, make sure you think about developing Plan B.
✓ Make sure you consider the risks and the ways to minimize them.

Action Steps

ACTION STEP 63

Write a cover letter for your plan.

Address your letter to a specific person who can help your business. Be brief; aim for about 200 words.

State the reason you are sending the plan. If you are asking for money, tell the person what you want it for and how much you need. One well-written paragraph should be all you need to do this.

Your purpose in writing the cover letter is to open the door gently and prepare the way for further negotiations. The cover letter is bait on your hook.

If you are putting money into the business, indicate how much.

The tone you are after in this opening move is confident and slightly formal. You want to appear neat, bright, organized, and in control of your venture. Be certain to explain briefly how you will repay the money.

Refer to the sample letter in Box 15.1.

ACTION STEP 64

Write an executive summary.

Imagine that you have two minutes to explain your business venture to a stranger. This approach gives you an idea of what information you need to put into writing for your executive summary.

Practise explaining your venture to friends and strangers, limiting yourself to two minutes. Ask them to raise questions, and use their questions to guide you as you revise and hone your presentation.

When you are satisfied with your oral summary, write it down and type it up. It should not exceed three typed pages. (The Software School's executive summary, which serves as our example, was less than one page, single spaced.)

This aspect of your Business Plan likely constitutes only a small piece, but it could well be the most important.

ACTION STEP 65

Describe your product or service.

Excite your reader about your business. Excitement is contagious. If you can get your reader going, there's a good chance you'll be offered money. Investors love hot ideas.

If this is a start-up, explain your product or service fully. What makes it unique? What industry is it in? Where does the industry fit in the big picture?

Mention numbers wherever you can. Percentages and dollar amounts are more meaningful than subjective words such as "lots" and "many."

If this is an ongoing business, your records of sales, costs, and profit and loss will substantiate your need for money.

ACTION STEP 66

Describe the market and the target customer.

Bring all of your marketing research into this section, and wow your reader with a description of your target customer utterly wanting your product or service.

Use data from secondary sources to give greater credibility to the picture you are painting.

ACTION STEP 67

Describe your major competitors.

Briefly profile the businesses that compete with you directly (direct competitors). Try to be objective as you assess their operations. Who are your indirect competitors?

What are their strengths? What are their weaknesses? What can you learn from them?

Why is your product or service unique in the eyes of your customer?

After you've described your competitors, provide your competitive positioning strategy. Back this up with primary and secondary research on your competition.

ACTION STEP 68

Describe your marketing strategy.

Now that you've profiled your target customer and assessed your competition, take some time to develop the thrust of your market strategy. Which techniques will produce the best and most cost-effective response?

Because pricing is such an important consideration, you might start with what your target customer sees as a good value and then develop your marketing mix.

ACTION STEP 69

Show off your location.

The great thing about a location is that it's so tangible. A potential lender can visit your site and get a feel for what's going on.

Often, a prospective banker will visit your business site. That's good news for you, because now the banker is on your turf. Clean up the place before the banker arrives.

You will want to persuade potential lenders to visit your site. Describe what goes on there. Use photographs, diagrams, and illustrations.

ACTION STEP 70

Introduce your management team.

Almost every study you read on small-business failure puts the blame on management. Use this section to highlight the positive qualities of your management team.

Focus on quality first: their experience, accomplishments, education, training, flexibility, imagination, and tenacity. Be sure you weave in experience that relates to your particular business. Because the key to a great team is balance, show how each person complements the others.

ACTION STEP 71

Describe your personnel.

Describe the kinds of people you will need as employees and how they fit into your plan.

What skills will they need? How much will you have to pay them? Will there be a training period? If so, for how long? What benefits will you offer? How will you handle overtime?

If you haven't yet written job descriptions, do that now. Job descriptions will help you hire people who best match the skills required.

ACTION STEP 72

Project your cash flow.

Get used to doing cash flow. Once a month is not too often. If you prepared a cash flow for your business back in Chapter 10, bring those numbers forward. If you skipped that step, do it now. Here's how it's done.
1. Write down all the cash you will have for one year.
2. Add net profit.
3. Add any loans.
4. Figure your total cash needs for the year.
5. Spread these numbers out across the year. You might have a lot of cash at the start of the year; you want to make sure you have enough to get all the way through.
6. Now list all disbursements. Spread these out too.
7. Now examine the figures. Is there any time during the year when you will run short of cash? It's better to know the truth now, when you're still working on paper.
8. If your cash picture looks good, drop in a couple of "what ifs." (Let's say you've budgeted $300 for utilities, and the air conditioner goes out. It will cost $200 to repair it, and the lease says it is your expense. Or let's say you see an opportunity for a sale, but you would have to hire someone to handle it for you. Can your cash flow handle such surprises?)

ACTION STEP 73

Project your income statement.

What you're driving at here is net profit—what's left after deducting all expenses—for each month and for the year.

First, you figure your sales. The first big bite out of the figure is the cost of goods sold. (In a service business, the big cost is labour). Subtracting that gives you a figure called "gross margin."

Now add up all your expenses (rent, utilities, insurance) and subtract them from the gross margin. Doing this gives you your net profit before taxes. (Businesses pay quarterly installments.)

Subtract taxes. There's your net profit.

ACTION STEP 74

Project your balance sheet.

A projected balance sheet is simply a prediction, on paper, of what your business will be worth at the end of a certain time. This prediction allows you to figure your actual and projected return on owner investment, which is the real bottom line.

1. Add up your assets. For convenience, divide these into current (e.g., cash, notes, receivables), fixed (e.g., land, equipment, buildings), and other (intangibles, such as patents, royalty deals, copyrights, goodwill, and contracts for exclusive use). You'll need to depreciate fixed assets that wear out. For value, show the net of cost minus the accumulated depreciation.
2. Add up your liabilities. For convenience, divide these into current (e.g., accounts payable, notes payable, accrued expenses, interest on loans) and long-term (e.g., trust deeds, bank loans, equipment loans, balloon payments).
3. Subtract the smaller figure from the larger one.
   You now have a prediction of your net worth. Will you be in the red or in the black?

ACTION STEP 75

Construct a PERT chart, and go for it!

The rehearsal is over. Now it's time to step onto the stage and get the drama under way. To shift from planning into action, develop your own personal PERT chart to serve as a script. The chart also will tell you and the other members of your team how long certain jobs should take.

List the tasks you need to accomplish—befriending a banker, filing for a business name, taking a lawyer to lunch, ordering business letterhead, selecting a site, contacting vendors, and so on—and set your deadlines.

As you already know, a successful package comprises many details. If you take the details one at a time, you'll get there without being overwhelmed. The sample PERT chart in Table 15.4 can guide you.

Checklist Questions and Actions to Develop Your Business Plan

Pulling the Plan Together

❏ How will your business idea contribute to society in general?

❏ In what way does your product or service differ from that of your competitors?

❏ What are the critical success factors for your business?

❏ How would your customers define your quality and level of customer service?

❏ In completing your Business Plan, ask yourself this question: Have I been consistent in my thinking that the quality of sales staff fits the image I wish to convey, and that money is set aside for appropriate training?

❏ What socially responsible practices do you intend to follow?

❏ If your business is successful, what is your long-term growth plan?

❏ Will you achieve your personal vision?

Note

1. Statistics Canada, *Canadian Internet Use Survey 2010*, http://www.statcan.gc.ca/daily-quotidien/110525/dq110525b-eng.htm.

Glossary

(Numbers in parentheses refer to the page number on which the term is defined)

24/7 Adventure Notebook A storage place in which to organize your personal and business ideas (11)

ability-to-pay valuation A valuation approach based on the ability of a business to pay off its business loan and provide a reasonable return on the owner's investment over a specified period (385)

adjusted book value The book value amended to reflect market values (385)

advisory board A group of individuals with expertise in various areas who provide advice but are not normally associated with the day-to-day operations of your business (264)

aftermarket The marketplace where replacement items, such as auto tires and sewing machine belts, can be purchased (53)

agent An intermediary, working on commission, who sells an exporter's products to foreign customers (M1-12)

anchor tenant A business in a commercial area that attracts customers (179)

angels Wealthy individuals from the informal venture capital market who are willing to risk their money in someone else's business (322)

application of funds Expenses you pay before starting your business (265)

asset-based valuation The purchase price of a business determined, in large part, by the assets of the business (384)

assets The dollar value of what the business owns (265)

baby boomers Those born between 1947 and 1966 (about 10 million Canadians, or about 30 percent of the total population) (45)

balance sheet A financial snapshot of what the business owns and what it owes at a given point in time (265)

bankruptcy A legal process, regulated by the *Bankruptcy and Insolvency Act*, by which you may be discharged from most of your debts (251)

book value Owner's equity, or total assets minus total liabilities (385)

bootstrapping Relying entirely on one's efforts and resources (315)

brainstorming A free and open exchange of ideas (37)

brand A name, sign, symbol, design, or combination of these used to identify the products of a firm (159)

bulk sales escrow An examination process intended to protect buyers from unknown liabilities (381)

business broker (business intermediary) Someone who sells a business on behalf of the owner (375)

business-to-business (B2B) company A firm whose target market is other businesses (105)

business-to-consumer (B2C) company A firm whose "heavy" target customer is the consumer, or end user (99)

business format franchise A type of franchise in which the product, method of distribution, and sales and management procedures are highly controlled (399)

business location The place where you distribute the goods and services for your business (175)

business model A framework of how all the different interrelated parts of a business work together to create value in the marketplace (84)

business mission statement A statement of your company's purpose and aims (80)

business plan A blueprint or road map for operating your business start-up and measuring progress (19)

business strategy The broad program for achieving an organization's objectives and implementing its vision (82)

business vision A mental picture of your business, product, or service at some time in the future (111)

buy-sell option A statement in a shareholders agreement that spells out how the shares will be transferred in an event such as the death, resignation, dismissal, personal bankruptcy, or divorce of a shareholder (211)

Canada Small Business Financing (CSBF) loan A loan guaranteed by the federal government under the *Canada Small Business Financing Act* (329)

cash in advance A short-term financing method in which a foreign buyer pays an exporter cash before goods are delivered (M1-20)

ceiling, or premium, pricing Setting the highest price target consumers will pay for a product or service, given their needs and values and the competitive options (148)

collateral Something of value—such as property or assets—that is pledged as a guarantee to support the repayment of a loan or debt (310)

common shares Equity investments that confer part ownership of the company but are not as safe as preferred shares should the company fail (333)

competition Those companies or individuals that provide similar products, services, or benefits, as perceived by your target customer (122)

competitive intelligence (CI) The process of learning, collecting, and using information about your competitors for the purpose of growing your business (123)

competitive positioning The process of establishing unique benefits and features that the target customer values relative to the competition (133)

competitive SWOT An analysis of the internal strengths and weaknesses, and external opportunities and threats for perceived competitors (128)

competitive test matrix A grid that allows you to evaluate the strengths and weaknesses of your competitors' products, services, and benefits (128)

competitive touchpoint analysis Analyzing customers' perceptions of the competition to find out what benefits and features are important to them (123)

competitor-based, or market-based, pricing Setting a price range acceptable to your customer that takes into consideration your competitors' prices (146)

completion bonds Insurance coverage to ensure that work on a contract is completed as agreed (245)

convertible debentures Loans that can be exchanged for common shares at a stated price and are better protected than common and preferred shares (333)

cooperative An organization owned by the members who use its services (212)

copyright The exclusive right to copy a creative work or allow someone else to do so (219)

core benefit proposition A statement about the benefits of your product or service to your target market (164)

corporation A legal entity with the authority to act and have liability separate and apart from its owners (204)

cost of goods sold (CGS) The cost of materials or inventory that you use up over a specified period (usually one year) (286)

credit Money loaned or the ability of an individual or company to borrow money (310)

current asset conversion cycle The time, in days, it takes to purchase a product or materials, produce and sell an item, and then collect on that item (274)

current assets Assets or holdings of a business that can be converted into cash or consumed in the production of income in a short period of time (usually one year) (267)

current liabilities Outstanding debts or obligations that are expected to come due within one year of the date of the balance sheet (270)

customer relationship marketing (CRM) The development of long-term, mutually beneficial, and cost-effective relationships with your customers (95)

dealership relationship franchise Also called a "licensing or associate relationship," a type of franchise in which the franchisee buys the right to distribute a franchisor's product or service (399)

debt financing An obligation of a business to repay a lender the full amount of a debt (loan) in addition to interest charges (327)

demographics Key characteristics of a group of people, such as age, sex, income, and where they live (99)

direct compensation The wage or salary received by the employee (357)

direct (first-level) competitors Those companies or individuals that offer the same types of products or services, as perceived by your target customer (122)

direct contact Foreign visits and participation in foreign trade shows and fairs provide many opportunities for direct contact (M1-13)

direct franchising A business arrangement in which a franchisee deals directly with the franchisor (400)

direct mail Advertisement or sales pitch that is mailed directly to target customers (154)

direct merchant (intermediary) Business that works directly with manufacturers in an attempt to eliminate the markups of middlemen (94)

direct selling 1. The sale of a consumer product or service by an independent sales contractor in a face-to-face manner away from a fixed retail location (156) 2. Selling to foreign markets without an intermediary (M1-13)

distinctive competency Unique features and benefits that attract customers and encourage customer loyalty (125)

distribution channel The method or way in that a producer makes a product or service available to the consumer (176)

dividend An amount distributed out of a corporation's retained earnings (accumulated profits) to shareholders (225)

documentary collection An unconditional order from the exporter requiring the buyer to pay on demand or at a determined time a specified amount to a specified person (M1-21)

domestic cost plus markup Simplest pricing approach that adds domestic costs and a markup to include export costs (M1-17)

due diligence The level of care, judgment, and caution that an employer would reasonably be expected to provide in order to prevent injuries or accidents in the workplace (251)

e-commerce Any business function or business process performed over electronic networks (43)

earnings-assets valuation A business valuation approach that takes into consideration both earning potential and asset value (387)

earnout A contractual arrangement in which the purchase price is stated in terms of a minimum, and the buyer of the business agrees to make future payments to the seller based on the achievement of predefined financial goals after the closing (381)

echo boomers (Millennials, or Y Generation) Those born between 1980 and 1995 (about 6 million Canadians, or about 20 percent of the total population) (46)

economy, or limit, pricing Setting "no-frills" low prices to increase volume and discourage competition (148)

elevator pitch A clear, concise description of your business idea that can hook your listener into responding, "Tell me more" (58)

employee selection The process of determining which persons in the applicant pool possess the qualifications necessary to be successful on the job (356)

encroachment Situation in which franchisors compete with franchisees by putting an outlet nearby or setting up alternative distribution channels, such as mail order or Internet sales (406)

equity The dollar value of what the business owes the owner (265)

escrow company A neutral third party (usually a lawyer) that holds deposits and deeds until all agreed-on conditions are met (381)

export shock The difficulty of opening an export market (M1-4)

fidelity bonds Insurance that protects an employer against employee dishonesty (245)

fixed assets Longer-term (more than one year) holdings or assets of a business that are used to earn revenue or produce products or services (269)

fixed rate Interest rate that remains the same over the period of a loan (332)

floating rate Interest rate that changes with changes in the prime rate (332)

foreign distributor An intermediary that purchases products from an exporter and resells them (M1-13)

four Cs of credit Capital, character, capacity, and collateral (313)

franchise fee Fee paid by a franchisee for the rights to represent the franchisor in a given geographic area for a specified length of time, commonly 5 to 10 years (401)

franchisee The individual operator who is licensed to operate under the franchisor's rules and directives (399)

franchising A special kind of distribution system in which one company (termed the franchisor) grants the right to sell its products or services to another company or individual (termed the franchisee) (177)

franchisor The firm that sells the rights to do business under its name and continues to control the business (399)

free ink and free air Information about a business that is published or broadcast free of charge (155)

full-cost pricing A pricing approach that includes fixed and variable costs and a profit margin (M1-17)

general partnership A partnership in which each partner has a hand in managing the business and assuming unlimited personal liability for any debts (202)

goodwill The dollar value obtained when you subtract the total value of the tangible assets from the purchase price (380)

gross margin return on inventory investment (GMROI) An income statement ratio (gross profit margin × sales-to-stock ratio) that takes into consideration both gross profit and inventory turnover (291)

gross profit Total sales minus your cost of goods sold (286)

gross profit margin (contribution margin) Gross profit divided by total sales (288)

gross rent A rental where the landlord provides all services and utilities, including tenant janitorial services (192)

growth industry An industry whose annual sales increase is well above average (54)

growth segment An identifiable slice of an industry that is expanding more rapidly than the industry as a whole (54)

guerrilla marketing Small business promotional strategy that involves unconventional methods of getting the customer's attention at minimal cost (145)

high-context culture A culture in which communication depends not only on the message itself but also on everything that surrounds it (M1-25)

impact marketing Conducting special events designed to attract the attention of target customers (158)

indirect compensation (fringe benefits) Employee benefits and services that are given entirely or partly at the expense of the company (357)

indirect (second-level) competitors Those companies or individuals that provide the same benefit, as perceived by your target customers (122)

industry norm, or keystone, pricing Setting a price that depends on generally accepted industry standards (147)

innovation A new idea, method or device; the process of creating, changing, modifying, or improving a product, service or business process with the purpose of creating value (24)

intrapreneurs Agents of change who own or work in small, medium-sized, or large organizations (14)

inventory Items carried in the normal course of doing business that are intended for sale (378)

inventory turnover The number of times each year a company turns over or replaces its inventory (289)

invisible competition People or businesses that have the capacity or desire to provide the same products, services, or benefits that you do (122)

invisible customer A person, type of person, or business you don't anticipate but has a need for your product or service (98)

joint health and safety committee (JHSC) A group consisting of labour and management representatives who meet on a regular basis to deal with health and safety issues (250)

joint venture Partnership formed for a specific undertaking, resulting in the formation of a new legal entity (350)

just-in-time team A group of individuals who are hired on a contract basis to perform a specific function (349)

labour pool Qualified people who are available for employmennear one's business location (179)

leadership The act of motivating others to do what is expected of them because they believe in what you are doing and share your vision (341)

lease Obtain a new or modified contract for occupancy (189)

letter of credit Sometimes called "documentary credit," a document issued by a bank at the request of an importer, in favour of a supplier or exporter, to finance theimportation of goods and services (M1-20)

liabilities The dollar value of what the business owes to parties other than the owner (265)

lien A legal obligation filed against a piece of property (392)

life cycle Four stages, from birth to death, of a product, business, service, industry, or location (52)

limited partnership A partnership composed of at least one or more limited partners and at least one general partner (202)

location escape hatch A way to cancel or modify your lease if the landlord fails to meet the specified terms (190)

long-term liabilities (deferred liabilities) Debts or financial obligations that are due after one year (270)

love money Investment from friends, relatives, and business associates (308)

low-context culture A culture in which communication tends to rely on explicit written and verbal messages (M1-25)

marginal-cost pricing A pricing approach that includes floor price (unit cost) and marginal, or export, costs (M1-17)

manufacturer's representative A specialized agent, working on commission, who sells a manufacturer's products to a specific group of customers within a given geographic area (M1-13)

market gap An area of the market where needs are not being met (76)

market segmentation Breaking down potential markets into homogeneous groups with similar characteristics and qualities (55)

market-pull approach Determining what the customer wants through a customer profile, and then adapting or creating a product or service to satisfy this want or need (96)

marketing mix A blend of product offering, pricing, promotion, and place (location) (145)

marketing strategy An analysis of four major elements: external market and trends, target market, product/service uniqueness and competitive advantage, and the marketing mix (145)

markup A percentage of your cost of sales (sometimes the selling price) that is added to the cost to determine your selling price (147)

mass customization The ability of companies to customize products and services efficiently and cost-effectively in large quantities (48)

master franchising A business arrangement in which a franchisor sells the rights of an area or territory to a franchisee, who is normally required to sell (or establish) and service a specified number of franchises in its area within a specified time period (400)

matrix grid A screen through which ideas are passed in order to find solutions (79)

mentoring A mutually beneficial partnership between a more experienced entrepreneur or businessperson, and an entrepreneur who is in the infant, or start-up, phase of a venture (351)

micro business Usually refers to a businesses with one to four employees (16)

mind map An idea-generating sketch—also known as a spoke diagram, a thought web, or a cluster diagram—that features circled words connected by lines to form units (151)

neighbour mix The industrial/commercial makeup of nearby businesses (179)

net profit (before taxes) Gross profit minus total operating and other expenses (288)

net rent A rental whereby the tenant also pays, in addition to the rent, its pro rata of all utilities, services, and real estate taxes (192)

net worth (personal equity) The market value of your personal assets minus your total personal liabilities (313)

networking Communicating through person-to-person channels in an attempt to sell or gain information; talking to people with the purpose of doing business (163)

new-eyes research Using your intuition and powers of observation to learn about the marketplace (20)

nonprofit organization (NPO) Club, society, or association that's organized and operated solely for social welfare, civic improvement, pleasure or recreation, or any other purpose except profit (214)

one-to-one (one-2-one) marketing The process of identifying the specific needs of each customer, repeatedly satisfying those needs, and creating a long-term value-added relationship (96)

open account transaction A form of collection that involves few or no conditions of payment (M1-21)

operating loan (line of credit) Money lent to help finance short-term business needs, such as inventory and accounts receivables (331)

outsourcing Contracting outside specialists to perform functions that are or could be performed by company employees (36)

partnership An association of two or more individuals carrying on a business to earn income (202)

patent A federal government grant that gives an inventor exclusive rights to his or her invention (217)

penetration pricing Setting the initial or introductory price artificially low to increase sales volume (148)

percentage lease Lease that specifies that the tenant will pay a base rate plus a percentage of the gross sales (191)

periodicals Various Canadian and U.S. trade and business magazines that regularly run features on specific foreign markets (M1-10)

personal balance sheet A list of the market value of assets (what you own) and liabilities (what you owe) that will show your net worth or personal equity (313)

personal selling The selling and taking of orders by an individual salesperson (157)

PERT Program Evaluation and Review Technique (444)

PEST forces An abbreviation referring to four macro environmental factors: **p**olitical, **e**conomic, **s**ociocultural/environmental, and **t**echnological (M1-8)

Plan B An alternative strategy for bailing the business out of a tight spot created by some unforeseen or unfortunate situation (240)

point-of-purchase (P-O-P) display A display that acts as a silent salesperson for a specific product (153)

positioning The process of establishing in the mind of the consumer a unique image or perception of a company, product, or service (127)

preferred shares Equity investments that confer part ownership of the company, earn investors dividends at a fixed rate, and are safer than common shares (333)

price skimming Setting prices high initially to appeal to consumers who are not price sensitive, then lowering prices as competitors enter the market (148)

price/earnings (P/E) ratio The market price of a common stock divided by its annual earnings per share for the latest 12-month period (380)

primary, or target, customer A person, type of person, or business that has the highest probability of buying your product or service (97)

primary research Interacting with the world directly by talking to people (networking) (20)

prime rate The lowest rate of interest charged by banks on commercial loans to their most preferred customers (331)

pro forma (or projected) income statement An itemized statement of sales (or revenues) and corresponding expenses (284)

product penetration A calculated thrust into the market (132)

profiling Describing the needs and behaviour of your customer (97)

profit-based, or cost plus, pricing Setting a price that covers all costs plus a profit (146)

projected (pro forma) cash flow A financial statement that helps you control the money that comes into your business (receipts) and the money that is spent (disbursements) (273)

promotion The art or science of moving the image of your business into the forefront of a prospective customer's mind (149)

promotional campaign A sales program designed to sell a specific product or service or to establish an image, benefit, or point (164)

promotional mix All the elements that you blend to maximize communication with your customer (149)

psychographics Segmenting of the population by lifestyle behaviour, buying habits, patterns of consumption, and attitudes (99)

restrictive covenants Things that your landlord cannot do that are written into your lease to protect you (191)

retailing Selling goods and services directly to the consumer, or end user (176)

return on owner's investment Net profit to owner's investment (437)

royalty fee Ongoing obligation to pay the franchisor a percentage of the gross sales (401)

secondary customer A person, type of person, or business that needs to be convinced to buy your product or service (98)

secondary research Reading about someone else's primary research (21)

shareholder loan Owner investment in the form of a loan (329)

shareholders agreement A legal document that establishes the rights of shareholders (owners) and the duties and powers of the board of directors and management (210)

shotgun clause A provision stating that one partner or shareholder can make a buyout offer to the other partner for her or his share of the business. The receiving partner has the option (within a set period of time) of either accepting this offer or buying out the partner who proposed the offer under the exact same terms (204)

small business Any venture with spirit, any business you want to start, or any idea you want to bring into the marketplace (15)

small business entrepreneurs Agents of change—doers who see a market need and satisfy that need by translating it into a successful business (81)

SME (small and medium-sized enterprise) Normally refers to a business with fewer than 500 employees (16)

social entrepreneurs Agents of social change; doers with innovative solutions to society's most pressing social challenges (14)

social entrepreneurship Not-for-profit businesses that are adapting creative "profit" approaches to satisfy social and community needs (212)

sole proprietorship A business that is owned by one person (200)

strategic alliance 1. A partnership between one or more organizations that is formed to create a competitive advantage (135) 2. Goal-oriented partnership formed between companies to create a competitive advantage (350)

strategic business units Independent teams or small businesses that support the functional needs of the main organization (345)

succession planning The process of establishing the procedures to change or transfer ownership or control of a business (230)

SWOT An abbreviation that refers to an analysis of internal strengths and weaknesses, and external opportunities and threats (82)

tangible assets Things your business owns that you can see and touch, such as real estate, equipment, and inventory (378)

target customers Customers with the highest probability of buying your product or service (21)

term loan Loan used for medium- to long-term financing of fixed assets, such as equipment, furniture, expansion, or renovation (332)

trade-mark A word, symbol, or design, or a combination of these, used to distinguish the goods or services of one person or organization from those of others in the marketplace (221)

trading houses Domestically based intermediaries that-market exporters' goods abroad (M1-13)

unsecured credit Credit extended to a borrower on the promise to repay the debt with no collateral required (310)

values The things in life that are important to you (71)

vendor statement A personally designed form that allows you to negotiate with each vendor from a position of informed strength (324)

viral marketing A marketing technique that uses social networks to produce increases in brand awareness (161)

virtual organization (or network organization) Organizational structure in which the major functions are broken up into strategic business units (345)

vision A mental picture of yourself or an event at some time in the future (70)

wholesaling The selling of products to retailers for resale to the end user, or consumer (177)

Workplace Hazardous Materials Information System (WHMIS) A comprehensive national plan for providing information on the safe use of hazardous materials used in Canadian workplaces (251)

Index

Note: page numbers followed by a "b" indicate boxes; "f" indicates figures; "t" indicates tables.

A

abilities and interests, assessment of, 15, 27
ability-to-pay valuation, 385–387
About.com, 20b
accountants, 228–229, 233–234
accounts payable, 293
accounts receivable, 269, 291, 330t
Adidas, 94, 98, 139
adjusted book value, 385, 396
Adventure Travel Company, 40
advertising, 151–152, 242b–243b
advertising budget, 280
advertising profile, 103, 104, 112
advisors, for start-up businesses, 241b, 301
advisory board, 264
advisory team, 346–347
aftermarket, 170
age groups, shifting sizes of, 47
agricultural wave, 47
alternative energy, 39
Amazon, 34
amiable personality type, 367
analytical personality type, 367
anchor tenant, 179, 189, 190
angels, 322
Angus, Ross, 98
anti-theft/fraud measures, 252b
ANZ, 297b
application of funds, 265, 266t–267t, 303
approvals, 181, 184
A. P. Reid Insurance Stores Ltd, 413
Arbour Environmental Shoppe, 11–12
Armstrong, Adrienne, 11–12, 107
asking price, 379–381
asset-based valuation, 384–385
assets, 267–268
  autos/trucks as, 144, 269, 293, 335
  in closing balance sheet, 265–266, 291–293
  current, 268, 269, 291
  defined, 265
  earnings-assets valuation, 387–390
  fixed, 269
  intangible, 269
  liquid, 271, 314t
  in opening balance sheets, 268t
  other, 293
  purchases of, 277t, 281, 324, 331, 332
  tangible, 378–379

associates, 350
association journals, 126
associations, 115
Associations Canada, 75, 113
Atlantic Canada Opportunities Agency (ACOA), 39b, 83b, 329, 413
auto insurance, 245b, 246b 247b
autos/trucks
  as assets, 144, 269, 293, 335
  for guerrilla marketing, 145, 158
  for start-up businesses, 242b

B

B2B company. See business-to-business (B2B) company
B2C company. See business-to-consumer (B2C) company
baby boomers, 45–46, 50
balance sheet, 265–267
  case study, 303–305
  closing, 291–293
  current ratio, 271
  debt-to-equity ratio, 273
  defined, 266
  ending, 283b, 285t, 294, 303, 305
  example, 272t, 388–389
  liquidity ratios, 271–273
  opening, 265–267, 268t
  personal, 313–315, 335
  proprietorship ratio, 273
  quick ratio, 271, 273
  ratios, 271–273, 294
  solvency ratios, 273
  types of, 265
bank loans 317–322. See also bankers; financing; loans
  application fees, 321–322
  collateral, 310, 320–321
  covenants, 321
  current portion of debt, 293
  demand loans, 320
  discretionary limits, 320
  insurance, 321
  loan management fees, 321
  negotiations, 319–320
  personal guarantees, 319
  premium rates, 320
  spousal guarantee, 320
bankers, 318–319, 334, 378
banking, 243b, 266t, 319
Bankrate.com, 297

bankruptcy, 230–232b
Bankruptcy and Insolvency Act, 231, 232b
banks, 22, 309b, 317–318
Barletta, Martha, 41
Barnard, Robert, 102
BDC (Business Development Bank of Canada), 20b, 22–23, 24
Beacon score, 335
Beatty, Mick, 188–189
Beck, Nuala, 41
before-you-buy checklist, 382b–383b
Bender, Peter Urs, 342, 360
Better Business Bureau, 375, 409b
Bezos, Jeff, 34
Big Micro Computer Instruction, 430b
BlackBerry®, 41
Blueprint Public Relations, 151
BN (business number), 223–224
board of directors, 209, 346–347
Body Shop, 406
bonds, 245, 248t, 252, 314t, 388. See also specific types
bookstores, 190, 233, 289, 290, 291
book value, 385, 396
boomers. See baby boomers; echo boomers
boomer trend, 38–39, 45–46
bootstrapping, 315–316
BOP (business owners policy), 247b
Bosum, Hugo, 308
Bplans.com, 297b
brain-to-brain telepathy, 37
brainstorming
  case study, 64, 174, 259
  defined, 37
  embryonic stage and, 133b
  encourage, 14
  for meetings, 38
  overview, 37–38
  rules, 78b
  solutions and, 78–79, 88
  tips, 37
  uniqueness and, 135
brand, 85f, 121, 132f, 159, 414
brand-driven social media, 49
branding, 159
brand loyalty, 132b, 133, 400
brand-name recognition, 121, 400, 414
Branson, Richard, 10

break-even analysis, 294–299. *See also* balance sheet
 calculators, 297b
 chart, 298f
 defined, 294
 example, 297
 overview, 294–295
 revenue method (gross profit margin), 296
 unit method, 295–296t
breweries, 34–35
bridge financing, 330t
Brookstone, Gloria, 174–175
Brown, James, 322
budget, 170, 254b. *See also* specific types
building gross area, 192
buildings, 293
bulk sales escrow, 381
Burgoyne, Doug, 68
business. *See also* business purchase; small business
 analyzing, 373–379, 391–393
 asking price for, 379–381, 384–390
 business number, 223–224
 decision to buy, 382–384
 defined, 57–57t
 federal income taxes, 225–226
 goods and services taxes, 223, 226–228
 green, 17–18
 harmonized sales taxes, 223, 227–228
 name, 216–217
 overview, 55–56
 payroll deductions, 224–225
 protection, 197, 384
 provincial sales taxes, 227–228
 purchasing, 370–373
 requirement checklist, 224b
 sales contract for, 391
 start-up guides, 243b
 successful actions, 86
 succession planning, 229–230
business advisors, 264, 382. *See also* financial advisor
Business Book Press, 375
business brokers, 375–376
business cards, 152
Business Development Bank of Canada (BDC), 22–23, 24
 angels and, 322
 break-even calculators, 297b
 business plan resources, 20
 earnings-assets valuation, 387
 financing sources, 323b
 opportunity trends, 39b
 ratio calculators, 297b
business establishments, 7t

business failures, 230, 329, 333, 447. *See also* bankruptcy
business format franchise, 399
business goals, identifying, 73–74, 87
business insurance, 184, 245b, 246b, 247. *See also* risk management
business intermediaries, 375. *See also* business brokers
business interruption insurance, 245b
business location, 175–176, 177–178. *See also* location
business mission statement, 80–81, 88–89, 91
business model, 84–86
Business Model Canvas, 84–85f
business models, stage 5 of e-commerce, 43
business name, 216–217
Businessnation.com, 402b
business number (BN), 223–224
business owners policy (BOP), 247b
Business Owner's Toolkit (CCH), 283b, 387
business plan, 18–20
 advertisement, 169
 assistance with, 423
 associations and partnerships, 115
 balance sheet, 302, 443t, 448
 business description, 19, 427b–428b
 cash flow description, 437b, 438t–439t, 447
 case study, 30–31, 90–91
 checklist for, 448
 competition assessment, 430–431
 competitors, description, 430b, 446
 cover letter, 423–424, 445
 customer profile, 115
 defined, 19
 description, 63, 257, 427–435b
 development checklist, 30, 90
 equity, 336b–337b
 example, 3
 executive summary, 425–426, 445
 fast-start, 19, 420
 financial section, 336b–337, 435–443
 format, 19, 275, 399
 future outlook, 62–63, 89
 human resources, 362, 434–435b
 income statement description, 440t–441t, 442b, 447–448
 industry overview, 62
 insurance, 257
 locations, 195–196, 197, 432–433, 447
 legal structures, 234
 lending sources, 336b–337b
 management and ownership, 63, 361–362, 433–434b

 management team description, 433–434b, 447
 marketing strategy description, 170, 428–429b, 431–432, 446, 446
 market opportunities, 139
 notes, 435–436, 437b, 442b
 numbers, 302, 435
 online resources, 20, 24, 29, 104, 154, 157, 243b
 opportunities and, 62, 89–90
 outline, 17b
 overview, 30, 255, 256, 420–421, 445
 personnel, 447
 PERT, 444–445, 448
 pricing products, 169
 products provided, description, 446
 projected balance sheet, 302, 436–437, 443t
 projected cash flow, 273, 302, 436, 437b, 438t–439t
 projected income statement, 274–275, 278–279, 302, 436, 440t–441t, 442b
 promotion, 169
 public relations, 169
 reasons for, 19
 red tape, 223, 234. *See also* specific government regulations
 reminders, 423
 resources, 20
 reviewers, 421
 services provided, 169–170, 427–428, 446
 sales projections, 302
 start-up appendix, 257
 start-up checklist, 253b–255b, 257, 302
 structure, 422
 successful actions, 25–26
 target customer description, 428–429b, 446
 table of contents, 425
 uniqueness and differentiation, 89
 words, 422, 427, 445, 446
 writing, 18–20, 30, 421–444
Business Planning and Financial Forecasting: A Start-Up Guide, 283b
business plan development checklists, 30, 448
 business purchase, 394
 competition, 139
 financing, 337
 franchises, 416
 legal issues, 234
 locations, 183, 196
 market opportunities, 64, 90
 market strategies and promotion, 170
 numbers, 302

success, 28
target customer profiling, 115
team building and management, 363
trends, 64
business protection, 197. *See also* security
auto, 245b
case study, 235, 236
for creative works, 219, 220
fire, 180
home, 39, 246b
Internet, 39
liability, 213
leases and, 190
name, 208, 216
patent, 217, 218–219
police, 180
for purchase offers, 384
for social media IP, 223
from unknown liabilities, 381
business purchase, 369–396
ability-to-pay valuation, 385–387
adjusted book value, 385
asset-based valuation, 384–385
book value, 385
bulk sales escrow, 381
business brokers, 375–376
buyer protection, 384
case study, 395–396
checklist for, 382b–383b, 394
contract, 391
decision making process, 381–384
earnings-assets valuation, 387–390
earnouts, 381
escrow company, 381, 383, 392
financial history, 376–377
GST/HST payments on, 377b
goodwill, 380
ill will, 394
investigating from inside, 375–376, 394
investigating from outside, 373–375, 393–394
inventory, 378
learning from others' mistakes, 373
liens, 392
letter of inquiry, 373, 393
loans, 386, 392, 386
negotiations, 383–384, 384–390
noncompetition covenant, 379
outside help for, 374–375
overview, 369–371, 393
price/earnings (P/E) ratios, 380
price of, 379–381, 384–390
profit returns on, 378, 391–392
process for, 372–373
reasons for, 371–372
red flags in, 381–382b

running own ad, 372
sellers' motives, 379
tangible assets, 378–379
tips, 375
valuation in, 377, 390b
Business Start-Up Quiz, 13
business strategy, 82–84
business-to-business (B2B) company
B2C versus, 107–108
case study, 116
defined, 105
example, 106–108
joint ventures, 106b, 350
Internet commerce in Canada, 76b
online catalogues and, 154
profiling, 105–108, 115
research for, 108
sales, 76b
strategic alliances, 106b, 134–136, 350
target customers, 98, 100–101
business-to-consumer (B2C) company, 99
B2B versus, 107–108
case study, 116
defined, 99
Internet commerce in Canada, 76b
profiling, 105–108, 115
sales, 76
target customers, 100–101
business vision, 111
Butterick®, 36
buy-sell option, 211

C

Calmeadow, 322, 326
Campbell, Derek, 433b
CampusCrow.com, 161b
Canada
e-commerce in, 24, 34, 42, 43–45
entrepreneurs in, 6, 40, 94, 116, 139, 398, 401–402, 413, 416, 433b–434b
ethnocultural profile, 47b–48b
exports, 35b, 40
franchises in, 126
Internet users in, 43
minority population, 47b
online consumers in, 44b, 76b. *See also* 1-800-GOT-JUNK?
population, 46t
small businesses in, 23, 38, 40, 177, 226b, 243b, 355b, 377b
Canada Business, 20b, 226b, 243b, 416
Canada Business Corporations Act, 207, 208, 211
Canada Business Network, 23, 179, 326, 377b, 402b

Canada Corporations Act, 207, 208, 211
Canada Pension Plan (CPP), 224b, 225, 262
Canada Revenue Agency, 205, 214–215, 223, 377, 379
Canada Savings Bonds, 267, 271
Canada Small Business Financing Act, 16, 329
Canada Small Business Financing Program (CSBF), 323b, 329–331
Canada's Information Resource Centre (CIRC), 24
Canadian Advertising Rates and Data (CARD), 157
Canadian Bankers' Association, 15
Canadian Business, 21, 60, 402b
Canadian Business Index, 75
Canadian Business Online, 70b, 171
Canadian Business Network, 402b, 403b
Canadian Centre for Occupational Health and Safety (CCOHS), 250b
Canadian Chamber of Commerce, 17, 241b, 322, 361
Canadian Company Capabilities, 23, 24, 106–107, 114
Canadian Demographics, 101
Canadian Federation of Independent Business (CFIB), 11, 18
Canadian Foundation for Economic Education (CFEE), 13b
Canadian Franchise Association (CFA), 126, 398, 402b
Canadian Franchise Directory, 402b
Canadian Importers Database, 24
Canadian Industry Shows and Exhibitions, 157
Canadian Industry Statistics, 24
Canadian Intellectual Property Office (CIPO), 64, 217, 218, 222, 236
Canadian Restaurant and Foodservice Association, 75
Canadian Revenue Agency (CRA), 205, 214–215, 223, 377, 379
Canadian Tax and Financial Information, 226b
Canadian Technology Network, 24
Canadian Tire, 135
Canada's Venture Capital & Private Equity Association, 323b, 326
Canadian Youth Business Foundation, 325b
capital, sources of, 213, 313. *See also* specific types
Carpenter, Philu, 434b
cash, 261, 265, 266t, 267
cash flow, 273, 274f

cash flow projection, 273–275, 275–284
   available, from loans, 386–387
   case study, 305
   cost deductions and, 387
   defined, 273
   drafting, 301
   factors in, 284b
   forecasting disbursements, 280–281
   forecasting receipts, 279, 385–386
   in opening balance, 275–277t
   overview, 299
   projected (pro forma) statement, 273, 282t–283t
   projected monthly sales, 274–275, 278–279
   resources for, 283b
   summary, 281
   value estimation, 385–387
   worksheet, 282t–283
cash reserve fund, 265, 266t, 267t
Castillo, Chris, 2, 435
CATA*Alliance*, 60
catalogues, 54, 153–156
CBI (Certified Business Intermediary), 376
CCOHS (Canadian Centre for Occupational Health and Safety), 249–250
ceiling pricing, 148
census data, 99–100b
Census of Population, 99–100
Centre for Small Business Financing, 323b
Ceridian Canada Limited, 105
Certified Business Intermediary (CBI), 376
CFEE (Canadian Foundation For Economic Education), 13b
CFIB (Canadian Federation of Independent Business), 11, 18, 32
CGS (cost of goods sold), 285t, 286, 287t, 289–290
charities, 214–216
CharityVillage, 326
chartered banks, 309b
Chilton, David, 70
CIPO (Canadian Intellectual Property Office), 64, 217, 218, 222, 236
Clark, Mary, 56–57
Clark's Stables, 57
Clemmer, Jim, 151
Close Connections, 177–178
closing balance sheet, 291–293
   assets, 291–293
   example, 292t
   liabilities, 293
   owner's equity, 287, 293
coaching, 342

cocooning, 39
Cohen, Mina, 103, 104, 134–135
collateral, 310, 320–321
collection timelines, 280b
college reports, 22
commercial leases, 192
common area, 192
common shares, 333
communicating, stage 1 of e-commerce, 43
company profile, 23, 105b, 107, 429b
company website analysis, 23, 126, 193
compensation, 357–358
competition, 122–125. *See also* competitors
   case study, 139–140
   defined, 122
   description in business plan, 137–138, 139
   direct (first-level) competitors, 122
   indirect (second-level) competitors, 122
   invisible, 98–99, 122–123
   life cycle, 131–134
   location of competitors, 179
   opportunities and, 49
   overview, 136
   product life cycle and, 131–132
competitive, as entrepreneur characteristic, 11
competitive intelligence (CI), 123
   case studies, 120–121
   defined, 123
   goals of, 123
   resource centres, 126, 127
   scouting competitive landscape in, 125–127
   touchpoint analysis, 123–125, 137
competitive positioning strategy, 132–134, 138
competitive pricing strategy, 129–131
competitive strategies, 127–131
   competitive pricing strategy, 129–131
   competitor analysis, 128–129, 139
   cost leadership strategy, 128
   differentiation strategy, 128
   factors, 84–85
   focus strategy, 127
   niches, 127
   positioning strategy, 127
competitive SWOT analysis, 128–129
competitive test matrix, 128–129, 138
competitive touchpoint analysis, 123–125, 137
competitor analysis, 128–129
competitor-based pricing, 129–131, 146
competitor review sheet, 137

competitors. *See also* competition
   defined, 122
   direct (first-level), 122
   description in business plan, 446
   identification, 379
   indirect (second-level) competitors, 122
   literature, 126
   location checklist, 183b
   overview, 137
   mature stage and, 133b
   niche, 127
   pricing review sheet, 130b–131
   profiling, 120, 122–125, 126–127
   researching, 120
   review sheet for, 137
   strategic alliances with, 134–136
   touchpoints, 123–125, 137
completion bonds, 245
Compusearch, 101
computer databases, 23–24
computerization, 182
concierge service agent, 50
conditional sale, 330t
conferences, 126
connected society, as social media trend, 48
connectivity, 48
consequential loss insurance, 245b, 247, 248t
consumer price index (CPI), 191
consumer profile, 99
consumers. *See* customers
Contact! The Canadian Management Network, 23–24
contracts, 391
contribution margin, 285t, 286, 288–289
convertible debentures, 333
cooperative partnership, 327
cooperatives, 212–214. *See also* small business
   advantages of, 213
   capital, 213
   defined, 212
   disadvantages of, 214
   incorporation, 212
   liability, 213
   organization, 212–213
   principles for, 212
   priorities, 213
   shares, 213
   social entrepreneurship, 212
   voting in, 213
copyright, 219–221
copyright infringement, 221
Copyright Office, 220, 221
core benefit proposition, 164
corporate seal, 211

corporations, 204–212
- board of directors, 209, 346–347
- buy-sell option, 211
- continuity, 206
- defined, 204
- disadvantages, 207–208
- estate planning, 207
- expenses, managing, 206
- incorporation process, 208–209
- internal incentives, 206–207
- liability, 204–205
- multiple ownership in, 206
- paperwork for, 207–208
- public image, 206
- reasons for incorporating, 204–208
- seals, 211
- shareholders, 209–212
- start-up costs, 207
- tax advantages, 205–206
- writeoffs, 207

cost leadership strategy, 128
Cost of Borrowing Calculator, 312
cost of goods sold (CGS), 285t, 286, 287t, 289–290
cost-of-living cap, 191
cost plus pricing, 146–147
costs
- business location, 180
- of employees, 358
- fixed, 85f, 286, 294–296, 298f
- of goods, 285t, 286, 287t, 289–290
- operating, 285t, 286–288, 387
- of recruitment, 358
- start-up, 265–267, 241b, 301
- total, 146, 285t, 287t, 295
- of training employees, 293, 336b, 348b, 358, 362
- variable, 280, 286, 294–296t

cost structure, 84
courtesy, 162–163
CPI (consumer price index), 191
CPP (Canada Pension Plan), 224b, 225, 262
CRA (Canadian Revenue Agency), 205, 214–215, 223, 377, 379
Crazy Plates, 70
Crazy's Roadhouse, 110–111, 125, 186
credit, 310. *See also* debt financing; financing
- applying for, 312b–313
- collateral, 310, 320–321
- decision process, 310
- defined, 310
- factors influencing, 311–313
- from family and friends, 316–317
- four Cs of credit, 313, 334
- lines of, 331–332

micro lending, 325–326
- projected income and, 437b, 442b
- rating, 335–336
- reports, 309–310, 334, 335
- risk tolerance, 315
- sources of, 311t
- unsecured, 310–313
- tips for, 312b
- types of, 330t

Credit Bureau Services Canada Inc., 309–310, 335
Credit Counseling Canada, 263b
credit history, 309–310, 312b
credit rating, 310, 312, 335–336
credit reports, 309–310, 334, 335
CreditGuru.com, 297b
crime insurance, 245b, 248t
critical illness insurance, 245b, 248t
Critical Mass, 95–96, 97, 140
CRM (customer relationship marketing), 95–96, 116
Cunnington-Taylor, Kimberley, 215–215
current asset conversion cycle, 274
current assets, 267–268, 269. *See also* assets
current debt, 293
current liabilities, 293
current ratio, 271
customer relationship marketing (CRM), 95–96, 116
customers
- invisible, 98–99
- loyalty, 125, 371
- primary, 94, 97, 115
- questions to, 20, 62, 109–110, 114, 124, 165
- relationships, 84, 95
- secondary, 98
- segments, 84
- as source of credit, 323
- specialized consumer tastes, 55
- success factors for, 151
- target, 99, 100–101, 105–108
- touchpoints, 123–125, 137
- types, 98
- vigilant, 183
customers, target, 99, 100–101, 105–108
- business-to-business (B2B) profile, 100–101
- defined, 21
- description in business plan, 115
- example, 103
- field interviewing, 108–109
- location and, 42t
- media sources, 103–104
- one-to-one marketing, 96–97

overview, 112
profiling, 5, 21, 97–98, 99–101, 116–117
surveying, 109–111
visualizing business and, 111

D

Dalglish, Peter, 14
D'Angelo, Gena, 163
databases, 21, 23, 75, 185, 402
D-Code, 102
dealership relationship franchise, 399
debt financing, 327–328, 329–323. *See also* financing; loans
- advantages of, 328
- Canada Small Business Financing (CSBF) loans, 329–331
- defined, 327
- disadvantages of, 328
- fixed rate, 332
- floating rate, 332
- long-term, 293
- operating loans, 331–332
- overview, 327
- primary types of, 329–323
- secondary types of, 330b
- shareholder loans, 281, 329
- term loans, 332
debts, managing, 230
debt-to-equity ratio, 273, 327
Decode, Inc., 101, 102
decline stage, 132, 133, 382
deferred liabilities, 270
de-layering, 39
DeLuca, Fred, 413
democratization of information, 39
demographic change, 39
demographic profile, 49, 99–101
demographics, 49, 99
dental insurance, 311
depreciation, 281, 293
Dickenson, Arlene, 9
differentiation strategy, 128
diffusion quick, 161
Digital Opportunity Trust, 214
DINKs (Double Income No Kids), 101
Dinkytown.net, 297b
direct compensation, 357
direct competitors, 122, 144, 171, 446
direct franchising, 400
direct mail, 154
direct merchant (intermediary), 94
Direct Sellers Association of Canada (DSA)156b
direct selling, 156b
directors, 209
directors' and officers' liability insurance, 245b

disability and critical illness insurance, 245b
disbursements, 275
    defined, 273
    depreciation, 281
    dividends, 205, 213, 225, 281
    fixed, 280
    forecasting, 280–281
    loan payments, 280–281
    management salaries, 281
    principal draw, 281
    purchases of fixed assets, 281
    shareholder loans, 281, 329
    variable, 280
discount coupons, 158–159
DISCovery Books and Magazines, 275, 276t–277t, 285t, 303
distinctive competency, 125, 129f, 136
distribution channels, 84, 176–178, 196–197
dividends, 205, 213, 225, 281
Domm, Perri, 120–121
Double Income No Kids (DINKs), 101
downsizing, 39b, 61, 183, 349
driver personality type, 367
Drucker, Peter, 8
due diligence, 251
dynamic partnerships, 39

E
early adopters, 94, 421
earnings-assets pricing formula, 388–390
earnings-assets valuation, 387–390
earnouts, 381
eBay, 6
e-books, 41
e-business planning, 45b
echo boomers, 46, 47, 49
Ecometrix Incorporated, 359
e-commerce, 43–45. See also Internet resources
    case study, 34, 90–91
    defined, 43
    functions of, 43
    individual usage, 42b
    Internet and, 42
    order statistics, 43b
    personalization of, 96b
    revolution, 45b
    strategies for, 43–45
    types of products, 44b
    websites, for success, 69, 94
economic change, 49
economy pricing, 148–149
ecoretailing, 50
e-forms, 45b
electronic cottages, 39b
elevator pitch, 58

Elgin, Jeff, 402b
e-module 3, 283b
embryonic stage, 131, 133b
employee dishonesty, 252
    examples of, 252
    fidelity bonds and, 245
    legal consequences, education of, 252
    measures to prevent, 252b
employees
    aging, 358–359
    compensation, 357–358
    cost of, 358
    fringe benefits, 357
    hiring, 352–354, 359, 360
    leasing, 351
    Master Entrepreneur thinking versus, 10t
    mentoring relationships, 351–352
    multicultural, 358–359
    private sector, 9t
    selection, 356–357
    as source of credit, 323
    as source of inside information, 378
    start-up businesses and, 243b
    training, 357
employers, as source of credit, 323
Employers' Guide to Payroll Deductions, 225
Employment Insurance (EI), 225–226, 350, 358
employment practices liability insurance (EPLI), 245b
employment trends, 50
encroachment, 406
end-user profile, 99, 105b
energy conservation trend, 50
Entrepreneur.com, 170, 398, 402b, 415, 416
entrepreneurs, 6–8. See also innovation; leases
    in Canada, 6, 40, 94, 116, 139–140, 398, 401–402, 413, 416, 433b–434b
    characteristics of, 8, 10–11, 13, 370
    goals, 30
    increased interest in, 39
    interviews, of experienced, 28–29
    intrapreneurs, 14–15
    "lifestylers," 12
    mechanic example, 2, 420
    as networkers, 31
    opportunity seeking, 3
    overview, 6, 25
    passion, 3, 68, 70, 91
    persistence, 3
    personality exercise, 13b
    reasons for becoming, 6, 12–13, 26
    roadblocks, 18, 31
    road map, 4–6
    self-assessment, 13, 27

self employment readiness quizzes, 13
    serial, 6, 36, 370
    skills, 31, 196
    small business, 8, 15–17
    social, 14
    social media and, 161
    statistics, 6–8
    success rate, 18
    tools for. See innovation
    types of, 13
    typeE quiz, 13
    websites for, 11, 12, 13b
    women, 54–55, 174–175, 323b, 340–341, 370, 407
environmental trend, 39, 50
EPLI (employment practices liability insurance), 245b
Equifax Canada Inc., 309, 335
equipment and fixtures, 242b, 291, 378
equity, 268t, 327. See also debt financing
    advantages of, 328
    in closing balance sheets, 292t
    common shares, 333
    convertible debentures, 333
    defined, 265
    disadvantages of, 328–329
    in opening balance sheet and, 268t
    owner's, 270–271
    preferred shares, 333
    types of, 332–333
equity financing, 332–333. See also specific types
    common shares, 333
    convertible debentures, 333
    overview, 333
    preferred shares, 333
    pros and cons of, 328–329
    SMEs and, 309b
    types of, 332–333
errors and omissions insurance, 245b
escape clause, 190–191
escrow company, 381, 383, 392
e-services, 45b
estate planning, 207
ethnic groups, 47–48b
ethnic trend, 50
Evans, Dan, 95
Eventful.com, 160
expenses, 206. See also costs
export, 40b
expressive personality type, 367
external recruitment, 354–355
extra equipment insurance, 245b

F
Facebook, 48, 160, 161b, 223
factoring, 330t

family-owned businesses, succession planning in, 229–230

Farthington, Don, 240

Fast4Cast, 297b

Fast-Start Business Plan, 20

Federal Corporations Data Online, 24

federal e-forms and services, 45b

federal income taxes, 225–226

federal requirements, 208, 224b

FedEx, 40

FICO score, 335

fidelity bonds, 245

field interview, 108–109

finances
  advisors for, 50, 241b, 264, 301, 319, 371
  balance sheets, 265–267
  fitness characteristics, 263b
  personal, 262, 263–264
  start-up costs, 207, 265–267, 301

financial advisor, 50, 241b, 264, 301

financial history, 376–377. *See also* credit history

financial institutions, 317–322
  advisors, 50, 241b, 264, 301, 319, 371
  bankers and, 318–320, 378
  in business plan description, 336–337
  fees of, 321–322
  guarantees to, 320
  negotiations with, 319–320
  overview, 317–318
  regulations of, 321
  teamwork and, 318
  types of, 320–321

financial instruments, 309b

Financial Post, 402b

financing, 308–309
  case study, 303–305, 338
  checklist for, 337
  debt, 327–332
  external sources of, 309b
  formal sources of, 317–322
  informal sources of, 315–316
  money IQ, 263b
  planning resources, 283b
  self-financing, 316
  sources of, 308–309

fire and general property insurance, 245

first-level competitors, 122

first wave, 35–36

Fisher, Andy, 240

Fisher, Patty, 240

fitness trend, 50

fixed assets, 269, 281, 293

fixed costs, 286, 294–296, 298f

fixed disbursements, 280

fixed rate, 332

fixtures, 242b

floating rate, 332

floating rent scale, 191

floor plan loan, 330t

focus strategy, 127

"the follower", target customer type, 98

Foot, David, 41

Form T1044, 215t

Form T2125, Statement of Business or Professional Activities, 225

Form T3010, 215t

founding team, 346

four Cs of credit, 313, 334

foursquare, 160

"4th P," 175–176

FP Markets, 101

franchise, 126

Franchise Comparison Worksheet, 402b

Franchise Direct, 403b

franchisees, 398, 399, 401, 416. *See also* franchises; franchisors

Franchise Magazine, 402b

FranchiseOpportunities.com, 402b

franchise purchase, 400–405. *See also* franchising, pitfalls of
  application form, 405f
  benefits to customers, 400
  benefits to franchisees, 400–401
  benefits to franchisors, 401
  investigation before, 401–403
  process of, 403–405
  reasons against, 412
  reasons for, 400, 414
  signing personally for, 407

franchises
  agreements for, 403–405
  business format, 399
  case study, 416–416
  in Canada, 399, 402B–403b, 407–408
  checklist for, 409b–412b, 416
  choosing product or services, 412
  databases and directories, 402b
  defined, 399
  dealership relationship, 399
  encroachment, 406
  evaluating, 408–412
  fees, 401
  "ground-floor," 406
  ideas for, 412–413
  information on, 126, 402b, 407–408
  insiders first in, 408
  insurance for, 403
  investigating, 401–403, 415–416
  member-owned buying group, 414
  networks, 400
  nonrefundable deposits in, 408

overview, 397–399, 413–415
  personal guarantees, 407
  poor training, 408
  regulation of, 407
  renewal period, 406
  resources for, 401b
  royalty fees, 401
  saturated markets, 408
  shows, 298
  supplies, 408
  systems, 399–400
  types of, 399–400
  verbal regulation, 406–407

Franchise Show, 398

franchising, 177
  defined, 177
  direct, 400
  global trend in, 399, 402b, 416
  master franchising, 400, 402b, 416
  overview, 177
  pitfalls of, 406–408
  profitability of, 407–408
  process in, 403–405
  research of, 415

franchisors, 399, 412–413

FranNet, 403b

fraud prevention, 252

free ink and free air, 155

freebies, 155

fringe benefits, 357–358

Frogbox.com, 68

furniture, 192, 231, 269, 291

Futurist, The, 51b

G

gap analysis, 55, 62

Garneau, Louis, 12

general partnership, 202

Generation X, 102b

Generation Y, 47

Gibson, Shane, 161–162

globalization, 40, 49. *See also* e-commerce
  defined, 40
  exports and, 40
  forcasts for, 51b
  of franchises, 399, 402b, 416
  need for, 39b, 40
  technology and the Internet, 39
  trends in, 49, 399, 402b, 416

Global Positioning System (GPS), 41

GMROI (gross margin return on inventory investment), 291

goal-oriented partnerships, 350

goals, 8, 73–74, 80f

GoDaddy.com, 223

gold-collar workers, 176

Goldfarb model, 101

Gonzales, Julia, 108–109

Good and Services Tax (GST), 226–227
Goodbye Graffiti, 120–121
goodwill, 371, 380, 383–384, 385
Google™, 41, 48, 60, 103, 160
1-800-GOT-JUNK?, 144–145, 170–172
government lending programs, 326
GPS (Global Positioning System), 41
Grameen Bank, 14
Green business, 17–18
Grenchik, James, 135
gross margin return on inventory investment (GMROI), 291
gross profit, 286, 288
gross profit margin, 285t, 286, 288–289
gross rent, 192
"ground-floor" franchises, 406
Government and Community-Based Financing Programs (Canada Business), 323b
growth industry, 54, 59
growth segment, 54–55
growth stage, 133b, 382b
GST (Good and Services Tax), 226–227
Guay, Louise, 94–95, 111, 116, 139
guerilla marketing, 145, 171
Guide for Canadian Small Businesses, 226b

H
H&R Block, 406
hard data, 21–24
hard working, as entrepreneur characteristic, 11
Harmonized Sales Tax (HST), 223, 227–228
Hastings, Reed, 34
hazardous materials, 250, 251
HBS Toolkit, 297b
health and safety, 249–251. See also OH&S
  case study, 258
  due diligence, 251
  hazardous materials, 251
  joint committees for, 250–251
  overview, 249–250
  policies, 256–257
  regulations, 250b
  responsibility for, 250
  workplace, 249–251
health care industry, mind map analysis, 56f
health-consciousness trend, 50
health insurance, 245b
Hellard, Ted, 95, 98
Herold, Cameron, 144
hiring, 352–354, 360. See also employees
H.M.A. Tires & Accessories, 308

home-based businesses, 181–184. See also small business
  case study, 197
  insuring, 184b, 246b–247b
  list of, 183
  location, 39b, 183b–184b
  reasons for, 182–183
  security, 39
  trends, 183
home equity line of credit, 310, 313
home equity loan, 313
Home Hardware, 399
homeowner's liability endorsement, 246b
homeowner's policy endorsement, 246b
home security, 50. See also business protection, security
hours of operation, 180
HR Best Practices Report (2009), 359
HST (Harmonized Sales Tax), 223, 227–228
human resources, 347, 348b, 359, 362–363. See also employees; hiring
Human Resources and Skills Development Canada (HRSDC), 250b

I
iD Configurator (Nike), 96b
ideas. See also brainstorming; mind mapping
  generation, 8, 15, 78, 83b, 342
  guide for, 243b
  risks and, 243b
  segmentation and, 77f
  selecting, 37, 52b, 79
  testing, 83b
immigrants, 39b, 358
impact marketing, 158
income statement ratios, 288–291. See also balance sheet; cash flow projection
  case study, 305
  gross margin return on inventory investment (GMROI), 291
  gross profit margin, 285t, 286, 288–289
  inventory turnover, 289–290
  overview, 300
  profit margin, 289
Income Tax Act, 216
income taxes, 225–226
incorporation, 204–207
"Inc." yourself, 15, 28 See also mind map
independence, 8, 16f, 212
independent contractor, 350
indirect compensation, 357
indirect (second-level) competitors, 122

indirect expenses, 294–295
industrial age, 35, 59, 102
industry analysis, 75–76, 126
Industry Canada, 15, 23, 24
industry journals, 126
industry norm pricing, 147–148
industry profile, 105b
industry segments, identification, 76–78
information access, 48
information, democratization of, 39
information wave, 35
in-home business policy, 246b–247b
in-home service provider, 50
innovation, 24, 31
inspiring behaviour, 341–342
Instagram.com, 160
insurance planning, 244–249
  completion bonds, 245
  costs, 256
  fidelity bonds, 245
  for franchises, 403
  for home business, 246b–247b
  legal agreements and, 245, 247, 249
  for loans, 321
  overview, 244, 247
  types of, 234b, 248
  worksheet, 248t
intellectual property (IP), 223
  in Canada, 64, 217–218
  case study, 236
  forms of, 217
  protection for, 223
  registration websites for, 223, 236
interests and abilities, assessment, 15, 27
interest payments, 280, 281, 287, 329, 333
intermediaries, 375. See also business brokers
internal recruitment, 354
International Business Brokers Association (IBBA), 376
international change, 49
Internet resources
  advertisements, free, 432
  analysis, 83, 140
  bankruptcy, 230, 231
  brokers, 375, 376
  as business connectivity, 42
  business information, 23–24, 75, 375
  business model, 84
  business plans, 20, 23–24, 165
  business purchase, 375, 377b, 390b
  CFA Disclosure Document Guide, 408
  cooperatives, 212, 216
  credit, 312, 335
  customer profiles, 47, 95, 100, 104, 106, 113, 114, 115
  data mining, 185
  direct sales, 156b

earnings-assets valuation, 387
e-commerce in Canada, 42–45, 76b
email, free, 161
employees' information on, 9t, 356, 359
employers' information on, 355
entrepreneurs, 9t, 11, 12, 13, 31
financial fitness, 263b
financial planning, 264, 283
financial statements, 305
financing, 126, 309, 322, 323, 325, 326, 331
franchise information on, 170, 398, 402, 403, 404, 407, 416, 417
globalization, 40
health and safety plans, 249, 250, 251, 257
home-based business, 7t, 182
industry analysis, 75–76, 126
information on, 23–24, 29, 185
insurance, 248
leadership, 348, 364–365
leases, 187, 192b
loan calculators, 281, 387
locations, 7t, 197
marketing strategies, 96, 151, 152
Master Entrepreneur®, 11
member-owned buying group, 414
mentors, 351, 361
mobile apps, 97b
net present value (NVP), 390
nonprofit organizations, 215t, 216
outsourcing, 65
partnerships, 202, 203, 365
patent applications tutorial, 233
patents, copyrights, and trademarks, 218, 233, 236
personal values, 71, 87
profit guide, 90
ratio calculators on, 288, 289, 297b
real estate, 41
as resources, 23–24
risk management, 257
sales, monthly, 279
security, 39
self-employed, 7t
shareholder agreements, 210, 235
small businesses, 52, 90, 243b, 244, 377b
SME Benchmarking Tool, 127, 283, 289, 290, 291
start-up costs, 301
surfing, 60
taxes, 205, 224, 225, 226, 227
technology, 60
trade shows, 157
trends and opportunities, 39, 64
value of business, 377b
websites, building, 45b, 65

intrapreneurs, 14–15
inventory, 242b, 269, 291, 378
inventory financing, 330t
inventory turnover, 289–290
investment firms, reports from, 22
invisible competition, 122–123
invisible customer, 98–99
IP. See intellectual property (IP), 223
iPhone™, 41

J
Jericho, Roberta, 433b
JHSC (joint health and safety committee), 250–251
job analysis, 353
job qualifications, 353
job requirements, 353
JobShark Corporation, 42
Jobs, Steve, 8
joint health and safety committee (JHSC), 250–251
joint ventures, 106b, 350
Jones, Vivienne, 82
just-in-time team, 349, 360

K
Keirsey Temperament Sorter II, 348b
key activities, 84
key employee insurance, 244, 245b
key partners, 84
key resources, 84
keystone pricing, 147–148
Kinnikinnick Foods Inc., 68–69
KJE Computer Solutions, 390b
Knowem, 223
knowledge-based era, 35, 101, 121, 176
Komatsu, Kazuko, 34–35, 49

L
labour pool, 179
land, 293
landlord, 180
Land's End, 94
lawyers, 228–229, 233–234
leadership, 341–343
    behaviour styles, 341–342
    defined, 341
    inspirational, 342b
    overview, 341–343
    motivation assessment, 348b
    resources for, 364
    types, 342b, 364
Leadership from Within (Bender), 342
Leadership Motivation Assessment, Mind Tools, 348

lenders, 335–336
leaseholder improvements, 191, 291
leases, 187–193
    checklist for, 191–192
    commercial, 192
    overview, 187–188, 193
    researching, 192b–193b
    rewriting, 190–192
    terminologies, 192b
    terms of, 188–189
    provisions for unexpected circumstances, 189–190
    questions before signing, 192b–193b
    successful actions, 193–194
leasing companies, 309b, 323b, 325b
LeBlanc, Ken, 128, 177, 325
legal changes, 49
legal representation, 371
legal structures, 200, 201t. See also cooperatives; corporations; partnerships; sole proprietorships
    in business plan description, 234
    case study, 234–236
    characteristics, of main forms, 201t
    charities versus non-profits, 215t
    corporation. See corporations
    development checklist, 234
    disbanding businesses, 203–204
    nonprofit organizations, 214–216
    overview, 232, 233
    partnerships, 202–204
    shotgun clause, 203–204
    for small businesses, 200
    social entrepreneurs and, 214–216
    for sole proprietorships, 200–202
letter of credit, 330t
Lewington, Trevor, 105
liabilities, 201t, 204–205, 208, 213
    categories, 269
    in closing balance sheets, 292t, 293
    current, 270, 304t
    defined, 265
    in opening balance sheets, 268t, 272t, 304t
    overview, 269
    in personal balance sheets, 313, 314t
    long-term, 270, 293, 304t
    other debt, 270
licences and permits, for start-up businesses, 241b. See also specific types
lien, 392
life cycle, 52, 131–134
    competition and, 131–134
    defined, 51
    home-based businesses and, 184
    overview, 131–132
    positioning, 132–134

life cycle (*Cont.*)
    stages, 52–53, 61, 133b
    strategies, 132
life insurance, 245b, 248t
lifestyle coach, 50
"lifestylers," 12
limited partnership, 202
limit pricing, 148–149
Lindsay, Bette, 189–190
line of credit, 331–332
Linkedin.com, 160, 161
linking externally, stage 4 of
    e-commerce, 45
linking internally, stage 3 of
    e-commerce, 44
liquid assets, 271, 314t
liquidity ratios, 271–273
living arrangements, 47
L.L. Bean, 47, 94, 98, 139
loan management fees, 321–322
loans, 331–332
    for available cash flow, 386–387
    business purchase, 386
    collateral, 310f, 320–321
    from family and friends, 316–317
    lenders, 335–336
    operating, 331–332
    payments, 274, 280–281
    term, 293, 332
    types of, 293
    unsecured, 310–313
local licensing, 179, 184
local markets, 49
location, 177–178, 178–181
    accessibility, 180
    approvals for, 181, 184
    description in business plan,
        195–196, 197
    case study, 196–197
    checklist, 196
    choosing, 177–181
    of competitors, 179, 183
    costs, 180
    description in business plan,
        195–196, 197, 432–433, 447
    escape hatch, 190–191
    evaluation, 194
    of home-based businesses,
        183b–184b, 195
    ideal, 194–195
    image, 180, 184
    leases and, 187–193
    life-cycle stage of, 180, 181f, 183
    lifestyles and, 184
    ownership, 180
    physical visibility, 180, 183
    professional advice, 180
    rating importance checklist, 179–181
    researching, 179–180, 184–187
    space, 180, 184

    for start-up businesses, 241b
    taxes, 181
    utilities, 180, 184
    work habits or behaviors and, 184
    zoning, 180
location escape hatch, 190–191
location filter, 178–181
logo, 152, 204
long-term debt, 270, 293
long-term liabilities, 270, 293
loss factor, 192
Lütke, Tobias, 34
Louis Garneau Group, 12
love money, 308

M
M&M Meatshops, 401–402, 404, 415
Maclean's magazine, 60
magazines, 21–22, 113, 168
mail advertising, 124
maintenance, of leases, 191–192
malpractice insurance, 245b,
    248t
Managing Money, 263b
management, 341–343, 346, 359, 361
management team, 346
market-based pricing, 146
market gap, 76–77, 87
market research, 113
Market Research Handbook (2008 edi-
    tion), 100
market segmentation, 55, 62, 91
market signals, 53–54
marketable securities, 267, 271, 275
marketing, 96–97, 144–155. *See also*
    promotion; specific types
    advertising, 151–152, 242b–243b
    branding, 159
    budget, 161b
    business cards, 152
    description in business plan, 170
    case study, 170–172
    catalogues, 153–154
    courtesy as promotion, 162–163
    customer-relationship, 95–96, 116
    direct mail, 154, 168
    direct selling, 156b
    discount coupons, 158–159
    example, 431b
    free ink and free air, 155
    freebies, 155
    guerilla, 145, 171
    impact, 158
    industry literature, 126, 158
    media advertising, 151–152, 168,
        242b–243b
    mix, 145
    money-back guarantees, 154
    networking, 163–164, 167–168

    one-to-one, 96–97
    online, 159–162, 172
    opportunities, 79–80
    overview, 165–166
    packaging, 153
    paid media advertising, 151–152,
        242b–243b
    personal selling, 155–157, 169, 431b
    point-of-purchase displays, 153
    sales reps, 162
    social media and networks, 160–161
    strategy, 151–152, 159–162,
        170, 171
    student classifieds, 161
    successful actions, 166
    trade shows, 157
    viral, 161–162
    websites, 159–160
marketing mix, 145
marketing strategy, 145, 169–170
market-pull approach, 96–97
markets. *See also* target customers
    competitive strategy for, 127–131b
    diversified, 85f
    emerging, 89, 139
    export, 40b, 49
    foreign, 40
    local, 49
    mass, 47–48
    multi-sided platform, 85f
    niche (focus), 127
    saturated, 408
    segmented, 55, 84
    signals, 53–54
    vertical, 49
markups, 147
mass customization, 48
mass market, 47–48
Master Entrepreneur®, 10t–11
master franchising, 400, 402b
Masters, Dan, 434b
material safety data sheets (MSDS), 251
matrix grid, 79–80, 88
mature stage, 133b, 382b
McCall's®, 36
McCarron, Mike, 82, 346, 347, 363,
    364, 365
McLachlan, Lorraine, 398
McDonald's, 122, 144, 376, 399
McKee, Mike, 144
Mechanic To You®, 2–3, 420, 428
mechanistic organizational structure,
    343t
media advertising, 151–152, 169,
    242b–243b, 431b
media change, 39
MegaDox.com, 402b
member-owned buying group, 414
mentors, 351–352, 353t, 361
Mercedes-Benz, 95, 97, 98, 105

mezzanine financing, 330t
micro business, 16
microchips, 41
microcredit, 14
Micro Credit (Canada Business), 323b
Micro Hut Computer Centre, 430b
micro lending programs, 325–326
middle class, 47
Millennials, 46
Milner, Craig, 105
mind map, 15, 16f, 31
    case study, 31, 37, 38f, 64
    defined, 15
    example, 16f, 56f
    health-care industry, 56f
    "Inc." yourself and, 15, 28
    snowboard express, 38f
Mind Tools, 140, 348, 365
Minister, David, 153
minorities, 47b–48b
mission, 68–69, 91. *See also* business
    mission statement
mobile apps, 96–97
money
    debtor help, 263b. *See also* bank-
        ruptcy
    financial IQ, 263b
    love, 308
    overview, 334
    management, 263b
    personal chart, 313–315
    profit comparison, 378
    quiz, 263b
money-back guarantees, 154
Moss, Geoff, 153
MSDS (material safety data sheets),
    251
MSM Transportation, 83b,
    363–365
multiple ownerships, 206
municipal licensing, 179, 184
municipal requirements, 184, 224b
Murray, Robert, 346, 348, 363–364
My Virtual Model (MVM),
    94–95, 105
    B2B clients, 139
    case study, 116, 139, 140
    example, 111
    "the follower", 98
    resources for, 140
    target customer of, 97
    "mystery shopper," 21

N

National Angel Capital Organization
    (NACO), 323b
National Geographic Traveler,
    103, 113
neighbourhood, 179, 183

Netflix, 34
net present value valuation
    (NPV), 390b
net profit, before taxes, 288
net rent, 192
net worth, 313, 314t, 335
networking, 163–164, 167–168
network organization, 345
new-eyes research, 20–21, 29
Newing, David J., 214, 215
Newly Upgraded Automated Name
    Search (NUANS), 217
newspapers, 21
Nexus generation, 102b
Nexus group, 102b
niches, 127
Nielsen, 24
Nike, 95–96, 105
NikeiD, 96
Nintendo Generation, 47
noncompetition covenant, 379
nonprofit funding, 326
non-profit organization (NPO),
    214–216
NUANS (Newly Upgraded Automated
    Name Search), 217

O

occupational health and safety, 249,
    250b, 251, 257
office supplies, 242b, 269, 291
one-to-one marketing (one-2-one),
    96–97
online business workshops, 243
online marketing, 160–162
    sales reps as connectors, 162
    social media, 48–49, 160–161
    social networks, 160–161
    viral marketing, 161–162
    website, 126, 159–160
online resources, 126–127, 243b. *See*
    also Internet resources
online sales, 42, 69, 76b
operating budges, 254
operating expenses, 285t,
    286–288, 387
operating loans, 331–332
opportunities, 35–39
    brainstorming, 37–38, 78–79,
        88, 168
    case study, 64–65
    goals and, 73–74, 80f
    overview, 72
    marketplace and, 79–80,
        89–90, 139
    problems and solutions and, 76–77,
        88. *See also* brainstorming
    recognition of, 35–39
    research for, 75–7680

seeking, 3, 8, 35
    segmentation and, 77f
    selection, 72–80
    trends and, 39b, 49–50, 61,
        91, 196
    watching for, 38–39, 41
orders, 42–44, 124
organic organizational structure, 343t
organization (business), 212–213. *See*
    also non-profit organization
    cooperatives and, 212–213
    network, 345
    plan B checklist for, 241b
    for teams, 343–346
    standards, 35
    for start-up businesses, 241b
    virtual, 345
organizational costs, 293, 336b. *See*
    also start-up costs
organizational structures. *See also* legal
    structures
    charting, 63, 344b, 361
    defined, 345
    key to, 343
    overview, 345, 359, 365
    ownership, 346
    types of, 343t–344b, 345
outsourcing, 36, 39, 65
owner's draw, 281
owner's equity, 270–271, 293
ownership, 180, 206, 346

P

Pacific Western Brewing Company,
    34–35
packaging, 153
paid media advertising, 151–152,
    242b–243b
parking, 180
partner, death of, 228–229
partnerships, 202–204, 350, 365
    advantages, 202–203
    agreement, 203
    dynamic, 39
    general, 202
    goal-oriented, 350
    limited, 202
    as marketing strategy, 115
    overview, 202–203, 349
    shotgun clause, 203–204
    strategic, 365
passion, 8, 35, 68b, 91, 395
past tenants, 180
patents, 217–219, 233
Pathfinders, 23
payments
    cash flow and, 274, 284, 437b
    dividend, 329, 333
    GST/HST payments, 377b

payments (*Cont.*)
    interest, 280–281, 287, 329, 333
    loans, 280–281, 448
    principal, 280–281, 286–287, 293, 296
    timelines, 280b
payroll, 9t, 105, 225, 350
payroll deductions, 224–225
payroll taxes, 437b, 438t, 442b
PDAs (personal digital assistants), 26, 41
P/E (price/earnings) ratio, 380
peer lending, 326
penetration pricing, 148–149
people orientation, 8
percentage lease, 191
permits and licences, for start-up businesses, 241b
persistence, 3, 8
personal balance sheet, 313–315, 335
personal budget, 315. *See also* personal balance sheet
personal digital assistants (PDAs), 26, 41
personal equity, 270–271, 313
personality analysis, 360, 366–367
    grid, 366–367
    groups, 366
    interpretation, 367
    profile, 348b
    strengths and weaknesses, 360
    traits, 367
personality profile, 348b
personal line of credit, 243b, 311t, 313, 319–320
personal selling, 155–157, 169, 431b
personal values, 83, 86–87
personnel. *See* employees
PERT (Program Evaluation and Review Technique), 444–445
Philips Electronics, 95, 98
phones, 96, 97, 103
Pinterest, 48, 160
pitch, 58
plan B, 240–244
    case study, 189–190, 258
    checklist, 241b–243b, 256
    online resources for, 243b
    overview, 240, 244
    solutions, 258t–259t
    suppliers, 244b
planning offices, 22
Podleski, Greta, 70
Podleski, Janet, 70
point-of-purchase (P-O-P) displays, 153
political change, 49
POP (Passionate, Opportunity seeking, and Persistent), 3, 8, 31
P-O-P (point-of-purchase) displays, 153
Popcorn, Faith, 41
Poptech, 153
population, 46t

Porter, Michael E., 83, 84
positioning, 127, 132–134
positioning strategy. *See* competitive positioning strategy
The Potter's Wheel Inc., 308
poverty of time, 39
preferred shares, 333
premium pricing, 148
prepaid expenses, 269, 291
prepaid legal, 233
press releases, 168
price, 130b–131b, 278, 295
price/earnings (P/E) ratio, 380
price skimming, 148–149
pricing, 145–146. *See also* marketing
    calculation and justification for, 167
    case study, 170–172
    ceiling (premium), 148
    competitor-based (market-based), 129–131, 146
    cost considerations, 167
    description in business plan, 169
    earnings-assets formula, 388–390
    economy (limit), 148–149
    estimates, 167
    industry norm (keystone), 147–148
    markups, 147
    overview, 145–146
    penetration, 148–149
    profit-based (cost plus), 146–147
    skimming, 148–149
    strategies, 167, 171
price tags and, 165, 168
primary customers, 94, 97, 115
primary research, 20
    in competitive intelligence, 123
    defined, 20
    of location information, 185–187
    news-eyes, 20–21
    target customers, 108, 120
    touchpoint analysis, 124, 137
prime rates, 320, 331
private sector employees, 9t
private sector funding, 323b
Procter & Gamble, 95, 98, 105
productivity, 132
product liability insurance, 245b, 248t
product life cycle, 131–134
product penetration, 148–149
profiling
    advertising, 103–104
    business-to-business, 105–108
    case study, 116–117
    company, 105b
    competitors, 446
    consumer, 99
    defined, 97
    demographic, 49, 99–101
    development checklist, 115
    end-user, 99, 105b

    example, 103–104
    importance of, 112
    industry, 105b
    invisible customer, 98–99
    overview, 97, 112
    media sources, 103–104
    primary customer, 97
    psychographic, 101
    secondary customer, 98
profit, 288
profit-based pricing, 146–147
PROFIT Hot 50 CEOs, 151, 153, 163
PROFIT magazine, 11, 21, 151
profit margin, 289
PROFIT 100 companies, 106
pro forma cash flow, 273, 282t–283t
pro forma income statement, 284–288
    cost of goods sold, 285t, 286, 287t
    defined, 284
    draft, 284, 301, 302
    example, 285t
    gross margin return, 291
    gross profit, 285t, 286, 287t, 288–289
    income statement ratios, 288–291
    inventory turnover, 289–290
    operating expenses, 285t, 286–288
    overview, 284–285, 300
    net profit, 287t, 288
    profit margin, 289
    sales, 286, 287t
    worksheet, 282t–283t
Program Evaluation and Review Technique (PERT), 444–445
projected cash flow, 273, 301
projected income statement, 274–275, 278–279
promoting, stage 2 of e-commerce, 43–44
promotion, 43–44, 149–150. *See also* marketing
    brainstorming, 168
    budget plan, 170, 425b, 431b
    description in business plan, 169
    case study, 170–172
    cornerstones for, 151
    courtesy as, 162–163
    customer service and quality, 151
    defined, 149
    example, 431b
    market research and, 164
    overview, 149–150
    planning steps, 149–150, 164–165
    price tags and, 165, 168
    questions for market strategy, 165
    websites and, 43–44, 126, 159–160
promotional campaign, 164
promotional mix, 150–151
property owner, 180

PropertyGuys.com, 128, 177, 325, 399, 400
proprietorship ratio, 273
provincial requirements, 208, 224b
provincial sales taxes (PST), 227–228
psychographic profiling, 101, 113
psychographics, 99, 112
public image, 180, 184, 206
public liability insurance, 245b, 248t
public relations, 169

Q

quality, 151
Quebec Pension Plan (QPP), 357, 358
QuestVest, 174–175, 196–197
quick ratio, 271, 273

R

ratio calculators, 288, 289, 297b
Raymundo, Ben, 370
Raymundo, Sally, 370
RBC. *See* Royal Bank Business Planning Resources (RBC)
reader profile, 103, 113, 168
reading, 160
real estate, 378
real estate firms, 22, 189
receipts, 22, 273, 276t
    cash in, 275, 279, 282t, 438t
    donation, 215t
    forecasting, 279
    from operations or sales, 190, 279
    tax, 215t
recruitment, 355–358. *See also* employees; human resources
    compensation, 357–358
    cost of, 358
    employee selection, 356–357
    external, 354–355
    hiring process, 352–354
    internal, 354
    non-financial compensation and, 355b
    overview, 355
    selection process, 356–357
    training and development, 357
Red Hat, 6
red tape file, 234
Reid, Aileen, 412–413
relevance, 161
renewal period
    in franchises, 401, 406
    in leases, 191, 379
    trade-mark, 221
rentable area, 192
Rescan Environmental Services Ltd. 359
research, 20–24

hard data, 21–24, 113–114
    industry, 29, 126
    for locations, 179–180, 184–187
    new-eyes, 20–21
    primary, 20, 108
    secondary, 21, 233
Research In Motion, 6
resource centres, 126–127
restrictive covenants, 191
retailing, 176
retail sales, 12, 156b, 176, 227, 399
retirement planner, 50
return on investment (ROI), 294
return on owner investment, 294, 386, 437, 442, 448
revenue method, 295–296
revenue streams, 84
revolving loans, 331
rewards, 29, 74, 80f
Richmond, Janice, 177–178
risk management, 239–259
    checklist of suppliers, 244b
    due diligence, 251
    employee responsibilities, 250
    employer responsibilities, 250
    insurance planning, 244–249, 256
    hazardous materials, 251
    joint health and safety, 250–251, 256–257
    committee, 250–251
    OH&S government responsibilities, 250
    plan B, 240–244
    theft and fraud prevention, 252
    workplace health and safety, 249–251
risk taking, 10, 243, 244–245
risk tolerance, 315
road map, 4–6
Robbinex Intermediaries, 376
ROI (return on investment), 294
Royal Bank Business Planning Resources (RBC), 20
royalty fee, 401
The Rubbish Boys, 144

S

safety and health regulations, 250b
salaries, 281
sales, 11, 129f, 156b, 278, 286
sales forecasting, 278–279
sales method, 156b, 278–279
sales reps, 162
sales-to-stock ratio, 291
sample business plans and templates, 283t
savings bonds, 267, 271
Schmitt, Paul, 41
Scudamore, Brian, 144
Sears, 94, 98, 139

secondary data. *See* secondary research
secondary customer, 98
secondary research, 21, 75, 76, 87
    benchmarking tools for, 147
    on corporations, 233
    defined, 21
    on franchising, 415
    of location information, 184–185
    online sources, 24
Second Cup, 415
second-level competitors, 122
second wave, 35
security, 39, 179, 197
segmentation
    customer, 84
    defined, 55
    gap analysis and, 55, 62
    idea generation and, 77f
    market, 55, 62, 91
    uses, 112
Selectyourfranchise.com, 402b
self-assessment, 13
self-employed persons, 6–7t, 15, 225, 226b
self-financing, 316
serial entrepreneurs, 6, 36, 370
service industry, 182
services, 169, 170, 180
sex, trends in, 55
Shamrock Model, 345f
shareholder loans, 281, 329
shareholders, 209–210
shareholders agreement, 203–204, 210–211
shares, 213
Sharing, as entrepreneur characteristic, 10
Shopify, 34
shotgun clause, 204
Sierra Wireless, 6
Siskinds Franchise Law Group, 402b
small and medium-sized enterprises (SMEs), 16
small business. *See also* business
    brainstorming, 37
    checklist of requirements, 224b
    deductions, 205
    description, 15–17
    distribution channels, 177–178
    entrepreneurs, 8, 13, 15, 25
    example, 95
    export trends, 40
    financing, 329
    globalization, 38
    guerrilla marketing, 145
    guide for, 226b, 243b, 377b
    ideas for, 77f
    legal forms, 200
    mentors, 352, 353t, 361
    pricing methods, 146–148

small business(*Cont.*)
   recruitment, 355b
   road map, 4–6
   serial, 6
   statistics, 6, 8, 9t
   success rate, 18
   tips, 74b
   valuation of, 376–377b
small business entrepreneurs, 8, 13,
   15, 25
SMART objectives, 74b
SME Benchmarking Tool, 127, 147, 165,
   283b
SMEs (small and medium-sized enterprises), 16, 309, 317
Smith, C. Hughes, 433b–434b
Snowboard Express, 37–38f, 53f
Sociable (Gibson), 160–161
social/cultural changes, 49
social entrepreneurship, 14, 212
social media, 48–49
   entrepreneurs and, 161
   globalization and, 49
   Internet and, 42t
   promotion and, 6, 160–161, 432
   protection for, 223
   websites, 223
   trends, 48–49
   viral marketing and, 161
Software School Inc.
   balance sheet description example,
      443t
   business description example,
      427b–428b
   business plan, 423
   cash flow description example, 437b,
      438t–439t
   competition description example,
      430b
   cover letter, 423–424b
   executive summary, 426b
   human resources description example,
      435b
   income statement description
      example, 440t–441t, 442b
   location description example, 432b
   management team description
      example, 433b, 434b
   marketing strategy description
      example, 429b, 431b
   table of contents page, 425b
   team management description, 433b
sole proprietorships, 200–202
solvency ratios, 273
Source for Sports, 414
Sources of Private Sector
   Financing, 323b
Spence, Rick, 11, 106, 309
Spending Patterns in Canada, 100
spoke diagram, 15

The Sports Factory, 274
Squires-Hutchings, Susan, 308
SRI Consulting Business Intelligence,
   113
SRI International, 101
staffing decisions, 354
St-Arnaud, Jean-François, 94–95, 111,
   116, 139, 140
start-up capital, 322–327
   angels, 322
   Canadian Youth Business Foundation,
      325b
   cooperative partnership, 327
   costs. *See* start-up costs
   customers, 323
   employees and employers, 323
   government lending programs, 326
   micro-lending programs, 325–326
   nonprofit funding, 326
   sources of, 323b
   suppliers, 322–323
   vendor statement form, 324–325
   venture capitalists, 326
start-up costs, 191, 207, 265–267,
   241b. *See also* costs
Start-up Quiz, Business, 13
Statistics Canada, 23, 24,
   99–100
Statistics Canada Catalogue, 23
Stewart, Joan, 262
Stewart, Ray, 262
stimulating behaviour, 342
strategic alliances, 134–136, 350
strategic business units, 345
Stratos Inc., 359
Street Kids International, 14
substituters, 182
Subway, 399, 404, 413
success checklist, 28
succession planning, 229–230
success rate, 18
Sunbelt Business Brokers, 376
Sunshine Generation, 47
supplementers, 182
suppliers, 126, 378
   checklist of, 244b
   competition research and, 126
   plan b checklist, 241b
   as source of funding, 322–323, 337
   start-up agenda and, 253b
   as tangible assets, 378
   for used equipment, 378
supply, 169
surveys, 109–111
SWOT analysis, 82–83, 91

T
T1 form, 225, 285t
T2 form, 215t, 225

tangible assets, 378–379
TANRO, 297b
Tapscott, Don, 41
target customers, 97. *See also* demographic profile
   business-to-business profile, 99,
      100–101, 105–108
   defined, 97
   description in business plan, 17b, 19,
      428–429b
   field interviewing, 108–109
   "the follower", 98
   as Generation X, 102b
   home-based businesses and, 183
   location and, 63, 178, 196, 429b
   markets and, 428
   media sources, 103–104
   as Nexus Generation, 102b
   one-to-one marketing, 96–97
   overview, 112
   profiling, 5, 21, 97–98
   research, 5, 114
   road map, 4f
   successful actions, 93, 96
   surveying, 109–111
   visualizing business and, 111
taxes, 181. *See also* specific types
   advantages for, 205–206
   federal income taxes, 225–226
   GST and HST, 223, 226–228
   for legal structures, 201t
   provincial sales, 227–228
   resources for, 226b
   writeoffs, 207
tax shelter, 202
Taxtips.ca, 205, 226, 227
Taylor, Ron, 120
Taylor, Sam, 94
Teams, 341–346
   advisory, 346–347
   associates, 350
   balance of, 347–348
   board of directors and, 346–347
   building, 342
   in business plan description, 363
   case study, 363–365
   employee leasing, 352
   founding, 346
   goal-oriented partnerships, 350
   human resources requirements,
      347, 348b
   independent contractor, 350
   joint ventures, 350
   just-in-time, 349, 360
   leading, 341–343, 359
   management profiles, 346
   managing, 341–343
   mentoring relationship,
      351–352, 361
   non-traditional, 349–352

organic versus mechanistic structure, 343t
organizing, 343–346
ownership structure and, 346
partnerships, 349, 350, 365
personality profile and, 348b
Shamrock Model, 345
strategic alliances, 350
strategic business units, 345
teamwork, 346–348
traditional approaches, 344f
virtual (network) organizations, 345–346
technology, 41–45. *See also* Internet resources
business mission statement, 81
as competitive edge, 41
computerization, 182
current, 60
e-commerce, 43–45
high-, 55
overview, 41
trends, 41, 49–50
technology coach, 50
telecommuting, 39
term loans, 332
Terrapex Environmental Ltd., 359
theft prevention, 252
time, 39
Tim Hortons coffee, 406
Tire Pro, 135
total costs, 146, 285t, 287t, 295
touchpoint analysis, 123–125, 137
trade associations
databases and information from, 21, 22, 59, 75
insurance and, 248, 311
joining for visibility, 165
locating, 29
as promotional activities, 165, 372
target markets and, 104
Trade Data Online, 24
trade journals, 22, 126
trade magazines, 127
trade-marks, 217, 221–223, 224b, 236
agent, 222
as intellectual property, 236
Canadian, 222
conflicting, 222
defined, 221
federal requirements, 224b
journal, 222
NUANS and, 217
registered, 221–222
trade name versus, 222
unregistered, 221–222
users of, 223
trade media, 104
trade shows, 126, 157

Trade Show News Network, 157
traffic direction, 162
Traherne Schools, 430b
training
from the business seller, 371
computer, 81, 426b, 427b, 429b
cost of training, 293, 336b, 348b, 358, 362
employee, 28, 243b, 354, 356, 357, 362, 401, 403, 413, 415, 428b, 430b, 448
Internet, 80f
Microsoft program, 433b
poor, 408
transfers, of leases, 191
transformational leadership, 341–342, 364
transportation
approvals for, 184b
business use of, 181
costs for, 128, 157, 177, 178, 244b, 325
as expense, 313, 338
as green business, 17
home business and, 182
living arrangements and, 47
Trashbusters, 144, 171
TransUnion, 309, 335
travel advisor/agent, 50, 59, 103, 163, 183
Treliving, Jim, 68
trends
baby boomers, 45–46
employment, 50
energy conservation, 50
environmental categories, 49, 50
ethnic, 47, 50
fitness, 50
forecasts, 51b–52b
gap analysis, 55, 62
globalization, 40
growth industry segments, 54–55
health-consciousness, 50
life-cycle stages, 52–53
market signals, 53–54
markets and opportunities, 39b
in the new millennium, 36, 39b
opportunities in, 35–39, 49–50, 60–61, 64–65, 91, 196
overview, 59
segmentation, 55, 62
sources for, 41
splintering of mass market, 47–53
technology, 41–45, 60
watching for, 38–39, 41
Turner, Matt, 2, 31–32, 428, 435
Type-Entrepreneurial personality, 13. *See also* entrepreneurs
tweens, 47

24/7 Adventure Notebook, 11–12, 26
Twitter, 48, 160, 161b, 432
two-income families, 182
Twomey, Sean, 107–108
Twubs, 223

U
unforeseen death, 228–229
uniqueness, 135
Unique Solutions Design, 36, 40, 41, 46, 48, 140
unit method, 278, 295–296t
university reports, 22
unsecured credit, 310–313
upmarket travel advisor/agent, 50
UPS, 40
usable building area, 192
utilities, 180, 184

V
VALS (value and lifestyle model), 101, 113
valuation, 377, 390b
ability-to-pay, 385–387
asset-based, 384–385
earnings-assets, 387–390
value
-added benefits, 81
of business, 71b, 91, 387
clarification of, 86
creation of, 24, 84
driven, 85f
of intangibles, 390, 396
market, 314t, 336–337
on online sales, 76b
of orders, 43t
personal, 71b, 91
propositions, 84, 85f
success and, 72f
of time per hour, 380
value and lifestyle model (VALS), 101, 113
value propositions, 84
values, 69, 70–71, 72f, 73f. *See also* personal values
variable costs, 280, 286, 294–296t
variable disbursements, 280
vendor statement, 324–325
venture capital, 326, 323b, 326
verbal regulation
in franchises, 406–407
promises, legality of, 324b
vendors, 324b
vertical markets, 49
viral marketing, 161–162
Virtual Causeway, 151

virtual organization, 345–346
The Virtual You™, 140
vision, 68–69, 70–72f, 90, 91
    business, 71b, 72, 73f, 80, 81, 82, 86, 89
    entrepreneurs characteristic, 8
    financial, 262, 300
    power of, 70b
    values and, 70–72f, 90, 91
visioning, 341
von Selzam, Ted Wolff, 69, 76
von Teichman, Matthew, 42
VR Business Brokers, 376

W

Wacker, Watts, 41
Wade, P.J., 41
wages, 201, 350, 354, 357, 358
The Wealthy Barber (Chilton), 70, 229
Webb, Charlene, 340, 347 353
Webber, Paul, 228–229
websites, 126, 159–160
Webview 360, 41, 42
Weeks, Tanya Shaw, 36, 41, 46, 48, 65

WHMIS (Workplace Hazardous Materials Information Systems), 251
wholesaling, 177
will, 229
Wilson, Sam, 381
Wilson, W. Brett, 68
Wired magazine, 60
Wood, Elizabeth, 109–110, 125
Woolett's Hardware, 391–392
women-owned businesses, 323b, 370, 407. *See also* entrepreneurs, women
Workers' Compensation, 250b
workforce, 358–359. *See also* employees
working capital, 271, 330. *See also* current ratio
Workplace Hazardous Materials Information Systems (WHMIS), 251
workplace health and safety, 249–251
Wozniak, Steve, 8

X
XZEL Designs, 36

Y
Yahoo!, 6
Y generation, 46
Yellow Pages
    advertising in, 151, 169, 235, 254b, 444
    brokers in, 375
    insertion dates, 256, 444
    direct mail and, 168, 169
    name, records or trade-mark agent searches, 217
Your Micro and You (YMAY), 430b
YourMoney Network (YMN), 263b
Youtube.com, 6, 160, 161b
Yunus, Muhammad, 14

Z
Zacks, 283b
Ziglar, Zig, 11
zoning, 180, 184